The Vicomte de

Alexandre Dumas, Auguste Maquet

Alpha Editions

This edition published in 2024

ISBN : 9789362925497

Design and Setting By
Alpha Editions
www.alphaedis.com
Email - info@alphaedis.com

As per information held with us this book is in Public Domain.
This book is a reproduction of an important historical work. Alpha Editions uses the best technology to reproduce historical work in the same manner it was first published to preserve its original nature. Any marks or number seen are left intentionally to preserve its true form.

Contents

Chapter I. The Letter. .... - 1 -
Chapter II. The Messenger. .... - 9 -
Chapter III. The Interview. .... - 17 -
Chapter IV. Father and Son. .... - 25 -
Chapter V. In which Something will be said of Cropoli. .... - 30 -
Chapter VI. The Unknown. .... - 35 -
Chapter VII. Parry. .... - 41 -
Chapter VIII. What his Majesty King Louis XIV. was at the Age of Twenty-Two. .... - 47 -
Chapter IX. In which the Unknown of the Hostelry of Les Medici loses his Incognito. .... - 57 -
Chapter X. The Arithmetic of M. de Mazarin. .... - 67 -
Chapter XI. Mazarin's Policy. .... - 75 -
Chapter XII. The King and the Lieutenant. .... - 82 -
Chapter XIII. Mary de Mancini. .... - 87 -
Chapter XIV. In which the King and the Lieutenant each give Proofs of Memory. .... - 92 -
Chapter XV. The Proscribed. .... - 100 -
Chapter XVI. "Remember!" .... - 105 -
Chapter XVII. In which Aramis is sought, and only Bazin is found. .... - 114 -
Chapter XVIII. In which D'Artagnan seeks Porthos, and only finds Mousqueton. .... - 122 -
Chapter XIX. What D'Artagnan went to Paris for. .... - 130 -
Chapter XX. Of the Society which was formed in the Rue des Lombards. .... - 135 -
Chapter XXI. In which D'Artagnan prepares to travel. .... - 145 -

Chapter XXII. D'Artagnan travels for the House of Planchet and Company. ....- 151 -

Chapter XXIII. In which the Author is forced to write a Little History. ....- 157 -

Chapter XXIV. The Treasure. ....- 168 -

Chapter XXV. The Marsh. ....- 175 -

Chapter XXVI. Heart and Mind. ....- 183 -

Chapter XXVII. The Next Day. ....- 191 -

Chapter XXVIII. Smuggling. ....- 197 -

Chapter XXIX. Fear he has placed his Money and that of Planchet in the Sinking Fund. ....- 204 -

Chapter XXX. The Shares of Planchet and Company rise again to Par. ....- 211 -

Chapter XXXI. Monk reveals Himself. ....- 217 -

Chapter XXXII. Athos and D'Artagnan meet once more at the Hostelry of the Corne du Cerf. ....- 221 -

Chapter XXXIII. The Audience. ....- 232 -

Chapter XXXIV. Of the Embarrassment of Riches. ....- 238 -

Chapter XXXV. On the Canal. ....- 244 -

Chapter XXXVI. How D'Artagnan drew a Country-Seat from a Deal Box. ....- 251 -

Chapter XXXVII. How D'Artagnan regulated the "Assets" of the Company. ....- 259 -

Chapter XXXVIII. the French Grocer had already been established in the Seventeenth Century. ....- 265 -

Chapter XXXIX. Mazarin's Gaming Party. ....- 271 -

Chapter XL. An Affair of State. ....- 275 -

Chapter XLI. The Recital. ....- 280 -

Chapter XLII. In which Mazarin becomes Prodigal. ....- 285 -

Chapter XLIII. Guenaud. ....- 289 -

Chapter XLIV. Colbert. ....- 293 -

Chapter XLV. Confession of a Man of Wealth. ....- 297 -
Chapter XLVI. The Donation. ....- 303 -
Chapter XLVII. How Anne of Austria gave one Piece of Advice to Louis XIV. ....- 308 -
Chapter XLVIII. Agony. ....- 316 -
Chapter XLIX. The First Appearance of Colbert. ....- 324 -
Chapter L: The First Day of the Royalty of Louis XIV. ....- 332 -
Chapter LI. A Passion. ....- 337 -
Chapter LII. D'Artagnan's Lesson. ....- 344 -
Chapter LIII. The King. ....- 351 -
Chapter LIV. The Houses of M. Fouquet. ....- 369 -
Chapter LV. The Abbe Fouquet. ....- 380 -
Chapter LVI. M. de la Fontaine's Wine. ....- 387 -
Chapter LVII. The Gallery of Saint-Mande. ....- 391 -
Chapter LVIII. Epicureans. ....- 396 -
Chapter LIX. A Quarter of an Hour's Delay. ....- 401 -
Chapter LX. Plan of Battle. ....- 407 -
Chapter LXI. The Cabaret of the Image-de-Notre-Dame. ......- 412 -
Chapter LXII. Vive Colbert! ....- 419 -
Chapter LXIII. How M. d'Eymeris's Diamond passed into the Hands of M. d'Artagnan. ....- 424 -
Chapter LXIV. Difference D'Artagnan finds between the Intendant and the Superintendent. ....- 432 -
Chapter LXV. Philosophy of the Heart and Mind ....- 439 -
Chapter LXVI. The Journey. ....- 442 -
Chapter LXVII. How D'Artagnan became Acquainted with a Poet. ....- 446 -
Chapter LXVIII. D'Artagnan continues his Investigations .....- 454 -
Chapter LXIX. D'Artagnan was to meet an Old Acquaintance. ....- 462 -

Chapter LXX. Wherein the Ideas of D'Artagnan begin to clear up a little. ...... - 468 -

Chapter LXXI. A Procession at Vannes. ...... - 477 -

Chapter LXXII. The Grandeur of the Bishop of Vannes. ...... - 484 -

Chapter LXXIII. In which Porthos begins to be sorry for having come with D'Artagnan. ...... - 494 -

Chapter LXXIV. D'Artagnan makes all Speed, Porthos snores, and Aramis counsels. ...... - 506 -

Chapter LXXV. In which Monsieur Fouquet Acts. ...... - 513 -

Chapter I.
The Letter.

TOWARDS the middle of the month of May, in the year 1660, at nine o'clock in the morning, when the sun, already high in the heavens, was fast absorbing the dew from the ramparts of the castle of Blois, a little cavalcade, composed of three men and two pages, re-entered the city by the bridge, without producing any other effect upon the passengers of the quay beyond a first movement of the hand to the head, as a salute, and a second movement of the tongue to express, in the purest French then spoken in France: "There is Monsieur returning from hunting." And that was all.

Whilst, however, the horses were climbing the steep acclivity which leads from the river to the castle, several shop-boys approached the last horse, from whose saddle-bow a number of birds were suspended by the beak.

On seeing this, the inquisitive youths manifested with rustic freedom their contempt for such paltry sport, and, after a dissertation among themselves upon the disadvantages of hawking, they returned to their occupations; one only of the curious party, a stout, stubby, cheerful lad, having demanded how it was that Monsieur, who, from his great revenues, had it in his power to amuse himself so much better, could be satisfied with such mean diversions.

"Do you not know," one of the standers-by replied, "that Monsieur's principal amusement is to weary himself?"

The light-hearted boy shrugged his shoulders with a gesture which said as clear as day: "In that case I would rather be plain Jack than a prince." And all resumed their labors.

In the meanwhile, Monsieur continued his route with an air at once so melancholy and so majestic, that he certainly would have attracted the attention of spectators, if spectators there had been; but the good citizens of Blois could not pardon Monsieur for having chosen their gay city for an abode in which to indulge melancholy at his ease, and as often as they caught a glimpse of the illustrious ennuye, they stole away gaping, or drew back their heads into the interior of their dwellings, to escape the soporific influence of that long pale face, of those watery eyes, and that languid address; so that the worthy prince was almost certain to find the streets deserted whenever he chanced to pass through them.

Now, on the part of the citizens of Blois this was a culpable piece of disrespect, for Monsieur was, after the king—nay, even perhaps, before the king—the greatest noble of the kingdom. In fact, God, who had granted to Louis XIV., then reigning, the honor of being son of Louis XIII., had granted to Monsieur the honor of being son of Henry IV. It was not then, or, at least, it ought not to have been, a trifling source of pride for the city of Blois, that Gaston of Orleans had chosen it as his residence, and held his court in the ancient Castle of the States.

But it was the destiny of this great prince to excite the attention and admiration of the public in a very modified degree wherever he might be. Monsieur had fallen into this situation by habit.

It was not, perhaps, this which gave him that air of listlessness. Monsieur had already been tolerably busy in the course of his life. A man cannot allow the heads of a dozen of his best friends to be cut off without feeling a little excitement; and as, since the accession of Mazarin to power, no heads had been cut off, Monsieur's occupation was gone, and his morale suffered from it.

The life of the poor prince was then very dull. After his little morning hawking-party on the banks of the Beuvron, or in the woods of Cheverny, Monsieur crossed the Loire, went to breakfast at Chambord, with or without an appetite, and the city of Blois heard no more of its sovereign lord and master till the next hawking-day.

So much for the ennui extra muros; of the ennui of the interior we will give the reader an idea if he will with us follow the cavalcade to the majestic porch of the Castle of the States.

Monsieur rode a little steady-paced horse, equipped with a large saddle of red Flemish velvet, with stirrups in the shape of buskins; the horse was of a bay color; Monsieur's pourpoint of crimson velvet corresponded with the cloak of the same shade and the horse's equipment, and it was only by this red appearance of the whole that the prince could be known from his two companions, the one dressed in violet, the other in green. He on the left, in violet, was his equerry; he on the right, in green, was the grand veneur.

One of the pages carried two gerfalcons upon a perch, the other a hunting-horn, which he blew with a careless note at twenty paces from the castle. Every one about this listless prince did what he had to listlessly.

At this signal, eight guards, who were lounging in the sun in the square court, ran to their halberts, and Monsieur made his solemn entry into the castle.

When he had disappeared under the shades of the porch, three or four idlers, who had followed the cavalcade to the castle, after pointing out the suspended birds to each other, dispersed with comments upon what they saw: and, when they were gone, the street, the palace, and the court, all remained deserted alike.

Monsieur dismounted without speaking a word, went straight to his apartments, where his valet changed his dress, and as Madame had not yet sent orders respecting breakfast, Monsieur stretched himself upon a chaise longue, and was soon as fast asleep as if it had been eleven o'clock at night.

The eight guards, who concluded their service for the day was over, laid themselves down very comfortably in the sun upon some stone benches; the grooms disappeared with their horses into the stables, and, with the exception of a few joyous birds, startling each other with their sharp chirping in the tufted shrubberies, it might have been thought that the whole castle was as soundly asleep as Monsieur was.

All at once, in the midst of this delicious silence, there resounded a clear ringing laugh, which caused several of the halberdiers in the enjoyment of their siesta to open at least one eye.

This burst of laughter proceeded from a window of the castle, visited at this moment by the sun, that embraced it in one of those large angles which the profiles of the chimneys mark out upon the walls before mid-day.

The little balcony of wrought iron which advanced in front of this window was furnished with a pot of red gilliflowers, another pot of primroses, and an early rose-tree, the foliage of which, beautifully green, was variegated with numerous red specks announcing future roses.

In the chamber lighted by this window, was a square table, covered with an old large-flowered Haarlem tapestry; in the center of this table was a long-necked stone bottle, in which were irises and lilies of the valley; at each end of this table was a young girl.

The position of these two young people was singular; they might have been taken for two boarders escaped from a convent. One of them, with both elbows on the table, and a pen in her hand, was tracing characters upon a sheet of fine Dutch paper; the other, kneeling upon a chair, which allowed her to advance her head and bust over the back of it to the middle of the table, was watching her companion as she wrote, or rather hesitated to write.

Thence the thousand cries, the thousand railleries, the thousand laughs, one of which, more brilliant than the rest, had startled the birds in the gardens, and disturbed the slumbers of Monsieur's guards.

We are taking portraits now; we shall be allowed, therefore, we hope, to sketch the two last of this chapter.

The one who was leaning in the chair—that is to say, the joyous, laughing one—was a beautiful girl of from eighteen to twenty, with brown complexion and brown hair, splendid, from eyes which sparkled beneath strongly-marked brows, and particularly from her teeth, which seemed to shine like pearls between her red coral lips. Her every movement seemed the accent of a sunny nature; she did not walk—she bounded.

The other, she who was writing, looked at her turbulent companion with an eye as limpid, as pure, and as blue as the azure of the day. Her hair, of a shaded fairness, arranged with exquisite taste, fell in silky curls over her lovely mantling cheeks; she passed across the paper a delicate hand, whose thinness announced her extreme youth. At each burst of laughter that proceeded from her friend, she raised, as if annoyed, her white shoulders in a poetical and mild manner, but they were wanting in that richfulness of mold that was likewise to be wished in her arms and hands.

"Montalais! Montalais!" said she at length, in a voice soft and caressing as a melody, "you laugh too loud—you laugh like a man! You will not only draw the attention of messieurs the guards, but you will not hear Madame's bell when Madame rings."

This admonition neither made the young girl called Montalais cease to laugh nor gesticulate. She only replied: "Louise, you do not speak as you think, my dear; you know that messieurs the guards, as you call them, have only just commenced their sleep, and that a cannon would not waken them; you know that Madame's bell can be heard at the bridge of Blois, and that consequently I shall hear it when my services are required by Madame. What annoys you, my child, is that I laugh while you are writing; and what you are afraid of is that Madame de Saint-Remy, your mother, should come up here, as she does sometimes when we laugh too loud, that she should surprise us, and that she should see that enormous sheet of paper upon which, in a quarter of an hour, you have only traced the words Monsieur Raoul. Now, you are right, my dear Louise, because after these words, 'Monsieur Raoul', others may be put so significant and incendiary as to cause Madame Saint-Remy to burst out into fire and flames! Hein! is not that true now?—say."

And Montalais redoubled her laughter and noisy provocations.

The fair girl at length became quite angry; she tore the sheet of paper on which, in fact, the words "Monsieur Raoul" were written in good characters; and crushing the paper in her trembling hands, she threw it out of the window.

"There! there!" said Mademoiselle de Montalais; "there is our little lamb, our gentle dove, angry! Don't be afraid, Louise—Madame de Saint-Remy will not come; and if she should, you know I have a quick ear. Besides, what can be more permissible than to write to an old friend of twelve years' standing, particularly when the letter begins with the words 'Monsieur Raoul'?"

"It is all very well—I will not write to him at all," said the young girl.

"Ah, ah! in good sooth, Montalais is properly punished," cried the jeering brunette, still laughing. "Come, come! let us try another sheet of paper, and finish our dispatch off-hand. Good! there is the bell ringing now. By my faith, so much the worse! Madame must wait, or else do without her first maid of honor this morning."

A bell, in fact, did ring; it announced that Madame had finished her toilette, and waited for Monsieur to give her his hand, and conduct her from the salon to the refectory.

This formality being accomplished with great ceremony, the husband and wife breakfasted, and then separated till the hour of dinner, invariably fixed at two o'clock.

The sound of this bell caused a door to be opened in the offices on the left hand of the court, from which filed two maitres d'hotel followed by eight scullions bearing a kind of hand-barrow loaded with dishes under silver covers.

One of the maitres d'hotel, the first in rank, touched one of the guards, who was snoring on his bench, slightly with his wand; he even carried his kindness so far as to place the halbert which stood against the wall in the hands of the man stupid with sleep, after which the soldier, without explanation, escorted the viande of Monsieur to the refectory, preceded by a page and the two maitres d'hotel.

Wherever the viande passed, the soldiers ported arms.

Mademoiselle de Montalais and her companion had watched from their window the details of this ceremony, to which, by the bye, they must have been pretty well accustomed. But they did not look so much from curiosity as to be assured they should not be disturbed. So, guards, scullions, maitres d'hotel, and pages having passed, they resumed their places at the table; and the sun, which, through the window-frame, had for an instant fallen upon those two charming countenances, now only shed its light upon the gilliflowers, primroses, and rose-tree.

"Bah!" said Mademoiselle de Montalais, taking her place again; "Madame will breakfast very well without me!"

"Oh! Montalais, you will be punished!" replied the other girl, sitting down quietly in hers.

"Punished, indeed!—that is to say, deprived of a ride! That is just the way in which I wish to be punished. To go out in the grand coach, perched upon a doorstep; to turn to the left, twist round to the right, over roads full of ruts, where we cannot exceed a league in two hours; and then to come back straight towards the wing of the castle in which is the window of Mary de

Medici, so that Madame never fails to say: 'Could one believe it possible that Mary de Medici should have escaped from that window—forty-seven feet high? The mother of two princes and three princesses!' If you call that relaxation, Louise, all I ask is to be punished every day; particularly when my punishment is to remain with you and write such interesting letters as we write!"

"Montalais! Montalais! there are duties to be performed."

"You talk of them very much at your ease, dear child!—you, who are left quite free amidst this tedious court. You are the only person that reaps the advantages of them without incurring the trouble,—you, who are really more one of Madame's maids of honor than I am, because Madame makes her affection for your father-in-law glance off upon you; so that you enter this dull house as the birds fly into yonder court, inhaling the air, pecking the flowers, picking up the grain, without having the least service to perform, or the least annoyance to undergo. And you talk to me of duties to be performed! In sooth, my pretty idler, what are your own proper duties, unless to write to the handsome Raoul? And even that you don't do; so that it looks to me as if you likewise were rather negligent of your duties!"

Louise assumed a serious air, leant her chin upon her hand, and, in a tone full of candid remonstrance, "And do you reproach me with my good fortune?" said she. "Can you have the heart to do it? You have a future; you will belong to the court; the king, if he should marry, will require Monsieur to be near his person; you will see splendid fetes, you will see the king, who they say is so handsome, so agreeable!"

"Ay, and still more, I shall see Raoul, who attends upon M. le Prince," added Montalais, maliciously.

"Poor Raoul!" sighed Louise.

"Now is the time to write to him, my pretty dear! Come, begin again, with that famous 'Monsieur Raoul' which figures at the top of the poor torn sheet."

She then held the pen toward her, and with a charming smile encouraged her hand, which quickly traced the words she named.

"What next?" asked the younger of the two girls.

"Why, now write what you think, Louise," replied Montalais.

"Are you quite sure I think of anything?"

"You think of somebody, and that amounts to the same thing, or rather even more."

"Do you think so, Montalais?"

"Louise, Louise, your blue eyes are as deep as the sea I saw at Boulogne last year! No, no, I mistake—the sea is perfidious: your eyes are as deep as the azure yonder—look!—over our heads!"

"Well, since you can read so well in my eyes, tell me what I am thinking about, Montalais."

"In the first place, you don't think, Monsieur Raoul; you think, My dear Raoul."

"Oh!—"

"Never blush for such a trifle as that! 'My dear Raoul,' we will say—'You implore me to write you at Paris, where you are detained by your attendance on M. le Prince. As you must be very dull there, to seek for amusement in the remembrance of a provinciale—'"

Louise rose up suddenly. "No, Montalais," said she, with a smile; "I don't think a word of that. Look, this is what I think;" and she seized the pen boldly, and traced, with a firm hand, the following words:

"I should have been very unhappy if your entreaties to obtain a remembrance of me had been less warm. Everything here reminds me of our early days, which so quickly passed away, which so delightfully flew by, that no others will ever replace the charm of them in my heart."

Montalais, who watched the flying pen, and read, the wrong way upwards, as fast as her friend wrote, here interrupted by clapping her hands. "Capital!" cried she; "there is frankness—there is heart—there is style! Show these Parisians, my dear, that Blois is the city for fine language!"

"He knows very well that Blois was a Paradise to me," replied the girl.

"That is exactly what you mean to say; and you speak like an angel."

"I will finish, Montalais," and she continued as follows: "You often think of me, you say, Monsieur Raoul: I thank you; but that does not surprise me, when I recollect how often our hearts have beaten close to each other."

"Oh! oh!" said Montalais. "Beware, my lamb! You are scattering your wool, and there are wolves about."

Louise was about to reply, when the gallop of a horse resounded under the porch of the castle.

"What is that?" said Montalais, approaching the window. "A handsome cavalier, by my faith!"

"Oh!—Raoul!" exclaimed Louise, who had made the same movement as her friend, and, becoming pale as death, sunk back beside her unfinished letter.

"Now, he is a clever lover, upon my word!" cried Montalais; "he arrives just at the proper moment."

"Come in, come in, I implore you!" murmured Louise.

"Bah! he does not know me. Let me see what he has come here for."

Chapter II.
The Messenger.

MADEMOISELLE de Montalais was right; the young cavalier was goodly to look upon.

He was a young man of from twenty-four to twenty-five years of age, tall and slender, wearing gracefully the picturesque military costume of the period. His large boots contained a foot which Mademoiselle de Montalais might not have disowned if she had been transformed into a man. With one of his delicate but nervous hands he checked his horse in the middle of the court, and with the other raised his hat, whose long plumes shaded his at once serious and ingenuous countenance.

The guards, roused by the steps of the horse, awoke, and were on foot in a minute. The young man waited till one of them was close to his saddle-bow: then, stooping towards him, in a clear, distinct voice, which was perfectly audible at the window where the two girls were concealed, "A message for his royal highness," he said.

"Ah, ah!" cried the soldier. "Officer, a messenger!"

But this brave guard knew very well that no officer would appear, seeing that the only one who could have appeared dwelt at the other side of the castle, in an apartment looking into the gardens. So he hastened to add: "The officer, monsieur, is on his rounds; but, in his absence, M. de Saint-Remy, the maitre d'hotel, shall be informed."

"M. de Saint-Remy?" repeated the cavalier, slightly blushing.

"Do you know him?"

"Why, yes; but request him, if you please, that my visit be announced to his royal highness as soon as possible."

"It appears to be pressing," said the guard, as if speaking to himself, but really in the hope of obtaining an answer.

The messenger made an affirmative sign with his head.

"In that case," said the guard, "I will go and seek the maitre d'hotel myself."

The young man, in the meantime, dismounted; and whilst the others were making their remarks upon the fine horse the cavalier rode, the soldier returned.

"Your pardon, young gentleman; but your name, if you please?"

"The Vicomte de Bragelonne, on the part of his highness M. le Prince de Conde."

The soldier made a profound bow, and, as if the name of the conqueror of Rocroi and Lens had given him wings, he stepped lightly up the steps leading to the ante-chamber.

A. de Bragelonne had not had time to fasten his horse to the iron bars of the perron, when M. de Saint-Remy came running, out of breath, supporting his capacious body with one hand, whilst with the other he cut the air as a fisherman cleaves the waves with his oar.

"Ah, Monsieur le Vicomte! You at Blois!" cried he. "Well, that is a wonder. Good-day to you—good-day, Monsieur Raoul."

"I offer you a thousand respects, M. de Saint-Remy."

"How Madame de la Vall—I mean, how delighted Madame de Saint-Remy will be to see you! But come in. His royal highness is at breakfast—must he be interrupted? Is the matter serious?"

"Yes, and no, Monsieur de Saint-Remy. A moment's delay, however, would be disagreeable to his royal highness."

"If that is the case, we will force the consigne, Monsieur le Vicomte. Come in. Besides, Monsieur is in an excellent humor to-day. And then you bring news, do you not?"

"Great news, Monsieur de Saint-Remy."

"And good, I presume?"

"Excellent."

"Come quickly, come quickly then!" cried the worthy man, putting his dress to rights as he went along.

Raoul followed him, hat in hand, and a little disconcerted at the noise made by his spurs in these immense salons.

As soon as he had disappeared in the interior of the palace, the window of the court was repeopled, and an animated whispering betrayed the emotion of the two girls. They soon appeared to have formed a resolution, for one of the two faces disappeared from the window. This was the brunette; the other remained behind the balcony, concealed by the flowers, watching attentively through the branches the perron by which M. de Bragelonne had entered the castle.

In the meantime the object of so much laudable curiosity continued his route, following the steps of the maitre d'hotel. The noise of quick steps, an odor of wine and viands, a clinking of crystal and plates, warned them that they were coming to the end of their course.

The pages, valets and officers, assembled in the office which led up to the refectory, welcomed the newcomer with the proverbial politeness of the country; some of them were acquainted with Raoul, and all knew that he came from Paris. It might be said that his arrival for a moment suspended the service. In fact, a page, who was pouring out wine for his royal highness, on hearing the jingling of spurs in the next chamber, turned round like a child, without perceiving that he was continuing to pour out, not into the glass, but upon the tablecloth.

Madame, who was not so preoccupied as her glorious spouse was, remarked this distraction of the page.

"Well?" exclaimed she.

"Well!" repeated Monsieur; "what is going on then?"

A. de Saint-Remy, who had just introduced his head through the doorway, took advantage of the moment.

"Why am I to be disturbed?" said Gaston, helping himself to a thick slice of one of the largest salmon that had ever ascended the Loire to be captured between Paimboeuf and Saint-Nazaire.

"There is a messenger from Paris. Oh! but after monseigneur has breakfasted will do; there is plenty of time."

"From Paris!" cried the prince, letting his fork fall. "A messenger from Paris, do you say? And on whose part does this messenger come?"

"On the part of M. le Prince," said the maitre d'hotel promptly.

Every one knows that the Prince de Conde was so called.

"A messenger from M. le Prince!" said Gaston, with an inquietude that escaped none of the assistants, and consequently redoubled the general curiosity.

Monsieur, perhaps, fancied himself brought back again to the happy times when the opening of a door gave him an emotion, in which every letter might contain a state secret,—in which every message was connected with a dark and complicated intrigue. Perhaps, likewise, that great name of M. le Prince expanded itself, beneath the roofs of Blois, to the proportions of a phantom.

Monsieur pushed away his plate.

"Shall I tell the envoy to wait?" asked M. de Saint-Remy.

A glance from Madame emboldened Gaston, who replied: "No, no! let him come in at once, on the contrary. A propos, who is he?"

"A gentleman of this country, M. le Vicomte de Bragelonne."

"Ah, very well! Introduce him, Saint-Remy—introduce him."

And when he had let fall these words, with his accustomed gravity, Monsieur turned his eyes, in a certain manner, upon the people of his suite, so that all, pages, officers, and equerries, quitted the service, knives and goblets, and made towards the second chamber door a retreat as rapid as it was disorderly.

This little army had dispersed in two files when Raoul de Bragelonne, preceded by M. de Saint-Remy, entered the refectory.

The short interval of solitude which this retreat had left him, permitted Monsieur the time to assume a diplomatic countenance. He did not turn round, but waited till the maitre d'hotel should bring the messenger face to face with him.

Raoul stopped even with the lower end of the table, so as to be exactly between Monsieur and Madame. From this place he made a profound bow to Monsieur, and a very humble one to Madame; then, drawing himself up into military pose, he waited for Monsieur to address him.

On his part the prince waited till the doors were hermetically closed; he would not turn round to ascertain the fact, as that would have been derogatory to his dignity, but he listened with all his ears for the noise of the lock, which would promise him at least an appearance of secrecy.

The doors being closed, Monsieur raised his eyes towards the vicomte, and said, "It appears that you come from Paris, monsieur?"

"This minute, monseigneur."

"How is the king?"

"His majesty is in perfect health, monseigneur."

"And my sister-in-law?"

"Her majesty the queen-mother still suffers from the complaint in her chest, but for the last month she has been rather better."

"Somebody told me you came on the part of M. le Prince. They must have been mistaken, surely?"

"No, monseigneur; M. le Prince has charged me to convey this letter to your royal highness, and I am to wait for an answer to it."

Raoul had been a little annoyed by this cold and cautious reception, and his voice insensibly sank to a low key.

The prince forgot that he was the cause of this apparent mystery, and his fears returned.

He received the letter from the Prince de Conde with a haggard look, unsealed it as he would have unsealed a suspicious packet, and in order to read it so that no one should remark the effects of it upon his countenance, he turned round.

Madame followed, with an anxiety almost equal to that of the prince, every maneuver of her august husband.

Raoul, impassible, and a little disengaged by the attention of his hosts, looked from his place through the open window at the gardens and the statues which peopled them.

"Well!" cried Monsieur, all at once, with a cheerful smile; "here is an agreeable surprise, and a charming letter from M. le Prince. Look, Madame!"

The table was too large to allow the arm of the prince to reach the hand of Madame; Raoul sprang forward to be their intermediary, and did it with so good a grace as to procure a flattering acknowledgement from the princess.

"You know the contents of this letter, no doubt?" said Gaston to Raoul.

"Yes, monseigneur; M. le Prince at first gave me the message verbally, but upon reflection his highness took up his pen."

"It is beautiful writing," said Madame, "but I cannot read it."

"Will you read it to Madame, M. de Bragelonne?" said the duke.

"Yes; read it, if you please, monsieur."

Raoul began to read, Monsieur giving again all his attention. The letter was conceived in these terms:

"MONSEIGNEUR—The king is about to set out for the frontiers. You are aware the marriage of his majesty is concluded upon. The king has done me the honor to appoint me his marechal-des-logis for this journey, and as I knew with what joy his majesty would pass a day at Blois, I venture to ask your royal highness's permission to mark the house you inhabit as our quarters. If, however, the suddenness of this request should create to your royal highness any embarrassment, I entreat you to say so by the messenger I send, a gentleman of my suite, M. le Vicomte de Bragelonne. My itinerary will depend on your royal highness's determination, and instead of passing through Blois, we shall come through Vendome or Romorantin. I venture to hope that your royal highness will be pleased with my arrangement, it being the expression of my boundless desire to make myself agreeable to you."

"Nothing can be more gracious toward us," said Madame, who had more than once consulted the looks of her husband during the reading of the letter. "The king here!" exclaimed she, in a rather louder tone than would have been necessary to preserve secrecy.

"Monsieur," said his royal highness in his turn, "you will offer my thanks to M. de Conde, and express to him my gratitude for the honor he has done me." Raoul bowed.

"On what day will his majesty arrive?" continued the prince.

"The king, monseigneur, will in all probability arrive this evening."

"But how, then, could he have known my reply if it had been in the negative?"

"I was desired, monseigneur, to return in all haste to Beaugency, to give counter-orders to the courier, who was himself to go back immediately with counter-orders to M. le Prince."

"His majesty is at Orleans, then?"

"Much nearer, monseigneur; his majesty must by this time have arrived at Meung."

"Does the court accompany him?"

"Yes, monseigneur."

"A propos, I forgot to ask you after M. le Cardinal."

"His eminence appears to enjoy good health, monseigneur."

"His nieces accompany him, no doubt?"

"No, monseigneur; his eminence has ordered the Mesdemoiselles de Mancini to set out for Brouage. They will follow the left bank of the Loire, while the court will come by the right."

"What! Mademoiselle Mary de Mancini quit the court in that manner?" asked Monsieur, his reserve beginning to diminish.

"Mademoiselle Mary de Mancini in particular," replied Raoul discreetly.

A fugitive smile, an imperceptible vestige of his ancient spirit of intrigue, shot across the pale face of the prince.

"Thanks, M. de Bragelonne," then said Monsieur. "You would, perhaps, not be willing to carry M. le Prince the commission with which I would charge you, and that is, that his messenger has been very agreeable to me; but I will tell him so myself."

Raoul bowed his thanks to Monsieur for the honor he had done him.

Monsieur made a sign to Madame, who struck a bell which was placed at her right hand; M. de Saint-Remy entered, and the room was soon filled with people.

"Messieurs," said the prince, "his majesty is about to pay me the honor of passing a day at Blois; I depend on the king, my nephew, not having to repent of the favor he does my house."

"Vive le Roi!" cried all the officers of the household with frantic enthusiasm, and M. de Saint-Remy louder than the rest.

Gaston hung down his head with evident chagrin. He had all his life been obliged to hear, or rather to undergo, this cry of "Vive le Roi!" which passed over him. For a long time, being unaccustomed to hear it, his ear had had rest, and now a younger, more vivacious, and more brilliant royalty rose up before him, like a new and more painful provocation.

Madame perfectly understood the sufferings of that timid, gloomy heart; she rose from the table, Monsieur imitated her mechanically, and all the domestics, with a buzzing like that of several bee-hives, surrounded Raoul for the purpose of questioning him.

Madame saw this movement, and called M. de Saint-Remy.

"This is not the time for gossiping, but working," said she, with the tone of an angry housekeeper.

A. de Saint-Remy hastened to break the circle formed by the officers round Raoul, so that the latter was able to gain the ante-chamber.

"Care will be taken of that gentleman, I hope," added Madame, addressing M. de Saint-Remy.

The worthy man immediately hastened after Raoul. "Madame desires refreshments to be offered to you," said he; "and there is, besides, a lodging for you in the castle."

"Thanks, M. de Saint-Remy," replied Raoul; "but you know how anxious I must be to pay my duty to M. le Comte, my father."

"That is true, that is true, Monsieur Raoul; present him, at the same time, my humble respects, if you please."

Raoul thus once more got rid of the old gentleman, and pursued his way. As he was passing under the porch, leading his horse by the bridle, a soft voice called him from the depths of an obscure path.

"Monsieur Raoul!" said the voice.

The young man turned round, surprised, and saw a dark complexioned girl, who, with a finger on her lip, held out her other hand to him. This young lady was an utter stranger.

Chapter III.
The Interview.

RAOUL made one step towards the girl who thus called him.

"But my horse, madame?" said he.

"Oh! you are terribly embarrassed! Go yonder way—there is a shed in the outer court: fasten your horse, and return quickly!"

"I obey, madame."

Raoul was not four minutes in performing what he had been directed to do; he returned to the little door, where, in the gloom, he found his mysterious conductress waiting for him, on the first steps of a winding staircase.

"Are you brave enough to follow me, monsieur knight errant?" asked the girl, laughing at the momentary hesitation Raoul had manifested.

The latter replied by springing up the dark staircase after her. They thus climbed up three stories, he behind her, touching with his hands, when he felt for the banister, a silk dress which rubbed against each side of the staircase. At every false step made by Raoul, his conductress cried, "Hush!" and held out to him a soft perfumed hand.

"One would mount thus to the belfry of the castle without being conscious of fatigue," said Raoul.

"All of which means, monsieur, that you are very much perplexed, very tired, and very uneasy. But be of good cheer, monsieur; here we are, at our destination."

The girl threw open a door, which immediately, without any transition, filled with a flood of light the landing of the staircase, at the top of which Raoul appeared, holding fast by the balustrade.

The girl continued to walk on—he followed her; she entered a chamber—he did the same.

As soon as he was fairly in the net he heard a loud cry, and, turning round, saw at two paces from him, with her hands clasped and her eyes closed, that beautiful fair girl with blue eyes and white shoulders, who, recognizing him, called him Raoul.

He saw her, and divined at once so much love and so much joy in the expression of her countenance, the he sank on his knees in the middle of the chamber, murmuring, on his part, the name of Louise.

"Ah! Montalais!—Montalais!" she sighed, "it is very wicked to deceive me so."

"Who, I? I have deceived you?"

"Yes; you told me you would go down to inquire the news, and you have brought up monsieur!"

"Well, I was obliged to do so—how else could he have received the letter you wrote him?" And she pointed with her finger to the letter which was still upon the table.

Raoul made a step to take it; Louise, more rapid, although she had sprung forward with a sufficiently remarkable physical hesitation, reached out her hand to stop him. Raoul came in contact with that trembling hand, took it within his own, and carried it so respectfully to his lips, that he might have been said to have deposited a sigh upon it rather than a kiss.

In the meantime, Mademoiselle de Montalais had taken the letter, folded it carefully, as women do, in three folds, and slipped it into her bosom.

"Don't be afraid, Louise," said she; "monsieur will no more venture to take it hence than the defunct king Louis XIII. ventured to take billets from the corsage of Mademoiselle de Hautefort."

Raoul blushed at seeing the smile of the two girls; and he did not remark that the hand of Louise remained in his.

"There!" said Montalais, "you have pardoned me, Louise, for having brought monsieur to you; and you, monsieur, bear me no malice for having followed me to see mademoiselle. Now, then, peace being made, let us chat like old friends. Present me, Louise, to M. de Bragelonne."

"Monsieur le Vicomte," said Louise, with her quiet grace and ingenuous smile, "I have the honor to present to you Mademoiselle Aure de Montalais, maid of honor to her royal highness MADAME, and moreover my friend—my excellent friend."

Raoul bowed ceremoniously.

"And me, Louise," said he—"will you not present me also to mademoiselle?"

"Oh, she knows you—she knows all!"

This unguarded expression made Montalais laugh and Raoul sigh with happiness, for he interpreted it thus: "She knows all our love."

"The ceremonies being over, Monsieur le Vicomte," said Montalais, "take a chair, and tell us quickly the news you bring flying thus."

"Mademoiselle, it is no longer a secret; the king, on his way to Poitiers, will stop at Blois, to visit his royal highness."

"The king here!" exclaimed Montalais, clapping her hands. "What! are we going to see the court? Only think, Louise—the real court from Paris! Oh, good heavens! But when will this happen, monsieur?"

"Perhaps this evening, mademoiselle; at latest, to-morrow."

Montalais lifted her shoulders in a sigh of vexation.

"No time to get ready! No time to prepare a single dress! We are as far behind the fashions as the Poles. We shall look like portraits from the time of Henry IV. Ah, monsieur! this is sad news you bring us!"

"But, mesdemoiselles, you will be still beautiful!"

"That's no news! Yes, we shall always be beautiful, because nature has made us passable; but we shall be ridiculous, because the fashion will have forgotten us. Alas! ridiculous! I shall be thought ridiculous—I!"

"And by whom?" said Louise, innocently.

"By whom? You are a strange girl, my dear. Is that a question to put to me? I mean everybody; I mean the courtiers, the nobles; I mean the king."

"Pardon me, my good friend; but as here every one is accustomed to see us as we are—"

"Granted; but that is about to change, and we shall be ridiculous, even for Blois; for close to us will be seen the fashions from Paris, and they will perceive that we are in the fashion of Blois! It is enough to make one despair!"

"Console yourself, mademoiselle."

"Well, so let it be! After all, so much the worse for those who do not find me to their taste!" said Montalais, philosophically.

"They would be very difficult to please," replied Raoul, faithful to his regular system of gallantry.

"Thank you, Monsieur le Vicomte. We were saying, then, that the king is coming to Blois?"

"With all the court."

"Mesdemoiselles de Mancini, will they be with them?"

"No, certainly not."

"But as the king, it is said, cannot do without Mademoiselle Mary?"

"Mademoiselle, the king must do without her. M. le Cardinal will have it so. He has exiled his nieces to Brouage."

"He!—the hypocrite!"

"Hush!" said Louise, pressing a finger on her friend's rosy lips.

"Bah! nobody can hear me. I say that old Mazarino Mazarini is a hypocrite, who burns impatiently to make his niece Queen of France."

"That cannot be, mademoiselle, since M. le Cardinal, on the contrary, had brought about the marriage of his majesty with the Infanta Maria Theresa."

Montalais looked Raoul full in the face, and said, "And do you Parisians believe in these tales? Well! we are a little more knowing than you, at Blois."

"Mademoiselle, if the king goes beyond Poitiers and sets out for Spain; if the articles of the marriage contract are agreed upon by Don Luis de Haro and his eminence, you must plainly perceive that it is not child's play."

"All very fine! but the king is king, I suppose?"

"No doubt, mademoiselle; but the cardinal is the cardinal."

"The king is not a man, then! And he does not love Mary Mancini?"

"He adores her."

"Well, he will marry her then. We shall have war with Spain. M. Mazarin will spend a few of the millions he has put away; our gentlemen will perform prodigies of valor in their encounters with the proud Castilians, and many of them will return crowned with laurels, to be recrowned by us with myrtles. Now, that is my view of politics."

"Montalais, you are wild!" said Louise, "and every exaggeration attracts you as light does a moth."

"Louise, you are so extremely reasonable, that you will never know how to love."

"Oh!" said Louise, in a tone of tender reproach, "don't you see, Montalais? The queen-mother desires to marry her son to the Infanta; would you wish him to disobey his mother? Is it for a royal heart like his to set such a bad example? When parents forbid love, love must be banished."

And Louise sighed: Raoul cast down his eyes, with an expression of constraint. Montalais, on her part, laughed aloud.

"Well, I have no parents!" said she.

"You are acquainted, without doubt, with the state of health of M. le Comte de la Fere?" said Louise, after breathing that sigh which had revealed so many griefs in its eloquent utterance.

"No, mademoiselle," replied Raoul, "I have not let paid my respects to my father; I was going to his house when Mademoiselle de Montalais so kindly stopped me. I hope the comte is well. You have heard nothing to the contrary, have you?"

"No, M. Raoul—nothing, thank God!"

Here, for several instants, ensued a silence, during which two spirits, which followed the same idea, communicated perfectly, without even the assistance of a single glance.

"Oh, heavens!" exclaimed Montalais in a fright; "there is somebody coming up."

"Who can it be?" said Louise, rising in great agitation.

"Mesdemoiselles, I inconvenience you very much. I have, without doubt, been very indiscreet," stammered Raoul, very ill at ease.

"It is a heavy step," said Louise.

"Ah! if it is only M. Malicorne," added Montalais, "do not disturb yourselves."

Louise and Raoul looked at each other to inquire who M. Malicorne could be.

"There is no occasion to mind him," continued Montalais; "he is not jealous."

"But, mademoiselle—" said Raoul.

"Yes, I understand. Well, he is discreet as I am."

"Good heavens!" cried Louise, who had applied her ear to the door, which had been left ajar; "it is my mother's step!"

"Madame de Saint-Remy! Where shall I hide myself?" exclaimed Raoul, catching at the dress of Montalais, who looked quite bewildered.

"Yes," said she; "yes, I know the clicking of those pattens! It is our excellent mother. M. le Vicomte, what a pity it is the window looks upon a stone pavement, and that fifty paces below it."

Raoul glanced at the balcony in despair. Louise seized his arm and held it tight.

"Oh, how silly I am!" said Montalais; "have I not the robe-of-ceremony closet? It looks as if it were made on purpose."

It was quite time to act; Madame de Saint-Remy was coming up at a quicker pace than usual. She gained the landing at the moment when Montalais, as in all scenes of surprises, shut the closet by leaning with her back against the door.

"Ah!" cried Madame de Saint-Remy, "you are here, are you, Louise?"

"Yes, madame," replied she, more pale than if she had committed a great crime.

"Well, well!"

"Pray be seated, madame," said Montalais, offering her a chair, which she placed so that the back was towards the closet.

"Thank you, Mademoiselle Aure—thank you. Come, my child, be quick."

"Where do you wish me to go, madame?"

"Why, home, to be sure; have you not to prepare your toilette?"

"What did you say?" cried Montalais, hastening to affect surprise, so fearful was she that Louise would in some way commit herself.

"You don't know the news, then?" said Madame de Saint-Remy.

"What news, madame, is it possible for two girls to learn up in this dove-cote?"

"What! have you seen nobody?"

"Madame, you talk in enigmas, and you torment us at a slow fire!" cried Montalais, who, terrified at seeing Louise become paler and paler, did not know to what saint to put up her vows.

At length she caught an eloquent look of her companion's, one of those looks which would convey intelligence to a brick wall. Louise directed her attention to a hat—Raoul's unlucky hat, which was set out in all its feathery splendor upon the table.

Montalais sprang towards it, and, seizing it with her left hand, passed it behind her into the right, concealing it as she was speaking.

"Well," said Madame de Saint-Remy, "a courier has arrived, announcing the approach of the king. There, mesdemoiselles; there is something to make you put on your best looks."

"Quick, quick!" cried Montalais. "Follow Madame your mother, Louise; and leave me to get ready my dress of ceremony."

Louise arose; her mother took her by the hand, and led her out on to the landing.

"Come along," said she; then adding in a low voice, "When I forbid you to come the apartment of Montalais, why do you do so?"

"Madame, she is my friend. Besides, I had but just come."

"Did you see nobody concealed while you were there?"

"Madame!"

"I saw a man's hat, I tell you—the hat of that fellow, that good-for-nothing!"

"Madame!" repeated Louise.

"Of that do-nothing Malicorne! A maid of honor to have such company—fie! fie!" and their voices were lost in the depths of the narrow staircase.

Montalais had not missed a word of this conversation, which echo conveyed to her as if through a tunnel. She shrugged her shoulders on seeing Raoul, who had listened likewise, issue from the closet.

"Poor Montalais!" said she, "the victim of friendship! Poor Malicorne, the victim of love!"

She stopped on viewing the tragic-comic face of Raoul, who was vexed at having, in one day, surprised so many secrets.

"Oh, mademoiselle!" said he; "how can we repay your kindness?"

"Oh, we will balance accounts some day," said she. "For the present, begone, M. de Bragelonne, for Madame de Saint-Remy is not over indulgent; and any indiscretion on her part might bring hither a domiciliary visit, which would be disagreeable to all parties."

"But Louise—how shall I know—"

"Begone! begone! King Louis XI. knew very well what he was about when he invented the post."

"Alas!" sighed Raoul.

"And am I not here—I, who am worth all the posts in the kingdom? Quick, I say, to horse! so that if Madame de Saint-Remy should return for the purpose of preaching me a lesson on morality, she may not find you here."

"She would tell my father, would she not?" murmured Raoul.

"And you would be scolded. Ah, vicomte, it is very plain you come from court; you are as timid as the king. Peste! at Blois we contrive better than that, to do without papa's consent. Ask Malicorne else!"

And at these words the girl pushed Raoul out of the room by the shoulders. He glided swiftly down to the porch, regained his horse, mounted, and set off as if he had had Monsieur's guards at his heels.

Chapter IV.
Father and Son.

RAOUL followed the well-known road, so dear to his memory, which led from Blois to the residence of the Comte de la Fere.

The reader will dispense with a second description of that habitation: he, perhaps, has been with us there before, and knows it. Only, since our last journey thither, the walls had taken on a grayer tint, and the brick-work assumed a more harmonious copper tone; the trees had grown, and many that then only stretched their slender branches along the tops of the hedges, now, bushy, strong, and luxuriant, cast around, beneath boughs swollen with sap, great shadows of blossoms or fruit for the benefit of the traveler.

Raoul perceived, from a distance, the two little turrets, the dove-cote in the elms, and the flights of pigeons, which wheeled incessantly around that brick cone, seemingly without power to quit it, like the sweet memories which hover round a spirit at peace.

As he approached, he heard the noise of the pulleys which grated under the weight of the heavy pails; he also fancied he heard the melancholy moaning of the water which falls back again into the wells—a sad, funereal, solemn sound, which strikes the ear of the child and the poet—both dreamers—which the English call splash; Arabian poets gasgachau; and which we Frenchmen, who would be poets, can only translate by a paraphrase—the noise of water falling into water.

It was more than a year since Raoul had been to visit his father. He had passed the whole time in the household of M. le Prince. In fact, after all the commotions of the Fronde, of the early period of which we formerly attempted to give a sketch, Louis de Conde had made a public, solemn and frank reconciliation with the court. During all the time that the rupture between the king and the prince had lasted, the prince, who had long entertained a great regard for Bragelonne, had in vain offered him advantages of the most dazzling kind for a young man. The Comte de la Fere, still faithful to his principles of loyalty, and royalty, one day developed before his son in the vaults of Saint Denis,—the Comte de la Fere, in the name of his son, had always declined them. Moreover, instead of following M. de Conde in his rebellion, the vicomte had followed M. de Turenne, fighting for the king. Then when M. de Turenne, in his turn, had appeared to abandon the royal cause, he had quitted M. de Turenne, as he had quitted M. de Conde. It resulted from this invariable line of conduct, that, as Conde and Turenne had never been conquerors of each other but under the standard of the king, Raoul, however young, had ten victories inscribed on his list of services, and not one defeat from which his bravery or conscience had to suffer.

Raoul, therefore, had, in compliance with the wish of his father, served obstinately and passively the fortunes of Louis XIV., in spite of the tergiversations which were endemic, and, it might be said, inevitable, at that period.

A. de Conde; on being restored to favor, had at once availed himself of all the privileges of the amnesty to ask for many things back again which had been granted to him before, and among others, Raoul. M. de la Fere, with his invariable good sense, had immediately sent him again to the prince.

A year, then, had passed away since the separation of the father and son; a few letters had softened, but not removed, the pain of absence. We have seen that Raoul had left at Blois another love in addition to filial love. But let us do him this justice—if it had not been for chance and Mademoiselle de Montalais, two great temptations, Raoul, after delivering his message, would have galloped off towards his father's house, turning his head round, perhaps, but without stopping for a single instant, even if Louise had held out her arms to him.

So the first part of the journey was given by Raoul to regretting the past which he had been forced to quit so quickly, that is to say, his lady-love; and the other part to the friend he was about to join, so much too slowly for his wishes.

Raoul found the garden-gate open, and rode straight in, without regarding the long arms, raised in anger, of an old man dressed in a jacket of violet-colored wool, and a large cap of faded velvet.

The old man, who was weeding with his hands a bed of dwarf roses and arguerites, was indignant at seeing a horse thus traversing his sanded and nicely-raked walks. He even ventured a vigorous "Humph!" which made the cavalier turn round. Then there was a change of scene; for no sooner had he caught sight of Raoul's face, than the old man sprang up and set off in the direction of the house, amidst interrupted growlings, which appeared to be paroxysms of wild delight.

When arrived at the stables, Raoul gave his horse to a little lackey, and sprang up the perron with an ardor that would have delighted the heart of his father.

He crossed the ante-chamber, the dining-room, and the salon, without meeting any one; at length, on reaching the door of M. de la Fere's apartment, he rapped impatiently, and entered almost without waiting for the word "Enter!" which was vouchsafed him by a voice at once sweet and serious. The comte was seated at a table covered with papers and books; he was still the noble, handsome gentleman of former days, but time had given to this nobleness and beauty a more solemn and distinct character. A brow white and void of wrinkles, beneath his long hair, now more white than black; an eye piercing and mild, under the lids of a young man; his mustache, fine but slightly grizzled, waved over lips of a pure and delicate model, as if they had never been curled by mortal passions; a form straight and supple; an irreproachable but thin hand—this was what remained of the illustrious gentleman whom so many illustrious mouths had praised under the name of Athos. He was engaged in correcting the pages of a manuscript book, entirely filled by his own hand.

Raoul seized his father by the shoulders, by the neck, as he could, and embraced him so tenderly and so rapidly, that the comte had neither strength nor time to disengage himself, or to overcome his paternal emotions.

"What! you here, Raoul—you! Is it possible?" said he.

"Oh, monsieur, monsieur, what joy to see you once again!"

"But you don't answer me, vicomte. Have you leave of absence, or has some misfortune happened at Paris?"

"Thank God, monsieur," replied Raoul, calming himself by degrees, "nothing has happened but what is fortunate. The king is going to be married, as I had the honor of informing you in my last letter, and, on his way to Spain, he will pass through Blois."

"To pay a visit to Monsieur?"

"Yes, monsieur le comte. So, fearing to find him unprepared, or wishing to be particularly polite to him, monsieur le prince sent me forward to have the lodgings ready."

"You have seen Monsieur?" asked the comte, eagerly.

"I have had that honor."

"At the castle?"

"Yes, monsieur," replied Raoul, casting down his eyes, because, no doubt, he had felt there was something more than curiosity in the comte's inquiries.

"Ah, indeed, vicomte? Accept my compliments thereupon."

Raoul bowed.

"But you have seen some one else at Blois?"

"Monsieur, I saw her royal highness, Madame."

"That's very well: but it is not Madame that I mean."

Raoul colored deeply, but made no reply.

"You do not appear to understand me, monsieur le vicomte," persisted M. de la Fere, without accenting his words more strongly, but with a rather severer look.

"I understand you quite plainly, monsieur," replied Raoul, "and if I hesitate a little in my reply, you are well assured I am not seeking for a falsehood."

"No, you cannot tell a lie; and that makes me so astonished you should be so long in saying yes or no."

"I cannot answer you without understanding you very well; and if I have understood you, you will take my first words in ill part. You will displeased, no doubt, monsieur le comte, because I have seen—"

"Mademoiselle de la Valliere—have you not?"

"It was of her you meant to speak, I know very well, monsieur," said Raoul, with inexpressible sweetness.

"And I asked you if you have seen her."

"Monsieur, I was ignorant, when I entered the castle, that Mademoiselle de la Valliere was there; it was only on my return, after I had performed my mission, that chance brought us together. I have had the honor of paying my respects to her."

"But what do you call the chance that led you into the presence of Mademoiselle de la Valliere?"

"Mademoiselle de Montalais, monsieur."

"And who is Mademoiselle de Montalais?"

"A young lady I did not know before, whom I had never seen. She is maid of honor to Madame."

"Monsieur le vicomte, I will push my interrogatory no further, and reproach myself with having carried it so far. I had desired you to avoid Mademoiselle de la Valliere, and not to see her without my permission. Oh, I am quite sure you have told me the truth, and that you took no measures to approach her. Chance has done me this injury; I do not accuse you of it. I will be content, then, with what I formerly said to you concerning this young lady. I do not reproach her with anything—God is my witness! only it is not my intention or wish that you should frequent her place of residence. I beg you once more, my dear Raoul, to understand that."

It was plain the limpid eyes of Raoul were troubled at this speech.

"Now, my friend," said the comte, with his soft smile, and in his customary tone, "let us talk of other matters. You are returning, perhaps, to your duty?"

"No, monsieur, I have no duty for to-day, except the pleasure of remaining with you. The prince kindly appointed me no other: which was so much in accord with my wish."

"Is the king well?"

"Perfectly."

"And monsieur le prince also?"

"As usual, monsieur."

The comte forgot to inquire after Mazarin; that was an old habit.

"Well, Raoul, since you are entirely mine, I will give up my whole day to you. Embrace me—again, again! You are at home, vicomte! Ah, there is our old Grimaud! Come in, Grimaud: monsieur le vicomte is desirous of embracing you likewise."

The good old man did not require to be twice told; he rushed in with open arms, Raoul meeting him half-way.

"Now, if you please, we will go into the garden, Raoul. I will show you the new lodging I have had prepared for you during your leave of absence; and whilst examining the last winter's plantations, and two saddle-horses I have just acquired, you will give me all the news of our friends in Paris."

The comte closed his manuscript, took the young man's arm, and went out into the gardens with him.

Grimaud looked at Raoul with a melancholy air as the young man passed out; observing that his head nearly touched the traverse of the doorway, stroking his white royale, he slowly murmured:—"How he has grown!"

Chapter V.
In which Something will be said of Cropoli.

WHILST the Comte de la Fere with Raoul visits the new buildings he has erected, and the new horses he has bought, with the reader's permission we will lead him back to the city of Blois, and make him a witness of the unaccustomed activity which pervades that city.

It was in the hotels that the surprise of the news brought by Raoul was most sensibly felt.

In fact, the king and the court at Blois, that is to say, a hundred horsemen, ten carriages, two hundred horses, as many lackeys as masters—where was this crowd to be housed? Where were to be lodged all the gentry of the neighborhood, who would gather in two or three hours after the news had enlarged the circle of its report, like the increasing circumferences produced by a stone thrown into a placid lake?

Blois, as peaceful in the morning, as we have seen, as the calmest lake in the world, at the announcement of the royal arrival, was suddenly filled with the tumult and buzzing of a swarm of bees.

All the servants of the castle, under the inspection of the officers, were sent into the city in quest of provisions, and ten horsemen were dispatched to the preserves of Chambord to seek for game, to the fisheries of Beuvron for fish, and to the gardens of Cheverny for fruits and flowers.

Precious tapestries, and lusters with great gilt chains, were drawn from the cupboards; an army of the poor were engaged in sweeping the courts and washing the stone fronts, whilst their wives went in droves to the meadows beyond the Loire, to gather green boughs and field-flowers. The whole city, not to be behind in this luxury of cleanliness, assumed its best toilette with the help of brushes, brooms, and water. The gutters of the upper town, swollen by these continued ablutions, became rivers at the bottom of the city, and the pavement, generally very muddy, it must be allowed, took a clean face, and absolutely shone in the friendly rays of the sun.

Next the music was to be provided; drawers were emptied; the shop-keepers did a glorious trade in wax, ribbons, and sword-knots; housekeepers laid in stores of bread, meat, and spices. Already numbers of the citizens whose houses were furnished as if for a siege, having nothing more to do, donned their festive clothes, and directed their course towards the city gate, in order to be the first to signal or see the cortege. They knew very well that the king would not arrive before night, perhaps not before the next morning. Yet what is expectation but a kind of folly, and what is that folly but an excess of hope?

In the lower city, at scarcely a hundred paces from the Castle of the States, between the mall and the castle, in a sufficiently handsome street, then called the Rue Vieille, and which must, in fact, have been very old, stood a venerable edifice, with pointed gables, of squat but large dimensions, ornamented with three windows looking into the street on the first floor, with two in the second, and with a little oeil de boeuf in the third.

On the sides of this triangle had recently been constructed a parallelogram of considerable size, which encroached upon the street remorselessly, according to the familiar uses of the building of that period. The street was narrowed by a quarter by it, but then the house was enlarged by a half; and was not that a sufficient compensation?

Tradition said that this house with the pointed gables was inhabited, in the time of Henry III., by a councilor of state whom Queen Catherine came, some say to visit, and others to strangle. However that may be, the good lady must have stepped with a circumspect foot over the threshold of this building.

After the councilor had died—whether by strangulation or naturally is of no consequence—the house had been sold, then abandoned, and lastly isolated from the other houses of the street. Towards the middle of the reign of Louis XIII. only, an Italian named Cropoli, escaped from the kitchens of the Marechal d'Ancre, came and took possession of this house. There he established a little hostelry, in which was fabricated a macaroni so delicious that people came from miles round to fetch it or eat it.

So famous had the house become for it, that when Mary de Medici was a prisoner, as we know, in the castle of Blois, she once sent for some.

It was precisely on the day she had escaped by the famous window. The dish of macaroni was left upon the table, only just tasted by the royal mouth.

This double favor, of a strangulation and a macaroni, conferred upon the triangular house, gave poor Cropoli a fancy to grace his hostelry with a pompous title. But his quality of an Italian was no recommendation in these times, and his small, well-concealed fortune forbade attracting too much attention.

When he found himself about to die, which happened in 1643, just after the death of Louis XIII., he called to him his son, a young cook of great promise, and with tears in his eyes, he recommended him to preserve carefully the secret of the macaroni, to Frenchify his name, and at length, when the political horizon should be cleared from the clouds which obscured it—this was practiced then as in our day, to order of the nearest smith a handsome sign, upon which a famous painter, whom he named, should design two queens' portraits, with these words as a legend: "TO THE MEDICI."

The worthy Cropoli, after these recommendations, had only sufficient time to point out to his young successor a chimney, under the slab of which he had hidden a thousand ten-franc pieces, and then expired.

Cropoli the younger, like a man of good heart, supported the loss with resignation, and the gain without insolence. He began by accustoming the public to sound the final i of his name so little, that by the aid of general complaisance, he was soon called nothing but M. Cropole, which is quite a French name. He then married, having had in his eye a little French girl, from whose parents he extorted a reasonable dowry by showing them what there was beneath the slab of the chimney.

These two points accomplished, he went in search of the painter who was to paint the sign; and he was soon found. He was an old Italian, a rival of the Raphaels and the Caracci, but an unfortunate rival. He said he was of the Venetian school, doubtless from his fondness for color. His works, of which he had never sold one, attracted the eye at a distance of a hundred paces; but they so formidably displeased the citizens, that he had finished by painting no more.

He boasted of having painted a bath-room for Madame la Marechale d'Ancre, and mourned over this chamber having been burnt at the time of the marechal's disaster.

Cropoli, in his character of a compatriot, was indulgent towards Pittrino, which was the name of the artist. Perhaps he had seen the famous pictures of the bath-room. Be this as it may, he held in such esteem, we may say in such friendship, the famous Pittrino, that he took him in his own house.

Pittrino, grateful, and fed with macaroni, set about propagating the reputation of this national dish, and from the time of its founder, he had rendered, with his indefatigable tongue, signal services to the house of Cropoli.

As he grew old he attached himself to the son as he had done to the father, and by degrees became a kind of over-looker of a house in which his remarkable integrity, his acknowledged sobriety, and a thousand other virtues useless to enumerate, gave him an eternal place by the fireside, with a right of inspection over the domestics. Besides this, it was he who tasted the macaroni, to maintain the pure flavor of the ancient tradition; and it must be allowed that he never permitted a grain of pepper too much, or an atom of parmesan too little. His joy was at its height on that day when called upon to share the secret of Cropoli the younger, and to paint the famous sign.

He was seen at once rummaging with ardor in an old box, in which he found some brushes, a little gnawed by the rats, but still passable; some linseed-oil in a bottle, and a palette which had formerly belonged to Bronzino, that dieu de la pittoure, as the ultramontane artist, in his ever young enthusiasm, always called him.

Pittrino was puffed up with all the joy of a rehabilitation.

He did as Raphael had done—he changed his style, and painted, in the fashion of Albani, two goddesses rather than two queens. These illustrious ladies appeared so lovely on the sign,—they presented to the astonished eyes such an assemblage of lilies and roses, the enchanting result of the changes of style in Pittrino—they assumed the poses of sirens so Anacreontically— that the principal echevin, when admitted to view this capital piece in the salle of Cropole, at once declared that these ladies were too handsome, of too animated a beauty, to figure as a sign in the eyes of passers-by.

To Pittrino he added, "His royal highness, Monsieur, who often comes into our city, will not be much pleased to see his illustrious mother so slightly clothed, and he will send you to the oubliettes of the state; for, remember, the heart of that glorious prince is not always tender. You must efface either the two sirens or the legend, without which I forbid the exhibition of the sign. I say this for your sake, Master Cropole, as well for yours, Signor Pittrino."

What answer could be made to this? It was necessary to thank the echevin for his kindness, which Cropole did. But Pittrino remained downcast and said he felt assured of what was about to happen.

The visitor was scarcely gone when Cropole, crossing his arms, said: "Well, master, what is to be done?"

"We must efface the legend," said Pittrino, in a melancholy tone. "I have some excellent ivory-black; it will be done in a moment, and we will replace the Medici by the nymphs or the sirens, whichever you prefer."

"No," said Cropole, "the will of my father must be carried out. My father considered—"

"He considered the figures of the most importance," said Pittrino.

"He thought most of the legend," said Cropole.

"The proof of the importance in which he held the figures," said Pittrino, "is that he desired they should be likenesses, and they are so."

"Yes; but if they had not been so, who would have recognized them without the legend? At the present day even, when the memory of the Blaisois begins to be faint with regard to these two celebrated persons, who would recognize Catherine and Mary without the words 'To the Medici'?"

"But the figures?" said Pittrino, in despair; for he felt that young Cropole was right. "I should not like to lose the fruit of my labor."

"And I should not wish you to be thrown into prison, and myself into the oubliettes."

"Let us efface 'Medici'," said Pittrino, supplicatingly.

"No," replied Cropole, firmly. "I have got an idea, a sublime idea—your picture shall appear, and my legend likewise. Does not 'Medici' mean doctor, or physician, in Italian?"

"Yes, in the plural."

"Well, then, you shall order another sign-frame of the smith; you shall paint six physicians, and write underneath 'Aux Medici' which makes a very pretty play upon words."

"Six physicians! impossible! And the composition?" cried Pittrino.

"That is your business—but so it shall be—I insist upon it—it must be so—my macaroni is burning."

This reasoning was peremptory—Pittrino obeyed. He composed the sign of six physicians, with the legend; the echevin applauded and authorized it.

The sign produced an extravagant success in the city, which proves that poetry has always been in the wrong, before citizens, as Pittrino said.

Cropole, to make amends to his painter-in-ordinary, hung up the nymphs of the preceding sign in his bedroom, which made Madame Cropole blush every time she looked at it, when she was undressing at night.

This is the way in which the pointed-gable house got a sign; and this is how the hostelry of the Medici, making a fortune, was found to be enlarged by a quarter, as we have described. And this is how there was at Blois a hostelry of that name, and had for a painter-in-ordinary Master Pittrino.

Chapter VI.
The Unknown.

THUS founded and recommended by its sign, the hostelry of Master Cropole held its way steadily on towards a solid prosperity.

It was not an immense fortune that Cropole had in perspective; but he might hope to double the thousand louis d'or left by his father, to make another thousand louis by the sale of his house and stock, and at length to live happily like a retired citizen.

Cropole was anxious for gain, and was half-crazy with joy at the news of the arrival of Louis XIV.

Himself, his wife, Pittrino, and two cooks, immediately laid hands upon all the inhabitants of the dove-cote, the poultry-yard, and the rabbit-hutches; so that as many lamentations and cries resounded in the yards of the hostelry of the Medici as were formerly heard in Rama.

Cropole had, at the time, but one single traveler in his house.

This was a man of scarcely thirty years of age, handsome, tall, austere, or rather melancholy, in all his gestures and looks.

He was dressed in black velvet with jet trimmings; a white collar, as plain as that of the severest Puritan, set off the whiteness of his youthful neck; a small dark-colored mustache scarcely covered his curled, disdainful lip.

He spoke to people looking them full in the face, without affectation, it is true, but without scruple; so that the brilliancy of his black eyes became so insupportable, that more than one look had sunk beneath his, like the weaker sword in a single combat.

At this time, in which men, all created equal by God, were divided, thanks to prejudices, into two distinct castes, the gentlemen and the commoner, as they are really divided into two races, the black and the white,—at this time, we say, he whose portrait we have just sketched could not fail of being taken for a gentleman, and of the best class. To ascertain this, there was no necessity to consult anything but his hands, long, slender, and white, of which every muscle, every vein, became apparent through the skin at the least movement, and eloquently spoke of good descent.

This gentleman, then, had arrived alone at Cropole's house. He had taken, without hesitation, without reflection even, the principal apartment which the hotelier had pointed out to him with a rapacious aim, very praiseworthy, some will say, very reprehensible will say others, if they admit that Cropole was a physiognomist, and judged people at first sight.

This apartment was that which composed the whole front of the ancient triangular house; a large salon, lighted by two windows on the first stage, a small chamber by the side of it, and another above it.

Now, from the time he had arrived, this gentleman had scarcely touched any repast that had been served up to him in his chamber. He had spoken but two words to the host, to warn him that a traveler of the name of Parry would arrive, and to desire that, when he did, he should be shown up to him immediately.

He afterwards preserved so profound a silence, that Cropole was almost offended, so much did he prefer people who were good company.

This gentleman had risen early the morning of the day on which this history begins, and had placed himself at the window of his salon, seated upon the ledge, and leaning upon the rail of the balcony, gazing sadly but persistently on both sides of the street, watching, no doubt, for the arrival of the traveler he had mentioned to the host.

In this way he had seen the little cortege of Monsieur return from hunting, then had again partaken of the profound tranquillity of the street, absorbed in his own expectations.

All at once the movement of the crowd going to the meadows, couriers setting out, washers of pavement, purveyors of the royal household, gabbling, scampering shop-boys, chariots in motion, hair-dressers on the run, and pages toiling along, this tumult and bustle had surprised him, but without losing any of that impassible and supreme majesty which gives to the eagle and the lion that serene and contemptuous glance amidst the hurrahs and shouts of hunters or the curious.

Soon the cries of the victims slaughtered in the poultry-yard, the hasty steps of Madame Cropole up that little wooden staircase, so narrow and so echoing; the bounding pace of Pittrino, who only that morning was smoking at the door with all the phlegm of a Dutchman; all this communicated something like surprise and agitation to the traveler.

As he was rising to make inquiries, the door of his chamber opened. The unknown concluded they were about to introduce the impatiently expected traveler, and made three precipitate steps to meet him.

But, instead of the person he expected, it was Master Cropole who appeared, and behind him, in the half-dark staircase, the pleasant face of Madame Cropole, rendered trivial by curiosity. She only gave one furtive glance at the handsome gentleman, and disappeared.

Cropole advanced, cap in hand, rather bent than bowing.

A gesture of the unknown interrogated him, without a word being pronounced.

"Monsieur," said Cropole, "I come to ask how—what ought I to say: your lordship, monsieur le comte, or monsieur le marquis?"

"Say monsieur, and speak quickly," replied the unknown, with that haughty accent which admits of neither discussion nor reply.

"I came, then, to inquire how monsieur had passed the night, and if monsieur intended to keep this apartment?"

"Yes."

"Monsieur, something has happened upon which we could not reckon."

"What?"

"His majesty Louis XIV. will enter our city to-day, and will remain here one day, perhaps two."

Great astonishment was painted on the countenance of the unknown.

"The King of France is coming to Blois?"

"He is on the road, monsieur."

"Then there is the stronger reason for my remaining," said the unknown.

"Very well; but will monsieur keep all the apartments?"

"I do not understand you. Why should I require less to-day than yesterday?"

"Because, monsieur, your lordship will permit me to say, yesterday I did not think proper, when you chose your lodging, to fix any price that might have made your lordship believe that I prejudged your resources; whilst to-day—"

The unknown colored; the idea at once struck him that he was supposed to be poor, and was being insulted.

"Whilst to-day," replied he, coldly, "you do not prejudge."

"Monsieur, I am a well-meaning man, thank God! and simple hotelier as I am, there is in me the blood of a gentleman. My father was a servant and officer of the late Marechal d'Ancre. God rest his soul!"

"I do not contest that point with you; I only wish to know, and that quickly, to what your questions tend?"

"You are too reasonable, monsieur, not to comprehend that our city is small, that the court is about to invade it, that the houses will be overflowing with inhabitants, and that lodgings will consequently obtain considerable prices."

Again the unknown colored. "Name your terms," said he.

"I name them with scruple, monsieur, because I seek an honest gain, and that I wish to carry on my business without being uncivil or extravagant in my demands. Now the room you occupy is considerable, and you are alone."

"That is my business."

"Oh! certainly. I do not mean to turn monsieur out."

The blood rushed to the temples of the unknown; he darted at poor Cropole, the descendant of one of the officers of the Marechal d'Ancre, a glance that would have crushed him down to beneath that famous chimney-slab, if Cropole had not been nailed to the spot by the question of his own proper interests.

"Do you desire me to go?" said he. "Explain yourself—but quickly."

"Monsieur, monsieur, you do not understand me. It is very critical—I know—that which I am doing. I express myself badly, or perhaps, as monsieur is a foreigner, which I perceive by his accent—"

In fact, the unknown spoke with that impetuosity which is the principal character of English accentuation, even among men who speak the French language with the greatest purity.

"As monsieur is a foreigner, I say, it is perhaps he who does not catch my exact meaning. I wish for monsieur to give up one or two of the apartments he occupies, which would diminish his expenses and ease my conscience. Indeed, it is hard to increase unreasonably the price of the chambers, when one has had the honor to let them at a reasonable price."

"How much does the hire amount to since yesterday?"

"Monsieur, to one louis, with refreshments and the charge for the horse."

"Very well; and that of to-day?"

"Ah! there is the difficulty. This is the day of the king's arrival; if the court comes to sleep here, the charge of the day is reckoned. From that it results that three chambers, at two louis each, make six louis. Two louis, monsieur, are not much; but six louis make a great deal."

The unknown, from red, as we have seen him, became very pale.

He drew from his pocket, with heroic bravery, a purse embroidered with a coat-of-arms, which he carefully concealed in the hollow of his hand. This purse was of a thinness, a flabbiness, a hollowness, which did not escape the eye of Cropole.

The unknown emptied the purse into his hand. It contained three double louis, which amounted to the six louis demanded by the host.

But it was seven that Cropole had required.

He looked, therefore, at the unknown, as much as to say, "And then?"

"There remains one louis, does there not, master hotelier?"

"Yes, monsieur, but—"

The unknown plunged his hand into the pocket of his haut-de-chausses, and emptied it. It contained a small pocket-book, a gold key, and some silver. With this change, he made up a louis.

"Thank you, monsieur," said Cropole. "It now only remains for me to ask whether monsieur intends to occupy his apartments to-morrow, in which case I will reserve them for him; whereas, if monsieur does not mean to do so, I will promise them to some of the king's people who are coming."

"That is but right," said the unknown, after a long silence; "but as I have no more money, as you have seen, and as I yet must retain the apartments, you must either sell this diamond in the city, or hold it in pledge."

Cropole looked at the diamond so long, that the unknown said, hastily:

"I prefer your selling it, monsieur; for it is worth three hundred pistoles. A Jew—are there any Jews in Blois?—would give you two hundred or a hundred and fifty for it—take whatever may be offered for it, if it be no more than the price of your lodging. Begone!"

"Oh! monsieur," replied Cropole, ashamed of the sudden inferiority which the unknown reflected upon him by this noble and disinterested confidence, as well as by the unalterable patience opposed to so many suspicions and evasions. "Oh, monsieur, I hope people are not so dishonest at Blois as you seem to think; and that the diamond, being worth what you say—"

The unknown here again darted at Cropole one of his withering glances.

"I really do not understand diamonds, monsieur, I assure you," cried he.

"But the jewelers do: ask them," said the unknown. "Now I believe our accounts are settled, are they not, monsieur l'hote?"

"Yes, monsieur, and to my profound regret; for I fear I have offended monsieur."

"Not at all!" replied the unknown, with ineffable majesty.

"Or have appeared to be extortionate with a noble traveler. Consider, monsieur, the peculiarity of the case."

"Say no more about it, I desire; and leave me to myself."

Cropole bowed profoundly, and left the room with a stupefied air, which announced that he had a good heart, and felt genuine remorse.

The unknown himself shut the door after him, and, when left alone, looked mournfully at the bottom of the purse, from which he had taken a small silken bag containing the diamond, his last resource.

He dwelt likewise upon the emptiness of his pockets, turned over the papers in his pocket-book, and convinced himself of the state of absolute destitution in which he was about to be plunged.

He raised his eyes towards heaven, with a sublime emotion of despairing calmness, brushed off with his hand some drops of sweat which trickled over his noble brow, and then cast down upon the earth a look which just before had been impressed with almost divine majesty.

That the storm had passed far from him, perhaps he had prayed in the bottom of his soul.

He drew near to the window, resumed his place in the balcony, and remained there, motionless, annihilated, dead, till the moment when, the heavens beginning to darken, the first flambeaux traversed the enlivened street, and gave the signal for illumination to all the windows of the city.

Chapter VII.
Parry.

WHILST the unknown was viewing these lights with interest, and lending an ear to the various noises, Master Cropole entered his apartment, followed by two attendants, who laid the cloth for his meal.

The stranger did not pay them the least attention; but Cropole approaching him respectfully, whispered, "Monsieur, the diamond has been valued."

"Ah!" said the traveler. "Well?"

"Well, monsieur, the jeweler of S. A. R. gives two hundred and eighty pistoles for it."

"Have you them?"

"I thought it best to take them, monsieur; nevertheless, I made it a condition of the bargain, that if monsieur wished to keep his diamond, it should be held till monsieur was again in funds."

"Oh, no, not at all: I told you to sell it."

"Then I have obeyed, or nearly so, since, without having definitely sold it, I have touched the money."

"Pay yourself," added the unknown.

"I will do so, monsieur, since you so positively require it."

A sad smile passed over the lips of the gentleman.

"Place the money on that trunk," said he, turning round and pointing to the piece of furniture.

Cropole deposited a tolerably large bag as directed, after having taken from it the amount of his reckoning.

"Now," said he, "I hope monsieur will not give me the pain of not taking any supper. Dinner has already been refused; this is affronting to the house of les Medici. Look, monsieur, the supper is on the table, and I venture to say that it is not a bad one."

The unknown asked for a glass of wine, broke off a morsel of bread, and did not stir from the window whilst he ate and drank.

Shortly after was heard a loud flourish of trumpets; cries arose in the distance, a confused buzzing filled the lower part of the city, and the first distinct sound that struck the ears of the stranger was the tramp of advancing horses.

"The king! the king!" repeated a noisy and eager crowd.

"The king!" cried Cropole, abandoning his guest and his ideas of delicacy, to satisfy his curiosity.

With Cropole were mingled, and jostled, on the staircase, Madame Cropole, Pittrino, and the waiters and scullions.

The cortege advanced slowly, lighted by a thousand flambeaux, in the streets and from the windows.

After a company of musketeers, a closely ranked troop of gentlemen, came the litter of monsieur le cardinal, drawn like a carriage by four black horses. The pages and people of the cardinal marched behind.

Next came the carriage of the queen-mother, with her maids of honor at the doors, her gentlemen on horseback at both sides.

The king then appeared, mounted upon a splendid horse of Saxon breed, with a flowing mane. The young prince exhibited, when bowing to some windows from which issued the most animated acclamations, a noble and handsome countenance, illuminated by the flambeaux of his pages.

By the side of the king, though a little in the rear, the Prince de Conde, M. Dangeau, and twenty other courtiers, followed by their people and their baggage, closed this veritably triumphant march. The pomp was of a military character.

Some of the courtiers—the elder ones, for instance—wore traveling dresses; but all the rest were clothed in warlike panoply. Many wore the gorget and buff coat of the times of Henry IV. and Louis XIII.

When the king passed before him, the unknown, who had leant forward over the balcony to obtain a better view, and who had concealed his face by leaning on his arm, felt his heart swell and overflow with a bitter jealousy.

The noise of the trumpets excited him—the popular acclamations deafened him: for a moment he allowed his reason to be absorbed in this flood of lights, tumult, and brilliant images.

"He is a king!" murmured he, in an accent of despair.

Then, before he had recovered from his sombre reverie, all the noise, all the splendor, had passed away. At the angle of the street there remained nothing beneath the stranger but a few hoarse, discordant voices, shouting at intervals "Vive le Roi!"

There remained likewise the six candles held by the inhabitants of the hostelry des Medici; that is to say, two for Cropole, two for Pittrino, and one for each scullion. Cropole never ceased repeating, "How good-looking the king is! How strongly he resembles his illustrious father!"

"A handsome likeness!" said Pittrino.

"And what a lofty carriage he has!" added Madame Cropole, already in promiscuous commentary with her neighbors of both sexes.

Cropole was feeding their gossip with his own personal remarks, without observing that an old man on foot, but leading a small Irish horse by the bridle, was endeavoring to penetrate the crowd of men and women which blocked up the entrance to the Medici. But at that moment the voice of the stranger was heard from the window.

"Make way, monsieur l'hotelier, to the entrance of your house!"

Cropole turned around, and, on seeing the old man, cleared a passage for him.

The window was instantly closed.

Pittrino pointed out the way to the newly-arrived guest, who entered without uttering a word.

The stranger waited for him on the landing; he opened his arms to the old man, and led him to a seat.

"Oh, no, no, my lord!" said he. "Sit down in your presence?—never!"

"Parry," cried the gentleman, "I beg you will; you come from England—you come so far. Ah! it is not for your age to undergo the fatigues my service requires. Rest yourself."

"I have my reply to give your lordship, in the first place."

"Parry, I conjure you to tell me nothing; for if your news had been good, you would not have begun in such a manner; you go about, which proves that the news is bad."

"My lord," said the old man, "do not hasten to alarm yourself; all is not lost, I hope. You must employ energy, but more particularly resignation."

"Parry," said the young man, "I have reached this place through a thousand snares and after a thousand difficulties; can you doubt my energy? I have meditated this journey ten years, in spite of all counsels and all obstacles—have you faith in my perseverance? I have this evening sold the last of my father's diamonds; for I had nothing wherewith to pay for my lodgings and my host was about to turn me out."

Parry made a gesture of indignation, to which the young man replied by a pressure of the hand and a smile.

"I have still two hundred and seventy-four pistoles left and I feel myself rich. I do not despair, Parry; have you faith in my resignation?"

The old man raised his trembling hands towards heaven.

"Let me know," said the stranger,—"disguise nothing from me—what has happened?"

"My recital will be short, my lord; but in the name of Heaven do not tremble so."

"It is impatience, Parry. Come, what did the general say to you?"

"At first the general would not receive me."

"He took you for a spy?"

"Yes, my lord; but I wrote him a letter."

"Well?"

"He read it, and received me, my lord."

"Did that letter thoroughly explain my position and my views?"

"Oh, yes!" said Parry, with a sad smile; "it painted your very thoughts faithfully."

"Well—then, Parry."

"Then the general sent me back the letter by an aide-de-camp, informing me that if I were found the next day within the circumscription of his command, he would have me arrested."

"Arrested!" murmured the young man. "What! arrest you, my most faithful servant?"

"Yes, my lord."

"And notwithstanding you had signed the name Parry?"

"To all my letters, my lord; and the aide-de-camp had known me at St. James's and at Whitehall, too," added the old man with a sigh.

The young man leaned forward, thoughtful and sad.

"Ay, that's what he did before his people," said he, endeavoring to cheat himself with hopes. "But, privately—between you and him—what did he do? Answer!"

"Alas! my lord, he sent to me four cavaliers, who gave me the horse with which you just now saw me come back. These cavaliers conducted me, in great haste, to the little port of Tenby, threw me, rather than embarked me, into a little fishing-boat, about to sail for Brittany, and here I am."

"Oh!" sighed the young man, clasping his neck convulsively with his hand, and with a sob. "Parry, is that all?—is that all?"

"Yes, my lord; that is all."

After this brief reply ensued a long interval of silence, broken only by the convulsive beating of the heel of the young man on the floor.

The old man endeavored to change the conversation; it was leading to thoughts much too sinister.

"My lord," said he, "what is the meaning of all the noise which preceded me? What are these people crying 'Vive le Roi!' for? What king do they mean? and what are all these lights for?"

"Ah! Parry," replied the young man ironically, "don't you know that this is the King of France visiting his good city of Blois? All these trumpets are his, all those gilded housings are his, all those gentlemen wear swords that are his. His mother precedes him in a carriage magnificently encrusted with silver and gold. Happy mother! His minister heaps up millions, and conducts him to a rich bride. Then all these people rejoice; they love their king, they hail him with their acclamations, and they cry, 'Vive le Roi! Vive le Roi!'"

"Well, well, my lord," said Parry, more uneasy at the turn the conversation had taken than at the other.

"You know," resumed the unknown, "that my mother and my sister, whilst all this is going on in honor of the King of France, have neither money nor bread; you know that I myself shall be poor and degraded within a fortnight, when all Europe will become acquainted with what you have told me. Parry, are there not examples in which a man of my condition should himself—"

"My lord, in the name of Heaven—"

"You are right, Parry; I am a coward, and if I do nothing for myself, what will God do? No, no; I have two arms, Parry, and I have a sword." And he struck his arm violently with his hand, and took down his sword, which hung against the wall.

"What are you going to do, my lord?"

"What am I going to do, Parry? What every one in my family does. My mother lives on public charity, my sister begs for my mother; I have, somewhere or other, brothers who equally beg for themselves; and I, the eldest, will go and do as all the rest do—I will go and ask charity!"

And with these words, which he finished sharply with a nervous and terrible laugh, the young man girded on his sword, took his hat from the trunk, fastened to his shoulder a black cloak, which he had worn all during his journey, and pressing the two hands of the old man, who watched his proceedings with a look of anxiety,—

"My good Parry," said he, "order a fire, drink, eat, sleep, and be happy; let us both be happy, my faithful friend, my only friend. We are rich, as rich as kings!"

He struck the bag of pistoles with his clenched hand as he spoke, and it fell heavily to the ground. He resumed that dismal laugh that had so alarmed Parry; and whilst the whole household was screaming, singing, and preparing to install the travelers who had been preceded by their lackeys, he glided out by the principal entrance into the street, where the old man, who had gone to the window, lost sight of him in a moment.

Chapter VIII.
What his Majesty King Louis XIV. was at the Age of Twenty-Two.

IT has been seen, by the account we have endeavored to give of it, that the entree of King Louis XIV. into the city of Blois had been noisy and brilliant; his young majesty had therefore appeared perfectly satisfied with it.

On arriving beneath the porch of the Castle of the States, the king met, surrounded by his guards and gentlemen, with S. A. R. the duke, Gaston of Orleans, whose physiognomy, naturally rather majestic, had borrowed on this solemn occasion a fresh luster and a fresh dignity. On her part, Madame, dressed in her robes of ceremony, awaited, in the interior balcony, the entrance of her nephew. All the windows of the old castle, so deserted and dismal on ordinary days, were resplendent with ladies and lights.

It was then to the sound of drums, trumpets, and vivats, that the young king crossed the threshold of that castle in which, seventy-two years before, Henry III. had called in the aid of assassination and treachery to keep upon his head and in his house a crown which was already slipping from his brow, to fall into another family.

All eyes, after having admired the young king, so handsome and so agreeable, sought for that other king of France, much otherwise king than the former, and so old, so pale, so bent, that people called the Cardinal Mazarin.

Louis was at this time endowed with all the natural gifts which make the perfect gentleman; his eye was brilliant, mild, and of a clear azure blue. But the most skillful physiognomists, those divers into the soul, on fixing their looks upon it, if it had been possible for a subject to sustain the glance of the king,—the most skillful physiognomists, we say, would never have been able to fathom the depths of that abyss of mildness. It was with the eyes of the king as with the immense depths of the azure heavens, or with those more terrific, and almost as sublime, which the Mediterranean reveals under the keels of its ships in a clear summer day, a gigantic mirror in which heaven delights to reflect sometimes its stars, sometimes its storms.

The king was short of stature—he was scarcely five feet two inches: but his youth made up for this defect, set off likewise by great nobleness in all his movements, and by considerable address in all bodily exercises.

Certes, he was already quite a king, and it was a great thing to be a king in that period of traditional devotedness and respect; but as, up to that time, he had been but seldom and always poorly shown to the people, as they to whom he was shown saw him by the side of his mother, a tall woman, and monsieur le cardinal, a man of commanding presence, many found him so little of a king as to say,—

"Why, the king is not so tall as monsieur le cardinal!"

Whatever may be thought of these physical observations, which were principally made in the capital, the young king was welcomed as a god by the inhabitants of Blois, and almost like a king by his uncle and aunt, Monsieur and Madame, the inhabitants of the castle.

It must, however, be allowed, that when he saw, in the hall of reception, chairs of equal height for himself, his mother, the cardinal, and his uncle and aunt, a disposition artfully concealed by the semi-circular form of the assembly, Louis XIV. became red with anger, and looked around him to ascertain by the countenances of those that were present, if this humiliation had been prepared for him. But as he saw nothing upon the impassible visage of the cardinal, nothing on that of his mother, nothing on those of the assembly, he resigned himself, and sat down, taking care to be seated before anybody else.

The gentlemen and ladies were presented to their majesties and monsieur le cardinal.

The king remarked that his mother and he scarcely knew the names of any of the persons who were presented to them; whilst the cardinal, on the contrary, never failed, with an admirable memory and presence of mind, to talk to every one about his estates, his ancestors, or his children, some of whom he named, which enchanted those worthy country gentlemen, and confirmed them in the idea that he alone is truly king who knows his subjects, from the same reason that the sun has no rival, because the sun alone warms and lightens.

The study of the young king, which had begun a long time before, without anybody suspecting it, was continued then, and he looked around him attentively to endeavor to make out something in the physiognomies which had at first appeared the most insignificant and trivial.

A collation was served. The king, without daring to call upon the hospitality of his uncle, had waited for it impatiently. This time, therefore, he had all the honors due, if not to his rank, at least to his appetite.

As to the cardinal, he contented himself with touching with his withered lips a bouillon, served in a golden cup. The all-powerful minister, who had taken her regency from the queen, and his royalty from the king, had not been able to take a good stomach from nature.

Anne of Austria, already suffering from the cancer which six or eight years after caused her death, ate very little more than the cardinal.

For Monsieur, already puffed up with the great event which had taken place in his provincial life, he ate nothing whatever.

Madame alone, like a true Lorrainer, kept pace with his majesty; so that Louis XIV., who, without this partner, might have eaten nearly alone, was at first much pleased with his aunt, and afterwards with M. de Saint-Remy, her maitre d'hotel, who had really distinguished himself.

The collation over, at a sign of approbation from M. de Mazarin, the king arose, and, at the invitation of his aunt, walked about among the ranks of the assembly.

The ladies then observed—there are certain things for which women are as good observers at Blois as at Paris—the ladies then observed that Louis XIV. had a prompt and bold look, which premised a distinguished appreciator of beauty. The men, on their part, observed that the prince was proud and haughty, that he loved to look down those who fixed their eyes upon him too long or too earnestly, which gave presage of a master.

Louis XIV. had accomplished about a third of his review when his ears were struck with a word which his eminence pronounced whilst conversing with Monsieur.

This word was the name of a woman.

Scarcely had Louis XIV. heard this word than he heard, or rather listening to nothing else; and neglecting the arc of the circle which awaited his visit, his object seemed to be to come as quickly as possible to the extremity of the curve.

Monsieur, like a good courtier, was inquiring of monsieur le cardinal after the health of his nieces; he regretted, he said, not having the pleasure of receiving them at the same time with their uncle; they must certainly have grown in stature, beauty and grace, as they had promised to do the last time Monsieur had seen them.

What had first struck the king was a certain constraint in the voices of the two interlocutors. The voice of Monsieur was calm and natural when he spoke thus; while that of M. de Mazarin jumped by a note and a half to reply above the diapason of his usual voice. It might have been said that he wished that voice to strike, at the end of the salon, any ear that was too distant.

"Monseigneur," replied he, "Mesdemoiselles de Mazarin have still to finish their education: they have duties to fulfill, and a position to make. An abode in a young and brilliant court would dissipate them a little."

Louis, at this last sentence, smiled sadly. The court was young, it was true, but the avarice of the cardinal had taken good care that it should not be brilliant.

"You have nevertheless no intention," replied Monsieur, "to cloister them or make them borgeoises?"

"Not at all," replied the cardinal, forcing his Italian pronunciation in such a manner that, from soft and velvety as it was, it became sharp and vibrating; "not at all: I have a full and fixed intention to marry them, and that as well as I shall be able."

"Parties will not be wanting, monsieur le cardinal," replied Monsieur, with a bonhomie worthy of one tradesman congratulating another.

"I hope not, monseigneur, and with reason, as God has been pleased to give them grace, intelligence, and beauty."

During this conversation, Louis XIV., conducted by Madame, accomplished, as we have described, the circle of presentations.

"Mademoiselle Auricule," said the princess, presenting to his majesty a fat, fair girl of two-and-twenty, who at a village fete might have been taken for a peasant in Sunday finery,—"the daughter of my music-mistress."

The king smiled. Madame had never been able to extract four correct notes from either viol or harpsichord.

"Mademoiselle Aure de Montalais," continued Madame; "a young lady of rank, and my good attendant."

This time it was not the king that smiled; it was the young lady presented, because, for the first time in her life, she heard, given to her by Madame, who generally showed no tendency to spoil her, such an honorable qualification.

Our old acquaintance Montalais, therefore, made his majesty a profound courtesy, the more respectful from the necessity she was under of concealing certain contractions of her laughing lips, which the king might not have attributed to their real cause.

It was just at this moment that the king caught the word which startled him.

"And the name of the third?" asked Monsieur.

"Mary, monseigneur," replied the cardinal.

There was doubtless some magical influence in that word, for, as we have said, the king started in hearing it, and drew Madame towards the middle of the circle, as if he wished to put some confidential question to her, but, in reality, for the sake of getting nearer to the cardinal.

"Madame, my aunt," said he, laughing, and in a suppressed voice, "my geography-master did not teach me that Blois was at such an immense distance from Paris."

"What do you mean, nephew?" asked Madame.

"Why, because it would appear that it requires several years, as regards fashion, to travel the distance!—Look at those young ladies!"

"Well; I know them all."

"Some of them are pretty."

"Don't say that too loud, monsieur my nephew; you will drive them wild."

"Stop a bit, stop a bit, dear aunt!" said the king, smiling; "for the second part of my sentence will serve as a corrective to the first. Well, my dear aunt, some of them appear old and others ugly, thanks to their ten-year-old fashions."

"But, sire, Blois is only five days' journey from Paris."

"Yes, that is it," said the king: "two years behind for each day."

"Indeed! do you really think so? Well, that is strange! It never struck me."

"Now, look, aunt," said Louis XIV., drawing still nearer to Mazarin, under the pretext of gaining a better point of view, "look at that simple white dress by the side of those antiquated specimens of finery, and those pretentious coiffures. She is probably one of my mother's maids of honor, though I don't know her."

"Ah! ah! my dear nephew!" replied Madame, laughing; "permit me to tell you that your divinatory science is at fault for once. The young lady you honor with your praise is not a Parisian, but a Blaisoise."

"Oh, aunt!" replied the king with a look of doubt.

"Come here, Louise," said Madame.

And the fair girl, already known to you under that name, approached them, timid, blushing, and almost bent beneath the royal glance.

"Mademoiselle Louise Francoise de la Beaume le Blanc, the daughter of the Marquise de la Valliere," said Madame, ceremoniously.

The young girl bowed with so much grace, mingled with the profound timidity inspired by the presence of the king, that the latter lost, while looking at her, a few words of the conversation of Monsieur and the cardinal.

"Daughter-in-law," continued Madame, "of M. de Saint-Remy, my maitre d'hotel, who presided over the confection of that excellent daube truffee which your majesty seemed so much to appreciate."

No grace, no youth, no beauty, could stand out against such a presentation. The king smiled. Whether the words of Madame were a pleasantry, or uttered in all innocency, they proved the pitiless immolation of everything that Louis had found charming or poetic in the young girl. Mademoiselle de la Valliere, for Madame and, by rebound, for the king, was, for a moment, no more than the daughter of a man of a superior talent over dindes truffees.

But princes are thus constituted. The gods, too, were just like this in Olympus. Diana and Venus, no doubt, abused the beautiful Alcmena and poor Io, when they condescended for distraction's sake, to speak, amidst nectar and ambrosia, of mortal beauties, at the table of Jupiter.

Fortunately, Louise was so bent in her reverential salute, that she did not catch either Madame's words or the king's smile. In fact, if the poor child, who had so much good taste as alone to have chosen to dress herself in white amidst all her companions—if that dove's heart, so easily accessible to painful emotions, had been touched by the cruel words of Madame, or the egotistical cold smile of the king, it would have annihilated her.

And Montalais herself, the girl of ingenious ideas, would not have attempted to recall her to life; for ridicule kills beauty even.

But fortunately, as we have said, Louise, whose ears were buzzing, and her eyes veiled by timidity,—Louise saw nothing and heard nothing; and the king, who had still his attention directed to the conversation of the cardinal and his uncle, hastened to return to them.

He came up just at the moment Mazarin terminated by saying: "Mary, as well as her sisters, has just set off for Brouage. I make them follow the opposite bank of the Loire to that along which we have traveled; and if I calculate their progress correctly, according to the orders I have given, they will to-morrow be opposite Blois."

These words were pronounced with that tact—that measure, that distinctness of tone, of intention, and reach—which made del Signor Giulio Mazarini the first comedian in the world.

It resulted that they went straight to the heart of Louis XIV., and the cardinal, on turning round at the simple noise of the approaching footsteps of his majesty, saw the immediate effect of them upon the countenance of his pupil, an effect betrayed to the keen eyes of his eminence by a slight increase of color. But what was the ventilation of such a secret to him whose craft had for twenty years deceived all the diplomatists of Europe?

From the moment the young king heard these last words, he appeared as if he had received a poisoned arrow in his heart. He could not remain quiet in a place, but cast around an uncertain, dead, and aimless look over the assembly. He with his eyes interrogated his mother more than twenty times: but she, given up to the pleasure of conversing with her sister-in-law, and likewise constrained by the glance of Mazarin, did not appear to comprehend any of the supplications conveyed by the looks of her son.

From this moment, music, lights, flowers, beauties, all became odious and insipid to Louis XIV. After he had a hundred times bitten his lips, stretched his legs and his arms like a well-brought-up child, who, without daring to gape, exhausts all the modes of evincing his weariness—after having uselessly again implored his mother and the minister, he turned a despairing look towards the door, that is to say, towards liberty.

At this door, in the embrasure of which he was leaning, he saw, standing out strongly, a figure with a brown and lofty countenance, an aquiline nose, a stern but brilliant eye, gray and long hair, a black mustache, the true type of military beauty, whose gorget, more sparkling than a mirror, broke all the reflected lights which concentrated upon it, and sent them back as lightning. This officer wore his gray hat with its long red plumes upon his head, a proof that he was called there by his duty, and not by his pleasure. If he had been brought thither by his pleasure—if he had been a courtier instead of a soldier, as pleasure must always be paid for at the same price—he would have held his hat in his hand.

That which proved still better that this officer was upon duty, and was accomplishing a task to which he was accustomed, was, that he watched, with folded arms, remarkable indifference, and supreme apathy, the joys and ennuis of this fete. Above all, he appeared, like a philosopher, and all old soldiers are philosophers,—he appeared above all to comprehend the ennuis infinitely better than the joys; but in the one he took his part, knowing very well how to do without the other.

Now, he was leaning, as we have said, against the carved door-frame when the melancholy, weary eyes of the king, by chance, met his.

It was not the first time, as it appeared, that the eyes of the officer had met those eyes, and he was perfectly acquainted with the expression of them; for, as soon as he had cast his own look upon the countenance of Louis XIV., and had read by it what was passing in his heart—that is to say, all the ennui that oppressed him—all the timid desire to go out which agitated him,—he perceived he must render the king a service without his commanding it,— almost in spite of himself. Boldly, therefore, as if he had given the word of command to cavalry in battle, "On the king's service!" cried he, in a clear, sonorous voice.

At these words, which produced the effect of a peal of thunder, prevailing over the orchestra, the singing and the buzz of the promenaders, the cardinal and the queen-mother looked at each other with surprise.

Louis XIV., pale, but resolved, supported as he was by that intuition of his own thought which he had found in the mind of the officer of musketeers, and which he had just manifested by the order given, arose from his chair, and took a step towards the door.

"Are you going, my son?" said the queen, whilst Mazarin satisfied himself with interrogating by a look which might have appeared mild if it had not been so piercing.

"Yes, madame," replied the king; "I am fatigued, and, besides, wish to write this evening."

A smile stole over the lips of the minister, who appeared, by a bend of the head, to give the king permission.

Monsieur and Madame hastened to give orders to the officers who presented themselves.

The king bowed, crossed the hall, and gained the door, where a hedge of twenty musketeers awaited him. At the extremity of this hedge stood the officer, impassible, with his drawn sword in his hand. The king passed, and all the crowd stood on tip-toe, to have one more look at him.

Ten musketeers, opening the crowd of the ante-chambers and the steps, made way for his majesty. The other ten surrounded the king and Monsieur, who had insisted upon accompanying his majesty. The domestics walked behind. This little cortege escorted the king to the chamber destined for him. The apartment was the same that had been occupied by Henry III. during his sojourn in the States.

Monsieur had given his orders. The musketeers, led by their officer, took possession of the little passage by which one wing of the castle communicates with the other. This passage was commenced by a small square ante-chamber, dark even in the finest days. Monsieur stopped Louis XIV.

"You are passing now, sire," said he, "the very spot where the Duc de Guise received the first stab of the poniard."

The king was ignorant of all historical matters; he had heard of the fact, but he knew nothing of the localities or the details.

"Ah!" said he with a shudder.

And he stopped. The rest, both behind and before him, stopped likewise.

"The duc, sire," continued Gaston, "was nearly were I stand: he was walking in the same direction as your majesty; M. de Loignac was exactly where your lieutenant of musketeers is; M. de Saint-Maline and his majesty's ordinaries were behind him and around him. It was here that he was struck."

The king turned towards his officer, and saw something like a cloud pass over his martial and daring countenance.

"Yes, from behind!" murmured the lieutenant, with a gesture of supreme disdain. And he endeavored to resume the march, as if ill at ease at being between walls formerly defiled by treachery.

But the king, who appeared to wish to be informed, was disposed to give another look at this dismal spot.

Gaston perceived his nephew's desire.

"Look, sire," said he, taking a flambeaux from the hands of M. de Saint-Remy, "this is where he fell. There was a bed there, the curtains of which he tore with catching at them."

"Why does the floor seem hollowed out at this spot?" asked Louis.

"Because it was here the blood flowed," replied Gaston; "the blood penetrated deeply into the oak, and it was only by cutting it out that they succeeded in making it disappear. And even then," added Gaston, pointing the flambeaux to the spot, "even then this red stain resisted all the attempts made to destroy it."

Louis XIV. raised his head. Perhaps he was thinking of that bloody trace that had once been shown him at the Louvre, and which, as a pendant to that of Blois, had been made there one day by the king his father with the blood of Concini.

"Let us go on," said he.

The march was resumed promptly; for emotion, no doubt, had given to the voice of the young prince a tone of command which was not customary with him. When he arrived at the apartment destined for the king, which communicated not only with the little passage we have passed through, but further with the great staircase leading to the court,—

"Will your majesty," said Gaston, "condescend to occupy this apartment, all unworthy as it is to receive you?"

"Uncle," replied the young king, "I render you my thanks for your cordial hospitality."

Gaston bowed to his nephew, embraced him, and then went out.

Of the twenty musketeers who had accompanied the king, ten reconducted Monsieur to the reception-rooms, which were not yet empty, notwithstanding the king had retired.

The ten others were posted by their officer, who himself explored, in five minutes, all the localities, with that cold and certain glance which not even habit gives unless that glance belongs to genius.

Then, when all were placed, he chose as his headquarters the ante-chamber, in which he found a large fauteuil, a lamp, some wine, some water, and some dry bread.

He refreshed his lamp, drank half a glass of wine, curled his lip with a smile full of expression, installed himself in his large armchair, and made preparations for sleeping.

Chapter IX.
In which the Unknown of the Hostelry of Les Medici loses his Incognito.

THIS officer, who was sleeping, or preparing to sleep, was, notwithstanding his careless air, charged with a serious responsibility.

Lieutenant of the king's musketeers, he commanded all the company which came from Paris, and that company consisted of a hundred and twenty men; but, with the exception of the twenty of whom we have spoken, the other hundred were engaged in guarding the queen-mother, and more particularly the cardinal.

Monsignor Giulio Mazarini economized the traveling expenses of his guards; he consequently used the king's, and that largely, since he took fifty of them for himself—a peculiarity which would not have failed to strike any one unacquainted with the usages of that court.

That which would still further have appeared, if not inconvenient, at least extraordinary, to a stranger, was, that the side of the castle destined for monsieur le cardinal was brilliant, light and cheerful. The musketeers there mounted guard before every door, and allowed no one to enter, except the couriers, who, even while he was traveling, followed the cardinal for the carrying on of his correspondence.

Twenty men were on duty with the queen-mother; thirty rested, in order to relieve their companions the next day.

On the king's side, on the contrary, were darkness, silence, and solitude. When once the doors were closed, there was no longer an appearance of royalty. All the servitors had by degrees retired. Monsieur le Prince had sent to know if his majesty required his attendance; and on the customary "No" of the lieutenant of musketeers, who was habituated to the question and the reply, all appeared to sink into the arms of sleep, as if in the dwelling of a good citizen.

And yet it was possible to hear from the side of the house occupied by the young king the music of the banquet, and to see the windows of the great hall richly illuminated.

Ten minutes after his installation in his apartment, Louis XIV. had been able to learn, by movement much more distinguished than marked his own leaving, the departure of the cardinal, who, in his turn, sought his bedroom, accompanied by a large escort of ladies and gentlemen.

Besides, to perceive this movement, he had nothing to do but look out at his window, the shutters of which had not been closed.

His eminence crossed the court, conducted by Monsieur, who himself held a flambeau; then followed the queen-mother, to whom Madame familiarly gave her arm; and both walked chatting away, like two old friends.

Behind these two couples filed nobles, ladies, pages and officers; the flambeaux gleamed over the whole court, like the moving reflections of a conflagration. Then the noise of steps and voices became lost in the upper floors of the castle.

No one was then thinking of the king, who, leaning on his elbow at his window, had sadly seen pass away all that light, and heard that noise die off—no, not one, if it was not that unknown of the hostelry des Medici, whom we have seen go out, enveloped in his cloak.

He had come straight up to the castle, and had, with his melancholy countenance, wandered round and round the palace, from which the people had not yet departed; and finding that on one guarded the great entrance, or the porch, seeing that the soldiers of Monsieur were fraternizing with the royal soldiers—that is to say, swallowing Beaugency at discretion, or rather indiscretion—the unknown penetrated through the crowd, then ascended to the court, and came to the landing of the staircase leading to the cardinal's apartment.

What, according to all probability, induced him to direct his steps that way, was the splendor of the flambeaux, and the busy air of the pages and domestics. But he was stopped short by a presented musket and the cry of the sentinel.

"Where are you going, my friend?" asked the soldier.

"I am going to the king's apartment," replied the unknown, haughtily, but tranquilly.

The soldier called one of his eminence's officers, who, in the tone in which a youth in office directs a solicitor to a minister, let fall these words: "The other staircase, in front."

And the officer, without further notice of the unknown, resumed his interrupted conversation.

The stranger, without reply, directed his steps towards the staircase pointed out to him. On this side there was no noise, there were no more flambeaux.

Obscurity, through which a sentinel glided like a shadow; silence, which permitted him to hear the sound of his own footsteps, accompanied with the jingling of his spurs upon the stone slabs.

This guard was one of the twenty musketeers appointed for attendance upon the king, and who mounted guard with the stiffness and consciousness of a statue.

"Who goes there?" said the guard.

"A friend," replied the unknown.

"What do you want?"

"To speak to the king."

"Do you, my dear monsieur? That's not very likely."

"Why not?"

"Because the king has gone to bed."

"Gone to bed already?"

"Yes."

"No matter: I must speak to him."

"And I tell you that is impossible."

"And yet—"

"Go back!"

"Do you require the word?"

"I have no account to render to you. Stand back!"

And this time the soldier accompanied his word with a threatening gesture; but the unknown stirred no more than if his feet had taken root.

"Monsieur le mousquetaire," said he, "are you a gentleman?"

"I have that honor."

"Very well! I also am one; and between gentlemen some consideration ought to be observed."

The soldier lowered his arms, overcome by the dignity with which these words were pronounced.

"Speak, monsieur," said he; "and if you ask me anything in my power—"

"Thank you. You have an officer, have you not?"

"Our lieutenant? Yes, monsieur."

"Well, I wish to speak to him."

"Oh, that's a different thing. Come up, monsieur."

The unknown saluted the soldier in a lofty fashion, and ascended the staircase; whilst a cry, "Lieutenant, a visit!" transmitted from sentinel to sentinel, preceded the unknown, and disturbed the slumbers of the officer.

Dragging on his boot, rubbing his eyes, and hooking his cloak, the lieutenant made three steps towards the stranger.

"What can I do to serve you, monsieur?" asked he.

"You are the officer on duty, lieutenant of the musketeers, are you?"

"I have that honor," replied the officer.

"Monsieur, I must absolutely speak to the king."

The lieutenant looked attentively at the unknown, and in that look, he saw all he wished to see—that is to say, a person of high distinction in an ordinary dress.

"I do not suppose you to be mad," replied he; "and yet you seem to me to be in a condition to know, monsieur, that people do not enter a king's apartments in this manner without his consent."

"He will consent."

"Monsieur, permit me to doubt that. The king has retired this quarter of an hour; he must be now undressing. Besides, the word is given."

"When he knows who I am, he will recall the word."

The officer was more and more surprised, more and more subdued.

"If I consent to announce you, may I at least know whom to announce, monsieur?"

"You will announce His Majesty Charles II., King of England, Scotland, and Ireland."

The officer uttered a cry of astonishment, drew back, and there might be seen upon his pallid countenance one of the most poignant emotions that ever an energetic man endeavored to drive back to his heart.

"Oh, yes, sire; in fact," said he, "I ought to have recognized you."

"You have seen my portrait, then?"

"No, sire."

"Or else you have seen me formerly at court, before I was driven from France?"

"No, sire, it is not even that."

"How then could you have recognized me, if you have never seen my portrait or my person?"

"Sire, I saw his majesty your father at a terrible moment."

"The day—"

"Yes."

A dark cloud passed over the brow of the prince; then, dashing his hand across it, "Do you see any difficulty in announcing me?" said he.

"Sire, pardon me," replied the officer, "but I could not imagine a king under so simple an exterior; and yet I had the honor to tell your majesty just now that I had seen Charles I. But pardon me, monsieur; I will go and inform the king."

But returning after going a few steps, "Your majesty is desirous, without doubt, that this interview should be a secret?" said he.

"I do not require it; but if it were possible to preserve it—"

"It is possible, sire, for I can dispense with informing the first gentleman on duty; but, for that, your majesty must please to consent to give up your sword."

"True, true; I had forgotten that no one armed is permitted to enter the chamber of a king of France."

"Your majesty will form an exception, if you wish it; but then I shall avoid my responsibility by informing the king's attendant."

"Here is my sword, monsieur. Will you now please to announce me to his majesty?"

"Instantly, sire." And the officer immediately went and knocked at the door of communication, which the valet opened to him.

"His Majesty the King of England!" said the officer.

"His Majesty the King of England!" replied the valet de chambre.

At these words a gentleman opened the folding-doors of the king's apartment, and Louis XIV. was seen, without hat or sword, and his pourpoint open, advancing with signs of the greatest surprise.

"You, my brother—you at Blois!" cried Louis XIV., dismissing with a gesture both the gentlemen and the valet de chambre, who passed out into the next apartment.

"Sire," replied Charles II., "I was going to Paris, in the hope of seeing your majesty, when report informed me of your approaching arrival in this city. I therefore prolonged my abode here, having something very particular to communicate to you."

"Will this closet suit you, my brother?"

"Perfectly well, sire; for I think no one can hear us here."

"I have dismissed my gentleman and my watcher; they are in the next chamber. There, behind that partition, is a solitary closet, looking into the ante-chamber, and in that ante-chamber you found nobody but a solitary officer, did you?"

"No, sire."

"Well, then, speak, my brother; I listen to you."

"Sire, I commence, and entreat your majesty to have pity on the misfortunes of our house."

The king of France colored, and drew his chair closer to that of the king of England.

"Sire," said Charles II., "I have no need to ask if your majesty is acquainted with the details of my deplorable history."

Louis XIV. blushed, this time more strongly than before; then, stretching forth his hand to that of the king of England, "My brother," said he, "I am ashamed to say so, but the cardinal scarcely ever speaks of political affairs before me. Still more, formerly I used to get Laporte, my valet de chambre, to read historical subjects to me; but he put a stop to these readings, and took away Laporte from me. So that I beg my brother Charles to tell me all those matters as to a man who knows nothing."

"Well, sire, I think that by taking things from the beginning I shall have a better chance of touching the heart of your majesty."

"Speak on, my brother—speak on."

"You know, sire, that being called in 1650 to Edinburgh, during Cromwell's expedition into Ireland, I was crowned at Scone. A year after, wounded in one of the provinces he had usurped, Cromwell returned upon us. To meet him was my object; to leave Scotland was my wish."

"And yet," interrupted the young king, "Scotland is almost your native country, is it not, my brother?"

"Yes, but the Scots were cruel compatriots for me, sire; they had forced me to forsake the religion of my fathers; they had hung Lord Montrose, the most devoted of my servants, because he was not a Covenanter; and as the poor martyr, to whom they had offered a favor when dying, had asked that his body might be cut into as many pieces as there are cities in Scotland, in order that evidence of his fidelity might be met with everywhere, I could not leave one city, or go into another, without passing under some fragments of a body which had acted, fought, and breathed for me.

"By a bold, almost desperate march, I passed through Cromwell's army, and entered England. The Protector set out in pursuit of this strange flight, which had a crown for its object. If I had been able to reach London before him, without doubt the prize of the race would have been mine; but he overtook me at Worcester.

"The genius of England was no longer with us, but with him. On the 3rd of September, 1651, sire, the anniversary of the other battle of Dunbar, so fatal to the Scots, I was conquered. Two thousand men fell around me before I thought of retreating a step. At length I was obliged to fly.

"From that moment my history became a romance. Pursued with persistent inveteracy, I cut off my hair, I disguised myself as a woodman. One day spent amidst the branches of an oak gave to that tree the name of the royal oak, which it bears to this day. My adventures in the county of Stafford, whence I escaped with the daughter of my host on a pillion behind me, still fill the tales of the country firesides, and would furnish matter for ballads. I will some day write all this, sire, for the instruction of my brother kings.

"I will first tell how, on arriving at the residence of Mr. Norton, I met with a court chaplain, who was looking on at a party playing at skittles, and an old servant who named me, bursting into tears, and who was as near and as certainly killing me by his fidelity as another might have been by treachery. Then I will tell of my terrors—yes, sire, of my terrors—when, at the house of Colonel Windham, a farrier who came to shoe our horses declared they had been shod in the north."

"How strange!" murmured Louis XIV. "I never heard anything of all that; I was only told of your embarkation at Brighelmstone and your landing in Normandy."*

* The correct name of the city is Brighthelmstone. The mistake is Dumas's.

"Oh!" exclaimed Charles, "if Heaven permits kings to be thus ignorant of the histories of each other, how can they render assistance to their brothers who need it?"

"But tell me," continued Louis XIV., "how, after being so roughly received in England, you can still hope for anything from that unhappy country and that rebellious people?"

"Oh, sire! since the battle of Worcester, everything is changed there. Cromwell is dead, after having signed a treaty with France, in which his name is placed above yours. He died on the 3rd of September, 1658, a fresh anniversary of the battles of Dunbar and Worcester."

"His son has succeeded him."

"But certain men have a family, sire, and no heir. The inheritance of Oliver was too heavy for Richard. Richard was neither a republican nor a royalist; Richard allowed his guards to eat his dinner, and his generals to govern the republic; Richard abdicated the protectorate on the 22nd of April, 1659, more than a year ago, sire.

"From that time England is nothing but a tennis-court, in which the players throw dice for the crown of my father. The two most eager players are Lambert and Monk. Well, sire, I, in my turn, wish to take part in this game, where the stakes are thrown upon my royal mantle. Sire, it only requires a million to corrupt one of these players and make an ally of him, or two hundred of your gentlemen to drive them out of my palace at Whitehall, as Christ drove the money-changers from the temple."

"You come, then," replied Louis XIV., "to ask me—"

"For your assistance; that is to say, not only for that which kings owe to each other, but that which simple Christians owe to each other—your assistance, sire, either in money or men. Your assistance, sire, and within a month, whether I oppose Lambert to Monk, or Monk to Lambert, I shall have reconquered my paternal inheritance, without having cost my country a guinea, or my subjects a drop of blood, for they are now all drunk with revolutions, protectorates, and republics, and ask nothing better than to fall staggering to sleep in the arms of royalty. Your assistance, sire, and I shall owe you more than I owe my father,—my poor father, who bought at so dear a rate the ruin of our house! You may judge, sire, whether I am unhappy, whether I am in despair, for I accuse my own father!"

And the blood mounted to the pale face of Charles II., who remained for an instant with his head between his hands, and as if blinded by that blood which appeared to revolt against the filial blasphemy.

The young king was not less affected than his elder brother; he threw himself about in his fauteuil, and could not find a single word of reply.

Charles II., to whom ten years in age gave a superior strength to master his emotions, recovered his speech the first.

"Sire," said he, "your reply? I wait for it as a criminal waits for his sentence. Must I die?"

"My brother," replied the French prince, "you ask of me for a million—me, who was never possessed of a quarter of that sum! I possess nothing. I am no more king of France than you are king of England. I am a name, a cipher dressed in fleur-de-lised velvet,—that is all. I am upon a visible throne; that is my only advantage over your majesty. I have nothing—I can do nothing."

"Can it be so?" exclaimed Charles II.

"My brother," said Louis, sinking his voice, "I have undergone miseries with which my poorest gentlemen are unacquainted. If my poor Laporte were here, he would tell you that I have slept in ragged sheets, through the holes of which my legs have passed; he would tell you that afterwards, when I asked for carriages, they brought me conveyances half-destroyed by the rats of the coach-houses; he would tell you that when I asked for my dinner, the servants went to the cardinal's kitchen to inquire if there were any dinner for the king. And look! to-day, this very day even, when I am twenty-two years of age,—to-day, when I have attained the grade of the majority of kings,—to-day, when I ought to have the key of the treasury, the direction of the policy, the supremacy in peace and war,—cast your eyes around me, see how I am left! Look at this abandonment—this disdain—this silence!—Whilst yonder—look yonder! View the bustle, the lights, the homage! There!—there you see the real king of France, my brother!"

"In the cardinal's apartments?"

"Yes, in the cardinal's apartments."

"Then I am condemned, sire?"

Louis XIV. made no reply.

"Condemned is the word; for I will never solicit him who left my mother and sister to die with cold and hunger—the daughter and grand-daughter of Henry IV.—as surely they would have if M. de Retz and the parliament had not sent them wood and bread."

"To die?" murmured Louis XIV.

"Well!" continued the king of England, "poor Charles II., grandson of Henry IV., as you are, sire having neither parliament nor Cardinal de Retz to apply to, will die of hunger, as his mother and sister had nearly done."

Louis knitted his brow, and twisted violently the lace of his ruffles.

This prostration, this immobility, serving as a mark to an emotion so visible, struck Charles II., and he took the young man's hand.

"Thanks!" said he, "my brother. You pity me, and that is all I can require of you in your present situation."

"Sire," said Louis XIV., with a sudden impulse, and raising his head, "it is a million you require, or two hundred gentlemen, I think you say?"

"Sire, a million would be quite sufficient."

"That is very little."

"Offered to a single man it is a great deal. Convictions have been purchased at a much lower price; and I should have nothing to do but with venalities."

"Two hundred gentlemen! Reflect!—that is little more than a single company."

"Sire, there is in our family a tradition, and that is, that four men, four French gentlemen, devoted to my father, were near saving my father, though condemned by a parliament, guarded by an army and surrounded by a nation."

"Then if I can procure you a million, or two hundred gentlemen, you will be satisfied; and you will consider me your well-affectioned brother?"

"I shall consider you as my saviour; and if I recover the throne of my father, England will be, as long as I reign it, a sister to France, as you will have been a brother to me."

"Well, my brother," said Louis, rising, "what you hesitate to ask for, I will myself demand; that which I have never done on my own account, I will do on yours. I will go and find the king of France—the other—the rich, the powerful one, I mean. I will myself solicit this million, or these two hundred gentlemen; and—we will see."

"Oh!" cried Charles; "you are a noble friend, sire—a heart created by God! You save me, my brother; and if you should ever stand in need of the life you restored me, demand it."

"Silence, my brother,—silence!" said Louis, in a suppressed voice. "Take care that no one hears you! We have not obtained our end yet. To ask money of Mazarin—that is worse than traversing the enchanted forest, each tree of which inclosed a demon. It is more than setting out to conquer a world."

"But yet, sire, when you ask it—"

"I have already told you that I never asked," replied Louis with a haughtiness that made the king of England turn pale.

And the latter, like a wounded man, made a retreating movement—"Pardon me, my brother," replied he. "I have neither a mother nor a sister who are suffering. My throne is hard and naked, but I am firmly seated on my throne. Pardon me that expression, my brother; it was that of an egotist. I will retract it, therefore, by a sacrifice,—I will go to monsieur le cardinal. Wait for me, if you please—I will return."

Chapter X.
The Arithmetic of M. de Mazarin.

WHILST the king was directing his course rapidly towards the wing of the castle occupied by the cardinal, taking nobody with him but his valet de chambre, the officer of musketeers came out, breathing like a man who has for a long time been forced to hold his breath, from the little cabinet of which we have already spoken, and which the king believed to be quite solitary. This little cabinet had formerly been part of the chamber, from which it was only separated by a thin partition. It resulted that this partition, which was only for the eye, permitted the ear the least indiscreet to hear every word spoken in the chamber.

There was no doubt, then, that this lieutenant of musketeers had heard all that passed in his majesty's apartment.

Warned by the last words of the young king, he came out just in time to salute him on his passage, and to follow him with his eyes till he had disappeared in the corridor.

Then as soon as he had disappeared, he shook his head after a fashion peculiarly his own, and in a voice which forty years' absence from Gascony had not deprived of its Gascon accent, "A melancholy service," said he, "and a melancholy master!"

These words pronounced, the lieutenant resumed his place in his fauteuil, stretched his legs and closed his eyes, like a man who either sleeps or meditates.

During this short monologue and the mise en scene that had accompanied it, whilst the king, through the long corridors of the old castle, proceeded to the apartment of M. de Mazarin, a scene of another sort was being enacted in those apartments.

Mazarin was in bed, suffering a little from the gout. But as he was a man of order, who utilized even pain, he forced his wakefulness to be the humble servant of his labor. He had consequently ordered Bernouin, his valet de chambre, to bring him a little traveling-desk, so that he might write in bed. But the gout is not an adversary that allows itself to be conquered so easily; therefore, at each movement he made, the pain from dull became sharp.

"Is Brienne there?" asked he of Bernouin.

"No, monseigneur," replied the valet de chambre; "M. de Brienne, with your permission, is gone to bed. But if it is the wish of your eminence, he can speedily be called."

"No, it is not worth while. Let us see, however. Cursed ciphers!"

And the cardinal began to think, counting on his fingers the while.

"Oh, ciphers is it?" said Bernouin. "Very well! if your eminence attempts calculations, I will promise you a pretty headache to-morrow! And with that please to remember M. Guenaud is not here."

"You are right, Bernouin. You must take Brienne's place, my friend. Indeed, I ought to have brought M. Colbert with me. That young man goes on very well, Bernouin, very well; a very orderly youth."

"I do not know," said the valet de chambre, "but I don't like the countenance of your young man who goes on so well."

"Well, well, Bernouin! We don't stand in need of your advice. Place yourself there: take the pen and write."

"I am ready, monseigneur; what am I to write?"

"There, that's the place: after the two lines already traced."

"I am there."

"Write seven hundred and sixty thousand livres."

"That is written."

"Upon Lyons—" The cardinal appeared to hesitate.

"Upon Lyons," repeated Bernouin.

"Three millions nine hundred thousand livres."

"Well, monseigneur?"

"Upon Bordeaux, seven millions."

"Seven?" repeated Bernouin.

"Yes," said the cardinal, pettishly, "seven." Then, recollecting himself, "You understand, Bernouin," added he, "that all this money is to be spent?"

"Eh! monseigneur; whether it be spent or put away is of very little consequence to me, since none of these millions are mine."

"These millions are the king's; it is the king's money I am reckoning. Well, what were we saying? You always interrupt me!"

"Seven millions upon Bordeaux."

"Ah! yes; that's right. Upon Madrid four millions. I give you to understand plainly to whom this money belongs, Bernouin, seeing that everybody has the stupidity to believe me rich in millions. I repel the silly idea. A minister, besides, has nothing of his own. Come, go on. Rentrees generales, seven millions; properties, nine millions. Have you written that, Bernouin?"

"Yes, monseigneur."

"Bourse, six hundred thousand livres; various property, two millions. Ah! I forgot—the furniture of the different chateaux—"

"Must I put of the crown?" asked Bernouin.

"No, no; it is of no use doing that—that is understood. Have you written that, Bernouin?"

"Yes, monseigneur."

"And the ciphers?"

"Stand straight under one another."

"Cast them up, Bernouin."

"Thirty-nine millions two hundred and sixty thousand livres, monseigneur."

"Ah!" cried the cardinal, in a tone of vexation; "there are not yet forty millions!"

Bernouin recommenced the addition.

"No, monseigneur; there want seven hundred and forty thousand livres."

Mazarin asked for the account, and revised it carefully.

"Yes, but," said Bernouin, "thirty-nine millions two hundred and sixty thousand livres make a good round sum."

"Ah, Bernouin; I wish the king had it."

"Your eminence told me that this money was his majesty's."

"Doubtless, as clear, as transparent as possible. These thirty-nine millions are bespoken, and much more."

Bernouin smiled after his own fashion—that is, like a man who believes no more than he is willing to believe—whilst preparing the cardinal's night draught, and putting his pillow to rights.

"Oh!" said Mazarin, when the valet had gone out; "not yet forty millions! I must, however, attain that sum, which I had set down for myself. But who knows whether I shall have time? I sink, I am going, I shall never reach it! And yet, who knows that I may not find two or three millions in the pockets of my good friends the Spaniards? They discovered Peru, those people did, and—what the devil! they must have something left."

As he was speaking thus, entirely occupied with his ciphers, and thinking no more of his gout, repelled by a preoccupation which, with the cardinal, was the most powerful of all preoccupations, Bernouin rushed into the chamber, quite in a fright.

"Well!" asked the cardinal, "what is the matter now?"

"The king, monseigneur,—the king!"

"How?—the king!" said Mazarin, quickly concealing his paper. "The king here! the king at this hour! I thought he was in bed long ago. What is the matter, then?"

The king could hear these last words, and see the terrified gesture of the cardinal rising up in his bed, for he entered the chamber at that moment.

"It is nothing, monsieur le cardinal, or at least nothing which can alarm you. It is an important communication which I wish to make to your eminence to-night,—that is all."

Mazarin immediately thought of that marked attention which the king had given to his words concerning Mademoiselle de Mancini, and the communication appeared to him probably to refer to this source. He recovered his serenity then instantly, and assumed his most agreeable air, a change of countenance which inspired the king with the greatest joy; and when Louis was seated,—

"Sire," said the cardinal, "I ought certainly to listen to your majesty standing, but the violence of my complaint—"

"No ceremony between us, my dear monsieur le cardinal," said Louis kindly: "I am your pupil, and not the king, you know very well, and this evening in particular, as I come to you as a petitioner, as a solicitor, and one very humble, and desirous to be kindly received, too."

Mazarin, seeing the heightened color of the king, was confirmed in his first idea; that is to say, that love thoughts were hidden under all these fine words. This time, political cunning, as keen as it was, made a mistake; this color was not caused by the bashfulness of a juvenile passion, but only by the painful contraction of the royal pride.

Like a good uncle, Mazarin felt disposed to facilitate the confidence.

"Speak, sire," said he, "and since your majesty is willing for an instant to forget that I am your subject, and call me your master and instructor, I promise your majesty my most devoted and tender consideration."

"Thanks, monsieur le cardinal," answered the king; "that which I have to ask of your eminence has but little to do with myself."

"So much the worse!" replied the cardinal; "so much the worse! Sire, I should wish your majesty to ask of me something of importance, even a sacrifice; but whatever it may be that you ask me, I am ready to set your heart at rest by granting it, my dear sire."

"Well, this is what brings me here," said the king, with a beating of the heart that had no equal except the beating of the heart of the minister; "I have just received a visit from my brother, the king of England."

Mazarin bounded in his bed as if he had been put in relation with a Leyden jar or a voltaic pile, at the same time that a surprise, or rather a manifest disappointment, inflamed his features with such a blaze of anger, that Louis XIV., little diplomatist as he was, saw that the minister had hoped to hear something else.

"Charles II.?" exclaimed Mazarin, with a hoarse voice and a disdainful movement of his lips. "You have received a visit from Charles II.?"

"From King Charles II.," replied Louis, according in a marked manner to the grandson of Henry IV. the title which Mazarin had forgotten to give him. "Yes, monsieur le cardinal, that unhappy prince has touched my heart with the relation of his misfortunes. His distress is great, monsieur le cardinal, and it has appeared painful to me, who have seen my own throne disputed, who have been forced in times of commotion to quit my capital,—to me, in short, who am acquainted with misfortune,—to leave a deposed and fugitive brother without assistance."

"Eh!" said the cardinal, sharply; "why had he not, as you have, a Jules Mazarin by his side? His crown would then have remained intact."

"I know all that my house owes to your eminence," replied the king, haughtily, "and you may well believe that I, on my part, shall never forget it. It is precisely because my brother, the king of England has not about him the powerful genius who has saved me, it is for that, I say, that I wish to conciliate the aid of that same genius, and beg you to extend your arm over his head, well assured, monsieur le cardinal, that your hand, by touching him only, would know how to replace upon his brow the crown which fell at the foot of his father's scaffold."

"Sire," replied Mazarin, "I thank you for your good opinion with regard to myself, but we have nothing to do yonder: they are a set of madmen who deny God, and cut off the heads of their kings. They are dangerous, observe, sire, and filthy to the touch after having wallowed in royal blood and covenantal murder. That policy has never suited me,—I scorn it and reject it."

"Therefore you ought to assist in establishing a better."

"What is that?"

"The restoration of Charles II., for example."

"Good heavens!" cried Mazarin, "does the poor prince flatter himself with that chimera?"

"Yes, he does," replied the young king, terrified at the difficulties opposed to this project, which he fancied he could perceive in the infallible eye of his minister; "he only asks for a million to carry out his purpose."

"Is that all—a little million, if you please!" said the cardinal, ironically, with an effort to conquer his Italian accent. "A little million, if you please, brother! Bah! a family of mendicants!"

"Cardinal," said Louis, raising his head, "that family of mendicants is a branch of my family."

"Are you rich enough to give millions to other people, sire? Have you millions to throw away?"

"Oh!" replied Louis XIV., with great pain, which he, however, by a strong effort, prevented from appearing on his countenance;—"oh! yes, monsieur le cardinal, I am well aware I am poor, and yet the crown of France is worth a million, and to perform a good action I would pledge my crown if it were necessary. I could find Jews who would be willing to lend me a million."

"So, sire, you say you want a million?" said Mazarin.

"Yes, monsieur, I say so."

"You are mistaken, greatly mistaken, sire; you want much more than that,—Bernouin!—you shall see, sire, how much you really want."

"What, cardinal!" said the king, "are you going to consult a lackey about my affairs?"

"Bernouin!" cried the cardinal again, without appearing to remark the humiliation of the young prince. "Come here, Bernouin, and tell me the figures I gave you just now."

"Cardinal, cardinal! did you not hear me?" said Louis, turning pale with anger.

"Do not be angry, sire; I deal openly with the affairs of your majesty. Every one in France knows that; my books are as open as day. What did I tell you to do just now, Bernouin?"

"Your eminence commanded me to cast up an account."

"You did it, did you not?"

"Yes, my lord."

"To verify the amount of which his majesty, at this moment, stands in need. Did I not tell you so? Be frank, my friend."

"Your eminence said so."

"Well, what sum did I say I wanted?"

"Forty-five millions, I think."

"And what sum could we find, after collecting all our resources?"

"Thirty-nine millions two hundred and sixty thousand."

"That is correct, Bernouin; that is all I wanted to know. Leave us now," said the cardinal, fixing his brilliant eye upon the young king, who sat mute with stupefaction.

"However—" stammered the king.

"What, do you still doubt, sire?" said the cardinal. "Well, here is a proof of what I said."

And Mazarin drew from under his bolster the paper covered with figures, which he presented to the king, who turned away his eyes, his vexation was so deep.

"Therefore, as it is a million you want, sire, and that million is not set down here, it is forty-six millions your majesty stands in need of. Well, I don't think that any Jews in the world would lend such a sum, even upon the crown of France."

The king, clenching his hands beneath his ruffles, pushed away his chair.

"So it must be then!" said he; "my brother the king of England will die of hunger."

"Sire," replied Mazarin, in the same tone, "remember this proverb, which I give you as the expression of the soundest policy: 'Rejoice at being poor when your neighbor is poor likewise.'"

Louis meditated this for a few moments, with an inquisitive glance directed to the paper, one end of which remained under the bolster.

"Then," said he, "it is impossible to comply with my demand for money, my lord cardinal, is it?"

"Absolutely, sire."

"Remember, this will secure me a future enemy, if he succeed in recovering his crown without my assistance."

"If your majesty only fears that, you may be quite at ease," replied Mazarin, eagerly.

"Very well, I say no more about it," exclaimed Louis XIV.

"Have I at least convinced you, sire?" placing his hand upon that of the young king.

"Perfectly."

"If there be anything else, ask it, sire; I shall most happy to grant it to you, having refused this."

"Anything else, my lord?"

"Why yes; am I not devoted body and soul to your majesty? Hola! Bernouin!—lights and guards for his majesty! His majesty is returning to his own chamber."

"Not yet, monsieur: since you place your good-will at my disposal, I will take advantage of it."

"For yourself, sire?" asked the cardinal, hoping that his niece was at length about to be named.

"No, monsieur, not for myself," replied Louis, "but still for my brother Charles."

The brow of Mazarin again became clouded, and he grumbled a few words that the king could not catch.

Chapter XI.
Mazarin's Policy.

INSTEAD of the hesitation with which he had accosted the cardinal a quarter of an hour before, there might be read in the eyes of the young king that will against which a struggle might be maintained, and which might be crushed by its own impotence, but which, at least, would preserve, like a wound in the depth of the heart, the remembrance of its defeat.

"This time, my lord cardinal, we have to deal with something more easily found than a million."

"Do you think so, sire?" said Mazarin, looking at the king with that penetrating eye which was accustomed to read to the bottom of hearts.

"Yes, I think so; and when you know the object of my request—"

"And do you think I do not know it, sire?"

"You know what remains for me to say to you?"

"Listen, sire; these are King Charles's own words—"

"Oh, impossible!"

"Listen. 'And if that miserly, beggarly Italian,' said he—"

"My lord cardinal!"

"That is the sense, if not the words. Eh! Good heavens! I wish him no ill on that account; one is biased by his passions. He said to you: 'If that vile Italian refuses the million we ask of him, sire,—if we are forced, for want of money, to renounce diplomacy, well, then, we will ask him to grant us five hundred gentlemen.'"

The king started, for the cardinal was only mistaken in the number.

"Is not that it, sire?" cried the minister, with a triumphant accent. "And then he added some fine words: he said, 'I have friends on the other side of the channel, and these friends only want a leader and a banner. When they see me, when they behold the banner of France, they will rally around me, for they will comprehend that I have your support. The colors of the French uniform will be worth as much to me as the million M. de Mazarin refuses us,'—for he was pretty well assured I should refuse him that million.—'I shall conquer with these five hundred gentlemen, sire, and all the honor will be yours.' Now, that is what he said, or to that purpose, was it not?—turning those plain words into brilliant metaphors and pompous images, for they are fine talkers in that family! The father talked even on the scaffold."

The perspiration of shame stood on the brow of Louis. He felt that it was inconsistent with his dignity to hear his brother thus insulted, but he did not yet know how to act with him to whom every one yielded, even his mother. At last he made an effort.

"But," said he, "my lord cardinal, it is not five hundred men, it is only two hundred."

"Well, but you see I guessed what he wanted."

"I never denied that you had a penetrating eye, and that was why I thought you would not refuse my brother Charles a thing so simple and so easy to grant him as what I ask of you in his name, my lord cardinal, or rather in my own."

"Sire," said Mazarin, "I have studied policy thirty years; first, under the auspices of M. le Cardinal Richelieu; and then alone. This policy has not always been over-honest, it must be allowed, but it has never been unskillful. Now that which is proposed to your majesty is dishonest and unskillful at the same time."

"Dishonest, monsieur!"

"Sire, you entered into a treaty with Cromwell."

"Yes, and in that very treaty Cromwell signed his name above mine."

"Why did you sign yours so lo down, sire? Cromwell found a good place, and he took it; that was his custom. I return, then, to M. Cromwell. You have a treaty with him, that is to say, with England, since when you signed that treaty M. Cromwell was England."

"M. Cromwell is dead."

"Do you think so, sire?"

"No doubt he is, since his son Richard has succeeded him, and has abdicated."

"Yes, that is it exactly. Richard inherited after the death of his father, and England at the abdication of Richard. The treaty formed part of the inheritance, whether in the hands of M. Richard or in the hands of England. The treaty is, then, still as good, as valid as ever. Why should you evade it, sire? What is changed? Charles wants to-day what we were not willing to grant him ten years ago; but that was foreseen and provided against. You are the ally of England, sire, and not of Charles II. It was doubtless wrong, from a family point of view, to sign a treaty with a man who had cut off the head of the king your father's brother-in-law, and to contract an alliance with a parliament which they call yonder the Rump Parliament; it was unbecoming,

I acknowledge, but it was not unskillful from a political point of view, since, thanks to that treaty, I saved your majesty, then a minor, the trouble and danger of a foreign war, which the Fronde—you remember the Fronde, sire?"—the young king hung his head—"which the Fronde might have fatally complicated. And thus I prove to your majesty that to change our plan now, without warning our allies, would be at once unskillful and dishonest. We should make war with the aggression on our side; we should make it, deserving to have it made against us; and we should have the appearance of fearing it whilst provoking it, for a permission granted to five hundred men, to two hundred men, to fifty men, to ten men, is still a permission. One Frenchman, that is the nation; one uniform, that is the army. Suppose, sire, for example, that you should have war with Holland, which, sooner or later, will certainly happen; or with Spain, which will perhaps ensue if your marriage fails" (Mazarin stole a furtive glance at the king), "and there are a thousand causes that might yet make your marriage fail,—well, would you approve of England's sending to the United Provinces or to Spain a regiment, a company, a squadron even, of English gentlemen? Would you think that they kept within the limits of their treaty of alliance?"

Louis listened; it seemed so strange to him that Mazarin should invoke good faith, and he the author of so many political tricks, called Mazarinades. "And yet," said the king, "without manifest of my authorization, I cannot prevent gentlemen of my states from passing over into England, if such should be their good pleasure."

"You should compel them to return, sire, or at least protest against their presence as enemies in a allied country."

"But come, my lord cardinal, you who are so profound a genius, try if you cannot find a means to assist this poor king, without compromising ourselves."

"And that is exactly what I am not willing to do, my dear sire," said Mazarin. "If England were to act exactly according to my wishes, she could not act better than she does; if I directed the policy of England from this place, I should not direct it otherwise. Governed as she is governed, England is an eternal nest of contention for all Europe. Holland protects Charles II., let Holland do so; they will quarrel, they will fight. Let them destroy each other's navies, we can construct ours with the wrecks of their vessels; when we shall save our money to buy nails."

"Oh, how paltry and mean is all this that you are telling me, monsieur le cardinal!"

"Yes, but nevertheless it is true, sire; you must confess that. Still further. Suppose I admit, for a moment, the possibility of breaking your word, and evading the treaty—such a thing as sometimes happens, but that is when some great interest is to be promoted by it, or when the treaty is found to be too troublesome—well, you will authorize the engagement asked of you: France—her banner, which is the same thing—will cross the Straits and will fight; France will be conquered."

"Why so?"

"Ma foi! we have a pretty general to fight under—this Charles II.! Worcester gave us proofs of that."

"But he will no longer have to deal with Cromwell, monsieur."

"But he will have to deal with Monk, who is quite as dangerous. The brave brewer of whom we are speaking, was a visionary; he had moments of exaltation, of inflation, during which he ran over like an over-filled cask; and from the chinks there always escaped some drops of his thoughts, and by the sample the whole of his thought was to be made out. Cromwell has thus allowed us more than ten times to penetrate into his very soul, when one would have conceived that soul to be enveloped in triple brass, as Horace had it. But Monk! Oh, sire, God defend you from ever having anything to transact politically with Monk. It is he who has given me, in one year, all the gray hairs I have. Monk is no fanatic; unfortunately he is a politician; he does not overflow, he keeps close together. For ten years he has had his eyes fixed upon one object, and nobody has yet been able to ascertain what. Every morning, as Louis XI. advised, he burns his nightcap. Therefore, on the day when this plan, slowly and solitarily ripened, shall break forth, it will break forth with all the conditions of success which always accompany an unforeseen event. That is Monk, sire, of whom, perhaps, you have never even heard—of whom, perhaps, you did not even know the name, before your brother, Charles II., who knows what he is, pronounced it before you. He is a marvel of depth and tenacity, the two only things against which intelligence and ardor are blunted. Sire, I had ardor when I was young; I always was intelligent. I may safely boast of it, because I am reproached with it. I have done very well with these two qualities, since, from the son of a fisherman of Piscina, I have become prime minister to the king of France; and in that position your majesty will perhaps acknowledge I have rendered some service to the throne of your majesty. Well, sire, if I had met with Monk on my way, instead of Monsieur de Beaufort, Monsieur de Retz, or Monsieur le Prince—well, we should have been ruined. If you engage yourself rashly, sire, you will fall into the talons of this politic soldier. The casque of Monk, sire, is an iron coffer, and no one has the key of it. Therefore, near him, or rather before him, I bow, sire, for I have nothing but a velvet cap."

"What do you think Monk wishes to do, then?"

"Eh! sire, if I knew that, I would not tell you to mistrust him, for I should be stronger than he; but with him, I am afraid to guess—to guess!—you understand my word?—for if I thought I had guessed, I should stop at an idea, and, in spite of myself, should pursue that idea. Since that man has been in power yonder, I am like one of the damned in Dante whose neck Satan has twisted, and who walk forward looking around behind them. I am traveling towards Madrid, but I never lose sight of London. To guess, with that devil of a man, is to deceive one's self and to deceive one's self is to ruin one's self. God keep me from ever seeking to guess what he aims at; I confine myself to watching what he does, and that is well enough. Now I believe— you observe the meaning of the word I believe?—I believe, with respect to Monk, ties one to nothing—I believe that he has a strong inclination to succeed Cromwell. Your Charles II. has already caused proposals to be made to him by ten persons; he has satisfied himself with driving these ten meddlers from his presence, without saying anything to them but, 'Begone, or I will have you hung.' That man is a sepulcher! At this moment Monk is affecting devotion to the Rump Parliament; of this devotion, I am not the dupe. Monk has no wish to be assassinated,—an assassination would stop him in the middle of his operations; and his work must be accomplished;— so I believe—but do not believe what I believe, sire: for as I say I believe from habit—I believe that Monk is keeping on friendly terms with the parliament till the day comes for dispersing it. You are asked for swords, but they are to fight against Monk. God preserve you from fighting against Monk, sire; for Monk would beat us, and I should never console myself after being beaten by Monk. I should say to myself, Monk has foreseen that victory ten years. For God's sake, sire, out of friendship for you, if not out of consideration for himself, let Charles II. keep quiet. Your majesty will give him a little income here; give him one of your chateaux. Yes, yes—wait awhile. But I forget the treaty—that famous treaty of which we were just now speaking. Your majesty has not even the right to give him a chateau."

"How is that?"

"Yes, yes; your majesty is bound not to grant hospitality to King Charles, and to compel him to leave France even. It was on this account we forced him to quit you, and yet here he is again. Sire, I hope you will give your brother to understand that he cannot remain with us; that it is impossible he should be allowed to compromise us; or I myself—"

"Enough, my lord," said Louis XIV., rising. "In refusing me a million, perhaps you may be right; your millions are your own. In refusing me two hundred gentlemen, you are still further in the right; for you are prime minister, and you have, in the eyes of France, the responsibility of peace and war. But that you should pretend to prevent me, who am king, from extending my hospitality to the grandson of Henry IV., to my cousin-german, to the companion of my childhood—there your power stops, and there begins my will."

"Sire," said Mazarin, delighted at being let off so cheaply, and who had, besides, only fought so earnestly to arrive at that,—"sire, I shall always bend before the will of my king. Let my king, then, keep near him, or in one of his chateaux, the king of England; let Mazarin know it, but let not the minister know it."

"Good-night, my lord," said Louis XIV., "I go away in despair."

"But convinced, and that is all I desire, sire," replied Mazarin.

The king made no answer, and retired quite pensive, convinced, not of all Mazarin had told him, but of one thing which he took care not to mention to him; and that was, that it was necessary for him to study seriously both his own affairs and those of Europe, for he found them very difficult and very obscure. Louis found the king of England seated in the same place where he had left him. On perceiving him, the English prince arose; but at the first glance he saw discouragement written in dark letters upon his cousin's brow. Then, speaking first, as if to facilitate the painful avowal that Louis had to make to him,—

"Whatever it may be," said he, "I shall never forget all the kindness, all the friendship you have exhibited towards me."

"Alas!" replied Louis, in a melancholy tone, "only barren good-will, my brother."

Charles II. became extremely pale; he passed his cold hand over his brow, and struggled for a few instants against a faintness that made him tremble. "I understand," said he at last; "no more hope!"

Louis seized the hand of Charles II. "Wait, my brother," said he; "precipitate nothing; everything may change; hasty resolutions ruin all causes; add another year of trial, I implore you, to the years you have already undergone. You have, to induce you to act now rather than at another time, neither occasion nor opportunity. Come with me, my brother; I will give you one of my residences, whichever you prefer, to inhabit. I, with you, will keep my eyes upon events; we will prepare. Come, then, my brother, have courage!"

Charles II. withdrew his hand from that of the king, and drawing back, to salute him with more ceremony, "With all my heart, thanks!" replied he, "sire; but I have prayed without success to the greatest king on earth; now I will go and ask a miracle of God." And he went out without being willing to hear any more, his head carried loftily, his hand trembling, with a painful contraction of his noble countenance, and that profound gloom which, finding no more hope in the world of men, appeared to go beyond it, and ask it in worlds unknown. The officer of musketeers, on seeing him pass by thus pale, bowed almost to his knees as he saluted him. He then took a flambeau, called two musketeers, and descended the deserted staircase with the unfortunate king, holding in his left hand his hat, the plume of which swept the steps. Arrived at the door, the musketeer asked the king which way he was going, that he might direct the musketeers.

"Monsieur," replied Charles II., in a subdued voice, "you who have known my father, say, did you ever pray for him? If you have done so, do not forget me in your prayers. Now, I am going alone, and beg of you not to accompany me, or have me accompanied any further."

The officer bowed and sent away the musketeers into the interior of the palace. But he himself remained an instant under the porch watching the departing Charles II., till he was lost in the turn of the next street. "To him as to his father formerly," murmured he, "Athos, if he were here, would say with reason,—'Salute fallen majesty!'" Then, reascending the staircase: "Oh! the vile service that I follow!" said he at every step. "Oh! my pitiful master! Life thus carried on is no longer tolerable, and it is at length time that I should do something! No more generosity, no more energy! The master has succeeded, the pupil is starved forever. Mordioux! I will not resist. Come, you men," continued he, entering the ante-chamber, "why are you all looking at me so? Extinguish these torches and return to your posts. Ah! you were guarding me? Yes, you watch over me, do you not, worthy fellows? Brave fools! I am not the Duc de Guise. Begone! They will not assassinate me in the little passage. Besides," added he, in a low voice, "that would be a resolution, and no resolutions have been formed since Monsieur le Cardinal Richelieu died. Now, with all his faults, that was a man! It is settled: to-morrow I will throw my cassock to the nettles."

Then, reflecting: "No," said he, "not yet! I have one great trial to make and I will make it; but that, and I swear it, shall be the last, Mordioux!"

He had not finished speaking when a voice issued from the king's chamber. "Monsieur le lieutenant!" said this voice.

"Here I am," replied he.

"The king desires to speak to you."

"Humph!" said the lieutenant; "perhaps of what I was thinking about." And he went into the king's apartment.

Chapter XII.
The King and the Lieutenant.

AS soon as the king saw the officer enter, he dismissed his valet de chambre and his gentleman.

"Who is on duty to-morrow, monsieur?" asked he.

The lieutenant bowed his head with military politeness, and replied, "I am, sire."

"What! still you?"

"Always I, sire."

"How can that be, monsieur?"

"Sire, when traveling, the musketeers supply all the posts of your majesty's household; that is to say, yours, her majesty the queen's, and monsieur le cardinal's, the latter of whom borrows of the king the best part, or rather the numerous part, of the royal guard."

"But in the interims?"

"There are no interims, sire, but for twenty or thirty men who rest out of a hundred and twenty. At the Louvre it is very different, and if I were at the Louvre I should rely upon my brigadier; but, when traveling, sire, no one knows what may happen, and I prefer doing my duty myself."

"Then you are on guard every day?"

"And every night. Yes, sire."

"Monsieur, I cannot allow that—I will have you rest."

"That is very kind, sire; but I will not."

"What do you say?" said the king, who did not at first comprehend the full meaning of this reply.

"I say, sire, that I will not expose myself to the chance of a fault. If the devil had a trick to play on me, you understand, sire, as he knows the man with whom he has to deal, he would chose the moment when I should not be there. My duty and the peace of my conscience before everything, sire."

"But such duty will kill you, monsieur."

"Eh! sire, I have performed it for thirty years, and in all France and Navarre there is not a man in better health than I am. Moreover, I entreat you, sire, not to trouble yourself about me. That would appear very strange to me, seeing that I am not accustomed to it."

The king cut short the conversation by a fresh question. "Shall you be here, then, to-morrow morning?"

"As at present? yes, sire."

The king walked several times up and down his chamber; it was very plain that he burned with a desire to speak, but that he was restrained by some fear or other. The lieutenant, standing motionless, hat in hand, watched him making these evolutions, and, whilst looking at him, grumbled to himself, biting his mustache:

"He has not half a crown worth of resolution! Parole d'honneur! I would lay a wager he does not speak at all!"

The king continued to walk about, casting from time to time a side glance at the lieutenant. "He is the very image of his father," continued the latter, in is secret soliloquy, "he is at once proud, avaricious, and timid. The devil take his master, say I."

The king stopped. "Lieutenant," said he.

"I am here, sire."

"Why did you cry out this evening, down below in the salons—'The king's service! His majesty's musketeers!'"

"Because you gave me the order, sire."

"I?" "Yourself."

"Indeed, I did not say a word, monsieur."

"Sire, an order is given by a sign, by a gesture, by a glance, as intelligibly, as freely, and as clearly as by word of mouth. A servant who has nothing but ears is not half a good servant."

"Your eyes are very penetrating, then, monsieur."

"How is that, sire?"

"Because they see what is not."

"My eyes are good, though, sire, although they have served their master long and much: when they have anything to see, they seldom miss the opportunity. Now, this evening, they saw that your majesty colored with endeavoring to conceal the inclination to yawn, that your majesty looked with eloquent supplications, first to his eminence, and then at her majesty, the queen-mother, and at length to the entrance door, and they so thoroughly remarked all I have said, that they saw your majesty's lips articulate these words: 'Who will get me out of this?'"

- 83 -

"Monsieur!"

"Or something to this effect, sire—'My musketeers!' I could then no longer hesitate. That look was for me. I cried out instantly, 'His majesty's musketeers!' And, besides, that was shown to be true, sire, not only by your majesty's not saying I was wrong, but proving I was right by going out at once."

The king turned away to smile; then, after a few seconds, he again fixed his limpid eye upon that countenance, so intelligent, so bold, and so firm, that it might have been said to be the proud and energetic profile of the eagle facing the sun. "That is all very well," said he, after a short silence, during which he endeavored, in vain, to make his officer lower his eyes.

But seeing the king said no more, the latter pirouetted on his heels, and took three steps towards the door, muttering, "He will not speak! Mordioux! he will not speak!"

"Thank you, monsieur," said the king at last.

"Humph!" continued the lieutenant; "there was only wanting that. Blamed for having been less of a fool than another might have been." And he went to the door, allowing his spurs to jingle in true military style. But when he was on the threshold, feeling the king's desire drew him back, he returned.

"Has your majesty told me all?" asked he, in a tone we cannot describe, but which, without appearing to solicit the royal confidence, contained so much persuasive frankness, that the king immediately replied:

"Yes; but draw near, monsieur."

"Now then," murmured the officer, "he is coming to it at last."

"Listen to me."

"I shall not lose a word, sire."

"You will mount on horseback to-morrow, at about half-past four in the morning, and you will have a horse saddled for me."

"From your majesty's stables?"

"No; one of your musketeers' horses."

"Very well, sire. Is that all?"

"And you will accompany me."

"Alone?"

"Alone."

"Shall I come to seek your majesty, or shall I wait?"

"You will wait for me."

"Where, sire?"

"At the little park-gate."

The lieutenant bowed, understanding that the king had told him all he had to say. In fact, the king dismissed him with a gracious wave of the hand. The officer left the chamber of the king, and returned to place himself philosophically in his fauteuil, where, far from sleeping, as might have been expected, considering how late it was, he began to reflect more deeply than he had ever reflected before. The result of these reflections was not so melancholy as the preceding ones had been.

"Come, he has begun," said he. "Love urges him on, and he goes forward— he goes forward! The king is nobody in his own palace; but the man perhaps may prove to be worth something. Well, we shall see to-morrow morning. Oh! oh!" cried he, all at once starting up, "that is a gigantic idea, mordioux! and perhaps my fortune depends, at least, upon that idea!" After this exclamation, the officer arose and marched, with his hands in the pockets of his justaucorps, about the immense ante-chamber that served him as an apartment. The wax-light flamed furiously under the effects of a fresh breeze, which stole in through the chinks of the door and the window, and cut the salle diagonally. It threw out a reddish, unequal light, sometimes brilliant, sometimes dull, and the tall shadow of the lieutenant was seen marching on the wall, in profile, like a figure by Callot, with his long sword and feathered hat.

"Certainly!" said he, "I am mistaken if Mazarin is not laying a snare for this amorous boy. Mazarin, this evening, gave an address, and made an appointment as complacently as M. Daangeau himself could have done—I heard him, and I know the meaning of his words. 'To-morrow morning,' said he, 'they will pass opposite the bridge of Blois.' Mordioux! that is clear enough, and particularly for a lover. That is the cause of this embarrassment; that is the cause of this hesitation; that is the cause of this order—'Monsieur the lieutenant of my musketeers, be on horseback to-morrow at four o'clock in the morning.' Which is as clear as if he had said,—'Monsieur the lieutenant of my musketeers, to-morrow, at four, at the bridge of Blois,—do you understand?' Here is a state secret, then, which I, humble as I am, have in my possession, while it is in action. And how do I get it? Because I have good eyes, as his majesty just now said. They say he loves this little Italian doll furiously. They say he threw himself at his mother's feet, to beg her to allow him to marry her. They say the queen went so far as to consult the court of Rome, whether such a marriage, contracted against her will, would be valid. Oh, if I were but twenty-five! If I had by my side those I no longer have! If I did not despise the whole world most profoundly, I would embroil Mazarin with the queen-mother, France with Spain, and I would make a queen after my own fashion. But let that pass." And the lieutenant snapped his fingers in disdain.

"This miserable Italian—this poor creature—this sordid wretch—who has just refused the king of England a million, would not perhaps give me a thousand pistoles for the news I would carry him. Mordioux! I am falling into second childhood—I am becoming stupid indeed! The idea of Mazarin giving anything! ha! ha! ha!" and he laughed in a subdued voice.

"Well, let us go to sleep—let us go to sleep; and the sooner the better. My mind is wearied with my evening's work, and will see things to-morrow more clearly than to-day."

And upon this recommendation, made to himself, he folded his cloak around him, looking with contempt upon his royal neighbor. Five minutes after this he was asleep, with his hands clenched and his lips apart, giving escape, not to his secret, but to a sonorous sound, which rose and spread freely beneath the majestic roof of the ante-chamber.

Chapter XIII.
Mary de Mancini.

THE sun had scarcely shed its first beams on the majestic trees of the park and the lofty turrets of the castle, when the young king, who had been awake more than two hours, possessed by the sleeplessness of love, opened his shutters himself, and cast an inquiring look into the courts of the sleeping palace. He saw that it was the hour agreed upon: the great court clock pointed to a quarter past four. He did not disturb his valet de chambre, who was sleeping soundly at some distance; he dressed himself, and the valet, in a great fright, sprang up, thinking he had been deficient in his duty; but the king sent him back again, commanding him to preserve the most absolute silence. He then descended the little staircase, went out at a lateral door, and perceived at the end of the wall a mounted horseman, holding another horse by the bridle. This horseman could not be recognized in his cloak and slouched hat. As to the horse, saddled like that of a rich citizen, it offered nothing remarkable to the most experienced eye. Louis took the bridle: the officer held the stirrup without dismounting, and asked his majesty's orders in a low voice.

"Follow me," replied the king.

The officer put his horse to the trot, behind that of his master, and they descended the hill towards the bridge. When they reached the other side of the Loire,—

"Monsieur," said the king, "you will please to ride on till you see a carriage coming; then return and inform me. I will wait here."

"Will your majesty deign to give me some description of the carriage I am charged to discover?"

"A carriage in which you will see two ladies, and probably their attendants likewise."

"Sire, I should not wish to make a mistake; is there no other sign by which I may know this carriage?"

"It will bear, in all probability, the arms of monsieur le cardinal."

"That is sufficient, sire," replied the officer, fully instructed in the object of his search. He put his horse to the trot, and rode sharply on in the direction pointed out by the king. But he had scarcely gone five hundred paces when he saw four mules, and then a carriage, loom up from behind a little hill. Behind this carriage came another. It required only one glance to assure him that these were the equipages he was in search of; he therefore turned his bridle, and rode back to the king.

"Sire," said he, "here are the carriages. The first, as you said, contains two ladies with their femmes de chambre; the second contains the footmen, provisions, and necessaries."

"That is well," replied the king in an agitated voice. "Please to go and tell those ladies that a cavalier of the court wishes to pay his respects to them alone."

The officer set off at a gallop. "Mordioux!" said he, as he rode on, "here is a new and honorable employment, I hope! I complained of being nobody. I am the king's confidant: that is enough to make a musketeer burst with pride."

He approached the carriage, and delivered his message gallantly and intelligently. There were two ladies in the carriage: one of great beauty, although rather thin; the other less favored by nature, but lively, graceful, and uniting in the delicate lines of her brow all the signs of a strong will. Her eyes, animated and piercing, in particular, spoke more eloquently than all the amorous phrases in fashion in those days of gallantry. It was to her D'Artagnan addressed himself, without fear of being mistaken, although the other was, as we have said, the more handsome of the two.

"Madame," said he, "I am the lieutenant of the musketeers, and there is on the road a horseman who awaits you, and is desirous of paying his respects to you."

At these words, the effect of which he watched closely, the lady with the black eyes uttered a cry of joy, leant out of the carriage window, and seeing the cavalier approaching, held out her arms, exclaiming:

"Ah, my dear sire!" and the tears gushed from her eyes.

The coachman stopped his team; the women rose in confusion from the back of the carriage, and the second lady made a slight curtsey, terminated by the most ironical smile that jealousy ever imparted to the lips of woman.

"Marie, dear Marie," cried the king, taking the hand of the black-eyed lady in both his. And opening the heavy door himself, he drew her out of the carriage with so much ardor, that she was in his arms before she touched the ground. The lieutenant, posted on the other side of the carriage, saw and heard all without being observed.

The king offered his arm to Mademoiselle de Mancini, and made a sign to the coachman and lackeys to proceed. It was nearly six o'clock; the road was fresh and pleasant; tall trees with their foliage still inclosed in the golden down of their buds, let the dew of morning filter from their trembling branches, like liquid diamonds; the grass was bursting at the foot of the hedges; the swallows having returned only a few days since, described their graceful curves between the heavens and the water; a breeze, laden with the perfumes of the blossoming woods, sighed along the road, and wrinkled the surface of the waters of the river; all these beauties of the day, all these perfumes of the plants, all these aspirations of the earth towards heaven, intoxicated the two lovers, walking side by side, leaning upon each other, eyes fixed upon eyes, hand clasping hand, and who, lingering as by a common desire, did not dare to speak, they had so much to say.

The officer saw that the king's horse, in wandering this way and that, annoyed Mademoiselle de Mancini. He took advantage of the pretext of securing the horse to draw near them, and dismounting, walked between the two horses he led; he did not lose a single word or gesture of the lovers. It was Mademoiselle de Mancini who at length began.

"Ah, my dear sire!" said she, "you do not abandon me, then?"

"No, Marie," replied the king; "you see I do not."

"I had so often been told, though, that as soon as we should be separated you would no longer think of me."

"Dear Marie, is it then to-day only that you have discovered we are surrounded by people interested in deceiving us?"

"But then, sire, this journey, this alliance with Spain? They are going to marry you off!"

Louis hung his head. At the same time the officer could see the eyes of Marie de Mancini shine in the sun with the brilliancy of a dagger starting from its sheath. "And you have done nothing in favor of our love?" asked the girl, after a silence of a moment.

"Ah! mademoiselle, how could you believe that? I threw myself at the feet of my mother; I begged her, I implored her; I told her all my hopes of happiness were in you; I even threatened—"

"Well?" asked Marie, eagerly.

"Well, the queen-mother wrote to the court of Rome, and received as answer, that a marriage between us would have no validity, and would be dissolved by the holy father. At length, finding there was no hope for us, I requested to have my marriage with the infanta at least delayed."

"And yet that does not prevent your being on the road to meet her?"

"How can I help it? To my prayers, to my supplications, to my tears, I received no answer but reasons of state."

"Well, well?"

"Well, what is to be done, mademoiselle, when so many wills are leagued against me?"

It was now Marie's turn to hang her head. "Then I must bid you adieu forever," said she. "You know that I am being exiled; you know that I am going to be buried alive; you know still more that they want to marry me off, too."

Louis became very pale, and placed his hand upon his heart.

"If I had thought that my life only had been at stake, I have been so persecuted that I might have yielded; but I thought yours was concerned, my dear sire, and I stood out for the sake of preserving your happiness."

"Oh, yes! my happiness, my treasure!" murmured the king, more gallantly than passionately, perhaps.

"The cardinal might have yielded," said Marie, "if you had addressed yourself to him, if you had pressed him. For the cardinal to call the king of France his nephew! do you not perceive, sire? He would have made war even for that honor; the cardinal, assured of governing alone, under the double pretext of having brought up the king and given his niece to him in marriage—the cardinal would have fought all antagonists, overcome all obstacles. Oh, sire! I can answer for that. I am a woman, and I see clearly into everything where love is concerned."

These words produced a strange effect upon the king. Instead of heightening his passion, they cooled it. He stopped, and said hastily,—

"What is to be said, mademoiselle? Everything has failed."

"Except your will, I trust, my dear sire?"

"Alas!" said the king, coloring, "have I a will?"

"Oh!" said Mademoiselle de Mancini mournfully, wounded by that expression.

"The king has no will but that which policy dictates, but that which reasons of state impose upon him."

"Oh! it is because you have no love," cried Mary; "if you loved, sire, you would have a will."

On pronouncing these words, Mary raised her eyes to her lover, whom she saw more pale and more cast down than an exile who is about to quit his native land forever. "Accuse me," murmured the king, "but do not say I do not love you."

A long silence followed these words, which the young king had pronounced with a perfectly true and profound feeling. "I am unable to think that to-morrow, and after to-morrow, I shall see you no more; I cannot think that I am going to end my sad days at a distance from Paris; that the lips of an old man, of an unknown, should touch that hand which you hold within yours; no, in truth, I cannot think of all that, my dear sire, without having my poor heart burst with despair."

And Marie de Mancini did shed floods of tears. On his part, the king, much affected, carried his handkerchief to his mouth, and stifled a sob.

"See," said she, "the carriages have stopped, my sister waits for me, the time is come; what you are about to decide upon will be decided for life. Oh, sire! you are willing, then, that I should lose you? You are willing, then, Louis, that she to whom you have said 'I love you,' should belong to another than to her king, to her master, to her lover? Oh! courage, Louis! courage! One word, a single word! Say 'I will!' and all my life is enchained to yours, and all my heart is yours forever."

The king made no reply. Mary then looked at him as Dido looked at Aeneas in the Elysian fields, fierce and disdainful.

"Farewell, then," said she; "farewell life! love! heaven!"

And she took a step away. The king detained her, seizing her hand, which he pressed to his lips, and despair prevailing over the resolution he appeared to have inwardly formed, he let fall upon that beautiful hand a burning tear of regret, which made Mary start, so really had that tear burnt her. She saw the humid eyes of the king, his pale brow, his convulsed lips, and cried, with an accent that cannot be described,—

"Oh, sire! you are a king, you weep, and yet I depart!"

As his sole reply, the king hid his face in his handkerchief. The officer uttered something so like a roar that it frightened the horses. Mademoiselle de Mancini, quite indignant, quitted the king's arm, hastily entered the carriage, crying to the coachman, "Go on, go on, and quick!"

The coachman obeyed, flogging his mules, and the heavy carriage rocked upon its creaking axle, whilst the king of France, alone, cast down, annihilated, did not dare to look either behind or before him.

Chapter XIV.
In which the King and the Lieutenant each give Proofs of Memory.

WHEN the king, like all the people in the world who are in love, had long and attentively watched disappear in the distance the carriage which bore away his mistress; when he had turned and turned again a hundred times to the same side and had at length succeeded in somewhat calming the agitation of his heart and thoughts, he recollected that he was not alone. The officer still held the horse by the bridle, and had not lost all hope of seeing the king recover his resolution. He had still the resource of mounting and riding after the carriage; they would have lost nothing by waiting a little. But the imagination of the lieutenant of the musketeers was too rich and too brilliant; it left far behind it that of the king, who took care not to allow himself to be carried away to such excess. He contented himself with approaching the officer, and in a doleful voice, "Come," said he, "let us be gone; all is ended. To horse!"

The officer imitated this carriage, this slowness, this sadness, and leisurely mounted his horse. The king pushed on sharply, the lieutenant followed him. At the bridge Louis turned around for the last time. The lieutenant, patient as a god who has eternity behind and before him, still hoped for a return of energy. But it was groundless, nothing appeared. Louis gained the street which led to the castle, and entered as seven was striking. When the king had returned, and the musketeer, who saw everything, had seen a corner of the tapestry over the cardinal's window lifted up, he breathed a profound sigh, like a man unloosed from the tightest bonds, and said in a low voice:

"Now then, my officer, I hope that it is over."

The king summoned his gentleman. "Please to understand I shall receive nobody before two o'clock," said he.

"Sire," replied the gentleman, "there is, however, some one who requests admittance."

"Who is that?"

"Your lieutenant of musketeers."

"He who accompanied me?"

"Yes, sire."

"Ah," said the king, "let him come in."

The officer entered. The king made a sign, and the gentleman and the valet retired. Louis followed them with his eyes until they had shut the door, and when the tapestries had fallen behind them,—"You remind me by your presence, monsieur, of something I had forgotten to recommend to you, that is to say, the most absolute discretion."

"Oh! sire, why does your majesty give yourself the trouble of making me such a recommendation? It is plain you do not know me."

"Yes, monsieur, that is true. I know that you are discreet; but as I had prescribed nothing—"

The officer bowed. "Has your majesty nothing else to say to me?"

"No, monsieur; you may retire."

"Shall I obtain permission not to do so till I have spoken to the king, sire?"

"What do you have to say to me? Explain yourself, monsieur."

"Sire, a thing without importance to you, but which interests me greatly. Pardon me, then, for speaking of it. Without urgency, without necessity, I never would have done it, and I would have disappeared, mute and insignificant as I always have been."

"How! Disappeared! I do not understand you, monsieur."

"Sire, in a word," said the officer, "I am come to ask for my discharge from your majesty's service."

The king made a movement of surprise, but the officer remained as motionless as a statue.

"Your discharge—yours, monsieur? and for how long a time, I pray?"

"Why, forever, sire."

"What, you are desirous of quitting my service, monsieur?" said Louis, with an expression that revealed something more than surprise.

"Sire, I regret to say that I am."

"Impossible!"

"It is so, however, sire. I am getting old; I have worn harness now thirty-five years; my poor shoulders are tired; I feel that I must give place to the young. I don't belong to this age; I have still one foot in the old one; it results that everything is strange in my eyes, everything astonishes and bewilders me. In short, I have the honor to ask your majesty for my discharge."

"Monsieur," said the king, looking at the officer, who wore his uniform with an ease that would have caused envy in a young man, "you are stronger and more vigorous than I am."

"Oh!" replied the officer, with an air of false modesty, "your majesty says so because I still have a good eye and a tolerably firm foot—because I can still ride a horse, and my mustache is black; but, sire, vanity of vanities all that—illusions all that—appearance, smoke, sire! I have still a youthful air, it is true, but I feel old, and within six months I am certain I shall be broken down, gouty, impotent. Therefore, then, sire—"

"Monsieur," interrupted the king, "remember your words of yesterday. You said to me in this very place where you now are, that you were endowed with the best health of any man in France; that fatigue was unknown to you! that you did not mind spending whole days and nights at your post. Did you tell me that, monsieur, or not? Try and recall, monsieur."

The officer sighed. "Sire," said he, "old age is boastful; and it is pardonable for old men to praise themselves when others no longer do it. It is very possible I said that; but the fact is, sire, I am very much fatigued, an request permission to retire."

"Monsieur," said the king, advancing towards the officer with a gesture full of majesty, "you are not assigning me the true reason. You wish to quit my service, it may be true, but you disguise from me the motive of your retreat."

"Sire, believe that—"

"I believe what I see, monsieur; I see a vigorous, energetic man, full of presence of mind, the best soldier in France, perhaps; and this personage cannot persuade me the least in the world that he stands in need of rest."

"Ah! sire," said the lieutenant, with bitterness, "what praise! Indeed, your majesty confounds me! Energetic, vigorous, brave, intelligent, the best soldier in the army! But, sire, your majesty exaggerates my small portion of merit to such a point, that however good an opinion I may have of myself, I do not recognize myself; in truth I do not. If I were vain enough to believe only half of your majesty's words, I should consider myself a valuable, indispensable man. I should say that a servant possessed of such brilliant qualities was a treasure beyond all price. Now, sire, I have been all my life—I feel bound to say it—except at the present time, appreciated, in my opinion, much below my value. I therefore repeat, your majesty exaggerates."

The king knitted his brow, for he saw a bitter raillery beneath the words of the officer. "Come, monsieur," said he, "let us meet the question frankly. Are you dissatisfied with my service, say? No evasions; speak boldly, frankly—I command you to do so."

The officer, who had been twisting his hat about in his hands, with an embarrassed air, for several minutes, raised his head at these words. "Oh! sire," said he, "that puts me a little more at my ease. To a question put so frankly, I will reply frankly. To tell the truth is a good thing, as much from the pleasure one feels in relieving one's heart, as on account of the rarity of the fact. I will speak the truth, then, to my king, at the same time imploring him to excuse the frankness of an old soldier."

Louis looked at his officer with anxiety, which he manifested by the agitation of his gesture. "Well, then, speak," said he, "for I am impatient to hear the truths you have to tell me."

The officer threw his hat upon a table, and his countenance, always so intelligent and martial, assumed, all at once, a strange character of grandeur and solemnity. "Sire," said he, "I quit the king's service because I am dissatisfied. The valet, in these times, can approach his master as respectfully as I do, can give him an account of his labor, bring back his tools, return the funds that have been intrusted to him, and say 'Master, my day's work is done. Pay me, if you please, and let us part.'"

"Monsieur! monsieur!" exclaimed the king, crimson with rage.

"Ah! sire," replied the officer, bending his knee for a moment, "never was servant more respectful than I am before your majesty; only you commanded me to tell the truth. Now I have begun to tell it, it must come out, even if you command me to hold my tongue."

There was so much resolution expressed in the deep-sunk muscles of the officer's countenance, that Louis XIV. had no occasion to tell him to continue; he continued, therefore, whilst the king looked at him with a curiosity mingled with admiration.

"Sire, I have, as I have said, now served the house of France thirty-five years; few people have worn out so many swords in that service as I have, and the swords I speak of were good swords, too, sire. I was a boy, ignorant of everything except courage, when the king your father guessed that there was a man in me. I was a man, sire, when the Cardinal de Richelieu, who was a judge of manhood, discovered an enemy in me. Sire, the history of that enmity between the ant and the lion may be read from the first to the last line, in the secret archives of your family. If ever you feel an inclination to know it, do so, sire; the history is worth the trouble—it is I who tell you so. You will there read that the lion, fatigued, harassed, out of breath, at length cried for quarter, and the justice must be rendered him to say, that he gave as much as he required. Oh! those were glorious times, sire, strewed over with battles like one of Tasso's or Ariosto's epics. The wonders of those times, to which the people of ours would refuse belief, were every-day occurrences. For five years together, I was a hero every day; at least, so I was told by persons of judgment; and that is a long period for heroism, trust me, sire, a period of five years. Nevertheless, I have faith in what these people told me, for the were good judges. They were named M. de Richelieu, M. de Buckingham, M. de Beaufort, M. de Retz, a mighty genius himself in street warfare,—in short, the king, Louis XIII., and even the queen, your noble mother, who one day condescended to say, 'Thank you.' I don't know what service I had had the good fortune to render her. Pardon me, sire, for speaking so boldly; but what I relate to you, as I have already had the honor to tell your majesty, is history." The king bit his lips, and threw himself violently on a chair.

"I appear importunate to your majesty," said the lieutenant. "Eh! sire, that is the fate of truth; she is a stern companion; she bristles all over with steel; she wounds those whom she attacks, and sometimes him who speaks her."

"No, monsieur," replied the king: "I bade you speak—speak then."

"After the service of the king and the cardinal, came the service of the regency, sire; I fought pretty well in the Fronde—much less, though, than the first time. The men began to diminish in stature. I have, nevertheless, led your majesty's musketeers on some perilous occasions, which stand upon the orders of the day of the company. Mine was a beautiful luck at that time. I was the favorite of M. de Mazarin. Lieutenant here! lieutenant there! lieutenant to the right! lieutenant to the left! There was not a buffet dealt in France, of which your humble servant did not have the dealing; but soon France was not enough. The cardinal sent me to England on Cromwell's account; another gentleman who was not over gentle, I assure you, sire. I had the honor of knowing him, and I was well able to appreciate him. A great deal was promised me on account of that mission. So, as I did much more than I had been bidden to do, I was generously paid, for I was at length appointed captain of the musketeers; that is to say, the most envied position in court, which takes precedence over the marshals of France, and justly; for who says captain of the musketeers says the flower of chivalry and king of the brave."

"Captain, monsieur!" interrupted the king; "you make a mistake. Lieutenant, you mean."

"Not at all, sire—I make no mistake; your majesty may rely upon me in that respect. Monsieur le cardinal gave me the commission himself."

"Well!"

"But M. de Mazarin, as you know better than anybody, does not often give, and sometimes takes back what he has given; he took it back again as soon as peace was made and he was no longer in want of me. Certainly I was not worthy to replace M. de Treville, of illustrious memory; but they had promised me, and they had given me; they ought to have stopped there."

"Is that what dissatisfies you monsieur? Well, I shall make inquiries. I love justice; and your claim, though made in military fashion, does not displease me."

"Oh, sire!" said the officer, "your majesty has ill understood me; I no longer claim anything now."

"Excess of delicacy, monsieur; but I will keep my eye upon your affairs, and later—"

"Oh, sire! what a word!—later! Thirty years have I lived upon that promising word, which has been pronounced by so many great personages, and which your mouth has, in its turn, just pronounced. Later—that is how I have received a score of wounds, and how I have reached fifty-four years of age without ever having had a louis in my purse, and without ever having met with a protector on my way,—I who have protected so many people! So I change my formula, sire; and when any one says to me 'Later,' I reply 'Now.' It is rest that I solicit, sire. That may be easily granted me. That will cost nobody anything."

"I did not look for this language, monsieur, particularly from a man who has always lived among the great. You forget you are speaking to the king, to a gentleman who is, I suppose, as of good a house as yourself; and when I say later, I mean a certainty."

"I do not at all doubt it, sire; but this is the end of the terrible truth I had to tell you. If I were to see upon that table a marshal's stick, the sword of constable, the crown of Poland, instead of later, I swear to you, sire, that I should still say Now! Oh, excuse me, sire! I am from the country of your grandfather, Henry IV. I do not speak often: but when I do speak, I speak all."

"The future of my reign has little temptation for you, monsieur, it appears," said Louis, haughtily.

"Forgetfulness, forgetfulness everywhere!" cried the officer, with a noble air; "the master has forgotten the servant, so the servant is reduced to forget his master. I live in unfortunate times, sire. I see youth full of discouragement and fear, I see it timid and despoiled, when it ought to be rich and powerful. I yesterday evening, for example, open the door to a king of England, whose father, humble as I am, I was near saving, if God had not been against me— God, who inspired His elect, Cromwell! I open, I said, the door, that is to say, the palace of one brother to another brother, and I see—stop, sire, that is a load on my heart!—I see the minister of that king drive away the proscribed prince, and humiliate his master by condemning to want another king, his equal. Then I see my prince, who is young, handsome and brave, who has courage in his heart and lightening in his eye,—I see him tremble before a priest, who laughs at him behind the curtain of his alcove, where he digests all the gold of France, which he afterwards stuffs into secret coffers. Yes—I understand your looks, sire. I am bold to madness; but what is to be said? I am an old man, and I tell you here, sire, to you, my king, things which I would cram down the throat of any one who should dare to pronounce them before me. You have commanded me, to pour out the bottom of my heart before you, sire, and I cast at the feet of your majesty the pent-up indignation of thirty years, as I would pour out all my blood, if your majesty commanded me to do so."

The king, without speaking a word, wiped the drops of cold and abundant perspiration which trickled from his temples. The moment of silence which followed this vehement outbreak represented for him who had spoken, and for him who had listened, ages of suffering.

"Monsieur," said the king at length, "you spoke the word forgetfulness. I have heard nothing but that word; I will reply, then, to it alone. Others have perhaps been able to forget, but I have not, and the proof is, that I remember that one day of riot, that one day when the furious people, raging and roaring as the sea, invaded the royal palace; that one day when I feigned sleep in my bed, one man alone, naked sword in hand, concealed behind my curtain, watched over my life, ready to risk his own for me, as he had before risked it twenty times for the lives of my family. Was not the gentleman, whose name I then demanded, called M. d'Artagnan? say, monsieur."

"Your majesty has a good memory," replied the officer, coldly.

"You see, then," continued the king, "if I have such remembrances of my childhood, what an amount I may gather in the age of reason."

"Your majesty has been richly endowed by God," said the officer, in the same tone.

"Come, Monsieur d'Artagnan," continued Louis, with feverish agitation, "ought you not to be patient as I am? Ought you not to do as I do? Come!"

"And what do you do, sire?"

"I wait."

"Your majesty may do so, because you are young; but I, sire, have not time to wait; old age is at my door, and death is behind it, looking into the very depths of my house. Your majesty is beginning life, its future is full of hope and fortune; but I, sire, I am on the other side of the horizon, and we are so far from each other, that I should never have time to wait till your majesty came up to me."

Louis made another turn in his apartment, still wiping the moisture from his brow, in a manner that would have terrified his physicians, if his physicians had witnessed the state his majesty was in.

"It is very well, monsieur," said Louis XIV., in a sharp voice; "you are desirous of having your discharge, and you shall have it. You offer me your resignation of the rank of lieutenant of the musketeers?"

"I deposit it humbly at your majesty's feet, sire."

"That is sufficient. I will order your pension."

"I shall have a thousand obligations to your majesty."

"Monsieur," said the king, with a violent effort, "I think you are losing a good master."

"And I am sure of it, sire."

"Shall you ever find such another?"

"Oh, sire! I know that your majesty is alone in the world; therefore will I never again take service with any other king upon earth, and will never again have other master than myself."

"You say so?"

"I swear so, your majesty."

"I shall remember that word, monsieur."

D'Artagnan bowed.

"And you know I have a good memory," said the king.

"Yes, sire; and yet I should desire that that memory should fail your majesty in this instance, in order that you might forget all the miseries I have been forced to spread before your eyes. Your majesty is so much above the poor and the mean, that I hope—"

"My majesty, monsieur, will act like the sun, which looks upon all, great and small, rich and poor, giving luster to some, warmth to others, and life to all. Adieu, Monsieur d'Artagnan—adieu: you are free."

And the king, with a hoarse sob, which was lost in his throat, passed quickly into the next room. D'Artagnan took up his hat from the table on which he had thrown in, and went out.

Chapter XV.
The Proscribed.

D'ARTAGNAN had not reached the bottom of the staircase, when the king called his gentleman. "I have a commission to give you, monsieur," said he.

"I am at your majesty's commands."

"Wait, then." And the young king began to write the following letter, which cost him more than one sigh, although, at the same time, something like a feeling of triumph glittered in his eyes:

"MY LORD CARDINAL,—Thanks to your good counsels, and, above all, thanks to your firmness, I have succeeded in overcoming a weakness unworthy of a king. You have too ably arranged my destiny to allow gratitude not to stop me at the moment when I was about to destroy your work. I felt I was wrong to wish to make my life turn from the course you had marked out for it. Certainly it would have been a misfortune to France and my family if a misunderstanding had taken place between me and my minister. This, however, would certainly have happened if I had made your niece my wife. I am perfectly aware of this, and will henceforth oppose nothing to the accomplishment of my destiny. I am prepared, then, to wed the infanta, Maria Theresa. You may at once open the conference.—Your affectionate LOUIS."

The king, after reperusing the letter, sealed it himself.

"This letter for my lord cardinal," said he.

The gentleman took it. At Mazarin's door he found Bernouin waiting with anxiety.

"Well?" asked the minister's valet de chambre.

"Monsieur," said the gentleman, "here is a letter for his eminence."

"A letter! Ah! we expected one after the little journey of the morning."

"Oh! you know, then, that his majesty—"

"As first minister, it belongs to the duties of our charge to know everything. And his majesty prays and implores, I presume."

"I don't know, but he sighed frequently whilst he was writing."

"Yes, yes, yes; we understand all that; people sigh sometimes from happiness as well as from grief, monsieur."

"And yet the king did not look very happy when he returned, monsieur."

"You did not see clearly. Besides, you only saw his majesty on his return, for he was only accompanied by the lieutenant of the guards. But I had his eminence's telescope; I looked through it when he was tired, and I am sure they both wept."

"Well! was it for happiness they wept?"

"No, but for love, and they vowed to each other a thousand tendernesses, which the king asks no better to keep. Now this letter is a beginning of the execution."

"And what does his eminence think of this love, which is, by the bye, no secret to anybody?"

Bernouin took the gentleman by the arm, and whilst ascending the staircase,—"In confidence," said he, in a low voice, "his eminence looks for success in the affair. I know very well we shall have war with Spain; but, bah! war will please the nobles. My lord cardinal, besides, can endow his niece royally, nay, more than royally. There will be money, festivities, and fireworks—everybody will be delighted."

"Well, for my part," replied the gentleman, shaking his head, "it appears to me that this letter is very light to contain all that."

"My friend," replied Bernouin, "I am certain of what I tell you. M. d'Artagnan related all that passed to me."

"Ay, ay! and what did he tell you? Let us hear."

"I accosted him by asking him, on the part of the cardinal, if there were any news, without discovering my designs, observe, for M. d'Artagnan is a cunning hand. 'My dear Monsieur Bernouin,' he replied, 'the king is madly in love with Mademoiselle de Mancini, that is all I have to tell you.' And then I asked him: 'Do you think, to such a degree that it will urge him to act contrary to the designs of his eminence?' 'Ah! don't ask me,' said he; 'I think the king capable of anything; he has a will of iron, and what he wills he wills in earnest. If he takes it into his head to marry Mademoiselle de Mancini, he will marry her, depend upon it.' And thereupon he left me and went straight to the stables, took a horse, saddled it himself, jumped upon its back, and set off as if the devil were at his heels."

"So that you believe, then——"

"I believe that monsieur the lieutenant of the guards knew more than he was willing to say."

"In you opinion, then, M. d'Artagnan——"

"Is gone, according to all probability, after the exiles, to carry out all that can facilitate the success of the king's love."

Chatting thus, the two confidants arrived at the door of his eminence's apartment. His eminence's gout had left him; he was walking about his chamber in a state of great anxiety, listening at doors and looking out of windows. Bernouin entered, followed by the gentleman, who had orders from the king to place the letter in the hands of the cardinal himself. Mazarin took the letter, but before opening it, he got up a ready smile, a smile of circumstance, able to throw a veil over emotions of whatever sort they might be. So prepared, whatever was the impression received from the letter, no reflection of that impression was allowed to transpire upon his countenance.

"Well," said he, when he had read and reread the letter, "very well, monsieur. Inform the king that I thank him for his obedience to the wishes of the queen-mother, and that I will do everything for the accomplishment of his will."

The gentleman left the room. The door had scarcely closed before the cardinal, who had no mask for Bernouin, took off that which had so recently covered his face, and with a most dismal expression,—"Call M. de Brienne," said he. Five minutes afterward the secretary entered.

"Monsieur," said Mazarin, "I have just rendered a great service to the monarchy, the greatest I have ever rendered it. You will carry this letter, which proves it, to her majesty the queen-mother, and when she shall have returned it to you, you will lodge it in portfolio B., which is filed with documents and papers relative to my ministry."

Brienne went as desired, and, as the letter was unsealed, did not fail to read it on his way. There is likewise no doubt that Bernouin, who was on good terms with everybody, approached so near to the secretary as to be able to read the letter over his shoulder; so that the news spread with such activity through the castle, that Mazarin might have feared it would reach the ears of the queen-mother before M. de Brienne could convey Louis XIV.'s letter to her. A moment after orders were given for departure, and M. de Conde having been to pay his respects to the king on his pretended rising, inscribed the city of Poitiers upon his tablets, as the place of sojourn and rest for their majesties.

Thus in a few instants was unraveled an intrigue which had covertly occupied all the diplomacies of Europe. It had nothing, however, very clear as a result, but to make a poor lieutenant of musketeers lose his commission and his fortune. It is true, that in exchange he gained his liberty. We shall soon know how M. d'Artagnan profited by this. For the moment, if the reader will permit us, we shall return to the hostelry of les Medici, of which one of the windows opened at the very moment the orders were given for the departure of the king.

The window that opened was that of one of the rooms of Charles II. The unfortunate prince had passed the night in bitter reflections, his head resting on his hands, and his elbows on the table, whilst Parry, infirm and old, wearied in body and in mind, had fallen asleep in a corner. A singular fortune was that of this faithful servant, who saw beginning for the second generation the fearful series of misfortunes which had weighed so heavily on the first. When Charles II. had well thought over the fresh defeat he had experienced, when he perfectly comprehended the complete isolation into which he had just fallen, on seeing his fresh hope left behind him, he was seized as with a vertigo, and sank back into the large armchair in which he was seated. Then God took pity on the unhappy prince, and sent to console him sleep, the innocent brother of death. He did not wake till half-past six, that is to say, till the sun shone brightly into his chamber, and Parry, motionless with fear of waking him, was observing with profound grief the eyes of the young man already red with wakefulness, and his cheeks pale with suffering and privations.

At length the noise of some heavy carts descending towards the Loire awakened Charles. He arose, looked around him like a man who has forgotten everything, perceived Parry, shook him by the hand, and commanded him to settle the reckoning with Master Cropole. Master Cropole, being called upon to settle his account with Parry, acquitted himself, it must be allowed, like an honest man; he only made his customary remark, that the two travelers had eaten nothing, which had the double disadvantage of being humiliating for his kitchen, and of forcing him to ask payment for a repast not consumed, but not the less lost. Parry had nothing to say to the contrary, and paid.

"I hope," said the king, "it has not been the same with the horses. I don't see that they have eaten at your expense, and it would be a misfortune for travelers like us, who have a long journey to make, to have our horses fail us."

But Cropole, at this doubt, assumed his majestic air, and replied that the stables of les Medici were not less hospitable than its refectory.

The king mounted his horse; his old servant did the same, and both set out towards Paris, without meeting a single person on their road, in the streets or the faubourgs of the city. For the prince the blow was the more severe, as it was a fresh exile. The unfortunates cling to the smallest hopes, as the happy do to the greatest good; and when they are obliged to quit the place where that hope has soothed their hearts, they experience the mortal regret which the banished man feels when he places his foot upon the vessel which is to bear him into exile. It appears that the heart already wounded so many times suffers from the least scratch; it appears that it considers as a good the momentary absence of evil, which is nothing but the absence of pain; and that God, into the most terrible misfortunes, has thrown hope as the drop of water which the rich sinner in hell entreated of Lazarus.

For one instant even the hope of Charles II. had been more than a fugitive joy;—that was when he found himself so kindly welcomed by his brother king; then it had taken a form that had become a reality; then, all at once, the refusal of Mazarin had reduced the fictitious reality to the state of a dream. This promise of Louis XIV., so soon retracted, had been nothing but a mockery; a mockery like his crown—like his scepter—like his friends—like all that had surrounded his royal childhood, and which had abandoned his proscribed youth. Mockery! everything was a mockery for Charles II. except the cold, black repose promised by death.

Such were the ideas of the unfortunate prince while sitting listlessly upon his horse, to which he abandoned the reins: he rode slowly along beneath the warm May sun, in which the somber misanthropy of the exile perceived a last insult to his grief.

Chapter XVI.
"Remember!"

A HORSEMAN going rapidly along the road leading towards Blois, which he had left nearly half an hour before, passed the two travelers, and, though apparently in haste, raised his hat as he passed them. The king scarcely observed this young man, who was about twenty-five years of age, and who, turning round several times, made friendly signals to a man standing before the gate of a handsome white-and-red house; that is to say, built of brick and stone, with a slated roof, situated on the left hand of the road the prince was traveling.

This man, old, tall, and thin, with white hair,—we speak of the one standing by the gate;—this man replied to the farewell signals of the young one by signs of parting as tender as could have been made by a father. The young man disappeared at the first turn of the road, bordered by fine trees, and the old man was preparing to return to the house, when the two travelers, arriving in front of the gate, attracted his attention.

The king, as we have said, was riding with his head cast down, his arms inert, leaving his horse to go what pace he liked, whilst Parry, behind him, the better to imbibe the genial influence of the sun, had taken off his hat, and was looking about right and left. His eyes encountered those of the old man leaning against the gate; the latter, as if struck by some strange spectacle, uttered an exclamation, and made one step towards the two travelers. From Parry his eyes immediately turned towards the king, upon whom they rested for an instant. This examination, however rapid, was instantly reflected in a visible manner upon the features of the tall old man. For scarcely had he recognized the younger of the travelers—and we said recognized, for nothing but a perfect recognition could have explained such an act—scarcely, we say, had he recognized the younger of the two travelers, than he clapped his hands together, with respectful surprise, and, raising his hat from his head, bowed so profoundly that it might have been said he was kneeling. This demonstration, however absent, or rather, however absorbed was the king in his reflections, attracted his attention instantly; and checking his horse and turning towards Parry, he exclaimed, "Good God, Parry, who is that man who salutes me in such a marked manner? Can he know me, think you?"

Parry, much agitated and very pale, had already turned his horse towards the gate. "Ah, sire!" said he, stopping suddenly at five or six paces' distance from the still bending old man: "sire, I am seized with astonishment, for I think I recognize that brave man. Yes, it must be he! Will your majesty permit me to speak to him?"

"Certainly."

"Can it be you, Monsieur Grimaud?" asked Parry.

"Yes, it is I," replied the tall old man, drawing himself up, but without losing his respectful demeanor.

"Sire," then said Parry, "I was not deceived. This good man is the servant of the Comte de la Fere, and the Comte de la Fere, if you remember, is the worthy gentleman of whom I have so often spoken to your majesty that the remembrance of him must remain, not only in your mind, but in your heart."

"He who assisted my father at his last moments?" asked Charles, evidently affected at the remembrance.

"The same, sire."

"Alas!" said Charles; and then addressing Grimaud, whose penetrating and intelligent eyes seemed to search and divine his thoughts.—"My friend," said he, "does your master, Monsieur le Comte de la Fere, live in this neighborhood?"

"There," replied Grimaud, pointing with his outstretched arm to the white-and-red house behind the gate.

"And is Monsieur le Comte de la Fere at home at present?"

"At the back, under the chestnut trees."

"Parry," said the king, "I will not miss this opportunity, so precious for me, to thank the gentleman to whom our house is indebted for such a noble example of devotedness and generosity. Hold my horse, my friend, if you please." And, throwing the bridle to Grimaud, the king entered the abode of Athos, quite alone, as one equal enters the dwelling of another. Charles had been informed by the concise explanation of Grimaud,—"At the back, under the chestnut trees;" he left, therefore, the house on the left, and went straight down the path indicated. The thing was easy; the tops of those noble trees, already covered with leaves and flowers, rose above all the rest.

On arriving under the lozenges, by turns luminous and dark, which checkered the ground of this path according as the trees were more or less in leaf, the young prince perceived a gentleman walking with his arms behind him, apparently plunged in a deep meditation. Without doubt, he had often had this gentleman described to himself, for, without hesitating, Charles II. walked straight up to him. At the sound of his footsteps, the Comte de la Fere raised his head, and seeing an unknown man of noble and elegant carriage coming towards him, he raised his hat and waited. At some paces from him, Charles II. likewise took off his hat. Then, as if in reply to the comte's mute interrogation,—

"Monsieur le Comte," said he, "I come to discharge a debt towards you. I have, for a long time, had the expression of a profound gratitude to bring you. I am Charles II., son of Charles Stuart, who reigned in England, and died on the scaffold."

On hearing this illustrious name, Athos felt a kind of shudder creep through his veins, but at the sight of the young prince standing uncovered before him, and stretching out his hand towards him, two tears, for an instant, dimmed his brilliant eyes. He bent respectfully, but the prince took him by the hand.

"See how unfortunate I am, my lord count; it is only due to chance that I have met with you. Alas! I ought to have people around me whom I love and honor, whereas I am reduced to preserve their services in my heart, and their names in my memory: so that if your servant had not recognized mine, I should have passed by your door as by that of a stranger."

"It is but too true," said Athos, replying with his voice to the first part of the king's speech, and with a bow to the second; "it is but too true, indeed, that your majesty has seen many evil days."

"And the worst, alas!" replied Charles, "are perhaps still to come."

"Sire, let us hope."

"Count, count," continued Charles, shaking his head, "I entertained hope till last night, and that of a good Christian, I swear."

Athos looked at the king as if to interrogate him.

"Oh, the history is soon related," said Charles. "Proscribed, despoiled, disdained, I resolved, in spite of all my repugnance, to tempt fortune one last time. Is it not written above, that, for our family, all good fortune and all bad fortune shall eternally come from France? You know something of that, monsieur,—you, who are one of the Frenchmen whom my unfortunate father found at the foot of his scaffold, on the day of his death, after having found them at his right hand on the day of battle."

"Sire," said Athos modestly, "I was not alone. My companions and I did, under the circumstances, our duty as gentlemen, and that was all. Your majesty was about to do me the honor to relate—"

"That is true, I had the protection,—pardon my hesitation, count, but, for a Stuart, you, who understand everything, you will comprehend that the word is hard to pronounce;—I had, I say, the protection of my cousin the stadtholder of Holland; but without the intervention, or at least without the authorization of France, the stadtholder would not take the initiative. I came, then, to ask this authorization of the king of France, who has refused me."

"The king has refused you, sire!"

"Oh, not he; all justice must be rendered to my younger brother Louis; but Monsieur de Mazarin—"

Athos bit his lips.

"You perhaps think I should have expected this refusal?" said the king, who had noticed the movement.

"That was, in truth, my thought, sire," replied Athos, respectfully; "I know that Italian of old."

"Then I determined to come to the test, and know at once the last word of my destiny. I told my brother Louis, that, not to compromise either France or Holland, I would tempt fortune myself in person, as I had already done, with two hundred gentlemen, if he would give them to me; and a million, if he would lend it me."

"Well, sire?"

"Well, monsieur, I am suffering at this moment something strange, and that is, the satisfaction of despair. There is in certain souls,—and I have just discovered that mine is of the number,—a real satisfaction in the assurance that all is lost, and the time is come to yield."

"Oh, I hope," said Athos, "that your majesty is not come to that extremity."

"To say so, my lord count, to endeavor to revive hope in my heart, you must have ill understood what I have just told you. I came to Blois to ask of my brother Louis the alms of a million, with which I had the hopes of re-establishing my affairs; and my brother Louis has refused me. You see, then, plainly, that all is lost."

"Will your majesty permit me to express a contrary opinion?"

"How is that, count? Do you think my heart of so low an order that I do not know how to face my position?"

"Sire, I have always seen that it was in desperate positions that suddenly the great turns of fortune have taken place."

"Thank you, count: it is some comfort to meet with a heart like yours; that is to say, sufficiently trustful in God and in monarchy, never to despair of a royal fortune, however low it may be fallen. Unfortunately, my dear count, your words are like those remedies they call 'sovereign,' and which, though able to cure curable wounds or diseases, fail against death. Thank you for your perseverance in consoling me, count, thanks for your devoted remembrance, but I know in what I must trust—nothing will save me now. And see, my friend, I was so convinced, that I was taking the route of exile, with my old Parry; I was returning to devour my poignant griefs in the little hermitage offered me by Holland. There, believe me, count, all will soon be over, and death will come quickly; it is called so often by this body, eaten up by its soul, and by this soul, which aspires to heaven."

"Your majesty has a mother, a sister, and brothers; your majesty is the head of the family, and ought, therefore, to ask a long life of God, instead of imploring Him for a prompt death. Your majesty is an exile, a fugitive, but you have right on your side; you ought to aspire to combats, dangers, business, and not to rest in heavens."

"Count," said Charles II., with a smile of indescribable sadness, "have you ever heard of a king who reconquered his kingdom with one servant the age of Parry, and with three hundred crowns which that servant carried in his purse?"

"No, sire; but I have heard—and that more than once—that a dethroned king has recovered his kingdom with a firm will, perseverance, some friends, and a million skillfully employed."

"But you cannot have understood me. The million I asked of my brother Louis was refused me."

"Sire," said Athos, "will your majesty grant me a few minutes, and listen attentively to what remains for me to say to you?"

Charles II. looked earnestly at Athos. "Willingly, monsieur," said he.

"Then I will show your majesty the way," resumed the count, directing his steps towards the house. He then conducted the king to his study, and begged him to be seated. "Sire," said he, "your majesty just now told me that, in the present state of England, a million would suffice for the recovery of your kingdom."

"To attempt it at least, monsieur; and to die as a king if I should not succeed."

"Well, then, sire, let your majesty, according to the promise you have made me, have the goodness to listen to what I have to say." Charles made an affirmative sign with his head. Athos walked straight up to the door, the bolts of which he drew, after looking to see if anybody was near, and then returned. "Sire," said he, "your majesty has kindly remembered that I lent assistance to the very noble and very unfortunate Charles I., when his executioners conducted him from St. James's to Whitehall."

"Yes, certainly I do remember it, and always shall remember it."

"Sire, it is a dismal history to be heard by a son who no doubt has had it related to him many times; and yet I ought to repeat it to your majesty without omitting one detail."

"Speak on, monsieur."

"When the king your father ascended the scaffold, or rather when he passed from his chamber to the scaffold, on a level with his window, everything was prepared for his escape. The executioner was got out of the way; a hole contrived under the floor of his apartment; I myself was beneath the funeral vault, which I heard all at once creak beneath his feet."

"Parry has related to me all these terrible details, monsieur."

Athos bowed and resumed. "But here is something he had not related to you, sire, for what follows passed between God, your father, and myself; and never has the revelation of it been made even to my dearest friends. 'Go a little further off,' said the august prisoner to the executioner; 'it is but for an instant, and I know that I belong to you; but remember not to strike till I give the signal. I wish to offer up my prayers in freedom.'"

"Pardon me," said Charles II., turning very pale, "but you, count, who know so many details of this melancholy event,—details which, as you said just now, have never been revealed to any one,—do you know the name of that infernal executioner, of that base wretch who concealed his face that he might assassinate a king with impunity?"

Athos became slightly pale. "His name?" said he, "yes, I know it, but cannot tell it."

"And what is become of him, for nobody in England knows his destiny?"

"He is dead."

"But he did not die in his bed; he did not die a calm and peaceful death; he did not die the death of the good?"

"He died a violent death, in a terrible night, rendered so by the passions of man and a tempest from God. His body, pierced by a dagger, sank to the depths of the ocean. God pardon his murderer!"

"Proceed, then," said Charles II., seeing that the count was unwilling to say more.

"The king of England, after having, as I have said, spoken thus to the masked executioner, added,—'Observe, you will not strike till I shall stretch out my arms, saying—REMEMBER!'"

"I was aware," said Charles, in an agitated voice, "that that was the last word pronounced by my unfortunate father. But why and for whom?"

"For the French gentleman placed beneath his scaffold."

"For you, then, monsieur?"

"Yes, sire; and every one of the words which he spoke to me, through the planks of the scaffold covered with a black cloth, still sounds in my ears. The king knelt down on one knee: 'Comte de la Fere,' said he, 'are you there?' 'Yes, sire,' replied I. Then the king stooped towards the boards."

Charles II., also palpitating with interest, burning with grief, stooped towards Athos, to catch, one by one, every word that escaped from him. His head touched that of the comte.

"Then," continued Athos, "the king stooped. 'Comte de la Fere,' said he, 'I could not be saved by you: it was not to be. Now, even though I commit a sacrilege, I must speak to you. Yes, I have spoken to men—yes, I have spoken to God, and I speak to you the last. To sustain a cause which I thought sacred, I have lost the throne of my fathers and the heritage of my children.'"

Charles II. concealed his face in his hands, and a bitter tear glided between his white and slender fingers.

"'I have still a million in gold,' continued the king. 'I buried it in the vaults of the castle of Newcastle, a moment before I left that city.'" Charles raised his head with an expression of such painful joy that it would have drawn tears from any one acquainted with his misfortunes.

"A million!" murmured he, "Oh, count!"

"'You alone know that this money exists: employ it when you think it can be of the greatest service to my eldest son. And now, Comte de la Fere, bid me adieu!'

"'Adieu, adieu, sire!' cried I."

Charles arose, and went and leant his burning brow against the window.

"It was then," continued Athos, "that the king pronounced the word 'REMEMBER!' addressed to me. You see, sire, that I have remembered."

The king could not resist or conceal his emotion. Athos beheld the movement of his shoulders, which undulated convulsively; he heard the sobs which burst from his over-charged breast. He was silent himself, suffocated by the flood of bitter remembrances he had just poured upon that royal head. Charles II., with a violent effort, left the window, devoured his tears, and came and sat by Athos. "Sire," said the latter, "I thought till to-day that the time had not yet arrived for the employment of that last resource; but, with my eyes fixed upon England, I felt it was approaching. To-morrow I meant to go and inquire in what part of the world your majesty was, and then I purposed going to you. You come to me, sire; that is an indication that God is with us."

"My lord," said Charles, in a voice choked by emotion, "you are, for me, what an angel sent from heaven would be,—you are a preserver sent to me from the tomb of my father himself; but, believe me, for ten years' civil war has passed over my country, striking down men, tearing up soil, it is no more probable that gold should remain in the entrails of the earth, than love in the hearts of my subjects."

"Sire, the spot in which his majesty buried the million is well known to me, and no one, I am sure, has been able to discover it. Besides, is the castle of Newcastle quite destroyed? Have they demolished it stone by stone, and uprooted the soil to the last tree?"

"No, it is still standing: but at this moment General Monk occupies it and is encamped there. The only spot from which I could look for succor, where I possess a single resource, you see, is invaded by my enemies."

"General Monk, sire, cannot have discovered the treasure which I speak of."

"Yes, but can I go and deliver myself up to Monk, in order to recover this treasure? Ah! count, you see plainly I must yield to destiny, since it strikes me to the earth every time I rise. What can I do with Parry as my only servant, with Parry, whom Monk has already driven from his presence? No, no, no, count, we must yield to this last blow."

"But what your majesty cannot do, and what Parry can no more attempt, do you not believe that I could succeed in accomplishing?"

"You—you, count—you would go?"

"If it please your majesty," said Athos, bowing to the king, "yes, I will go, sire."

"What! you so happy here, count?"

"I am never happy when I have a duty left to accomplish, and it is an imperative duty which the king your father left me to watch over your fortunes, and make a royal use of his money. So, if your majesty honors me with a sign, I will go with you."

"Ah, monsieur!" said the king, forgetting all royal etiquette and throwing his arms around the neck of Athos, "you prove to me that there is a God in heaven, and that this God sometimes sends messengers to the unfortunate who groan on the earth."

Athos, exceedingly moved by this burst of feeling of the young man, thanked him with profound respect, and approached the window. "Grimaud!" cried he, "bring out my horses."

"What, now—immediately!" said the king. "Ah, monsieur, you are indeed a wonderful man!"

"Sire," said Athos, "I know nothing more pressing than your majesty's service. Besides," added he, smiling, "it is a habit contracted long since, in the service of the queen your aunt, and of the king your father. How is it possible for me to lose it at the moment your majesty's service calls for it?"

"What a man!" murmured the king.

Then, after a moment's reflection,—"But no, count, I cannot expose you to such privations. I have no means of rewarding such services."

"Bah!" said Athos, laughing. "Your majesty is joking; have you not a million? Ah! why am I not possessed of half such a sum! I would already have raised a regiment. But, thank God! I have still a few rolls of gold and some family diamonds left. Your majesty will, I hope, deign to share with a devoted servant."

"With a friend—yes, count, but on condition that, in his turn, that friend will share with me hereafter!"

"Sire!" said Athos, opening a casket, form which he drew both gold and jewels, "you see, sire, we are too rich. Fortunately, there are four of us, in the event of our meeting with thieves."

Joy made the blood rush to the pale cheeks of Charles II., as he saw Athos's two horses, led by Grimaud, already booted for the journey, advance towards the porch.

"Blaisois, this letter for the Vicomte de Bragelonne. For everybody else I am gone to Paris. I confide the house to you, Blaisois." Blaisois bowed, shook hands with Grimaud, and shut the gate.

Chapter XVII.
In which Aramis is sought, and only Bazin is found.

TWO hours had scarcely elapsed since the departure of the master of the house, who, in Blaisois's sight, had taken the road to Paris, when a horseman, mounted on a good pied horse, stopped before the gate, and with a sonorous "hola!" called the stable-boys, who, with the gardeners, had formed a circle round Blaisois, the historian-in-ordinary to the household of the chateau. This "hola," doubtless well known to Master Blaisois, made him turn his head and exclaim—"Monsieur d'Artagnan! run quickly, you chaps, and open the gate."

A swarm of eight brisk lads flew to the gate, which was opened as if it had been made of feathers; and every one loaded him with attentions, for they knew the welcome this friend was accustomed to receive from their master; and for such remarks the eye of the valet may always be depended upon.

"Ah!" said M. d'Artagnan, with an agreeable smile, balancing himself upon his stirrup to jump to the ground, "where is that dear count?"

"Ah! how unfortunate you are, monsieur!" said Blaisois: "and how unfortunate will monsieur le comte, our master, think himself when he hears of your coming! As ill luck will have it, monsieur le comte left home two hours ago."

D'Artagnan did not trouble himself about such trifles. "Very good!" said he. "You always speak the best French in the world; you shall give me a lesson in grammar and correct language, whilst I wait the return of your master."

"That is impossible, monsieur," said Blaisois; "you would have to wait too long."

"Will he not come back to-day, then?"

"No, nor to-morrow, nor the day after to-morrow. Monsieur le comte has gone on a journey."

"A journey!" said D'Artagnan, surprised; "that's a fable, Master Blaisois."

"Monsieur, it is no more than the truth. Monsieur has done me the honor to give me the house in charge; and he added, with his voice so full of authority and kindness—that is all one to me: 'You will say I have gone to Paris.'"

"Well!" cried D'Artagnan, "since he is gone towards Paris, that is all I wanted to know! you should have told me so at first, booby! He is then two hours in advance?"

"Yes, monsieur."

"I shall soon overtake him. Is he alone?"

"No, monsieur."

"Who is with him, then?"

"A gentleman whom I don't know, an old man, and M. Grimaud."

"Such a party cannot travel as fast as I can—I will start."

"Will monsieur listen to me an instant?" said Blaisois, laying his hand gently on the reins of the horse.

"Yes, if you don't favor me with fine speeches, and make haste."

"Well, then, monsieur, that word Paris appears to me to be only an excuse."

"Oh, oh!" said D'Artagnan, seriously, "an excuse, eh?"

"Yes, monsieur: and monsieur le comte is not going to Paris, I will swear."

"What makes you think so?"

"This,—M. Grimaud always knows where our master is going; and he had promised me that the first time he went to Paris, he would take a little money for me to my wife."

"What, have you a wife, then?"

"I had one—she was of this country; but monsieur thought her a noisy scold, and I sent her to Paris; it is sometimes inconvenient, but very agreeable at others."

"I understand; but go on. You do not believe the count gone to Paris?"

"No, monsieur; for then M. Grimaud would have broken his word; he would have perjured himself, and that is impossible."

"That is impossible," repeated D'Artagnan, quite in a study, because he was quite convinced. "Well, my brave Blaisois, many thanks to you."

Blaisois bowed.

"Come, you know I am not curious—I have serious business with your master. Could you not, by a little bit of a word—you who speak so well—give me to understand—one syllable only—I will guess the rest."

"Upon my word, monsieur, I cannot. I am quite ignorant where monsieur le comte is gone. As to listening at doors, that is contrary to my nature; and besides, it is forbidden here."

"My dear fellow," said D'Artagnan, "this is a very bad beginning for me. Never mind; you know when monsieur le comte will return, at least?"

"As little, monsieur, as the place of his destination."

"Come, Blaisois, come, search."

"Monsieur doubts my sincerity? Ah, monsieur, that grieves me much."

"The devil take his gilded tongue!" grumbled D'Artagnan. "A clown with a word would be worth a dozen of him. Adieu!"

"Monsieur, I have the honor to present you my respects."

"Cuistre!" said D'Artagnan to himself, "the fellow is unbearable." He gave another look up to the house, turned his horse's head, and set off like a man who has nothing either annoying or embarrassing in his mind. When he was at the end of the wall, and out of sight,—"Well, now, I wonder," said he, breathing quickly, "whether Athos was at home. No; all those idlers, standing with their arms crossed, would have been at work if the eye of the master was near. Athos gone on a journey?—that is incomprehensible. Bah! it is all devilish mysterious! And then—no—he is not the man I want. I want one of a cunning, patient mind. My business is at Melun, in a certain presbytery I am acquainted with. Forty-five leagues—four days and a half! Well, it is fine weather, and I am free. Never mind the distance!"

And he put his horse into a trot, directing his course towards Paris. On the fourth day he alighted at Melun, as he had intended.

D'Artagnan was never in the habit of asking any one on the road for any common information. For these sorts of details, unless in very serious circumstances, he confided in his perspicacity, which was so seldom at fault, in his experience of thirty years, and in a great habit of reading the physiognomies of houses, as well as those of men. At Melun, D'Artagnan immediately found the presbytery—a charming house, plastered over red brick, with vines climbing along the gutters, and a cross, in carved stone, surmounting the ridge of the roof. From the ground-floor of this house came a noise, or rather a confusion of voices, like the chirping of young birds when the brood is just hatched under the down. One of these voices was spelling the alphabet distinctly. A voice thick, yet pleasant, at the same time scolded the talkers and corrected the faults of the reader. D'Artagnan recognized that voice, and as the window of the ground-floor was open, he leant down from his horse under the branches and red fibers of the vine and cried, "Bazin, my dear Bazin! good-day to you."

A short, fat man, with a flat face, a cranium ornamented with a crown of gray hairs, cut short, in imitation of a tonsure, and covered with an old black velvet cap, arose as soon as he heard D'Artagnan—we ought not to say arose, but bounded up. In fact, Bazin bounded up, carrying with him his little low chair, which the children tried to take away, with battles more fierce than those of the Greeks endeavoring to recover the body of Patroclus from the hands of the Trojans. Bazin did more than bound; he let fall both his alphabet and his ferule. "You!" said he; "you, Monsieur D'Artagnan?"

"Yes, myself! Where is Aramis—no, M. le Chevalier d'Herblay—no, I am still mistaken—Monsieur le Vicaire-General?"

"Ah, monsieur," said Bazin, with dignity, "monseigneur is at his diocese."

"What did you say?" said D'Artagnan. Bazin repeated the sentence.

"Ah, ah! but has Aramis a diocese?"

"Yes, monsieur. Why not?"

"Is he a bishop, then?"

"Why, where can you come from," said Bazin, rather irreverently, "that you don't know that?"

"My dear Bazin, we pagans, we men of the sword, know very well when a man is made a colonel, or maitre-de-camp, or marshal of France; but if he be made a bishop, arch-bishop, or pope—devil take me if the news reaches us before the three quarters of the earth have had the advantage of it!"

"Hush! hush!" said Bazin, opening his eyes: "do not spoil these poor children, in whom I am endeavoring to inculcate such good principles." In fact, the children had surrounded D'Artagnan, whose horse, long sword, spurs, and martial air they very much admired. But above all, they admired his strong voice; so that, when he uttered his oath, the whole school cried out, "The devil take me!" with fearful bursts of laughter, shouts, and bounds, which delighted the musketeer, and bewildered the old pedagogue.

"There!" said he, "hold your tongues, you brats! You have come, M. d'Artagnan, and all my good principles fly away. With you, as usual, comes disorder. Babel is revived. Ah! Good Lord! Ah! the wild little wretches!" And the worthy Bazin distributed right and left blows which increased the cries of his scholars by changing the nature of them.

"At least," said he, "you will no longer decoy any one here."

"Do you think so?" said D'Artagnan, with a smile which made a shudder creep over the shoulders of Bazin.

"He is capable of it," murmured he.

"Where is your master's diocese?"

"Monseigneur Rene is bishop of Vannes."

"Who had him nominated?"

"Why, monsieur le surintendant, our neighbor."

"What! Monsieur Fouquet?"

"To be sure he did."

"Is Aramis on good terms with him, then?"

"Monseigneur preached every Sunday at the house of monsieur le surintendant at Vaux; then they hunted together."

"Ah!"

"And monseigneur composed his homilies—no, I mean his sermons—with monsieur le surintendant."

"Bah! he preached in verse, then, this worthy bishop?"

"Monsieur, for the love of heaven, do not jest with sacred things."

"There, Bazin, there! So, then, Aramis is at Vannes?"

"At Vannes, in Bretagne."

"You are a deceitful old hunks, Bazin; that is not true."

"See, monsieur, if you please; the apartments of the presbytery are empty."

"He is right there," said D'Artagnan, looking attentively at the house, the aspect of which announced solitude.

"But monseigneur must have written you an account of his promotion."

"When did it take place?"

"A month back."

"Oh! then there is no time lost. Aramis cannot yet have wanted me. But how is it, Bazin, you do not follow your master?"

"Monsieur, I cannot; I have occupations."

"Your alphabet?"

"And my penitents."

"What, do you confess, then? Are you a priest?"

"The same as one. I have such a call."

"But the orders?"

"Oh," said Bazin, without hesitation, "now that monseigneur is a bishop, I shall soon have my orders, or at least my dispensations." And he rubbed his hands.

"Decidedly," said D'Artagnan to himself, "there will be no means of uprooting these people. Get me some supper, Bazin."

"With pleasure, monsieur."

"A fowl, a bouillon, and a bottle of wine."

"This is Saturday night, monsieur—it is a day of abstinence."

"I have a dispensation," said D'Artagnan.

Bazin looked at him suspiciously.

"Ah, ah, master hypocrite!" said the musketeer, "for whom do you take me? If you, who are the valet, hope for dispensation to commit a crime, shall not I, the friend of your bishop, have dispensation for eating meat at the call of my stomach? Make yourself agreeable with me, Bazin, or by heavens! I will complain to the king, and you shall never confess. Now you know that the nomination of bishops rests with the king,—I have the king, I am the stronger."

Bazin smiled hypocritically. "Ah, but we have monsieur le surintendant," said he.

"And you laugh at the king, then?"

Bazin made no reply; his smile was sufficiently eloquent.

"My supper," said D'Artagnan, "it is getting towards seven o'clock."

Bazin turned round and ordered the eldest of the pupils to inform the cook. In the meantime, D'Artagnan surveyed the presbytery.

"Phew!" said he, disdainfully, "monseigneur lodged his grandeur very meanly here."

"We have the Chateau de Vaux," said Bazin.

"Which is perhaps equal to the Louvre?" said D'Artagnan, jeeringly.

"Which is better," replied Bazin, with the greatest coolness imaginable.

"Ah, ah!" said D'Artagnan.

He would perhaps have prolonged the discussion, and maintained the superiority of the Louvre, but the lieutenant perceived that his horse remained fastened to the bars of a gate.

"The devil!" said he. "Get my horse looked after; your master the bishop has none like him in his stables."

Bazin cast a sidelong glance at the horse, and replied, "Monsieur le surintendant gave him four from his own stables; and each of the four is worth four of yours."

The blood mounted to the face of D'Artagnan. His hand itched and his eye glanced over the head of Bazin, to select the place upon which he should discharge his anger. But it passed away; reflection came, and D'Artagnan contented himself with saying,—

"The devil! the devil! I have done well to quit the service of the king. Tell me, worthy Master Bazin," added he, "how many musketeers does monsieur le surintendant retain in his service?"

"He could have all there are in the kingdom with his money," replied Bazin, closing his book, and dismissing the boys with some kindly blows of his cane.

"The devil! the devil!" repeated D'Artagnan, once more, as if to annoy the pedagogue. But as supper was now announced, he followed the cook, who introduced him into the refectory, where it awaited him. D'Artagnan placed himself at the table, and began a hearty attack upon his fowl.

"It appears to me," said D'Artagnan, biting with all his might at the tough fowl they had served up to him, and which they had evidently forgotten to fatten,—"it appears that I have done wrong in not seeking service with that master yonder. A powerful noble this intendant, seemingly! In good truth, we poor fellows know nothing at the court, and the rays of the sun prevent our seeing the large stars, which are also suns, at a little greater distance from our earth,—that is all."

As D'Artagnan delighted, both from pleasure and system, in making people talk about things which interested him, he fenced in his best style with Master Bazin, but it was pure loss of time; beyond the tiresome and hyperbolical praises of monsieur le surintendant of the finances, Bazin, who, on his side, was on his guard, afforded nothing but platitudes to the curiosity of D'Artagnan, so that our musketeer, in a tolerably bad humor, desired to go to bed as soon as he had supped. D'Artagnan was introduced by Bazin into a mean chamber, in which there was a poor bed; but D'Artagnan was not fastidious in that respect. He had been told that Aramis had taken away the key of his own private apartment, and as he knew Aramis was a very particular man, and had generally many things to conceal in his apartment, he had not been surprised. He, therefore, although it seemed comparatively even harder, attacked the bed as bravely as he had done the fowl; and, as he had as good an inclination to sleep as he had had to eat, he took scarcely longer time to be snoring harmoniously than he had employed in picking the last bones of the bird.

Since he was no longer in the service of any one, D'Artagnan had promised himself to indulge in sleeping as soundly as he had formerly slept lightly; but with whatever good faith D'Artagnan had made himself this promise, and whatever desire he might have to keep it religiously, he was awakened in the middle of the night by a loud noise of carriages, and servants on horseback. A sudden illumination flashed over the walls of his chamber; he jumped out of bed and ran to the window in his shirt. "Can the king be coming this way?" he thought, rubbing his eyes; "in truth, such a suite can only be attached to royalty."

"Vive le monsieur le surintendant!" cried, or rather vociferated, from a window on the ground-floor, a voice which he recognized as Bazin's, who at the same time waved a handkerchief with one hand, and held a large candle in the other. D'Artagnan then saw something like a brilliant human form leaning out of the principal carriage; at the same time loud bursts of laughter, caused, no doubt, by the strange figure of Bazin, and issuing from the same carriage, left, as it were, a train of joy upon the passage of the rapid cortege.

"I might easily see it was not the king," said D'Artagnan; "people don't laugh so heartily when the king passes. Hola, Bazin!" cried he to his neighbor, three-quarters of whose body still hung out of the window, to follow the carriage with his eyes as long as he could. "What is all that about?"

"It is M. Fouquet," said Bazin, in a patronizing tone.

"And all those people?"

"That is the court of M. Fouquet."

"Oh, oh!" said D'Artagnan; "what would M. de Mazarin say to that if he heard it?" And he returned to his bed, asking himself how Aramis always contrived to be protected by the most powerful personages in the kingdom. "Is it that he has more luck than I, or that I am a greater fool than he? Bah!" That was the concluding word by the aid of which D'Artagnan, having become wise, now terminated every thought and every period of his style. Formerly he said, "Mordioux!" which was a prick of the spur, but now he had become older, and he murmured that philosophical "Bah!" which served as a bridle to all the passions.

Chapter XVIII.
In which D'Artagnan seeks Porthos, and only finds Mousqueton.

WHEN D'Artagnan had perfectly convinced himself that the absence of the Vicar-General d'Herblay was real, and that his friend was not to be found at Melun or in its vicinity, he left Bazin without regret, cast an ill-natured glance at the magnificent Chateau de Vaux, which was beginning to shine with that splendor which brought on its ruin, and, compressing his lips like a man full of mistrust and suspicion, he put spurs to his pied horse, saying, "Well, well! I have still Pierrefonds left, and there I shall find the best man and the best filled coffer. And that is all I want, for I have an idea of my own."

We will spare our readers the prosaic incidents of D'Artagnan's journey, which terminated on the morning of the third day within sight of Pierrefonds. D'Artagnan came by the way of Nanteuil-le-Haudouin and Crepy. At a distance he perceived the Castle of Louis of Orleans, which, having become part of the crown domain, was kept by an old concierge. This was one of those marvelous manors of the middle ages, with walls twenty feet in thickness, and a hundred in height.

D'Artagnan rode slowly past its walls, measured its towers with his eye and descended into the valley. From afar he looked down upon the chateau of Porthos, situated on the shores of a small lake, and contiguous to a magnificent forest. It was the same place we have already had the honor of describing to our readers; we shall therefore satisfy ourselves with naming it. The first thing D'Artagnan perceived after the fine trees, the May sun gilding the sides of the green hills, the long rows of feather-topped trees which stretched out towards Compiegne, was a large rolling box, pushed forward by two servants and dragged by two others. In this box there was an enormous green-and-gold thing, which went along the smiling glades of the park, thus dragged and pushed. This thing, at a distance, could not be distinguished, and signified absolutely nothing; nearer, it was a hogshead muffled in gold-bound green cloth; when close, it was a man, or rather a poussa, the inferior extremity of whom, spreading over the interior of the box, entirely filled it; when still closer, the man was Mousqueton—Mousqueton, with gray hair and a face as red as Punchinello's.

"Pardieu!" cried D'Artagnan; "why, that's my dear Monsieur Mousqueton!"

"Ah!" cried the fat man—"ah! what happiness! what joy! There's M. d'Artagnan. Stop, you rascals!" These last words were addressed to the lackeys who pushed and dragged him. The box stopped, and the four lackeys, with a precision quite military, took off their laced hats and ranged themselves behind it.

"Oh, Monsieur d'Artagnan!" said Mousqueton, "why can I not embrace your knees? But I have become impotent, as you see."

"Dame! my dear Mousqueton, it is age."

"No, monsieur, it is not age; it is infirmities—troubles."

"Troubles! you, Mousqueton?" said D'Artagnan, making the tour of the box; "are you out of your mind, my dear friend? Thank God! you are as hearty as a three-hundred-year-old oak."

"Ah! but my legs, monsieur, my legs!" groaned the faithful servant.

"What's the matter with your legs?"

"Oh, they will no longer bear me!"

"Ah, the ungrateful things! And yet you feed them well, Mousqueton, apparently."

"Alas, yes! They can reproach me with nothing in that respect," said Mousqueton, with a sigh; "I have always done what I could for my poor body; I am not selfish." And Mousqueton sighed afresh.

"I wonder whether Mousqueton wants to be a baron, too, as he sighs after that fashion?" thought D'Artagnan.

"Mon Dieu, monsieur!" said Mousqueton, as if rousing himself from a painful reverie; "how happy monseigneur will be that you have thought of him!"

"Kind Porthos!" cried D'Artagnan, "I am anxious to embrace him."

"Oh!" said Mousqueton, much affected, "I shall certainly write to him."

"What!" cried D'Artagnan, "you will write to him?"

"This very day; I shall not delay it an hour."

"Is he not here, then?"

"No, monsieur."

"But is he near at hand?—is he far off?"

"Oh, can I tell, monsieur, can I tell?"

"Mordioux!" cried the musketeer, stamping with his foot, "I am unfortunate. Porthos is such a stay-at-home!"

"Monsieur, there is not a more sedentary man that monseigneur, but—"

"But what?"

"When a friend presses you—"

"A friend?"

"Doubtless—the worthy M. d'Herblay."

"What, has Aramis pressed Porthos?"

"This is how the thing happened, Monsieur d'Artagnan. M. d'Herblay wrote to monseigneur—"

"Indeed!"

"A letter, monsieur, such a pressing letter that it threw us all into a bustle."

"Tell me all about it, my dear friend," said D'Artagnan; "but remove these people a little further off first."

Mousqueton shouted, "Fall back, you fellows," with such powerful lungs that the breath, without the words, would have been sufficient to disperse the four lackeys. D'Artagnan seated himself on the shaft of the box and opened his ears. "Monsieur," said Mousqueton, "monseigneur, then, received a letter from M. le Vicaire-General d'Herblay, eight or nine days ago; it was the day of the rustic pleasures, yes, it must have been Wednesday."

"What do you mean?" said D'Artagnan. "The day of rustic pleasures?"

"Yes, monsieur; we have so many pleasures to take in this delightful country, that we were encumbered by them; so much so, that we have been forced to regulate the distribution of them."

"How easily do I recognize Porthos's love of order in that! Now, that idea would never have occurred to me; but then I am not encumbered with pleasures."

"We were, though," said Mousqueton.

"And how did you regulate the matter, let me know?" said D'Artagnan.

"It is rather long, monsieur."

"Never mind, we have plenty of time; and you speak so well, my dear Mousqueton, that it is really a pleasure to hear you."

"It is true," said Mousqueton, with a sigh of satisfaction, which emanated evidently from the justice which had been rendered him, "it is true I have made great progress in the company of monseigneur."

"I am waiting for the distribution of the pleasures, Mousqueton, and with impatience. I want to know if I have arrived on a lucky day."

"Oh, Monsieur d'Artagnan," said Mousqueton in a melancholy tone, "since monseigneur's departure all the pleasures have gone too!"

"Well, my dear Mousqueton, refresh your memory."

"With what day shall I begin?"

"Eh, pardieux! begin with Sunday; that is the Lord's day."

"Sunday, monsieur?"

"Yes."

"Sunday pleasures are religious: monseigneur goes to mass, makes the bread-offering, and has discourses and instructions made to him by his almoner-in-ordinary. That is not very amusing, but we expect a Carmelite from Paris who will do the duty of our almonry, and who, we are assured, speaks very well, which will keep us awake, whereas our present almoner always sends us to sleep. These are Sunday religious pleasures. On Monday, worldly pleasures."

"Ah, ah!" said D'Artagnan, "what do you mean by that? Let us have a glimpse at your worldly pleasures."

"Monsieur, on Monday we go into the world; we pay and receive visits, we play on the lute, we dance, we make verses, and burn a little incense in honor of the ladies."

"Peste! that is the height of gallantry," said the musketeer, who was obliged to call to his aid all the strength of his facial muscles to suppress an enormous inclination to laugh.

"Tuesday, learned pleasures."

"Good!" cried D'Artagnan. "What are they? Detail them, my dear Mousqueton."

"Monseigneur has bought a sphere or globe, which I shall show you; it fills all the perimeter of the great tower, except a gallery which he has had built over the sphere: there are little strings and brass wires to which the sun and moon are hooked. It all turns; and that is very beautiful. Monseigneur points out to me the seas and distant countries. We don't intend to visit them, but it is very interesting."

"Interesting! yes, that's the word," repeated D'Artagnan. "And Wednesday?"

"Rustic pleasures, as I have had the honor to tell you, monsieur le chevalier. We look over monseigneur's sheep and goats; we make the shepherds dance to pipes and reeds, as is written in a book monseigneur has in his library, which is called 'Bergeries.' The author died about a month ago."

"Monsieur Racan, perhaps," said D'Artagnan.

"Yes, that was his name—M. Racan. But that is not all: we angle in the little canal, after which we dine, crowned with flowers. That is Wednesday."

"Peste!" said D'Artagnan; "you don't divide your pleasures badly. And Thursday?—what can be left for poor Thursday?"

"It is not very unfortunate, monsieur," said Mousqueton, smiling. "Thursday, Olympian pleasures. Ah, monsieur, that is superb! We get together all monseigneur's young vassals, and we make them throw the disc, wrestle, and run races. Monseigneur can't run now, no more can I; but monseigneur throws the disc as nobody else can throw it. And when he does deal a blow, oh, that proves a misfortune!"

"How so?"

"Yes, monsieur, we were obliged to renounce the cestus. He cracked heads; he broke jaws—beat in ribs. It was charming sport; but nobody was willing to play with him."

"Then his wrist—"

"Oh, monsieur, firmer than ever. Monseigneur gets a trifle weaker in his legs,—he confesses that himself; but his strength has all taken refuge in his arms, so that—"

"So that he can knock down bullocks, as he used to formerly."

"Monsieur, better than that—he beats in walls. Lately, after having supped with one of our farmers—you know how popular and kind monseigneur is—after supper, as a joke, he struck the wall a blow. The wall crumbled away beneath his hand, the roof fell in, and three men and an old woman were stifled."

"Good God, Mousqueton! And your master?"

"Oh, monseigneur, a little skin was rubbed off his head. We bathed the wounds with some water which the monks gave us. But there was nothing the matter with his hand."

"Nothing?"

"No, nothing, monsieur."

"Deuce take the Olympic pleasures! They must cost your master too dear; for widows and orphans—"

"They all had pensions, monsieur; a tenth of monseigneur's revenue was spent in that way."

"Then pass on to Friday," said D'Artagnan.

"Friday, noble and warlike pleasures. We hunt, we fence, we dress falcons and break horses. Then, Saturday is the day for intellectual pleasures: we adorn our minds; we look at monseigneur's pictures and statues; we write, even, and trace plans: and then we fire monseigneur's cannon."

"You draw plans, and fire cannon?"

"Yes, monsieur."

"Why, my friend," said D'Artagnan, "M. du Vallon, in truth, possesses the most subtle and amiable mind that I know. But there is one kind of pleasure you have forgotten, it appears to me."

"What is that, monsieur?" asked Mousqueton, with anxiety.

"The material pleasures."

Mousqueton colored. "What do you mean by that, monsieur?" said he, casting down his eyes.

"I mean the table—good wine—evenings occupied in passing the bottle."

"Ah, monsieur, we don't reckon those pleasures,—we practice them every day."

"My brave Mousqueton," resumed D'Artagnan, "pardon me, but I was so absorbed in your charming recital that I have forgotten the principal object of our conversation, which was to learn what M. le Vicaire-General d'Herblay could have to write to your master about."

"That is true, monsieur," said Mousqueton; "the pleasures have misled us. Well, monsieur, this is the whole affair."

"I am all attention, Mousqueton."

"On Wednesday—"

"The day of the rustic pleasures?"

"Yes—a letter arrived; he received it from my hands. I had recognized the writing."

"Well?"

Monseigneur read it and cried out, 'Quick, my horses! my arms!'"

"Oh, good Lord! then it was for some duel?" said D'Artagnan.

"No, monsieur, there were only these words: 'Dear Porthos, set out, if you would wish to arrive before the Equinox. I expect you.'"

"Mordioux!" said D'Artagnan, thoughtfully, "that was pressing, apparently."

"I think so; therefore," continued Mousqueton, "monseigneur set out the very same day with his secretary, in order to endeavor to arrive in time."

"And did he arrive in time?"

"I hope so. Monseigneur, who is hasty, as you know, monsieur, repeated incessantly, 'Tonne Dieu! What can this mean? The Equinox? Never mind, a fellow must be well mounted to arrive before I do.'"

"And you think Porthos will have arrived first, do you?" asked D'Artagnan.

"I am sure of it. This Equinox, however rich he may be, has certainly no horses so good as monseigneur's."

D'Artagnan repressed his inclination to laugh, because the brevity of Aramis's letter gave rise to reflection. He followed Mousqueton, or rather Mousqueton's chariot, to the castle. He sat down to a sumptuous table, of which they did him the honors as to a king. But he could draw nothing from Mousqueton,—the faithful servant seemed to shed tears at will, but that was all.

D'Artagnan, after a night passed in an excellent bed, reflected much upon the meaning of Aramis's letter; puzzled himself as to the relation of the Equinox with the affairs of Porthos; and being unable to make anything out unless it concerned some amour of the bishopp's, for which it was necessary that the days and nights should be equal, D'Artagnan left Pierrefonds as he had left Melun, as he had left the chateau of the Comte de la Fere. It was not, however, without a melancholy, which might in good sooth pass for one of the most dismal of D'Artagnan's moods. His head cast down, his eyes fixed, he suffered his legs to hang on each side of his horse, and said to himself, in that vague sort of reverie which ascends sometimes to the sublimest eloquence:

"No more friends! no more future! no more anything! My energies are broken like the bonds of our ancient friendship. Oh, old age is coming, cold and inexorable; it envelopes in its funeral crepe all that was brilliant, all that was embalming in my youth; then it throws that sweet burthen on its shoulders and carries it away with the rest into the fathomless gulf of death."

A shudder crept through the heart of the Gascon, so brave and so strong against all the misfortunes of life; and during some moments the clouds appeared black to him, the earth slippery and full of pits as that of cemeteries.

"Whither am I going?" said he to himself. "What am I going to do! Alone, quite alone—without family, without friends! Bah!" cried he all at once. And he clapped spurs to his horse, who, having found nothing melancholy in the heavy oats of Pierrefonds, profited by this permission to show his gayety in a gallop which absorbed two leagues. "To Paris!" said D'Artagnan to himself. And on the morrow he alighted in Paris. He had devoted ten days to this journey.

Chapter XIX.
What D'Artagnan went to Paris for.

THE lieutenant dismounted before a shop in the Rue des Lombards, at the sign of the Pilon d'Or. A man of good appearance, wearing a white apron, and stroking his gray mustache with a large hand, uttered a cry of joy on perceiving the pied horse. "Monsieur le chevalier," said he, "ah, is that you?"

"Bon jour, Planchet," replied D'Artagnan, stooping to enter the shop.

"Quick, somebody," cried Planchet, "to look after Monsieur d'Artagnan's horse,—somebody to get ready his room,—somebody to prepare his supper."

"Thanks, Planchet. Good-day, my children!" said D'Artagnan to the eager boys.

"Allow me to send off this coffee, this treacle, and these raisins," said Planchet; "they are for the store-room of monsieur le surintendant."

"Send them off, send them off!"

"That is only the affair of a moment, then we shall sup."

"Arrange it that we may sup alone; I want to speak to you."

Planchet looked at his old master in a significant manner.

"Oh, don't be uneasy, it is nothing unpleasant," said D'Artagnan.

"So much the better—so much the better!" And Planchet breathed freely again, whilst D'Artagnan seated himself quietly down in the shop, upon a bale of corks, and made a survey of the premises. The shop was well stocked; there was a mingled perfume of ginger, cinnamon, and ground pepper, which made D'Artagnan sneeze. The shop-boy, proud of being in company with so renowned a warrior, of a lieutenant of musketeers, who approached the person of the king, began to work with an enthusiasm which was something like delirium, and to serve the customers with a disdainful haste that was noticed by several.

Planchet put away his money, and made up his accounts, amidst civilities addressed to his former master. Planchet had with his equals the short speech and haughty familiarity of the rich shopkeeper who serves everybody and waits for nobody. D'Artagnan observed this habit with a pleasure which we shall analyze presently. He saw night come on by degrees, and at length Planchet conducted him to a chamber on the first story, where, amidst bales and chests, a table very nicely set out awaited the two guests.

D'Artagnan took advantage of a moment's pause to examine the countenance of Planchet, whom he had not seen for a year. The shrewd Planchet had acquired a slight protuberance in front, but his countenance was not puffed. His keen eye still played with facility in its deep-sunk orbit; and fat, which levels all the characteristic saliences of the human face, had not yet touched either his high cheek-bones, the sign of cunning and cupidity, or his pointed chin, the sign of acuteness and perseverance. Planchet reigned with as much majesty in his dining-room as in his shop. He set before his master a frugal, but perfectly Parisian repast: roast meat, cooked at the baker's, with vegetables, salad, and a dessert borrowed from the shop itself. D'Artagnan was pleased that the grocer had drawn from behind the fagots a bottle of that Anjou wine which during all his life had been D'Artagnan's favorite wine.

"Formerly, monsieur," said Planchet, with a smile full of bonhomie, "it was I who drank your wine; now you do me the honor to drink mine."

"And, thank God, friend Planchet, I shall drink it for a long time to come, I hope; for at present I am free."

"Free? You have a leave of absence, monsieur?"

"Unlimited."

"You are leaving the service?" said Planchet, stupefied.

"Yes, I am resting."

"And the king?" cried Planchet, who could not suppose it possible that the king could do without the services of such a man as D'Artagnan.

"The king will try his fortune elsewhere. But we have supped well, you are disposed to enjoy yourself; you invite me to confide in you. Open your ears, then."

"They are open." And Planchet, with a laugh more frank than cunning, opened a bottle of white wine.

"Leave me my reason, at least."

"Oh, as to you losing your head—you, monsieur!"

"Now my head is my own, and I mean to take better care of it than ever. In the first place we shall talk business. How fares our money-box?"

"Wonderfully well, monsieur. The twenty thousand livres I had of you are still employed in my trade, in which they bring me nine per cent. I give you seven, so I gain two by you."

"And you are still satisfied?"

"Delighted. Have you brought me any more?"

"Better than that. But do you want any?"

"Oh! not at all. Every one is willing to trust me now. I am extending my business."

"That was your intention."

"I play the banker a little. I buy goods of my needy brethren; I lend money to those who are not ready for their payments."

"Without usury?"

"Oh! monsieur, in the course of the last week I have had two meetings on the boulevards, on account of the word you have just pronounced."

"What?"

"You shall see: it concerned a loan. The borrower gives me in pledge some raw sugars, on condition that I should sell if repayment were not made within a fixed period. I lend a thousand livres. He does not pay me, and I sell the sugars for thirteen hundred livres. He learns this and claims a hundred crowns. Ma foi! I refused, pretending that I could not sell them for more than nine hundred livres. He accused me of usury. I begged him to repeat that word to me behind the boulevards. He was an old guard, and he came: and I passed your sword through his left thigh."

"Tu dieu! what a pretty sort of banker you make!" said D'Artagnan.

"For above thirteen per cent I fight," replied Planchet; "that is my character."

"Take only twelve," said D'Artagnan, "and call the rest premium and brokerage."

"You are right, monsieur; but to your business."

"Ah! Planchet, it is very long and very hard to speak."

"Do speak it, nevertheless."

D'Artagnan twisted his mustache like a man embarrassed with the confidence he is about to make and mistrustful of his confidant.

"Is it an investment?" asked Planchet.

"Why, yes."

"At good profit?"

"A capital profit,—four hundred per cent, Planchet."

Planchet gave such a blow with his fist upon the table, that the bottles bounded as if they had been frightened.

"Good heavens! is that possible?"

"I think it will be more," replied D'Artagnan coolly; "but I like to lay it at the lowest!"

"The devil!" said Planchet, drawing nearer. "Why, monsieur, that is magnificent! Can one put much money in it?"

"Twenty thousand livres each, Planchet."

"Why, that is all you have, monsieur. For how long a time?"

"For a month."

"And that will give us—"

"Fifty thousand livres each, profit."

"It is monstrous! It is worth while to fight for such interest as that!"

"In fact, I believe it will be necessary to fight not a little," said D'Artagnan, with the same tranquillity; "but this time there are two of us, Planchet, and I shall take all the blows to myself."

"Oh! monsieur, I will not allow that."

"Planchet, you cannot be concerned in it; you would be obliged to leave your business and your family."

"The affair is not in Paris, then."

"No."

"Abroad?"

"In England."

"A speculative country, that is true," said Planchet,—"a country that I know well. What sort of an affair, monsieur, without too much curiosity?"

"Planchet, it is a restoration."

"Of monuments?"

"Yes, of monuments; we shall restore Whitehall."

"That is important. And in a month, you think?"

"I shall undertake it."

"That concerns you, monsieur, and when once you are engaged—"

"Yes, that concerns me. I know what I am about; nevertheless, I will freely consult with you."

"You do me great honor; but I know very little about architecture."

"Planchet, you are wrong; you are an excellent architect, quite as good as I am, for the case in question."

"Thanks, monsieur. But your old friends of the musketeers?"

"I have been, I confess, tempted to speak of the thing to those gentlemen, but they are all absent from their houses. It is vexatious, for I know none more bold or able."

"Ah! then it appears there will be an opposition, and the enterprise will be disputed?"

"Oh, yes, Planchet, yes."

"I burn to know the details, monsieur."

"Here they are, Planchet—close all the doors tight."

"Yes, monsieur." And Planchet double-locked them.

"That is well; now draw near." Planchet obeyed.

"And open the window, because the noise of the passers-by and the carts will deafen all who might hear us." Planchet opened the window as desired, and the gust of tumult which filled the chamber with cries, wheels, barkings, and steps deafened D'Artagnan himself, as he had wished. He then swallowed a glass of white wine, and began in these terms: "Planchet, I have an idea."

"Ah! monsieur, I recognize you so well in that!" replied Planchet, panting with emotion.

Chapter XX.
Of the Society which was formed in the Rue des Lombards.

AFTER a moment's silence, in which D'Artagnan appeared to be collecting, not one idea but all his ideas,—"It cannot be, my dear Planchet," said he, "that you have not heard of his majesty Charles I. of England?"

"Alas! yes, monsieur, since you left France in order to assist him, and that, in spite of that assistance, he fell, and was near dragging you down in his fall."

"Exactly so; I see you have a good memory, Planchet."

"Peste! the astonishing thing would be, if I could have lost that memory, however bad it might have been. When one has heard Grimaud, who, you know, is not given to talking, relate how the head of King Charles fell, how you sailed the half of a night in a scuttled vessel, and saw floating on the water that good M. Mordaunt with a certain gold-hafted dagger buried in his breast, one is not very likely to forget such things."

"And yet there are people who forget them, Planchet."

"Yes, such as have not seen them, or have not heard Grimaud relate them."

"Well, it is all the better that you recollect all that; I shall only have to remind you of one thing, and that is that Charles I. had a son."

"Without contradicting you, monsieur, he had two," said Planchet; "for I saw the second one in Paris, M. le Duke of York, one day, as he was going to the Palais Royal, and I was told that he was not the eldest son of Charles I. As to the eldest, I have the honor of knowing him by name, but not personally."

"That is exactly the point, Planchet, we must come to: it is to this eldest son, formerly called the Prince of Wales, and who is now styled Charles II., king of England."

"A king without a kingdom, monsieur," replied Planchet, sententiously.

"Yes, Planchet, and you may add an unfortunate prince, more unfortunate than the poorest man of the people lost in the worst quarter of Paris."

Planchet made a gesture full of that sort of compassion which we grant to strangers with whom we think we can never possibly find ourselves in contact. Besides, he did not see in this politico-sentimental operation any sign of the commercial idea of M. d'Artagnan, and it was in this idea that

D'Artagnan, who was, from habit, pretty well acquainted with men and things, had principally interested Planchet.

"I am come to our business. This young Prince of Wales, a king without a kingdom, as you have so well said, Planchet, has interested me. I, D'Artagnan, have seen him begging assistance of Mazarin, who is a miser, and the aid of Louis, who is a child, and it appeared to me, who am acquainted with such things, that in the intelligent eye of the fallen king, in the nobility of his whole person, a nobility apparent above all his miseries, I could discern the stuff of a man and the heart of a king."

Planchet tacitly approved of all this; but it did not at all, in his eyes at least, throw any light upon D'Artagnan's idea. The latter continued: "This, then, is the reasoning which I made with myself. Listen attentively, Planchet, for we are coming to the conclusion."

"I am listening."

"Kings are not so thickly sown upon the earth, that people can find them whenever they want them. Now, this king without a kingdom is, in my opinion, a grain of seed which will blossom in some season or other, provided a skillful, discreet, and vigorous hand sow it duly and truly, selecting soil, sky, and time."

Planchet still approved by a nod of his head, which showed that he did not perfectly comprehend all that was said.

"'Poor little seed of a king,' said I to myself, and really I was affected, Planchet, which leads me to think I am entering upon a foolish business. And that is why I wished to consult you, my friend."

Planchet colored with pleasure and pride.

"'Poor little seed of a king! I will pick you up and cast you into good ground.'"

"Good God!" said Planchet, looking earnestly at his old master, as if in doubt as to the state of his reason.

"Well, what is it?" said D'Artagnan; "who hurts you?"

"Me! nothing, monsieur."

"You said, 'Good God!'"

"Did I?"

"I am sure you did. Can you already understand?"

"I confess, M. d'Artagnan, that I am afraid—"

"To understand?"

"Yes."

"To understand that I wish to replace upon his throne this King Charles II., who has no throne? Is that it?"

Planchet made a prodigious bound in his chair. "Ah, ah!" said he, in evident terror, "that is what you call a restoration!"

"Yes, Planchet; is it not the proper term for it?"

"Oh, no doubt, no doubt! But have you reflected seriously?"

"Upon what?"

"Upon what is going on yonder."

"Where?"

"In England."

"And what is that? Let us see, Planchet."

"In the first place, monsieur, I ask you pardon for meddling in these things, which have nothing to do with my trade; but since it is an affair that you propose to me—for you are proposing an affair, are you not?—"

"A superb one, Planchet."

"But as it is business you propose to me, I have the right to discuss it."

"Discuss it, Planchet; out of discussion is born light."

"Well, then, since I have monsieur's permission, I will tell him that there is yonder, in the first place, the parliament."

"Well, next?"

"And then the army."

"Good! Do you see anything else?"

"Why, then the nation."

"Is that all?"

"The nation which consented to the overthrow and death of the late king, the father of this one, and which will not be willing to belie its acts."

"Planchet," said D'Artagnan, "you argue like a cheese! The nation—the nation is tired of these gentlemen who give themselves such barbarous names, and who sing songs to it. Chanting for chanting, my dear Planchet; I have remarked that nations prefer singing a merry chant to the plain chant.

Remember the Fronde; what did they sing in those times? Well, those were good times."

"Not too good, not too good! I was near being hung in those times."

"Well, but you were not."

"No."

"And you laid the foundations of your fortune in the midst of all those songs?"

"That is true."

"Then you have nothing to say against them."

"Well, I return, then, to the army and parliament."

"I say that I borrow twenty thousand livres of M. Planchet, and that I put twenty thousand livres of my own to it; and with these forty thousand livres I raise an army."

Planchet clasped his hands; he saw that D'Artagnan was in earnest, and, in good truth, he believed his master had lost his senses.

"An army!—ah, monsieur," said he, with his most agreeable smile, for fear of irritating the madman, and rendering him furious,—"an army!—how many?"

"Of forty men," said D'Artagnan.

"Forty against forty thousand! that is not enough. I know very well that you, M. d'Artagnan, alone, are equal to a thousand men; but where are we to find thirty-nine men equal to you? Or, if we could find them, who would furnish you with money to pay them?"

"Not bad, Planchet. Ah, the devil! you play the courtier."

"No, monsieur, I speak what I think, and that is exactly why I say that, in the first pitched battle you fight with your forty men, I am very much afraid—"

"Therefore I shall fight no pitched battles, my dear Planchet," said the Gascon, laughing. "We have very fine examples in antiquity of skillful retreats and marches, which consisted in avoiding the enemy instead of attacking them. You should know that, Planchet, you who commanded the Parisians the day on which they ought to have fought against the musketeers, and who so well calculated marches and countermarches, that you never left the Palais Royal."

Planchet could not help laughing. "It is plain," replied he, "that if your forty men conceal themselves, and are not unskillful, they may hope not to be beaten: but you propose obtaining some result, do you not?"

"No doubt. This, then, in my opinion, is the plan to be proceeded upon in order quickly to replace his majesty Charles II. on his throne."

"Good!" said Planchet, increasing his attention; "let us see your plan. But in the first place it seems to me we are forgetting something."

"What is that?"

"We have set aside the nation, which prefers singing merry songs to psalms, and the army, which we will not fight; but the parliament remains, and that seldom sings."

"Nor does it fight. How is it, Planchet, that an intelligent man like yourself should take any heed of a set of brawlers who call themselves Rumps and Barebones? The parliament does not trouble me at all, Planchet."

"As soon as it ceases to trouble you, monsieur, let us pass on."

"Yes, and arrive at the result. You remember Cromwell, Planchet?"

"I have heard a great deal of talk about him."

"He was a rough soldier."

"And a terrible eater, moreover."

"What do you mean by that?"

"Why, at one gulp he swallowed all England."

"Well, Planchet, the evening before the day on which he swallowed England, if any one had swallowed M. Cromwell?"

"Oh, monsieur, it is one of the axioms of mathematics that the container must be greater than the contained."

"Very well! That is our affair, Planchet."

"But M. Cromwell is dead, and his container is now the tomb."

"My dear Planchet, I see with pleasure that you have not only become a mathematician, but a philosopher."

"Monsieur, in my grocery business I use much printed paper, and that instructs me."

"Bravo! You know then, in that case—for you have not learnt mathematics and philosophy without a little history—that after this Cromwell so great, there came one who was very little."

"Yes; he was named Richard, and he as done as you have, M. d'Artagnan—he has tendered his resignation."

"Very well said—very well! After the great man who is dead, after the little one who tendered his resignation, there came a third. This one is named Monk; he is an able general, considering he has never fought a battle; he is a skillful diplomatist, considering that he never speaks in public, and that having to say 'good-day' to a man, he meditates twelve hours, and ends by saying 'good night;' which makes people exclaim 'miracle!' seeing that it falls out correctly."

"That is rather strong," said Planchet; "but I know another political man who resembles him very much."

"M. Mazarin you mean?"

"Himself."

"You are right, Planchet; only M. Mazarin does not aspire to the throne of France; and that changes everything. Do you see? Well, this M. Monk, who has England ready-roasted in his plate, and who is already opening his mouth to swallow it—this M. Monk, who says to the people of Charles II., and to Charles II. himself, 'Nescio vos'—"

"I don't understand English," said Planchet.

"Yes, but I understand it," said D'Artagnan. "'Nescio vos' means 'I do not know you.' This M. Monk, the most important man in England, when he shall have swallowed it—"

"Well?" asked Planchet.

"Well, my friend, I shall go over yonder, and with my forty men I shall carry him off, pack him up, and bring him into France, where two modes of proceeding present themselves to my dazzled eyes."

"Oh! and to mine too," cried Planchet, transported with enthusiasm. "We will put him in a cage and show him for money."

"Well, Planchet, that is a third plan, of which I had not thought."

"Do you think it a good one?"

"Yes, certainly, but I think mine better."

"Let us see yours, then."

"In the first place, I shall set a ransom on him."

"Of how much?"

"Peste! a fellow like that must be well worth a hundred thousand crowns."

"Yes, yes!"

"You see, then—in the first place, a ransom of a hundred thousand crowns."

"Or else—"

"Or else, what is much better, I deliver him up to King Charles, who, having no longer either a general or an army to fear, nor a diplomatist to trick him, will restore himself, and when once restored, will pay down to me the hundred thousand crowns in question. That is the idea I have formed; what do you say to it, Planchet?"

"Magnificent, monsieur!" cried Planchet, trembling with emotion. "How did you conceive that idea?"

"It came to me one morning on the banks of the Loire, whilst our beloved king, Louis XIV., was pretending to weep upon the hand of Mademoiselle de Mancini."

"Monsieur, I declare the idea is sublime. But—"

"Ah! is there a but?"

"Permit me! But this is a little like the skin of that fine bear—you know—that they were about to sell, but which it was necessary to take from the back of the living bear. Now, to take M. Monk, there will be a bit of a scuffle, I should think."

"No doubt; but as I shall raise an army to—"

"Yes, yes—I understand, parbleu!—a coup-de-main. Yes, then, monsieur, you will triumph, for no one equals you in such sorts of encounters."

"I certainly am lucky in them," said D'Artagnan, with a proud simplicity. "You know that if for this affair I had my dear Athos, my brave Porthos, and my cunning Aramis, the business would be settled; but they are all lost, as it appears, and nobody knows where to find them. I will do it, then, alone. Now, do you find the business good, and the investment advantageous?"

"Too much so—too much so."

"How can that be?"

"Because fine things never reach the expected point."

"This is infallible, Planchet, and the proof is that I undertake it. It will be for you a tolerably pretty gain, and for me a very interesting stroke. It will be said, 'Such was the old age of M. d'Artagnan,' and I shall hold a place in tales and even in history itself, Planchet. I am greedy of honor."

"Monsieur," cried Planchet, "when I think that it is here, in my home, in the midst of my sugar, my prunes, and my cinnamon, that this gigantic project is ripened, my shop seems a palace to me."

"Beware, beware, Planchet! If the least report of this escapes, there is the Bastile for both of us. Beware, my friend, for this is a plot we are hatching. M. Monk is the ally of M. Mazarin—beware!"

"Monsieur, when a man has had the honor to belong to you, he knows nothing of fear; and when he has had the advantage of being bound up in interests with you, he holds his tongue."

"Very well; that is more your affair than mine, seeing that in a week I shall be in England."

"Depart, monsieur, depart—the sooner the better."

"Is the money, then, ready?"

"It will be to-morrow; to-morrow you shall receive it from my own hands. Will you have gold or silver?"

"Gold; that is most convenient. But how are we going to arrange this? Let us see."

"Oh, good Lord! in the simplest way possible. You shall give me a receipt, that is all."

"No, no," said D'Artagnan, warmly; "we must preserve order in all things."

"That is likewise my opinion; but with you, M. d'Artagnan—"

"And if I should die yonder—if I should be killed by a musket-ball—if I should burst from drinking beer?"

"Monsieur, I beg you to believe that in that case I should be so much afflicted at your death, that I should not think about the money."

"Thank you, Planchet; but no matter. We shall, like two lawyers' clerks, draw up together an agreement, a sort of act, which may be called a deed of company."

"Willingly, monsieur."

"I know it is difficult to draw such a thing up, but we can try."

"Let us try, then." And Planchet went in search of pens, ink, and paper. D'Artagnan took the pen and wrote:—"Between Messire d'Artagnan, ex-lieutenant of the king's musketeers, at present residing in the Rue Tiquetonne, Hotel de la Chevrette; and the Sieur Planchet, grocer, residing in the Rue des Lombards, at the sign of the Pilon d'Or, it has been agreed as follows:—A company, with a capital of forty thousand livres, and formed for the purpose of carrying out an idea conceived by M. d'Artagnan, and the said Planchet approving of it in all points, will place twenty thousand livres in the hands of M. d'Artagnan. He will require neither repayment nor interest before the return of M. d'Artagnan from a journey he is about to take into England. On his part, M. d'Artagnan undertakes it to find twenty thousand livres, which he will join to the twenty thousand already laid down by the Sieur Planchet. He will employ the said sum of forty thousand livres according to his judgment in an undertaking which is described below. On the day when M. d'Artagnan shall have re-established, by whatever means, his majesty King Charles II. upon the throne of England, he will pay into the hands of M. Planchet the sum of—"

"The sum of a hundred and fifty thousand livres," said Planchet, innocently, perceiving that D'Artagnan hesitated.

"Oh, the devil, no!" said D'Artagnan, "the division cannot be made by half; that would not be just."

"And yet, monsieur, we each lay down half," objected Planchet, timidly.

"Yes; but listen to this clause, my dear Planchet, and if you do not find if equitable in every respect when it is written, well, we can scratch it out again:—'Nevertheless, as M. d'Artagnan brings to the association, besides his capital of twenty thousand livres, his time, his idea, his industry, and his skin,—things which he appreciates strongly, particularly the last,—M. d'Artagnan will keep, of the three hundred thousand livres, two hundred thousand livres for himself, which will make his share two-thirds.'"

"Very well," said Planchet.

"Is it just?" asked D'Artagnan.

"Perfectly just, monsieur."

"And you will be contented with a hundred thousand livres?"

"Peste! I think so. A hundred thousand for twenty thousand!"

"And in a month, understand."

"How, in a month?"

"Yes, I only ask one month."

"Monsieur," said Planchet, generously, "I give you six weeks."

"Thank you," replied the musketeer, politely; after which the two partners reperused their deed.

"That is perfect, monsieur," said Planchet; "and the late M. Coquenard, the first husband of Madame la Baronne du Vallon, could not have done it better."

"Do you find it so? Let us sign it then." And both affixed their signatures.

"In this fashion," said D'Artagnan, "I shall be under obligations to no one."

"But I shall be under obligations to you," said Planchet.

"No; for whatever store I set by it, Planchet, I may lose my skin yonder, and you will lose all. A propos—peste!—that makes me think of the principal, an indispensable clause. I shall write it:—'In case of M. d'Artagnan dying in this enterprise, liquidation will be considered made, and the Sieur Planchet will give quittance from that moment to the shade of Messire d'Artagnan for the twenty thousand livres paid by him into the hands of the said company.'"

This last clause made Planchet knit his brows a little, but when he saw the brilliant eye, the muscular hand, the supple and strong back of his associate, he regained his courage, and, without regret, he at once added another stroke to his signature. D'Artagnan did the same. Thus was drawn the first known company contract; perhaps such things have been abused a little since, both in form and principle.

"Now," said Planchet, pouring out the last glass of Anjou wine for D'Artagnan,—"now go to sleep, my dear master."

"No," replied D'Artagnan; "for the most difficult part now remains to be done, and I will think over that difficult part."

"Bah!" said Planchet; "I have such great confidence in you, M. d'Artagnan, that I would not give my hundred thousand livres for ninety thousand livres down."

"And devil take me if I don't think you are right!" Upon which D'Artagnan took a candle and went up to his bedroom.

Chapter XXI.
In which D'Artagnan prepares to travel.

D'ARTAGNAN reflected to such good purpose during the night that his plan was settled by morning. "This is it," said he, sitting up in bed, supporting his elbow on his knee, and his chin in his hand;—"this is it. I shall seek out forty steady, firm men, recruited among people a little compromised, but having habits of discipline. I shall promise them five hundred livres for a month if they return; nothing if they do not return, or half for their kindred. As to food and lodging, that concerns the English, who have cattle in their pastures, bacon in their bacon-racks, fowls in their poultry-yards, and corn in their barns. I will present myself to General Monk with my little body of troops. He will receive me. I shall win his confidence, and take advantage of it, as soon as possible."

But without going further, D'Artagnan shook his head and interrupted himself. "No," said he; "I should not dare to relate this to Athos; the way is therefore not honorable. I must use violence," continued he,—"very certainly I must, but without compromising my loyalty. With forty men I will traverse the country as a partisan. But if I fall in with, not forty thousand English, as Planchet said, but purely and simply with four hundred, I shall be beaten. Supposing that among my forty warriors there should be found at least ten stupid ones—ten who will allow themselves to be killed one after the other, from mere folly? No; it is, in fact, impossible to find forty men to be depended upon—they do not exist. I must learn how to be contented with thirty. With ten men less I should have the right of avoiding any armed encounter, on account of the small number of my people; and if the encounter should take place, my chance is better with thirty men than forty. Besides, I should save five thousand francs; that is to say, the eighth of my capital; that is worth the trial. This being so, I should have thirty men. I shall divide them into three bands,—we will spread ourselves about over the country, with an injunction to reunite at a given moment; in this fashion, ten by ten, we should excite no suspicion—we should pass unperceived. Yes, yes, thirty—that is a magic number. There are three tens—three, that divine number! And then, truly, a company of thirty men, when all together, will look rather imposing. Ah! stupid wretch that I am!" continued D'Artagnan, "I want thirty horses. That is ruinous. Where the devil was my head when I forgot the horses? We cannot, however, think of striking such a blow without horses. Well, so be it, that sacrifice must be made; we can get the horses in the country—they are not bad, besides. But I forgot—peste! Three bands—that necessitates three leaders; there is the difficulty. Of the three commanders I have already one—that is myself;—yes, but the two others will of themselves cost almost as much money as all the rest of the troop.

No; positively I must have but one lieutenant. In that case, then, I should reduce my troop to twenty men. I know very well that twenty men is but very little; but since with thirty I was determined not to seek to come to blows, I should do so more carefully still with twenty. Twenty—that is a round number; that, besides, reduces the number of the horses by ten, which is a consideration; and then, with a good lieutenant—Mordioux! what things patience and calculation are! Was I not going to embark with forty men, and I have now reduced them to twenty for an equal success? Ten thousand livres saved at one stroke, and more safety; that is well! Now, then, let us see; we have nothing to do but to find this lieutenant—let him be found, then; and after—That is not so easy; he must be brave and good, a second myself. Yes, but a lieutenant must have my secret, and as that secret is worth a million, and I shall only pay my man a thousand livres, fifteen hundred at the most, my man will sell the secret to Monk. Mordioux! no lieutenant. Besides, this man, were he as mute as a disciple of Pythagoras,—this man would be sure to have in the troop some favorite soldier, whom he would make his sergeant; the sergeant would penetrate the secret of the lieutenant, in case the latter should be honest and unwilling to sell it. Then the sergeant, less honest and less ambitious, will give up the whole for fifty thousand livres. Come, come! that is impossible. The lieutenant is impossible. But then I must have no fractions; I cannot divide my troop in two, and act upon two points, at once, without another self, who—But what is the use of acting upon two points, as we have only one man to take? What can be the use of weakening a corps by placing the right here, and the left there? A single corps—Mordioux! a single one, and that commanded by D'Artagnan. Very well. But twenty men marching in one band are suspected by everybody; twenty horsemen must not be seen marching together, or a company will be detached against them and the password will be required; the which company, upon seeing them embarrassed to give it, would shoot M. d'Artagnan and his men like so many rabbits. I reduce myself then to ten men; in this fashion I shall act simply and with unity; I shall be forced to be prudent, which is half the success in an affair of the kind I am undertaking; a greater number might, perhaps, have drawn me into some folly. Ten horses are not many, either, to buy or take. A capital idea; what tranquillity it infuses into my mind! no more suspicions—no passwords—no more dangers! Ten men, they are valets or clerks. Ten men, leading ten horses laden with merchandise of whatever kind, are tolerated, well received everywhere. Ten men travel on account of the house of Planchet & Co., of France,—nothing can be said against that. These ten men, clothed like manufacturers, have a good cutlass or a good musket at their saddle-bow, and a good pistol in the holster. They never allow themselves to be uneasy, because they have no evil designs. They are, perhaps, in truth, a little disposed to be smugglers, but what harm is in that? Smuggling is not, like polygamy, a hanging offense. The worst that can happen to us is the confiscation of our merchandise. Our merchandise confiscated—a fine affair that! Come, come! it is a superb plan. Ten men only—ten men, whom I will engage for my service; ten men who shall be as resolute as forty, who would cost me four times as much, and to whom, for greater security, I will never open my mouth as to my designs, and to whom I shall only say 'My friends, there is a blow to be struck.' Things being after this fashion, Satan will be very malicious if he plays me one of his tricks. Fifteen thousand livres saved—that's superb—out of twenty!"

Thus fortified by his laborious calculations, D'Artagnan stopped at this plan, and determined to change nothing in it. He had already on a list furnished by his inexhaustible memory, ten men illustrious amongst the seekers of adventure, ill-treated by fortune, and not on good terms with justice. Upon this D'Artagnan rose, and instantly set off on the search, telling Planchet not to expect him to breakfast, and perhaps not to dinner. A day and a half spent in rummaging amongst certain dens of Paris sufficed for his recruiting; and, without allowing his adventurers to communicate with each other, he had picked up and got together, in less than thirty hours, a charming collection of ill-looking faces, speaking a French less pure than the English they were about to attempt. These men were, for the most part, guards, whose merit D'Artagnan had had an opportunity of appreciating in various encounters, whom drunkenness, unlucky sword-thrusts, unexpected winnings at play, or the economical reforms of Mazarin, had forced to seek shade and solitude, those two great consolers of irritated and chafing spirits. They bore upon their countenances and in their vestments the traces of the heartaches they had undergone. Some had their visages scarred,—all had their clothes in rags. D'Artagnan comforted the most needy of these brotherly miseries by a prudent distribution of the crowns of the company; then, having taken care that these crowns should be employed in the physical improvement of the troop, he appointed a trysting place in the north of France, between Bergues and Saint Omer. Six days were allowed as the utmost term, and D'Artagnan was sufficiently acquainted with the good-will, the good-humor, and the relative probity of these illustrious recruits, to be certain that not one of them would fail in his appointment. These orders given, this rendezvous fixed, he went to bid farewell to Planchet, who asked news of his army. D'Artagnan did not think it proper to inform him of the reduction he had made in his personnel. He feared that the confidence of his associate would be abated by such an avowal. Planchet was delighted to learn that the army was levied, and that he (Planchet) found himself a kind of half king, who from his throne-counter kept in pay a body of troops destined to make war against perfidious Albion, that enemy of all true French hearts. Planchet paid down in double louis, twenty thousand livres to D'Artagnan, on the part of himself (Planchet), and twenty thousand livres, still in double louis, in account with D'Artagnan. D'Artagnan placed each of the twenty thousand francs in a bag, and weighing a bag in each hand,—"This money is very embarrassing, my dear Planchet," said he. "Do you know this weighs thirty pounds?"

"Bah! your horse will carry that like a feather."

D'Artagnan shook his head. "Don't tell me such things, Planchet: a horse overloaded with thirty pounds, in addition to the rider and his portmanteau, cannot cross a river so easily—cannot leap over a wall or ditch so lightly; and the horse failing, the horseman fails. It is true that you, Planchet, who have served in the infantry, may not be aware of all that."

"Then what is to be done, monsieur?" said Planchet, greatly embarrassed.

"Listen to me," said D'Artagnan. "I will pay my army on its return home. Keep my half of twenty thousand livres, which you can use during that time."

"And my half?" said Planchet.

"I shall take that with me."

"Your confidence does me honor," said Planchet: "but supposing you should not return?"

"That is possible, though not very probable. Then, Planchet, in case I should not return—give me a pen; I will make my will." D'Artagnan took a pen and some paper, and wrote upon a plain sheet,—"I, D'Artagnan, possess twenty thousand livres, laid up cent per cent during thirty years that I have been in the service of his majesty the king of France. I leave five thousand to Athos, five thousand to Porthos, and five thousand to Aramis, that they may give the said sums in my name and their own to my young friend Raoul, Vicomte de Bragelonne. I give the remaining five thousand to Planchet, that he may distribute the fifteen thousand with less regret among my friends. With which purpose I sign these presents.—D'ARTAGNAN."

Planchet appeared very curious to know what D'Artagnan had written.

"Here," said the musketeer, "read it."

On reading the last lines the tears came into Planchet's eyes. "You think, then, that I would not have given the money without that? Then I will have none of your five thousand francs."

D'Artagnan smiled. "Accept it, accept it, Planchet; and in that way you will only lose fifteen thousand francs instead of twenty thousand, and you will not be tempted to disregard the signature of your master and friend, by losing nothing at all."

How well that dear Monsieur d'Artagnan knew the hearts of men and grocers! They who have pronounced Don Quixote mad because he rode out to the conquest of an empire with nobody but Sancho his squire, and they who have pronounced Sancho mad because he accompanied his master in his attempt to conquer the said empire,—they certainly will have no hesitation in extending the same judgment to D'Artagnan and Planchet. And yet the first passed for one of the most subtle spirits among the astute spirits of the court of France. As to the second, he had acquired by good right the reputation of having one of the longest heads among the grocers of the Rue des Lombards; consequently of Paris, and consequently of France. Now, to consider these two men from the point of view from which you would consider other men, and the means by the aid of which they contemplated to restore a monarch to his throne, compared with other means, the shallowest brains of the country where brains are most shallow must have revolted against the presumptuous madness of the lieutenant and the stupidity of his associate. Fortunately, D'Artagnan was not a man to listen to the idle talk of those around him, or to the comments that were made on himself. He had adopted the motto, "Act well, and let people talk." Planchet, on his part had adopted this, "Act and say nothing." It resulted from this, that, according to the custom of all superior geniuses, these two men flattered themselves, intra pectus, with being in the right against all who found fault with them.

As a beginning, D'Artagnan set out in the finest of possible weather, without a cloud in the heavens—without a cloud on his mind, joyous and strong, calm and decided, great in his resolution, and consequently carrying with him a tenfold dose of that potent fluid which the shocks of mind cause to spring from the nerves, and which procure for the human machine a force and an influence of which future ages will render, according to all probability, a more arithmetical account than we can possibly do at present. He was again, as in times past, on that same road of adventures which had led him to Boulogne, and which he was now traveling for the fourth time. It appeared to him that he could almost recognize the trace of his own steps upon the road, and that of his fist upon the doors of the hostelries;—his memory, always active and present, brought back that youth which neither thirty years later his great heart nor his wrist of steel would have belied. What a rich nature was that of this man! He had all the passions, all the defects, all the weaknesses, and the spirit of contradiction familiar to his understanding changed all these imperfections into corresponding qualities. D'Artagnan, thanks to his ever active imagination, was afraid of a shadow, and ashamed of being afraid, he marched straight up to that shadow, and then became extravagant in his bravery, if the danger proved to be real. Thus everything in him was emotion, and therefore enjoyment. He loved the society of others, but never became tired of his own; and more than once, if he could have been heard when he was alone, he might have been seen laughing at the jokes he related to himself or the tricks his imagination created just five minutes before ennui might have been looked for. D'Artagnan was not perhaps so gay this time as he would have been with the prospect of finding some good friends at Calais, instead of joining the ten scamps there; melancholy, however, did not visit him more than once a day, and it was about five visits that he received from that somber deity before he got sight of the sea at Boulogne, and then these visits were indeed but short. But when once D'Artagnan found himself near the field of action, all other feelings but that of confidence disappeared never to return. From Boulogne he followed the coast to Calais. Calais was the place of general rendezvous, and at Calais he had named to each of his recruits the hostelry of "Le Grande Monarque," where living was not extravagant, where sailors messed, and where men of the sword, with sheath of leather, be it understood, found lodging, table, food, and all the comforts of life, for thirty sous per diem. D'Artagnan proposed to himself to take them by surprise in flagrante delicto of wandering life, and to judge by the first appearance if he could count on them as trusty companions.

He arrived at Calais at half past four in the afternoon.

Chapter XXII.
D'Artagnan travels for the House of Planchet and Company.

THE hostelry of "Le Grand Monarque" was situated in a little street parallel to the port without looking out upon the port itself. Some lanes cut—as steps cut the two parallels of the ladder—the two great straight lines of the port and the street. By these lanes passengers came suddenly from the port into the street, or from the street on to the port. D'Artagnan, arrived at the port, took one of these lanes, and came out in front of the hostelry of "Le Grand Monarque." The moment was well chosen and might remind D'Artagnan of his start in life at the hostelry of the "Franc-Meunier" at Meung. Some sailors who had been playing at dice had started a quarrel, and were threatening each other furiously. The host, hostess, and two lads were watching with anxiety the circle of these angry gamblers, from the midst of which war seemed ready to break forth, bristling with knives and hatchets. The play, nevertheless, was continued. A stone bench was occupied by two men, who appeared thence to watch the door; four tables, placed at the back of the common chamber, were occupied by eight other individuals. Neither the men at the door, nor those at the tables took any part in the play or the quarrel. D'Artagnan recognized his ten men in these cold, indifferent spectators. The quarrel went on increasing. Every passion has, like the sea, its tide which ascends and descends. Reaching the climax of passion, one sailor overturned the table and the money which was upon it. The table fell, and the money rolled about. In an instant all belonging to the hostelry threw themselves upon the stakes, and many a piece of silver was picked up by people who stole away whilst the sailors were scuffling with each other.

The two men on the bench and the eight at the tables, although they seemed perfect strangers to each other, these ten men alone, we say, appeared to have agreed to remain impassible amidst the cries of fury and the chinking of money. Two only contented themselves with pushing with their feet combatants who came under their table. Two others, rather than take part in this disturbance, buried their hands in their pockets; and another two jumped upon the table they occupied, as people do to avoid being submerged by overflowing water.

"Come, come," said D'Artagnan to himself, not having lost one of the details we have related, "this is a very fair gathering—circumspect, calm, accustomed to disturbance, acquainted with blows! Peste! I have been lucky."

All at once his attention was called to a particular part of the room. The two men who had pushed the strugglers with their feet, were assailed with abuse by the sailors, who had become reconciled. One of them, half drunk with passion, and quite drunk with beer, came, in a menacing manner, to demand of the shorter of these two sages by what right he had touched with his foot creatures of the good God, who were not dogs. And whilst putting this question, in order to make it more direct, he applied his great fist to the nose of D'Artagnan's recruit.

This man became pale, without its being to be discerned whether his pallor arose from anger or fear; seeing which, the sailor concluded it was from fear, and raised his fist with the manifest intention of letting it fall upon the head of the stranger. But though the threatened man did not appear to move, he dealt the sailor such a severe blow in the stomach that he sent him rolling and howling to the other side of the room. At the same instant, rallied by the espirit de corps, all the comrades of the conquered man fell upon the conqueror.

The latter, with the same coolness of which he had given proof, without committing the imprudence of touching his weapons, took up a beer-pot with a pewter-lid, and knocked down two or three of his assailants; then, as he was about to yield to numbers, the seven other silent men at the tables, who had not yet stirred, perceived that their cause was at stake, and came to the rescue. At the same time, the two indifferent spectators at the door turned round with frowning bows, indicating their evident intention of taking the enemy in the rear, if the enemy did not cease their aggressions.

The host, his helpers, and two watchmen who were passing, and who from the curiosity had penetrated too far into the room, were mixed up in the tumult and showered with blows. The Parisians hit like Cyclops, with an ensemble and a tactic delightful to behold. At length, obliged to beat a retreat before superior numbers, they formed an intrenchment behind the large table, which they raised by main force; whilst the two others, arming themselves each with a trestle, and using it like a great sledge-hammer, knocked down at a blow eight sailors upon whose heads they had brought their monstrous catapult in play. The floor was already strewn with wounded, and the room filled with cries and dust, when D'Artagnan, satisfied with the test, advanced, sword in hand, and striking with the pommel every head that came in his way, he uttered a vigorous hola! which put an instantaneous end to the conflict. A great back-flood directly took place from the center to the sides of the room, so that D'Artagnan found himself isolated and dominator.

"What is this all about?" then demanded he of the assembly, with the majestic tone of Neptune pronouncing the Quos ego.

At the very instant, at the first sound of his voice, to carry on the Virgilian metaphor, D'Artagnan's recruits, recognizing each his sovereign lord, discontinued their plank-fighting and trestle blows. On their side, the sailors, seeing that long naked sword, that martial air, and the agile arm which came to the rescue of their enemies, in the person of a man who seemed accustomed to command, the sailors picked up their wounded and their pitchers. The Parisians wiped their brows, and viewed their leader with respect. D'Artagnan was loaded with thanks by the host of "Le Grand Monarque." He received them like a man who knows that nothing is being offered that does not belong to him, and then said he would go and walk upon the port till supper was ready. Immediately each of the recruits, who understood the summons, took his hat, brushed the dust off his clothes, and followed D'Artagnan. But D'Artagnan, whilst walking and observing, took care not to stop; he directed his course towards the downs, and the ten men—surprised at finding themselves going in the track of each other, uneasy at seeing on their right, on their left, and behind them, companions upon whom they had not reckoned—followed him, casting furtive glances at each other. It was not till he had arrived at the hollow part of the deepest down that D'Artagnan, smiling to see them outdone, turned towards them, making a friendly sign with his hand.

"Eh! come, come, gentlemen," said he, "let us not devour each other; you are made to live together, to understand each other in all respects, and not to devour one another."

Instantly all hesitation ceased; the men breathed as if they had been taken out of a coffin, and examined each other complacently. After this examination they turned their eyes towards their leader, who had long been acquainted with the art of speaking to men of that class, and who improvised the following little speech, pronounced with an energy truly Gascon:

"Gentlemen, you all know who I am. I have engaged you from knowing you to be brave, and willing to associate you with me in a glorious enterprise. Imagine that in laboring for me you labor for the king. I only warn you that if you allow anything of this supposition to appear, I shall be forced to crack your skulls immediately, in the manner most convenient to me. You are not ignorant, gentlemen, that state secrets are like a mortal poison: as long as that poison is in its box and the box is closed, it is not injurious; out of the box, it kills. Now draw near, and you shall know as much of this secret as I am able to tell you." All drew close to him with an expression of curiosity. "Approach," continued D'Artagnan, "and let not the bird which passes over our heads, the rabbit which sports on the downs, the fish which bounds from the waters, hear us. Our business is to learn and to report to monsieur le surintendant of the finances to what extent English smuggling is injurious to the French merchants. I shall enter every place, and see everything. We are poor Picard fishermen, thrown upon the coast by a storm. It is certain that we must sell fish, neither more nor less, like true fishermen. Only people might guess who we are, and might molest us; it is therefore necessary that we should be in a condition to defend ourselves. And this is why I have selected men of spirit and courage. We shall lead a steady life, and not incur much danger, seeing that we have behind us a powerful protector, thanks to whom no embarrassment is possible. One thing alone puzzles me; but I hope that after a short explanation, you will relieve me from that difficulty. The thing which puzzles me is taking with me a crew of stupid fishermen, which crew will annoy me immensely, whilst if, by chance, there were among you any who have seen the sea—"

"Oh! don't let that trouble you," said one of the recruits; "I was a prisoner among the pirates of Tunis three years, and can maneuver a boat like an admiral."

"See," said D'Artagnan, "what an admirable thing chance is!" D'Artagnan pronounced these words with an indefinable tone of feigned bonhomie, for he knew very well that the victim of the pirates was an old corsair, and had engaged him in consequence of that knowledge. But D'Artagnan never said more than there was need to say, in order to leave people in doubt. He paid himself with the explanation, and welcomed the effect, without appearing to be preoccupied with the cause.

"And I," said a second, "I, by chance, had an uncle who directed the works of the port of La Rochelle. When quite a child, I played about the boats, and I know how to handle an oar or a sail as well as the best Ponantais sailor." The latter did not lie much more than the first, for he had rowed on board his majesty's galleys six years, at Ciotat. Two others were more frank: they confessed honestly that they had served on board a vessel as soldiers as punishment, and did not blush for it. D'Artagnan found himself, then, the leader of ten men of war and four sailors, having at once an land army and a sea force, which would have carried the pride of Planchet to its height, if Planchet had known the details.

Nothing was now left but arranging the general orders, and D'Artagnan gave them with precision. He enjoined his men to be ready to set out for the Hague, some following the coast which leads to Breskens, others the road to Antwerp. The rendezvous was given, by calculating each day's march, a fortnight from that time, upon the chief place at the Hague. D'Artagnan recommended his men to go in couples, as they liked best, from sympathy. He himself selected from among those with the least disreputable look, two guards whom he had formerly known, and whose only faults were being drunkards and gamblers. These men had not entirely lost all ideas of civilization, and under proper garments their hearts would beat again. D'Artagnan, not to create any jealousy with the others, made the rest go forward. He kept his two selected ones, clothed them from his own wardrobe, and set out with them.

It was to these two, whom he seemed to honor with an absolute confidence, that D'Artagnan imparted a false secret, destined to secure the success of the expedition. He confessed to them that the object was not to learn to what extent French merchants were injured by English smuggling, but to learn how far French smuggling could annoy English trade. These men appeared convinced; they were effectively so. D'Artagnan was quite sure that at the first debauch, when thoroughly drunk, one of the two would divulge the secret to the whole band. His game appeared infallible.

A fortnight after all we have said had taken place at Calais, the whole troop assembled at the Hague.

Then D'Artagnan perceived that all his men, with remarkable intelligence, had already travestied themselves into sailors, more or less ill-treated by the sea. D'Artagnan left them to sleep in a den in Newkerke street, whilst he lodged comfortably upon the Grand Canal. He learned that the king of England had come back to his old ally, William II. of Nassau, stadtholder of Holland. He learned also that the refusal of Louis XIV. had a little cooled the protection afforded him up to that time, and in consequence he had gone to reside in a little village house at Scheveningen, situated in the downs, on the sea-shore, about a league from the Hague.

There, it was said, the unfortunate banished king consoled himself in his exile, by looking, with the melancholy peculiar to the princes of his race, at that immense North Sea, which separated him from his England, as it had formerly separated Mary Stuart from France. There, behind the trees of the beautiful wood of Scheveningen, on the fine sand upon which grows the golden broom of the down, Charles II. vegetated as it did, more unfortunate, for he had life and thought, and he hoped and despaired by turns.

D'Artagnan went once as far as Scheveningen, in order to be certain that all was true that was said of the king. He beheld Charles II., pensive and alone, coming out of a little door opening into the wood, and walking on the beach in the setting sun, without even attracting the attention of the fishermen, who, on their return in the evening, drew, like the ancient mariners of the Archipelago, their barks up upon the sand of the shore.

D'Artagnan recognized the king; he saw him fix his melancholy look upon the immense extent of the waters, and absorb upon his pale countenance the red rays of the sun already cut by the black line of the horizon. Then Charles returned to his isolated abode, always alone, slow and sad, amusing himself with making the friable and moving sand creak beneath his feet.

That very evening D'Artagnan hired for a thousand livres a fishing-boat worth four thousand. He paid a thousand livres down, and deposited the three thousand with a Burgomaster, after which he brought on board, without their being seen, the six men who formed his land army; and with the rising tide, at three o'clock in the morning, he got into the open sea, maneuvering ostensibly with the four others, and depending upon the science of his galley slave as upon that of the first pilot of the port.

Chapter XXIII.
In which the Author is forced to write a Little History.

WHILE kings and men were thus occupied with England, which governed itself quite alone, and which, it must be said in its praise, had never been so badly governed, a man upon whom God had fixed his eye, and placed his finger, a man predestined to write his name in brilliant letters upon the page of history, was pursuing in the face of the world a work full of mystery and audacity. He went on, and no one knew whither he meant to go, although not only England, but France, and Europe, watched him marching with a firm step and head held high. All that was known of this man we are about to tell.

Monk had just declared himself in favor of the liberty of the Rump Parliament, a parliament which General Lambert, imitating Cromwell, whose lieutenant he had been, had just blocked up so closely, in order to bring it to his will, that no member, during all the blockade, was able to go out, and only one, Peter Wentworth, had been able to get in.

Lambert and Monk—everything was summed up in these two men; the first representing military despotism, the second pure republicanism. These men were the two sole political representatives of that revolution in which Charles I. had first lost his crown, and afterwards his head. As regarded Lambert, he did not dissemble his views; he sought to establish a military government, and to be himself the head of that government.

Monk, a rigid republican, some said, wished to maintain the Rump Parliament, that visible though degenerated representative of the republic. Monk, artful and ambitious, said others, wished simply to make of this parliament, which he affected to protect, a solid step by which to mount the throne which Cromwell had left empty, but upon which he had never dared to take his seat.

Thus Lambert by persecuting the parliament, and Monk by declaring for it, had mutually proclaimed themselves enemies of each other. Monk and Lambert, therefore, had at first thought of creating an army each for himself: Monk in Scotland, where were the Presbyterians and the royalists, that is to say, the malcontents; Lambert in London, where was found, as is always the case, the strongest opposition to the existing power which it had beneath its eyes.

Monk had pacified Scotland, he had there formed for himself an army, and found an asylum. The one watched the other. Monk knew that the day was not yet come, the day marked by the Lord for a great change; his sword, therefore, appeared glued to the sheath. Inexpugnable in his wild and mountainous Scotland, an absolute general, king of an army of eleven thousand old soldiers, whom he had more than once led on to victory; as well informed, nay, even better, of the affairs of London, than Lambert, who held garrison in the city,—such was the position of Monk, when, at a hundred leagues from London, he declared himself for the parliament. Lambert, on the contrary, as we have said, lived in the capital. That was the center of all his operations, and he there collected all around him all his friends, and all the people of the lower class, eternally inclined to cherish the enemies of constituted power.

It was then in London that Lambert learnt the support that, from the frontiers of Scotland, Monk lent to the parliament. He judged there was no time to be lost, and that the Tweed was not so far distant from the Thames that an army could not march from one river to the other, particularly when it was well commanded. He knew, besides, that as fast as the soldiers of Monk penetrated into England, they would form on their route that ball of snow, the emblem of the globe of fortune, which is for the ambitious nothing but a step growing unceasingly higher to conduct him to his object. He got together, therefore, his army, formidable at the same time for its composition and its numbers, and hastened to meet Monk, who, on his part, like a prudent navigator sailing amidst rocks, advanced by very short marches, listening to the reports which came from London.

The two armies came in sight of each other near Newcastle; Lambert, arriving first, encamped in the city itself. Monk, always circumspect, stopped where he was, and placed his general quarters at Coldstream, on the Tweed. The sight of Lambert spread joy through Monk's army, whilst, on the contrary, the sight of Monk threw disorder into Lambert's army. It might have been thought that these intrepid warriors, who had made such a noise in the streets of London, had set out with the hopes of meeting no one, and that now seeing that they had met an army, and that that army hoisted before them not only a standard, but still further, a cause and a principle,—it might have been believed, we say, that these intrepid warriors had begun to reflect that they were less good republicans than the soldiers of Monk, since the latter supported the parliament; whilst Lambert supported nothing, not even himself.

As to Monk, if he had had to reflect, or if he did reflect, it must have been after a sad fashion, for history relates—and that modest dame, it is well known, never lies—history relates, that the day of his arrival at Coldstream search was made in vain throughout the place for a single sheep.

If Monk had commanded an English army, that was enough to have brought about a general desertion. But it is not with the Scots as it is with the English, to whom that fluid flesh which is called blood is a paramount necessity; the

Scots, a poor and sober race, live upon a little barley crushed between two stones, diluted with the water of the fountain, and cooked upon another stone, heated.

The Scots, their distribution of barley being made, cared very little whether there was or was not any meat in Coldstream. Monk, little accustomed to barley-cakes, was hungry, and his staff, at least as hungry as himself, looked with anxiety right and left, to know what was being prepared for supper.

Monk ordered search to be made; his scouts had on arriving in the place found it deserted and the cupboards empty; upon butchers and bakers it was of no use depending in Coldstream. The smallest morsel of bread, then, could not be found for the general's table.

As accounts succeeded each other, all equally unsatisfactory, Monk, seeing terror and discouragement upon every face, declared that he was not hungry; besides, they should eat on the morrow, since Lambert was there probably with the intention of giving battle, and consequently would give up his provisions, if he were forced from Newcastle, or forever to relieve Monk's soldiers from hunger if he conquered.

This consolation was only efficacious upon a very small number; but of what importance was it to Monk? for Monk was very absolute, under the appearance of the most perfect mildness. Every one, therefore, was obliged to be satisfied, or at least to appear so. Monk, quite as hungry as his people, but affecting perfect indifference for the absent mutton, cut a fragment of tobacco, half an inch long, from the carotte of a sergeant who formed part of his suite, and began to masticate the said fragment, assuring his lieutenant that hunger was a chimera, and that, besides, people were never hungry when they had anything to chew.

This joke satisfied some of those who had resisted Monk's first deduction drawn from the neighborhood of Lambert's army; the number of the dissentients diminished greatly; the guard took their posts, the patrols began, and the general continued his frugal repast beneath his open tent.

Between his camp and that of the enemy stood an old abbey, of which, at the present day, there only remain some ruins, but which then was in existence, and was called Newcastle Abbey. It was built upon a vast site, independent at once of the plain and of the river, because it was almost a marsh fed by springs and kept up by rains. Nevertheless, in the midst of these pools of water, covered with long grass, rushes, and reeds, were seen solid spots of ground, formerly used as the kitchen-garden, the park, the pleasure-gardens, and other dependencies of the abbey, looking like one of those great sea-spiders, whose body is round, whilst the claws go diverging round from this circumference.

The kitchen-garden, one of the longest claws of the abbey, extended to Monk's camp. Unfortunately it was, as we have said, early in June, and the kitchen-garden, being abandoned, offered no resources.

Monk had ordered this spot to be guarded, as most subject to surprises. The fires of the enemy's general were plainly to be perceived on the other side of the abbey. But between these fires and the abbey extended the Tweed, unfolding its luminous scales beneath the thick shade of tall green oaks. Monk was perfectly well acquainted with this position, Newcastle and its environs having already more than once been his headquarters. He knew that by this day his enemy might without doubt throw a few scouts into these ruins and promote a skirmish, but that by night he would take care to abstain from such a risk. He felt himself, therefore, in security.

Thus his soldiers saw him, after what he boastingly called his supper—that is to say, after the exercise of mastication reported by us at the commencement of this chapter—like Napoleon on the eve of Austerlitz, seated asleep in his rush chair, half beneath the light of his lamp, half beneath the reflection of the moon, commencing its ascent in the heavens, which denoted that it was nearly half past nine in the evening. All at once Monk was roused from his half sleep, fictitious perhaps, by a troop of soldiers, who came with joyous cries, and kicked the poles of his tent with a humming noise as if on purpose to wake him. There was no need of so much noise; the general opened his eyes quickly.

"Well, my children, what is going on now?" asked the general.

"General!" replied several voices at once, "General! you shall have some supper."

"I have had my supper, gentlemen," replied he quietly, "and was comfortably digesting it, as you see. But come in, and tell me what brings you hither."

"Good news, general."

"Bah! Has Lambert sent us word that he will fight to-morrow?"

"No; but we have just captured a fishing-boat conveying fish to Newcastle."

"And you have done very wrong, my friends. These gentlemen from London are delicate, must have their first course; you will put them sadly out of humor this evening, and to-morrow they will be pitiless. It would really be in good taste to send back to Lambert both his fish and his fishermen, unless—" and the general reflected an instant.

"Tell me," continued he, "what are these fishermen, if you please?"

"Some Picard seamen who were fishing on the coasts of France or Holland, and who have been thrown upon ours by a gale of wind."

"Do any among them speak our language?"

"The leader spoke some few words of English."

The mistrust of the general was awakened in proportion as fresh information reached him. "That is well," said he. "I wish to see these men; bring them to me."

An officer immediately went to fetch them.

"How many are there of them?" continued Monk; "and what is their vessel?"

"There are ten or twelve of them, general, and they were aboard of a kind of chasse-maree, as it is called—Dutch-built, apparently."

"And you say they were carrying fish to Lambert's camp?"

"Yes, general, and they seem to have had good luck in their fishing."

"Humph! We shall see that," said Monk.

At this moment the officer returned, bringing the leader of the fishermen with him. He was a man from fifty to fifty-five years old, but good-looking for his age. He was of middle height, and wore a justaucorps of coarse wool, a cap pulled down over his eyes, a cutlass hung from his belt, and he walked with the hesitation peculiar to sailors, who, never knowing, thanks to the movement of the vessel, whether their foot will be placed upon the plank or upon nothing, give to every one of their steps a fall as firm as if they were driving a pile. Monk, with an acute and penetrating look, examined the fisherman for some time, while the latter smiled, with that smile, half cunning, half silly, peculiar to French peasants.

"Do you speak English?" asked Monk, in excellent French.

"Ah! but badly, my lord," replied the fisherman.

This reply was made much more with the lively and sharp accentuation of the people beyond the Loire, than with the slightly-drawling accent of the countries of the west and north of France.

"But you do speak it?" persisted Monk, in order to examine his accent once more.

"Eh! we men of the sea," replied the fisherman, "speak a little of all languages."

"Then you are a sea fisherman?"

"I am at present, my lord—a fisherman, and a famous fisherman, too. I have taken a barbel that weighs at least thirty pounds, and more than fifty mullets; I have also some little whitings that will fry beautifully."

"You appear to me to have fished more frequently in the Gulf of Gascony than in the Channel," said Monk, smiling.

"Well, I am from the south; but does that prevent me from being a good fisherman, my lord?"

"Oh! not at all; I shall buy your fish. And now speak frankly; for whom did you destine them?"

"My lord, I will conceal nothing from you. I was going to Newcastle, following the coast, when a party of horsemen who were passing along in an opposite direction made a sign to my bark to turn back to your honor's camp, under penalty of a discharge of musketry. As I was not armed for fighting," added the fisherman, smiling, "I was forced to submit."

"And why did you go to Lambert's camp in preference to mine?"

"My lord, I will be frank; will your lordship permit me?"

"Yes, and even if need be shall command you to be so."

"Well, my lord, I was going to M. Lambert's camp because those gentlemen from the city pay well—whilst your Scotchmen, Puritans, Presbyterians, Covenanters, or whatever you chose to call them, eat but little, and pay for nothing."

Monk shrugged his shoulders, without, however, being able to refrain from smiling at the same time. "How is it that, being from the south, you come to fish on our coasts?"

"Because I have been fool enough to marry in Picardy."

"Yes; but even Picardy is not England."

"My lord, man shoves his boat into the sea, but God and the wind do the rest, and drive the boat where they please."

"You had, then, no intention of landing on our coasts?"

"Never."

"And what route were you steering?"

"We were returning from Ostend, where some mackerel had already been seen, when a sharp wind from the south drove us from our course; then, seeing that it was useless to struggle against it, we let it drive us. It then became necessary, not to lose our fish, which were good, to go and sell them at the nearest English port, and that was Newcastle. We were told the opportunity was good, as there was an increase of population in the camp, an increase of population in the city; both, we were told, were full of gentlemen, very rich and very hungry. So we steered our course towards Newcastle."

"And your companions, where are they?"

"Oh, my companions have remained on board; they are sailors without the least instruction."

"Whilst you—" said Monk.

"Who, I?" said the patron, laughing; "I have sailed about with my father; and I know what is called a sou, a crown, a pistole, a louis, and a double louis, in all the languages of Europe; my crew, therefore, listen to me as they would to an oracle, and obey me as if I were an admiral."

"Then it was you who preferred M. Lambert as the best customer?"

"Yes, certainly. And, to be frank, my lord, was I wrong?"

"You will see that by and by."

"At all events, my lord, if there is a fault, the fault is mine; and my comrades should not be dealt hardly with on that account."

"This is decidedly an intelligent, sharp fellow," thought Monk. Then, after a few minutes' silence employed in scrutinizing the fisherman,—"You come from Ostend, did you not say?" asked the general.

"Yes, my lord, in a straight line."

"You have then heard of the affairs of the day; for I have no doubt that both in France and Holland they excite interest. What is he doing who calls himself king of England?"

"Oh, my lord!" cried the fisherman, with loud and expansive frankness, "that is a lucky question, and you could not put it to anybody better than to me, for in truth I can make you a famous reply. Imagine, my lord, that when putting into Ostend to sell the few mackerel we had caught, I saw the ex-king walking on the downs waiting for his horses, which were to take him to the Hague. He is a rather tall, pale man, with black hair, and somewhat hard-featured. He looks ill, and I don't think the air of Holland agrees with him."

Monk followed with the greatest attention the rapid, heightened, and diffuse conversation of the fisherman, in a language which was not his own, but which, as we have said, he spoke with great facility. The fisherman, on his part, employed sometimes a French word, sometimes an English word, and sometimes a word which appeared not to belong to any language, but was, in truth, pure Gascon. Fortunately his eyes spoke for him, and that so eloquently, that it was possible to lose a word from his mouth, but not a single intention from his eyes. The general appeared more and more satisfied with his examination. "You must have heard that this ex-king, as you call him, was going to the Hague for some purpose?"

"Oh, yes," said the fisherman, "I heard that."

"And what was his purpose?"

"Always the same," said the fisherman. "Must he not always entertain the fixed idea of returning to England?"

"That is true," said Monk, pensively.

"Without reckoning," added the fisherman, "that the stadtholder—you know, my lord, William II.?—"

"Well?"

"He will assist him with all his power."

"Ah! did you hear that said?"

"No, but I think so."

"You are quite a politician, apparently," said Monk.

"Why, we sailors, my lord, who are accustomed to study the water and the air—that is to say, the two most changeable things in the world—are seldom deceived as to the rest."

"Now, then," said Monk, changing the conversation, "I am told you are going to provision us."

"I shall do my best, my lord."

"How much do you ask for your fish in the first place?"

"Not such a fool as to name a price, my lord."

"Why not?"

"Because my fish is yours."

"By what right?"

"By that of the strongest."

"But my intention is to pay you for it."

"That is very generous of you, my lord."

"And the worth of it—"

"My lord, I fix no price."

"What do you ask, then?"

"I only ask to be permitted to go away."

"Where?—to General Lambert's camp?"

"I!" cried the fisherman; "what should I go to Newcastle for, now I have no longer any fish?"

"At all events, listen to me."

"I do, my lord."

"I shall give you some advice."

"How, my lord!—pay me and give me good advice likewise! You overwhelm me, my lord."

Monk looked more earnestly than ever at the fisherman, about whom he still appeared to entertain some suspicion. "Yes, I shall pay you, and give you a piece of advice; for the two things are connected. If you return, then, to General Lambert—"

The fisherman made a movement of his head and shoulders, which signified, "If he persists in it, I won't contradict him."

"Do not cross the marsh," continued Monk: "you will have money in your pocket, and there are in the marsh some Scottish ambuscaders I have placed there. Those people are very intractable; they understand but very little of the language which you speak, although it appears to me to be composed of three languages. They might take from you what I have given you, and, on your return to your country, you would not fail to say that General Monk has two hands, the one Scottish, and the other English; and that he takes back with the Scottish hand what he has given with the English hand."

"Oh! general, I shall go where you like, be sure of that," said the fisherman, with a fear too expressive not to be exaggerated. "I only wish to remain here, if you will allow me to remain."

"I readily believe you," said Monk, with an imperceptible smile, "but I cannot, nevertheless, keep you in my tent."

"I have no such wish, my lord, and desire only that your lordship should point out where you will have me posted. Do not trouble yourself about us—with us a night soon passes away."

"You shall be conducted to your bark."

"As your lordship pleases. Only, if your lordship would allow me to be taken back by a carpenter, I should be extremely grateful."

"Why so?"

"Because the gentlemen of your army, in dragging my boat up the river with a cable pulled by their horses, have battered it a little upon the rocks of the shore, so that I have at least two feet of water in my hold, my lord."

"The greater reason why you should watch your boat, I think."

"My lord, I am quite at your orders," said the fisherman; "I shall empty my baskets where you wish; then you will pay me, if you please to do so; and you will send me away, if it appears right to you. You see I am very easily managed and pleased, my lord."

"Come, come, you are a very good sort of fellow," said Monk, whose scrutinizing glance had not been able to find a single shade in the clear eye of the fisherman. "Holloa, Digby!" An aid-de-camp appeared. "You will conduct this good fellow and his companions to the little tents of the canteens, in front of the marshes, so that they will be near their bark, and yet will not sleep on board to-night. What is the matter, Spithead?"

Spithead was the sergeant from whom Monk had borrowed a piece of tobacco for his supper. Spithead having entered the general's tent without being sent for, had drawn this question from Monk.

"My lord," said he, "a French gentleman has just presented himself at the outposts and wishes to speak to your honor."

All this was said, be it understood, in English; but, notwithstanding, it produced a slight emotion in the fisherman, which Monk, occupied with his sergeant, did not remark.

"Who is the gentleman?" asked Monk.

"My lord," replied Spithead, "he told it me; but those devils of French names are so difficult to pronounce for a Scottish throat, that I could not retain it. I believe, however, from what the guards say, that it is the same gentleman who presented himself yesterday at the halt, and whom your honor would not receive."

"That is true; I was holding a council of officers."

"Will your honor give any orders respecting this gentleman?"

"Yes, let him be brought here."

"Must we take any precautions?"

"Such as what?"

"Blinding his eyes, for instance?"

"To what purpose? He can only see what I desire should be seen; that is to say, that I have around me eleven thousand brave men, who ask no better than to have their throats cut in honor of the parliament of Scotland and England."

"And this man, my lord?" said Spithead, pointing to the fisherman, who, during this conversation, had remained standing and motionless, like a man who sees but does not understand.

"Ah, that is true," said Monk. Then turning towards the fisherman,—"I shall see you again, my brave fellow," said he; "I have selected a lodging for you. Digby, take him to it. Fear nothing; your money shall be sent to you presently."

"Thank you, my lord," said the fisherman, and after having bowed, he left the tent, accompanied by Digby. Before he had gone a hundred paces he found his companions, who were whispering with a volubility which did not appear exempt from uneasiness, but he made them a sign which seemed to reassure them. "Hola, you fellows!" said the patron, "come this way. His lordship, General Monk, has the generosity to pay us for our fish, and the goodness to give us hospitality for to-night."

The fishermen gathered round their leader, and, conducted by Digby, the little troop proceeded towards the canteens, the post, as may be remembered, which had been assigned them. As they went along in the dark, the fishermen passed close to the guards who were conducting the French gentleman to General Monk. This gentleman was on horseback and enveloped in a large cloak, which prevented the patron from seeing him, however great his curiosity might be. As to the gentleman, ignorant that he was elbowing compatriots, he did not pay any attention to the little troop.

The aid-de-camp settled his guests in a tolerably comfortable tent, from which was dislodged an Irish canteen woman, who went, with her six children, to sleep where she could. A large fire was burning in front of this tent, and threw its purple light over the grassy pools of the marsh, rippled by a fresh breeze. The arrangements made, the aid-de-camp wished the fishermen good-night, calling to their notice that they might see from the door of the tent the masts of their bark, which was tossing gently on the Tweed, a proof that it had not yet sunk. The sight of this appeared to delight the leader of the fishermen infinitely.

Chapter XXIV.
The Treasure.

THE French gentleman whom Spithead had announced to Monk, and who, closely wrapped in his cloak, had passed by the fishermen who left the general's tent five minutes before he entered it,—the French gentleman went through the various posts without even casting his eyes around him, for fear of appearing indiscreet. As the order had been given, he was conducted to the tent of the general. The gentleman was left alone in the sort of antechamber in front of the principal body of the tent, where he awaited Monk, who only delayed till he had heard the report of his people, and observed through the opening of the canvas the countenance of the person who solicited an audience.

Without doubt, the report of those who had accompanied the French gentleman established the discretion with which he had behaved, for the first impression the stranger received of the welcome made him by the general was more favorable than he could have expected at such a moment, and on the part of so suspicious a man. Nevertheless, according to his custom, when Monk found himself in the presence of a stranger, he fixed upon him his penetrating eyes, which scrutiny, the stranger, on his part, sustained without embarrassment or notice. At the end of a few seconds, the general made a gesture with his hand and head in sign of attention.

"My lord," said the gentleman, in excellent English, "I have requested an interview with your honor, for an affair of importance."

"Monsieur," replied Monk, in French, "you speak our language well for a son of the continent. I ask your pardon—for doubtless the question is indiscreet—do you speak French with the same purity?"

"There is nothing surprising, my lord, in my speaking English tolerably; I resided for some time in England in my youth, and since then I have made two voyages to this country." These words were spoken in French, and with a purity of accent that bespoke not only a Frenchman, but a Frenchman from the vicinity of Tours.

"And what part of England have you resided in, monsieur?"

"In my youth, London, my lord; then, about 1635, I made a pleasure trip to Scotland; and lastly, in 1648, I lived for some time at Newcastle, particularly in the convent, the gardens of which are now occupied by your army."

"Excuse me, monsieur; but you must comprehend that these questions are necessary on my part—do you not?"

"It would astonish me, my lord, if they were not asked."

"Now, then, monsieur, what can I do to serve you? What do you wish?"

"This, my lord;—but, in the first place, are we alone?"

"Perfectly so, monsieur, except, of course, the post which guards us." So saying, Monk pulled open the canvas with his hand, and pointed to the soldier placed at ten paces from the tent, and who, at the first call, could have rendered assistance in a second.

"In that case, my lord," said the gentleman, in as calm a tone as if he had been for a length of time in habits of intimacy with his interlocutor, "I have made up my mind to address myself to you, because I believe you to be an honest man. Indeed, the communication I am about to make to you will prove to you the esteem in which I hold you."

Monk, astonished at this language, which established between him and the French gentleman equality at least, raised his piercing eye to the stranger's face, and with a sensible irony conveyed by the inflection of his voice alone, for not a muscle of his face moved,—"I thank you, monsieur," said he; "but, in the first place, to whom have I the honor of speaking?"

"I sent you my name by your sergeant, my lord."

"Excuse him, monsieur, he is a Scotsman,—he could not retain it."

"I am called the Comte de la Fere, monsieur," said Athos, bowing.

"The Comte de la Fere?" said Monk, endeavoring to recollect the name. "Pardon me, monsieur, but this appears to be the first time I have ever heard that name. Do you fill any post at the court of France?"

"None; I am a simple gentleman."

"What dignity?"

"King Charles I. made me a knight of the Garter, and Queen Anne of Austria has given me the cordon of the Holy Ghost. These are my only dignities."

"The Garter! the Holy Ghost! Are you a knight of those two orders, monsieur?"

"Yes."

"And on what occasions have such favors been bestowed upon you?"

"For services rendered to their majesties."

Monk looked with astonishment at this man, who appeared to him so simple and so great at the same time. Then, as if he had renounced endeavoring to penetrate this mystery of a simplicity and grandeur upon which the stranger did not seem disposed to give him any other information than that which he had already received,—"Did you present yourself yesterday at our advanced posts?"

"And was sent back? Yes, my lord."

"Many officers, monsieur, would permit no one to enter their camp, particularly on the eve of a probable battle. But I differ from my colleagues, and like to leave nothing behind me. Every advice is good to me; all danger is sent to me by God, and I weigh it in my hand with the energy He has given me. So, yesterday, you were only sent back on account of the council I was holding. To-day I am at liberty,—speak."

"My lord, you have done much better in receiving me, for what I have to say has nothing to do with the battle you are about to fight with General Lambert, or with your camp; and the proof is, that I turned away my head that I might not see your men, and closed my eyes that I might not count your tents. No, I came to speak to you, my lord, on my own account."

"Speak then, monsieur," said Monk.

"Just now," continued Athos, "I had the honor of telling your lordship that for a long time I lived in Newcastle; it was in the time of Charles I., and when the king was given up to Cromwell by the Scots."

"I know," said Monk, coldly.

"I had at that time a large sum in gold, and on the eve of the battle, from a presentiment perhaps of the turn which things would take on the morrow, I concealed it in the principal vault of the covenant of Newcastle, in the tower whose summit you now see silvered by the moonbeams. My treasure has then remained interred there, and I have come to entreat your honor to permit me to withdraw it before, perhaps, the battle turning that way, a mine or some other war engine has destroyed the building and scattered my gold, or rendered it so apparent that the soldiers will take possession of it."

Monk was well acquainted with mankind; he saw in the physiognomy of this gentleman all the energy, all the reason, all the circumspection possible; he could therefore only attribute to a magnanimous confidence the revelation the Frenchman had made him, and he showed himself profoundly touched by it.

"Monsieur," said he, "you have augured well of me. But is the sum worth the trouble to which you expose yourself? Do you even believe that it can be in the same place where you left it?"

"It is there monsieur, I do not doubt."

"That is a reply to one question; but to the other. I asked you if the sum was so large as to warrant your exposing yourself thus."

"It is really large; yes, my lord, for it is a million I inclosed in two barrels."

"A million!" cried Monk, at whom this time, in turn, Athos looked earnestly and long. Monk perceived this, and his mistrust returned.

"Here is a man," said he to himself, "who is laying a snare for me. So you wish to withdraw this money, monsieur," replied he, "as I understand?"

"If you please, my lord."

"To-day?"

"This very evening, and that on account of the circumstances I have named."

"But, monsieur," objected Monk, "General Lambert is as near the abbey where you have to act as I am. Why, then, have you not addressed yourself to him?"

"Because, my lord, when one acts in important matters, it is best to consult one's instinct before everything. Well, General Lambert does not inspire with me so much confidence as you do."

"Be it so, monsieur. I shall assist you in recovering your money, if, however, it can still be there; for that is far from likely. Since 1648 twelve years have rolled away, and many events have taken place." Monk dwelt upon this point to see if the French gentleman would seize the evasions that were open to him, but Athos did not hesitate.

"I assure you, my lord," he said firmly, "that my conviction is, that the two barrels have neither changed place nor master." This reply had removed one suspicion from the mind of Monk, but it had suggested another. Without doubt this Frenchman was some emissary sent to entice into error the protector of the parliament; the gold was nothing but a lure; and by the help of this lure they thought to excite the cupidity of the general. This gold might not exist. It was Monk's business, then, to seize the Frenchman in the act of falsehood and trick, and to draw from the false step itself in which his enemies wished to entrap him, a triumph for his renown. When Monk was determined how to act,—

"Monsieur," said he to Athos, "without doubt you will do me the honor to share my supper this evening?"

"Yes, my lord," replied Athos, bowing; "for you do me an honor of which I feel myself worthy, by the inclination which drew me towards you."

"It is so much the more gracious on your part to accept my invitation with such frankness, as my cooks are but few and inexperienced, and my providers have returned this evening empty-handed; so that if it had not been for a fisherman of your nation who strayed into our camp, General Monk would have gone to bed without his supper to-day; I have, then, some fresh fish to offer you, as the vendor assures me."

"My lord, it is principally for the sake of having the honor to pass an hour with you."

After this exchange of civilities, during which Monk had lost nothing of his circumspection, the supper, or what was to serve for one, had been laid upon a deal table. Monk invited the Comte de la Fere to be seated at this table, and took his place opposite to him. A single dish of boiled fish, set before the two illustrious guests, was more tempting to hungry stomachs than to delicate palates.

Whilst supping, that is, while eating the fish, washed down with bad ale, Monk got Athos to relate to him the last events of the Fronde, the reconciliation of M. de Conde with the king, and the probable marriage of the infanta of Spain; but he avoided, as Athos himself avoided it, all allusion to the political interests which united, or rather which disunited at this time, England, France and Holland.

Monk, in this conversation, convinced himself of one thing, which he must have remarked after the first words exchanged: that was, that he had to deal with a man of high distinction. He could not be an assassin, and it was repugnant to Monk to believe him to be a spy; but there was sufficient finesse and at the same time firmness in Athos to lead Monk to fancy he was a conspirator. When they had quitted the table, "You still believe in your treasure, then, monsieur?" asked Monk.

"Yes, my lord."

"Quite seriously?"

"Seriously."

"And you think you can find the place again where it was buried?"

"At the first inspection."

"Well, monsieur, from curiosity I shall accompany you. And it is so much the more necessary that I should accompany you, that you would find great difficulties in passing through the camp without me or one of my lieutenants."

"General, I would not suffer you to inconvenience yourself if I did not, in fact, stand in need of your company; but as I recognize that this company is not only honorable, but necessary, I accept it."

"Do you desire we should take any people with us?" asked Monk.

"General, I believe that would be useless, if you yourself do not see the necessity for it. Two men and a horse will suffice to transport the two casks on board the felucca which brought me hither."

"But it will be necessary to pick, dig, and remove the earth, and split stones; you don't intend doing this work yourself, monsieur, do you?"

"General, there is no picking or digging required. The treasure is buried in the sepulchral vault of the convent, under a stone in which is fixed a large iron ring, and under which there are four steps leading down. The two casks are there, placed end to end, covered with a coat of plaster in the form of a bier. There is, besides, an inscription, which will enable me to recognize the stone; and as I am not willing, in an affair of delicacy and confidence, to keep the secret from your honor, here is the inscription:—'Hic jacet venerabilis, Petrus Gulielmus Scott, Canon Honorab. Conventus Novi Castelli. Obiit quarta et decima Feb. ann. Dom. MCCVIII. Requiescat in pace.'"

Monk did not lose a single word. He was astonished either at the marvelous duplicity of this man and the superior style in which he played his part, or at the good loyal faith with which he presented his request, in a situation in which concerning a million of money, risked against the blow from a dagger, amidst an army that would have looked upon the theft as a restitution.

"Very well," said he; "I shall accompany you; and the adventure appears to me so wonderful, that I shall carry the torch myself." And saying these words, he girded on a short sword, placed a pistol in his belt, disclosing in this movement, which opened his doublet a little, the fine rings of a coat of mail, destined to protect him from the first dagger-thrust of an assassin. After which he took a Scottish dirk in his left hand, and then turning to Athos, "Are you ready, monsieur?" said he.

"I am."

Athos, as if in opposition to what Monk had done, unfastened his poniard, which he placed upon the table; unhooked his sword-belt, which he laid close to his poniard; and, without affectation, opening his doublet as if to look for his handkerchief, showed beneath his fine cambric shirt his naked breast, without weapons either offensive or defensive.

"This is truly a singular man," said Monk; "he is without any arms; he has an ambuscade placed somewhere yonder."

"General," said he, as if he had divined Monk's thought, "you wish we should be alone; that is very right, but a great captain ought never to expose himself with temerity. It is night, the passage of the marsh may present dangers; be accompanied."

"You are right," replied he, calling Digby. The aid-de-camp appeared. "Fifty men with swords and muskets," said he, looking at Athos.

"That is too few if there is danger, too many if there is not."

"I will go alone," said Monk; "I want nobody. Come, monsieur."

Chapter XXV.
The Marsh.

ATHOS and Monk passed over, in going from the camp towards the Tweed, that part of the ground which Digby had traversed with the fishermen coming from the Tweed to the camp. The aspect of this place, the aspect of the changes man had wrought in it, was of a nature to produce a great effect upon a lively and delicate imagination like that of Athos. Athos looked at nothing but these desolate spots; Monk looked at nothing but Athos—at Athos, who, with his eyes sometimes directed towards heaven, and sometimes towards the earth, sought, thought, and sighed.

Digby, whom the last orders of the general, and particularly the accent with which he had given them, had at first a little excited, Digby followed the pair at about twenty paces, but the general having turned round as if astonished to find his orders had not been obeyed, the aid-de-camp perceived his indiscretion, and returned to his tent.

He supposed that the general wished to make, incognito, one of those reviews of vigilance which every experienced captain never fails to make on the eve of a decisive engagement: he explained to himself the presence of Athos in this case as an inferior explains all that is mysterious on the part of his leader. Athos might be, and, indeed, in the eyes of Digby, must be, a spy, whose information was to enlighten the general.

At the end of a walk of about ten minutes among the tents and posts, which were closer together near the headquarters, Monk entered upon a little causeway which diverged into three branches. That on the left led to the river, that in the middle to Newcastle Abbey on the marsh, that on the right crossed the first lines of Monk's camp; that is to say, the lines nearest to Lambert's army. Beyond the river was an advanced post, belonging to Monk's army, which watched the enemy; it was composed of one hundred and fifty Scots. They had swum across the Tweed, and, in case of attack, were to recross it in the same manner, giving the alarm; but as there was no post at that spot, and as Lambert's soldiers were not so prompt at taking to the water as Monk's were, the latter appeared not to have as much uneasiness on that side. On this side of the river, at about five hundred paces from the old abbey, the fishermen had taken up their abode amidst a crowd of small tents raised by soldiers of the neighboring clans, who had with them their wives and children. All this confusion, seen by the moon's light, presented a striking coup d'oeil; the half shadow enlarged every detail, and the light, that flatterer which only attaches itself to the polished side of things, courted upon each rusty musket the point still left intact, and upon every rag of canvas the whitest and least sullied part.

Monk arrived then with Athos, crossing this spot, illumined with a double light, the silver splendor of the moon, and the red blaze of the fires at the meeting of these three causeways; there he stopped, and addressing his companion,—"Monsieur," said he, "do you know your road?"

"General, if I am not mistaken, the middle causeway leads straight to the abbey."

"That is right; but we shall want lights to guide us in the vaults." Monk turned round.

"Ah! I thought Digby was following us!" said he. "So much the better; he will procure us what we want."

"Yes, general, there is a man yonder who has been walking behind us for some time."

"Digby!" cried Monk. "Digby! come here, if you please."

But instead of obeying, the shadow made a motion of surprise, and, retreating instead of advancing, it bent down and disappeared along the jetty on the left, directing its course towards the lodging of the fishermen.

"It appears not to be Digby," said Monk.

Both had followed the shadow which had vanished. But it was not so rare a thing for a man to be wandering about at eleven o'clock at night, in a camp in which are reposing ten or eleven thousand men, as to give Monk and Athos any alarm at his disappearance.

"As it is so," said Monk, "and we must have a light, a lantern, a torch, or something by which we may see where to see our feet; let us seek this light."

"General, the first soldier we meet will light us."

"No," said Monk, in order to discover if there were not any connivance between the Comte de la Fere and the fisherman. "No, I should prefer one of these French sailors who came this evening to sell me their fish. They leave to-morrow, and the secret will be better kept by them; whereas, if a report should be spread in the Scottish army, that treasures are to be found in the abbey of Newcastle, my Highlanders will believe there is a million concealed beneath every slab, and they will not leave stone upon stone in the building."

"Do as you think best, general," replied Athos, in a natural tone of voice, making evident that soldier or fisherman was the same to him, and that he had no preference.

Monk approached the causeway behind which had disappeared the person he had taken for Digby, and met a patrol who, making the tour of the tents, was going towards headquarters; he was stopped with his companion, gave the password, and went on. A soldier, roused by the noise, unrolled his plaid, and looked up to see what was going forward. "Ask him," said Monk to Athos, "where the fishermen are; if I were to speak to him, he would know me."

Athos went up to the soldier, who pointed out the tent to him; immediately Monk and Athos turned towards it. It appeared to the general that at the moment they came up, a shadow like that they had already seen, glided into this tent; but on drawing nearer he perceived he must have been mistaken, for all of them were asleep pele mele, and nothing was seen but arms and legs joined, crossed, and mixed. Athos, fearing lest he should be suspected of connivance with some of his compatriots, remained outside the tent.

"Hola!" said Monk, in French, "wake up here." Two or three of the sleepers got up.

"I want a man to light me," continued Monk.

"Your honor may depend on us," said a voice which made Athos start. "Where do you wish us to go?"

"You shall see. A light! come, quickly!"

"Yes, your honor. Does it please your honor that I should accompany you?"

"You or another; it is of very little consequence, provided I have a light."

"It is strange!" thought Athos; "what a singular voice that man has!"

"Some fire, you fellows!" cried the fisherman; "come, make haste!"

Then addressing his companion nearest to him in a low voice:—"Get ready a light, Menneville," said he, "and hold yourself ready for anything."

One of the fishermen struck light from a stone, set fire to some tinder, and by the aid of a match lit a lantern. The light immediately spread all over the tent.

"Are you ready, monsieur?" said Monk to Athos, who had turned away, not to expose his face to the light.

"Yes, general," replied he.

"Ah! the French gentleman!" said the leader of the fishermen to himself. "Peste! I have a great mind to charge you with the commission, Menneville; he may know me. Light! light!" This dialogue was pronounced at the back of the tent, and in so low a voice that Monk could not hear a syllable of it; he was, besides, talking with Athos. Menneville got himself ready in the meantime, or rather received the orders of his leader.

"Well?" said Monk.

"I am ready, general," said the fisherman.

Monk, Athos, and the fisherman left the tent.

"It is impossible!" thought Athos. "What dream could put that into my head?"

"Go forward; follow the middle causeway, and stretch out your legs," said Monk to the fisherman.

They were not twenty paces on their way when the same shadow that had appeared to enter the tent came out of it again, crawled along as far as the piles, and, protected by that sort of parapet placed along the causeway, carefully observed the march of the general. All three disappeared in the night haze. They were walking towards Newcastle, the white stones of which appeared to them like sepulchers. After standing for a few seconds under the porch, they penetrated into the interior. The door had been broken open by hatchets. A post of four men slept in safety in a corner, so certain were they that the attack would not take place on that side.

"Will not these men be in your way?" said Monk to Athos.

"On the contrary, monsieur, they will assist in rolling out the barrels, if your honor will permit them."

"You are right."

The post, though fast asleep, roused up at the first steps of the three visitors amongst the briars and grass that invaded the porch. Monk gave the password, and penetrated into the interior of the convent, preceded by the light. He walked last, watching the least movement of Athos, his naked dirk in his sleeve, and ready to plunge it into the back of the gentleman at the first suspicious gesture he should see him make. But Athos, with a firm and sure step, crossed the chambers and courts.

Not a door, not a window was left in the building. The doors had been burnt, some on the spot, and the charcoal of them was still jagged with the action of the fire, which had gone out of itself, powerless, no doubt, to get to the heart of those massive joints of oak fastened together with iron nails. As to the windows, all the panes having been broken, night birds, alarmed by the torch, flew away through their holes. At the same time, gigantic bats began to trace their vast, silent circles around the intruders, whilst the light of the torch made their shadows tremble on the high stone walls. Monk concluded that there could be no man in the convent, since wild beasts and birds were there still, and fled away at his approach.

After having passed the rubbish, and torn away more than one branch of ivy that had made itself a guardian of the solitude, Athos arrived at the vaults situated beneath the great hall, but the entrance of which was from the chapel. There he stopped. "Here we are, general," said he.

"This, then, is the slab?"

"Yes."

"Ay, and here is the ring—but the ring is sealed into the stone."

"We must have a lever."

"That's a very easy thing to find."

Whilst looking around them, Athos and Monk perceived a little ash of about three inches in diameter, which had shot up in an angle of the wall, reaching a window, concealed by its branches.

"Have you a knife?" said Monk to the fisherman.

"Yes, monsieur."

"Cut down this tree, then."

The fisherman obeyed, but not without notching his cutlass. When the ash was cut and fashioned into the shape of a lever, the three men penetrated into the vault.

"Stop where you are," said Monk to the fisherman. "We are going to dig up some powder; your light may be dangerous."

The man drew back in a sort of terror, and faithfully kept to the post assigned him, whilst Monk and Athos turned behind a column at the foot of which, penetrating through a crack, was a moonbeam, reflected exactly on the stone which the Comte de la Fere had come so far in search.

"This is it," said Athos, pointing out to the general the Latin inscription.

"Yes," said Monk.

Then, as if still willing to leave the Frenchman one means of evasion,—

"Do you not observe that this vault has already been broken into," continued he, "and that several statues have already been knocked down?"

"My lord, you have, without doubt, heard that the religious respect of your Scots loves to confide to the statues of the dead the valuable objects they have possessed during their lives. Therefore, the soldiers had reason to think that under the pedestals of the statues which ornament most of these tombs, a treasure was hidden. They have consequently broken down pedestal and statue: but the tomb of the venerable cannon, with which we have to do, is not distinguished by any monument. It is simple, therefore it has been protected by the superstitious fear which your Puritans have always had of sacrilege. Not a morsel of the masonry of this tomb has been chipped off."

"That is true," said Monk.

Athos seized the lever.

"Shall I help you?" said Monk.

"Thank you, my lord; but I am not willing that your honor should lend your hand to a work of which, perhaps, you would not take the responsibility if you knew the probable consequences of it."

Monk raised his head.

"What do you mean by that, monsieur?"

"I mean—but that man—"

"Stop," said Monk; "I perceive what you are afraid of. I shall make a trial." Monk turned towards the fisherman, the whole of whose profile was thrown upon the wall.

"Come here, friend!" said he in English, and in a tone of command.

The fisherman did not stir.

"That is well," continued he: "he does not know English. Speak to me, then, in English, if you please, monsieur."

"My lord," replied Athos, "I have frequently seen men in certain circumstances have sufficient command over themselves not to reply to a question put to them in a language they understood. The fisherman is perhaps more learned than we believe him to be. Send him away, my lord, I beg you."

"Decidedly," said Monk, "he wishes to have me alone in this vault. Never mind, we shall go through with it; one man is as good as another man; and we are alone. My friend," said Monk to the fisherman, "go back up the stairs we have just descended, and watch that nobody comes to disturb us." The fisherman made a sign of obedience. "Leave your torch," said Monk; "it would betray your presence, and might procure you a musket-ball."

The fisherman appeared to appreciate the counsel; he laid down the light, and disappeared under the vault of the stairs. Monk took up the torch, and brought it to the foot of the column.

"Ah, ah!" said he; "money, then, is concealed under this tomb?"

"Yes, my lord; and in five minutes you will no longer doubt it."

At the same time Athos struck a violent blow upon the plaster, which split, presenting a chink for the point of the lever. Athos introduced the bar into this crack, and soon large pieces of plaster yielded, rising up like rounded slabs. Then the Comte de la Fere seized the stones and threw them away with a force that hands so delicate as his might not have been supposed capable of having.

"My lord," said Athos, "this is plainly the masonry of which I told your honor."

"Yes; but I do not yet see the casks," said Monk.

"If I had a dagger," said Athos, looking round him, "you should soon see them, monsieur. Unfortunately, I left mine in your tent."

"I would willingly offer you mine," said Monk, "but the blade is too thin for such work."

Athos appeared to look around him for a thing of some kind that might serve as a substitute for the weapon he desired. Monk did not lose one of the movements of his hands, or one of the expressions of his eyes. "Why do you not ask the fisherman for his cutlass?" said Monk; "he has a cutlass."

"Ah! that is true," said Athos; "for he cut the tree down with it." And he advanced towards the stairs.

"Friend," said he to the fisherman, "throw me down your cutlass, if you please; I want it."

The noise of the falling weapon sounded on the steps.

"Take it," said Monk; "it is a solid instrument, as I have seen, and a strong hand might make good use of it."

Athos appeared only to give to the words of Monk the natural and simple sense under which they were to be heard and understood. Nor did he remark, or at least appear to remark, that when he returned with the weapon, Monk drew back, placing his left hand on the stock of his pistol; in the right he already held his dirk. He went to work then, turning his back to Monk, placing his life in his hands, without possible defense. He then struck, during several seconds, so skillfully and sharply upon the intermediary plaster, that it separated into two parts, and Monk was able to discern two barrels placed end to end, and which their weight maintained motionless in their chalky envelope.

"My lord," said Athos, "you see that my presentiments have not been disappointed."

"Yes, monsieur," said Monk, "and I have good reason to believe you are satisfied; are you not?"

"Doubtless I am; the loss of this money would have been inexpressibly great to me: but I was certain that God, who protects the good cause, would not have permitted this gold, which should procure its triumph, to be diverted to baser purposes."

"You are, upon my honor, as mysterious in your words as in your actions, monsieur," said Monk. "Just now as I did not perfectly understand you when you said that you were not willing to throw upon me the responsibility of the work we were accomplishing."

"I had reason to say so, my lord."

"And now you speak to me of the good cause. What do you mean by the words 'the good cause?' We are defending at this moment, in England, five or six causes, which does not prevent every one from considering his own not only as the good cause, but as the best. What is yours, monsieur? Speak boldly, that we may see if, upon this point, to which you appear to attach a great importance, we are of the same opinion."

Athos fixed upon Monk one of those penetrating looks which seemed to convey to him to whom they are directed a challenge to conceal a single one of his thoughts; then, taking off his hat, he began in a solemn voice, while his interlocutor, with one hand upon his visage, allowed that long and nervous hand to compress his mustache and beard, while his vague and melancholy eye wandered about the recesses of the vaults.

Chapter XXVI.
Heart and Mind.

My lord," said the Comte de la Fere, "you are an noble Englishman, you are a loyal man; you are speaking to a noble Frenchman, to a man of heart. The gold contained in these two casks before us, I have told you was mine. I was wrong—it is the first lie I have pronounced in my life, a temporary lie, it is true. This gold is the property of King Charles II., exiled from his country, driven from his palaces, the orphan at once of his father and his throne, and deprived of everything, even of the melancholy happiness of kissing on his knees the stone upon which the hands of his murderers have written that simple epitaph which will eternally cry out for vengeance upon them:—'HERE LIES CHARLES I.'"

Monk grew slightly pale, and an imperceptible shudder crept over his skin and raised his gray mustache.

"I," continued Athos, "I, Comte de la Fere, the last, only faithful friend the poor abandoned prince has left, I have offered him to come hither to find the man upon whom now depends the fate of royalty and of England; and I have come, and placed myself under the eye of this man, and have placed myself naked and unarmed in his hands, saying:—'My lord, here are the last resources of a prince whom God made your master, whom his birth made your king; upon you, and you alone, depend his life and future. Will you employ this money in consoling England for the evils it must have suffered from anarchy; that is to say, will you aid, and if not aid, will you allow King Charles II. to act? You are master, you are king, all-powerful master and king, for chance sometimes defeats the work of time and God. I am here alone with you, my lord: if divided success alarms you, if my complicity annoys you, you are armed, my lord, and here is a grave ready dug; if, on the contrary, the enthusiasm of your cause carries you away, if you are what you appear to be, if your hand in what it undertakes obeys your mind, and your mind your heart, here are the means of ruining forever the cause of your enemy, Charles Stuart. Kill, then, the man you have before you, for that man will never return to him who has sent him without bearing with him the deposit which Charles I., his father, confided to him, and keep the gold which may assist in carrying on the civil war. Alas! my lord, it is the fate of this unfortunate prince. He must either corrupt or kill, for everything resists him, everything repulses him, everything is hostile to him; and yet he is marked with divine seal, and he must, not to belie his blood, reascend the throne, or die upon the sacred soil of his country.'

"My lord, you have heard me. To any other but the illustrious man who listens to me, I would have said: 'My lord, you are poor; my lord, the king offers you this million as an earnest of an immense bargain; take it, and serve Charles II. as I served Charles I., and I feel assured that God, who listens to us, who sees us, who alone reads in your heart, shut up from all human eyes,—I am assured God will give you a happy eternal life after death.' But to General Monk, to the illustrious man of whose standard I believe I have taken measure, I say: 'My lord, there is for you in the history of peoples and kings a brilliant place, an immortal, imperishable glory, if alone, without any other interest but the good of your country and the interests of justice, you become the supporter of your king. Many others have been conquerors and glorious usurpers; you, my lord, you will be content with being the most virtuous, the most honest, and the most incorruptible of men: you will have held a crown in your hand, and instead of placing it upon your own brow, you will have deposited it upon the head of him for whom it was made. Oh, my lord, act thus, and you will leave to posterity the most enviable of names, in which no human creature can rival you.'"

Athos stopped. During the whole time that the noble gentleman was speaking, Monk had not given one sign of either approbation or disapprobation; scarcely even, during this vehement appeal, had his eyes been animated with that fire which bespeaks intelligence. The Comte de la Fere looked at him sorrowfully, and on seeing that melancholy countenance, felt discouragement penetrate to his very heart. At length Monk appeared to recover, and broke the silence.

"Monsieur," said he, in a mild, calm tone, "in reply to you, I will make use of your own words. To any other but yourself I would reply by expulsion, imprisonment, or still worse, for, in fact, you tempt me and you force me at the same time. But you are one of those men, monsieur, to whom it is impossible to refuse the attention and respect they merit; you are a brave gentleman, monsieur—I say so, and I am a judge. You just now spoke of a deposit which the late king transmitted through you to his son—are you, then, one of those Frenchmen who, as I have heard, endeavored to carry off Charles I. from Whitehall?"

"Yes, my lord; it was I who was beneath the scaffold during the execution; I, who had not been able to redeem it, received upon my brow the blood of the martyred king. I received, at the same time, the last word of Charles I.; it was to me he said, 'REMEMBER!' and in saying, 'Remember!' he alluded to the money at your feet, my lord."

"I have heard much of you, monsieur," said Monk, "but I am happy to have, in the first place, appreciated you by my own observations, and not by my remembrances. I will give you, then, explanations that I have given to no other, and you will appreciate what a distinction I make between you and the persons who have hitherto been sent to me."

Athos bowed and prepared to absorb greedily the words which fell, one by one, from the mouth of Monk,—those words rare and precious as the dew in the desert.

"You spoke to me," said Monk, "of Charles II.; but pray, monsieur, of what consequence to me is that phantom of a king? I have grown old in a war and in a policy which are nowadays so closely linked together, that every man of the sword must fight in virtue of his rights or his ambition with a personal interest, and not blindly behind an officer, as in ordinary wars. For myself, I perhaps desire nothing, but I fear much. In the war of to-day rests the liberty of England, and, perhaps, that of every Englishman. How can you expect that I, free in the position I have made for myself, should go willingly and hold out my hands to the shackles of a stranger? That is all Charles is to me. He has fought battles here which he has lost, he is therefore a bad captain; he has succeeded in no negotiation, he is therefore a bad diplomatist; he has paraded his wants and his miseries in all the courts of Europe, he has therefore a weak and pusillanimous heart. Nothing noble, nothing great, nothing strong has hitherto emanated from that genius which aspires to govern one of the greatest kingdoms of the earth. I know this Charles, then, under none but bad aspects, and you would wish me, a man of good sense, to go and make myself gratuitously the slave of a creature who is inferior to me in military capacity, in politics, and in dignity! No, monsieur. When some great and noble action shall have taught me to value Charles, I shall perhaps recognize his rights to a throne from which we cast the father because he wanted the virtues which his son has hitherto lacked, but, in fact of rights, I only recognize my own; the revolution made me a general, my sword will make me protector, if I wish it. Let Charles show himself, let him present himself, let him enter the competition open to genius, and, above all, let him remember that he is of a race from whom more will be expected than from any other. Therefore, monsieur, say no more about him. I neither refuse nor accept: I reserve myself—I wait."

Athos knew Monk to be too well informed of all concerning Charles to venture to urge the discussion further; it was neither the time nor the place. "My lord," then said he, "I have nothing to do but thank you."

"And why, monsieur? Because you have formed a correct opinion of me, or because I have acted according to your judgment? Is that, in truth, worthy of thanks? This gold which you are about to carry to Charles will serve me as a test for him, by seeing the use he will make of it. I shall have an opinion which now I have not."

"And yet does not your honor fear to compromise yourself by allowing such a sum to be carried away for the service of your enemy?"

"My enemy, say you? Eh, monsieur, I have no enemies. I am in the service of the parliament, which orders me to fight General Lambert and Charles Stuart—its enemies, and not mine. I fight them. If the parliament, on the contrary, ordered me to unfurl my standards on the port of London, and to assemble my soldiers on the banks to receive Charles II.—"

"You would obey?" cried Athos, joyfully.

"Pardon me," said Monk, smiling, "I was going on—I, a gray-headed man—in truth, how could I forget myself? was going to speak like a foolish young man."

"Then you would not obey?" said Athos.

"I do not say that either, monsieur. The welfare of my country before everything. God, who has given me the power, has, no doubt, willed that I should have that power for the good of all, and He has given me, at the same time, discernment. If the parliament were to order such a thing, I should reflect."

The brow of Athos became clouded. "Then I may positively say that your honor is not inclined to favor King Charles II.?"

"You continue to question me, monsieur le comte; allow me to do so in turn, if you please."

"Do, monsieur; and may God inspire you with the idea of replying to me as frankly as I shall reply to you."

"When you shall have taken this money back to your prince, what advice will you give him?"

Athos fixed upon Monk a proud and resolute look.

"My lord," said he, "with this million, which others would perhaps employ in negotiating, I would advise the king to rise two regiments, to enter Scotland, which you have just pacified: to give to the people the franchises which the revolution promised them, and in which it has not, in all cases, kept its word. I should advise him to command in person this little army, which would, believe me, increase, and to die, standard in hand, and sword in sheath, saying, 'Englishmen! I am the third king of my race you have killed; beware of the justice of God!'"

Monk hung down his head, and mused for an instant. "If he succeeded," said he, "which is very improbable, but not impossible—for everything is possible in this world—what would you advise him to do?"

"To think that by the will of God he lost his crown, by the good will of men he recovered it."

An ironical smile passed over the lips of Monk.

"Unfortunately, monsieur," said he, "kings do not know how to follow good advice."

"Ah, my lord, Charles II. is not a king," replied Athos, smiling in his turn, but with a very different expression from Monk.

"Let us terminate this, monsieur le comte,—that is your desire, is it not?"

Athos bowed.

"I shall give orders to have these two casks transported whither you please. Where are you lodging, monsieur?"

"In a little hamlet at the mouth of the river, your honor."

"Oh, I know the hamlet; it consists of five or six houses, does it not?"

"Exactly. Well, I inhabit the first,—two net-makers occupy it with me; it is their bark which brought me ashore."

"But your own vessel, monsieur?"

"My vessel is at anchor, a quarter of a mile at sea, and waits for me."

"You do not think, however, of setting out immediately?"

"My lord, I shall try once more to convince your honor."

"You will not succeed," replied Monk; "but it is of consequence that you should depart from Newcastle without leaving of your passage the least suspicion that might prove injurious to me or you. To-morrow my officers think Lambert will attack me. I, on the contrary, am convinced he will not stir; it is in my opinion impossible. Lambert leads an army devoid of homogeneous principles, and there is no possible army with such elements. I have taught my soldiers to consider my authority subordinate to another, therefore, after me, round me, and beneath me, they still look for something. It would result that if I were dead, whatever might happen, my army would not be demoralized all at once; it results, that if I choose to absent myself, for instance, as it does please me to do sometimes, there would not be in the camp the shadow of uneasiness or disorder. I am the magnet—the sympathetic and natural strength of the English. All those scattered irons that will be sent against me I shall attract to myself. Lambert, at this moment, commands eighteen thousand deserters; but I have never mentioned that to my officers, you may easily suppose. Nothing is more useful to an army than the expectation of a coming battle; everybody is awake—everybody is on guard. I tell you this that you may live in perfect security. Do not be in a hurry, then, to cross the seas; within a week there will be something fresh, either a battle or an accommodation. Then, as you have judged me to be an honorable man, and confided your secret to me, I have to thank you for this confidence, and I shall come and pay you a visit or send for you. Do not go before I send word. I repeat the request."

"I promise you, general," cried Athos, with a joy so great, that in spite of all his circumspection, he could not prevent its sparkling in his eyes.

Monk surprised this flash, and immediately extinguished it by one of those silent smiles which always caused his interlocutors to know they had made no inroad on his mind.

"Then, my lord, it is a week that you desire me to wait?"

"A week? yes, monsieur."

"And during those days what shall I do?"

"If there should be a battle, keep at a distance from it, I beseech you. I know the French delight in such amusements;—you might take a fancy to see how we fight, and you might receive some chance shot. Our Scotsmen are very bad marksmen, and I do not wish that a worthy gentleman like you should return to France wounded. Nor should I like to be obliged, myself, to send to your prince his million left here by you; for then it would be said, and with some reason, that I paid the Pretender to enable him to make war against the parliament. Go, then, monsieur, and let it be done as has been agreed upon."

"Ah, my lord," said Athos, "what joy it would give me to be the first that penetrated to the noble heart which beats beneath that cloak!"

"You think, then, that I have secrets," said Monk, without changing the half cheerful expression of his countenance. "Why, monsieur, what secret can you expect to find in the hollow head of a soldier? But it is getting late, and our torch is almost out; let us call our man."

"Hola!" cried Monk in French, approaching the stairs; "hola! fisherman!"

The fisherman, benumbed by the cold night air, replied in a hoarse voice, asking what they wanted of him.

"Go to the post," said Monk, "and order a sergeant, in the name of General Monk, to come here immediately."

This was a commission easily performed; for the sergeant, uneasy at the general's being in that desolate abbey, had drawn nearer by degrees, and was not much further off than the fisherman. The general's order was therefore heard by him, and he hastened to obey it.

"Get a horse and two men," said Monk.

"A horse and two men?" repeated the sergeant.

"Yes," replied Monk. "Have you got any means of getting a horse with a pack-saddle or two panniers?"

"No doubt, at a hundred paces off, in the Scottish camp."

"Very well."

"What shall I do with the horse, general."

"Look here."

The sergeant descended the three steps which separated him from Monk, and came into the vault.

"You see," said Monk, "that gentleman yonder?"

"Yes, general."

"And you see these two casks?"

"Perfectly."

"They are two casks, one containing powder, and the other balls; I wish these casks to be transported to the little hamlet at the mouth of the river, and which I intend to occupy to-morrow with two hundred muskets. You understand that the commission is a secret one, for it is a movement that may decide the fate of the battle."

"Oh, general!" murmured the sergeant.

"Mind, then! Let these casks be fastened on to the horse, and let them be escorted by two men and you to the residence of this gentleman, who is my friend. But take care that nobody knows it."

"I would go by the marsh if I knew the road," said the sergeant.

"I know one myself," said Athos; "it is not wide, but it is solid, having been made upon piles; and with care we shall get over safely enough."

"Do everything this gentleman shall order you to do."

"Oh! oh! the casks are heavy," said the sergeant, trying to lift one.

"They weigh four hundred pounds each, if they contain what they ought to contain, do they not, monsieur."

"Thereabouts," said Athos.

The sergeant went in search of the two men and the horse. Monk, left alone with Athos, affected to speak to him on nothing but indifferent subjects while examining the vault in a cursory manner. Then, hearing the horse's steps,—

"I leave you with your men, monsieur," said he, "and return to the camp. You are perfectly safe."

"I shall see you again, then, my lord?" asked Athos.

"That is agreed upon, monsieur, and with much pleasure."

Monk held out his hand to Athos.

"Ah! my lord, if you would!" murmured Athos.

"Hush! monsieur, it is agreed that we shall speak no more of that." And bowing to Athos, he went up the stairs, meeting about half-way his men, who were coming down. He had not gone twenty paces, when a faint but prolonged whistle was heard at a distance. Monk listened, but seeing nothing and hearing nothing, he continued his route. Then he remembered the fisherman, and looked about for him; but the fisherman had disappeared. If he had, however, looked with more attention, he might have seen that man, bent double, gliding like a serpent along the stones and losing himself in the mist that floated over the surface of the marsh. He might equally have seen, had he attempted to pierce that mist, a spectacle that might have attracted his attention; and that was the rigging of the vessel, which had changed place, and was now nearer the shore. But Monk saw nothing; and thinking he had nothing to fear, he entered the deserted causeway which led to his camp. It was then that the disappearance of the fisherman appeared strange, and that a real suspicion began to take possession of his mind. He had just placed at the orders of Athos the only post that could protect him. He had a mile of causeway to traverse before he could regain his camp. The fog increased with such intensity that he could scarcely distinguish objects at ten paces' distance. Monk then thought he heard the sound of an oar over the marsh on the right. "Who goes there?" said he.

But nobody answered; then he cocked his pistol, took his sword in his hand, and quickened his pace, without, however, being willing to call anybody. Such a summons, for which there was no absolute necessity, appeared unworthy of him.

Chapter XXVII.
The Next Day.

IT was seven o'clock in the morning, the first rays of day lightened the pools of the marsh, in which the sun was reflected like a red ball, when Athos, awakening and opening the window of his bed-chamber, which looked out upon the banks of the river, perceived, at fifteen paces' distance from him, the sergeant and the men who had accompanied him the evening before, and who, after having deposited the casks at his house, had returned to the camp by the causeway on the right.

Why had these men come back after having returned to the camp? That was the question which first presented itself to Athos. The sergeant, with his head raised, appeared to be watching the moment when the gentleman should appear to address him. Athos, surprised to see these men, whom he had seen depart the night before, could not refrain from expressing his astonishment to them.

"There is nothing surprising in that, monsieur," said the sergeant; "for yesterday the general commanded me to watch over your safety, and I thought it right to obey that order."

"Is the general at the camp?" asked Athos.

"No doubt he is, monsieur; as when he left you he was going back."

"Well, wait for me a moment; I am going thither to render an account of the fidelity with which you fulfilled your duty, and to get my sword, which I left upon the table in the tent."

"This happens very well," said the sergeant, "for we were about to request you to do so."

Athos fancied he could detect an air of equivocal bonhomie upon the countenance of the sergeant; but the adventure of the vault might have excited the curiosity of the man, and it was not surprising that he allowed some of the feelings which agitated his mind to appear in his face. Athos closed the doors carefully, confiding the keys to Grimaud, who had chosen his domicile beneath the shed itself, which led to the cellar where the casks had been deposited. The sergeant escorted the Comte de la Fere to the camp. There a fresh guard awaited him, and relieved the four men who had conducted Athos.

This fresh guard was commanded by the aid-de-camp Digby, who, on their way, fixed upon Athos looks so little encouraging, that the Frenchman asked himself whence arose, with regard to him, this vigilance and this severity, when the evening before he had been left perfectly free. He nevertheless continued his way to the headquarters, keeping to himself the observations which men and things forced him to make. He found in the general's tent, to which he had been introduced the evening before, three superior officers: these were Monk's lieutenant and two colonels. Athos perceived his sword; it was still on the table where he left it. Neither of the officers had seen Athos, consequently neither of them knew him. Monk's lieutenant asked, at the appearance of Athos, if that were the same gentleman with whom the general had left the tent.

"Yes, your honor," said the sergeant; "it is the same."

"But," said Athos, haughtily, "I do not deny it, I think; and now, gentlemen, in turn, permit me to ask you to what purpose these questions are asked, and particularly some explanations upon the tone in which you ask them?"

"Monsieur," said the lieutenant, "if we address these questions to you, it is because we have a right to do so, and if we make them in a particular tone, it is because that tone, believe me, agrees with the circumstances."

"Gentlemen," said Athos, "you do not know who I am; but I must tell you that I acknowledge no one here but General Monk as my equal. Where is he? Let me be conducted to him, and if he has any questions to put to me, I will answer him and to his satisfaction, I hope. I repeat, gentlemen, where is the general?"

"Eh! good God! you know better than we do where he is," said the lieutenant.

"I?" "Yes, you."

"Monsieur," said Athos; "I do not understand you."

"You will understand me—and, in the first place, do not speak so loudly."

Athos smiled disdainfully.

"We don't ask you to smile," said one of the colonels warmly; "we require you to answer."

"And I, gentlemen, declare to you that I will not reply until I am in the presence of the general."

"But," replied the same colonel who had already spoken, "you know very well that is impossible."

"This is the second time I have received this strange reply to the wish I express," said Athos. "Is the general absent?"

This question was made with such apparent good faith, and the gentleman wore an air of such natural surprise, that the three officers exchanged a meaning look. The lieutenant, by a tacit convention with the other two, was spokesman.

"Monsieur, the general left you last night on the borders of the monastery."

"Yes, monsieur."

"And you went—"

"It is not for me to answer you, but for those who have accompanied me. They were your soldiers, ask them."

"But if we please to question you?"

"Then it will please me to reply, monsieur, that I do not recognize any one here, that I know no one here but the general, and that it is to him alone I will reply."

"So be it, monsieur; but as we are the masters, we constitute ourselves a council of war, and when you are before judges you must reply."

The countenance of Athos expressed nothing but astonishment and disdain, instead of the terror the officers expected to read in it at this threat.

"Scottish or English judges upon me, a subject of the king of France; upon me, placed under the safeguard of British honor! You are mad, gentlemen!" said Athos, shrugging his shoulders.

The officers looked at each other. "Then, monsieur," said one of them, "do you pretend not to know where the general is?"

"To that, monsieur, I have already replied."

"Yes, but you have already replied an incredible thing."

"It is true, nevertheless, gentlemen. Men of my rank are not generally liars. I am a gentleman, I have told you, and when I have at my side the sword which, by an excess of delicacy, I left last night upon the table whereon it still lies, believe me, no man says that to me which I am unwilling to hear. I am at this moment disarmed; if you pretend to be my judges, try me; if you are but my executioners, kill me."

"But, monsieur—" asked the lieutenant, in a more courteous voice, struck with the lofty coolness of Athos.

"Sir, I came to speak confidentially with your general about affairs of importance. It was not an ordinary welcome that he gave me. The accounts your soldiers can give you may convince you of that. If, then, the general received me in that manner, he knew my titles to his esteem. Now, you do not suspect, I should think, that I should reveal my secrets to you, and still less his."

"But these casks, what do they contain?"

"Have you not put that question to your soldiers? What was their reply?"

"That they contained powder and ball."

"From whom had they that information? They must have told you that."

"From the general; but we are not dupes."

"Beware, gentlemen; it is not to me you are now giving the lie, it is to your leader."

The officers again looked at each other. Athos continued: "Before your soldiers the general told me to wait a week, and at the expiration of that week he would give me the answer he had to make me. Have I fled away? No; I wait."

"He told you to wait a week!" cried the lieutenant.

"He told me that so clearly, sir, that I have a sloop at the mouth of the river, which I could with ease have joined yesterday, and embarked. Now, if I have remained, it was only in compliance with the desire of your general; his honor having requested me not to depart without a last audience, which he fixed at a week hence. I repeat to you, then, I am waiting."

The lieutenant turned towards the other officers, and said, in a low voice: "If this gentleman speaks truth, there may still be some hope. The general may be carrying out some negotiations so secret, that he thought it imprudent to inform even us. Then the time limited for his absence would be a week." Then, turning towards Athos: "Monsieur," said he, "your declaration is of the most serious importance; are you willing to repeat it under the seal of an oath?"

"Sir," replied Athos, "I have always lived in a world where my simple word was regarded as the most sacred of oaths."

"This time, however, monsieur, the circumstance is more grave than any you may have been placed in. The safety of the whole army is at stake. Reflect; the general has disappeared, and our search for him has been in vain. Is this disappearance natural? Has a crime been committed? Are we not bound to carry our investigations to extremity? Have we any right to wait with patience? At this moment, everything, monsieur, depends upon the words you are about to pronounce."

"Thus questioned, gentlemen, I no longer hesitate," said Athos. "Yes, I came hither to converse confidentially with General Monk, and ask him for an answer regarding certain interests; yes, the general being, doubtless, unable to pronounce before the expected battle, begged me to remain a week in the house I inhabit, promising me that in a week I should see him again. Yes, all this is true, and I swear it by God who is the absolute master of my life and yours." Athos pronounced these words with so much grandeur and solemnity, that the three officers were almost convinced. Nevertheless, one of the colonels made a last attempt.

"Monsieur," said he, "although we may now be persuaded of the truth of what you say, there is yet a strange mystery in all this. The general is too prudent a man to have thus abandoned his army on the eve of a battle without having at least given notice of it to one of us. As for myself, I cannot believe but some strange event has been the cause of this disappearance. Yesterday some foreign fishermen came to sell their fish here; they were lodged yonder among the Scots; that is to say, on the road the general took with this gentleman, to go to the abbey, and to return from it. It was one of these fishermen that accompanied the general with a light. And this morning, bark and fishermen have all disappeared, carried away by the night's tide."

"For my part," said the lieutenant, "I see nothing in that that is not quite natural, for these people were not prisoners."

"No; but I repeat it was one of them who lighted the general and this gentleman to the abbey, and Digby assures us that the general had strong suspicions concerning those people. Now, who can say whether these people were not connected with this gentleman; and that, the blow being struck, the gentleman, who is evidently brave, did not remain to reassure us by his presence, and to prevent our researches being made in a right direction?"

This speech made an impression upon the other two officers.

"Sir," said Athos, "permit me to tell you, that your reasoning, though specious in appearance, nevertheless wants consistency, as regards me. I have remained, you say, to divert suspicion. Well! on the contrary, suspicions arise in me as well as in you; and I say, it is impossible, gentlemen, that the general, on the eve of a battle, should leave his army without saying anything to at least one of his officers. Yes, there is some strange event connected with this; instead of being idle and waiting, you must display all the activity and all the vigilance possible. I am your prisoner, gentlemen, upon parole or otherwise. My honor is concerned in ascertaining what has become of General Monk, and to such a point, that if you were to say to me, 'Depart!' I should reply: 'No, I will remain!' And if you were to ask my opinion, I should add: 'Yes, the general is the victim of some conspiracy, for, if he had intended to leave the camp he would have told me so.' Seek, then, search the land, search the sea; the general has not gone of his own good will."

The lieutenant made a sign to the two other officers.

"No, monsieur," said he, "no; in your turn you go too far. The general has nothing to suffer from these events, and, no doubt, has directed them. What Monk is now doing he has often done before. We are wrong in alarming ourselves; his absence will, doubtless, be of short duration; therefore, let us beware, lest by a pusillanimity which the general would consider a crime, of making his absence public, and by that means demoralize the army. The general gives a striking proof of his confidence in us; let us show ourselves worthy of it. Gentlemen, let the most profound silence cover all this with an impenetrable veil; we will detain this gentleman, not from mistrust of him with regard to the crime, but to assure more effectively the secret of the general's absence by keeping among ourselves; therefore, until fresh orders, the gentleman will remain at headquarters."

"Gentlemen," said Athos, "you forget that last night the general confided to me a deposit over which I am bound to watch. Give me whatever guard you like, chain me if you like, but leave me the house I inhabit for my prison. The general, on his return, would reproach you, I swear on the honor of a gentleman, for having displeased him in this."

"So be it, monsieur," said the lieutenant; "return to your abode."

Then they placed over Athos a guard of fifty men, who surrounded his house, without losing sight of him for a minute.

The secret remained secure, but hours, days passed away without the general's returning, or without anything being heard of him.

Chapter XXVIII.
Smuggling.

TWO days after the events we have just related, and while General Monk was expected every minute in the camp to which he did not return, a little Dutch felucca, manned by eleven men, cast anchor upon the coast of Scheveningen, nearly within cannon-shot of the port. It was night, the darkness was great, the tide rose in the darkness; it was a capital time to land passengers and merchandise.

The road of Scheveningen forms a vast crescent; it is not very deep and not very safe; therefore, nothing is seen stationed there but large Flemish hoys, or some of those Dutch barks which fishermen draw up on the sand on rollers, as the ancients did, according to Virgil. When the tide is rising, and advancing on land, it is not prudent to bring the vessels too close in shore, for, if the wind is fresh, the prows are buried in the sand; and the sand of that coast is spongy; it receives easily, but does not yield so well. It was on this account, no doubt, that a boat was detached from the bark, as soon as the latter had cast anchor, and came with eight sailors, amidst whom was to be seen an object of an oblong form, a sort of large pannier or bale.

The shore was deserted; the few fishermen inhabiting the down were gone to bed. The only sentinel that guarded the coast (a coast very badly guarded, seeing that a landing from large ships was impossible), without having been able to follow the example of the fishermen, who were gone to bed, imitated them so far, that he slept at the back of his watch-box as soundly as they slept in their beds. The only noise to be heard, then, was the whistling of the night breeze among the bushes and the brambles of the downs. But the people who were approaching were doubtless mistrustful people, for this real silence and apparent solitude did not satisfy them. Their boat, therefore, scarcely as visible as a dark speck upon the ocean, gilded along noiselessly, avoiding the use of their oars for fear of being heard, and gained the nearest land.

Scarcely had it touched the ground when a single man jumped out of the boat, after having given a brief order, in a manner which denoted the habit of commanding. In consequence of this order, several muskets immediately glittered in the feeble light reflected from that mirror of the heavens, the sea; and the oblong bale of which we spoke, containing no doubt some contraband object, was transported to land, with infinite precautions. Immediately after that, the man who had landed first, set off at a rapid pace diagonally towards the village of Scheveningen, directing his course to the nearest point of the wood. When there, he sought for that house already described as the temporary residence—and a very humble residence—of him who was styled by courtesy king of England.

All were asleep there, as everywhere else, only a large dog, of the race of those which the fishermen of Scheveningen harness to little carts to carry fish to the Hague, began to bark formidably as soon as the stranger's steps were audible beneath the windows. But the watchfulness, instead of alarming the newly-landed man, appeared, on the contrary, to give him great joy, for his voice might perhaps have proved insufficient to rouse the people of the house, whilst, with an auxiliary of that sort, his voice became almost useless. The stranger waited, then, till these reiterated and sonorous barkings should, according to all probability, have produced their effect, and then he ventured a summons. On hearing his voice, the dog began to roar with such violence that another voice was soon heard from the interior, quieting the dog. With that the dog was quieted.

"What do you want?" asked that voice, at the same time weak, broken, and civil.

"I want his majesty King Charles II., king of England," said the stranger.

"What do you want with him?"

"I want to speak with him."

"Who are you?"

"Ah! Mordioux! you ask too much; I don't like talking through doors."

"Only tell me your name."

"I don't like to declare my name in the open air, either; besides, you may be sure I shall not eat your dog, and I hope to God he will be as reserved with respect to me."

"You bring news, perhaps, monsieur, do you not?" replied the voice, patient and querulous as that of an old man.

"I will answer for it, I bring you news you little expect. Open the door, then, if you please, hein!"

"Monsieur," persisted the old man, "do you believe, upon your soul and conscience, that your news is worth waking the king?"

"For God's sake, my dear monsieur, draw your bolts; you will not be sorry, I swear, for the trouble it will give you. I am worth my weight in gold, parole d'honneur!"

"Monsieur, I cannot open the door till you have told me your name."

"Must I, then?"

"It is by the order of my master, monsieur."

"Well, my name is—but, I warn you, my name will tell you absolutely nothing."

"Never mind, tell it, notwithstanding."

"Well, I am the Chevalier d'Artagnan."

The voice uttered an exclamation.

"Oh! good heavens!" said a voice on the other side of the door. "Monsieur d'Artagnan. What happiness! I could not help thinking I knew that voice."

"Humph!" said D'Artagnan. "My voice is known here! That's flattering."

"Oh! yes, we know it," said the old man, drawing the bolts; "and here is the proof." And at these words he let in D'Artagnan, who, by the light of the lantern he carried in his hand, recognized his obstinate interlocutor.

"Ah! Mordioux!" cried he: "why, it is Parry! I ought to have known that."

"Parry, yes, my dear Monsieur d'Artagnan, it is I. What joy to see you once again!"

"You are right there, what joy!" said D'Artagnan, pressing the old man's hand. "There, now you'll go and inform the king, will you not?"

"But the king is asleep, my dear monsieur."

"Mordioux! then wake him. He won't scold you for having disturbed him, I will promise you."

"You come on the part of the count, do you not?"

"The Comte de la Fere?"

"From Athos?"

"Ma foi! no; I come on my own part. Come, Parry, quick! The king—I want the king."

Parry did not think it his duty to resist any longer; he knew D'Artagnan of old; he knew that, although a Gascon, his words never promised more than they could stand to. He crossed a court and a little garden, appeased the dog, that seemed most anxious to taste of the musketeer's flesh, and went to knock at the window of a chamber forming the ground-floor of a little pavilion. Immediately a little dog inhabiting that chamber replied to the great dog inhabiting the court.

"Poor king!" said D'Artagnan to himself, "these are his body-guards. It is true he is not the worse guarded on that account."

"What is wanted with me?" asked the king, from the back of the chamber.

"Sire, it is M. le Chevalier d'Artagnan, who brings you some news."

A noise was immediately heard in the chamber, a door was opened, and a flood of light inundated the corridor and the garden. The king was working by the light of a lamp. Papers were lying about upon his desk, and he had commenced the first copy of a letter which showed, by the numerous erasures, the trouble he had had in writing it.

"Come in, monsieur le chevalier," said he, turning around. Then perceiving the fisherman, "What do you mean, Parry? Where is M. le Chevalier d'Artagnan?" asked Charles.

"He is before you, sire," said M. d'Artagnan.

"What, in that costume?"

"Yes; look at me, sire; do you not remember having seen me at Blois, in the ante-chamber of King Louis XIV.?"

"Yes, monsieur, and I remember I was much pleased with you."

D'Artagnan bowed. "It was my duty to behave as I did, the moment I knew that I had the honor of being near your majesty."

"You bring me news, do you say?"

"Yes, sire."

"From the king of France?"

"Ma foi! no, sire," replied D'Artagnan. "Your majesty must have seen yonder that the king of France is only occupied with his own majesty."

Charles raised his eyes towards heaven.

"No, sire, no," continued D'Artagnan. "I bring news entirely composed of personal facts. Nevertheless, I hope that your majesty will listen to the facts and news with some favor."

"Speak, monsieur."

"If I am not mistaken, sire, your majesty spoke a great deal at Blois, of the embarrassed state in which the affairs of England are."

Charles colored. "Monsieur," said he, "it was to the king of France I related—"

"Oh! your majesty is mistaken," said the musketeer, coolly; "I know how to speak to kings in misfortune. It is only when they are in misfortune that they speak to me; once fortunate, they look upon me no more. I have, then, for your majesty, not only the greatest respect, but, still more, the most absolute devotion; and that, believe me, with me, sire, means something. Now, hearing your majesty complain of fate, I found that you were noble and generous, and bore misfortune well."

"In truth!" said Charles, much astonished, "I do not know which I ought to prefer, your freedoms or your respects."

"You will choose presently, sire," said D'Artagnan. "Then your majesty complained to your brother, Louis XIV., of the difficulty you experienced in returning to England and regaining your throne for want of men and money."

Charles allowed a movement of impatience to escape him.

"And the principal object your majesty found in your way," continued D'Artagnan, "was a certain general commanding the armies of the parliament, and who was playing yonder the part of another Cromwell. Did not your majesty say so?"

"Yes; but I repeat to you, monsieur, those words were for the king's ears alone."

"And you will see, sire, that it is very fortunate that they fell into those of his lieutenant of musketeers. That man so troublesome to your majesty was one General Monk, I believe; did I not hear his name correctly, sire?"

"Yes, monsieur, but once more, to what purpose are all these questions."

"Oh! I know very well, sire, that etiquette will not allow kings to be questioned. I hope, however, presently you will pardon my want of etiquette. Your majesty added that, notwithstanding, if you could see him, confer with him, and meet him face to face, you would triumph, either by force or persuasion, over that obstacle—the only serious one, the only insurmountable one, the only real one you met with on your road."

"All that is true, monsieur: my destiny, my future, my obscurity, or my glory depend upon that man; but what do you draw from that?"

"One thing alone, that if this General Monk is troublesome to the point your majesty describes, it would be expedient to get rid of him or make an ally of him."

"Monsieur, a king who has neither army nor money, as you have heard my conversation with my brother Louis, has no means of acting against a man like Monk."

"Yes, sire, that was your opinion, I know very well: but, fortunately for you, it was not mine."

"What do you mean by that?"

"That, without an army and without a million, I have done—I, myself—what your majesty thought could alone be done with an army and a million."

"How! What do you say? What have you done?"

"What have I done? Eh! well, sire, I went yonder to take this man who is so troublesome to your majesty."

"In England?"

"Exactly, sire."

"You went to take Monk in England?"

"Should I by chance have done wrong, sire?"

"In truth, you are mad, monsieur!"

"Not the least in the world, sire."

"You have taken Monk?"

"Yes, sire."

"Where?"

"In the midst of his camp."

The king trembled with impatience.

"And having taken him on the causeway of Newcastle, I bring him to your majesty," said D'Artagnan, simply.

"You bring him to me!" cried the king, almost indignant at what he considered a mystification.

"Yes, sire," replied D'Artagnan, in the same tone, "I bring him to you; he is down below yonder, in a large chest pierced with holes, so as to allow him to breathe."

"Good God!"

"Oh! don't be uneasy, sire, we have taken the greatest possible care of him. He comes in good state, and in perfect condition. Would your majesty please to see him, to talk with him, or to have him thrown into the sea?"

"Oh, heavens!" repeated Charles, "oh, heavens! do you speak the truth, monsieur? Are you not insulting me with some unworthy joke? You have accomplished this unheard-of act of audacity and genius—impossible!"

"Will your majesty permit me to open the window?" said D'Artagnan, opening it.

The king had not time to reply yes or no. D'Artagnan gave a shrill and prolonged whistle, which he repeated three times through the silence of the night.

"There!" said he, "he will be brought to your majesty."

Chapter XXIX.
Fear he has placed his Money and that of Planchet in the Sinking Fund.

THE king could not overcome his surprise, and looked sometimes at the smiling face of the musketeer, and sometimes at the dark window which opened into the night. But before he had fixed his ideas, eight of D'Artagnan's men, for two had remained to take care of the bark, brought to the house, where Parry received him, that object of an oblong form, which, for the moment, inclosed the destinies of England. Before he left Calais, D'Artagnan had had made in that city a sort of coffin, large and deep enough for a man to turn in it at his ease. The bottom and sides, properly upholstered, formed a bed sufficiently soft to prevent the rolling of the ship turning this kind of cage into a rat-trap. The little grating, of which D'Artagnan had spoken to the king, like the visor of the helmet, was placed opposite to the man's face. It was so constructed that, at the least cry, a sudden pressure would stifle that cry, and, if necessary, him who had uttered that cry.

D'Artagnan was so well acquainted with his crew and his prisoner, that during the whole voyage he had been in dread of two things: either that the general would prefer death to this sort of imprisonment, and would smother himself by endeavoring to speak, or that his guards would allow themselves to be tempted by the offers of the prisoner, and put him, D'Artagnan, into the box instead of Monk.

D'Artagnan, therefore, had passed the two days and the two nights of the voyage close to the coffin, alone with the general, offering him wine and food, which the latter had refused, and constantly endeavoring to reassure him upon the destiny which awaited him at the end of this singular captivity. Two pistols on the table and his naked sword made D'Artagnan easy with regard to indiscretions from without.

When once at Scheveningen he had felt completely reassured. His men greatly dreaded any conflict with the lords of the soil. He had, besides, interested in his cause him who had morally served him as lieutenant, and whom we have seen reply to the name of Menneville. The latter, not being a vulgar spirit, had more to risk than the others, because he had more conscience. He believed in a future in the service of D'Artagnan, and consequently would have allowed himself to be cut to pieces, rather than violate the order given by his leader. Thus it was that, once landed, it was to him that D'Artagnan had confided the care of the chest and the general's breathing. It was he, too, he had ordered to have the chest brought by the seven men as soon as he should hear the triple whistle. We have seen that the lieutenant obeyed. The coffer once in the house, D'Artagnan dismissed his men with a gracious smile, saying, "Messieurs, you have rendered a great service to King Charles II., who in less than six weeks will be king of England. Your gratification will then be doubled. Return to the boat and wait for me." Upon which they departed with such shouts of joy as terrified even the dog himself.

D'Artagnan had caused the coffer to be brought as far as the king's antechamber. He then, with great care, closed the door of this ante-chamber, after which he opened the coffer, and said to the general:

"General, I have a thousand excuses to make to you; my manner of acting has not been worthy of such a man as you, I know very well; but I wished you to take me for the captain of a bark. And then England is a very inconvenient country for transports. I hope, therefore, you will take all that into consideration. But now, general, you are at liberty to get up and walk." This said, he cut the bonds which fastened the arms and hands of the general. The latter got up, and then sat down with the countenance of a man who expects death. D'Artagnan opened the door of Charles's study, and said, "Sire, here is your enemy, M. Monk; I promised myself to perform this service for your majesty. It is done; now order as you please. M. Monk," added he, turning towards the prisoner, "you are in the presence of his majesty Charles II., sovereign lord of Great Britain."

Monk raised towards the prince his coldly stoical look, and replied: "I know no king of Great Britain; I recognize even here no one worthy of bearing the name of gentleman: for it is in the name of King Charles II. that an emissary, whom I took for an honest man, came and laid an infamous snare for me. I have fallen into that snare; so much the worse for me. Now, you the tempter," said he to the king; "you the executor," said he to D'Artagnan; "remember what I am about to say to you: you have my body, you may kill it, and I advise you to do so, for you shall never have my mind or my will. And now, ask me not a single word, as from this moment I will not open my mouth even to cry out. I have said."

And he pronounced these words with the savage, invincible resolution of the most mortified Puritan. D'Artagnan looked at his prisoner like a man who knows the value of every word, and who fixes that value according to the accent with which it has been pronounced.

"The fact is," said he, in a whisper to the king, "the general is an obstinate man; he would not take a mouthful of bread, nor swallow a drop of wine, during the two days of our voyage. But as from this moment it is your majesty who must decide his fate, I wash my hands of him."

Monk, erect, pale, and resigned, waited with his eyes fixed and his arms folded. D'Artagnan turned towards him. "You will please to understand perfectly," said he, "that your speech, otherwise very fine, does not suit anybody, not even yourself. His majesty wished to speak to you, you refused an interview; why, now that you are face to face, that you are here by a force independent of your will, why do you confine yourself to the rigors which I consider useless and absurd? Speak! what the devil! speak, if only to say 'No.'"

Monk did not unclose his lips; Monk did not turn his eyes; Monk stroked his mustache with a thoughtful air, which announced that matters were going on badly.

During all this time Charles II. had fallen into a profound reverie. For the first time he found himself face to face with Monk; with the man he had so much desired to see; and, with that peculiar glance which God has given to eagles and kings, he had fathomed the abyss of his heart. He beheld Monk, then, resolved positively to die rather than speak, which was not to be wondered at in so considerable a man, the wound in whose mind must at the moment have been cruel. Charles II. formed, on the instant, one of those resolutions upon which an ordinary man risks his life, a general his fortune, and a king his kingdom. "Monsieur," said he to Monk, "you are perfectly right upon certain points; I do not, therefore, ask you to answer me, but to listen to me."

There was a moment's silence, during which the king looked at Monk, who remained impassible.

"You have made me just now a painful reproach, monsieur," continued the king; "you said that one of my emissaries had been to Newcastle to lay a snare for you, and that, parenthetically, cannot be understood by M. d'Artagnan here, and to whom, before everything, I owe sincere thanks for his generous, his heroic devotion."

D'Artagnan bowed with respect; Monk took no notice.

"For M. d'Artagnan—and observe, M. Monk, I do not say this to excuse myself—for M. d'Artagnan," continued the king, "went to England of his free will, without interest, without orders, without hope, like a true gentleman as he is, to render a service to an unfortunate king, and to add to the illustrious actions of an existence, already so well filled, one glorious deed more."

D'Artagnan colored a little, and coughed to keep his countenance. Monk did not stir.

"You do not believe what I tell you, M. Monk," continued the king. "I can understand that,—such proofs of devotion are so rare, that their reality may well be put in doubt."

"Monsieur would do wrong not to believe you, sire," cried D'Artagnan: "for that which your majesty has said is the exact truth, and the truth so exact that it seems, in going to fetch the general, I have done something which sets everything wrong. In truth, if it be so, I am in despair."

"Monsieur d'Artagnan," said the king, pressing the hand of the musketeer, "you have obliged me as much as if you had promoted the success of my cause, for you have revealed to me an unknown friend, to whom I shall ever be grateful, and whom I shall always love." And the king pressed his hand cordially. "And," continued he, bowing to Monk, "an enemy whom I shall henceforth esteem at his proper value."

The eyes of the Puritan flashed, but only once, and his countenance, for an instant, illuminated by that flash, resumed its somber impassibility.

"Then, Monsieur d'Artagnan," continued Charles, "this is what was about to happen: M. le Comte de la Fere, who you know, I believe, has set out for Newcastle."

"What, Athos!" exclaimed D'Artagnan.

"Yes, that was his nom de guerre, I believe. The Comte de la Fere had then set out for Newcastle, and was going, perhaps, to bring the general to hold a conference with me or with those of my party, when you violently, as it appears, interfered with the negotiation."

"Mordioux!" replied D'Artagnan, "he entered the camp the very evening in which I succeeded in getting into it with my fishermen—"

An almost imperceptible frown on the brow of Monk told D'Artagnan that he had surmised rightly.

"Yes, yes," muttered he; "I thought I knew his person; I even fancied I knew his voice. Unlucky wretch that I am! Oh! sire, pardon me! I thought I had so successfully steered my bark."

"There is nothing ill in it, sir," said the king, "except that the general accuses me of having laid a snare for him, which is not the case. No, general, those are not the arms which I contemplated employing with you, as you will soon see. In the meanwhile, when I give you my word upon the honor of a gentleman, believe me, sir, believe me! Now, Monsieur d'Artagnan, a word with you, if you please."

"I listen on my knees, sire."

"You are truly at my service, are you not?"

"Your majesty has seen that I am, too much so."

"That is well; from a man like you one word suffices. In addition to that word you bring actions. General, have the goodness to follow me. Come with us, M. d'Artagnan."

D'Artagnan, considerably surprised, prepared to obey. Charles II. went out, Monk followed him, D'Artagnan followed Monk. Charles took the path by which D'Artagnan had come to his abode; the fresh sea breezes soon caressed the faces of the three nocturnal travelers, and, at fifty paces from the little gate which Charles opened, they found themselves upon the down in the face of the ocean, which, having ceased to rise, reposed upon the shore like a wearied monster. Charles II. walked pensively along, his head hanging down and his hand beneath his cloak. Monk followed him, with crossed arms and an uneasy look. D'Artagnan came last, with his hand on the hilt of his sword.

"Where is the boat in which you came, gentlemen?" said Charles to the musketeer.

"Yonder, sire; I have seven men and an officer waiting me in that little bark which is lighted by a fire."

"Yes, I see; the boat is drawn upon the sand; but you certainly did not come from Newcastle in that frail bark?"

"No, sire; I freighted a felucca, at my own expense, which is at anchor within cannon-shot of the downs. It was in that felucca we made the voyage."

"Sir," said the king to Monk, "you are free."

However firm his will, Monk could not suppress an exclamation. The king added an affirmative motion of his head, and continued: "We shall waken a fisherman of the village, who will put his boat to sea immediately, and will take you back to any place you may command him. M. d'Artagnan here will escort your honor. I place M. d'Artagnan under the safeguard of your loyalty, M. Monk."

Monk allowed a murmur of surprise to escape him, and D'Artagnan a profound sigh. The king, without appearing to notice either, knocked against the deal trellis which inclosed the cabin of the principal fisherman inhabiting the down.

"Hey! Keyser!" cried he, "awake!"

"Who calls me?" asked the fisherman.

"I, Charles the king."

"Ah, my lord!" cried Keyser, rising ready dressed from the sail in which he slept, as people sleep in a hammock. "What can I do to serve you?"

"Captain Keyser," said Charles, "you must set sail immediately. Here is a traveler who wishes to freight your bark, and will pay you well; serve him well." And the king drew back a few steps to allow Monk to speak to the fisherman.

"I wish to cross over into England," said Monk, who spoke Dutch enough to make himself understood.

"This minute," said the patron, "this very minute, if you wish it."

"But will that be long?" said Monk.

"Not half an hour, your honor. My eldest son is at this moment preparing the boat, as we were going out fishing at three o'clock in the morning."

"Well, is all arranged?" asked the king, drawing near.

"All but the price," said the fisherman; "yes, sire."

"That is my affair," said Charles, "the gentleman is my friend."

Monk started and looked at Charles on hearing this word.

"Very well, my lord," replied Keyser. And at that moment they heard Keyser's son, signaling form the shore with the blast of a bull's horn.

"Now, gentlemen," said the king, "depart."

"Sire," said D'Artagnan, "will it please your majesty to grant me a few minutes? I have engaged men, and I am going without them; I must give them notice."

"Whistle to them," said Charles, smiling.

D'Artagnan, accordingly, whistled, whilst the patron Keyser replied to his son; and four men, led by Menneville, attended the first summons.

"Here is some money in account," said D'Artagnan, putting into their hands a purse containing two thousand five hundred livres in gold. "Go and wait for me at Calais, you know where." And D'Artagnan heaved a profound sigh, as he let the purse fall into the hands of Menneville.

"What, are you leaving us?" cried the men.

"For a short time," said D'Artagnan, "or for a long time, who knows? But with 2,500 livres, and the 2,500 you have already received, you are paid according to our agreement. We are quits, then, my friend."

"But the boat?"

"Do not trouble yourself about that."

"Our things are on board the felucca."

"Go and seek them, and then set off immediately."

"Yes, captain."

D'Artagnan returned to Monk, saying,—"Monsieur, I await your orders, for I understand we are to go together, unless my company be disagreeable to you."

"On the contrary, monsieur," said Monk.

"Come, gentlemen, on board," cried Keyser's son.

Charles bowed to the general with grace and dignity, saying,—"You will pardon me this unfortunate accident, and the violence to which you have been subjected, when you are convinced that I was not the cause of them."

Monk bowed profoundly without replying. On his side, Charles affected not to say a word to D'Artagnan in private, but aloud,—"Once more, thanks, monsieur le chevalier," said he, "thanks for your services. They will be repaid you by the Lord God, who, I hope, reserves trials and troubles for me alone."

Monk followed Keyser and his son embarked with them. D'Artagnan came after, muttering to himself,—"Poor Planchet! poor Planchet! I am very much afraid we have made a bad speculation."

Chapter XXX.
The Shares of Planchet and Company rise again to Par.

DURING the passage, Monk only spoke to D'Artagnan in cases of urgent necessity. Thus, when the Frenchman hesitated to come and take his meals, poor meals, composed of salt fish, biscuit, and Hollands gin, Monk called him, saying,—"To table, monsieur, to table!"

This was all. D'Artagnan, from being himself on all great occasions, extremely concise, did not draw from the general's conciseness a favorable augury of the result of his mission. Now, as D'Artagnan had plenty of time for reflection, he battered his brains during this time in endeavoring to find out how Athos had seen King Charles, how he had conspired his departure with him, and lastly, how he had entered Monk's camp; and the poor lieutenant of musketeers plucked a hair from his mustache every time that he reflected that the horseman who accompanied Monk on the night of the famous abduction must have been Athos.

At length, after a passage of two nights and two days, the patron Keyser touched at the point where Monk, who had given all the orders during the voyage, had commanded they should land. It was exactly at the mouth of the little river, near where Athos had chosen his abode.

Daylight was waning, a splendid sun, like a red steel buckler, was plunging the lower extremity of its disc beneath the blue line of the sea. The felucca was making fair way up the river, tolerably wide in that part, but Monk, in his impatience, desired to be landed, and Keyser's boat set him and D'Artagnan upon the muddy bank, amidst the reeds. D'Artagnan, resigned to obedience, followed Monk exactly as a chained bear follows his master; but the position humiliated him not a little, and he grumbled to himself that the service of kings was a bitter one, and that the best of them was good for nothing. Monk walked with long and hasty strides; it might be thought that he did not yet feel certain of having reached English land. They had already begun to perceive distinctly a few of the cottages of the sailors and fishermen spread over the little quay of this humble port, when, all at once, D'Artagnan cried out,—"God pardon me, there is a house on fire!"

Monk raised his eyes, and perceived there was, in fact, a house which the flames were beginning to devour. It had begun at a little shed belonging to the house, the roof of which had caught. The fresh evening breeze agitated the fire. The two travelers quickened their steps, hearing loud cries, and seeing, as they drew nearer, soldiers with their glittering arms pointed towards the house on fire. It was doubtless this menacing occupation which had made them neglect to signal the felucca. Monk stopped short for an instant, and, for the first time, formulated his thoughts into words. "Eh! but," said he, "perhaps they are not my soldiers but Lambert's."

These words contained at once a sorrow, and apprehension, and a reproach perfectly intelligible to D'Artagnan. In fact, during the general's absence, Lambert might have given battle, conquered, and dispersed the parliament's army, and taken with his own the place of Monk's army, deprived of its strongest support. At this doubt, which passed from the mind of Monk to his own, D'Artagnan reasoned in this manner:—"One of two things is going to happen; either Monk has spoken correctly, and there are no longer any but Lambertists in the country—that is to say, enemies, who would receive me wonderfully well, since it is to me they owe their victory; or nothing is changed, and Monk, transported with joy at finding his camp still in the same place, will not prove too severe in his settlement with me." Whilst thinking thus, the two travelers advanced, and began to mingle with a little knot of sailors, who looked on with sorrow at the burning house, but did not dare to say anything on account of the threats of the soldiers. Monk addressed one of these sailors:—"What is going on here?" asked he.

"Sir," replied the man, not recognizing Monk as an officer, under the thick cloak which enveloped him, "that house was inhabited by a foreign gentleman, and this foreigner became suspected by the soldiers. They wanted to get into his house under pretense of taking him to the camp; but he, without being frightened by their number, threatened death to the first who should cross the threshold of his door; and as there was one who did venture, the Frenchman stretched him on the earth with a pistol-shot."

"Ah! he is a Frenchman, is he?" said D'Artagnan, rubbing his hands. "Good!"

"How good?" replied the fisherman.

"No, I don't mean that.—What then—my tongue slipped."

"What then, sir?—why, the other men became as enraged as so many lions: they fired more than a hundred shots at the house; but the Frenchman was sheltered by the wall, and every time they tried to enter by the door they met with a shot from his lackey, whose aim is deadly, d'ye see? Every time they threatened the window, they met with a pistol-shot from the master. Look and count—there are seven men down."

"Ah! my brave countryman," cried D'Artagnan, "wait a little, wait a little. I will be with you; and we will settle with this rabble."

"One instant, sir," said Monk, "wait."

"Long?"

"No; only the time to ask a question." Then, turning towards the sailor, "My friend," asked he, with an emotion which, in spite of all his self-command, he could not conceal, "whose soldiers are these, pray tell me?"

"Whose should they be but that madman, Monk's?"

"There has been no battle, then?"

"A battle, ah, yes! for what purpose? Lambert's army is melting away like snow in April. All come to Monk, officers and soldiers. In a week Lambert won't have fifty men left."

The fisherman was interrupted by a fresh discharge directed against the house, and by another pistol-shot which replied to the discharge and struck down the most daring of the aggressors. The rage of soldiers was at its height. The fire still continued to increase, and a crest of flame and smoke whirled and spread over the roof of the house. D'Artagnan could no longer contain himself. "Mordioux!" said he to Monk, glancing at him sideways: "you are a general, and allow your men to burn houses and assassinate people, while you look on and warm your hands at the blaze of the conflagration? Mordioux! you are not a man."

"Patience, sir, patience!" said Monk, smiling.

"Patience! yes, until that brave gentleman is roasted—is that what you mean?" And D'Artagnan rushed forward.

"Remain where you are, sir," said Monk, in a tone of command. And he advanced towards the house, just as an officer had approached it, saying to the besieged: "The house is burning, you will be roasted within an hour! There is still time—come, tell us what you know of General Monk, and we will spare your life. Reply, or by Saint Patrick—"

The besieged made no answer; he was no doubt reloading his pistol.

"A reinforcement is expected," continued the officer; "in a quarter of an hour there will be a hundred men around your house."

"I reply to you," said the Frenchman. "Let your men be sent away; I will come out freely and repair to the camp alone, or else I will be killed here!"

"Mille tonnerres!" shouted D'Artagnan; "why, that's the voice of Athos! Ah canailles!" and the sword of D'Artagnan flashed from its sheath. Monk stopped him and advanced himself, exclaiming, in a sonorous voice: "Hola! what is going on here? Digby, whence this fire? why these cries?"

"The general!" cried Digby, letting the point of his sword fall.

"The general!" repeated the soldiers.

"Well, what is there so astonishing in that?" said Monk, in a calm tone. Then, silence being re-established,—"Now," said he, "who lit this fire?"

The soldiers hung their heads.

"What! do I ask a question, and nobody answers me?" said Monk. "What! do I find a fault, and nobody repairs it? The fire is still burning, I believe."

Immediately the twenty men rushed forward, seizing pails, buckets, jars, barrels, and extinguishing the fire with as much ardor as they had, an instant before, employed in promoting it. But already, and before all the rest, D'Artagnan had applied a ladder to the house, crying, "Athos! it is I, D'Artagnan! Do not kill me, my dearest friend!" And in a moment the count was clasped in his arms. In the meantime, Grimaud, preserving his calmness, dismantled the fortification of the ground-floor, and after having opened the door, stood, with his arms folded, quietly on the sill. Only, on hearing the voice of D'Artagnan, he uttered an exclamation of surprise. The fire being extinguished, the soldiers presented themselves, Digby at their head.

"General," said he, "excuse us; what we have done was for love of your honor, whom we thought lost."

"You are mad, gentlemen. Lost! Is a man like me to be lost? Am I not permitted to be absent, according to my pleasure, without giving formal notice? Do you, by chance, take me for a citizen from the city? Is a gentleman, my friend, my guest, to be besieged, entrapped, and threatened with death, because he is suspected? What signifies the word, suspected? Curse me if I don't have every one of you shot like dogs, that the brave gentleman has left alive!

"General," said Digby, piteously, "there were twenty-eight of us, and see, there are eight on the ground."

"I authorize M. le Comte de la Fere to send the twenty to join the eight," said Monk, stretching out his hand to Athos. "Let them return to camp. Mr. Digby, you will consider yourself under arrest for a month."

"General—"

"That is to teach you, sir, not to act, another time, without orders."

"I had those of the lieutenant, general."

"The lieutenant had no such orders to give you, and he shall be placed under arrest, instead of you, if he has really commanded you to burn this gentleman."

"He did not command that, general; he commanded us to bring him to the camp; but the count was not willing to follow us."

"I was not willing that they should enter and plunder my house," said Athos to Monk, with a significant look.

"And you were quite right. To the camp, I say." The soldiers departed with dejected looks. "Now we are alone," said Monk to Athos, "have the goodness to tell me, monsieur, why you persisted in remaining here, whilst you had your felucca—"

"I waited for you, general," said Athos. "Had not your honor appointed to meet me in a week?"

An eloquent look from D'Artagnan made it clear to Monk that these two men, so brave and so loyal, had not acted in concert for his abduction. He knew already it could not be so.

"Monsieur," said he to D'Artagnan, "you were perfectly right. Have the kindness to allow me a moment's conversation with M. le Comte de la Fere?"

D'Artagnan took advantage of this to go and ask Grimaud how he was. Monk requested Athos to conduct him to the chamber he lived in.

This chamber was still full of smoke and rubbish. More than fifty balls had passed through the windows and mutilated the walls. They found a table, inkstand, and materials for writing. Monk took up a pen, wrote a single line, signed it, folded the paper, sealed the letter with the seal of his ring, and handed over the missive to Athos, saying, "Monsieur, carry, if you please, this letter to King Charles II., and set out immediately, if nothing detains you here any longer."

"And the casks?" said Athos.

"The fisherman who brought me hither will assist you in transporting them on board. Depart, if possible, within an hour."

"Yes, general," said Athos.

"Monsieur D'Artagnan!" cried Monk, from the window. D'Artagnan ran up precipitately.

"Embrace your friend and bid him adieu, sir; he is returning to Holland."

"To Holland!" cried D'Artagnan; "and I?"

"You are at liberty to follow him, monsieur; but I request you to remain," said Monk. "Will you refuse me?"

"Oh, no, general; I am at your orders."

D'Artagnan embraced Athos, and only had time to bid him adieu. Monk watched them both. Then he took upon himself the preparations for the departure, the transportation of the casks on board, and the embarking of

Athos; then, taking D'Artagnan by the arm, who was quite amazed and agitated, he led him towards Newcastle. Whilst going along, the general leaning on his arm, D'Artagnan could not help murmuring to himself,—"Come, come, it seems to me that the shares of the firm of Planchet and Company are rising."

Chapter XXXI.
Monk reveals Himself.

D'ARTAGNAN, although he flattered himself with better success, had, nevertheless, not too well comprehended his situation. It was a strange and grave subject for him to reflect upon—this voyage of Athos into England; this league of the king with Athos, and that extraordinary combination of his design with that of the Comte de la Fere. The best way was to let things follow their own train. An imprudence had been committed, and, whilst having succeeded, as he had promised, D'Artagnan found that he had gained no advantage by his success. Since everything was lost, he could risk no more.

D'Artagnan followed Monk through his camp. The return of the general had produced a marvelous effect, for his people had thought him lost. But Monk, with his austere look and icy demeanor, appeared to ask of his eager lieutenants and delighted soldiers the cause of all this joy. Therefore, to the lieutenants who had come to meet him, and who expressed the uneasiness with which they had learnt his departure,—

"Why is all this?" said he; "am I obliged to give you an account of myself?"

"But your honor, the sheep may well tremble without the shepherd."

"Tremble!" replied Monk, in his calm and powerful voice; "ah, monsieur, what a word! Curse me, if my sheep have not both teeth and claws; I renounce being their shepherd. Ah, you tremble, gentlemen, do you?"

"Yes, general, for you."

"Oh! pray meddle with your own concerns. If I have not the wit God gave to Oliver Cromwell, I have that which He has sent to me: I am satisfied with it, however little it may be."

The officer made no reply; and Monk, having imposed silence on his people, all remained persuaded that he had accomplished some important work or made some important trial. This was forming a very poor conception of his patience and scrupulous genius. Monk, if he had the good faith of the Puritans, his allies, must have returned fervent thanks to the patron saint who had taken him from the box of M. d'Artagnan. Whilst these things were going on, our musketeer could not help constantly repeating,—

"God grant that M. Monk may not have as much pride as I have; for I declare that if any one had put me into a coffer with that grating over my mouth, and carried me packed up, like a calf, across the seas, I should cherish such a memory of my piteous looks in that coffer, and such an ugly animosity against him who had inclosed me in it, I should dread so greatly to see a sarcastic smile blooming upon the face of the malicious wretch, or in his attitude any grotesque imitation of my position in the box, that, Mordioux! I should plunge a good dagger into his throat in compensation for the grating, and would nail him down in a veritable bier, in remembrance of the false coffin in which I had been left in to grow moldy for two days."

And D'Artagnan spoke honestly when he spoke thus; for the skin of our Gascon was a very thin one. Monk, fortunately, entertained other ideas. He never opened his mouth to his timid conqueror concerning the past; but he admitted him very near to his person in his labors, took him with him to several reconnoiterings, in such a way as to obtain that which he evidently warmly desired,—a rehabilitation in the mind of D'Artagnan. The latter conducted himself like a past-master in the art of flattery: he admired all Monk's tactics, and the ordering of his camp; he joked very pleasantly upon the circumvallations of Lambert's camp, who had, he said, very uselessly given himself the trouble to inclose a camp for twenty thousand men, whilst an acre of ground would have been quite sufficient for the corporal and fifty guards who would perhaps remain faithful to him.

Monk, immediately after his arrival, had accepted the proposition made by Lambert the evening before, for an interview, and which Monk's lieutenants had refused under the pretext that the general was indisposed. This interview was neither long nor interesting: Lambert demanded a profession of faith from his rival. The latter declared he had no other opinion than that of the majority. Lambert asked if it would not be more expedient to terminate the quarrel by an alliance than by a battle. Monk hereupon demanded a week for consideration. Now, Lambert could not refuse this: and Lambert, nevertheless, had come saying that he should devour Monk's army. Therefore, at the end of the interview, which Lambert's party watched with impatience, nothing was decided—neither treaty nor battle—the rebel army, as M. d'Artagnan had foreseen, began to prefer the good cause to the bad one, and the parliament, rumpish as it was, to the pompous nothings of Lambert's designs.

They remembered, likewise, the good feasts of London—the profusion of ale and sherry with which the citizens of London paid their friends the soldiers;—they looked with terror at the black war bread, at the troubled waters of the Tweed,—too salt for the glass, not enough so for the pot; and they said to themselves, "Are not the roast meats kept warm for Monk in London?" From that time nothing was heard of but desertion in Lambert's army. The soldiers allowed themselves to be drawn away by the force of principles, which are, like discipline, the obligatory tie in everybody constituted for any purpose. Monk defended the parliament—Lambert attacked it. Monk had no more inclination to support parliament than Lambert, but he had it inscribed on his standards, so that all those of the contrary party were reduced to write upon theirs, "Rebellion," which sounded ill to puritan ears. They flocked, then, from Lambert to Monk, as sinners flock from Baal to God.

Monk made his calculations; at a thousand desertions a day Lambert had men enough to last twenty days; but there is in sinking things such a growth of weight and swiftness, which combine with each other, that a hundred left the first day, five hundred the second, a thousand the third. Monk thought he had obtained his rate. But from one thousand the deserters increased to two thousand, then to four thousand, and, a week after, Lambert, perceiving that he had no longer the possibility of accepting battle, if it were offered to him, took the wise resolution of decamping during the night, returning to London, and being beforehand with Monk in constructing a power with the wreck of the military party.

But Monk, free and without uneasiness, marched towards London as a conqueror, augmenting his army with all the floating parties on the way. He encamped at Barnet, that is to say, within four leagues of the capital, cherished by the parliament, which thought it beheld in him a protector, and awaited by the people, who were anxious to see him reveal himself, that they might judge him. D'Artagnan himself had not been able to fathom his tactics; he observed—he admired. Monk could not enter London with a settled determination without bringing about civil war. He temporized for a short time.

Suddenly, when least expected, Monk drove the military party out of London, and installed himself in the city amidst the citizens, by order of the parliament; then, at the moment when the citizens were crying out against Monk—at the moment when the soldiers themselves were accusing their leader—Monk, finding himself certain of a majority, declared to the Rump Parliament that it must abdicate—be dissolved—and yield its place to a government which would not be a joke. Monk pronounced this declaration, supported by fifty thousand swords, to which, that same evening, were united, with shouts of delirious joy, the five thousand inhabitants of the good city of London. At length, at the moment when the people, after their triumphs and festive repasts in the open streets, were looking about for a master, it was affirmed that a vessel had left the Hague, bearing King Charles II. and his fortunes.

"Gentlemen," said Monk to his officers, "I am going to meet the legitimate king. He who loves me will follow me." A burst of acclamations welcomed these words, which D'Artagnan did not hear without the greatest delight.

"Mordioux!" said he to Monk, "that is bold, monsieur."

"You will accompany me, will you not?" said Monk.

"Pardieu! general. But tell me, I beg, what you wrote by Athos, that is to say, the Comte de la Fere—you know—the day of our arrival?"

"I have no secrets from you now," replied Monk. "I wrote these words: 'Sire, I expect your majesty in six weeks at Dover.'"

"Ah!" said D'Artagnan, "I no longer say it is bold; I say it is well played; it is a fine stroke!"

"You are something of a judge in such matters," replied Monk.

And this was the only time the general had ever made an allusion to his voyage to Holland.

Chapter XXXII.
Athos and D'Artagnan meet once more at the Hostelry of the Corne du Cerf.

THE king of England made his entree into Dover with great pomp, as he afterwards did in London. He had sent for his brothers; he had brought over his mother and sister. England had been for so long a time given up to herself—that is to say, to tyranny, mediocrity and nonsense—that this return of Charles II., whom the English only knew as the son of the man whose head they had cut off, was a festival for three kingdoms. Consequently, all the good wishes, all the acclamations which accompanied his return, struck the young king so forcibly that he stooped and whispered in the ear of James of York, his younger brother, "In truth, James, it seems to have been our own fault that we were so long absent from a country where we are so much beloved!" The pageant was magnificent. Beautiful weather favored the solemnity. Charles had regained all his youth, all his good humor; he appeared to be transfigured; hearts seemed to smile on him like the sun. Amongst this noisy crowd of courtiers and worshipers, who did not appear to remember they had conducted to the scaffold at Whitehall the father of the new king, a man, in the garb of a lieutenant of musketeers, looked, with a smile upon his thin, intellectual lips, sometimes at the people vociferating their blessings, and sometimes at the prince, who pretended emotion, and who bowed most particularly to the women, whose bouquets fell beneath his horse's feet.

"What a fine trade is that of king!" said this man, so completely absorbed in contemplation that he stopped in the middle of the road, leaving the cortege to file past. "Now, there is, in good truth, a prince all bespangled over with gold and diamonds, enamelled with flowers like a spring meadow; he is about to plunge his empty hands into the immense coffer in which his now faithful—but so lately unfaithful—subjects have amassed one or two cartloads of ingots of gold. They cast bouquets enough upon him to smother him; and yet, if he had presented himself to them two months ago, they would have sent as many bullets and balls at him as they now throw flowers. Decidedly it is worth something to be born in a certain sphere, with due respect to the lowly, who pretend that it is of very little advantage to them to be born lowly." The cortege continued to file on, and, with the king, the acclamations began to die away in the direction of the palace, which, however, did not prevent our officer from being pushed about.

"Mordioux!" continued the reasoner, "these people tread upon my toes and look upon me as of very little consequence, or rather of none at all, seeing that they are Englishmen and I am a Frenchman. If all these people were asked,—'Who is M. d'Artagnan?' they would reply, 'Nescio vos.' But let any one say to them, 'There is the king going by,' 'There is M. Monk going by,' they would run away, shouting,—'Vive le roi!' 'Vive M. Monk!' till their lungs were exhausted. And yet," continued he, surveying, with that look sometimes so keen and sometimes so proud, the diminishing crowd,—"and yet, reflect a little, my good people, on what your king has done, on what M. Monk has done, and then think what has been done by this poor unknown, who is called M. d'Artagnan! It is true you do not know him, since he is here unknown, and that prevents your thinking about the matter! But, bah! what matters it! All that does not prevent Charles II. from being a great king, although he has been exiled twelve years, or M. Monk from being a great captain, although he did make a voyage to Holland in a box. Well, then, since it is admitted that one is a great king and the other a great captain,—'Hurrah for King Charles II.!—Hurrah for General Monk!'" And his voice mingled with the voices of the hundreds of spectators, over which it sounded for a moment. Then, the better to play the devoted man, he took off his hat and waved it in the air. Some one seized his arm in the very height of his expansive loyalism. (In 1660 that was so termed which we now call royalism.)

"Athos!" cried D'Artagnan, "you here!" And the two friends seized each other's hands.

"You here!—and being here," continued the musketeer, "you are not in the midst of all these courtiers, my dear comte! What! you, the hero of the fete, you are not prancing on the left hand of the king, as M. Monk is prancing on the right? In truth, I cannot comprehend your character, nor that of the prince who owes you so much!"

"Always scornful, my dear D'Artagnan!" said Athos. "Will you never correct yourself of that vile habit?"

"But you do not form part of the pageant?"

"I do not, because I was not willing to do so."

"And why were you not willing?"

"Because I am neither envoy nor ambassador, nor representative of the king of France; and it does not become me to exhibit myself thus near the person of another king than the one God has given me for a master."

"Mordioux! you came very near to the person of the king, his father."

"That was another thing, my friend; he was about to die."

"And yet that which you did for him—"

"I did it because it was my duty to do it. But you know I hate all ostentation. Let King Charles II., then, who no longer stands in need of me, leave me to my rest, and the shadow; that is all I claim of him."

D'Artagnan sighed.

"What is the matter with you?" said Athos. "One would say that this happy return of the king to London saddens you, my friend; you who have done at least as much for his majesty as I have."

"Have I not," replied D'Artagnan, with his Gascon laugh, "have I not done much for his majesty, without any one suspecting it?"

"Yes, yes, but the king is well aware of it, my friend," cried Athos.

"He is aware of it!" said the musketeer bitterly. "By my faith! I did not suspect so, and I was even a moment ago trying to forget it myself."

"But he, my friend, will not forget it, I will answer for him."

"You tell me that to console me a little, Athos."

"For what?"

"Mordioux! for all the expense I incurred. I have ruined myself, my friend, ruined myself for the restoration of this young prince who has just passed, cantering on his isabelle colored horse."

"The king does not know you have ruined yourself, my friend; but he knows he owes you much."

"And say, Athos, does that advance me in any respect? for, to do you justice, you have labored nobly. But I—I who in appearance marred your combinations, it was I who really made them succeed. Follow my calculations closely; you might not have, by persuasions or mildness, convinced General Monk, whilst I so roughly treated this dear general, that I furnished your prince with an opportunity of showing himself generous: this generosity was inspired in him by the fact of my fortunate mistake, and Charles is paid by the restoration which Monk has brought about."

"All that, my dear friend, is strikingly true," replied Athos.

"Well, strikingly true as it may be, it is not less true, my friend, that I shall return—greatly beloved by M. Monk, who calls me dear captain all day long, although I am neither dear to him nor a captain;—and much appreciated by the king, who has already forgotten my name;—it is not less true, I say, that I shall return to my beautiful country, cursed by the soldiers I had raised with the hopes of large pay, cursed by the brave Planchet, of who I have borrowed a part of his fortune."

"How is that? What the devil had Planchet to do in all this?"

"Ah, yes, my friend; but this king, so spruce, so smiling, so adored, M. Monk fancies he has recalled him, you fancy you have supported him, I fancy I have brought him back, the people fancy they have reconquered him, he himself fancies he has negotiated his restoration; and yet nothing of all this is true, for Charles II., king of England, Scotland, and Ireland, has been replaced upon the throne by a French grocer, who lives in the Rue des Lombards, and is named Planchet. And such is grandeur! 'Vanity!' says the Scripture: vanity, all is vanity.'"

Athos could not help laughing at this whimsical outbreak of his friend.

"My dear D'Artagnan," said he, pressing his hand affectionately, "should you not exercise a little more philosophy? Is it not some further satisfaction to you to have saved my life as you did by arriving so fortunately with Monk, when those damned parliamentarians wanted to burn me alive?"

"Well, but you, in some degree, deserved a little burning, my friend."

"How so? What, for having saved King Charles's million?"

"What million?"

"Ah, that is true! you never knew that, my friend; but you must not be angry, for it was my secret. That word 'REMEMBER' which the king pronounced upon the scaffold."

"And which means 'souviens-toi!'"

"Exactly. That was signified. 'Remember there is a million buried in the vaults of Newcastle Abbey, and that that million belongs to my son.'"

"Ah! very well, I understand. But what I understand likewise, and what is very frightful, is, that every time his majesty Charles II. will think of me, he will say to himself: 'There is the man who came very near to making me lose my crown. Fortunately I was generous, great, full of presence of mind.' That will be said by the young gentleman in a shabby black doublet, who came to the chateau of Blois, hat in hand, to ask me if I would give him access to the king of France."

"D'Artagnan! D'Artagnan!" said Athos, laying his hand on the shoulder of the musketeer, "you are unjust."

"I have a right to be so."

"No—for you are ignorant of the future."

D'Artagnan looked his friend full in the face, and began to laugh. "In truth, my dear Athos," said he, "you have some sayings so superb, that they only belong to you and M. le Cardinal Mazarin."

Athos frowned slightly.

"I beg your pardon," continued D'Artagnan, laughing, "I beg your pardon if I have offended you. The future! Nein! what pretty words are words that promise, and how well they fill the mouth in default of other things! Mordioux! After having met with so many who promised, when shall I find one who will give? But, let that pass!" continued D'Artagnan. "What are you doing here, my dear Athos? Are you the king's treasurer?"

"How—why the king's treasurer?"

"Well, since the king possess a million, he must want a treasurer. The king of France, although he is not worth a sou, has still a superintendent of finance, M. Fouquet. It is true, that, in exchange, M. Fouquet, they say, has a good number of millions of his own."

"Oh! our million was spent long ago," said Athos, laughing in his turn.

"I understand; it was frittered away in satin, precious stones, velvet, and feathers of all sorts and colors. All these princes and princesses stood in great need of tailors and dressmakers. Eh! Athos, do you remember what we fellows spent in equipping ourselves for the campaign of La Rochelle, and to make our appearance on horseback? Two or three thousand livres, by my faith! But a king's robe is the more ample; it would require a million to purchase the stuff. At least, Athos, if you are not treasurer, you are on good footing at court."

"By the faith of a gentleman, I know nothing about it," said Athos, simply.

"What! you know nothing about it?"

"No! I have not seen the king since we left Dover."

"Then he has forgotten you, too! Mordioux! That is shameful!"

"His majesty has had so much business to transact."

"Oh!" cried D'Artagnan, with one of those intelligent grimaces which he alone knew how to make, "that is enough to make me recover my love for Monseigneur Giulio Mazarini. What, Athos! the king has not seen you since then?"

"No."

"And you are not furious?"

"I! why should I be? Do you imagine, my dear D'Artagnan, that it was on the king's account I acted as I have done? I did not know the young man. I defended the father, who represented a principle—sacred in my eyes, and I allowed myself to be drawn towards the son from sympathy for this same principle. Besides, he was a worthy knight, a noble creature, that father; do you remember him?"

"Yes; that is true; he was a brave, an excellent man, who led a sad life, but made a fine end."

"Well, my dear D'Artagnan, understand this; to that king, to that man of heart, to that friend of my thoughts, if I durst venture to say so, I swore at the last hour to preserve faithfully the secret of a deposit which was to be transmitted to his son, to assist him in his hour of need. This young man came to me; he described his destitution; he was ignorant that he was anything to me save a living memory of his father. I have accomplished towards Charles II. what I promised Charles I.; that is all! Of what consequence is it to me, then, whether he be grateful or not? It is to myself I have rendered a service, by relieving myself of this responsibility, and not to him."

"Well, I have always said," replied D'Artagnan, with a sigh, "that disinterestedness was the finest thing in the world."

"Well, and you, my friend," resumed Athos, "are you not in the same situation as myself? If I have properly understood your words, you allowed yourself to be affected by the misfortunes of this young man; that, on your part, was much greater than it was upon mine, for I had a duty to fulfill; whilst you were under no obligation to the son of the martyr. You had not, on your part, to pay him the price of that precious drop of blood which he let fall upon my brow, through the floor of the scaffold. That which made you act was heart alone—the noble and good heart which you possess beneath your apparent skepticism and sarcastic irony; you have engaged the fortune of a servitor, and your own, I suspect, my benevolent miser! and your sacrifice is not acknowledged! Of what consequence is it? You wish to repay Planchet his money. I can comprehend that, my friend: for it is not becoming in a gentleman to borrow from his inferior, without returning to him principal and interest. Well, I will sell La Fere if necessary, and if not, some little farm. You shall pay Planchet, and there will be enough, believe me, of corn left in my granaries for us two and Raoul. In this way, my friend, you will be under obligations to nobody but yourself; and, if I know you well, it will not be a small satisfaction to your mind to be able to say, 'I have made a king!' Am I right?"

"Athos! Athos!" murmured D'Artagnan, thoughtfully, "I have told you more than once that the day on which you will preach I shall attend the sermon;

the day on which you will tell me there is a hell—Mordioux! I shall be afraid of the gridiron and the pitch-forks. You are better than I, or rather, better than anybody, and I only acknowledge the possession of one quality, and that is, of not being jealous. Except that defect, damme, as the English say, if I have not all the rest."

"I know no one equal to D'Artagnan," replied Athos; "but here we are, having quietly reached the house I inhabit. Will you come in, my friend?"

"Eh! why this is the tavern of the Corne du Cerf, I think," said D'Artagnan.

"I confess I chose it on purpose. I like old acquaintances; I like to sit down on that place, whereon I sank, overcome by fatigue, overwhelmed by despair, when you returned on the 31st of January."

"After having discovered the abode of the masked executioner? Yes, that was a terrible day!"

"Come in, then," said Athos, interrupting him.

They entered the large apartment, formerly the common one. The tavern, in general, and this room in particular, had undergone great changes; the ancient host of the musketeers, having become tolerably rich for an innkeeper, had closed his shop, and make of this room of which we were speaking, a store-room for colonial provisions. As for the rest of the house, he let it ready furnished to strangers. It was with unspeakable emotion D'Artagnan recognized all the furniture of the chamber of the first story; the wainscoting, the tapestries, and even that geographical chart which Porthos had so fondly studied in his moments of leisure.

"It is eleven years ago," cried D'Artagnan. "Mordioux! it appears to me a century!"

"And to me but a day," said Athos. "Imagine the joy I experience, my friend, in seeing you there, in pressing your hand, in casting from me sword and dagger, and tasting without mistrust this glass of sherry. And, oh! what still further joy it would be, if our two friends were there, at the two corners of the table, and Raoul, my beloved Raoul, on the threshold, looking at us with his large eyes, at once so brilliant and so soft!"

"Yes, yes," said D'Artagnan, much affected, "that is true. I approve particularly of the first part of your thought; it is very pleasant to smile there where we have so legitimately shuddered in thinking that from one moment to another M. Mordaunt might appear upon the landing."

At this moment the door opened, and D'Artagnan, brave as he was, could not restrain a slight movement of fright. Athos understood him, and, smiling,—

"It is our host," said he, "bringing me a letter."

"Yes, my lord," said the good man; "here is a letter for your honor."

"Thank you," said Athos, taking the letter without looking at it. "Tell me, my dear host, if you do not remember this gentleman?"

The old man raised his head, and looked attentively at D'Artagnan.

"No," said he.

"It is," said Athos, "one of those friends of whom I have spoken to you, and who lodged here with me eleven years ago."

"Oh! but," said the old man, "so many strangers have lodged here!"

"But we lodged here on the 30th of January, 1649," added Athos, believing he should stimulate the lazy memory of the host by this remark.

"That is very possible," replied he, smiling; "but it is so long ago!" and he bowed, and went out.

"Thank you," said D'Artagnan—"perform exploits, accomplish revolutions, endeavor to engrave your name in stone or bronze with strong swords! there is something more rebellious, more hard, more forgetful than iron, bronze, or stone, and that is, the brain of a lodging-house keeper who has grown rich in the trade;—he does not know me! Well, I should have known him, though."

Athos, smiling at his friend's philosophy, unsealed his letter.

"Ah!" said he, "a letter from Parry."

"Oh! oh!" said D'Artagnan; "read it, my friend, read it! No doubt it contains news."

Athos shook his head, and read:

"MONSIEUR LE COMTE.—The king has experienced much regret at not seeing you to-day beside him, at his entrance. His majesty commands me to say so, and to recall him to your memory. His majesty will expect you this evening, at the palace of St. James, between nine and ten o'clock.

"I am, respectfully, monsieur le comte, your honor's very humble and very obedient servant,—PARRY."

"You see, my dear D'Artagnan," said Athos, "we must not despair of the hearts of kings."

"Not despair! you are right to say so!" replied D'Artagnan.

"Oh! my dear, very dear friend," resumed Athos, whom the almost imperceptible bitterness of D'Artagnan had not escaped. "Pardon me! can I have unintentionally wounded my best comrade?"

"You are mad, Athos, and to prove it, I shall conduct you to the palace; to the very gate, I mean; the walk will do me good."

"You shall go in with me, my friend; I will speak to his majesty."

"No, no!" replied D'Artagnan, with true pride, free from all mixture; "if there is anything worse than begging yourself, it is making others beg for you. Come, let us go, my friend, the walk will be charming; on the way I shall show you the house of M. Monk, who has detained me with him. A beautiful house, by my faith. Being a general in England is better than being a marechal in France, please to know."

Athos allowed himself to be led along, quite saddened by D'Artagnan's forced attempts at gayety. The whole city was in a state of joy; the two friends were jostled at every moment by enthusiasts who required them, in their intoxication, to cry out, "Long live good King Charles!" D'Artagnan replied by a grunt, and Athos by a smile. They arrived thus in front of Monk's house, before which, as we have said, they had to pass on their way to St. James's.

Athos and D'Artagnan said but little on the road, for the simple reason that they would have had so many things to talk about if they had spoken. Athos thought that by speaking he should evince satisfaction, and that might wound D'Artagnan. The latter feared that in speaking he should allow some little bitterness to steal into his words which would render his company unpleasant to his friend. It was a singular emulation of silence between contentment and ill-humor. D'Artagnan gave way first to that itching at the tip of his tongue which he so habitually experienced.

"Do you remember, Athos," said he, "the passage of the 'Memoires de D'Aubigny,' in which that devoted servant, a Gascon like myself, poor as myself, and, I was going to add, brave as myself, relates instances of the meanness of Henry IV.? My father always told me, I remember, that D'Aubigny was a liar. But, nevertheless, examine how all the princes, the issue of the great Henry, keep up the character of the race."

"Nonsense!" said Athos, "the kings of France misers? You are mad, my friend."

"Oh! you are so perfect yourself, you never agree to the faults of others. But, in reality, Henry IV. was covetous, Louis XIII., his son, was so likewise; we know something of that, don't we? Gaston carried this vice to exaggeration, and has made himself, in this respect, hated by all who surround him. Henriette, poor woman, might well be avaricious, she who did not eat every day, and could not warm herself every winter; and that is an example she has given to her son Charles II., grandson of the great Henry IV., who is as covetous as his mother and his grandfather. See if I have well traced the genealogy of the misers?"

"D'Artagnan, my friend," cried Athos, "you are very rude towards that eagle race called the Bourbons."

"Eh! and I have forgotten the best instance of all—the other grandson of the Bernais, Louis XIV., my ex-master. Well, I hope he is miserly enough, he who would not lend a million to his brother Charles! Good! I see you are beginning to be angry. Here we are, by good luck, close to my house, or rather that of my friend, M. Monk."

"My dear D'Artagnan, you do not make me angry, you make me sad; it is cruel, in fact, to see a man of your deserts out of the position his services ought to have acquired; it appears to me, my dear friend, that your name is as radiant as the greatest names in war and diplomacy. Tell me if the Luynes, the Ballegardes, and the Bassompierres have merited, as we have, fortunes and honors? You are right, my friend, a hundred times right."

D'Artagnan sighed, and preceded his friend under the porch of he mansion Monk inhabited, at the extremity of the city. "Permit me," said he, "to leave my purse at home; for if in the crowd those clever pickpockets of London, who are much boasted of, even in Paris, were to steal from me the remainder of my poor crowns, I should not be able to return to France. Now, content I left France, and wild with joy I should return to it, seeing that all my prejudices of former days against England have returned, accompanied by many others."

Athos made no reply.

"So, then, my dear friend, one second, and I will follow you," said D'Artagnan. "I know you are in a hurry to go yonder to receive your reward, but, believe me, I am not less eager to partake of your joy, although from a distance. Wait for me." And D'Artagnan was already passing through the vestibule, when a man, half servant, half soldier, who filled in Monk's establishment the double function of porter and guard, stopped our musketeer, saying to him in English:

"I beg your pardon, my Lord d'Artagnan!"

"Well," replied the latter: "what is it? Is the general going to dismiss me? I only needed to be expelled by him."

These words, spoken in French, made no impression upon the person to whom they were addressed, and who himself only spoke an English mixed with the rudest Scots. But Athos was grieved at them, for he began to think D'Artagnan was not wrong.

The Englishman showed D'Artagnan a letter: "From the general," said he.

"Aye! that's it, my dismissal!" replied the Gascon. "Must I read it, Athos?"

"You must be deceived," said Athos, "or I know no more honest people in the world but you and myself."

D'Artagnan shrugged his shoulders and unsealed the letter, while the impassible Englishman held for him a large lantern, by the light of which he was enabled to read it.

"Well, what is the matter?" said Athos, seeing the countenance of the reader change.

"Read it yourself," said the musketeer.

Athos took the paper and read:

"MONSIEUR D'ARTAGNAN.—The king regrets very much you did not come to St. Paul's with his cortege. He missed you, as I also have missed you, my dear captain. There is but one means of repairing all this. His majesty expects me at nine o'clock at the palace of St. James's: will you be there at the same time with me? His gracious majesty appoints that hour for an audience he grants you."

This letter was from Monk.

Chapter XXXIII.
The Audience.

WELL?" CRIED Athos with a mild look of reproach, when D'Artagnan had read the letter addressed to him by Monk.

"Well!" said D'Artagnan, red with pleasure, and a little with shame, at having so hastily accused the king and Monk. "This is a politeness,—which leads to nothing, it is true, but yet it is a politeness."

"I had great difficulty in believing the young prince ungrateful," said Athos.

"The fact is, that his present is still too near his past," replied D'Artagnan; "after all, everything to the present moment proved me right."

"I acknowledge it, my dear friend, I acknowledge it. Ah! there is your cheerful look returned. You cannot think how delighted I am."

"Thus you see," said D'Artagnan, "Charles II. receives M. Monk at nine o'clock; he will receive me at ten; it is a grand audience, of the sort which at the Louvre are called 'distributions of court holy water.' Come, let us go and place ourselves under the spout, my dear friend! Come along."

Athos replied nothing; and both directed their steps, at a quick pace, towards the palace of St. James's, which the crowd still surrounded, to catch, through the windows, the shadows of the courtiers, and the reflection of the royal person. Eight o'clock was striking when the two friends took their places in the gallery filled with courtiers and politicians. Every one looked at these simply-dressed men in foreign costumes, at these two noble heads so full of character and meaning. On their side, Athos and D'Artagnan, having with two glances taken the measure of the whole assembly, resumed their chat.

A great noise was suddenly heard at the extremity of the gallery,—it was General Monk, who entered, followed by more than twenty officers, all eager for a smile, as only the evening before he was master of all England, and a glorious to-morrow was looked to, for the restorer of the Stuart family.

"Gentlemen," said Monk, turning round, "henceforward I beg you to remember that I am no longer anything. Lately I commanded the principal army of the republic; now that army is the king's, into whose hands I am about to surrender, at his command, my power of yesterday."

Great surprise was painted on all the countenances, and the circle of adulators and suppliants which surrounded Monk an instant before, was enlarged by degrees, and ended by being lost in the large undulations of the crowd. Monk was going into the ante-chamber as others did. D'Artagnan could not help remarking this to the Comte de la Fere, who frowned on beholding it. Suddenly the door of the royal apartment opened, and the young king appeared, preceded by two officers of his household.

"Good evening, gentlemen," said he. "Is General Monk here?"

"I am here, sire," replied the old general.

Charles stepped hastily towards him, and seized his hand with the warmest demonstration of friendship. "General," said the king, aloud, "I have just signed your patent,—you are Duke of Albemarle; and my intention is that no one shall equal you in power and fortune in this kingdom, where—the noble Montrose excepted—no one has equaled you in loyalty, courage, and talent. Gentlemen, the duke is commander of our armies of land and sea; pay him your respects, if you please, in that character."

Whilst every one was pressing round the general, who received all this homage without losing his impassibility for an instant, D'Artagnan said to Athos: "When one thinks that this duchy, this commander of the land and sea forces, all these grandeurs, in a word, have been shut up in a box six feet long and three feet wide—"

"My friend," replied Athos, "much more imposing grandeurs are confined in boxes still smaller,—and remain there forever."

All at once Monk perceived the two gentlemen, who held themselves aside until the crowd had diminished; he made himself a passage towards them, so that he surprised them in the midst of their philosophical reflections. "Were you speaking of me?" sad he, with a smile.

"My lord," replied Athos, "we were speaking likewise of God."

Monk reflected for a moment, and then replied gayly: "Gentlemen, let us speak a little of the king likewise, if you please; for you have, I believe, an audience of his majesty."

"At nine o'clock," said Athos.

"At ten o'clock," said D'Artagnan.

"Let us go into this closet at once," replied Monk, making a sign to his two companions to precede him; but to that neither would consent.

The king, during this discussion so characteristic of the French, had returned to the center of the gallery.

"Oh! my Frenchmen!" said he, in that tone of careless gayety which, in spite of so much grief and so many crosses, he had never lost. "My Frenchmen! my consolation!" Athos and D'Artagnan bowed.

"Duke, conduct these gentlemen into my study. I am at your service, messieurs," added he in French. And he promptly expedited his court, to return to his Frenchmen, as he called them. "Monsieur d'Artagnan," said he, as he entered his closet, "I am glad to see you again."

"Sire, my joy is at its height, at having the honor to salute your majesty in your own palace of St. James's."

"Monsieur, you have been willing to render me a great service, and I owe you my gratitude for it. If I did not fear to intrude upon the rights of our command general, I would offer you some post worthy of you near our person."

"Sire," replied D'Artagnan, "I have quitted the service of the king of France, making a promise to my prince not to serve any other king."

"Humph!" said Charles, "I am sorry to hear that; I should like to do much for you; I like you very much."

"Sire—"

"But, let us see," said Charles with a smile, "if we cannot make you break your word. Duke, assist me. If you were offered, that is to say, if I offered you the chief command of my musketeers?" D'Artagnan bowed lower than before.

"I should have the regret to refuse what your gracious majesty would offer me," said he; "a gentleman has but his word, and that word, as I have had the honor to tell your majesty, is engaged to the king of France."

"We shall say no more about it, then," said the king, turning towards Athos, and leaving D'Artagnan plunged in the deepest pangs of disappointment.

"Ah! I said so!" muttered the musketeer. "Words! words! Court holy water! Kings have always a marvelous talent for offering us that which they know we will not accept, and in appearing generous without risk. So be it!—triple fool that I was to have hoped for a moment!"

During this time, Charles took the hand of Athos. "Comte," said he, "you have been to me a second father; the services you have rendered to me are above all price. I have, nevertheless, thought of a recompense. You were created by my father a Knight of the Garter—that is an order which all the kings of Europe cannot bear; by the queen regent, Knight of the Holy Ghost—which is an order not less illustrious; I join to it that of the Golden Fleece sent me by the king of France, to whom the king of Spain, his father-in-law, gave two on the occasion of his marriage; but in return, I have a service to ask of you."

"Sire," said Athos, with confusion, "the Golden Fleece for me! when the king of France is the only person in my country who enjoys that distinction?"

"I wish you to be in your country and all others the equal of all those whom sovereigns have honored with their favor," said Charles, drawing the chain from his neck; "and I am sure, comte, my father smiles on me from his grave."

"It is unaccountably strange," said D'Artagnan to himself, whilst his friend, on his knees, received the eminent order which the king conferred on him— "it is almost incredible that I have always seen showers of prosperity fall upon all who surrounded me, and that not a drop ever reached me! If I were a jealous man, it would be enough to make one tear one's hair, parole d'honneur!"

Athos rose from his knees, and Charles embraced him tenderly. "General!" said he to Monk—then stopping, with a smile, "pardon me, duke, I mean. No wonder if I make a mistake; the word duke is too short for me, I always seek some title to lengthen it. I should wish to see you so near my throne, that I might say to you, as to Louis XIV., my brother! Oh! I have it; and you will almost be my brother, for I make you viceroy of Ireland and Scotland, my dear duke. So, after that fashion, henceforward I shall not make a mistake."

The duke seized the hand of the king, but without enthusiasm, without joy, as he did everything. His heart, however, had been moved by this last favor. Charles, by skillfully husbanding his generosity, had given the duke time to wish, although he might not have wished for so much as was given him.

"Mordioux!" grumbled D'Artagnan, "there is the shower beginning again! Oh! it is enough to turn one's brain!" and he turned away with an air so sorrowful and so comically piteous, that the king, who caught it, could not restrain a smile. Monk was preparing to leave the room, to take leave of Charles.

"What! my trusty and well-beloved!" said the king to the duke, "are you going?"

"With your majesty's permission, for in truth I am weary. The emotions of the day have worn me out; I stand in need of rest."

"But," said the king, "you are not going without M. d'Artagnan, I hope."

"Why not, sire?" said the old warrior.

"Well! you know very well why," said the king.

Monk looked at Charles with astonishment.

"Oh! it may be possible; but if you forget, you, M. d'Artagnan, do not."

Astonishment was painted on the face of the musketeer.

"Well, then, duke," said the king, "do you not lodge with M. d'Artagnan?"

"I had the honor of offering M. d'Artagnan a lodging; yes, sire."

"That idea is your own, and yours solely?"

"Mine and mine only; yes, sire."

"Well! but it could not be otherwise—the prisoner always lodges with his conqueror."

Monk colored in his turn. "Ah! that is true," said he; "I am M. d'Artagnan's prisoner."

"Without doubt, duke, since you are not yet ransomed; but have no care of that; it was I who took you out of M. d'Artagnan's hands, and it is I who will pay your ransom."

The eyes of D'Artagnan regained their gayety and their brilliancy. The Gascon began to understand. Charles advanced towards him.

"The general," said he, "is not rich, and cannot pay you what he is worth. I am richer, certainly; but now that he is a duke, and if not a king, almost a king, he is worth a sum I could not perhaps pay. Come, M. d'Artagnan, be moderate with me; how much do I owe you?"

D'Artagnan, delighted at the turn things were taking, but not for a moment losing his self-possession, replied,—"Sire, your majesty has no occasion to be alarmed. When I had the good fortune to take his grace, M. Monk was only a general; it is therefore only a general's ransom that is due to me. But if the general will have the kindness to deliver me his sword, I shall consider myself paid; for there is nothing in the world but the general's sword which is worth as much as himself."

"Odds fish! as my father said," cried Charles. "That is a gallant proposal, and a gallant man, is he not, duke?"

"Upon my honor, yes, sire," and he drew his sword. "Monsieur," said he to D'Artagnan, "here is what you demand. Many have handled a better blade; but however modest mine may be, I have never surrendered it to any one."

D'Artagnan received with pride the sword which had just made a king.

"Oh! oh!" cried Charles II.; "what a sword that has restored me to my throne—to go out of the kingdom—and not, one day, to figure among the crown jewels! No, on my soul! that shall not be! Captain d'Artagnan, I will give you two hundred thousand livres for your sword! If that is too little, say so."

"It is too little, sire," replied D'Artagnan, with inimitable seriousness. "In the first place, I do not at all wish to sell it; but your majesty desires me to do so, and that is an order. I obey, then, but the respect I owe to the illustrious warrior who hears me, commands me to estimate a third more the reward of my victory. I ask then three hundred thousand livres for the sword, or I shall give it to your majesty for nothing." And taking it by the point he presented it to the king. Charles broke into hilarious laughter.

"A gallant man, and a merry companion! Odds fish! is he not, duke? is he not, comte? He pleases me! I like him! Here, Chevalier d'Artagnan, take this." And going to the table, he took a pen and wrote an order upon his treasurer for three hundred thousand livres.

D'Artagnan took it, and turning gravely towards Monk: "I have still asked too little, I know," said he, "but believe me, your grace, I would rather have died that allow myself to be governed by avarice."

The king began to laugh again, like the happiest cockney of his kingdom.

"You will come and see me again before you go, chevalier?" said he; "I shall want to lay in a stock of gayety now my Frenchmen are leaving me."

"Ah! sire, it will not be with the gayety as with the duke's sword; I will give it to your majesty gratis," replied D'Artagnan, whose feet scarcely seemed to touch the ground.

"And you, comte," added Charles, turning towards Athos, "come again, also; I have an important message to confide to you. Your hand, duke." Monk pressed the hand of the king.

"Adieu! gentlemen," said Charles, holding out each of his hands to the two Frenchmen, who carried them to their lips.

"Well," said Athos, when they were out of the palace, "are you satisfied?"

"Hush!" said D'Artagnan, wild with joy, "I have not yet returned from the treasurer's—a shutter may fall upon my head."

Chapter XXXIV.
Of the Embarrassment of Riches.

D'ARTAGNAN lost no time, and as soon as the thing was suitable and opportune, he paid a visit to the lord treasurer of his majesty. He had then the satisfaction to exchange a piece of paper, covered with very ugly writing, for a prodigious number of crowns, recently stamped with the effigies of his very gracious majesty Charles II.

D'Artagnan easily controlled himself: and yet, on this occasion, he could not help evincing a joy which the reader will perhaps comprehend, if he deigns to have some indulgence for a man who, since his birth, had never seen so many pieces and rolls of pieces juxta-placed in an order truly agreeable to the eye. The treasurer placed all the rolls in bags, and closed each bag with a stamp sealed with the arms of England, a favor which treasurers do not grant to everybody. Then, impassible, and just as polite as he ought to be towards a man honored with the friendship of the king, he said to D'Artagnan:

"Take away your money, sir." Your money! These words made a thousand chords vibrate in the heart of D'Artagnan, which he had never felt before. He had the bags packed in a small cart, and returned home meditating deeply. A man who possessed three hundred thousand livres can no longer expect to wear a smooth brow; a wrinkle for every hundred thousand livres is not too much.

D'Artagnan shut himself up, ate no dinner, closed his door to everybody, and, with a lighted lamp, and a loaded pistol on the table, he watched all night, ruminating upon the means of preventing these lovely crowns, which from the coffers of the king had passed into his coffers, from passing from his coffers into the pockets of any thief whatever. The best means discovered by the Gascon was to inclose his treasure, for the present, under locks so solid that no wrist could break them, and so complicated that no master-key could open them. D'Artagnan remembered that the English are masters in mechanics and conservative industry; and he determined to go in the morning in search of a mechanic who would sell him a strong box. He did not go far; Master Will Jobson, dwelling in Piccadilly, listened to his propositions, comprehended his wishes, and promised to make him a safety lock that should relieve him from all future fear.

"I will give you," said he, "a piece of mechanism entirely new. At the first serious attempt upon your lock, an invisible plate will open of itself and vomit forth a pretty copper bullet the weight of a mark—which will knock down the intruder, and not with a loud report. What do you think of it?"

"I think it very ingenuous," cried D'Artagnan; "the little copper bullet pleases me mightily. So now, sir mechanic, the terms?"

"A fortnight for the execution, and fifteen hundred livres payable on delivery," replied the artisan.

D'Artagnan's brow darkened. A fortnight was delay enough to allow the thieves of London time to remove all occasion for the strong box. As to the fifteen hundred livres—that would be paying too dear for what a little vigilance would procure him for nothing.

"I will think of it," said he; "thank you, sir." And he returned home at full speed; nobody had yet touched his treasure. That same day Athos paid a visit to his friend and found him so thoughtful that he could not help expressing his surprise.

"How is this?" said he, "you are rich and not gay—you, who were so anxious for wealth!"

"My friend, the pleasures to which we are not accustomed oppress us more than the griefs with which we are familiar. Give me your opinion, if you please. I can ask you, who have always had money: when we have money, what do we do with it?"

"That depends."

"What have you done with yours, seeing that it has not made you a miser or a prodigal? For avarice dries up the heart, and prodigality drowns it—is that not so?"

"Fabricius could not have spoken more justly. But in truth, my money has never been a burden to me."

"How so? Do you place it out at interest?"

"No; you know I have a tolerably handsome house; and that house composes the better part of my property."

"I know it does."

"So that you can be as rich as I am, and, indeed, more rich, whenever you like, by the same means."

"But your rents,—do you lay them by?"

"No."

"What do you think of a chest concealed in a wall?"

"I never made use of such a thing."

"Then you must have some confidant, some safe man of business who pays you interest at a fair rate."

"Not at all."

"Good heavens! what do you do with it, then?"

"I spend all I have, and I only have what I spend, my dear D'Artagnan."

"Ah! that may be. But you are something of a prince; fifteen or sixteen thousand livres melt away between your fingers; and then you have expenses and appearances—"

"Well, I don't see why you should be less of a noble than I am, my friend; your money would be quite sufficient."

"Three hundred thousand livres! Two-thirds too much!"

"I beg your pardon—did you not tell me?—I thought I heard you say—I fancied you had a partner—"

"Ah! Mordioux! that's true," cried D'Artagnan, coloring; "there is Planchet. I had forgotten Planchet, upon my life! Well! there are my three hundred thousand livres broken into. That's a pity! it was a round sum, and sounded well. That is true, Athos; I am no longer rich. What a memory you have!"

"Tolerably good; yes, thank God!"

"The worthy Planchet!" grumbled D'Artagnan; "his was not a bad dream! What a speculation! Peste! Well! what is said is said."

"How much are you to give him?"

"Oh!" said D'Artagnan, "he is not a bad fellow; I shall arrange matters with him. I have had a great deal of trouble, you see, and expenses; all that must be taken into account."

"My dear friend, I can depend on you, and have no fear for the worthy Planchet; his interests are better in your hands than in his own. But now that you have nothing more to do here, we shall depart, if you please. You can go and thank his majesty, ask if he has any commands, and in six days we may be able to get sight of the towers of Notre Dame."

"My friend, I am most anxious to be off, and will go at once and pay my respects to the king."

"I," said Athos, "am going to call upon some friends in the city, and shall then be at your service."

"Will you lend me Grimaud?"

"With all my heart. What do you want to do with him?"

"Something very simple, and which will not fatigue him; I shall only beg him to take charge of my pistols, which lie there on the table near that coffer."

"Very well!" replied Athos, imperturbably.

"And he will not stir, will he?"

"Not more than the pistols themselves."

"Then I shall go and take leave of his majesty. Au revoir!"

D'Artagnan arrived at St. James's, where Charles II., who was busy writing, kept him in the ante-chamber a full hour. Whilst walking about in the gallery, from the door to the window, from the window to the door, he thought he saw a cloak like Athos's cross the vestibule; but at the moment he was going to ascertain if it were he, the usher summoned him to his majesty's presence. Charles II. rubbed his hands while receiving the thanks of our friend.

"Chevalier," said he, "you are wrong to express gratitude to me; I have not paid you a quarter of the value of the history of the box into which you put the brave general—the excellent Duke of Albemarle, I mean." And the king laughed heartily.

D'Artagnan did not think it proper to interrupt his majesty, and he bowed with much modesty.

"A propos," continued Charles, "do you think my dear Monk has really pardoned you?"

"Pardoned me! yes, I hope so, sire!"

"Eh!—but it was a cruel trick! Odds fish! to pack up the first personage of the English revolution like a herring. In your place I would not trust him, chevalier."

"But, sire—"

"Yes, I know very well Monk calls you his friend, but he has too penetrating an eye not to have a memory, and too lofty a brow not to be very proud, you know, grande supercilium."

"I shall certainly learn Latin," said D'Artagnan to himself.

"But stop," cried the merry monarch, "I must manage your reconciliation; I know how to set about it; so—"

D'Artagnan bit his mustache. "Will your majesty permit me to tell you the truth?"

"Speak, chevalier, speak."

"Well, sire, you alarm me greatly. If your majesty undertakes the affair, as you seem inclined to do, I am a lost man; the duke will have me assassinated."

The king burst into a fresh roar of laughter, which changed D'Artagnan's alarm into downright terror.

"Sire, I beg you to allow me to settle this matter myself, and if your majesty has no further need of my services—"

"No, chevalier. What, do you want to leave us?" replied Charles, with a hilarity that grew more and more alarming.

"If your majesty has no more commands for me."

Charles became more serious.

"One single thing. See my sister, the Lady Henrietta. Do you know her?"

"No, sire, but—an old soldier like me is not an agreeable spectacle for a young and gay princess."

"Ah! but my sister must know you; she must in case of need have you to depend upon."

"Sire, every one that is dear to your majesty will be sacred to me."

"Very well!—Parry! Come here, Parry!"

The side door opened and Parry entered, his face beaming with pleasure as soon as he saw D'Artagnan.

"What is Rochester doing?" said the king.

"He is on the canal with the ladies," replied Parry.

"And Buckingham?"

"He is there also."

"That is well. You will conduct the chevalier to Villiers; that is the Duke of Buckingham, chevalier; and beg the duke to introduce M. d'Artagnan to the Princess Henrietta."

Parry bowed and smiled to D'Artagnan.

"Chevalier," continued the king, "this is your parting audience; you can afterwards set out as soon as you please."

"Sire, I thank you."

"But be sure you make your peace with Monk!"

"Oh, sire—"

"You know there is one of my vessels at your disposal?"

"Sire, you overpower me; I cannot think of putting your majesty's officers to inconvenience on my account."

The king slapped D'Artagnan upon the shoulder.

"Nobody will be inconvenienced on your account, chevalier, but for that of an ambassador I am about sending to France, and to whom you will willingly serve as a companion, I fancy, for you know him."

D'Artagnan appeared astonished.

"He is a certain Comte de la Fere,—whom you call Athos," added the king; terminating the conversation, as he had begun it, by a joyous burst of laughter. "Adieu, chevalier, adieu. Love me as I love you." And thereupon, making a sign to Parry to ask if there were any one waiting for him in the adjoining closet, the king disappeared into that closet, leaving the chevalier perfectly astonished by this singular audience. The old man took his arm in a friendly way, and led him towards the garden.

Chapter XXXV.
On the Canal.

UPON the green waters of the canal bordered with marble, upon which time had already scattered black spots and tufts of mossy grass, there glided majestically a long, flat bark adorned with the arms of England, surmounted by a dais, and carpeted with long damasked stuffs, which trailed their fringes in the water. Eight rowers, leaning lazily to their oars, made it move upon the canal with the graceful slowness of the swans, which, disturbed in their ancient possessions by the approach of the bark, looked from a distance at this splendid and noisy pageant. We say noisy—for the bark contained four guitar and lute players, two singers, and several courtiers, all sparkling with gold and precious stones, and showing their white teeth in emulation of each other, to please the Lady Henrietta Stuart, grand-daughter of Henry IV., daughter of Charles I., and sister of Charles II., who occupied the seat of honor under the dais of the bark. We know this young princess, we have seen her at the Louvre with her mother, wanting wood, wanting bread, and fed by the coadjuteur and the parliament. She had, therefore, like her brothers, passed through an uneasy youth; then, all at once, she had just awakened from a long and horrible dream, seated on the steps of a throne, surrounded by courtiers and flatterers. Like Mary Stuart on leaving prison, she aspired not only to life and liberty, but to power and wealth.

The Lady Henrietta, in growing, had attained remarkable beauty, which the recent restoration had rendered celebrated. Misfortune had taken from her the luster of pride, but prosperity had restored it to her. She was resplendent, then, in her joy and her happiness,—like those hot-house flowers which, forgotten during a frosty autumn night, have hung their heads, but which on the morrow, warmed once more by the atmosphere in which they were born, rise again with greater splendor than ever. Villiers, Duke of Buckingham, son of him who played so conspicuous a part in the early chapters of this history,—Villiers of Buckingham, a handsome cavalier, melancholy with women, a jester with men,—and Wilmot, Lord Rochester, a jester with both sexes, were standing at this moment before the Lady Henrietta, disputing the privilege of making her smile. As to that young and beautiful princess, reclining upon a cushion of velvet bordered with gold, her hands hanging listlessly so as to dip in the water, she listened carelessly to the musicians without hearing them, and heard the two courtiers without appearing to listen to them.

This Lady Henrietta—this charming creature—this woman who joined the graces of France to the beauties of England, not having yet loved, was cruel in her coquetry. The smile, then,—that innocent favor of young girls,—did not even lighten her countenance; and if, at times, she did raise her eyes, it was to fasten them upon one or other of the cavaliers with such a fixity, that their gallantry, bold as it generally was, took the alarm, and became timid.

In the meanwhile the boat continued its course, the musicians made a great noise, and the courtiers began, like them, to be out of breath. Besides, the excursion became doubtless monotonous to the princess, for all at once, shaking her head with an air of impatience,—"Come gentlemen,—enough of this;—let us land."

"Ah, madam," said Buckingham, "we are very unfortunate! We have not succeeded in making the excursion agreeable to your royal highness."

"My mother expects me," replied the princess; "and I must frankly admit, gentlemen, I am bored." And whilst uttering this cruel word, Henrietta endeavored to console by a look each of the two young men, who appeared terrified at such frankness. The look produced its effect—the two faces brightened; but immediately, as if the royal coquette thought she had done too much for simple mortals, she made a movement, turned her back on both her adorers, and appeared plunged in a reverie in which it was evident they had no part.

Buckingham bit his lips with anger, for he was truly in love with the Lady Henrietta, and, in that case, took everything in a serious light. Rochester bit his lips likewise; but his wit always dominated over his heart, it was purely and simply to repress a malicious smile. The princess was then allowing the eyes she turned from the young nobles to wander over the green and flowery turf of the park, when she perceived Parry and D'Artagnan at a distance.

"Who is coming yonder?" said she.

The two young men turned round with the rapidity of lightning.

"Parry," replied Buckingham; "nobody but Parry."

"I beg your pardon," said Rochester, "but I think he has a companion."

"Yes," said the princess, at first with languor, but then,—"What mean those words, 'Nobody but Parry;' say, my lord?"

"Because, madam," replied Buckingham, piqued, "because the faithful Parry, the wandering Parry, the eternal Parry, is not, I believe, of much consequence."

"You are mistaken, duke. Parry—the wandering Parry, as you call him—has always wandered in the service of my family, and the sight of that old man always gives me satisfaction."

The Lady Henrietta followed the usual progress of pretty women, particularly coquettish women; she passed from caprice to contradiction;—

the gallant had undergone the caprice, the courtier must bend beneath the contradictory humor. Buckingham bowed, but made no reply.

"It is true, madam," said Rochester, bowing in his turn, "that Parry is the model of servants; but, madam, he is no longer young, and we laugh only when we see cheerful objects. Is an old man a gay object?"

"Enough, my lord," said the princess, coolly; "the subject of conversation is unpleasant to me."

Then, as if speaking to herself, "It is really unaccountable," said she, "how little regard my brother's friends have for his servants."

"Ah, madam," cried Buckingham, "your royal highness pierces my heart with a dagger forged by your own hands."

"What is the meaning of that speech, which is turned so like a French madrigal, duke? I do not understand it."

"It means, madam, that you yourself, so good, so charming, so sensible, you have laughed sometimes—smiled, I should say—at the idle prattle of that good Parry, for whom your royal highness to-day entertains such a marvelous susceptibility."

"Well, my lord, if I have forgotten myself so far," said Henrietta, "you do wrong to remind me of it." And she made a sign of impatience. "The good Parry wants to speak to me, I believe: please order them to row to the shore, my Lord Rochester."

Rochester hastened to repeat the princess's command; and a moment later the boat touched the bank.

"Let us land, gentlemen," said Henrietta, taking the arm which Rochester offered her, although Buckingham was nearer to her, and had presented his. Then Rochester, with an ill-dissembled pride, which pierced the heart of the unhappy Buckingham through and through, led the princess across the little bridge which the rowers had cast from the royal boat to the shore.

"Which way will your highness go?" asked Rochester.

"You see, my lord, towards that good Parry, who is wandering, as my lord of Buckingham says, and seeking me with eyes weakened by the tears he has shed over our misfortunes."

"Good heavens!" said Rochester, "how sad your royal highness is to-day; in truth we seem ridiculous fools to you, madam."

"Speak for yourself, my lord," interrupted Buckingham with vexation; "for my part, I displease her royal highness to such a degree, that I appear absolutely nothing to her."

Neither Rochester nor the princess made any reply; Henrietta only urged her companion more quickly on. Buckingham remained behind, and took advantage of this isolation to give himself up to his anger; he bit his handkerchief so furiously that it was soon in shreds.

"Parry, my good Parry," said the princess, with her gentle voice, "come hither. I see you are seeking me, and I am waiting for you."

"Ah, madam," said Rochester, coming charitably to the help of his companion, who had remained, as we have said, behind, "if Parry cannot see your royal highness, the man who follows him is a sufficient guide, even for a blind man; for he has eyes of flame. That man is a double-lamped lantern."

"Lighting a very handsome martial countenance," said the princess, determined to be as ill-natured as possible. Rochester bowed. "One of those vigorous soldiers' heads seen nowhere but in France," added the princess, with the perseverance of a woman sure of impunity.

Rochester and Buckingham looked at each other, as much as to say,—"What can be the matter with her?"

"See, my lord of Buckingham, what Parry wants," said Henrietta. "Go!"

The young man, who considered this order as a favor, resumed his courage, and hastened to meet Parry, who, followed by D'Artagnan, advanced slowly on account of his age. D'Artagnan walked slowly but nobly, as D'Artagnan, doubled by the third of a million, ought to walk, that is to say, without conceit or swagger, but without timidity. When Buckingham, very eager to comply with the desire of the princess, who had seated herself on a marble bench, as if fatigued with the few steps she had gone,—when Buckingham, we say, was at a distance of only a few paces from Parry, the latter recognized him.

"Ah! my lord!" cried he, quite out of breath, "will your grace obey the king?"

"In what, Mr. Parry?" said the young man, with a kind of coolness tempered by a desire to make himself agreeable to the princess.

"Well, his majesty begs your grace to present this gentleman to her royal highness the Princess Henrietta."

"In the first place, what is the gentleman's name?" said the duke, haughtily.

D'Artagnan, as we know, was easily affronted, and the Duke of Buckingham's tone displeased him. He surveyed the courtier from head to foot, and two flashes beamed from beneath his bent brows. But, after a struggle,—"Monsieur le Chevalier d'Artagnan, my lord," replied he, quietly.

"Pardon me, sir, that teaches me your name, but nothing more."

"You mean—"

"I mean I do not know you."

"I am more fortunate than you, sir," replied D'Artagnan, "for I have had the honor of knowing your family, and particularly my lord Duke of Buckingham, your illustrious father."

"My father?" said Buckingham. "Well, I think I now remember. Monsieur le Chevalier d'Artagnan, do you say?"

D'Artagnan bowed. "In person," said he.

"Pardon me, but are you one of those Frenchmen who had secret relations with my father?"

"Exactly, my lord duke, I am one of those Frenchmen."

"Then, sir, permit me to say that it was strange my father never heard of you during his lifetime."

"No, monsieur, but he heard of me at the moment of his death: it was I who sent to him, through the hands of the valet de chambre of Anne of Austria, notice of the dangers which threatened him; unfortunately, it came too late."

"Never mind, monsieur," said Buckingham. "I understand now, that, having had the intention of rendering a service to the father, you have come to claim the protection of the son."

"In the first place, my lord," replied D'Artagnan, phlegmatically, "I claim the protection of no man. His majesty, Charles II., to whom I have had the honor of rendering some services—I may tell you, my lord, my life has been passed in such occupations—King Charles II., then, who wishes to honor me with some kindness, desires me to be presented to her royal highness the Princess Henrietta, his sister, to whom I shall, perhaps, have the good fortune to be of service hereafter. Now, the king knew that you at this moment were with her royal highness, and sent me to you. There is no other mystery, I ask absolutely nothing of you; and if you will not present me to her royal highness, I shall be compelled to do without you, and present myself."

"At least, sir," said Buckingham, determined to have the last word, "you will not refuse me an explanation provoked by yourself."

"I never refuse, my lord," said D'Artagnan.

"As you have had relations with my father, you must be acquainted with some private details?"

"These relations are already far removed from us, my lord—for you were not then born—and for some unfortunate diamond studs, which I received from his hands and carried back to France, it is really not worth while awakening so many remembrances."

"Ah! sir," said Buckingham, warmly, going up to D'Artagnan, and holding out his hand to him, "it is you, then—you whom my father sought everywhere and who had a right to expect so much from us."

"To expect, my lord, in truth, that is my forte; all my life I have expected."

At this moment, the princess, who was tired of not seeing the stranger approach her, arose and came towards them.

"At least, sir," said Buckingham, "you shall not wait for the presentation you claim of me."

Then turning towards the princess and bowing: "Madam," said the young man, "the king, your brother, desires me to have the honor of presenting to your royal highness, Monsieur le Chevalier d'Artagnan."

"In order that your royal highness may have, in case of need, a firm support and a sure friend," added Parry. D'Artagnan bowed.

"You have still something to say, Parry," replied Henrietta, smiling upon D'Artagnan, while addressing the old servant.

"Yes, madam, the king desires you to preserve religiously in your memory the name and merit of M. d'Artagnan, to whom his majesty owes, he says, the recovery of his kingdom." Buckingham, the princess, and Rochester looked at each other.

"That," said D'Artagnan, "is another little secret, of which, in all probability, I shall not boast to his majesty's son, as I have done to you with respect to the diamond studs."

"Madam," said Buckingham, "monsieur has just, for the second time, recalled to my memory an event which excites my curiosity to such a degree, that I shall venture to ask your permission to take him to one side for a moment, to converse in private."

"Do, my lord," said the princess; "but restore to the sister, as quickly as possible, this friend so devoted to the brother." And she took the arm of Rochester, whilst Buckingham took that of D'Artagnan.

"Oh! tell me, chevalier," said Buckingham, "all that affair of the diamonds, which nobody knows in England, not even the son of him who was the hero of it."

"My lord, one person alone had a right to relate all that affair, as you call it, and that was your father; he thought it proper to be silent, I must beg you to allow me to be so likewise." And D'Artagnan bowed like a man upon whom it was evident no entreaties could prevail.

"Since it is so, sir," said Buckingham, "pardon my indiscretion, I beg you; and if, at any time, I should go into France—" and he turned round to take a last look at the princess, who took but little notice of him, totally occupied as she was, or appeared to be, with Rochester. Buckingham sighed.

"Well?" said D'Artagnan.

"I was saying that if, any day, I were to go to France—"

"You will go, my lord," said D'Artagnan, "I shall answer for that."

"And how so?"

"Oh, I have strange powers of prediction; if I do predict anything I am seldom mistaken. If, then, you do come to France?"

"Well, then, monsieur, you, of whom kings ask that valuable friendship which restores crowns to them, I will venture to beg of you a little of that great interest you took in my father."

"My lord," replied D'Artagnan, "believe me, I shall deem myself highly honored if, in France, you remember having seen me here. And now permit—"

Then, turning towards the princess: "Madam," said he, "your royal highness is a daughter of France; and in that quality I hope to see you again in Paris. One of my happy days will be on that on which your royal highness shall give me any command whatever, thus proving to me that you have not forgotten the recommendations of your august brother." And he bowed respectfully to the young princess, who gave him her hand to kiss with a right royal grace.

"Ah! madam," said Buckingham, in a subdued voice, "what can a man do to obtain a similar favor from your royal highness?"

"Dame! my lord," replied Henrietta, "ask Monsieur d'Artagnan; he will tell you."

Chapter XXXVI.
How D'Artagnan drew a Country-Seat from a Deal Box.

THE king's words regarding the wounded pride of Monk had inspired D'Artagnan with no small portion of apprehension. The lieutenant had had, all his life, the great art of choosing his enemies; and when he had found them implacable and invincible, it was when he had not been able, under any pretense, to make them otherwise. But points of view change greatly in the course of a life. It is a magic lantern, of which the eye of man every year changes the aspects. It results that from the last day of a year on which we saw white, to the first day of the year on which we shall see black, there is the interval of but a single night.

Now, D'Artagnan, when he left Calais with his ten scamps, would have hesitated as little in attacking a Goliath, a Nebuchadnezzar, or a Holofernes, as he would in crossing swords with a recruit or caviling with a land-lady. Then he resembled the sparrow-hawk, which, when fasting, will attack a ram. Hunger is blind. But D'Artagnan satisfied—D'Artagnan rich—D'Artagnan a conqueror—D'Artagnan proud of so difficult a triumph—D'Artagnan had too much to lose not to reckon, figure by figure, with probable misfortune.

His thoughts were employed, therefore, all the way on the road from his presentation, with one thing, and that was, how he should conciliate a man like Monk, a man whom Charles himself, king as he was, conciliated with difficulty; for, scarcely established, the protected might again stand in need of the protector, and would, consequently, not refuse him, such being the case, the petty satisfaction of transporting M. d'Artagnan, or of confining him in one of the Middlesex prisons, or drowning him a little on his passage from Dover to Boulogne. Such sorts of satisfaction kings are accustomed to render to viceroys without disagreeable consequences.

It would not be at all necessary for the king to be active in that contrepartie of the play in which Monk should take his revenge. The part of the king would be confined to simply pardoning the viceroy of Ireland all he should undertake against D'Artagnan. Nothing more was necessary to place the conscience of the Duke of Albemarle at rest than a te absolvo said with a laugh, or the scrawl of "Charles the King," traced at the foot of a parchment; and with these two words pronounced, and these two words written, poor D'Artagnan was forever crushed beneath the ruins of his imagination.

And then, a thing sufficiently disquieting for a man with such foresight as our musketeer, he found himself alone; and even the friendship of Athos could not restore his confidence. Certainly if the affair had only concerned a free distribution of sword-thrusts, the musketeer would have counted upon his companion; but in delicate dealings with a king, when the perhaps of an unlucky chance should arise in justification of Monk or of Charles of England, D'Artagnan knew Athos well enough to be sure he would give the best possible coloring to the loyalty of the survivor, and would content himself with shedding floods of tears on the tomb of the dead, supposing the dead to be his friend, and afterwards composing his epitaph in the most pompous superlatives.

"Decidedly," thought the Gascon; and this thought was the result of the reflections which he had just whispered to himself and which we have repeated aloud—"decidedly, I must be reconciled with M. Monk, and acquire proof of his perfect indifference for the past. If, and God forbid it should be so! he is still sulky and reserved in the expression of this sentiment, I shall give my money to Athos to take away with him, and remain in England just long enough to unmask him, then, as I have a quick eye and a light foot, I shall notice the first hostile sign; to decamp or conceal myself at the residence of my lord Buckingham, who seems a good sort of devil at the bottom, and to whom, in return for his hospitality, I shall relate all that history of the diamonds, which can now compromise nobody but an old queen, who need not be ashamed, after being the wife of a miserly creature like Mazarin, of having formerly been the mistress of a handsome nobleman like Buckingham. Mordioux! that is the thing, and this Monk shall not get the better of me. Eh? and besides I have an idea!"

We know that, in general, D'Artagnan was not wanting in ideas; and during this soliloquy, D'Artagnan buttoned his vest up to the chin, and nothing excited his imagination like this preparation for a combat of any kind, called accinction by the Romans. He was quite heated when he reached the mansion of the Duke of Albemarle. He was introduced to the viceroy with a promptitude which proved that he was considered as one of the household. Monk was in his business-closet.

"My lord," said D'Artagnan, with that expression of frankness which the Gascon knew so well how to assume, "my lord, I have come to ask your grace's advice!"

Monk, as closely buttoned up morally as his antagonist was physically, replied: "Ask, my friend;" and his countenance presented an expression not less open than that of D'Artagnan.

"My lord, in the first place, promise me secrecy and indulgence."

"I promise you all you wish. What is the matter? Speak!"

"It is, my lord, that I am not quite pleased with the king."

"Indeed! And on what account, my dear lieutenant?"

"Because his majesty gives way sometimes to jests very compromising for his servants; and jesting, my lord, is a weapon that seriously wounds men of the sword, as we are."

Monk did all in his power not to betray his thought, but D'Artagnan watched him with too close attention not to detect an almost imperceptible flush upon his face. "Well, now, for my part," said he, with the most natural air possible, "I am not an enemy of jesting, my dear Monsieur d'Artagnan; my soldiers will tell you that even many times in camp, I listened very indifferently, and with a certain pleasure, to the satirical songs which the army of Lambert passed into mine, and which, certainly, would have caused the ears of a general more susceptible than I am to tingle."

"Oh, my lord," said D'Artagnan, "I know you are a complete man; I know you have been, for a long time, placed above human miseries; but there are jests and jests of a certain kind, which have the power of irritating me beyond expression."

"May I inquire what kind, my friend?"

"Such as are directed against my friends or against people I respect, my lord!"

Monk made a slight movement, which D'Artagnan perceived. "Eh! and in what," asked Monk, "in what can the stroke of a pin which scratches another tickle your skin? Answer me that."

"My lord, I can explain it to you in a single sentence; it concerns you."

Monk advanced a single step towards D'Artagnan. "Concerns me?" said he.

"Yes, and this is what I cannot explain; but that arises, perhaps, from my want of knowledge of his character. How can the king have the heart to jest about a man who has rendered him so many and such great services? How can one understand that he should amuse himself in setting by the ears a lion like you with a gnat like me?"

"I cannot conceive that in any way," said Monk.

"But so it is. The king, who owed me a reward, might have rewarded me as a soldier, without contriving that history of the ransom, which affects you, my lord."

"No," said Monk, laughing: "it does not affect me in any way, I can assure you."

"Not as regards me, I can understand; you know me, my lord, I am so discreet that the grave would appear a babbler compared to me; but—do you understand, my lord?"

"No," replied Monk, with persistent obstinacy.

"If another knew the secret which I know—"

"What secret?"

"Eh! my lord, why, that unfortunate secret of Newcastle."

"Oh! the million of the Comte de la Fere?"

"No, my lord, no; the enterprise made upon your grace's person."

"It was well played, chevalier, that is all, and no more is to be said about it: you are a soldier, both brave and cunning, which proves that you unite the qualities of Fabius and Hannibal. You employed your means, force and cunning: there is nothing to be said against that: I ought to have been on guard."

"Ah! yes; I know, my lord, and I expected nothing less from your partiality; so that if it were only the abduction in itself, Mordioux! that would be nothing; but there are—"

"What?"

"The circumstances of that abduction."

"What circumstances?"

"Oh! you know very well what I mean, my lord."

"No, curse me if I do."

"There is—in truth, it is difficult to speak it."

"There is?"

"Well, there is that devil of a box!"

Monk colored visibly. "Well, I have forgotten it."

"Deal box," continued D'Artagnan, "with holes for the nose and mouth. In truth, my lord, all the rest was well; but the box, the box! that was really a coarse joke." Monk fidgeted about in his chair. "And, notwithstanding my having done that," resumed D'Artagnan, "I, a soldier of fortune, it was quite simple, because by the side of that action, a little inconsiderate I admit, which I committed, but which the gravity of the case may excuse, I am circumspect and reserved."

"Oh!" said Monk, "believe me, I know you well, Monsieur d'Artagnan, and I appreciate you."

D'Artagnan never took his eyes off Monk; studying all which passed in the mind of the general, as he prosecuted his idea. "But it does not concern me," resumed he.

"Well, then, who does it concern?" said Monk, who began to grow a little impatient.

"It relates to the king, who will never restrain his tongue."

"Well! and suppose he should say all he knows?" said Monk, with a degree of hesitation.

"My lord," replied D'Artagnan, "do not dissemble, I implore you, with a man who speaks so frankly as I do. You have a right to feel your susceptibility excited, however benignant it may be. What, the devil! it is not the place for a man like you, a man who plays with crowns and scepters as a Bohemian plays with his balls; it is not the place of a serious man, I said, to be shut up in a box like some freak of natural history; for you must understand it would make all your enemies ready to burst with laughter, and you are so great, so noble, so generous, that you must have many enemies. This secret is enough to set half the human race laughing, if you were represented in that box. It is not decent to have the second personage in the kingdom laughed at."

Monk was quite out of countenance at the idea of seeing himself represented in this box. Ridicule, as D'Artagnan had judiciously foreseen, acted upon him in a manner which neither the chances of war, the aspirations of ambition, nor the fear of death had been able to do.

"Good," thought the Gascon, "he is frightened: I am safe."

"Oh! as to the king," said Monk, "fear nothing, my dear Monsieur d'Artagnan; the king will not jest with Monk, I assure you!"

The momentary flash of his eye was noticed by D'Artagnan. Monk lowered his tone immediately: "The king," continued he, "is of too noble a nature, the king's heart is too high to allow him to wish ill to those who do him good."

"Oh! certainly," cried D'Artagnan. "I am entirely of your grace's opinion with regard to his heart, but not as to his head—it is good, but it is trifling."

"The king will not trifle with Monk, be assured."

"Then you are quite at ease, my lord?"

"On that side, at least! yes, perfectly!"

"Oh! I understand you; you are at ease as far as the king is concerned?"

"I have told you I was."

"But you are not so much so on my account?"

"I thought I had told you that I had faith in your loyalty and discretion."

"No doubt, no doubt, but you must remember one thing—"

"What is that?"

"That I was not alone, that I had companions; and what companions!"

"Oh! yes, I know them."

"And, unfortunately, my lord, they know you, too!"

"Well?"

"Well; they are yonder, at Boulogne, waiting for me."

"And you fear—"

"Yes, I fear that in my absence—Parbleu! If I were near them, I could answer for their silence."

"Was I not right in saying that the danger, if there was any danger, would not come from his majesty, however disposed he may be to jest, but from your companions, as you say? To be laughed at by a king may be tolerable, but by the horse-boys and scamps of the army! Damn it!"

"Yes, I understand, that would be unbearable; that is why, my lord, I came to say,—do you not think it would be better for me to set out for France as soon as possible?"

"Certainly, if you think your presence—"

"Would impose silence upon those scoundrels? Oh! I am sure of that, my lord."

"Your presence will not prevent the report from spreading, if the tale has already transpired."

"Oh! it has not transpired, my lord, I will wager. At all events, be assured that I am determined upon one thing."

"What is that?"

"To blow out the brains of the first who shall have propagated that report, and of the first who has heard it. After which I shall return to England to seek an asylum, and perhaps employment with your grace."

"Oh, come back! come back!"

"Unfortunately, my lord, I am acquainted with nobody here but your grace, and if I should no longer find you, or if you should have forgotten me in your greatness?"

"Listen to me, Monsieur d'Artagnan," replied Monk; "you are a superior man, full of intelligence and courage; you deserve all the good fortune this world can bring you; come with me into Scotland, and, I swear to you, I shall arrange for you a fate which all may envy."

"Oh! my lord, that is impossible. At present I have a sacred duty to perform; I have to watch over your glory, I have to prevent a low jester from tarnishing in the eyes of our contemporaries—who knows? in the eyes of posterity—the splendor of your name."

"Of posterity, Monsieur d'Artagnan?"

"Doubtless. It is necessary, as regards posterity, that all the details of that history should remain a mystery; for, admit that this unfortunate history of the deal box should spread, and it should be asserted that you had not re-established the king loyally, and of your own free will, but in consequence of a compromise entered into at Scheveningen between you two. It would be vain for me to declare how the thing came about, for though I know I should not be believed, it would be said that I had received my part of the cake, and was eating it."

Monk knitted his brow.—"Glory, honor, probity!" said he, "you are but empty words."

"Mist!" replied D'Artagnan; "nothing but mist, through which nobody can see clearly."

"Well, then, go to France, my dear Monsieur d'Artagnan," said Monk; "go, and to render England more attractive and agreeable to you, accept a remembrance of me."

"What now?" thought D'Artagnan.

"I have on the banks of the Clyde," continued Monk, "a little house in a grove, cottage as it is called here. To this house are attached a hundred acres of land. Accept it as a souvenir."

"Oh, my lord!—"

"Faith! you will be there in your own home, and that will be the place of refuge you spoke of just now."

"For me to be obliged to your lordship to such an extent! Really, your grace, I am ashamed."

"Not at all, not at all, monsieur," replied Monk, with an arch smile; "it is I who shall be obliged to you. And," pressing the hand of the musketeer, "I shall go and draw up the deed of gift,"—and he left the room.

D'Artagnan looked at him as he went out with something of a pensive and even an agitated air.

"After all," said he, "he is a brave man. It is only a sad reflection that it is from fear of me, and not affection that he acts thus. Well, I shall endeavor that affection may follow." Then, after an instant's deeper reflection,— "Bah!" said he, "to what purpose? He is an Englishman." And he in turn went out, a little confused after the combat.

"So," said he, "I am a land-owner! But how the devil am I to share the cottage with Planchet? Unless I give him the land, and I take the chateau, or the he takes the house and I—nonsense! M. Monk will never allow me to share a house he has inhabited, with a grocer. He is too proud for that. Besides, why should I say anything about it to him? It was not with the money of the company I have acquired that property, it was with my mother-wit alone; it is all mine, then. So, now I will go and find Athos." And he directed his steps towards the dwelling of the Comte de la Fere.

Chapter XXXVII.
How D'Artagnan regulated the "Assets" of the Company.

"DECIDEDLY," said D'Artagnan to himself, "I have struck a good vein. That star which shines once in the life of every man, which shone for Job and Iris, the most unfortunate of the Jews and the poorest of the Greeks, is come at last to shine on me. I will commit no folly, I will take advantage of it; it comes quite late enough to find me reasonable."

He supped that evening, in very good humor, with his friend Athos; he said nothing to him about the expected donation, but he could not forbear questioning his friend, while eating, about country produce, sowing, and planting. Athos replied complacently, as he always did. His idea was that D'Artagnan wished to become a land-owner, only he could not help regretting, more than once, the absence of the lively humor and amusing sallies of the cheerful companion of former days. In fact, D'Artagnan was so absorbed, that, with his knife, he took advantage of the grease left at the bottom of his plate, to trace ciphers and make additions of surprising rotundity.

The order, or rather license, for their embarkation, arrived at Athos's lodgings that evening. While this paper was remitted to the comte, another messenger brought to D'Artagnan a little bundle of parchments, adorned with all the seals employed in setting off property deeds in England. Athos surprised him turning over the leaves of these different acts which established the transmission of property. The prudent Monk—others would say the generous Monk—had commuted the donation into a sale, and acknowledged the receipt of the sum of fifteen thousand crowns as the price of the property ceded. The messenger was gone. D'Artagnan still continued reading, Athos watched him with a smile. D'Artagnan, surprising one of those smiles over his shoulder, put the bundle in its wrapper.

"I beg your pardon," said Athos.

"Oh! not at all, my friend," replied the lieutenant, "I shall tell you—"

"No, don't tell me anything, I beg you; orders are things so sacred, that to one's brother, one's father, the person charged with such orders should never open his mouth. Thus I, who speak to you, and love you more tenderly than brother, father, or all the world—"

"Except your Raoul?"

"I shall love Raoul still better when he shall be a man, and I shall have seen him develop himself in all the phases of his character and his actions—as I have seen you, my friend."

"You said, then, that you had an order likewise, and that you would not communicate it to me."

"Yes, my dear D'Artagnan."

The Gascon sighed. "There was a time," said he, "when you would have placed that order open upon the table, saying, 'D'Artagnan, read this scrawl to Porthos, Aramis, and to me.'"

"That is true. Oh! that was the time of youth, confidence, the generous season when the blood commands, when it is warmed by feeling!"

"Well! Athos, will you allow me to tell you?"

"Speak, my friend!"

"That delightful time, that generous season, that ruling by warm blood, were all very fine things, no doubt: but I do not regret them at all. It is absolutely like the period of studies. I have constantly met with fools who would boast of the days of pensums, ferules, and crusts of dry bread. It is singular, but I never loved all that; for my part, however active and sober I might be (you know if I was so, Athos), however simple I might appear in my clothes, I would not the less have preferred the braveries and embroideries of Porthos to my little perforated cassock, which gave passage to the wind in winter and the sun in summer. I should always, my friend, mistrust him who would pretend to prefer evil to good. Now, in times past all went wrong with me, and every month found a fresh hole in my cassock and in my skin, a gold crown less in my poor purse; of that execrable time of small beer and seesaw, I regret absolutely nothing, nothing, nothing save our friendship; for within me I have a heart, and it is a miracle that heart has not been dried up by the wind of poverty which passed through all the holes of my cloak, or pierced by the swords of all shapes which passed through the holes in my poor flesh."

"Do not regret our friendship," said Athos, "that will only die with ourselves. Friendship is composed, above all things, of memories and habits, and if you have just now made a little satire upon mine, because I hesitate to tell you the nature of my mission into France—"

"Who! I?—Oh! heavens! if you knew, my dear friend, how indifferent all the missions of the world will henceforth become to me!" And he laid his hand upon the parchment in his vest pocket.

Athos rose from the table and called the host in order to pay the reckoning.

"Since I have known you, my friend," said D'Artagnan, "I have never discharged the reckoning. Porthos often did, Aramis sometimes, and you, you almost always drew out your purse with the dessert. I am now rich, and should like to try if it is heroic to pay."

"Do so," said Athos, returning his purse to his pocket.

The two friends then directed their steps towards the port, not, however, without D'Artagnan's frequently turning round to watch the transportation of his dear crowns. Night had just spread her thick veil over the yellow waters of the Thames; they heard those noises of casks and pulleys, the preliminaries of preparing to sail which had so many times made the hearts of the musketeers beat when the dangers of the sea were the least of those they were going to face. This time they were to embark on board a large vessel which awaited them at Gravesend, and Charles II., always delicate in small affairs, had sent one of his yachts, with twelve men of his Scots guard, to do honor to the ambassador he was sending to France. At midnight the yacht had deposited its passengers on board the vessel, and at eight o'clock in the morning, the vessel landed the ambassador and his friend on the wharf at Boulogne. Whilst the comte, with Grimaud, was busy procuring horses to go straight to Paris, D'Artagnan hastened to the hostelry where, according to his orders, his little army was to wait for him. These gentlemen were at breakfast upon oysters, fish, and spiced brandy, when D'Artagnan appeared. They were all very gay, but not one of them had yet exceeded the bounds of reason. A hurrah of joy welcomed the general. "Here I am," said D'Artagnan, "the campaign is ended. I am come to bring each his supplement of pay, as agreed upon." Their eyes sparkled. "I will lay a wager there are not, at this moment, a hundred crowns remaining in the purse of the richest among you."

"That is true!" cried they in chorus.

"Gentlemen," said D'Artagnan, "then, this is the last order. The treaty of commerce has been concluded, thanks to our coup-de-main which made us masters of the most skillful financier of England, for now I am at liberty to confess to you that the man we had to carry off was the treasurer of General Monk."

This word treasurer produced a certain effect on his army. D'Artagnan observed that the eyes of Menneville alone did not evince perfect faith. "This treasurer," he continued, "I conveyed to a neutral territory, Holland; I forced him to sign the treaty; I have even reconducted him to Newcastle, and he was obliged to be satisfied with our proceedings towards him—the deal coffer being always carried without jolting, and being lined softly, I asked a gratification for you. Here it is." He threw a respectable-looking purse upon the cloth; and all involuntarily stretched out their hands. "One moment, my lambs," said D'Artagnan; "if there are profits, there are also charges."

"Oh! oh!" murmured they.

"We are about to find ourselves, my friends, in a position which would not be tenable for people without brains. I speak plainly; we are between the gallows and the Bastile."

"Oh! Oh!" said the chorus.

"That is easily understood. It was necessary to explain to General Monk the disappearance of his treasurer. I waited, for that purpose, till the unhoped-for moment of the restoration of King Charles II., who is one of my friends."

This army exchanged a glance of satisfaction in reply to the sufficiently proud look of D'Artagnan. "The king being restored, I restored to Monk his man of business, a little plucked, it is true, but, in short, I restored him. Now, General Monk, when he pardoned me, for he has pardoned me, could not help repeating these words to me, which I charge every one of you to engrave deeply there, between the eyes, under the vault of the cranium:—'Monsieur, the joke has been a good one, but I don't naturally like jokes; if ever a word of what you have done' (you understand me, Menneville) 'escapes from your lips, or the lips of your companions, I have, in my government of Scotland and Ireland, seven hundred and forty-one wooden gibbets, of strong oak, clamped with iron, and freshly greased every week. I will make a present of one of these gibbets to each of you, and observe well, M. d'Artagnan,' added he (observe it also, M. Menneville), 'I shall still have seven hundred and thirty left for my private pleasure. And still further—'"

"Ah! ah!" said the auxiliaries, "is there still more?"

"A mere trifle. 'Monsieur d'Artagnan, I send to the king of France the treaty in question, with a request that he will cast into the Bastile provisionally, and then send to me, all who have taken part in this expedition; and that is a prayer with which the king will certainly comply.'"

A cry of terror broke from all corners of the table.

"There! there! there!" said D'Artagnan, "this brave M. Monk has forgotten one thing, and that is he does not know the name of any one of you; I alone know you, and it is not I, you well may believe, who will betray you. Why should I? As for you—I cannot suppose you will be silly enough to denounce yourselves, for then the king, to spare himself the expense of feeding and lodging you, will send you off to Scotland, where the seven hundred and forty-one gibbets are to be found. That is all, messieurs; I have not another word to add to what I have had the honor to tell you. I am sure you have understood me perfectly well, have you not, M. Menneville?"

"Perfectly," replied the latter.

"Now the crowns!" said D'Artagnan. "Shut the doors," he cried, and opened the bag upon the table, from which rolled several fine gold crowns. Every one made a movement towards the floor.

"Gently!" cried D'Artagnan. "Let no one stoop, and then I shall not be out in my reckoning." He found it all right, gave fifty of those splendid crowns to each man, and received as many benedictions as he bestowed pieces. "Now," said he, "if it were possible for you to reform a little, if you could become good and honest citizens—"

"That is rather difficult," said one of the troop.

"What then, captain?" said another.

"Because I might be able to find you again, and, who knows what other good fortune?" He made a sign to Menneville, who listened to all he said with a composed air. "Menneville," said he, "come with me. Adieu, my brave fellows! I need not warn you to be discreet."

Menneville followed him, whilst the salutations of the auxiliaries were mingled with the sweet sound of the money clinking in their pockets.

"Menneville," said D'Artagnan, when they were once in the street, "you were not my dupe; beware of being so. You did not appear to have any fear of the gibbets of Monk, or the Bastile of his majesty, King Louis XIV., but you will do me the favor of being afraid of me. Then listen; at the smallest word that shall escape you, I will kill you as I would a fowl. I have absolution from our holy father, the pope, in my pocket."

"I assure you I know absolutely nothing, my dear M. d'Artagnan, and that your words have all been to me so many articles of faith."

"I was quite sure you were an intelligent fellow," said the musketeer; "I have tried you for a length of time. These fifty crowns which I give you above the rest will prove the esteem I have for you. Take them."

"Thanks, Monsieur d'Artagnan," said Menneville.

"With that sum you can really become an honest man," replied D'Artagnan, in the most serious tone possible. "It would be disgraceful for a mind like yours, and a name you no longer dare to bear, to sink forever under the rust of an evil life. Become a gallant man, Menneville, and live for a year upon those hundred gold crowns: it is a good provision; twice the pay of a high officer. In a year come to me, and, Mordioux! I will make something of you."

Menneville swore, as his comrades had sworn, that he would be as silent as the grave. And yet some one must have spoken; and as, certainly, it was not one of the nine companions, and quite as certainly, it was not Menneville, it must have been D'Artagnan, who, in his quality of a Gascon, had his tongue very near to his lips. For, in short, if it were not he, who could it be? And how can it be explained that the secret of the deal coffer pierced with holes should come to our knowledge, and in so complete a fashion that we have, as has been seen, related the history of it in all its most minute details; details which, besides, throw a light as new as unexpected upon all that portion of the history of England which has been left, up to the present day, completely in darkness by the historian of our neighbors?

Chapter XXXVIII.
the French Grocer had already been established in the Seventeenth Century.

HIS accounts once settled, and his recommendations made, D'Artagnan thought of nothing but returning to Paris as soon as possible. Athos, on his part, was anxious to reach home and to rest a little. However whole the character and the man may remain after the fatigues of a voyage, the traveler perceives with pleasure, at the close of the day—even though the day has been a fine one—that night is approaching, and will bring a little sleep with it. So, from Boulogne to Paris, jogging on, side by side, the two friends, in some degree absorbed each in his individual thoughts, conversed of nothing sufficiently interesting for us to repeat to our readers. Each of them given up to his personal reflections, and constructing his future after his own fashion, was, above all, anxious to abridge the distance by speed. Athos and D'Artagnan arrived at the gates of Paris on the evening of the fourth day after leaving Boulogne.

"Where are you going, my friend?" asked Athos. "I shall direct my course straight to my hotel."

"And I straight to my partner's."

"To Planchet's?"

"Yes; at the Pilon d'Or."

"Well, but shall we not meet again?"

"If you remain in Paris, yes; for I shall stay here."

"No: after having embraced Raoul, with whom I have appointed a meeting at my hotel, I shall set out immediately for La Fere."

"Well, adieu, then, dear and true friend."

"Au revoir! I should rather say, for why can you not come and live with me at Blois? You are free, you are rich, I shall purchase for you, if you like, a handsome estate in the vicinity of Cheverny or of Bracieux. On the one side you will have the finest woods in the world, which join those of Chambord; on the other, admirable marshes. You who love sporting, and who, whether you admit it or not, are a poet, my dear friend, you will find pheasants, rail and teal, without counting sunsets and excursions on the water, to make you fancy yourself Nimrod and Apollo themselves. While awaiting the purchase, you can live at La Fere, and we shall go together to fly our hawks among the vines, as Louis XIII. used to do. That is a quiet amusement for old fellows like us."

D'Artagnan took the hands of Athos in his own. "Dear count," said he, "I shall say neither 'Yes' nor 'No.' Let me pass in Paris the time necessary for the regulation of my affairs, and accustom myself, by degrees, to the heavy and glittering idea which is beating in my brain and dazzles me. I am rich, you see, and from this moment until the time when I shall have acquired the habit of being rich, I know myself, and I shall be an insupportable animal. Now, I am not enough of a fool to wish to appear to have lost my wits before a friend like you, Athos. The cloak is handsome, the cloak is richly gilded, but it is new, and does not seem to fit me."

Athos smiled. "So be it," said he. "But a propos of this cloak, dear D'Artagnan, will you allow me to offer you a little advice?"

"Yes, willingly."

"You will not be angry?"

"Proceed."

"When wealth comes to a man late in life or all at once, that man, in order not to change, must most likely become a miser—that is to say, not spend much more money than he had done before; or else become a prodigal, and contract so many debts as to become poor again."

"Oh! but what you say looks very much like a sophism, my dear philosophic friend."

"I do not think so. Will you become a miser?"

"No, pardieu! I was one already, having nothing. Let us change."

"Then be prodigal."

"Still less, Mordioux! Debts terrify me. Creditors appear to me, by anticipation, like those devils who turn the damned upon the gridirons, and as patience is not my dominant virtue, I am always tempted to thrash those devils."

"You are the wisest man I know, and stand in no need of advice from any one. Great fools must they be who think they have anything to teach you. But are we not at the Rue Saint Honore?"

"Yes, dear Athos."

"Look yonder, on the left, that small, long white house is the hotel where I lodge. You may observe that it has but two stories; I occupy the first; the other is let to an officer whose duties oblige him to be absent eight or nine months in the year,—so I am in that house as in my own home, without the expense."

"Oh! how well you manage, Athos! What order and what liberality! They are what I wish to unite! But, of what use trying! that comes from birth, and cannot be acquired."

"You are a flatterer! Well! adieu, dear friend. A propos, remember me to Master Planchet; he always was a bright fellow."

"And a man of heart, too, Athos. Adieu."

And the separated. During all this conversation, D'Artagnan had not for a moment lost sight of a certain pack-horse, in whose panniers, under some hay, were spread the sacoches (messenger's bags) with the portmanteau. Nine o'clock was striking at Saint-Merri. Planchet's helps were shutting up his shop. D'Artagnan stopped the postilion who rode the pack-horse, at the corner of the Rue des Lombards, under a pent-house, and calling one of Planchet's boys, he desired him not only to take care of the two horses, but to watch the postilion; after which he entered the shop of the grocer, who had just finished supper, and who, in his little private room, was, with a degree of anxiety, consulting the calendar, on which, every evening, he scratched out the day that was past. At the moment when Planchet, according to his daily custom, with the back of his pen, erased another day, D'Artagnan kicked the door with his foot, and the blow made his steel spur jingle. "Oh! good Lord!" cried Planchet. The worthy grocer could say no more; he had just perceived his partner. D'Artagnan entered with a bent back and a dull eye: the Gascon had an idea with regard to Planchet.

"Good God!" thought the grocer, looking earnestly at the traveler, "he looks sad!" The musketeer sat down.

"My dear Monsieur d'Artagnan!" said Planchet, with a horrible palpitation of the heart. "Here you are! and your health?"

"Tolerably good, Planchet, tolerably good!" said D'Artagnan, with a profound sigh.

"You have not been wounded, I hope?"

"Phew!"

"Ah, I see," continued Planchet, more and more alarmed, "the expedition has been a trying one?"

"Yes," said D'Artagnan. A shudder ran down Planchet's back. "I should like to have something to drink," said the musketeer, raising his head piteously.

Planchet ran to the cupboard, and poured out to D'Artagnan some wine in a large glass. D'Artagnan examined the bottle.

"What wine is that?" asked he.

"Alas! that which you prefer, monsieur," said Planchet; "that good old Anjou wine, which was one day nearly costing us all so dear."

"Ah!" replied D'Artagnan, with a melancholy smile, "Ah! my poor Planchet, ought I still to drink good wine?"

"Come! my dear master," said Planchet, making a super-human effort, whilst all his contracted muscles, his pallor and his trembling betrayed the most acute anguish. "Come! I have been a soldier and consequently have some courage; do not make me linger, dear Monsieur d'Artagnan; our money is lost, is it not?"

Before he answered, D'Artagnan took his time, and that appeared an age to the poor grocer. Nevertheless he did nothing but turn about on his chair.

"And if that were the case," said he, slowly, moving his head up and down, "if that were the case, what would you say, my dear friend?"

Planchet, from being pale, turned yellow. It might have been thought he was going to swallow his tongue, so full became his throat, so red were his eyes!

"Twenty thousand livres!" murmured he. "Twenty thousand livres, and yet—"

D'Artagnan, with his neck elongated, his legs stretched out, and his hands hanging listlessly, looked like a statue of discouragement. Planchet drew up a sigh from the deepest cavities of his breast.

"Well," said he, "I see how it is. Let us be men! It is all over, is it not? The principal thing is, monsieur, that your life is safe."

"Doubtless! doubtless!—life is something—but I am ruined!"

"Cordieu! monsieur!" said Planchet, "If it is so, we must not despair for that; you shall become a grocer with me; I shall take you for my partner, we will share the profits, and if there should be no more profits, well, why then we shall share the almonds, raisins and prunes, and we will nibble together the last quarter of Dutch cheese."

D'Artagnan could hold out no longer. "Mordioux!" cried he, with great emotion, "thou art a brave fellow, on my honor, Planchet. You have not been playing a part, have you? You have not seen the pack-horse with the bags under the shed yonder?"

"What horse? What bags?" said Planchet, whose trembling heart began to suggest that D'Artagnan was mad.

"Why, the English bags, Mordioux!" said D'Artagnan, all radiant, quite transfigured.

"Ah! good God!" articulated Planchet, drawing back before the dazzling fire of his looks.

"Imbecile!" cried D'Artagnan, "you think me mad! Mordioux! On the contrary, never was my head more clear, or my heart more joyous. To the bags, Planchet, to the bags!"

"But to what bags, good heavens!"

D'Artagnan pushed Planchet towards the window.

"Under that shed yonder, don't you see a horse?"

"Yes."

"Don't you see how his back is laden?"

"Yes, yes!"

"Don't you see your lad talking with the postilion?"

"Yes, yes, yes!"

"Well, you know the name of that lad, because he is your own. Call him."

"Abdon! Abdon!" vociferated Planchet, from the window.

"Bring the horse!" shouted D'Artagnan.

"Bring the horse!" screamed Planchet.

"Now give ten livres to the postilion," said D'Artagnan, in the tone he would have employed in commanding a maneuver; "two lads to bring up the first two bags, two to bring up the two last,—and move, Mordioux! be lively!"

Planchet rushed down the stairs, as if the devil had been at his heels. A moment later the lads ascended the stairs, bending beneath their burden. D'Artagnan sent them off to their garrets, carefully closed the door, and addressing Planchet, who, in his turn, looked a little wild,—

"Now, we are by ourselves," said he; and he spread upon the floor a large cover, and emptied the first bag into it. Planchet did the same with the second; then D'Artagnan, all in a tremble, let out the precious bowels of the third with a knife. When Planchet heard the provoking sound of the silver and gold—when he saw bubbling out of the bags the shining crowns, which glittered like fish from the sweep-net—when he felt himself plunging his hands up to the elbows in that still rising tide of yellow and white coins, a giddiness seized him, and like a man struck by lightning, he sank heavily down upon the enormous heap, which his weight caused to roll away in all directions. Planchet, suffocated with joy, had lost his senses. D'Artagnan threw a glass of white wine in his face, which incontinently recalled him to life.

"Ah! good heavens! good heavens! good heavens!" said Planchet, wiping his mustache and beard.

At that time, as they do now, grocers wore the cavalier mustache and the lansquenet beard, only the money baths, already rare in those days, have become almost unknown now.

"Mordioux!" said D'Artagnan, "there are a hundred thousand livres for you, partner. Draw your share, if you please, and I will draw mine."

"Oh! the lovely sum! Monsieur d'Artagnan, the lovely sum!"

"I confess that half an hour ago I regretted that I had to give you so much; but now I no longer regret it; thou art a brave grocer, Planchet. There, let us close our accounts, for, as they say, short reckonings make long friends."

"Oh! rather, in the first place, tell me the whole history," said Planchet; "that must be better than the money."

"Ma foi!" said D'Artagnan, stroking his mustache, "I can't say no; and if ever the historian turns to me for information, he will be able to say he has not dipped his bucket into a dry spring. Listen, then, Planchet, I will tell you all about it."

"And I shall build piles of crowns," said Planchet. "Begin, my dear master."

"Well, this is it," said D'Artagnan, drawing his breath.

"And that is it," said Planchet, picking up his first handful of crowns.

Chapter XXXIX.
Mazarin's Gaming Party.

IN a large chamber of the Palais Royal, hung with a dark colored velvet, which threw into strong relief the gilded frames of a great number of magnificent pictures, on the evening of the arrival of the two Frenchmen, the whole court was assembled before the alcove of M. le Cardinal de Mazarin, who gave a card party to the king and queen.

A small screen separated three prepared tables. At one of these tables the king and the two queens were seated. Louis XIV., placed opposite to the young queen, his wife, smiled upon her with an expression of real happiness. Anne of Austria held the cards against the cardinal, and her daughter-in-law assisted her in the game, when she was not engaged in smiling at her husband. As for the cardinal, who was lying on his bed with a weary and careworn face, his cards were held by the Comtesse de Soissons, and he watched them with an incessant look of interest and cupidity.

The cardinal's face had been painted by Bernouin; but the rouge, which glowed only on his cheeks, threw into stronger contrast the sickly pallor of his countenance and the shining yellow of his brow. His eyes alone acquired a more brilliant luster from this auxiliary, and upon those sick man's eyes were, from time to time, turned the uneasy looks of the king, the queen, and the courtiers. The fact is, that the two eyes of the Signor Mazarin were the stars more or less brilliant in which the France of the seventeenth century read its destiny every evening and every morning.

Monseigneur neither won nor lost; he was, therefore, neither gay nor sad. It was a stagnation in which, full of pity for him, Anne of Austria would not have willingly left him; but in order to attract the attention of the sick man by some brilliant stroke, she must have either won or lost. To win would have been dangerous, because Mazarin would have changed his indifference into an ugly grimace; to lose would likewise have been dangerous, because she must have cheated, and the infanta, who watched her game, would, doubtless, have exclaimed against her partiality for Mazarin. Profiting by this calm, the courtiers were chatting. When not in a bad humor, M. de Mazarin was a very debonnaire prince, and he, who prevented nobody from singing, provided they paid, was not tyrant enough to prevent people from talking, provided they made up their minds to lose.

They were therefore chatting. At the first table, the king's younger brother, Philip, Duc d'Anjou, was admiring his handsome face in the glass of a box. His favorite, the Chevalier de Lorraine, leaning over the back of the prince's chair, was listening, with secret envy, to the Comte de Guiche, another of Philip's favorites, who was relating in choice terms the various vicissitudes of fortune of the royal adventurer Charles II. He told, as so many fabulous events, all the history of his perigrinations in Scotland, and his terrors when the enemy's party was so closely on his track; of nights spent in trees, and days spent in hunger and combats. By degrees, the fate of the unfortunate king interested his auditors so greatly, that the play languished even at the royal table, and the young king, with a pensive look and downcast eye, followed, without appearing to give any attention to it, the smallest details of this Odyssey, very picturesquely related by the Comte de Guiche.

The Comtesse de Soissons interrupted the narrator: "Confess, count, you are inventing."

"Madame, I am repeating like a parrot all the stories related to me by different Englishmen. To my shame I am compelled to say, I am as exact as a copy."

"Charles II. would have died before he could have endured all that."

Louis XIV. raised his intelligent and proud head. "Madame," said he, in a grave tone, still partaking something of the timid child, "monsieur le cardinal will tell you that during my minority the affairs of France were in jeopardy,— and that if I had been older, and obliged to take sword in hand, it would sometimes have been for the purpose of procuring the evening meal."

"Thanks to God," said the cardinal, who spoke for the first time, "your majesty exaggerates, and your supper has always been ready with that of your servants."

The king colored.

"Oh!" cried Philip, inconsiderately, from his place, and without ceasing to admire himself,—"I recollect once, at Melun, the supper was laid for nobody, and that the king ate two-thirds of a slice of bread, and abandoned to me the other third."

The whole assembly, seeing Mazarin smile, began to laugh. Courtiers flatter kings with the remembrance of past distresses, as with the hopes of future good fortune.

"It is not to be denied that the crown of France has always remained firm upon the heads of its kings," Anne of Austria hastened to say, "and that it has fallen off of that of the king of England; and when by chance that crown oscillated a little,—for there are throne-quakes as well as earthquakes,— every time, I say, that rebellion threatened it, a good victory restored tranquillity."

"With a few gems added to the crown," said Mazarin.

The Comte de Guiche was silent: the king composed his countenance, and Mazarin exchanged looks with Anne of Austria, as if to thank her for her intervention.

"It is of no consequence," said Philip, smoothing his hair; "my cousin Charles is not handsome, but he is very brave, and fought like a landsknecht; and if he continues to fight thus, no doubt he will finish by gaining a battle, like Rocroi—"

"He has no soldiers," interrupted the Chevalier de Lorraine.

"The king of Holland, his ally, will give him some. I would willingly have given him some if I had been king of France."

Louis XIV. blushed excessively. Mazarin affected to be more attentive to his game than ever.

"By this time," resumed the Comte de Guiche, "the fortune of this unhappy prince is decided. If he has been deceived by Monk, he is ruined. Imprisonment, perhaps death, will finish what exiles, battles, and privations have commenced."

Mazarin's brow became clouded.

"It is certain," said Louis XIV., "that his majesty Charles II., has quitted the Hague?"

"Quite certain, your majesty," replied the young man; "my father has received a letter containing all the details; it is even known that the king has landed at Dover; some fishermen saw him entering the port; the rest is still a mystery."

"I should like to know the rest," said Philip, impetuously. "You know,—you, my brother."

Louis XIV. colored again. That was the third time within an hour. "Ask my lord cardinal," replied he, in a tone which made Mazarin, Anne of Austria, and everybody else open their eyes.

"That means, my son," said Anne of Austria, laughing, "that the king does not like affairs of state to be talked of out of the council."

Philip received the reprimand with good grace, and bowed, first smiling at his brother, and then at his mother. But Mazarin saw from the corner of his eye that a group was about to be formed in the corner of the room, and that the Duc d'Anjou, with the Comte de Guiche, and the Chevalier de Lorraine, prevented from talking aloud, might say, in a whisper, what it was not convenient should be said. He was beginning, then, to dart at them glances full of mistrust and uneasiness, inviting Anne of Austria to throw perturbation in the midst of the unlawful assembly, when, suddenly, Bernouin, entering from behind the tapestry of the bedroom, whispered in the ear of Mazarin, "Monseigneur, an envoy from his majesty, the king of England."

Mazarin could not help exhibiting a slight emotion, which was perceived by the king. To avoid being indiscreet, rather than to appear useless, Louis XIV. rose immediately, and approaching his eminence, wished him good-night. All the assembly had risen with a great noise of rolling of chairs and tables being pushed away.

"Let everybody depart by degrees," said Mazarin in a whisper to Louis XIV., "and be so good as to excuse me a few minutes. I am going to dispatch an affair about which I wish to converse with your majesty this very evening."

"And the queens?" asked Louis XIV.

"And M. le Duc d'Anjou," said his eminence.

At the same time he turned round in his ruelle, the curtains of which, in falling, concealed the bed. The cardinal, nevertheless, did not lose sight of the conspirators.

"M. le Comte de Guiche," said he, in a fretful voice, whilst putting on, behind the curtain, his dressing-gown, with the assistance of Bernouin.

"I am here, my lord," said the young man, as he approached.

"Take my cards, you are lucky. Win a little money for me of these gentlemen."

"Yes, my lord."

The young man sat down at the table from which the king withdrew to talk with the two queens. A serious game was commenced between the comte and several rich courtiers. In the meantime Philip was discussing the questions of dress with the Chevalier de Lorraine, and they had ceased to hear the rustling of the cardinal's silk robe from behind the curtain. His eminence had followed Bernouin into the closet adjoining the bedroom.

Chapter XL.
An Affair of State.

THE cardinal, on passing into his cabinet, found the Comte de la Fere, who was waiting for him, engaged in admiring a very fine Raphael placed over a sideboard covered with a plate. His eminence came in softly, lightly, and as silently as a shadow, and surprised the countenance of the comte, as he was accustomed to do, pretending to divine by the simple expression of the face of his interlocutor what would be the result of the conversation.

But this time Mazarin was foiled in his expectation: he read nothing upon the face of Athos, not even the respect he was accustomed to see on all faces. Athos was dressed in black, with a simple lacing of silver. He wore the Holy Ghost, the Garter, and the Golden Fleece, three orders of such importance, that a king alone, or else a player, could wear them at once.

Mazarin rummaged a long time in his somewhat troubled memory to recall the name he ought to give to this icy figure, but he did not succeed. "I am told," said he, at length, "you have a message from England for me."

And he sat down, dismissing Bernouin, who, in his quality of secretary, was getting his pen ready.

"On the part of his majesty, the king of England, yes, your eminence."

"You speak very good French for an Englishman, monsieur," said Mazarin, graciously, looking through his fingers at the Holy Ghost, Garter, and Golden Fleece, but more particularly at the face of the messenger.

"I am not an Englishman, but a Frenchman, monsieur le cardinal," replied Athos.

"It is remarkable that the king of England should choose a Frenchman for his ambassador; it is an excellent augury. Your name, monsieur, if you please."

"Comte de la Fere," replied Athos, bowing more slightly than the ceremonial and pride of the all-powerful minister required.

Mazarin bent his shoulders, as if to say:—

"I do not know that name."

Athos did not alter his carriage.

"And you come, monsieur," continued Mazarin, "to tell me—"

"I come on the part of his majesty the king of Great Britain to announce to the king of France"—Mazarin frowned—"to announce to the king of

France," continued Athos, imperturbably, "the happy restoration of his majesty Charles II. to the throne of his ancestors."

This shade did not escape his cunning eminence. Mazarin was too much accustomed to mankind, not to see in the cold and almost haughty politeness of Athos, an index of hostility, which was not of the temperature of that hothouse called a court.

"You have powers, I suppose?" asked Mazarin, in a short, querulous tone.

"Yes, monseigneur." And the word "monseigneur" came so painfully from the lips of Athos that it might be said it skinned them.

Athos took from an embroidered velvet bag which he carried under his doublet a dispatch. The cardinal held out his hand for it. "Your pardon, monseigneur," said Athos. "My dispatch is for the king."

"Since you are a Frenchman, monsieur, you ought to know the position of a prime minister at the court of France."

"There was a time," replied Athos, "when I occupied myself with the importance of prime ministers; but I have formed, long ago, a resolution to treat no longer with any but the king."

"Then, monsieur," said Mazarin, who began to be irritated, "you will neither see the minister nor the king."

Mazarin rose. Athos replaced his dispatch in its bag, bowed gravely, and made several steps towards the door. This coolness exasperated Mazarin. "What strange diplomatic proceedings are these!" cried he. "Have we returned to the times when Cromwell sent us bullies in the guise of charges d'affaires? You want nothing, monsieur, but the steel cap on your head, and a Bible at your girdle."

"Monsieur," said Athos, dryly, "I have never had, as you have, the advantage of treating with Cromwell; and I have only seen his charges d'affaires sword in hand; I am therefore ignorant of how he treated with prime ministers. As for the king of England, Charles II., I know that when he writes to his majesty King Louis XIV., he does not write to his eminence the Cardinal Mazarin. I see no diplomacy in that distinction."

"Ah!" cried Mazarin, raising his attenuated hand, and striking his head, "I remember now!" Athos looked at him in astonishment. "Yes, that is it!" said the cardinal, continuing to look at his interlocutor; "yes, that is certainly it. I know you now, monsieur. Ah! diavolo! I am no longer astonished."

"In fact, I was astonished that, with your eminence's excellent memory," replied Athos, smiling, "you had not recognized me before."

"Always refractory and grumbling—monsieur—monsieur—What do they call you? Stop—a name of a river—Potamos; no—the name of an island—Naxos; no, per Giove!—the name of a mountain—Athos! now I have it. Delighted to see you again, and to be no longer at Rueil, where you and your damned companions made me pay ransom. Fronde! still Fronde! accursed Fronde! Oh, what grudges! Why, monsieur, have your antipathies survived mine? If any one has cause to complain, I think it could not be you, who got out of the affair not only in a sound skin, but with the cordon of the Holy Ghost around your neck."

"My lord cardinal," replied Athos, "permit me not to enter into considerations of that kind. I have a mission to fulfill. Will you facilitate the means of my fulfilling that mission, or will you not?"

"I am astonished," said Mazarin,—quite delighted at having recovered his memory, and bristling with malice,—"I am astonished, Monsieur—Athos—that a Frondeur like you should have accepted a mission for the Perfidious Mazarin, as used to be said in the good old times—" And Mazarin began to laugh, in spite of a painful cough, which cut short his sentences, converting them into sobs.

"I have only accepted the mission near the king of France, monsieur le cardinal," retorted the comte, though with less asperity, for he thought he had sufficiently the advantage to show himself moderate.

"And yet, Monsieur le Frondeur," said Mazarin, gayly, "the affair which you have taken in charge must, from the king—"

"With which I have been given in charge, monseigneur. I do not run after affairs."

"Be it so. I say that this negotiation must pass through my hands. Let us lose no precious time, then. Tell me the conditions."

"I have had the honor of assuring your eminence that only the letter of his majesty King Charles II. contains the revelation of his wishes."

"Pooh! you are ridiculous with your obstinacy, Monsieur Athos. It is plain you have kept company with the Puritans yonder. As to your secret, I know it better than you do; and you have done wrongly, perhaps, in not having shown some respect for a very old and suffering man, who has labored much during his life, and kept the field for his ideas as bravely as you have for yours. You will not communicate your letter to me? You will say nothing to me? Very well! Come with me into my chamber; you shall speak to the king—and before the king.—Now, then, one last word: who gave you the Fleece? I remember you passed for having the Garter; but as to the Fleece, I do not know—"

"Recently, my lord, Spain, on the occasion of the marriage of his majesty Louis XIV., sent King Charles II. a brevet of the Fleece in blank; Charles II. immediately transmitted it to me, filling up the blank with my name."

Mazarin arose, and leaning on the arm of Bernouin, he returned to his ruelle at the moment the name of M. le Prince was being announced. The Prince de Conde, the first prince of the blood, the conqueror of Rocroi, Lens, and Nordlingen, was, in fact, entering the apartment of Monseigneur de Mazarin, followed by his gentlemen, and had already saluted the king, when the prime minister raised his curtain. Athos had time to see Raoul pressing the hand of the Comte de Guiche, and send him a smile in return for his respectful bow. He had time, likewise, to see the radiant countenance of the cardinal, when he perceived before him, upon the table, an enormous heap of gold, which the Comte de Guiche had won in a run of luck, after his eminence had confided his cards to him. So forgetting ambassador, embassy and prince, his first thought was of the gold. "What!" cried the old man—"all that— won?"

"Some fifty thousand crowns; yes, monseigneur," replied the Comte de Guiche, rising. "Must I give up my place to your eminence, or shall I continue?"

"Give up! give up! you are mad. You would lose all you have won. Peste!"

"My lord!" said the Prince de Conde, bowing.

"Good-evening, monsieur le prince," said the minister, in a careless tone; "it is very kind of you to visit an old sick friend."

"A friend!" murmured the Comte de la Fere, at witnessing with stupor this monstrous alliance of words;—"friends! when the parties are Conde and Mazarin!"

Mazarin seemed to divine the thoughts of the Frondeur, for he smiled upon him with triumph, and immediately,—"Sire," said he to the king, "I have the honor of presenting to your majesty, Monsieur le Comte de la Fere, ambassador from his Britannic majesty. An affair of state, gentlemen," added he, waving his hand to all who filled the chamber, and who, the Prince de Conde at their head, all disappeared at the simple gesture. Raoul, after a last look cast at the comte, followed M. de Conde. Philip of Anjou and the queen appeared to be consulting about departing.

"A family affair," said Mazarin, suddenly, detaining them in their seats. "This gentleman is the bearer of a letter in which King Charles II., completely restored to his throne, demands an alliance between Monsieur, the brother of the king, and Mademoiselle Henrietta, grand-daughter of Henry IV. Will you remit your letter of credit to the king, monsieur le comte?"

Athos remained for a minute stupefied. How could the minister possibly know the contents of the letter, which had never been out of his keeping for a single instant? Nevertheless, always master of himself, he held out the dispatch to the young king, Louis XIV., who took it with a blush. A solemn silence reigned in the cardinal's chamber. It was only troubled by the dull sound of the gold, which Mazarin, with his yellow, dry hand, piled up in a casket, whilst the king was reading.

Chapter XLI.
The Recital.

THE maliciousness of the cardinal did not leave much for the ambassador to say; nevertheless, the word "restoration" had struck the king, who, addressing the comte, upon whom his eyes had been fixed since his entrance,—"Monsieur," said he, "will you have the kindness to give us some details concerning the affairs of England. You come from that country, you are a Frenchman, and the orders which I see glittering upon your person announce you to be a man of merit as well as a man of quality."

"Monsieur," said the cardinal, turning towards the queen-mother, "is an ancient servant of your majesty's, Monsieur le Comte de la Fere."

Anne of Austria was as oblivious as a queen whose life had been mingled with fine and stormy days. She looked at Mazarin, whose evil smile promised her something disagreeable; then she solicited from Athos, by another look, an explanation.

"Monsieur," continued the cardinal, "was a Treville musketeer, in the service of the late king. Monsieur is well acquainted with England, whither he has made several voyages at various periods; he is a subject of the highest merit."

These words made allusion to all the memories which Anne of Austria trembled to evoke. England, that was her hatred of Richelieu and her love for Buckingham; a Treville musketeer, that was the whole Odyssey of the triumphs which had made the heart of the young woman throb, and of the dangers which had been so near overturning the throne of the young queen. These words had much power, for they rendered mute and attentive all the royal personages, who, with very various sentiments, set about recomposing at the same time the mysteries which the young had not seen, and which the old had believed to be forever effaced.

"Speak, monsieur," said Louis XIV., the first to escape from troubles, suspicions, and remembrances.

"Yes, speak," added Mazarin, to whom the little malicious thrust directed against Anne of Austria had restored energy and gayety.

"Sire," said the comte, "a sort of miracle has changed the whole destiny of Charles II. That which men, till that time, had been unable to do, God resolved to accomplish."

Mazarin coughed while tossing about in his bed.

"King Charles II.," continued Athos, "left the Hague neither as a fugitive nor a conqueror, but as an absolute king, who, after a distant voyage from his kingdom, returns amidst universal benedictions."

"A great miracle, indeed," said Mazarin; "for, if the news was true, King Charles II., who has just returned amidst benedictions, went away amidst musket-shots."

The king remained impassible. Philip, younger and more frivolous, could not repress a smile, which flattered Mazarin as an applause of his pleasantry.

"It is plain," said the king, "there is a miracle; but God, who does so much for kings, monsieur le comte, nevertheless employs the hand of man to bring about the triumph of His designs. To what men does Charles II. principally owe his re-establishment?"

"Why," interrupted Mazarin, without any regard for the king's pride—"does not your majesty know that it is to M. Monk?"

"I ought to know it," replied Louis XIV., resolutely; "and yet I ask my lord ambassador, the causes of the change in this General Monk?"

"And your majesty touches precisely the question," replied Athos; "for without the miracle of which I have had the honor to speak, General Monk would probably have remained an implacable enemy of Charles II. God willed that a strange, bold, and ingenious idea should enter into the mind of a certain man, whilst a devoted and courageous idea took possession of the mind of another man. The combinations of these two ideas brought about such a change in the position of M. Monk, that, from an inveterate enemy, he became a friend to the deposed king."

"These are exactly the details I asked for," said the king. "Who and what are the two men of whom you speak?"

"Two Frenchmen, sire."

"Indeed! I am glad of that."

"And the two ideas," said Mazarin;—"I am more curious about ideas than about men, for my part."

"Yes," murmured the king.

"The second idea, the devoted, reasonable idea—the least important, sir—was to go and dig up a million in gold, buried by King Charles I. at Newcastle, and to purchase with that gold the adherence of Monk."

"Oh, oh!" said Mazarin, reanimated by the word million. "But Newcastle was at the time occupied by Monk."

"Yes, monsieur le cardinal, and that is why I venture to call the idea courageous as well as devoted. It was necessary, if Monk refused the offers of the negotiator, to reinstate King Charles II. in possession of this million, which was to be torn, as it were, from the loyalty and not the loyalism of General Monk. This was effected in spite of many difficulties: the general proved to be loyal, and allowed the money to be taken away."

"It seems to me," said the timid, thoughtful king, "that Charles II. could not have known of this million whilst he was in Paris."

"It seems to me," rejoined the cardinal, maliciously, "that his majesty the king of Great Britain knew perfectly well of this million, but that he preferred having two millions to having one."

"Sire," said Athos, firmly, "the king of England, whilst in France, was so poor that he had not even money to take the post; so destitute of hope that he frequently thought of dying. He was so entirely ignorant of the existence of the million at Newcastle, that but for a gentleman—one of your majesty's subjects—the moral depositary of the million, who revealed the secret to King Charles II., that prince would still be vegetating in the most cruel forgetfulness."

"Let us pass on to the strange, bold and ingenious idea," interrupted Mazarin, whose sagacity foresaw a check. "What was that idea?"

"This—M. Monk formed the only obstacle to the re-establishment of the fallen king. A Frenchman imagined the idea of suppressing this obstacle."

"Oh! oh! but he is a scoundrel, that Frenchman," said Mazarin; "and the idea is not so ingenious as to prevent its author being tied up by the neck at the Place de Greve, by decree of the parliament."

"Your eminence is mistaken," replied Athos, dryly; "I did not say that the Frenchman in question had resolved to assassinate M. Monk, but only to suppress him. The words of the French language have a value which the gentlemen of France know perfectly. Besides, this is an affair of war; and when men serve kings against their enemies they are not to be condemned by a parliament—God is their judge. This French gentleman, then, formed the idea of gaining possession of the person of Monk, and he executed his plan."

The king became animated at the recital of great actions. The king's younger brother struck the table with his hand, exclaiming, "Ah! that is fine!"

"He carried off Monk?" said the king. "Why, Monk was in his camp."

"And the gentleman was alone, sire."

"That is marvelous!" said Philip.

"Marvelous, indeed!" cried the king.

"Good! There are the two little lions unchained," murmured the cardinal. And with an air of spite, which he did not dissemble: "I am unacquainted with these details, will you guarantee their authenticity, monsieur?"

"All the more easily, my lord cardinal, from having seen the events."

"You have?"

"Yes, monseigneur."

The king had involuntarily drawn close to the count, the Duc d'Anjou had turned sharply round, and pressed Athos on the other side.

"What next? monsieur, what next?" cried they both at the same time.

"Sire, M. Monk, being taken by the Frenchman, was brought to King Charles II., at the Hague. The king gave back his freedom to Monk, and the grateful general, in return, gave Charles II. the throne of Great Britain, for which so many valiant men had fought in vain."

Philip clapped his hands with enthusiasm, Louis XIV., more reflective, turned towards the Comte de la Fere.

"Is this true," said he, "in all its details?"

"Absolutely true, sire."

"That one of my gentlemen knew the secret of the million, and kept it?"

"Yes, sire."

"The name of that gentleman?"

"It was your humble servant," said Athos, simply, and bowing.

A murmur of admiration made the heart of Athos swell with pleasure. He had reason to be proud, at least. Mazarin, himself, had raised his arms towards heaven.

"Monsieur," said the king, "I shall seek and find means to reward you." Athos made a movement. "Oh, not for your honesty, to be paid for that would humiliate you; but I owe you a reward for having participated in the restoration of my brother, King Charles II."

"Certainly," said Mazarin.

"It is the triumph of a good cause which fills the whole house of France with joy," said Anne of Austria.

"I continue," said Louis XIV.: "Is it also true that a single man penetrated to Monk, in his camp, and carried him off?"

"That man had ten auxiliaries, taken from a very inferior rank."

"And nothing more but them?"

"Nothing more."

"And he is named?"

"Monsieur d'Artagnan, formerly lieutenant of the musketeers of your majesty."

Anne of Austria colored; Mazarin became yellow with shame; Louis XIV. was deeply thoughtful, and a drop of moisture fell from his pale brow. "What men!" murmured he. And, involuntarily, he darted a glance at the minister which would have terrified him, if Mazarin, at the moment, had not concealed his head under his pillow.

"Monsieur," said the young Duc d'Anjou, placing his hand, delicate and white as that of a woman, upon the arm of Athos, "tell that brave man, I beg you, that Monsieur, brother of the king, will to-morrow drink his health before five hundred of the best gentlemen of France." And, on finishing those words, the young man, perceiving that his enthusiasm had deranged one of his ruffles, set to work to put it to rights with the greatest care imaginable.

"Let us resume business, sire," interrupted Mazarin, who never was enthusiastic, and who wore no ruffles.

"Yes, monsieur," replied Louis XIV. "Pursue your communication, monsieur le comte," added he, turning towards Athos.

Athos immediately began and offered in due form the hand of the Princess Henrietta Stuart to the young prince, the king's brother. The conference lasted an hour; after which the doors of the chamber were thrown open to the courtiers, who resumed their places as if nothing had been kept from them in the occupations of that evening. Athos then found himself again with Raoul, and the father and son were able to clasp each other's hands.

Chapter XLII.
In which Mazarin becomes Prodigal.

WHILST Mazarin was endeavoring to recover from the serious alarm he had just experienced, Athos and Raoul were exchanging a few words in a corner of the apartment. "Well, here you are at Paris, then, Raoul?" said the comte.

"Yes, monsieur, since the return of M. le Prince."

"I cannot converse freely with you here, because we are observed; but I shall return home presently, and shall expect you as soon as your duty permits."

Raoul bowed, and, at that moment, M. le Prince came up to them. The prince had that clear and keen look which distinguishes birds of prey of the noble species; his physiognomy itself presented several distinct traits of this resemblance. It is known that in the Prince de Conde, the aquiline nose rose out sharply and incisively from a brow slightly retreating, rather low than high, and according to the railers of the court,—a pitiless race without mercy even for genius,—constituted rather an eagle's beak than a human nose, in the heir of the illustrious princes of the house of Conde. This penetrating look, this imperious expression of the whole countenance, generally disturbed those to whom the prince spoke, more than either majesty or regular beauty could have done in the conqueror of Rocroi. Besides this, the fire mounted so suddenly to his projecting eyes, that with the prince every sort of animation resembled passion. Now, on account of his rank, everybody at the court respected M. le Prince, and many even, seeing only the man, carried their respect as far as terror.

Louis de Conde then advanced towards the Comte de la Fere and Raoul, with the marked intention of being saluted by the one, and of speaking with the other. No man bowed with more reserved grace than the Comte de la Fere. He disdained to put into a salutation all the shades which a courtier ordinarily borrows from the same color—the desire to please. Athos knew his own personal value, and bowed to the prince like a man, correcting by something sympathetic and undefinable that which might have appeared offensive to the pride of the highest rank in the inflexibility of his attitude. The prince was about to speak to Raoul. Athos forestalled him. "If M. le Vicomte de Bragelonne," said he, "were not one of the humble servants of your royal highness, I would beg him to pronounce my name before you—mon prince."

"I have the honor to address Monsieur le Comte de la Fere," said Conde, instantly.

"My protector," added Raoul, blushing.

"One of the most honorable men in the kingdom," continued the prince; "one of the first gentlemen of France, and of whom I have heard so much that I have frequently desired to number him among my friends."

"An honor of which I should be unworthy," replied Athos, "but for the respect and admiration I entertain for your royal highness."

"Monsieur de Bragelonne," said the prince, "is a good officer, and it is plainly seen that he has been to a good school. Ah, monsieur le comte, in your time, generals had soldiers!"

"That is true, my lord, but nowadays soldiers have generals."

This compliment, which savored so little of flattery, gave a thrill of joy to the man whom already Europe considered a hero; and who might be thought to be satiated with praise.

"I regret very much," continued the prince, "that you should have retired from the service, monsieur le comte; for it is more than probable that the king will soon have a war with Holland or England, and opportunities for distinguishing himself would not be wanting for a man who, like you, knows Great Britain as well as you do France."

"I believe I may say, monseigneur, that I have acted wisely in retiring from the service," said Athos, smiling. "France and Great Britain will henceforward live like two sisters, if I can trust my presentiments."

"Your presentiments?"

"Stop, monseigneur, listen to what is being said yonder, at the table of my lord the cardinal."

"Where they are playing?"

"Yes, my lord."

The cardinal had just raised himself on one elbow, and made a sign to the king's brother, who went to him.

"My lord," said the cardinal, "pick up, if you please, all those gold crowns." And he pointed to the enormous pile of yellow and glittering pieces which the Comte de Guiche had raised by degrees before him by a surprising run of luck at play.

"For me?" cried the Duc d'Anjou.

"Those fifty thousand crowns; yes, monseigneur, they are yours."

"Do you give them to me?"

"I have been playing on your account, monseigneur," replied the cardinal, getting weaker and weaker, as if this effort of giving money had exhausted all his physical and moral faculties.

"Oh, good heavens!" exclaimed Philip, wild with joy, "what a fortunate day!" And he himself, making a rake of his fingers, drew a part of the sum into his pockets, which he filled, and still full a third remained on the table.

"Chevalier," said Philip to his favorite, the Chevalier de Lorraine, "come hither, chevalier." The favorite quickly obeyed. "Pocket the rest," said the young prince.

This singular scene was considered by the persons present only as a touching kind of family fete. The cardinal assumed the airs of a father with the sons of France, and the two princes had grown up under his wing. No one then imputed to pride, or even impertinence, as would be done nowadays, this liberality on the part of the first minister. The courtiers were satisfied with envying the prince.—The king turned away his head.

"I never had so much money before," said the young prince, joyously, as he crossed the chamber with his favorite to go to his carriage. "No, never! What a weight these crowns are!"

"But why has monsieur le cardinal given away all this money at once?" asked M. le Prince of the Comte de la Fere. "He must be very ill, the dear cardinal!"

"Yes, my lord, very ill, without doubt; he looks very ill, as your royal highness may perceive."

"But surely he will die of it. A hundred and fifty thousand livres! Oh, it is incredible! But, comte, tell me a reason for it?"

"Patience, monseigneur, I beg of you. Here comes M. le Duc d'Anjou, talking with the Chevalier de Lorraine; I should not be surprised if they spared us the trouble of being indiscreet. Listen to them."

In fact the chevalier said to the prince in a low voice, "My lord, it is not natural for M. Mazarin to give you so much money. Take care! you will let some of the pieces fall, my lord. What design has the cardinal upon you to make him so generous?"

"As I said," whispered Athos in the prince's ear; "that, perhaps, is the best reply to your question."

"Tell me, my lord," repeated the chevalier impatiently, as he was calculating, by weighing them in his pocket, the quota of the sum which had fallen to his share by rebound.

"My dear chevalier, a wedding present."

"How a wedding present?"

"Eh! yes, I am going to be married," replied the Duc d'Anjou, without perceiving, at the moment, he was passing the prince and Athos, who both bowed respectfully.

The chevalier darted at the young duke a glance so strange, and so malicious, that the Comte de la Fere quite started on beholding it.

"You! you to be married!" repeated he; "oh! that's impossible. You would not commit such a folly!"

"Bah! I don't do it myself; I am made to do it," replied the Duc d'Anjou. "But come, quick! let us get rid of our money." Thereupon he disappeared with his companion, laughing and talking, whilst all heads were bowed on his passage.

"Then," whispered the prince to Athos, "that is the secret."

"It was not I who told you so, my lord."

"He is to marry the sister of Charles II.?"

"I believe so."

The prince reflected for a moment, and his eye shot forth one of its not infrequent flashes. "Humph!" said he slowly, as if speaking to himself; "our swords are once more to be hung on the wall—for a long time!" and he sighed.

All that sigh contained of ambition silently stifled, of extinguished illusions and disappointed hopes, Athos alone divined, for he alone heard that sigh. Immediately after, the prince took leave and the king left the apartment. Athos, by a sign made to Bragelonne, renewed the desire he had expressed at the beginning of the scene. By degrees the chamber was deserted, and Mazarin was left alone, a prey to suffering which he could no longer dissemble. "Bernouin! Bernouin!" cried he in a broken voice.

"What does monseigneur want?"

"Guenaud—let Guenaud be sent for," said his eminence. "I think I'm dying."

Bernouin, in great terror, rushed into the cabinet to give the order, and the piqueur, who hastened to fetch the physician, passed the king's carriage in the Rue Saint Honore.

Chapter XLIII.
Guenaud.

THE cardinal's order was pressing; Guenaud quickly obeyed it. He found his patient stretched on his bed, his legs swelled, his face livid, and his stomach collapsed. Mazarin had a severe attack of gout. He suffered tortures with the impatience of a man who has not been accustomed to resistances. On seeing Guenaud: "Ah!" said he; "now I am saved!"

Guenaud was a very learned and circumspect man, who stood in no need of the critiques of Boileau to obtain a reputation. When facing a disease, if it were personified in a king, he treated the patient as a Turk treats a Moor. He did not, therefore, reply to Mazarin as the minister expected: "Here is the doctor; good-bye disease!" On the contrary, on examining his patient, with a very serious air:

"Oh! oh!" said he.

"Eh! what! Guenaud! How you look at me!"

"I look as I should on seeing your complaint, my lord; it is a very dangerous one."

"The gout—oh! yes, the gout."

"With complications, my lord."

Mazarin raised himself upon his elbow, and, questioning by look and gesture: "What do you mean by that? Am I worse than I believe myself to be?"

"My lord," said Guenaud, seating himself beside the bed; "your eminence has worked very hard during your life; your eminence has suffered much."

"But I am not old, I fancy. The late M. de Richelieu was but seventeen months younger than I am when he died, and died of a mortal disease. I am young, Guenaud: remember, I am scarcely fifty-two."

"Oh! my lord, you are much more than that. How long did the Fronde last?"

"For what purpose do you put such a question to me?"

"For a medical calculation, monseigneur."

"Well, some ten years—off and on."

"Very well; be kind enough to reckon every year of the Fronde as three years—that makes thirty; now twenty and fifty-two makes seventy-two years. You are seventy-two, my lord; and that is a great age."

Whilst saying this, he felt the pulse of his patient. This pulse was full of such fatal indications, that the physician continued, notwithstanding the interruptions of the patient: "Put down the years of the Fronde at four each, and you have lived eighty-two years."

"Are you speaking seriously, Guenaud?"

"Alas! yes, monseigneur."

"You take a roundabout way, then, to inform me that I am very ill?"

"Ma foi! yes, my lord, and with a man of the mind and courage of your eminence, it ought not to be necessary to do so."

The cardinal breathed with such difficulty that he inspired pity even in a pitiless physician. "There are diseases and diseases," resumed Mazarin. "From some of them people escape."

"That is true, my lord."

"Is it not?" cried Mazarin, almost joyously; "for, in short, what else would be the use of power, of strength of will? What would the use of genius be—your genius, Guenaud? What would be the use of science and art, if the patient, who disposes of all that, cannot be saved from peril?"

Guenaud was about to open his mouth, but Mazarin continued:

"Remember," said he, "I am the most confiding of your patients; remember I obey you blindly, and that consequently—"

"I know all that," said Guenaud.

"I shall be cured, then?"

"Monseigneur, there is neither strength of will, nor power, nor genius, nor science that can resist a disease which God doubtless sends, or which He cast upon the earth at the creation, with full power to destroy and kill mankind. When the disease is mortal, and nothing can—"

"Is—my—disease—mortal?" asked Mazarin.

"Yes, my lord."

His eminence sank down for a moment, like an unfortunate wretch who is crushed by a falling column. But the spirit of Mazarin was a strong one, or rather his mind was a firm one. "Guenaud," said he, recovering from his first shock, "you will permit me to appeal from your judgment. I will call together the most learned men of Europe: I will consult them. I will live, in short, by the virtue of I care not what remedy."

"My lord must not suppose," said Guenaud, "that I have the presumption to pronounce alone upon an existence so valuable as yours. I have already assembled all the good physicians and practitioners of France and Europe. There were twelve of them."

"And they said—"

"They said that your eminence was suffering from a mortal disease; I have the consultation signed in my portfolio. If your eminence will please to see it, you will find the names of all the incurable diseases we have met with. There is first—"

"No, no!" cried Mazarin, pushing away the paper. "No, no, Guenaud, I yield! I yield!" And a profound silence, during which the cardinal resumed his senses and recovered his strength, succeeded to the agitation of this scene. "There is another thing," murmured Mazarin; "there are empirics and charlatans. In my country, those whom physicians abandon run the chance of a quack, who kills them ten times but saves them a hundred times."

"Has not your eminence observed, that during the last month I have changed my remedies ten times?"

"Yes. Well?"

"Well, I have spent fifty thousand crowns in purchasing the secrets of all these fellows: the list is exhausted, and so is my purse. You are not cured: and, but for my art, you would be dead."

"That ends it!" murmured the cardinal; "that ends it." And he threw a melancholy look upon the riches which surrounded him. "And must I quit all that?" sighed he. "I am dying, Guenaud! I am dying!"

"Oh! not yet, my lord," said the physician.

Mazarin seized his hand. "In what time?" asked he, fixing his two large eyes upon the impassible countenance of the physician.

"My lord, we never tell that."

"To ordinary men, perhaps not;—but to me—to me, whose every minute is worth a treasure. Tell me, Guenaud, tell me!"

"No, no, my lord."

"I insist upon it, I tell you. Oh! give me a month, and for every one of those thirty days I will pay you a hundred thousand crowns."

"My lord," replied Guenaud, in a firm voice, "it is God who can give you days of grace, and not I. God only allows you a fortnight."

The cardinal breathed a painful sigh, and sank back down upon his pillow, murmuring, "Thank you, Guenaud, thank you!"

The physician was about to depart; the dying man, raising himself up: "Silence!" said he, with flaming eyes, "silence!"

"My lord, I have known this secret two months; you see that I have kept it faithfully."

"Go, Guenaud; I will take care of your fortunes; go, and tell Brienne to send me a clerk called M. Colbert. Go!"

Chapter XLIV.
Colbert.

COLBERT was not far off. During the whole evening he had remained in one of the corridors, chatting with Bernouin and Brienne, and commenting, with the ordinary skill of people of court, upon the news which developed like air-bubbles upon the water, on the surface of each event. It is doubtless time to trace, in a few words, one of the most interesting portraits of the age, and to trace it with as much truth, perhaps, as contemporary painters have been able to do. Colbert was a man in whom the historian and the moralist have an equal right.

He was thirteen years older than Louis XIV., his future master. Of middle height, rather lean than otherwise, he had deep-set eyes, a mean appearance, his hair was coarse, black and thin, which, say the biographers of his time, made him take early to the skull-cap. A look of severity, of harshness even, a sort of stiffness, which, with inferiors, was pride, with superiors an affectation of superior virtue; a surly cast of countenance upon all occasions, even when looking at himself in a glass alone—such is the exterior of his personage. As to the moral part of his character, the depth of his talent for accounts, and his ingenuity in making sterility itself productive, were much boasted of. Colbert had formed the idea of forcing governors of frontier places to feed the garrisons without pay, with what they drew from contributions. Such a valuable quality made Mazarin think of replacing Joubert, his intendant, who had recently died, by M. Colbert, who had such skill in nibbling down allowances. Colbert by degrees crept into court, notwithstanding his lowly birth, for he was the son of a man who sold wine as his father had done, but who afterwards sold cloth, and then silk stuffs. Colbert, destined for trade, had been clerk in Lyons to a merchant, whom he had quitted to come to Paris in the office of a Chatlet procureur named Biterne. It was here he learned the art of drawing up an account, and the much more valuable one of complicating it.

This stiffness of manner in Colbert had been of great service to him; it is so true that Fortune, when she has a caprice, resembles those women of antiquity, who, when they had a fancy, were disgusted by no physical or moral defects in either men or things. Colbert, placed with Michel Letellier, secretary of state in 1648, by his cousin Colbert, Seigneur de Saint-Penange, who protected him, received one day from the minister a commission for Cardinal Mazarin. His eminence was then in the enjoyment of flourishing health, and the bad years of the Fronde had not yet counted triple and quadruple for him. He was at Sedan, very much annoyed at a court intrigue in which Anne of Austria seemed inclined to desert his cause.

Of this intrigue Letellier held the thread. He had just received a letter from Anne of Austria, a letter very valuable to him, and strongly compromising Mazarin; but, as he already played the double part which served him so well, and by which he always managed two enemies so as to draw advantage from both, either by embroiling them more and more or by reconciling them, Michel Letellier wished to send Anne of Austria's letter to Mazarin, in order that he might be acquainted with it, and consequently pleased with his having so willingly rendered him a service. To send the letter was an easy matter; to recover it again, after having communicated it, that was the difficulty. Letellier cast his eyes around him, and seeing the black and meager clerk with the scowling brow, scribbling away in his office, he preferred him to the best gendarme for the execution of this design.

Colbert was commanded to set out for Sedan, with positive orders to carry the letter to Mazarin, and bring it back to Letellier. He listened to his orders with scrupulous attention, required the instructions to be repeated twice, and was particular in learning whether the bringing back was as necessary as the communicating, and Letellier replied sternly, "More necessary." Then he set out, traveled like a courier, without any care for his body, and placed in the hands of Mazarin, first a letter from Letellier, which announced to the cardinal the sending of the precious letter, and then that letter itself. Mazarin colored greatly whilst reading Anne of Austria's letter, gave Colbert a gracious smile and dismissed him.

"When shall I have the answer, monseigneur?"

"To-morrow."

"To-morrow morning?"

"Yes, monsieur."

The clerk turned upon his heel, after making his very best bow. The next day he was at his post at seven o'clock. Mazarin made him wait till ten. He remained patiently in the ante-chamber; his turn having come, he entered; Mazarin gave him a sealed packet. On the envelope of this packet were these words:—Monsieur Michel Letellier, etc. Colbert looked at the packet with much attention; the cardinal put on a pleasant countenance and pushed him towards the door.

"And the letter of the queen-mother, my lord?" asked Colbert.

"It is in with the rest, in the packet," said Mazarin.

"Oh! very well," replied Colbert; and placing his hat between his knees, he began to unseal the packet.

Mazarin uttered a cry. "What are you doing?" said he, angrily.

"I am unsealing the packet, my lord."

"You mistrust me, then, master pedant, do you? Did any one ever see such impertinence?"

"Oh! my lord, do not be angry with me! It is certainly not your eminence's word I place in doubt, God forbid!"

"What then?"

"It is the carefulness of your chancery, my lord. What is a letter? A rag. May not a rag be forgotten? And look, my lord, look if I was not right. Your clerks have forgotten the rag; the letter is not in the packet."

"You are an insolent fellow, and you have not looked," cried Mazarin, very angrily; "begone and wait my pleasure." Whilst saying these words, with perfectly Italian subtlety he snatched the packet from the hands of Colbert, and re-entered his apartments.

But this anger could not last so long as to be replaced in time by reason. Mazarin, every morning, on opening his closet door, found the figure of Colbert like a sentinel behind the bench, and this disagreeable figure never failed to ask him humbly, but with tenacity, for the queen-mother's letter. Mazarin could hold out no longer, and was obliged to give it up. He accompanied this restitution with a most severe reprimand, during which Colbert contented himself with examining, feeling, even smelling, as it were, the paper, the characters, and the signature, neither more nor less than if he had to deal with the greatest forger in the kingdom. Mazarin behaved still more rudely to him, but Colbert, still impassible, having obtained a certainty that the letter was the true one, went off as if he had been deaf. This conduct obtained for him afterwards the post of Joubert; for Mazarin, instead of bearing malice, admired him, and was desirous of attaching so much fidelity to himself.

It may be judged by this single anecdote, what the character of Colbert was. Events, developing themselves, by degrees allowed all the powers of his mind to act freely. Colbert was not long in insinuating himself to the good graces of the cardinal: he became even indispensable to him. The clerk was acquainted with all his accounts without the cardinal's ever having spoken to him about them. This secret between them was a powerful tie, and this was why, when about to appear before the Master of another world, Mazarin was desirous of taking good counsel in disposing the wealth he was so unwillingly obliged to leave in this world. After the visit of Guenaud, he therefore sent for Colbert, desired him to sit down, and said to him: "Let us converse, Monsieur Colbert, and seriously, for I am very ill, and I may chance to die."

"Man is mortal," replied Colbert.

"I have always remembered that, M. Colbert, and I have worked with that end in view. You know that I have amassed a little wealth."

"I know you have, monseigneur."

"At how much do you estimate, as near as you can, the amount of this wealth, M. Colbert?"

"At forty millions, five hundred and sixty thousand, two hundred livres, nine cents, eight farthings," replied Colbert.

The cardinal heaved a deep sigh, and looked at Colbert with wonder, but he allowed a smile to steal across his lips.

"Known money," added Colbert, in reply to that smile.

The cardinal gave quite a start in bed. "What do you mean by that?" said he.

"I mean," said Colbert, "that besides those forty millions, five hundred and sixty thousand, two hundred livres, nine cents, eight farthings, there are thirteen millions that are not known."

"Ouf!" sighed Mazarin, "what a man!"

At this moment, the head of Bernouin appeared through the embrasure of the door.

"What is it?" asked Mazarin, "and why do you disturb me?"

"The Theatin father, your eminence's director, was sent for this evening; and he cannot come again to my lord till after to-morrow."

Mazarin looked a Colbert, who rose and took his hat, saying: "I shall come again, my lord."

Mazarin hesitated. "No, no," said he; "I have as much business to transact with you as with him. Besides, you are my other confessor—and what I have to say to one the other may hear. Remain where you are, Colbert."

"But my lord, if there be no secret of penitence, will the director consent to my being here?"

"Do not trouble yourself about that; come into the ruelle."

"I can wait outside, monseigneur."

"No, no, it will do you good to hear the confession of a rich man."

Colbert bowed and went into the ruelle.

"Introduce the Theatin father," said Mazarin, closing the curtains.

Chapter XLV.
Confession of a Man of Wealth.

THE Theatin entered deliberately, without being too much astonished at the noise and agitation which anxiety for the cardinal's health had raised in his household. "Come in, my reverend father," said Mazarin, after a last look at the ruelle, "come in and console me."

"That is my duty, my lord," replied the Theatin.

"Begin by sitting down, and making yourself comfortable, for I am going to begin with a general confession; you will afterwards give me a good absolution, and I shall believe myself more tranquil."

"My lord," said the father, "you are not so ill as to make a general confession urgent—and it will be very fatiguing—take care."

"You suspect, then, that it may be long, father?"

"How can I think it otherwise, when a man has lived so completely as your eminence has done?"

"Ah! that is true!—yes—the recital may be long."

"The mercy of God is great," snuffled the Theatin.

"Stop," said Mazarin; "there I begin to terrify myself with having allowed so many things to pass which the Lord might reprove."

"Is that not always so?" said the Theatin naively, removing further from the lamp his thin pointed face, like that of a mole. "Sinners are so forgetful beforehand, and scrupulous when it is too late."

"Sinners?" replied Mazarin. "Do you use that word ironically, and to reproach me with all the genealogies I have allowed to be made on my account—I—the son of a fisherman, in fact?"

[This is quite untranslatable—it being a play upon the words pecheur (with a grave over the first e), a sinner, and pecheur (with an accent circumflex over the first e), a fisherman. It is in very bad taste.—TRANS.]

"Hum!" said the Theatin.

"That is a first sin, father; for I have allowed myself made to descend from two old Roman consuls, S. Geganius Macerinus 1st, Macerinus 2d, and Proculus Macerinus 3d, of whom the Chronicle of Haolander speaks. From Macerinus to Mazarin the proximity was tempting. Macerinus, a diminutive, means leanish, poorish, out of case. Oh! reverend father! Mazarini may now be carried to the augmentative Maigre, thin as Lazarus. Look!"—and he showed his fleshless arms.

"In your having been born of a family of fishermen I see nothing injurious to you; for—St. Peter was a fisherman; and if you are a prince of the church, my lord, he was the supreme head of it. Pass on, if you please."

"So much the more for my having threatened with the Bastile a certain Bounet, a priest of Avignon, who wanted to publish a genealogy of the Casa Mazarini much too marvelous."

"To be probable?" replied the Theatin.

"Oh! if I had acted up to his idea, father, that would have been the vice of pride—another sin."

"It was an excess of wit, and a person is not to be reproached with such sorts of abuses. Pass on, pass on!"

"I was all pride. Look you, father, I will endeavor to divide that into capital sins."

"I like divisions, when well made."

"I am glad of that. You must know that in 1630—alas! that is thirty-one years ago—"

"You were then twenty-nine years old, monseigneur."

"A hot-headed age. I was then something of a soldier, and I threw myself at Casal into the arquebusades, to show that I rode on horseback as well as an officer. It is true, I restored peace between the French and the Spaniards. That redeems my sin a little."

"I see no sin in being able to ride well on horseback," said the Theatin; "that is in perfect good taste, and does honor to our gown. As a Christian, I approve of your having prevented the effusion of blood; as a monk, I am proud of the bravery a monk has exhibited."

Mazarin bowed his head humbly. "Yes," said he, "but the consequences?"

"What consequences?"

"Eh! that damned sin of pride has roots without end. From the time that I threw myself in that manner between two armies, that I had smelt powder and faced lines of soldiers, I have held generals a little in contempt."

"Ah!" said the father.

"There is the evil; so that I have not found one endurable since that time."

"The fact is," said the Theatin, "that the generals we have had have not been remarkable."

"Oh!" cried Mazarin, "there was Monsieur le Prince. I have tormented him thoroughly!"

"He is not much to be pitied: he has acquired sufficient glory, and sufficient wealth."

"That may be, for Monsieur le Prince; but M. Beaufort, for example—whom I held suffering so long in the dungeon of Vincennes?"

"Ah! but he was a rebel, and the safety of the state required that you should make a sacrifice. Pass on!"

"I believe I have exhausted pride. There is another sin which I am afraid to qualify."

"I can qualify it myself. Tell it."

"A great sin, reverend father!"

"We shall judge, monseigneur."

"You cannot fail to have heard of certain relations which I have had—with her majesty the queen-mother;—the malevolent—"

"The malevolent, my lord, are fools. Was it not necessary for the good of the state and the interests of the young king, that you should live in good intelligence with the queen? Pass on, pass on!"

"I assure you," said Mazarin, "you remove a terrible weight from my breast."

"These are all trifles!—look for something serious."

"I have had much ambition, father."

"That is the march of great minds and things, my lord."

"Even the longing for the tiara?"

"To be pope is to be the first of Christians. Why should you not desire that?"

"It has been printed that, to gain that object, I had sold Cambria to the Spaniards."

"You have, perhaps, yourself written pamphlets without severely persecuting pamphleteers."

"Then, reverend father, I have truly a clean breast. I feel nothing remaining but slight peccadilloes."

"What are they?"

"Play."

"That is rather worldly: but you were obliged by the duties of greatness to keep a good house."

"I like to win."

"No player plays to lose."

"I cheated a little."

"You took your advantage. Pass on."

"Well! reverend father, I feel nothing else upon my conscience. Give me absolution, and my soul will be able, when God shall please to call it, to mount without obstacle to the throne—"

The Theatin moved neither his arms nor his lips. "What are you waiting for, father?" said Mazarin.

"I am waiting for the end."

"The end of what?"

"Of the confession, monsieur."

"But I have ended."

"Oh, no; your eminence is mistaken."

"Not that I know of."

"Search diligently."

"I have searched as well as possible."

"Then I shall assist your memory."

"Do."

The Theatin coughed several times. "You have said nothing of avarice, another capital sin, nor of those millions," said he.

"What millions, father?"

"Why, those you possess, my lord."

"Father, that money is mine, why should I speak to you about that?"

"Because, you see, our opinions differ. You say that money is yours, whilst I—I believe it is rather the property of others."

Mazarin lifted his cold hand to his brow, which was beaded with perspiration. "How so?" stammered he.

"This way. Your excellency had gained much wealth—in the service of the king."

"Hum! much—that is, not too much."

"Whatever it may be, whence came that wealth?"

"From the state."

"The state; that is the king."

"But what do you conclude from that, father?" said Mazarin, who began to tremble.

"I cannot conclude without seeing a list of the riches you possess. Let us reckon a little, if you please. You have the bishopric of Metz?"

"Yes."

"The abbeys of St. Clement, St. Arnould, and St. Vincent, all at Metz?"

"Yes."

"You have the abbey of St. Denis, in France, magnificent property?"

"Yes, father."

"You have the abbey of Cluny, which is rich?"

"I have."

"That of St. Medard at Soissons, with a revenue of one hundred thousand livres?"

"I cannot deny it."

"That of St. Victor, at Marseilles,—one of the best in the south?"

"Yes father."

"A good million a year. With the emoluments of the cardinalship and the ministry, I say too little when I say two millions a year."

"Eh!"

"In ten years that is twenty millions—and twenty millions put out at fifty per cent. give, by progression, twenty-three millions in ten years."

"How well you reckon for a Theatin!"

"Since your eminence placed our order in the convent we occupy, near St. Germain des Pres, in 1644, I have kept the accounts of the society."

"And mine likewise, apparently, father."

"One ought to know a little of everything, my lord."

"Very well. Conclude, at present."

"I conclude that your baggage is too heavy to allow you to pass through the gates of Paradise."

"Shall I be damned?"

"If you do not make restitution, yes."

Mazarin uttered a piteous cry. "Restitution!—but to whom, good God?"

"To the owner of that money,—to the king."

"But the king did not give it all to me."

"One moment,—does not the king sign the ordonances?"

Mazarin passed from sighs to groans. "Absolution! absolution!" cried he.

"Impossible, my lord. Restitution! restitution!" replied the Theatin.

"But you absolve me from all other sins, why not from that?"

"Because," replied the father, "to absolve you for that motive would be a sin for which the king would never absolve me, my lord."

Thereupon the confessor quitted his penitent with an air full of compunction. He then went out in the same manner he had entered.

"Oh, good God!" groaned the cardinal. "Come here, Colbert, I am very, very ill indeed, my friend."

Chapter XLVI.
The Donation.

COLBERT reappeared beneath the curtains.

"Have you heard?" said Mazarin.

"Alas! yes, my lord."

"Can he be right? Can all this money be badly acquired?"

"A Theatin, monseigneur, is a bad judge in matters of finance," replied Colbert, coolly. "And yet it is very possible that, according to his theological views, your eminence has been, in a certain degree, in the wrong. People generally find they have been so,—when they die."

"In the first place, they commit the wrong of dying, Colbert."

"That is true, my lord. Against whom, however, did the Theatin make out that you had committed these wrongs? Against the king?"

Mazarin shrugged his shoulders. "As if I had not saved both his state and his finances."

"That admits of no contradiction, my lord."

"Does it? Then I have received a merely legitimate salary, in spite of the opinion of my confessor?"

"That is beyond doubt."

"And I might fairly keep for my own family, which is so needy, a good fortune,—the whole, even, of which I have earned?"

"I see no impediment to that, monseigneur."

"I felt assured that in consulting you, Colbert, I should have good advice," replied Mazarin, greatly delighted.

Colbert resumed his pedantic look. "My lord," interrupted he, "I think it would be quite as well to examine whether what the Theatin said is not a snare."

"Oh! no; a snare? What for? The Theatin is an honest man."

"He believed your eminence to be at death's door, because your eminence consulted him. Did I not hear him say—'Distinguish that which the king has given you from that which you have given yourself.' Recollect, my lord, if he did not say something a little like that to you?—that is quite a theatrical speech."

"That is possible."

"In which case, my lord, I should consider you as required by the Theatin to—"

"To make restitution!" cried Mazarin, with great warmth.

"Eh! I do not say no."

"What, of all! You do not dream of such a thing! You speak just as the confessor did."

"To make restitution of a part,—that is to say, his majesty's part; and that, monseigneur, may have its dangers. Your eminence is too skillful a politician not to know that, at this moment, the king does not possess a hundred and fifty thousand livres clear in his coffers."

"That is not my affair," said Mazarin, triumphantly; "that belongs to M. le Surintendant Fouquet, whose accounts I gave you to verify some months ago."

Colbert bit his lips at the name of Fouquet. "His majesty," said he, between his teeth, "has no money but that which M. Fouquet collects: your money, monseigneur, would afford him a delicious banquet."

"Well, but I am not the superintendent of his majesty's finances—I have my purse—surely I would do much for his majesty's welfare—some legacy—but I cannot disappoint my family."

"The legacy of a part would dishonor you and offend the king. Leaving a part to his majesty, is to avow that that part has inspired you with doubts as to the lawfulness of the means of acquisition."

"Monsieur Colbert!"

"I thought your eminence did me the honor to ask my advice?"

"Yes, but you are ignorant of the principal details of the question."

"I am ignorant of nothing, my lord; during ten years, all the columns of figures which are found in France, have passed into review before me; and if I have painfully nailed them into my brain, they are there now so well riveted, that, from the office of M. Letellier, who is sober, to the little secret largesses of M. Fouquet, who is prodigal, I could recite, figure by figure, all the money that is spent in France from Marseilles to Cherbourg."

"Then, you would have me throw all my money into the coffers of the king!" cried Mazarin, ironically; and from whom, at the same time the gout forced painful moans. "Surely the king would reproach me with nothing, but he would laugh at me, while squandering my millions, and with good reason."

"Your eminence has misunderstood me. I did not, the least in the world, pretend that his majesty ought to spend your money."

"You said so, clearly, it seems to me, when you advised me to give it to him."

"Ah," replied Colbert, "that is because your eminence, absorbed as you are by your disease, entirely loses sight of the character of Louis XIV."

"How so?"

"That character, if I may venture to express myself thus, resembles that which my lord confessed just now to the Theatin."

"Go on—that is?"

"Pride! Pardon me, my lord, haughtiness, nobleness; kings have no pride, that is a human passion."

"Pride,—yes, you are right. Next?"

"Well, my lord, if I have divined rightly, your eminence has but to give all your money to the king, and that immediately."

"But for what?" said Mazarin, quite bewildered.

"Because the king will not accept of the whole."

"What, and he a young man, and devoured by ambition?"

"Just so."

"A young man who is anxious for my death—"

"My lord!"

"To inherit, yes, Colbert, yes; he is anxious for my death, in order to inherit. Triple fool that I am! I would prevent him!"

"Exactly: if the donation were made in a certain form he would refuse it."

"Well; but how?"

"That is plain enough. A young man who has yet done nothing—who burns to distinguish himself—who burns to reign alone, will never take anything ready built, he will construct for himself. This prince, monseigneur, will never be content with the Palais Royal, which M. de Richelieu left him, nor with the Palais Mazarin, which you have had so superbly constructed, nor with the Louvre, which his ancestors inhabited; nor with St. Germain, where he was born. All that does not proceed from himself, I predict, he will disdain."

"And you will guarantee, that if I give my forty millions to the king—"

"Saying certain things to him at the same time, I guarantee he will refuse them."

"But those things—what are they?"

"I will write them, if my lord will have the goodness to dictate them."

"Well, but, after all, what advantage will that be to me?"

"An enormous one. Nobody will afterwards be able to accuse your eminence of that unjust avarice with which pamphleteers have reproached the most brilliant mind of the present age."

"You are right, Colbert, you are right; go, and seek the king, on my part, and take him my will."

"Your donation, my lord."

"But, if he should accept it; if he should even think of accepting it!"

"Then there would remain thirteen millions for your family, and that is a good round sum."

"But then you would be either a fool or a traitor."

"And I am neither the one nor the other, my lord. You appear to be much afraid that the king will accept; you have a deal more reason to fear that he will not accept."

"But, see you, if he does not accept, I should like to guarantee my thirteen reserved millions to him—yes, I will do so—yes. But my pains are returning, I shall faint. I am very, very ill, Colbert; I am near my end!"

Colbert started. The cardinal was indeed very ill; large drops of sweat flowed down upon his bed of agony, and the frightful pallor of a face streaming with water was a spectacle which the most hardened practitioner could not have beheld without much compassion. Colbert was, without doubt, very much affected, for he quitted the chamber, calling Bernouin to attend to the dying man, and went into the corridor. There, walking about with a meditative expression, which almost gave nobility to his vulgar head, his shoulders thrown up, his neck stretched out, his lips half open, to give vent to unconnected fragments of incoherent thoughts, he lashed up his courage to the pitch of the undertaking contemplated, whilst within ten paces of him, separated only by a wall, his master was being stifled by anguish which drew from him lamentable cries, thinking no more of the treasures of the earth, or of the joys of Paradise, but much of all the horrors of hell. Whilst burning-hot napkins, physic, revulsives, and Guenaud, who was recalled, were performing their functions with increased activity, Colbert, holding his great head in both his hands, to compress within it the fever of the projects engendered by the brain, was meditating the tenor of the donation he would make Mazarin write, at the first hour of respite his disease should afford him. It would appear as if all the cries of the cardinal, and all the attacks of death upon this representative of the past, were stimulants for the genius of this thinker with the bushy eyebrows, who was turning already towards the rising sun of a regenerated society. Colbert resumed his place at Mazarin's pillow at the first interval of pain, and persuaded him to dictate a donation thus conceived.

"About to appear before God, the Master of mankind, I beg the king, who was my master on earth, to resume the wealth which his bounty has bestowed upon me, and which my family would be happy to see pass into such illustrious hands. The particulars of my property will be found—they are drawn up—at the first requisition of his majesty, or at the last sigh of his most devoted servant,

"JULES, Cardinal de Mazarin."

The cardinal sighed heavily as he signed this; Colbert sealed the packet, and carried it immediately to the Louvre, whither the king had returned.

He then went back to his own home, rubbing his hands with the confidence of workman who has done a good day's work.

Chapter XLVII.
How Anne of Austria gave one Piece of Advice to Louis XIV.

THE news of the extreme illness of the cardinal had already spread, and attracted at least as much attention among the people of the Louvre as the news of the marriage of Monsieur, the king's brother, which had already been announced as an official fact. Scarcely had Louis XIV. returned home, with his thoughts fully occupied with the various things he had seen and heard in the course of the evening, when an usher announced that the same crowd of courtiers who, in the morning, had thronged his lever, presented themselves again at his coucher, a remarkable piece of respect which, during the reign of the cardinal, the court, not very discreet in its performance, had accorded to the minister, without caring about displeasing the king.

But the minister had had, as we have said, an alarming attack of gout, and the tide of flattery was mounting towards the throne. Courtiers have a marvelous instinct in scenting the turn of events; courtiers possess a supreme kind of science; they are diplomatists in throwing light upon the unraveling of complicated intrigues, captains in divining the issue of battles, and physicians in curing the sick. Louis XIV., to whom his mother had taught this axiom, together with many others, understood at once that the cardinal must be very ill.

Scarcely had Anne of Austria conducted the young queen to her apartments and taken from her brow the head-dress of ceremony, when she went to see her son in his cabinet, where, alone, melancholy, and depressed, he was indulging, as if to exercise his will, in one of those terrible inward passions—king's passions—which create events when they break out, and with Louis XIV., thanks to his astonishing command over himself, became such benign tempests, that his most violent, his only passion, that which Saint Simon mentions with astonishment, was that famous fit of anger which he exhibited fifty years later, on the occasion of a little concealment of the Duc de Maine's, and which had for result a shower of blows inflicted with a cane upon the back of a poor valet who had stolen a biscuit. The young king then was, as we have seen, a prey to a double excitement; and he said to himself as he looked in a glass, "O king!—king by name, and not in fact;—phantom, vain phantom art thou!—inert statue, which has no other power than that of provoking salutations from courtiers, when wilt thou be able to raise thy velvet arm, or clench thy silken hand? when wilt thou be able to open, for any purpose but to sigh, or smile, lips condemned to the motionless stupidity of the marbles in thy gallery?"

Then, passing his hand over his brow, and feeling the want of air, he approached a window, and looking down, saw below some horsemen talking together, and groups of timid observers. These horsemen were a fraction of the watch: the groups were busy portions of the people, to whom a king is always a curious thing, the same as a rhinoceros, a crocodile, or a serpent. He struck his brow with his open hand, crying,—"King of France! what a title! People of France! what a heap of creatures! I have just returned to my Louvre; my horses, just unharnessed, are still smoking, and I have created interest enough to induce scarcely twenty persons to look at me as I passed. Twenty! what do I say? no; there were not twenty anxious to see the king of France. There are not even ten archers to guard my palace of residence: archers, people, guards, all are at the Palais Royal! Why, my good God! have not I, the king, the right to ask of you all that?"

"Because," said a voice, replying to his, and which sounded from the other side of the door of the cabinet, "because at the Palais Royal lies all the gold,—that is to say, all the power of him who desires to reign."

Louis turned round sharply. The voice which had pronounced these words was that of Anne of Austria. The king started, and advanced towards her. "I hope," said he, "your majesty has paid no attention to the vain declamations which the solitude and disgust familiar to kings suggest to the happiest dispositions?"

"I only paid attention to one thing, my son, and that was, that you were complaining."

"Who! I? Not at all," said Louis XIV.; "no, in truth, you err, madame."

"What were you doing, then?"

"I thought I was under the ferule of my professor, and developing a subject of amplification."

"My son," replied Anne of Austria, shaking her head, "you are wrong not to trust my word; you are wrong not to grant me your confidence. A day will come, and perhaps quickly, wherein you will have occasion to remember that axiom:—'Gold is universal power; and they alone are kings who are all-powerful.'"

"Your intention," continued the king, "was not, however, to cast blame upon the rich men of this age, was it?"

"No," said the queen, warmly; "no, sire; they who are rich in this age, under your reign, are rich because you have been willing they should be so, and I entertain against them neither malice nor envy; they have, without doubt, served your majesty sufficiently well for your majesty to have permitted them to reward themselves. That is what I mean to say by the words for which you reproach me."

"God forbid, madame, that I should ever reproach my mother with anything!"

"Besides," continued Anne of Austria, "the Lord never gives the goods of this world but for a season; the Lord—as correctives to honor and riches—the Lord has placed sufferings, sickness, and death; and no one," added she, with a melancholy smile, which proved she made the application of the funeral precept to herself, "no man can take his wealth or greatness with him to the grave. It results, therefore, that the young gather the abundant harvest prepared for them by the old."

Louis listened with increased attention to the words which Anne of Austria, no doubt, pronounced with a view to console him. "Madame," said he, looking earnestly at his mother, "one would almost say in truth that you had something else to announce to me."

"I have absolutely nothing, my son; only you cannot have failed to remark that his eminence the cardinal is very ill."

Louis looked at his mother, expecting some emotion in her voice, some sorrow in her countenance. The face of Anne of Austria appeared a little changed, but that was from sufferings of quite a personal character. Perhaps the alteration was caused by the cancer which had begun to consume her breast. "Yes, madame," said the king; "yes, M. de Mazarin is very ill."

"And it would be a great loss to the kingdom if God were to summon his eminence away. Is not that your opinion as well as mine, my son?" said the queen.

"Yes, madame; yes, certainly, it would be a great loss for the kingdom," said Louis, coloring; "but the peril does not seem to me to be so great; besides, the cardinal is still young." The king had scarcely ceased speaking when an usher lifted the tapestry, and stood with a paper in his hand, waiting for the king to speak to him.

"What have you there?" asked the king.

"A message from M. de Mazarin," replied the usher.

"Give it to me," said the king; and he took the paper. But at the moment he was about to open it, there was a great noise in the gallery, the ante-chamber, and the court.

"Ah, ah," said Louis XIV., who doubtless knew the meaning of that triple noise. "How could I say there was but one king in France! I was mistaken, there are two."

As he spoke or thought thus, the door opened, and the superintendent of finances, Fouquet, appeared before his nominal master. It was he who made the noise in the ante-chamber, it was his horse that made the noise in the courtyard. In addition to all this, a loud murmur was heard along his passage, which did not die away till some time after he had passed. It was this murmur which Louis XIV. regretted so deeply not hearing as he passed, and dying away behind him.

"He is not precisely a king, as you fancy," said Anne of Austria to her son; "he is only a man who is much too rich—that is all."

Whilst saying these words, a bitter feeling gave to these words of the queen a most hateful expression; whereas the brow of the king, calm and self-possessed, on the contrary, was without the slightest wrinkle. He nodded, therefore, familiarly to Fouquet, whilst he continued to unfold the paper given to him by the usher. Fouquet perceived this movement, and with a politeness at once easy and respectful, advanced towards the queen, so as not to disturb the king. Louis had opened the paper, and yet he did not read it. He listened to Fouquet paying the most charming compliments to the queen upon her hand and arm. Anne of Austria's frown relaxed a little, she even almost smiled. Fouquet perceived that the king, instead of reading, was looking at him; he turned half round, therefore, and while continuing his conversation with the queen, faced the king.

"You know, Monsieur Fouquet," said Louis, "how ill M. Mazarin is?"

"Yes, sire, I know that," said Fouquet; "in fact, he is very ill. I was at my country-house of Vaux when the news reached me; and the affair seemed so pressing that I left at once."

"You left Vaux this evening, monsieur?"

"An hour and a half ago, yes, your majesty," said Fouquet, consulting a watch, richly ornamented with diamonds.

"An hour and a half!" said the king, still able to restrain his anger, but not to conceal his astonishment.

"I understand you, sire. Your majesty doubts my word, and you have reason to do so; but I have really come in that time, though it is wonderful! I received from England three pairs of very fast horses, as I had been assured. They were placed at distances of four leagues apart, and I tried them this evening. They really brought me from Vaux to the Louvre in an hour and a half, so your majesty sees I have not been cheated." The queen-mother smiled with something like secret envy. But Fouquet caught her thought. "Thus, madame," he promptly said, "such horses are made for kings, not for subjects; for kings ought never to yield to any one in anything."

The king looked up.

"And yet," interrupted Anne of Austria, "you are not a king, that I know of, M. Fouquet."

"Truly not, madame; therefore the horses only await the orders of his majesty to enter the royal stables; and if I allowed myself to try them, it was only for fear of offering to the king anything that was not positively wonderful."

The king became quite red.

"You know, Monsieur Fouquet," said the queen, "that at the court of France it is not the custom for a subject to offer anything to his king."

Louis started.

"I hoped, madame," said Fouquet, much agitated, "that my love for his majesty, my incessant desire to please him, would serve to compensate the want of etiquette. It was not so much a present that I permitted myself to offer, as the tribute I paid."

"Thank you, Monsieur Fouquet," said the king politely, "and I am gratified by your intention, for I love good horses; but you know I am not very rich; you, who are my superintendent of finances, know it better than any one else. I am not able, then, however willing I may be, to purchase such a valuable set of horses."

Fouquet darted a haughty glance at the queen-mother, who appeared to triumph at the false position in which the minister had placed himself, and replied:—

"Luxury is the virtue of kings, sire: it is luxury which makes them resemble God; it is by luxury they are more than other men. With luxury a king nourishes his subjects, and honors them. Under the mild heat of this luxury of kings springs the luxury of individuals, a source of riches for the people. His majesty, by accepting the gift of these six incomparable horses, would stimulate the pride of his own breeders, of Limousin, Perche, and Normandy; and this emulation would have been beneficial to all. But the king is silent, and consequently I am condemned."

During this speech, Louis was, unconsciously, folding and unfolding Mazarin's paper, upon which he had not cast his eyes. At length he glanced upon it, and uttered a faint cry at reading the first line.

"What is the matter, my son?" asked the queen, anxiously, and going towards the king.

"From the cardinal," replied the king, continuing to read; "yes, yes, it is really from him."

"Is he worse, then?"

"Read!" said the king, passing the parchment to his mother, as if he thought that nothing less than reading would convince Anne of Austria of a thing so astonishing as was conveyed in that paper.

Anne of Austria read in turn, and as she read, her eyes sparkled with joy all the greater from her useless endeavor to hide it, which attracted the attention of Fouquet.

"Oh! a regularly drawn up deed of gift," said she.

"A gift?" repeated Fouquet.

"Yes," said the king, replying pointedly to the superintendent of finances, "yes, at the point of death, monsieur le cardinal makes me a donation of all his wealth."

"Forty millions," cried the queen. "Oh, my son! this is very noble on the part of his eminence, and will silence all malicious rumors; forty millions scraped together slowly, coming back all in one heap to the treasury! It is the act of a faithful subject and a good Christian." And having once more cast her eyes over the act, she restored it to Louis XIV., whom the announcement of the sum greatly agitated. Fouquet had taken some steps backwards and remained silent. The king looked at him, and held the paper out to him, in turn. The superintendent only bestowed a haughty look of a second upon it; then bowing,—"Yes, sire," said he, "a donation, I see."

"You must reply to it, my son," said Anne of Austria; "you must reply to it, and immediately."

"But how, madame?"

"By a visit to the cardinal."

"Why, it is but an hour since I left his eminence," said the king.

"Write, then, sire."

"Write!" said the young king, with evident repugnance.

"Well!" replied Anne of Austria, "it seems to me, my son, that a man who has just made such a present, has a good right to expect to be thanked for it with some degree of promptitude." Then turning towards Fouquet: "Is not that likewise your opinion, monsieur?"

"That the present is worth the trouble? Yes, madame," said Fouquet, with a lofty air that did not escape the king.

"Accept, then, and thank him," insisted Anne of Austria.

"What says M. Fouquet?" asked Louis XIV.

"Does your majesty wish to know my opinion?"

"Yes."

"Thank him, sire—"

"Ah!" said the queen.

"But do not accept," continued Fouquet.

"And why not?" asked the queen.

"You have yourself said why, madame," replied Fouquet; "because kings cannot and ought not to receive presents from their subjects."

The king remained silent between these two contrary opinions.

"But forty millions!" said Anne of Austria, in the same tone as that in which, at a later period, poor Marie Antoinette replied, "You will tell me as much!"

"I know," said Fouquet, laughing, "forty millions makes a good round sum,—such a sum as could almost tempt a royal conscience."

"But, monsieur," said Anne of Austria, "instead of persuading the king not to receive this present, recall to his majesty's mind, you, whose duty it is, that these forty millions are a fortune to him."

"It is precisely, madame, because these forty millions would be a fortune that I will say to the king, 'Sire, if it be not decent for a king to accept from a subject six horses, worth twenty thousand livres, it would be disgraceful for him to owe a fortune to another subject, more or less scrupulous in the choice of the materials which contributed to the building up of that fortune.'"

"It ill becomes you, monsieur, to give your king a lesson," said Anne of Austria; "better procure for him forty millions to replace those you make him lose."

"The king shall have them whenever he wishes," said the superintendent of finances, bowing.

"Yes, by oppressing the people," said the queen.

"And were they not oppressed, madame," replied Fouquet, "when they were made to sweat the forty millions given by this deed? Furthermore, his majesty has asked my opinion, I have given it; if his majesty ask my concurrence, it will be the same."

"Nonsense! accept, my son, accept," said Anne of Austria. "You are above reports and interpretations."

"Refuse, sire," said Fouquet. "As long as a king lives, he has no other measure but his conscience,—no other judge than his own desires; but when dead, he has posterity, which applauds or accuses."

"Thank you, mother," replied Louis, bowing respectfully to the queen. "Thank you Monsieur, Fouquet," said he, dismissing the superintendent civilly.

"Do you accept?" asked Anne of Austria, once more.

"I shall consider of it," replied he, looking at Fouquet.

Chapter XLVIII.
Agony.

THE day that the deed of gift had been sent to the king, the cardinal caused himself to be transported to Vincennes. The king and the court followed him thither. The last flashes of this torch still cast splendor enough around to absorb all other lights in its rays. Besides, as it has been seen, the faithful satellite of his minister, young Louis XIV., marched to the last minute in accordance with his gravitation. The disease, as Guenaud had predicted, had become worse; it was no longer an attack of gout, it was an attack of death; then there was another thing which made that agony more agonizing still,— and that was the agitation brought into his mind by the donation he had sent to the king, and which, according to Colbert, the king ought to send back unaccepted to the cardinal. The cardinal had, as we have said, great faith in the predictions of his secretary; but the sum was a large one, and whatever might be the genius of Colbert, from time to time the cardinal thought to himself that the Theatin also might possibly have been mistaken, and there was at least as much chance of his not being damned, as there was of Louis XIV. sending back his millions.

Besides, the longer the donation was in coming back, the more Mazarin thought that forty millions were worth a little risk, particularly of so hypothetic a thing as the soul. Mazarin, in his character of cardinal and prime minister, was almost an atheist, and quite a materialist. Every time that the door opened, he turned sharply round towards that door, expecting to see the return of his unfortunate donation; then, deceived in his hope, he fell back again with a sigh, and found his pains so much the greater for having forgotten them for an instant.

Anne of Austria had also followed the cardinal; her heart, though age had made it selfish, could not help evincing towards the dying man a sorrow which she owed him as a wife, according to some; and as a sovereign, according to others. She had, in some sort, put on a mourning countenance beforehand, and all the court wore it as she did.

Louis, in order not to show on his face what was passing at the bottom of his heart, persisted in remaining in his own apartments, where his nurse alone kept him company; the more he saw the approach of the time when all constraint would be at an end, the more humble and patient he was, falling back upon himself, as all strong men do when they form great designs, in order to gain more spring at the decisive moment. Extreme unction had been administered to the cardinal, who, faithful to his habits of dissimulation, struggled against appearances, and even against reality, receiving company in his bed, as if he only suffered from a temporary complaint.

Guenaud, on his part, preserved profound secrecy; wearied with visits and questions, he answered nothing but "his eminence is still full of youth and strength, but God wills that which He wills, and when He has decided that man is to be laid low, he will be laid low." These words, which he scattered with a sort of discretion, reserve, and preference, were commented upon earnestly by two persons,—the king and the cardinal. Mazarin, notwithstanding the prophecy of Guenaud, still lured himself with a hope, or rather played his part so well, that the most cunning, when saying that he lured himself, proved that they were his dupes.

Louis, absent from the cardinal for two days; Louis, with his eyes fixed upon that same donation which so constantly preoccupied the cardinal; Louis did not exactly know how to make out Mazarin's conduct. The son of Louis XIII., following the paternal traditions, had, up to that time, been so little of a king that, whilst ardently desiring royalty, he desired it with that terror which always accompanies the unknown. Thus, having formed his resolution, which, besides, he communicated to nobody, he determined to have an interview with Mazarin. It was Anne of Austria, who, constant in her attendance upon the cardinal, first heard this proposition of the king's, and transmitted it to the dying man, whom it greatly agitated. For what purpose could Louis wish for an interview? Was it to return the deed, as Colbert had said he would? Was it to keep it, after thanking him, as Mazarin thought he would? Nevertheless, as the dying man felt that the uncertainty increased his torments, he did not hesitate an instant.

"His majesty will be welcome,—yes, very welcome," cried he, making a sign to Colbert, who was seated at the foot of the bed, and which the latter understood perfectly. "Madame," continued Mazarin, "will your majesty be good enough to assure the king yourself of the truth of what I have just said?"

Anne of Austria rose; she herself was anxious to have the question of the forty millions settled—the question which seemed to lie heavy on the mind of everyone. Anne of Austria went out; Mazarin made a great effort, and, raising himself up towards Colbert: "Well, Colbert," said he, "two days have passed away—two mortal days—and, you see, nothing has been returned from yonder."

"Patience, my lord," said Colbert.

"Are you mad, you wretch? You advise me to have patience! Oh, in sad truth, Colbert, you are laughing at me. I am dying and you call out to me to wait!"

"My lord," said Colbert, with his habitual coolness, "it is impossible that things should not come out as I have said. His majesty is coming to see you, and no doubt he brings back the deed himself."

"Do you think so? Well, I, on the contrary, am sure that his majesty is coming to thank me."

At this moment Anne of Austria returned. On her way to the apartments of her son she had met with a new empiric. This was a powder which was said to have power to save the cardinal; and she brought a portion of this powder with her. But this was not what Mazarin expected; therefore he would not even look at it, declaring that life was not worth the pains that were taken to preserve it. But, whilst professing this philosophical axiom, his long-confined secret escaped him at last.

"That, madame," said he, "that is not the interesting part of my situation. I made, two days ago, a little donation to the king; up to this time, from delicacy, no doubt, his majesty has not condescended to say anything about it; but the time for explanation is come, and I implore your majesty to tell me if the king has made up his mind on that matter."

Anne of Austria was about to reply, when Mazarin stopped her.

"The truth, madame," said he—"in the name of Heaven, the truth! Do not flatter a dying man with a hope that may prove vain." There he stopped, a look from Colbert telling him he was on the wrong track.

"I know," said Anne of Austria, taking the cardinal's hand, "I know that you have generously made, not a little donation, as you modestly call it, but a magnificent gift. I know how painful it would be to you if the king—"

Mazarin listened, dying as he was, as ten living men could not have listened.

"If the king—" replied he.

"If the king," continued Anne of Austria, "should not freely accept what you offer so nobly."

Mazarin allowed himself to sink back upon his pillow like Pantaloon; that is to say, with all the despair of a man who bows before the tempest; but he still preserved sufficient strength and presence of mind to cast upon Colbert one of those looks which are well worth ten sonnets, which is to say, ten long poems.

"Should you not," added the queen, "have considered the refusal of the king as a sort of insult?" Mazarin rolled his head about upon his pillow, without articulating a syllable. The queen was deceived, or feigned to be deceived, by this demonstration.

"Therefore," resumed she, "I have circumvented him with good counsels; and as certain minds, jealous, no doubt, of the glory you are about to acquire by this generosity, have endeavored to prove to the king that he ought not to accept this donation, I have struggled in your favor, and so well I have struggled, that you will not have, I hope, that distress to undergo."

"Ah!" murmured Mazarin, with languishing eyes, "ah! that is a service I shall never forget for a single minute of the few hours I still have to live."

"I must admit," continued the queen, "that it was not without trouble I rendered it to your eminence."

"Ah, peste! I believe that. Oh! oh!"

"Good God! what is the matter?"

"I am burning!"

"Do you suffer much?"

"As much as one of the damned."

Colbert would have liked to sink through the floor.

"So, then," resumed Mazarin, "your majesty thinks that the king—" he stopped several seconds—"that the king is coming here to offer me some small thanks?"

"I think so," said queen. Mazarin annihilated Colbert with his last look.

At that moment the ushers announced that the king was in the ante-chambers, which were filled with people. This announcement produced a stir of which Colbert took advantage to escape by the door of the ruelle. Anne of Austria arose, and awaited her son, standing. Louis XIV. appeared at the threshold of the door, with his eyes fixed upon the dying man, who did not even think it worth while to notice that majesty from whom he thought he had nothing more to expect. An usher placed an armchair close to the bed. Louis bowed to his mother, then to the cardinal, and sat down. The queen took a seat in her turn.

Then, as the king looked behind him, the usher understood that look, and made a sign to the courtiers who filled up the doorway to go out, which they instantly did. Silence fell upon the chamber with the velvet curtains. The king, still very young, and very timid in the presence of him who had been his master from his birth, still respected him much, particularly now, in the supreme majesty of death. He did not dare, therefore, to begin the conversation, feeling that every word must have its weight not only upon things of this world, but of the next. As to the cardinal, at that moment he had but one thought—his donation. It was not physical pain which gave him that air of despondency, and that lugubrious look; it was the expectation of the thanks that were about to issue from the king's mouth, and cut off all hope of restitution. Mazarin was the first to break the silence. "Is your majesty come to make any stay at Vincennes?" said he.

Louis made an affirmative sign with his head.

"That is a gracious favor," continued Mazarin, "granted to a dying man, and which will render death less painful to him."

"I hope," replied the king, "I am come to visit, not a dying man, but a sick man, susceptible of cure."

Mazarin replied by a movement of the head.

"Your majesty is very kind; but I know more than you on that subject. The last visit, sire," said he, "the last visit."

"If it were so, monsieur le cardinal," said Louis, "I would come a last time to ask the counsels of a guide to whom I owe everything."

Anne of Austria was a woman; she could not restrain her tears. Louis showed himself much affected, and Mazarin still more than his two guests, but from very different motives. Here the silence returned. The queen wiped her eyes, and the king resumed his firmness.

"I was saying," continued the king, "that I owed much to your eminence." The eyes of the cardinal had devoured the king, for he felt the great moment had come. "And," continued Louis, "the principal object of my visit was to offer you very sincere thanks for the last evidence of friendship you have kindly sent me."

The cheeks of the cardinal became sunken, his lips partially opened, and the most lamentable sigh he had ever uttered was about to issue from his chest.

"Sire," said he, "I shall have despoiled my poor family; I shall have ruined all who belong to me, which may be imputed to me as an error; but, at least, it shall not be said of me that I have refused to sacrifice everything to my king."

Anne of Austria's tears flowed afresh.

"My dear Monsieur Mazarin," said the king, in a more serious tone than might have been expected from his youth, "you have misunderstood me, apparently."

Mazarin raised himself upon his elbow.

"I have no purpose to despoil your dear family, nor to ruin your servants. Oh, no, that must never be!"

"Humph!" thought Mazarin, "he is going to restore me some scraps; let us get the largest piece we can."

"The king is going to be foolishly affected and play generous," thought the queen; "he must not be allowed to impoverish himself; such an opportunity for getting a fortune will never occur again."

"Sire," said the cardinal, aloud, "my family is very numerous, and my nieces will be destitute when I am gone."

"Oh," interrupted the queen, eagerly, "have no uneasiness with respect to your family, dear Monsieur Mazarin; we have no friends dearer than your friends; your nieces shall be my children, the sisters of his majesty; and if a favor be distributed in France, it shall be to those you love."

"Smoke!" thought Mazarin, who knew better than any one the faith that can be put in the promises of kings. Louis read the dying man's thought in his face.

"Be comforted, my dear Monsieur Mazarin," said he, with a half-smile, sad beneath its irony; "the Mesdemoiselles de Mancini will lose, in losing you, their most precious good; but they shall none the less be the richest heiresses of France; and since you have been kind enough to give me their dowry"— the cardinal was panting—"I restore it to them," continued Louis, drawing from his breast and holding towards the cardinal's bed the parchment which contained the donation that, during two days, had kept alive such tempests in the mind of Mazarin.

"What did I tell you, my lord?" murmured in the alcove a voice which passed away like a breath.

"Your majesty returns my donation!" cried Mazarin, so disturbed by joy as to forget his character of a benefactor.

"Your majesty rejects the forty millions!" cried Anne of Austria, so stupefied as to forget her character of an afflicted wife, or queen.

"Yes, my lord cardinal; yes, madame," replied Louis XIV., tearing the parchment which Mazarin had not yet ventured to clutch; "yes, I annihilate this deed, which despoiled a whole family. The wealth acquired by his eminence in my service is his own wealth and not mine."

"But, sire, does your majesty reflect," said Anne of Austria, "that you have not ten thousand crowns in your coffers?"

"Madame, I have just performed my first royal action, and I hope it will worthily inaugurate my reign."

"Ah! sire, you are right!" cried Mazarin; "that is truly great—that is truly generous which you have just done." And he looked, one after the other, at the pieces of the act spread over his bed, to assure himself that it was the original and not a copy that had been torn. At length his eyes fell upon the fragment which bore his signature, and recognizing it, he sunk back on his bolster in a swoon. Anne of Austria, without strength to conceal her regret, raised her hands and eyes towards heaven.

"Oh! sire," cried Mazarin, "may you be blessed! My God! May you be beloved by all my family. Per Baccho! If ever any of those belonging to me should cause your displeasure, sire, only frown, and I will rise from my tomb!"

This pantalonnade did not produce all the effect Mazarin had counted upon. Louis had already passed to considerations of a higher nature, and as to Anne of Austria, unable to bear, without abandoning herself to the anger she felt burning within her, the magnanimity of her son and the hypocrisy of the cardinal, she arose and left the chamber, heedless of thus betraying the extent of her grief. Mazarin saw all this, and fearing that Louis XIV. might repent his decision, in order to draw attention another way he began to cry out, as, at a later period, Scapin was to cry out, in that sublime piece of pleasantry with which the morose and grumbling Boileau dared to reproach Moliere. His cries, however, by degrees, became fainter; and when Anne of Austria left the apartment, they ceased altogether.

"Monsieur le cardinal," said the king, "have you any recommendations to make me?"

"Sire," replied Mazarin, "you are already wisdom itself, prudence personified; of your generosity I shall not venture to speak; that which you have just done exceeds all that the most generous men of antiquity or of modern times have ever done."

The king received this praise coldly.

"So you confine yourself," said he, "to your thanks—and your experience, much more extensive than my wisdom, my prudence, or my generosity, does not furnish you with a single piece of friendly advice to guide my future." Mazarin reflected for a moment. "You have just done much for me, sire," said he, "that is, for my family."

"Say no more about that," said the king.

"Well!" continued Mazarin, "I shall give you something in exchange for these forty millions you have refused so royally."

Louis XIV. indicated by a movement that these flatteries were displeasing to him. "I shall give you a piece of advice," continued Mazarin; "yes, a piece of advice—advice more precious than the forty millions."

"My lord cardinal!" interrupted Louis.

"Sire, listen to this advice."

"I am listening."

"Come nearer, sire, for I am weak!—nearer, sire, nearer!"

The king bent over the dying man. "Sire," said Mazarin, in so low a tone that the breath of his words arrived only like a recommendation from the tomb in the attentive ears of the king—"Sire, never have a prime minister."

Louis drew back astonished. The advice was a confession—a treasure, in fact, was that sincere confession of Mazarin. The legacy of the cardinal to the young king was composed of six words only, but those six words, as Mazarin had said, were worth forty millions. Louis remained for an instant bewildered. As for Mazarin, he appeared only to have said something quite natural. A little scratching was heard along the curtains of the alcove. Mazarin understood: "Yes, yes!" cried he, warmly, "yes, sire, I recommend to you a wise man, an honest man, and a clever man."

"Tell me his name, my lord."

"His name is yet almost unknown, sire; it is M. Colbert, my attendant. Oh! try him," added Mazarin, in an earnest voice; "all that he has predicted has come to pass; he has a safe glance, he is never mistaken either in things or in men—which is more surprising still. Sire, I owe you much, but I think I acquit myself of all towards you in giving you M. Colbert."

"So be it," said Louis, faintly, for, as Mazarin had said, the name of Colbert was quite unknown to him, and he thought the enthusiasm of the cardinal partook of the delirium of a dying man. The cardinal sank back on his pillows.

"For the present, adieu, sire! adieu," murmured Mazarin. "I am tired, and I have yet a rough journey to take before I present myself to my new Master. Adieu, sire!"

The young king felt the tears rise to his eyes; he bent over the dying man, already half a corpse, and then hastily retired.

Chapter XLIX.
The First Appearance of Colbert.

THE whole night was passed in anguish, common to the dying man and to the king: the dying man expected his deliverance, the king awaited his liberty. Louis did not go to bed. An hour after leaving the chamber of the cardinal, he learned that the dying man, recovering a little strength, had insisted upon being dressed, adorned and painted, and seeing the ambassadors. Like Augustus, he no doubt considered the world a great stage, and was desirous of playing out the last act of the comedy. Anne of Austria reappeared no more in the cardinal's apartments; she had nothing more to do there. Propriety was the pretext for her absence. On his part, the cardinal did not ask for her: the advice the queen had giver her son rankled in his heart.

Towards midnight, while still painted, Mazarin's mortal agony came on. He had revised his will, and as this will was the exact expression of his wishes, and as he feared that some interested influence might take advantage of his weakness to make him change something in it, he had given orders to Colbert, who walked up and down the corridor which led to the cardinal's bed-chamber, like the most vigilant of sentinels. The king, shut up in his own apartment, dispatched his nurse every hour to Mazarin's chamber, with orders to bring him back an exact bulletin of the cardinal's state. After having heard that Mazarin was dressed, painted, and had seen the ambassadors, Louis herd that the prayers for the dying were being read for the cardinal. At one o'clock in the morning, Guenaud had administered the last remedy. This was a relic of the old customs of that fencing time, which was about to disappear to give place to another time, to believe that death could be kept off by some good secret thrust. Mazarin, after having taken the remedy, respired freely for nearly ten minutes. He immediately gave orders that the news should be spread everywhere of a fortunate crisis. The king, on learning this, felt as if a cold sweat were passing over his brow;—he had had a glimpse of the light of liberty; slavery appeared to him more dark and less acceptable than ever. But the bulletin which followed entirely changed the face of things. Mazarin could no longer breathe at all, and could scarcely follow the prayers which the cure of Saint-Nicholas-des-Champs recited near him. The king resumed his agitated walk about his chamber, and consulted, as he walked, several papers drawn from a casket of which he alone had the key. A third time the nurse returned. M. de Mazarin had just uttered a joke, and had ordered his "Flora," by Titian, to be revarnished. At length, towards two o'clock in the morning, the king could no longer resist his weariness: he had not slept for twenty-four hours. Sleep, so powerful at his age, overcame him for about an hour. But he did not go to bed for that hour; he slept in a fauteuil. About four o'clock his nurse awoke him by entering the room.

"Well?" asked the king.

"Well, my dear sire," said the nurse, clasping her hands with an air of commiseration. "Well; he is dead!"

The king arose at a bound, as if a steel spring had been applied to his legs. "Dead!" cried he.

"Alas! yes."

"Is it quite certain?"

"Yes."

"Official?"

"Yes."

"Has the news been made public?"

"Not yet."

"Who told you, then, that the cardinal was dead?"

"M. Colbert."

"M. Colbert?"

"Yes."

"And he was sure of what he said?"

"He came out of the chamber, and had held a glass for some minutes before the cardinal's lips."

"Ah!" said the king. "And what is become of M. Colbert?"

"He has just left his eminence's chamber."

"Where is he?"

"He followed me."

"So that he is—"

"Sire, waiting at your door, till it shall be your good pleasure to receive him."

Louis ran to the door, opened it himself, and perceived Colbert standing waiting in the passage. The king started at sight of this statue, all clothed in black. Colbert, bowing with profound respect, advanced two steps towards his majesty. Louis re-entered his chamber, making Colbert a sign to follow. Colbert entered; Louis dismissed the nurse, who closed the door as she went out. Colbert remained modestly standing near that door.

"What do you come to announce to me, monsieur?" said Louis, very much troubled at being thus surprised in his private thoughts, which he could not completely conceal.

"That monsieur le cardinal has just expired, sire; and that I bring your majesty his last adieu."

The king remained pensive for a minute; and during that minute he looked attentively at Colbert;—it was evident that the cardinal's last words were in his mind. "Are you, then, M. Colbert?" asked he.

"Yes, sire."

"His faithful servant, as his eminence himself told me?"

"Yes, sire."

"The depositary of many of his secrets?"

"Of all of them."

"The friends and servants of his eminence will be dear to me, monsieur, and I shall take care that you are well placed in my employment."

Colbert bowed.

"You are a financier, monsieur, I believe?"

"Yes, sire."

"And did monsieur le cardinal employ you in his stewardship?"

"I had that honor, sire."

"You never did anything personally for my household, I believe?"

"Pardon me, sire, it was I who had the honor of giving monsieur le cardinal the idea of an economy which puts three hundred thousand francs a year into your majesty's coffers."

"What economy was that, monsieur?" asked Louis XIV.

"Your majesty knows that the hundred Swiss have silver lace on each side of their ribbons?"

"Doubtless."

"Well, sire, it was I who proposed that imitation silver lace should be placed upon these ribbons; it could not be detected, and a hundred thousand crowns serve to feed a regiment during six months; and is the price of ten thousand good muskets or the value of a vessel of ten guns, ready for sea."

"That is true," said Louis XIV., considering more attentively, "and, ma foi! that was a well placed economy; besides, it was ridiculous for soldiers to wear the same lace as noblemen."

"I am happy to be approved of by your majesty."

"Is that the only appointment you held about the cardinal?" asked the king.

"It was I who was appointed to examine the accounts of the superintendent, sire."

"Ah!" said Louis, who was about to dismiss Colbert, but whom that word stopped; "ah! it was you whom his eminence had charged to control M. Fouquet, was it? And the result of that examination?"

"Is that there is a deficit, sire; but if your majesty will permit me—"

"Speak, M. Colbert."

"I ought to give your majesty some explanations."

"Not at all, monsieur, it is you who have controlled these accounts; give me the result."

"That is very easily done, sire: emptiness everywhere, money nowhere."

"Beware, monsieur; you are roughly attacking the administration of M. Fouquet, who, nevertheless, I have heard say, is an able man."

Colbert colored, and then became pale, for he felt that from that minute he entered upon a struggle with a man whose power almost equaled the sway of him who had just died. "Yes, sire, a very able man," repeated Colbert, bowing.

"But if M. Fouquet is an able man, and, in spite of that ability, if money be wanting, whose fault is it?"

"I do not accuse, sire, I verify."

"That is well; make out your accounts, and present them to me. There is a deficit, you say? A deficit may be temporary; credit returns and funds are restored."

"No, sire."

"Upon this year, perhaps, I understand that; but upon next year?"

"Next year is eaten as bare as the current year."

"But the year after, then?"

"Will be just like next year."

"What do you tell me, Monsieur Colbert?"

"I say there are four years engaged beforehand."

"They must have a loan, then."

"They must have three, sire."

"I will create offices to make them resign, and the salary of the posts shall be paid into the treasury."

"Impossible, sire, for there have already been creations upon creations of offices, the provisions of which are given in blank, so that the purchasers enjoy them without filling them. That is why your majesty cannot make them resign. Further, upon each agreement M. Fouquet has made an abatement of a third, so that the people have been plundered, without your majesty profiting by it."

The king started. "Explain me that, M. Colbert," he said.

"Let your majesty set down clearly your thought, and tell me what you wish me to explain."

"You are right, clearness is what you wish, is it not?"

"Yes, sire, clearness. God is God above all things, because He made light."

"Well, for example," resumed Louis XIV., "if to-day, the cardinal being dead, and I being king, suppose I wanted money?"

"Your majesty would not have any."

"Oh! that is strange, monsieur! How! my superintendent would not find me any money?"

Colbert shook his large head.

"How is that?" said the king; "is the income of the state so much in debt that there is no longer any revenue?"

"Yes, sire."

The king frowned and said, "If it be so, I will get together the ordonnances to obtain a discharge from the holders, a liquidation at a cheap rate."

"Impossible, for the ordonnances have been converted into bills, which bills, for the convenience of return and facility of transaction, are divided into so many parts that the originals can no longer be recognized."

Louis, very much agitated, walked about, still frowning. "But, if this is as you say, Monsieur Colbert," said he, stopping all at once, "I shall be ruined before I begin to reign."

"You are, in fact, sire," said the impassible caster-up of figures.

"Well, but yet, monsieur, the money is somewhere?"

"Yes, sire, and even as a beginning, I bring your majesty a note of funds which M. le Cardinal Mazarin was not willing to set down in his testament, neither in any act whatever, but which he confided to me."

"To you?"

"Yes, sire, with an injunction to remit it to your majesty."

"What! besides the forty millions of the testament?"

"Yes, sire."

"M. de Mazarin had still other funds?"

Colbert bowed.

"Why, that man was a gulf!" murmured the king. "M. de Mazarin on one side, M. Fouquet on the other,—more than a hundred millions perhaps between them! No wonder my coffers should be empty!" Colbert waited without stirring.

"And is the sum you bring me worth the trouble?" asked the king.

"Yes, sire, it is a round sum."

"Amounting to how much?"

"To thirteen millions of livres, sire."

"Thirteen millions!" cried Louis, trembling with joy; "do you say thirteen millions, Monsieur Colbert?"

"I said thirteen millions, yes, your majesty."

"Of which everybody is ignorant?"

"Of which everybody is ignorant."

"Which are in your hands?"

"In my hands, yes, sire."

"And which I can have?"

"Within two hours, sire."

"But where are they, then?"

"In the cellar of a house which the cardinal possessed in the city, and which he was so kind as to leave me by a particular clause of his will."

"You are acquainted with the cardinal's will, then?"

"I have a duplicate of it, signed by his hand."

"A duplicate?"

"Yes, sire, and here it is." Colbert drew the deed quietly from his pocket, and showed it to the king. The king read the article relative to the donation of the house.

"But," said he, "there is no question here but of the house; there is nothing said of the money."

"Your pardon, sire, it is in my conscience."

"And Monsieur Mazarin has intrusted it to you?"

"Why not, sire?"

"He! a man mistrustful of everybody?"

"He was not so of me, sire, as your majesty may perceive."

Louis fixed his eyes with admiration upon that vulgar but expressive face. "You are an honest man, M. Colbert," said the king.

"That is not a virtue, it is a duty," replied Colbert, coolly.

"But," added Louis, "does not the money belong to the family?"

"If this money belonged to the family it would be disposed of in the testament, as the rest of the fortune is. If this money belonged to the family, I, who drew up the deed of donation in favor of your majesty, should have added the sum of thirteen millions to that of forty millions which was offered to you."

"How!" exclaimed Louis XIV., "was it you who drew up the deed of donation?"

"Yes, sire."

"And yet the cardinal was attached to you?" added the king, ingenuously.

"I had assured his eminence you would by no means accept the gift," said Colbert, in that same quiet manner we have described, and which, even in the common habits of life, had something solemn in it.

Louis passed his hand over his brow: "Oh! how young I am," murmured he, "to have command of men."

Colbert waited the end of this monologue. He saw Louis raise his head. "At what hour shall I send the money to your majesty?" asked he.

"To-night, at eleven o'clock; I desire that no one may know that I possess this money."

Colbert made no more reply than if the thing had not been said to him.

"Is the amount in ingots, or coined gold?"

"In coined gold, sire."

"That is well."

"Where shall I send it?"

"To the Louvre. Thank you, M. Colbert."

Colbert bowed and retired. "Thirteen millions!" exclaimed Louis, as soon as he was alone. "This must be a dream!" Then he allowed his head to sink between his hands, as if he were really asleep. But, at the end of a moment, he arose, and opening the window violently, he bathed his burning brow in the keen morning air, which brought to his senses the scent of the trees, and the perfume of the flowers. A splendid dawn was gilding the horizon, and the first rays of the sun bathed in flame the young king's brow. "This is the dawn of my reign," murmured Louis XIV. "It's a presage sent by the Almighty."

Chapter L:
The First Day of the Royalty of Louis XIV.

IN the morning, the news of the death of the cardinal was spread through the castle, and thence speedily reached the city. The ministers Fouquet, Lyonne, and Letellier entered la salle des seances, to hold a council. The king sent for them immediately. "Messieurs," said he, "as long as monsieur le cardinal lived, I allowed him to govern my affairs; but now I mean to govern them myself. You will give me your advice when I ask it. You may go."

The ministers looked at each other with surprise. If they concealed a smile it was with a great effort, for they knew that the prince, brought up in absolute ignorance of business, by this took upon himself a burden much too heavy for his strength. Fouquet took leave of his colleagues upon the stairs, saying:—"Messieurs! there will be so much the less labor for us."

And he gayly climbed into his carriage. The others, a little uneasy at the turn things had taken, went back to Paris together. Towards ten o'clock the king repaired to the apartment of his mother, with whom he had a long and private conversation. After dinner, he got into his carriage, and went straight to the Louvre. There he received much company, and took a degree of pleasure in remarking the hesitation of each, and the curiosity of all. Towards evening he ordered the doors of the Louvre to be closed, with the exception of only one, which opened on the quay. He placed on duty at this point two hundred Swiss, who did not speak a word of French, with orders to admit all who carried packages, but no others; and by no means to allow any one to go out. At eleven o'clock precisely, he heard the rolling of a heavy carriage under the arch, then of another, then of a third; after which the gate grated upon its hinges to be closed. Soon after, somebody scratched with his nail at the door of the cabinet. The king opened it himself, and beheld Colbert, whose first word was this:—"The money is in your majesty's cellar."

The king then descended and went himself to see the barrels of specie, in gold and silver, which, under the direction of Colbert, four men had just rolled into a cellar of which the king had given Colbert the key in the morning. This review completed, Louis returned to his apartments, followed by Colbert, who had not apparently warmed with one ray of personal satisfaction.

"Monsieur," said the king, "what do you wish that I should give you, as a recompense for this devotedness and probity?"

"Absolutely nothing, sire."

"How! nothing? Not even an opportunity of serving me?"

"If your majesty were not to furnish me with that opportunity, I should not the less serve you. It is impossible for me not to be the best servant of the king."

"You shall be intendant of the finances, M. Colbert."

"But there is already a superintendent, sire."

"I know that."

"Sire, the superintendent of the finances is the most powerful man in the kingdom."

"Ah!" cried Louis, coloring, "do you think so?"

"He will crush me in a week, sire. Your majesty gives me a controle for which strength is indispensable. An intendant under a superintendent,—that is inferiority."

"You want support—you do not reckon upon me?"

"I had the honor of telling your majesty, that during the lifetime of M. de Mazarin, M. Fouquet was the second man in the kingdom; now M. de Mazarin is dead, M. Fouquet is become the first."

"Monsieur, I agree to what you told me of all things up to to-day; but to-morrow, please to remember, I shall no longer suffer it."

"Then I shall be of no use to your majesty?"

"You are already, since you fear to compromise yourself in serving me."

"I only fear to be placed so that I cannot serve your majesty."

"What do you wish, then?"

"I wish your majesty to allow me assistance in the labors of the office of intendant."

"That post would lose its value."

"It would gain in security."

"Choose your colleagues."

"Messieurs Breteuil, Marin, Hervart."

"To-morrow the ordonnance shall appear."

"Sire, I thank you."

"Is that all you ask?"

"No, sire, one thing more."

"What is that?"

"Allow me to compose a chamber of justice."

"What would this chamber of justice do?"

"Try the farmers-general and contractors, who, during ten years, have been robbing the state."

"Well, but what would you do with them?"

"Hang two or three, and that would make the rest disgorge."

"I cannot commence my reign with executions, Monsieur Colbert."

"On the contrary, sire, you had better, in order not to have to end with them."

The king made no reply. "Does your majesty consent?" said Colbert.

"I will reflect upon it, monsieur."

"It will be too late when reflection may be made."

"Why?"

"Because you have to deal with people stronger than ourselves, if they are warned."

"Compose that chamber of justice, monsieur."

"I will, sire."

"Is that all?"

"No, sire; there is still another important affair. What rights does your majesty attach to this office of intendant?"

"Well—I do not know—the customary ones."

"Sire, I desire that this office be invested with the right of reading the correspondence with England."

"Impossible, monsieur, for that correspondence is kept from the council; monsieur le cardinal himself carried it on."

"I thought your majesty had this morning declared that there should no longer be a council?"

"Yes, I said so."

"Let your majesty then have the goodness to read all the letters yourself, particularly those from England; I hold strongly to this article."

"Monsieur, you shall have that correspondence, and render me an account of it."

"Now, sire, what shall I do with respect to the finances?"

"Everything M. Fouquet has not done."

"That is all I ask of your majesty. Thanks, sire, I depart in peace;" and at these words he took his leave. Louis watched his departure. Colbert was not yet a hundred paces from the Louvre when the king received a courier from England. After having looked at and examined the envelope, the king broke the seal precipitately, and found a letter from Charles II. The following is what the English prince wrote to his royal brother:—

"Your majesty must be rendered very uneasy by the illness of M. le Cardinal Mazarin; but the excess of danger can only prove of service to you. The cardinal is given over by his physician. I thank you for the gracious reply you have made to my communication touching the Princess Henrietta, my sister, and, in a week, the princess and her court will set out for Paris. It is gratifying to me to acknowledge the fraternal friendship you have evinced towards me, and to call you, more justly than ever, my brother. It is gratifying to me, above everything, to prove to your majesty how much I am interested in all that may please you. You are wrong in having Belle-Ile-en-Mer secretly fortified. That is wrong. We shall never be at war against each other. That measure does not make me uneasy, it makes me sad. You are spending useless millions; tell your ministers so; and rest assured that I am well informed; render me the same service, my brother, if occasion offers."

The king rang his bell violently, and his valet de chambre appeared. "Monsieur Colbert is just gone; he cannot be far off. Let him be called back!" exclaimed he.

The valet was about to execute the order, when the king stopped him.

"No," said he, "no; I see the whole scheme of that man. Belle-Isle belongs to M. Fouquet; Belle-Isle is being fortified: that is a conspiracy on the part of M. Fouquet. The discovery of that conspiracy is the ruin of the superintendent, and that discovery is the result of the correspondence with England: this is why Colbert wished to have that correspondence. Oh! but I cannot place all my dependence upon that man; he has a good head, but I must have an arm!" Louis, all at once, uttered a joyful cry. "I had," said he, "a lieutenant of musketeers!"

"Yes, sire—Monsieur d'Artagnan."

"He quitted the service for a time."

"Yes, sire."

"Let him be found, and be here to-morrow the first thing in the morning."

The valet de chambre bowed and went out.

"Thirteen millions in my cellar," said the king; "Colbert carrying my purse and D'Artagnan my sword—I am king."

Chapter LI.
A Passion.

THE day of his arrival, on returning from the Palais Royal, Athos, as we have seen, went straight to his hotel in the Rue Saint-Honore. He there found the Vicomte de Bragelonne waiting for him in his chamber, chatting with Grimaud. It was not an easy thing to talk with this old servant. Two men only possessed the secret, Athos and D'Artagnan. The first succeeded, because Grimaud sought to make him speak himself; D'Artagnan, on the contrary, because he knew how to make Grimaud talk. Raoul was occupied in making him describe the voyage to England, and Grimaud had related it in all its details, with a limited number of gestures and eight words, neither more nor less. He had, at first, indicated by an undulating movement of his hand, that his master and he had crossed the sea. "Upon some expedition?" Raoul had asked.

Grimaud by bending down his head had answered, "Yes."

"When monsieur le comte incurred much danger?" asked Raoul.

"Neither too much nor too little," was replied by a shrug of the shoulders.

"But still, what sort of danger?" insisted Raoul.

Grimaud pointed to the sword; he pointed to the fire and to a musket that was hanging on the wall.

"Monsieur le comte had an enemy there, then?" cried Raoul.

"Monk," replied Grimaud.

"It is strange," continued Raoul, "that monsieur le comte persists in considering me a novice, and not allowing me to partake the honor and danger of his adventure."

Grimaud smiled. It was at this moment Athos came in. The host was lighting him up the stairs, and Grimaud, recognizing the step of his master, hastened to meet him, which cut short the conversation. But Raoul was launched on the sea of interrogatories, and did not stop. Taking both hands of the comte, with warm, but respectful tenderness,—"How is it, monsieur," said he, "that you have set out upon a dangerous voyage without bidding me adieu, without commanding the aid of my sword, of myself, who ought to be your support, now I have the strength; whom you have brought up like a man? Ah! monsieur, can you expose me to the cruel trial of never seeing you again?"

"Who told you, Raoul," said the comte, placing his cloak and hat in the hands of Grimaud, who had unbuckled his sword, "who told you that my voyage was a dangerous one?"

"I," said Grimaud.

"And why did you do so?" said Athos, sternly.

Grimaud was embarrassed; Raoul came to his assistance, by answering for him. "It is natural, monsieur, that our good Grimaud should tell me the truth in what concerns you. By whom should you be loved an supported, if not by me?"

Athos did not reply. He made a friendly motion to Grimaud, which sent him out of the room; he then seated himself in a fauteuil, whilst Raoul remained standing before him.

"But it is true," continued Raoul, "that your voyage was an expedition, and that steel and fire threatened you?"

"Say no more about that, vicomte," said Athos, mildly. "I set out hastily, it is true: but the service of King Charles II. required a prompt departure. As to your anxiety, I thank you for it, and I know that I can depend on you. You have not wanted for anything, vicomte, in my absence, have you?"

"No, monsieur, thank you."

"I left orders with Blaisois to pay you a hundred pistoles, if you should stand in need of money."

"Monsieur, I have not seen Blaisois."

"You have been without money, then?"

"Monsieur, I had thirty pistoles left from the sale of the horses I took in my last campaign, and M. le Prince had the kindness to allow me to win two hundred pistoles at his play-table three months ago."

"Do you play? I don't like that, Raoul."

"I never play, monsieur; it was M. le Prince who ordered me to hold his cards at Chantilly—one night when a courier came to him from the king. I won, and M. le Prince commanded me to take the stakes."

"Is that a practice in the household, Raoul?" asked Athos with a frown.

"Yes, monsieur; every week M. le Prince affords, upon one occasion or another, a similar advantage to one of his gentlemen. There are fifty gentlemen in his highness's household; it was my turn."

"Very well! You went into Spain, then?"

"Yes, monsieur, I made a very delightful and interesting journey."

"You have been back a month, have you not?"

"Yes, monsieur."

"And in the course of that month?"

"In that month—"

"What have you done?"

"My duty, monsieur."

"Have you not been home, to La Fere?"

Raoul colored. Athos looked at him with a fixed but tranquil expression.

"You would be wrong not to believe me," said Raoul. "I feel that I colored, and in spite of myself. The question you did me the honor to ask me is of a nature to raise in me much emotion. I color, then, because I am agitated, not because I meditate a falsehood."

"I know, Raoul, you never lie."

"No, monsieur."

"Besides, my young friend, you would be wrong; what I wanted to say—"

"I know quite well, monsieur. You would ask me if I have not been to Blois?"

"Exactly so."

"I have not been there; I have not even seen the person to whom you allude."

Raoul's voice trembled as he pronounced these words. Athos, a sovereign judge in all matters of delicacy, immediately added, "Raoul, you answer me with a painful feeling; you are unhappy."

"Very, monsieur; you have forbidden me to go to Blois, or to see Mademoiselle de la Valliere again." Here the young man stopped. That dear name, so delightful to pronounce, made his heart bleed, although so sweet upon his lips.

"And I have acted rightly, Raoul." Athos hastened to reply. "I am neither an unjust nor a barbarous father; I respect true love; but I look forward for you to a future—an immense future. A new reign is about to break upon us like a fresh dawn. War calls upon a young king full of chivalric spirit. What is wanting to assist this heroic ardor is a battalion of young and free lieutenants who would rush to the fight with enthusiasm, and fall, crying: 'Vive le Roi!' instead of 'Adieu, my dear wife.' You understand that, Raoul. However brutal my reasoning may appear, I conjure you, then, to believe me, and to turn away your thoughts from those early days of youth in which you took up this habit of love—days of effeminate carelessness, which soften the heart and render it incapable of consuming those strong bitter draughts called glory and adversity. Therefore, Raoul, I repeat to you, you should see in my counsel only the desire of being useful to you, only the ambition of seeing you prosper. I believe you capable of becoming a remarkable man. March alone, and you will march better, and more quickly."

"You have commanded, monsieur," replied Raoul, "and I obey."

"Commanded!" cried Athos. "Is it thus you reply to me? I have commanded you! Oh! you distort my words as you misconceive my intentions. I do not command you; I request you."

"No, monsieur, you have commanded," said Raoul, persistently; "had you requested me, your request is even more effective than your order. I have not seen Mademoiselle de la Valliere again."

"But you are unhappy! you are unhappy!" insisted Athos.

Raoul made no reply.

"I find you pale; I find you dull. The sentiment is strong, then?"

"It is a passion," replied Raoul.

"No—a habit."

"Monsieur, you know I have traveled much, that I have passed two years far away from her. A habit would yield to an absence of two years, I believe; whereas, on my return, I loved not more, that was impossible, but as much. Mademoiselle de la Valliere is for me the one lady above all others; but you are for me a god upon earth—to you I sacrifice everything."

"You are wrong," said Athos; "I have no longer any right over you. Age has emancipated you; you no longer even stand in need of my consent. Besides, I will not refuse my consent after what you have told me. Marry Mademoiselle de la Valliere, if you like."

Raoul was startled, but suddenly: "You are very kind, monsieur," said he; "and your concession excites my warmest gratitude, but I will not accept it."

"Then you now refuse?"

"Yes, monsieur."

"I will not oppose you in anything, Raoul."

"But you have at the bottom of your heart an idea against this marriage: it is not your choice."

"That is true."

"That is sufficient to make me resist: I will wait."

"Beware, Raoul! What you are now saying is serious."

"I know it is, monsieur; as I said, I will wait."

"Until I die?" said Athos, much agitated.

"Oh! monsieur," cried Raoul, with tears in his eyes, "is it possible that you should wound my heart thus? I have never given you cause of complaint!"

"Dear boy, that is true," murmured Athos, pressing his lips violently together to conceal the emotion of which he was no longer master. "No, I will no longer afflict you; only I do not comprehend what you mean by waiting. Will you wait till you love no longer?"

"Ah! for that!—no, monsieur. I will wait till you change your opinion."

"I should wish to put the matter to a test, Raoul; I should like to see if Mademoiselle de la Valliere will wait as you do."

"I hope so, monsieur."

"But, take care, Raoul! suppose she did not wait? Ah, you are young, so confiding, so loyal! Women are changeable."

"You have never spoken ill to me of women, monsieur; you have never had to complain of them; why should you doubt of Mademoiselle de la Valliere?"

"That is true," said Athos, casting down his eyes; "I have never spoken ill to you of women; I have never had to complain of them; Mademoiselle de la Valliere never gave birth to a suspicion; but when we are looking forward, we must go even to exceptions, even to improbabilities! If, I say, Mademoiselle de la Valliere should not wait for you?"

"How, monsieur?"

"If she turned her eyes another way."

"If she looked favorably upon another, do you mean, monsieur?" said Raoul, pale with agony.

"Exactly."

"Well, monsieur, I would kill him," said Raoul, simply, "and all the men whom Mademoiselle de la Valliere should choose, until one of them had killed me, or Mademoiselle de la Valliere had restored me her heart."

Athos started. "I thought," resumed he, in an agitated voice, "that you called my just now your god, your law in this world."

"Oh!" said Raoul, trembling, "you would forbid me the duel?"

"Suppose I did forbid it, Raoul?"

"You would not forbid me to hope, monsieur; consequently you would not forbid me to die."

Athos raised his eyes toward the vicomte. He had pronounced these words with the most melancholy look. "Enough," said Athos, after a long silence, "enough of this subject, upon which we both go too far. Live as well as you are able, Raoul, perform your duties, love Mademoiselle de la Valliere; in a word, act like a man, since you have attained the age of a man; only do not forget that I love you tenderly, and that you profess to love me."

"Ah! monsieur le comte!" cried Raoul, pressing the hand of Athos to his heart.

"Enough, dear boy, leave me; I want rest. A propos, M. d'Artagnan has returned from England with me; you owe him a visit."

"I will pay it, monsieur, with great pleasure. I love Monsieur d'Artagnan exceedingly."

"You are right in doing so; he is a worthy man and a brave cavalier."

"Who loves you dearly."

"I am sure of that. Do you know his address?"

"At the Louvre, I suppose, or wherever the king is. Does he not command the musketeers?"

"No; at present M. d'Artagnan is absent on leave; he is resting for awhile. Do not, therefore, seek him at the posts of his service. You will hear of him at the house of a certain Planchet."

"His former lackey?"

"Exactly; turned grocer."

"I know; Rue des Lombards?"

"Somewhere thereabouts, or Rue des Arcis."

"I will find it, monsieur—I will find it."

"You will say a thousand kind things to him, on my part, and ask him to come and dine with me before I set out for La Fere."

"Yes, monsieur."

"Good-might, Raoul!"

"Monsieur, I see you wear an order I never saw you wear before; accept my compliments."

"The Fleece!—that is true. A bauble, my boy, which no longer amuses an old child like myself. Good-night, Raoul!"

Chapter LII.
D'Artagnan's Lesson.

RAOUL did not meet with D'Artagnan the next day, as he had hoped. He only met with Planchet, whose joy was great at seeing the young man again, and who contrived to pay him two or three little soldierly compliments, savoring very little of the grocer's shop. But as Raoul was returning the next day from Vincennes at the head of fifty dragoons confided to him by Monsieur le Prince, he perceived, in La Place Baudoyer, a man with his nose in the air, examining a house as we examine a horse we have a fancy to buy. This man, dressed in a citizen costume buttoned up like a military pourpoint, a very small hat on his head, but a long shagreen-mounted sword by his side, turned his head as soon as he heard the steps of the horses, and left off looking at the house to look at the dragoons. It was simply M. d'Artagnan; D'Artagnan on foot; D'Artagnan with his hands behind him, passing a little review upon the dragoons, after having reviewed the buildings. Not a man, not a tag, not a horse's hoof escaped his inspection. Raoul rode at the side of his troop; D'Artagnan perceived him the last. "Eh!" said he, "Eh! Mordioux!"

"I was not mistaken!" cried Raoul, turning his horse towards him.

"Mistaken—no! Good-day to you," replied the ex-musketeer; whilst Raoul eagerly pressed the hand of his old friend. "Take care, Raoul," said D'Artagnan, "the second horse of the fifth rank will lose a shoe before he gets to the Pont Marie; he has only two nails left in his off fore-foot."

"Wait a minute, I will come back," said Raoul.

"Can you quit your detachment?"

"The cornet is there to take my place."

"Then you will come and dine with me?"

"Most willingly, Monsieur d'Artagnan."

"Be quick, then; leave your horse, or make them give me one."

"I prefer coming back on foot with you."

Raoul hastened to give notice to the cornet, who took his post; he then dismounted, gave his horse to one of the dragoons, and with great delight seized the arm of M. d'Artagnan, who had watched him during all these little evolutions with the satisfaction of a connoisseur.

"What, do you come from Vincennes?" said he.

"Yes, monsieur le chevalier."

"And the cardinal?"

"Is very ill; it is even reported he is dead."

"Are you on good terms with M. Fouquet?" asked D'Artagnan, with a disdainful movement of the shoulders, proving that the death of Mazarin did not affect him beyond measure.

"With M. Fouquet?" said Raoul; "I do not know him."

"So much the worse! so much the worse! for a new king always seeks to get good men in his employment."

"Oh! the king means no harm," replied the young man.

"I say nothing about the crown," cried D'Artagnan; "I am speaking of the king—the king, that is M. Fouquet, if the cardinal is dead. You must contrive to stand well with M. Fouquet, if you do not wish to molder away all your life as I have moldered. It is true you have, fortunately, other protectors."

"M. le Prince, for instance."

"Worn out! worn out!"

"M. le Comte de la Fere?"

"Athos! Oh! that's different; yes, Athos—and if you have any wish to make your way in England, you cannot apply to a better person; I can even say, without too much vanity, that I myself have some credit at the court of Charles II. There is a king—God speed him!"

"Ah!" cried Raoul, with the natural curiosity of well-born young people, while listening to experience and courage.

"Yes, a king who amuses himself, it is true, but who has had a sword in his hand, and can appreciate useful men. Athos is on good terms with Charles II. Take service there, and leave these scoundrels of contractors and farmers-general, who steal as well with French hands as others have done with Italian hands; leave the little snivelling king, who is going to give us another reign of Francis II. Do you know anything of history, Raoul?"

"Yes, monsieur le chevalier."

"Do you know, then, that Francis II. had always the earache?"

"No, I did not know that."

"That Charles IV. had always the headache?"

"Indeed!"

"And Henry III. had always the stomach-ache?"

Raoul began to laugh.

"Well, my dear friend, Louis XIV. always has the heart-ache; it is deplorable to see a king sighing from morning till night without saying once in the course of the day, ventre-saint-gris! corboeuf! or anything to rouse one."

"Was that the reason why you quitted the service, monsieur le chevalier?"

"Yes."

"But you yourself, M. d'Artagnan, are throwing the handle after the axe; you will not make a fortune."

"Who? I?" replied D'Artagnan, in a careless tone; "I am settled—I had some family property."

Raoul looked at him. The poverty of D'Artagnan was proverbial. A Gascon, he exceeded in ill-luck all the gasconnades of France and Navarre; Raoul had a hundred times heard Job and D'Artagnan named together, as the twins Romulus and Remus. D'Artagnan caught Raoul's look of astonishment.

"And has not your father told you I have been in England?"

"Yes, monsieur le chevalier."

"And that I there met with a very lucky chance?"

"No, monsieur, I did not know that."

"Yes, a very worthy friend of mine, a great nobleman, the viceroy of Scotland and Ireland, has endowed me with an inheritance."

"An inheritance?"

"And a good one, too."

"Then you are rich?"

"Bah!"

"Receive my sincere congratulation."

"Thank you! Look, that is my house."

"Place de Greve?"

"Yes; don't you like this quarter?"

"On the contrary, the look-out over the water is pleasant. Oh! what a pretty old house!"

"The sign Notre Dame; it is an old cabaret, which I have transformed into a private house in two days."

"But the cabaret is still open?"

"Pardieu!"

"And where do you lodge, then?"

"I? I lodge with Planchet."

"You said, just now, 'This is my house.'"

"I said so, because, in fact, it is my house. I have bought it."

"Ah!" said Raoul.

"At ten years' purchase, my dear Raoul; a superb affair; I bought the house for thirty thousand livres; it has a garden which opens to the Rue de la Mortillerie; the cabaret lets for a thousand livres, with the first story; the garret, or second floor, for five hundred livres."

"Indeed!"

"Yes, indeed."

"Five hundred livres for a garret? Why, it is not habitable."

"Therefore no one inhabits it; only, you see, this garret has two windows which look out upon the Place."

"Yes, monsieur."

"Well, then, every time anybody is broken on the wheel or hung, quartered, or burnt, these two windows let for twenty pistoles."

"Oh!" said Raoul, with horror.

"It is disgusting, is it not?" said D'Artagnan.

"Oh!" repeated Raoul.

"It is disgusting, but so it is. These Parisian cockneys are sometimes real anthropophagi. I cannot conceive how men, Christians, can make such speculation.

"That is true."

"As for myself," continued D'Artagnan, "if I inhabited that house, on days of execution I would shut it up to the very keyholes; but I do not inhabit it."

"And you let the garret for five hundred livres?"

"To the ferocious cabaretier, who sub-lets it. I said, then, fifteen hundred livres."

"The natural interest of money," said Raoul,—"five per cent."

"Exactly so. I then have left the side of the house at the back, store-rooms, and cellars, inundated every winter, two hundred livres; and the garden, which is very fine, well planted, well shaded under the walls and the portal of Saint-Gervais-Saint-Protais, thirteen hundred livres."

"Thirteen hundred livres! why, that is royal!"

"This is the whole history. I strongly suspect some canon of the parish (these canons are all rich as Croesus)—I suspect some canon of having hired the garden to take his pleasure in. The tenant has given the name of M. Godard. That is either a false name or a real name; if true, he is a canon; if false, he is some unknown; but of what consequence is it to me? he always pays in advance. I had also an idea just now, when I met you, of buying a house in the Place Baudoyer, the back premises of which join my garden, and would make a magnificent property. Your dragoons interrupted my calculations. But come, let us take the Rue de la Vannerie: that will lead us straight to M. Planchet's." D'Artagnan mended his pace, and conducted Raoul to Planchet's dwelling, a chamber of which the grocer had given up to his old master. Planchet was out, but the dinner was ready. There was a remains of military regularity and punctuality preserved in the grocer's household. D'Artagnan returned to the subject of Raoul's future.

"Your father brings you up rather strictly?" said he.

"Justly, monsieur le chevalier."

"Oh, yes, I know Athos is just; but close, perhaps?"

"A royal hand, Monsieur d'Artagnan."

"Well, never want, my boy! If ever you stand in need of a few pistoles, the old musketeer is at hand."

"My dear Monsieur d'Artagnan!"

"Do you play a little?"

"Never."

"Successful with the ladies, then?—Oh! my little Aramis! That, my dear friend, costs even more than play. It is true we fight when we lose; that is a compensation. Bah! that little sniveller, the king, makes winners give him his revenge. What a reign! my poor Raoul, what a reign! When we think that, in my time, the musketeers were besieged in their houses like Hector and Priam in the city of Troy; and the women wept, and then the walls laughed, and then five hundred beggarly fellows clapped their hands and cried, 'Kill! kill!' when not one musketeer was hurt. Mordioux! you will never see anything like that."

"You are very hard upon the king, my dear Monsieur d'Artagnan and yet you scarcely know him."

"I! Listen, Raoul. Day by day, hour by hour,—take note of my words,—I will predict what he will do. The cardinal being dead, he will fret; very well, that is the least silly thing he will do, particularly if he does not shed a tear."

"And then?"

"Why, then he will get M. Fouquet to allow him a pension, and will go and compose verses at Fontainebleau, upon some Mancini or other, whose eyes the queen will scratch out. She is a Spaniard, you see,—this queen of ours; and she has, for mother-in-law, Madame Anne of Austria. I know something of the Spaniards of the house of Austria."

"And next?"

"Well, after having torn the silver lace from the uniforms of his Swiss, because lace is too expensive, he will dismount his musketeers, because oats and hay of a horse cost five sols a day."

"Oh! do not say that."

"Of what consequence is it to me? I am no longer a musketeer, am I? Let them be on horseback, let them be on foot, let them carry a larding-pin, a spit, a sword, or nothing—what is it to me?"

"My dear Monsieur d'Artagnan, I beseech you speak no more ill of the king. I am almost in his service, and my father would be very angry with me for having heard, even from your mouth, words injurious to his majesty."

"Your father, eh! He is a knight in every bad cause. Pardieu! yes, your father is a brave man, a Caesar, it is true—but a man without perception."

"Now, my dear chevalier," exclaimed Raoul, laughing, "are you going to speak ill of my father, of him you call the great Athos? Truly you are in a bad vein to-day; riches render you as sour as poverty renders other people."

"Pardieu! you are right. I am a rascal and in my dotage; I am an unhappy wretch grown old; a tent-cord untwisted, a pierced cuirass, a boot without a sole, a spur without a rowel;—but do me the pleasure to add one thing."

"What is that, my dear Monsieur d'Artagnan?"

"Simply say: 'Mazarin was a pitiful wretch.'"

"Perhaps he is dead."

"More the reason—I say was; if I did not hope that he was dead, I would entreat you to say: 'Mazarin is a pitiful wretch.' Come, say so, say so, for love of me."

"Well, I will."

"Say it!"

"Mazarin was a pitiful wretch," said Raoul, smiling at the musketeer, who roared with laughter, as in his best days.

"A moment," said the latter; "you have spoken my first proposition, here is the conclusion of it,—repeat, Raoul, repeat: 'But I regret Mazarin.'"

"Chevalier!"

"You will not say it? Well, then, I will say it twice for you."

"But you would regret Mazarin?"

And they were still laughing and discussing this profession of principles, when one of the shop-boys entered. "A letter, monsieur," said he, "for M. d'Artagnan."

"Thank you; give it me," cried the musketeer.

"The handwriting of monsieur le comte," said Raoul.

"Yes, yes." And D'Artagnan broke the seal.

"Dear friend," said Athos, "a person has just been here to beg me to seek for you, on the part of the king."

"Seek me!" said D'Artagnan, letting the paper fall upon the table. Raoul picked it up, and continued to read aloud:—

"Make haste. His majesty is very anxious to speak to you, and expects you at the Louvre."

"Expects me?" again repeated the musketeer.

"He, he, he!" laughed Raoul.

"Oh, oh!" replied D'Artagnan. "What the devil can this mean?"

Chapter LIII.
The King.

THE first moment of surprise over, D'Artagnan reperused Athos's note. "It is strange," said he, "that the king should send for me."

"Why so?" said Raoul; "do you not think, monsieur, that the king must regret such a servant as you?"

"Oh, oh!" cried the officer, laughing with all his might; "you are poking fun at me, Master Raoul. If the king had regretted me, he would not have let me leave him. No, no; I see in it something better, or worse, if you like."

"Worse! What can that be, monsieur le chevalier?"

"You are young, you are a boy, you are admirable. Oh, how I should like to be as you are! To be but twenty-four, with an unfortunate brow, under which the brain is void of everything but women, love, and good intentions. Oh, Raoul, as long as you have not received the smiles of kings, the confidence of queens; as long as you have not had two cardinals killed under you, the one a tiger, the other a fox; as long as you have not—But what is the good of all this trifling? We must part, Raoul."

"How you say the word! What a serious face!"

"Eh! but the occasion is worthy of it. Listen to me. I have a very good recommendation to tender you."

"I am all attention, Monsieur d'Artagnan."

"You will go and inform your father of my departure."

"Your departure?"

"Pardieu! You will tell him I am gone into England; and that I am living in my little country-house."

"In England, you!—And the king's orders?"

"You get more and more silly: do you imagine that I am going to the Louvre, to place myself at the disposal of that little crowned wolf-cub?"

"The king a wolf-cub? Why, monsieur le chevalier, you are mad!"

"On the contrary, I never was so sane. You do not know what he wants to do with me, this worthy son of Louis le Juste!—But, mordioux! that is policy. He wishes to ensconce me snugly in the Bastile—purely and simply, look you!"

"What for?" cried Raoul, terrified at what he heard.

"On account of what I told him one day at Blois. I was warm; he remembers it."

"You told him what?"

"That he was mean, cowardly, and silly."

"Good God!" cried Raoul, "is it possible that such words should have issued from your mouth?"

"Perhaps I don't give the letter of my speech, but I give the sense of it."

"But did not the king have you arrested immediately?"

"By whom? It was I who commanded the musketeers; he must have commanded me to convey myself to prison; I would never have consented: I would have resisted myself. And then I went into England—no more D'Artagnan. Now, the cardinal is dead, or nearly so, they learn that I am in Paris, and they lay their hands on me."

"The cardinal was your protector?"

"The cardinal knew me; he knew certain particularities of me; I also knew some of his; we appreciated each other mutually. And then, on rendering his soul to the devil, he would recommend Anne of Austria to make me the inhabitant of a safe place. Go, then, and find your father, relate the fact to him—and adieu!"

"My dear Monsieur d'Artagnan," said Raoul, very much agitated, after having looked out the window, "you cannot even fly!"

"Why not?"

"Because there is below an officer of the Swiss guards waiting for you."

"Well?"

"Well, he will arrest you."

D'Artagnan broke into a Homeric laugh.

"Oh! I know very well that you will resist, that you will fight, even; I know very well that you will prove the conqueror; but that amounts to rebellion, and you are an officer yourself, knowing what discipline is."

"Devil of a boy, how logical that is!" grumbled D'Artagnan.

"You approve of it, do you not?"

"Yes, instead of passing into the street, where that idiot is waiting for me, I will slip quietly out at the back. I have a horse in the stable, and a good one. I will ride him to death; my means permit me to do so, and by killing one horse after another, I shall arrive at Boulogne in eleven hours; I know the road. Only tell your father one thing."

"What is that?"

"That is—that the thing he knows about is placed at Planchet's house, except a fifth, and that—"

"But, my dear D'Artagnan, rest assured that if you fly, two things will be said of you."

"What are they, my dear friend?"

"The first, that you have been afraid."

"Ah! and who will dare to say that?"

"The king first."

"Well! but he will tell the truth,—I am afraid."

"The second, that you knew yourself guilty."

"Guilty of what?"

"Why, of the crimes they wish to impute to you."

"That is true again. So, then, you advise me to go and get myself made a prisoner in the Bastile?"

"M. le Comte de la Fere would advise you just as I do."

"Pardieu! I know he would," said D'Artagnan thoughtfully. "You are right, I shall not escape. But if they cast me into the Bastile?"

"We will get you out again," said Raoul, with a quiet, calm air.

"Mordioux! You said that after a brave fashion, Raoul," said D'Artagnan, seizing his hand; "that savors of Athos, distinctly. Well, I will go, then. Do not forget my last word."

"Except a fifth," said Raoul.

"Yes, you are a fine boy! and I wish you to add one thing to that last word."

"Speak, chevalier!"

"It is that if you cannot get me out of the Bastile, and I remain there—Oh! that will be so, and I shall be a detestable prisoner; I, who have been a passable man,—in that case, I give three-fifths to you, and the fourth to your father."

"Chevalier!"

"Mordioux! If you will have some masses said for me, you are welcome."

That being said, D'Artagnan took his belt from the hook, girded on his sword, took a hat the feather of which was fresh, and held his hand out to Raoul, who threw himself into his arms. When in the shop, he cast a quick glance at the shop-lads, who looked upon the scene with a pride mingled with some inquietude; then plunging his hands into a chest of currants, he went straight to the officer who was waiting for him at the door.

"Those features! Can it be you, Monsieur de Friedisch?" cried D'Artagnan, gayly. "Eh! eh! what, do we arrest our friends?"

"Arrest!" whispered the lads among themselves.

"Ja, it is I, Monsieur d'Artagnan! Good-day to you!" said the Swiss, in his mountain patois.

"Must I give you up my sword? I warn you that it is long and heavy; you had better let me wear if to the Louvre: I feel quite lost in the streets without a sword, and you would be more at a loss that I should, with two."

"The king has given me no orders about it," replied the Swiss, "so keep your sword."

"Well, that is very polite on the part of the king. Let us go, at once."

Monsieur Friedisch was not a talker, and D'Artagnan had too many things to think about to say much. From Planchet's shop to the Louvre was not far,—they arrived in ten minutes. It was a dark night. M. de Friedisch wanted to enter by the wicket. "No," said D'Artagnan, "you would lose time by that; take the little staircase."

The Swiss did as D'Artagnan advised, and conducted him to the vestibule of the king's cabinet. When arrived there, he bowed to his prisoner, and, without saying anything, returned to his post. D'Artagnan had not had time to ask why his sword was not taken from him, when the door of the cabinet opened, and a valet de chambre called, "M. d'Artagnan!" The musketeer assumed his parade carriage, and entered, with his large eyes wide open, his brow calm, his moustache stiff. The king was seated at a table writing. He did not disturb himself when the step of the musketeer resounded on the floor; he did not even turn his head. D'Artagnan advanced as far as the middle of the room, and seeing that the king paid no attention to him, and suspecting, besides, that this was nothing but affectation, a sort of tormenting preamble to the explanation that was preparing, he turned his back on the prince, and began to examine the frescoes on the cornices, and the cracks in the ceiling. This maneuver was accompanied by a little tacit monologue. "Ah! you want to humble me, do you?—you, whom I have seen so young—you, whom I have saved as I would my own child,—you, whom

I have served as I would a God—that is to say, for nothing. Wait awhile! wait awhile! you shall see what a man can do who has suffered the air of the fire of the Huguenots, under the beard of monsieur le cardinal—the true cardinal." At this moment Louis turned round.

"Ah! are you there, Monsieur d'Artagnan?" said he.

D'Artagnan saw the movement and imitated it. "Yes, sire," said he.

"Very well; have the goodness to wait till I have cast this up."

D'Artagnan made no reply; he only bowed. "That is polite enough," thought he; "I have nothing to say."

Louis made a violent dash with his pen, and threw it angrily away.

"Ah! go on, work yourself up!" thought the musketeer; "you will put me at my ease. You shall find I did not empty the bag, the other day, at Blois."

Louis rose from his seat, passed his hand over his brow, then, stopping opposite to D'Artagnan, he looked at him with an air at once imperious and kind, "What the devil does he want with me? I wish he would begin!" thought the musketeer.

"Monsieur," said the king, "you know, without doubt, that monsieur le cardinal is dead?"

"I suspected so, sire."

"You know that, consequently, I am master in my own kingdom?"

"That is not a thing that dates from the death of monsieur le cardinal, sire; a man is always master in his own house, when he wishes to be so."

"Yes; but do you not remember all you said to me at Blois?"

"Now we come to it," thought D'Artagnan; "I was not deceived. Well, so much the better, it is a sign that my scent is tolerably keen yet."

"You do not answer me," said Louis.

"Sire, I think I recollect."

"You only think?"

"It is so long ago."

"If you do not remember, I do. You said to me,—listen with attention."

"Ah! I shall listen with all my ears, sire; for it is very likely the conversation will turn in a fashion very interesting to me."

Louis once more looked at the musketeer. The latter smoothed the feather of his hat, then his mustache, and waited bravely. Louis XIV. continued: "You quitted my service, monsieur, after having told me the whole truth?"

"Yes, sire."

"That is, after having declared to me all you thought to be true, with regard to my mode of thinking and acting. That is always a merit. You began by telling me that you had served my family thirty years, and were fatigued."

"I said so; yes, sire."

"And you afterwards admitted that that fatigue was a pretext, and that discontent was the real cause."

"I was discontented, in fact; but that discontent has never betrayed itself, that I know of, and if, like a man of heart, I have spoken out before your majesty, I have not even thought of the matter before anybody else."

"Do not excuse yourself, D'Artagnan, but continue to listen to me. When making me the reproach that you were discontented, you received in reply a promise:—'Wait.'—Is that not true?"

"Yes, sire, as true as what I told you."

"You answered me, 'Hereafter! No, now, immediately.' Do not excuse yourself, I tell you. It was natural, but you had no charity for your poor prince, Monsieur d'Artagnan."

"Sire!—charity for a king, on the part of a poor soldier!"

"You understand me very well; you knew that I stood in need of it; you knew very well that I was not master; you knew very well that my hope was in the future. Now, you answered me when I spoke of the future, 'My discharge,—and that directly.'"

"That is true," murmured D'Artagnan, biting his mustache.

"You did not flatter me when I was in distress," added Louis.

"But," said D'Artagnan, raising his head nobly, "if I did not flatter your majesty when poor, neither did I betray you. I have shed my blood for nothing; I have watched like a dog at a door, knowing full well that neither bread nor bone would be thrown to me. I, although poor likewise, asked nothing of your majesty but the discharge you speak of."

"I know you are a brave man, but I was a young man, and you ought to have had some indulgence for me. What had you to reproach the king with?—that he left King Charles II. without assistance?—let us say further—that he did not marry Mademoiselle de Mancini?" When saying these words, the king fixed upon the musketeer a searching look.

"Ah! ah!" thought the latter, "he is doing far more than remembering, he divines. The devil!"

"Your sentence," continued Louis, "fell upon the king and fell upon the man. But, Monsieur d'Artagnan, that weakness, for you considered it a weakness?"—D'Artagnan made no reply—"you reproached me also with regard to monsieur, the defunct cardinal. Now, monsieur le cardinal, did he not bring me up, did he not support me?—elevating himself and supporting himself at the same time, I admit; but the benefit was discharged. As an ingrate or an egotist, would you, then, have better loved or served me?"

"Sire!"

"We will say no more about it, monsieur; it would only create in you too many regrets, and me too much pain."

D'Artagnan was not convinced. The young king, in adopting a tone of hauteur with him, did not forward his purpose.

"You have since reflected?" resumed Louis.

"Upon what, sire?" asked D'Artagnan, politely.

"Why, upon all that I have said to you, monsieur."

"Yes, sire, no doubt—"

"And you have only waited for an opportunity of retracting your words?"

"Sire!"

"You hesitate, it seems."

"I do not understand what your majesty did me the honor to say to me."

Louis's brow became cloudy.

"Have the goodness to excuse me, sire; my understanding is particularly thick; things do not penetrate it without difficulty; but it is true, once they get in, they remain there."

"Yes, yes; you appear to have a memory."

"Almost as good a one as your majesty's."

"Then give me quickly one solution. My time is valuable. What have you been doing since your discharge?"

"Making my fortune, sire."

"The expression is crude, Monsieur d'Artagnan."

"Your majesty takes it in bad part, certainly. I entertain nothing but the profoundest respect for the king; and if I have been impolite, which might be excused by my long sojourn in camps and barracks, your majesty is too much above me to be offended at a word that innocently escapes from a soldier."

"In fact, I know you performed a brilliant action in England, monsieur. I only regret that you have broken your promise."

"I!" cried D'Artagnan.

"Doubtless. You engaged your word not to serve any other prince on quitting my service. Now it was for King Charles II. that you undertook the marvelous carrying off of M. Monk."

"Pardon me, sire; it was for myself."

"And did you succeed?"

"Like the captains of the fifteenth century, coups-de-main and adventures."

"What do you call succeeding?—a fortune?"

"A hundred thousand crowns, sire, which I now possess—that is, in one week three times as much money as I ever had in fifty years."

"It is a handsome sum. But you are ambitious, I perceive."

"I, sire? The quarter of that would be a treasure; and I swear to you I have no thought of augmenting it."

"What! you contemplate remaining idle?"

"Yes, sire."

"You mean to drop the sword?"

"That I have already done."

"Impossible, Monsieur d'Artagnan," said Louis, firmly.

"But, sire—"

"Well?"

"And why, sire?"

"Because it is my wish you should not!" said the young prince, in a voice so stern and imperious that D'Artagnan evinced surprise and even uneasiness.

"Will your majesty allow me one word of reply?" said he.

"Speak."

"I formed that resolution when I was poor and destitute."

"So be it. Go on."

"Now, when by my energy I have acquired a comfortable means of subsistence, would your majesty despoil me of my liberty? Your majesty would condemn me to the lowest, when I have gained the highest?"

"Who gave you permission, monsieur, to fathom my designs, or to reckon with me?" replied Louis, in a voice almost angry; "who told you what I shall do or what you will yourself do?"

"Sire," said the musketeer, quietly, "as far as I see, freedom is not the order of the conversation, as it was on the day we came to an explanation at Blois."

"No, monsieur; everything is changed."

"I tender your majesty my sincere compliments upon that, but—"

"But you don't believe it?"

"I am not a great statesman, and yet I have my eye upon affairs; it seldom fails; now, I do not see exactly as your majesty does, sire. The reign of Mazarin is over, but that of the financiers is begun. They have the money; your majesty will not often see much of it. To live under the paw of these hungry wolves is hard for a man who reckoned upon independence."

At this moment someone scratched at the door of the cabinet; the king raised his head proudly. "Your pardon, Monsieur d'Artagnan," said he; "it is M. Colbert, who comes to make me a report. Come in, M. Colbert."

D'Artagnan drew back. Colbert entered with papers in his hand, and went up to the king. There can be little doubt that the Gascon did not lose the opportunity of applying his keen, quick glance to the new figure which presented itself.

"Is the inquiry made?"

"Yes, sire."

"And the opinion of the inquisitors?"

"Is that the accused merit confiscation and death."

"Ah! ah!" said the king, without changing countenance, and casting an oblique look at D'Artagnan. "And your own opinion, M. Colbert?" said he.

Colbert looked at D'Artagnan is his turn. That imposing countenance checked the words upon his lips. Louis perceived this. "Do not disturb yourself," said he; "it is M. d'Artagnan,—do you not know M. d'Artagnan again?"

These two men looked at each other—D'Artagnan, with eyes open and bright as the day—Colbert, with his half closed, and dim. The frank intrepidity of the financier annoyed the other; the circumspection of the financier disgusted the soldier. "Ah! ah! this is the gentleman who made that brilliant stroke in England," said Colbert. And he bowed slightly to D'Artagnan.

"Ah! ah!" said the Gascon, "this is the gentleman who clipped off the lace from the uniform of the Swiss! A praiseworthy piece of economy."

The financier thought to pierce the musketeer; but the musketeer ran the financier through.

"Monsieur d'Artagnan," resumed the king, who had not remarked all the shades of which Mazarin would have missed not one, "this concerns the farmers of the revenue who have robbed me, whom I am hanging, and whose death-warrants I am about to sign."

"Oh! oh!" said D'Artagnan, starting.

"What did you say?"

"Oh! nothing, sire. This is no business of mine."

The king had already taken up the pen, and was applying it to the paper. "Sire," said Colbert in a subdued voice, "I beg to warn your majesty, that if an example be necessary, there will be difficulty in the execution of your orders."

"What do you say?" said Louis.

"You must not conceal from yourself," continued Colbert quietly, "that attacking the farmers-general is attacking the superintendence. The two unfortunate guilty men in question are the particular friends of a powerful personage, and the punishment, which otherwise might be comfortably confined to the Chatlet, will doubtless be a signal for disturbances!"

Louis colored and turned towards D'Artagnan, who took a slight bite at his mustache, not without a smile of pity for the financier, and for the king who had to listen to him so long. But Louis seized the pen, and with a movement so rapid that his hand shook, he affixed his signature at the bottom of the two papers presented by Colbert,—then looking the latter in the face,— "Monsieur Colbert," said he, "when you speak to me on business, exclude more frequently the word difficulty from your reasonings and opinions; as to the word impossibility, never pronounce it."

Colbert bowed, much humiliated at having to undergo such a lesson before the musketeer; he was about to go out, but, jealous to repair his check: "I forgot to announce to your majesty," said he, "that the confiscations amount to the sum of five millions of livres."

"That's pretty well!" thought D'Artagnan.

"Which makes in my coffers?" said the king.

"Eighteen millions of livres, sire," replied Colbert, bowing.

"Mordioux!" growled D'Artagnan, "that's glorious!"

"Monsieur Colbert," added the king, "you will, if you please, go through the gallery where M. Lyonne is waiting, and will tell him to bring hither what he has drawn up—by my order."

"Directly, sire; if your majesty wants me no more this evening?"

"No, monsieur: good-night!" And Colbert went out.

"Now, let us return to our affair, M. d'Artagnan," said the king, as if nothing had happened. "You see that, with respect to money, there is already a notable change."

"Something to the tune of from zero to eighteen millions," replied the musketeer gayly. "Ah! that was what your majesty wanted the day King Charles II. came to Blois. The two states would not have been embroiled to-day; for I must say, that there also I see another stumbling-block."

"Well, in the first place," replied Louis, "you are unjust, monsieur; for, if Providence had made me able to give my brother the million that day, you would not have quitted my service, and, consequently, you would not have made your fortune, as you told me just now you have done. But, in addition to this, I have had another piece of good fortune; and my difference with Great Britain need not alarm you."

A valet de chambre interrupted the king by announcing M. Lyonne. "Come in, monsieur," said the king; "you are punctual; that is like a good servant. Let us see your letter to my brother Charles II."

D'Artagnan pricked up his ears. "A moment, monsieur," said Louis carelessly to the Gascon; "I must expedite to London my consent to the marriage of my brother, M. le Duc d'Anjou, with the Princess Henrietta Stuart."

"He is knocking me about, it seems," murmured D'Artagnan, whilst the king signed the letter, and dismissed M. de Lyonne; "but ma foi! the more he knocks me about in this manner, the better I like it."

The king followed M. de Lyonne with his eyes, till the door was closed behind him; he even made three steps, as if he would follow the minister; but, after these three steps, stopping, passing, and coming back to the musketeer,—"Now, monsieur," said he, "let us hasten to terminate our affair. You told me the other day, at Blois, that you were not rich?"

"But I am now, sire."

"Yes, but that does not concern me; you have your own money, not mine; that does not enter into my account."

"I do not well understand what your majesty means."

"Then, instead of leaving you to draw out words, speak spontaneously. Should you be satisfied with twenty thousand livres a year as a fixed income?"

"But, sire" said D'Artagnan, opening his eyes to the utmost.

"Would you be satisfied with four horses furnished and kept, and with a supplement of funds such as you might require, according to occasions and needs, or would you prefer a fixed sum which would be, for example, forty thousand livres? Answer."

"Sire, your majesty—"

"Yes, you are surprised; that is natural, and I expected it. Answer me, come! or I shall think you have no longer that rapidity of judgment I have so much admired in you."

"It is certain, sire, that twenty thousand livres a year make a handsome sum; but—"

"No buts! Yes or no, is it an honorable indemnity?"

"Oh! very certainly."

"You will be satisfied with it? That is well. It will be better to reckon the extra expenses separately; you can arrange that with Colbert. Now let us pass to something more important."

"But, sire, I told your majesty—"

"That you wanted rest, I know you did: only I replied that I would not allow it—I am master, I suppose?"

"Yes, sire."

"That is well. You were formerly in the way of becoming captain of the musketeers?"

"Yes, sire."

"Well, here is your commission signed. I place it in this drawer. The day on which you return from a certain expedition which I have to confide to you, on that day you may yourself take the commission from the drawer." D'Artagnan still hesitated, and hung down his head. "Come, monsieur," said the king, "one would believe, to look at you, that you did not know that at the court of the most Christian king, the captain-general of the musketeers takes precedence of the marechals of France."

"Sire, I know he does."

"Then, am I to think you do put no faith in my word?"

"Oh! sire, never—never dream of such a thing."

"I have wished to prove to you, that you, so good a servant, had lost a good master; am I anything like the master that will suit you?"

"I begin to think you are, sire."

"Then, monsieur, you will resume your functions. Your company is quite disorganized since your departure, and the men go about drinking and rioting in the cabarets, where they fight, in spite of my edicts, and those of my father. You will reorganize the service as soon as possible."

"Yes, sire."

"You will not again quit my person."

"Very well, sire."

"You will march with me to the army, you will encamp round my tent."

"Then, sire," said D'Artagnan, "if it is only to impose upon me a service like that, your majesty need not give me twenty thousand livres a year. I shall not earn them."

"I desire that you shall keep open house; I desire that you should keep a liberal table; I desire that my captain of musketeers should be a personage."

"And I," said D'Artagnan, bluntly; "I do not like easily found money; I like money won! Your majesty gives me an idle trade, which the first comer would perform for four thousand livres."

Louis XIV. began to laugh. "You are a true Gascon, Monsieur d'Artagnan; you will draw my heart's secret from me."

"Bah! has your majesty a secret, then?"

"Yes, monsieur."

"Well! then I accept the twenty thousand livres, for I will keep that secret, and discretion is above all price, in these times. Will your majesty speak now?"

"Boot yourself, Monsieur d'Artagnan, and to horse!"

"Directly, sire."

"Within two days."

"That is well, sire: for I have my affairs to settle before I set out; particularly if it is likely there should be any blows stirring."

"That may happen."

"We can receive them! But, sire, you have addressed yourself to avarice, to ambition; you have addressed yourself to the heart of M. d'Artagnan, but you have forgotten one thing."

"What is that?"

"You have said nothing to his vanity; when shall I be a knight of the king's orders?"

"Does that interest you?"

"Why, yes, sire. My friend Athos is quite covered with orders, and that dazzles me."

"You shall be a knight of my order a month after you have taken your commission of captain."

"Ah! ah!" said the officer, thoughtfully, "after the expedition."

"Precisely."

"Where is your majesty going to send me?"

"Are you acquainted with Bretagne?"

"No, sire."

"Have you any friends there?"

"In Bretagne? No, ma foi!"

"So much the better. Do you know anything about fortifications?"

"I believe I do, sire," said D'Artagnan, smiling.

"That is to say you can readily distinguish a fortress from a simple fortification, such as is allowed to chatelains or vassals?"

"I distinguish a fort from a rampart as I distinguish a cuirass from a raised pie-crust, sire. Is that sufficient?"

"Yes, monsieur. You will set out, then."

"For Bretagne?"

"Yes."

"Alone?"

"Absolutely alone. That is to say, you must not even take a lackey with you."

"May I ask your majesty for what reason?"

"Because, monsieur, it will be necessary to disguise yourself sometimes, as the servant of a good family. Your face is very well known in France, M. d'Artagnan."

"And then, sire?"

"And then you will travel slowly through Bretagne, and will examine the fortifications of that country."

"The coasts?"

"Yes, and the isles; commencing by Belle-Ile-en-Mer."

"Ah! which belongs to M. Fouquet!" said D'Artagnan, in a serious tone, raising his intelligent eye to Louis XIV.

"I fancy you are right, monsieur, and that Bell-Isle does belong to M. Fouquet, in fact."

"Then your majesty wishes me to ascertain if Belle-Isle is a strong place?"

"Yes."

"If the fortifications of it are new or old?"

"Precisely."

"And if the vassals of M. Fouquet are sufficiently numerous to form a garrison?"

"That is what I want to know; you have placed your finger on the question."

"And if they are not fortifying, sire?"

"You will travel about Bretagne, listening and judging."

"Then I am a king's spy?" said D'Artagnan, bluntly, twisting his mustache.

"No, monsieur."

"Your pardon sire; I spy on your majesty's account."

"You start on a voyage of discovery, monsieur. Would you march at the head of your musketeers, with your sword in your hand, to observe any spot whatever, or an enemy's position?"

At this word D'Artagnan started.

"Do you," continued the king, "imagine yourself to be a spy?"

"No, no," said D'Artagnan, but pensively; "the thing changes its face when one observes an enemy: one is but a soldier. And if they are fortifying Belle-Isle?" added he, quickly.

"You will take an exact plan of the fortifications."

"Will they permit me to enter?"

"That does not concern me; that is your affair. Did you not understand that I reserved for you a supplement of twenty thousand livres per annum, if you wished it?"

"Yes, sire; but if they are not fortifying?"

"You will return quietly, without fatiguing your horse."

"Sire, I am ready."

"You will begin to-morrow by going to monsieur le surintendant's to take the first quarter of the pension I give you. Do you know M. Fouquet?"

"Very little, sire; but I beg your majesty to observe that I don't think it immediately necessary that I should know him."

"Your pardon, monsieur; for he will refuse you the money I wish you to take; and it is that refusal I look for."

"Ah!" said D'Artagnan. "Then, sire?"

"The money being refused, you will go and seek it at M. Colbert's. A propos, have you a good horse?"

"An excellent one, sire."

"How much did it cost you?"

"A hundred and fifty pistoles."

"I will buy it of you. Here is a note for two hundred pistoles."

"But I want a horse for my journey, sire."

"Well!"

"Well, and you take mine from me."

"Not at all. On the contrary, I give it you. Only as it is now mine and not yours, I am sure you will not spare it."

"Your majesty is in a hurry, then?"

"A great hurry."

"Then what compels me to wait two days?"

"Reasons known to myself."

"That's a different affair. The horse may make up the two days, in the eight he has to travel; and then there is the post."

"No, no, the post compromises, Monsieur d'Artagnan. Begone and do not forget you are my servant."

"Sire, it is not my duty to forget it! At what hour to-morrow shall I take my leave of your majesty?"

"Whence do you lodge?"

"I must henceforward lodge at the Louvre."

"That must not be now—keep your lodgings in the city: I will pay for them. As to your departure, it must take place at night; you must set out without being seen by any one, or, if you are seen, it must not be known that you belong to me. Keep your mouth shut, monsieur."

"Your majesty spoils all you have said by that single word."

"I asked where you lodged, for I cannot always send to M. le Comte de la Fere to seek you."

"I lodge with M. Planchet, a grocer, Rue des Lombards, at the sign of the Pilon d'Or."

"Go out but little, show yourself less, and await my orders."

"And yet, sire, I must go for the money."

"That is true, but when going to the superintendence, where so many people are constantly going, you must mingle with the crowd."

"I want the notes, sire, for the money."

"Here they are." The king signed them, and D'Artagnan looked on, to assure himself of their regularity.

"Adieu! Monsieur d'Artagnan," added the king; "I think you have perfectly understood me."

"I? I understand that your majesty sends me to Belle-Ile-en-Mer, that is all."

"To learn?"

"To learn how M. Fouquet's works are going on; that is all."

"Very well: I admit you may be taken."

"And I do not admit it," replied the Gascon, boldly.

"I admit you may be killed," continued the king.

"That is not probable, sire."

"In the first case, you must not speak; in the second there must be no papers found upon you."

D'Artagnan shrugged his shoulders without ceremony, and took leave of the king, saying to himself:—"The English shower continues—let us remain under the spout!"

Chapter LIV.
The Houses of M. Fouquet.

WHILST D'Artagnan was returning to Planchet's house, his head aching and bewildered with all that had happened to him, there was passing a scene of quite a different character, and which, nevertheless, is not foreign to the conversation our musketeer had just had with the king; only this scene took place out of Paris, in a house possessed by the superintendent Fouquet in the village of Saint-Mande. The minister had just arrived at this country-house, followed by his principal clerk, who carried an enormous portfolio full of papers to be examined, and others waiting for signature. As it might be about five o'clock in the afternoon, the masters had dined: supper was being prepared for twenty subaltern guests. The superintendent did not stop: on alighting from his carriage, he, at the same bound, sprang through the doorway, traversed the apartments and gained his cabinet, where he declared he would shut himself up to work, commanding that he should not be disturbed for anything but an order from the king. As soon as this order was given, Fouquet shut himself up, and two footmen were placed as sentinels at his door. Then Fouquet pushed a bolt which displaced a panel that walled up the entrance, and prevented everything that passed in this apartment from being either seen or heard. But, against all probability, it was only for the sake of shutting himself up that Fouquet shut himself up thus, for he went straight to a bureau, seated himself at it, opened the portfolio, and began to make a choice amongst the enormous mass of papers it contained. It was not more than ten minutes after he had entered, and taken all the precautions we have described, when the repeated noise of several slight equal knocks struck his ear, and appeared to fix his utmost attention. Fouquet raised his head, turned his ear, and listened.

The strokes continued. Then the worker arose with a slight movement of impatience and walked straight up to a glass behind which the blows were struck by a hand, or by some invisible mechanism. It was a large glass let into a panel. Three other glasses, exactly similar to it, completed the symmetry of the apartment. Nothing distinguished that one from the others. Without doubt, these reiterated knocks were a signal; for, at the moment Fouquet approached the glass listening, the same noise was renewed, and in the same measure. "Oh! oh!" murmured the intendant, with surprise, "who is yonder? I did not expect anybody to-day." And without doubt, to respond to the signal, he pulled out a gilded nail near the glass, and shook it thrice. Then returning to his place, and seating himself again, "Ma foi! let them wait," said he. And plunging again into the ocean of papers unrolled before him, he appeared to think of nothing now but work. In fact, with incredible rapidity and marvelous lucidity, Fouquet deciphered the largest papers and most complicated writings, correcting them, annotating them with a pen moved as if by a fever, and the work melting under his hands, signatures, figures, references, became multiplied as if ten clerks—that is to say, a hundred fingers and ten brains had performed the duties, instead of the five fingers and single brain of this man. From time to time, only, Fouquet, absorbed by his work, raised his head to cast a furtive glance upon a clock placed before him. The reason of this was, Fouquet set himself a task, and when this task was once set, in one hour's work he, by himself, did what another would not have accomplished in a day; always certain, consequently, provided he was not disturbed, of arriving at the close in the time his devouring activity had fixed. But in the midst of his ardent labor, the soft strokes upon the little bell placed behind the glass sounded again, hasty, and, consequently, more urgent.

"The lady appears to be impatient," said Fouquet. "Humph! a calm! That must be the comtesse; but, no, the comtesse is gone to Rambouillet for three days. The presidente, then? Oh! no, the presidente would not assume such grand airs; she would ring very humbly, then she would wait my good pleasure. The greatest certainty is, that I do not know who it can be, but that I know who it cannot be. And since it is not you, marquise, since it cannot be you, deuce take the rest!" And he went on with his work in spite of the reiterated appeals of the bell. At the end of a quarter of an hour, however, impatience prevailed over Fouquet in his turn: he might be said to consume, rather than to complete the rest of his work; he thrust his papers into his portfolio, and giving a glance at the mirror, whilst the taps continued faster than ever: "Oh! oh!" said he, "whence comes all this racket? What has happened, and who can the Ariadne be who expects me so impatiently. Let us see!"

He then applied the tip of his finger to the nail parallel to the one he had drawn. Immediately the glass moved like a folding-door and discovered a secret closet, rather deep, into which the superintendent disappeared as if going into a vast box. When there, he touched another spring, which opened, not a board, but a block of the wall, and he went out by that opening, leaving the door to shut of itself. Then Fouquet descended about a score of steps which sank, winding, underground, and came to a long, subterranean passage, lighted by imperceptible loopholes. The walls of this vault were covered with slabs or tiles, and the floor with carpeting. This passage was under the street itself, which separated Fouquet's house from the Park of Vincennes. At the end of the passage ascended a winding staircase parallel with that by which Fouquet had entered. He mounted these other stairs, entered by means of a spring placed in a closet similar to that in his cabinet, and from this closet an untenanted chamber furnished with the utmost elegance. As soon as he entered, he examined carefully whether the glass closed without leaving any trace, and, doubtless satisfied with his observation, he opened by means of a small gold key the triple fastenings of a door in front of him. This time the door opened upon a handsome cabinet, sumptuously furnished, in which was seated upon cushions a lady of surpassing beauty, who at the sound of the lock sprang towards Fouquet. "Ah! good heavens!" cried the latter, starting back with astonishment. "Madame la Marquise de Belliere, you here?"

"Yes," murmured la marquise. "Yes; it is I, monsieur."

"Marquise! dear marquise!" added Fouquet, ready to prostrate himself. "Ah! my God! how did you come here? And I, to keep you waiting!"

"A long time, monsieur; yes, a very long time!"

"I am happy in thinking this waiting has appeared long to you, marquise!"

"Oh! an eternity, monsieur; oh! I rang more than twenty times. Did you not hear me?"

"Marquise, you are pale, you tremble."

"Did you not hear, then, that you were summoned?"

"Oh, yes; I heard plainly enough, madame; but I could not come. After your rigors and your refusals, how could I dream it was you? If I could have had any suspicion of the happiness that awaited me, believe me, madame, I would have quitted everything to fall at your feet, as I do at this moment."

"Are we quite alone, monsieur?" asked the marquise, looking round the room.

"Oh, yes, madame, I can assure you of that."

"Really?" said the marquise, in a melancholy tone.

"You sigh!" said Fouquet.

"What mysteries! what precautions!" said the marquise, with a slight bitterness of expression; "and how evident it is that you fear the least suspicion of your amours to escape."

"Would you prefer their being made public?"

"Oh, no; you act like a delicate man," said the marquise, smiling.

"Come, dear marquise, punish me not with reproaches, I implore you."

"Reproaches! Have I a right to make you any?"

"No, unfortunately, no; but tell me, you, who during a year I have loved without return or hope—"

"You are mistaken—without hope it is true, but not without return."

"What! for me, of my love! there is but one proof, and that proof I still want."

"I am here to bring it, monsieur."

Fouquet wished to clasp her in his arms, but she disengaged herself with a gesture.

"You persist in deceiving yourself, monsieur, and will never accept of me the only thing I am willing to give you—devotion."

"Ah, then, you do not love me? Devotion is but a virtue, love is a passion."

"Listen to me, I implore you: I should not have come hither without a serious motive: you are well assured of that, are you not?"

"The motive is of very little consequence, so that you are but here—so that I see you—so that I speak to you!"

"You are right; the principal thing is that I am here without any one having seen me, and that I can speak to you."—Fouquet sank on his knees before her. "Speak! speak, madame!" said he, "I listen to you."

The marquise looked at Fouquet, on his knees at her feet, and there was in the looks of the woman a strange mixture of love and melancholy. "Oh!" at length murmured she, "would that I were she who has the right of seeing you every minute, of speaking to you every instant! would that I were she who might watch over you, she who would have no need of mysterious springs to summon and cause to appear, like a sylph, the man she loves, to look at him for an hour, and then see him disappear in the darkness of a mystery, still more strange at his going out than at his coming in. Oh! that would be to live like a happy woman!"

"Do you happen, marquise," said Fouquet, smiling, "to be speaking of my wife?"

"Yes, certainly, of her I spoke."

"Well, you need not envy her lot, marquise; of all the women with whom I have had any relations, Madame Fouquet is the one I see the least of, and who has the least intercourse with me."

"At least, monsieur, she is not reduced to place, as I have done, her hand upon the ornament of a glass to call you to her; at least you do not reply to her by the mysterious, alarming sound of a bell, the spring of which comes from I don't know where; at least you have not forbidden her to endeavor to discover the secret of these communications under pain of breaking off forever your connections with her, as you have forbidden all who come here before me, and who will come after me."

"Dear marquise, how unjust you are, and how little do you know what you are doing in thus exclaiming against mystery; it is with mystery alone we can love without trouble; it is with love without trouble alone that we can be happy. But let us return to ourselves, to that devotion of which you were speaking, or rather let me labor under a pleasing delusion, and believe this devotion is love."

"Just now," repeated the marquise, passing over her eyes a hand that might have been a model for the graceful contours of antiquity; "just now I was prepared to speak, my ideas were clear and bold; now I am quite confused, quite troubled; I fear I bring you bad news."

"If it is to that bad news I owe your presence, marquise, welcome be even that bad news! or rather, marquise, since you allow that I am not quite indifferent to you, let me hear nothing of the bad news, but speak of yourself."

"No, no, on the contrary, demand it of me; require me to tell it to you instantly, and not to allow myself to be turned aside by any feeling whatever. Fouquet, my friend! it is of immense importance."

"You astonish me, marquise; I will even say you almost frighten me. You, so serious, so collected; you who know the world we live in so well. Is it, then, important?"

"Oh! very important."

"In the first place, how did you come here?"

"You shall know that presently; but first to something of more consequence."

"Speak, marquise, speak! I implore you, have pity on my impatience."

"Do you know that Colbert is made intendant of the finances?"

"Bah! Colbert, little Colbert."

"Yes, Colbert, little Colbert."

"Mazarin's factotum?"

"The same."

"Well! what do you see so terrific in that, dear marquise? little Colbert is intendant; that is astonishing I confess, but is not terrible."

"Do you think the king has given, without pressing motive, such a place to one you call a little cuistre?"

"In the first place, is it positively true that the king has given it to him?"

"It is so said."

"Ay, but who says so?"

"Everybody."

"Everybody, that's nobody; mention some one likely to be well informed who says so."

"Madame Vanel."

"Ah! now you begin to frighten me in earnest," said Fouquet, laughing; "if any one is well informed, or ought to be well informed, it is the person you name."

"Do not speak ill of poor Marguerite, Monsieur Fouquet, for she still loves you."

"Bah! indeed? That is scarcely credible. I thought little Colbert, as you said just now, had passed over that love, and left the impression upon it of a spot of ink or a stain of grease."

"Fouquet! Fouquet! Is this the way you always treat the poor creatures you desert?"

"Why, you surely are not going to undertake the defense of Madame Vanel?"

"Yes, I will undertake it; for, I repeat, she loves you still, and the proof is she saves you."

"But your interposition, marquise; that is very cunning on her part. No angel could be more agreeable to me, or could lead me more certainly to salvation. But, let me ask you, do you know Marguerite?"

"She was my convent friend."

"And you say that she has informed you that Monsieur Colbert was named intendant?"

"Yes, she did."

"Well, enlighten me, marquise; granted Monsieur Colbert is intendant—so be it. In what can an intendant, that is to say my subordinate, my clerk, give me umbrage or injure me, even if he is Monsieur Colbert?"

"You do not reflect, monsieur, apparently," replied the marquise.

"Upon what?"

"This: that Monsieur Colbert hates you."

"Hates me?" cried Fouquet. "Good heavens! marquise, whence do you come? where can you live? Hates me! why all the world hates me, he, of course, as others do."

"He more than others."

"More than others—let him."

"He is ambitious."

"Who is not, marquise."

"Yes, but with him ambition has no bounds."

"I am quite aware of that, since he made it a point to succeed me with Madame Vanel."

"And obtained his end; look at that."

"Do you mean to say he has the presumption to pass from intendant to superintendent?"

"Have you not yourself already had the same fear?"

"Oh! oh!" said Fouquet, "to succeed with Madame Vanel is one thing, to succeed me with the king is another. France is not to be purchased so easily as the wife of a maitre des comptes."

"Eh! monsieur, everything is to be bought; if not by gold, by intrigue."

"Nobody knows to the contrary better than you, madame, you to whom I have offered millions."

"Instead of millions, Fouquet, you should have offered me a true, only and boundless love: I might have accepted that. So you see, still, everything is to be bought, if not in one way, by another."

"So, Colbert, in your opinion, is in a fair way of bargaining for my place of superintendent. Make yourself easy on that head, my dear marquise; he is not yet rich enough to purchase it."

"But if he should rob you of it?"

"Ah! that is another thing. Unfortunately, before he can reach me, that is to say, the body of the place, he must destroy, must make a breach in the advanced works, and I am devilishly well fortified, marquise."

"What you call your advanced works are your creatures, are they not—your friends?"

"Exactly so."

"And is M. d'Eymeris one of your creatures?"

"Yes, he is."

"Is M. Lyodot one of your friends?"

"Certainly."

"M. de Vanin?"

"M. de Vanin! ah! they may do what they like with him, but—"

"But—"

"But they must not touch the others!"

"Well, if you are anxious they should not touch MM. d'Eymeris and Lyodot, it is time to look about you."

"Who threatens them?"

"Will you listen to me now?"

"Attentively, marquise."

"Without interrupting me?"

"Speak."

"Well, this morning Marguerite sent for me."

"And what did she want with you?"

"'I dare not see M. Fouquet myself,' said she."

"Bah! why should she think I would reproach her? Poor woman, she vastly deceives herself."

"'See him yourself,' said she, 'and tell him to beware of M. Colbert.'"

"What! she warned me to beware of her lover?"

"I have told you she still loves you."

"Go on, marquise."

"'M. Colbert,' she added, 'came to me two hours ago, to inform me he was appointed intendant.'"

"I have already told you, marquise, that M. Colbert would only be the more in my power for that."

"Yes, but that is not all: Marguerite is intimate, as you know, with Madame d'Eymeris and Madame Lyodot."

"I know it."

"Well, M. Colbert put many questions to her, relative to the fortunes of these two gentlemen, and as to the devotion they had for you."

"Oh, as to those two, I can answer for them; they must be killed before they will cease to be mine."

"Then, as Madame Vanel was obliged to quit M. Colbert for an instant to receive a visitor, and as M. Colbert is industrious, scarcely was the new intendant left alone, before he took a pencil from his pocket, and, there was paper on the table, began to make notes."

"Notes concerning d'Eymeris and Lyodot?"

"Exactly."

"I should like to know what those notes were about."

"And that is just what I have brought you."

"Madame Vanel has taken Colbert's notes and sent them to me?"

"No; but by a chance which resembles a miracle, she has a duplicate of those notes."

"How could she get that?"

"Listen; I told you that Colbert found paper on the table."

"Yes."

"That he took a pencil from his pocket."

"Yes."

"And wrote upon that paper."

"Yes."

"Well, this pencil was a lead-pencil, consequently hard; so, it marked in black upon the first sheet, and in white upon the second."

"Go on."

"Colbert, when tearing off the first sheet, took no notice of the second."

"Well?"

"Well, on the second was to be read what had been written on the first; Madame Vanel read it, and sent for me."

"Yes, yes."

"Then, when she was assured I was your devoted friend, she gave me the paper, and told me the secret of this house."

"And this paper?" said Fouquet, in some degree of agitation.

"Here it is, monsieur—read it," said the marquise.

Fouquet read:

"Names of the farmers of revenue to be condemned by the Chamber of Justice: D'Eymeris, friend of M. F.; Lyodot, friend of M. F.; De Vanin, indif."

"D'Eymeris and Lyodot!" cried Fouquet, reading the paper eagerly again.

"Friends of M. F.," pointed the marquise with her finger.

"But what is the meaning of these words: 'To be condemned by the Chamber of Justice'?"

"Dame!" said the marquise, "that is clear enough, I think. Besides, that is not all. Read on, read on;" and Fouquet continued,—"The two first to death, the third to be dismissed, with MM. d'Hautemont and de la Vallette, who will only have their property confiscated."

"Great God!" cried Fouquet, "to death, to death! Lyodot and D'Eymeris. But even if the Chamber of Justice should condemn them to death, the king will never ratify their condemnation, and they cannot be executed without the king's signature."

"The king has made M. Colbert intendant."

"Oh!" cried Fouquet, as if he caught a glimpse of the abyss that yawned beneath his feet, "impossible! impossible! But who passed a pencil over the marks made by Colbert?"

"I did. I was afraid the first would be effaced."

"Oh! I will know all."

"You will know nothing, monsieur; you despise your enemy too much for that."

"Pardon me, my dear marquise; excuse me; yes, M. Colbert is my enemy, I believe him to be so; yes, M. Colbert is a man to be dreaded, I admit. But I! I have time, and as you are here, as you have assured me of your devotion, as you have allowed me to hope for your love, as we are alone—"

"I came here to save you, Monsieur Fouquet, and not to ruin myself," said the marquise, rising—"therefore, beware!—"

"Marquise, in truth you terrify yourself too much at least, unless this terror is but a pretext—"

"He is very deep, very deep; this M. Colbert: beware!"

Fouquet, in his turn, drew himself up. "And I?" asked he.

"And you, you have only a noble heart. Beware! beware!"

"So?"

"I have done what was right, my friend, at the risk of my reputation. Adieu!"

"Not adieu, au revoir!"

"Perhaps," said the marquise, giving her hand to Fouquet to kiss, and walking towards the door with so firm a step, that he did not dare to bar her passage. As to Fouquet, he retook, with his head hanging down and a fixed cloud on his brow, the path of the subterranean passage along which ran the metal wires that communicated from one house to the other, transmitting, through two glasses, the wishes and signals of hidden correspondents.

Chapter LV.
The Abbe Fouquet.

FOUQUET hastened back to his apartment by the subterranean passage, and immediately closed the mirror with the spring. He was scarcely in his well-known voice crying:—"Open the door, monseigneur, I entreat you, open the door!" Fouquet quickly restored a little order to everything that might have revealed either his absence or his agitation: he spread his papers over the desk, took up a pen, and, to gain time, said, through the closed door,—"Who is there?"

"What, monseigneur, do you not know me?" replied the voice.

"Yes, yes," said Fouquet to himself, "yes, my friend, I know you well enough." And then, aloud: "Is it not Gourville?"

"Why, yes, monseigneur."

Fouquet arose, cast a look at one of his glasses, went to the door, pushed back the bolt, and Gourville entered. "Ah! monseigneur! monseigneur!" cried he, "what cruelty!"

"In what?"

"I have been a quarter of an hour imploring you to open the door, and you would not even answer me."

"Once and for all, you know that I will not be disturbed when I am busy. Now, although I might make you an exception, Gourville, I insist upon my orders being respected by others."

"Monseigneur, at this moment, orders, doors, bolts, locks, and walls I could have broken, forced and overthrown!"

"Ah! ah! it relates to some great event, then?" asked Fouquet.

"Oh! I assure you it does, monseigneur," replied Gourville.

"And what is this event?" said Fouquet, a little troubled by the evident agitation of his most intimate confidant.

"There is a secret chamber of justice instituted, monseigneur."

"I know there is, but do the members meet, Gourville?"

"They not only meet, but they have passed a sentence, monseigneur."

"A sentence?" said the superintendent, with a shudder and pallor he could not conceal. "A sentence!—and on whom?"

"Two of your best friends."

"Lyodot and D'Eymeris, do you mean? But what sort of a sentence?"

"Sentence of death."

"Passed? Oh! you must be mistaken, Gourville; that is impossible."

"Here is a copy of the sentence which the king is to sign to-day, if he has not already signed it."

Fouquet seized the paper eagerly, read it, and returned it to Gourville. "The king will never sign that," said he.

Gourville shook his head.

"Monseigneur, M. Colbert is a bold councilor: do not be too confident!"

"Monsieur Colbert again!" cried Fouquet. "How is it that that name rises upon all occasions to torment my ears, during the last two or three days? You make so trifling a subject of too much importance, Gourville. Let M. Colbert appear, I will face him; let him raise his head, I will crush him; but you understand, there must be an outline upon which my look may fall, there must be a surface upon which my feet may be placed."

"Patience, monseigneur; for you do not know what Colbert is—study him quickly; it is with this dark financier as it is with meteors, which the eye never sees completely before their disastrous invasion; when we feel them we are dead."

"Oh! Gourville, this is going too far," replied Fouquet, smiling; "allow me, my friend, not to be so easily frightened; M. Colbert a meteor! Corbleu, we confront the meteor. Let us see acts, and not words. What has he done?"

"He has ordered two gibbets of the executioner of Paris," answered Gourville.

Fouquet raised his head, and a flash gleamed from his eyes. "Are you sure of what you say?" cried he.

"Here is the proof, monseigneur." And Gourville held out to the superintendent a note communicated by a certain secretary of the Hotel de Ville, who was one of Fouquet's creatures.

"Yes, that is true," murmured the minister; "the scaffold may be prepared, but the king has not signed; Gourville, the king will not sign."

"I shall soon know," said Gourville.

"How?"

"If the king has signed, the gibbets will be sent this evening to the Hotel de Ville, in order to be got up and ready by to-morrow morning."

"Oh! no, no!" cried the superintendent, once again; "you are all deceived, and deceive me in my turn; Lyodot came to see me only the day before yesterday; only three days ago I received a present of some Syracuse wine from poor D'Eymeris."

"What does that prove?" replied Gourville, "except that the chamber of justice has been secretly assembled, has deliberated in the absence of the accused, and that the whole proceeding was complete when they were arrested."

"What! are they, then, arrested?"

"No doubt they are."

"But where, when, and how have they been arrested?"

"Lyodot, yesterday at daybreak; D'Eymeris, the day before yesterday, in the evening, as he was returning from the house of his mistress; their disappearances had disturbed nobody; but at length M. Colbert all at once raised the mask, and caused the affair to be published; it is being cried by sound of trumpet, at this moment in Paris, and, in truth, monseigneur, there is scarcely anybody but yourself ignorant of the event."

Fouquet began to walk about in his chamber with an uneasiness that became more and more serious.

"What do you decide upon, monseigneur?" said Gourville.

"If it were really as easy as you say, I would go to the king," cried Fouquet. "But as I go to the Louvre, I will pass by the Hotel de Ville. We shall see if the sentence is signed."

"Incredulity! thou art the pest of all great minds," said Gourville, shrugging his shoulders.

"Gourville!"

"Yes," continued he, "and incredulity! thou ruinest, as contagion destroys the most robust health; that is to say, in an instant."

"Let us go," cried Fouquet; "desire the door to be opened, Gourville."

"Be cautious," said the latter, "the Abbe Fouquet is there."

"Ah! my brother," replied Fouquet, in a tone of annoyance; "he is there, is he? he knows all the ill news, then, and is rejoiced to bring it to me, as usual. The devil! if my brother is there, my affairs are bad, Gourville; why did you not tell me that sooner: I should have been the more readily convinced."

"Monseigneur calumniates him," said Gourville, laughing; "if he is come, it is not with a bad intention."

"What, do you excuse him?" cried Fouquet; "a fellow without a heart, without ideas; a devourer of wealth."

"He knows you are rich."

"And would ruin me."

"No, but he would have your purse. That is all."

"Enough! enough! A hundred thousand crowns per month, during two years. Corbleu! it is I that pay, Gourville, and I know my figures." Gourville laughed in a silent, sly manner. "Yes, yes, you mean to say it is the king pays," said the superintendent. "Ah, Gourville, that is a vile joke; this is not the place."

"Monseigneur, do not be angry."

"Well, then, send away the Abbe Fouquet; I have not a sou." Gourville made a step towards the door. "He has been a month without seeing me," continued Fouquet, "why could he not be two months?"

"Because he repents of living in bad company," said Gourville, "and prefers you to all his bandits."

"Thanks for the preference! You make a strange advocate, Gourville, to-day—the advocate of the Abbe Fouquet!"

"Eh! but everything and every man has a good side—their useful side, monseigneur."

"The bandits whom the abbe keeps in pay and drink have their useful side, have they? Prove that, if you please."

"Let the circumstance arise, monseigneur, and you will be very glad to have these bandits under your hand."

"You advise me, then, to be reconciled to the abbe?" said Fouquet, ironically.

"I advise you, monseigneur, not to quarrel with a hundred or a hundred and twenty loose fellows, who, by putting their rapiers end to end, would form a cordon of steel capable of surrounding three thousand men."

Fouquet darted a searching glance at Gourville, and passing before him,— "That is all very well; let M. l'Abbe Fouquet be introduced," said he to the footman. "You are right, Gourville."

Two minutes after, the Abbe Fouquet appeared in the doorway, with profound reverence. He was a man of from forty to forty-five years of age, half churchman, half soldier,—a spadassin grafted upon an abbe; upon seeing that he had not a sword by his side, you might be sure he had pistols. Fouquet saluted him more as elder brother than as a minister.

"What can I do to serve you, monsieur l'abbe?" said he.

"Oh! oh! how coldly you speak to me, brother!"

"I speak like a man who is in a hurry, monsieur."

The abbe looked maliciously at Gourville, and anxiously at Fouquet, and said, "I have three hundred pistoles to pay to M. de Bregi this evening. A play debt, a sacred debt."

"What next?" said Fouquet bravely, for he comprehended that the Abbe Fouquet would not have disturbed him for such a want.

"A thousand to my butcher, who will supply no more meat."

"Next?"

"Twelve hundred to my tailor," continued the abbe; "the fellow has made me take back seven suits of my people's, which compromises my liveries, and my mistress talks of replacing me by a farmer of the revenue, which would be a humiliation for the church."

"What else?" said Fouquet.

"You will please to remark," said the abbe, humbly, "that I have asked nothing for myself."

"That is delicate, monsieur," replied Fouquet; "so, as you see, I wait."

"And I ask nothing, oh! no,—it is not for want of need, though, I assure you."

The minister reflected for a minute. "Twelve hundred pistoles to the tailor; that seems a great deal for clothes," said he.

"I maintain a hundred men," said the abbe, proudly; "that is a charge, I believe."

"Why a hundred men?" said Fouquet. "Are you a Richelieu or a Mazarin, to require a hundred men as a guard? What use do you make of these men?—speak."

"And do you ask me that?" cried the Abbe Fouquet; "ah! how can you put such a question,—why I maintain a hundred men? Ah!"

"Why, yes, I do put that question to you. What have you to do with a hundred men?—answer."

"Ingrate!" continued the abbe, more and more affected.

"Explain yourself."

"Why, monsieur the superintendent, I only want one valet de chambre, for my part, and even if I were alone, could help myself very well; but you, you who have so many enemies—a hundred men are not enough for me to defend you with. A hundred men!—you ought to have ten thousand. I maintain, then, these men in order that in public places, in assemblies, no voice may be raised against you; and without them, monsieur, you would be loaded with imprecations, you would be torn to pieces, you would not last a week; no, not a week, do you understand?"

"Ah! I did not know you were my champion to such an extent, monsieur le abbe."

"You doubt it!" cried the abbe. "Listen, then, to what happened, no longer ago than yesterday, in the Rue de la Hochette. A man was cheapening a fowl."

"Well, how could that injure me, abbe?"

"This way. The fowl was not fat. The purchaser refused to give eighteen sous for it, saying that he could not afford eighteen sous for the skin of a fowl from which M. Fouquet has sucked all the fat."

"Go on."

"The joke caused a deal of laughter," continued the abbe; "laughter at your expense, death to the devils! and the canaille were delighted. The joker added, 'Give me a fowl fed by M. Colbert, if you like! and I will pay all you ask.' And immediately there was a clapping of hands. A frightful scandal! you understand; a scandal which forces a brother to hide his face."

Fouquet colored. "And you veiled it?" said the superintendent.

"No, for so it happened I had one of my men in the crowd; a new recruit from the provinces, one M. Menneville, whom I like very much. He made his way through the press, saying to the joker: 'Mille barbes! Monsieur the false joker, here's a thrust for Colbert!' 'And one for Fouquet,' replied the joker. Upon which they drew in front of the cook's shop, with a hedge of the curious round them, and five hundred as curious at the windows."

"Well?" said Fouquet.

"Well, monsieur, my Menneville spitted the joker, to the great astonishment of the spectators, and said to the cook:—'Take this goose, my friend, for it is fatter than your fowl.' That is the way, monsieur," ended the abbe, triumphantly, "in which I spend my revenues; I maintain the honor of the family, monsieur." Fouquet hung his head. "And I have a hundred as good as he," continued the abbe.

"Very well," said Fouquet, "give the account to Gourville, and remain here this evening."

"Shall we have supper?"

"Yes, there will be supper."

"But the chest is closed."

"Gourville will open it for you. Leave us, monsieur l'abbe, leave us."

"Then we are friends?" said the abbe, with a bow.

"Oh, yes, friends. Come, Gourville."

"Are you going out? You will not stay to supper, then?"

"I shall be back in an hour; rest easy, abbe." Then aside to Gourville,—"Let them put to my English horses," said he, "and direct the coachman to stop at the Hotel de Ville de Paris."

Chapter LVI.
M. de la Fontaine's Wine.

CARRIAGES were already bringing the guests of Fouquet to Saint-Mande; already the whole house was getting warm with the preparations for supper, when the superintendent launched his fleet horses upon the roads to Paris, and going by the quays, in order to meet fewer people on the way, soon reached the Hotel de Ville. It wanted a quarter to eight. Fouquet alighted at the corner of the Rue de Long-Pont, and, on foot, directed his course towards the Place de Greve, accompanied by Gourville. At the turning of the Place they saw a man dressed in black and violet, of dignified mien, who was preparing to stop at Vincennes. He had before him a large hamper filled with bottles, which he had just purchased at the cabaret with the sign of "L'Image-de-Notre-Dame."

"Eh, but! that is Vatel! my maitre d'hotel!" said Fouquet to Gourville.

"Yes, monseigneur," replied the latter.

"What can he have been doing at the sign of L'Image-de-Notre-Dame?"

"Buying wine, no doubt."

"What! buy wine for me, at a cabaret?" said Fouquet. "My cellar, then, must be in a miserable condition!" and he advanced towards the maitre d'hotel, who was arranging his bottles in the carriage with the most minute care.

"Hola! Vatel," said he, in the voice of a master.

"Take care, monseigneur!" said Gourville, "you will be recognized."

"Very well! Of what consequence?—Vatel!"

The man dressed in black and violet turned round. He had a good and mild countenance, without expression—a mathematician minus the pride. A certain fire sparkled in the eyes of this personage, a rather sly smile played round his lips; but the observer might soon have remarked that this fire and this smile applied to nothing, enlightened nothing. Vatel laughed like an absent man, and amused himself like a child. At the sound of his master's voice he turned round, exclaiming: "Oh! monseigneur!"

"Yes, it is I. What the devil are you doing here, Vatel? Wine! You are buying wine at a cabaret in the Place de Greve!"

"But, monseigneur," said Vatel, quietly after having darted a hostile glance at Gourville, "why am I interfered with here? Is my cellar kept in bad order?"

"No, certes, Vatel, no; but—"

"But what?" replied Vatel. Gourville touched Fouquet's elbow.

"Don't be angry, Vatel; I thought my cellar—your cellar—sufficiently well stocked for us to be able to dispense with recourse to the cellar of L'Image-de-Notre-Dame."

"Eh, monsieur," said Vatel, shrinking from monseigneur to monsieur with a degree of disdain: "your cellar is so well stocked that when certain of your guests dine with you they have nothing to drink."

Fouquet, in great surprise, looked at Gourville. "What do you mean by that?"

"I mean that your butler had not wine for all tastes, monsieur; and that M. de la Fontaine, M. Pelisson, and M. Conrart, do not drink when they come to the house—these gentlemen do not like strong wine. What is to be done, then?"

"Well, and therefore?"

"Well, then, I have found here a vin de Joigny, which they like. I know they come here once a week to drink at the Image-de-Notre-Dame. That is the reason I am making this provision."

Fouquet had no more to say; he was convinced. Vatel, on his part, had much more to say, without doubt, and it was plain he was getting warm. "It is just as if you would reproach me, monseigneur, for going to the Rue Planche Milbray, to fetch, myself, the cider M. Loret drinks when he comes to dine at your house."

"Loret drinks cider at my house!" cried Fouquet, laughing.

"Certainly he does, monsieur, and that is the reason why he dines there with pleasure."

"Vatel," cried Fouquet, pressing the hand of his maitre d'hotel, "you are a man! I thank you, Vatel, for having understood that at my house M. de la Fontaine, M. Conrart, and M. Loret are as great as dukes and peers, as great as princes, greater than myself. Vatel, you are a good servant, and I double your salary."

Vatel did not even thank his master, he merely shrugged his shoulders a little, murmuring this superb sentiment: "To be thanked for having done one's duty is humiliating."

"He is right," said Gourville, as he drew Fouquet's attention, by a gesture, to another point. He showed him a low-built tumbrel, drawn by two horses, upon which rocked two strong gibbets, bound together, back to back, by chains, whilst an archer, seated upon the cross-beam, suffered, as well as he could, with his head cast down, the comments of a hundred vagabonds, who guessed the destination of the gibbets, and were escorting them to the Hotel de Ville. Fouquet started. "It is decided, you see," said Gourville.

"But it is not done," replied Fouquet.

"Oh, do not flatter yourself, monseigneur; if they have thus lulled your friendship and suspicions—if things have gone so far, you will be able to undo nothing."

"But I have not given my sanction."

"M. de Lyonne has ratified for you."

"I will go to the Louvre."

"Oh, no, you will not."

"Would you advise such baseness?" cried Fouquet, "would you advise me to abandon my friends? would you advise me, whilst able to fight, to throw the arms I hold in my hand to the ground?"

"I do not advise you to do anything of the kind, monseigneur. Are you in a position to quit the post of superintendent at this moment?"

"No."

"Well, if the king wishes to displace you—"

"He will displace me absent as well as present."

"Yes, but you will not have insulted him."

"Yes, but I shall have been base; now I am not willing that my friends should die; and they shall not die!"

"For that it is necessary you should go to the Louvre, is it not?"

"Gourville!"

"Beware! once at the Louvre, you will be forced to defend your friends openly, that is to say, to make a profession of faith; or you will be forced to abandon them irrevocably."

"Never!"

"Pardon me;—the king will propose the alternative to you, rigorously, or else you will propose it to him yourself."

"That is true."

"That is the reason why conflict must be avoided. Let us return to Saint-Mande, monseigneur."

"Gourville, I will not stir from this place, where the crime is to be carried out, where my disgrace is to be accomplished; I will not stir, I say, till I have found some means of combating my enemies."

"Monseigneur," replied Gourville, "you would excite my pity, if I did not know you for one of the great spirits of this world. You possess a hundred and fifty millions, you are equal to the king in position, and a hundred and fifty millions his superior in money. M. Colbert has not even had the wit to have the will of Mazarin accepted. Now, when a man is the richest person in a kingdom, and will take the trouble to spend the money, if things are done he does not like, it is because he is a poor man. Let us return to Saint-Mande, I say."

"To consult with Pelisson?—we will."

"No, monseigneur, to count your money."

"So be it," said Fouquet, with angry eyes;—"yes, yes, to Saint-Mande!" He got into his carriage again, and Gourville with him. Upon their road, at the end of the Faubourg Saint-Antoine, they overtook the humble equipage of Vatel, who was quietly conveying home his vin de Joigny. The black horses, going at a swift pace, alarmed, as they passed, the timid hack of the maitre d'hotel, who, putting his head out at the window, cried, in a fright, "Take care of my bottles!"*

* In the five-volume edition, Volume 1 ends here.

Chapter LVII.
The Gallery of Saint-Mande.

FIFTY persons were waiting for the superintendent. He did not even take the time to place himself in the hands of his valet de chambre for a minute, but from the perron went straight into the premier salon. There his friends were assembled in full chat. The intendant was about to order supper to be served, but, above all, the Abbe Fouquet watched for the return of his brother, and was endeavoring to do the honors of the house in his absence. Upon the arrival of the superintendent, a murmur of joy and affection was heard; Fouquet, full of affability, good humor, and munificence, was beloved by his poets, his artists, and his men of business. His brow, upon which his little court read, as upon that of a god, all the movements of his soul, and thence drew rules of conduct,—his brow, upon which affairs of state never impressed a wrinkle, was this evening paler than usual, and more than one friendly eye remarked that pallor. Fouquet placed himself at the head of the table, and presided gayly during supper. He recounted Vatel's expedition to La Fontaine, he related the history of Menneville and the skinny fowl to Pelisson, in such a manner that all the table heard it. A tempest of laughter and jokes ensued, which was only checked by a serious and even sad gesture from Pelisson. The Abbe Fouquet, not being able to comprehend why his brother should have led the conversation in that direction, listened with all his ears, and sought in the countenance of Gourville, or in that of his brother, an explanation which nothing afforded him. Pelisson took up the matter:— "Did they mention M. Colbert, then?" said he.

"Why not?" replied Fouquet; "if true, as it is said to be, that the king has made him his intendant?" Scarcely had Fouquet uttered these words, with a marked intention, than an explosion broke forth among the guests.

"The miser!" said one.

"The mean, pitiful fellow!" said another.

"The hypocrite!" said a third.

Pelisson exchanged a meaning look with Fouquet. "Messieurs," said he, "in truth we are abusing a man whom no one knows: it is neither charitable nor reasonable; and here is monsieur le surintendant, who, I am sure, agrees with me."

"Entirely," replied Fouquet. "Let the fat fowls of M. Colbert alone; our business to-day is with the faisans truffes of M. Vatel." This speech stopped the dark cloud which was beginning to throw its shade over the guests. Gourville succeeded so well in animating the poets with the vin de Joigny; the abbe, intelligent as a man who stands in need of his host's money, so enlivened the financiers and the men of the sword, that, amidst the vapors of this joy and the noise of conversation, inquietudes disappeared completely. The will of Cardinal Mazarin was the text of the conversation at the second course and dessert; then Fouquet ordered bowls of sweetmeats and fountains of liquor to be carried into the salon adjoining the gallery. He led the way thither, conducting by the hand a lady, the queen, by his preference, of the evening. The musicians then supped, and the promenades in the gallery and the gardens commenced, beneath a spring sky, mild and flower-scented. Pelisson then approached the superintendent, and said: "Something troubles monseigneur?"

"Greatly," replied the minister; "ask Gourville to tell you what it is." Pelisson, on turning round, found La Fontaine treading upon his heels. He was obliged to listen to a Latin verse, which the poet had composed upon Vatel. La Fontaine had, for an hour, been scanning this verse in all corners, seeking some one to pour it out upon advantageously. He thought he had caught Pelisson, but the latter escaped him; he turned towards Sorel, who had, himself, just composed a quatrain in honor of the supper, and the Amphytrion. La Fontaine in vain endeavored to gain attention to his verses; Sorel wanted to obtain a hearing for his quatrain. He was obliged to retreat before M. le Comte de Charost, whose arm Fouquet had just taken. L'Abbe Fouquet perceived that the poet, absent-minded, as usual, was about to follow the two talkers; and he interposed. La Fontaine seized upon him, and recited his verses. The abbe, who was quite innocent of Latin, nodded his head, in cadence, at every roll which La Fontaine impressed upon his body, according to the undulations of the dactyls and spondees. While this was going on, behind the confiture-basins, Fouquet related the event of the day to his son-in-law, M. de Charost. "We will send the idle and useless to look at the fireworks," said Pelisson to Gourville, "whilst we converse here."

"So be it," said Gourville, addressing four words to Vatel. The latter then led towards the gardens the major part of the beaux, the ladies and the chatterers, whilst the men walked in the gallery, lighted by three hundred wax-lights, in the sight of all; the admirers of fireworks all ran away towards the garden. Gourville approached Fouquet, and said: "Monsieur, we are here."

"All?" said Fouquet.

"Yes,—count." The superintendent counted; there were eight persons. Pelisson and Gourville walked arm in arm, as if conversing upon vague and frivolous subjects. Sorel and two officers imitated them, and in an opposite direction. The Abbe Fouquet walked alone. Fouquet, with M. de Charost, walked as if entirely absorbed in the conversation of his son-in-law. "Messieurs," said he, "let no one of you raise his head as he walks, or appear to pay attention to me; continue walking, we are alone, listen to me."

A perfect silence ensued, disturbed only by the distant cries of the joyous guests, from the groves whence they beheld the fireworks. It was a whimsical spectacle this, of these men walking in groups, as if each one was occupied about something, whilst lending attention really only to one amongst them, who, himself, seemed to be speaking only to his companion. "Messieurs," said Fouquet, "you have, without doubt, remarked the absence of two of my friends this evening, who were with us on Wednesday. For God's sake, abbe, do not stop,—it is not necessary to enable you to listen; walk on, carrying your head in a natural way, and as you have excellent sight, place yourself at the window, and if any one returns towards the gallery, give us notice by coughing."

The abbe obeyed.

"I have not observed their absence," said Pelisson, who, at this moment, was turning his back to Fouquet, and walking the other way.

"I do not see M. Lyodot," said Sorel, "who pays me my pension."

"And I," said the abbe, at the window, "do not see M. d'Eymeris, who owes me eleven hundred livres from our last game of brelan."

"Sorel," continued Fouquet, walking bent, and gloomily, "you will never receive your pension any more from M. Lyodot; and you, abbe, will never be paid you eleven hundred livres by M. d'Eymeris; for both are doomed to die."

"To die!" exclaimed the whole assembly, arrested, in spite of themselves, in the comedy they were playing, by that terrible word.

"Recover yourselves, messieurs," said Fouquet, "for perhaps we are watched—I said: to die!"

"To die!" repeated Pelisson; "what, the men I saw six days ago, full of health, gayety, and the spirit of the future! What then is man, good God! that disease should thus bring him down all at once!"

"It is not a disease," said Fouquet.

"Then there is a remedy," said Sorel.

"No remedy. Messieurs de Lyodot and D'Eymeris are on the eve of their last day."

"Of what are these gentlemen dying, then?" asked an officer.

"Ask of him who kills them," replied Fouquet.

"Who kills them? Are they being killed, then?" cried the terrified chorus.

"They do better still; they are hanging them," murmured Fouquet, in a sinister voice, which sounded like a funeral knell in that rich gallery, splendid with pictures, flowers, velvet, and gold. Involuntarily every one stopped; the abbe quitted his window; the first fuses of the fireworks began to mount above the trees. A prolonged cry from the gardens attracted the superintendent to enjoy the spectacle. He drew near to a window, and his friends placed themselves behind him, attentive to his least wish.

"Messieurs," said he, "M. Colbert has caused to be arrested, tried and will execute my two friends; what does it become me to do?"

"Mordieu!" exclaimed the abbe, the first one to speak, "run M. Colbert through the body."

"Monseigneur," said Pelisson, "you must speak to his majesty."

"The king, my dear Pelisson, himself signed the order for the execution."

"Well!" said the Comte de Charost, "the execution must not take place, then; that is all."

"Impossible," said Gourville, "unless we could corrupt the jailers."

"Or the governor," said Fouquet.

"This night the prisoners might be allowed to escape."

"Which of you will take charge of the transaction?"

"I," said the abbe, "will carry the money."

"And I," said Pelisson, "will be the bearer of the words."

"Words and money," said Fouquet, "five hundred thousand livres to the governor of the conciergerie that is sufficient; nevertheless, it shall be a million, if necessary."

"A million!" cried the abbe; "why, for less than half, I would have half Paris sacked."

"There must be no disorder," said Pelisson. "The governor being gained, the two prisoners escape; once clear of the fangs of the law, they will call together the enemies of Colbert, and prove to the king that his young justice, like all other monstrosities, is not infallible."

"Go to Paris, then, Pelisson," said Fouquet, "and bring hither the two victims; to-morrow we shall see."

Gourville gave Pelisson the five hundred thousand livres. "Take care the wind does not carry you away," said the abbe; "what a responsibility. Peste! Let me help you a little."

"Silence!" said Fouquet, "somebody is coming. Ah! the fireworks are producing a magical effect." At this moment a shower of sparks fell rustling among the branches of the neighboring trees. Pelisson and Gourville went out together by the door of the gallery; Fouquet descended to the garden with the five last plotters.

Chapter LVIII.
Epicureans.

AS Fouquet was giving, or appearing to give, all his attention to the brilliant illuminations, the languishing music of the violins and hautboys, the sparkling sheaves of the artificial fires, which, inflaming the heavens with glowing reflections, marked behind the trees the dark profile of the donjon of Vincennes; as, we say, the superintendent was smiling on the ladies and the poets, the fete was every whit as gay as usual; and Vatel, whose restless, even jealous look, earnestly consulted the aspect of Fouquet, did not appear dissatisfied with the welcome given to the ordering of the evening's entertainment. The fireworks over, the company dispersed about the gardens and beneath the marble porticoes with the delightful liberty which reveals in the master of the house so much forgetfulness of greatness, so much courteous hospitality, so much magnificent carelessness. The poets wandered about, arm in arm, through the groves; some reclined upon beds of moss, to the great damage of velvet clothes and curled heads, into which little dried leaves and blades of grass insinuated themselves. The ladies, in small numbers, listened to the songs of the singers and the verses of the poets; others listened to the prose, spoken with much art, by men who were neither actors nor poets, but to whom youth and solitude gave an unaccustomed eloquence, which appeared to them better than everything else in the world. "Why," said La Fontaine, "does not our master Epicurus descend into the garden? Epicurus never abandoned his pupils; the master is wrong."

"Monsieur," said Conrart, "you yourself are in the wrong persisting in decorating yourself with the name of an Epicurean; indeed, nothing here reminds me of the doctrine of the philosopher of Gargetta."

"Bah!" said La Fontaine, "is it not written that Epicurus purchased a large garden and lived in it tranquilly with his friends?"

"That is true."

"Well, has not M. Fouquet purchased a large garden at Saint-Mande, and do we not live here very tranquilly with him and his friends?"

"Yes, without doubt; unfortunately it is neither the garden nor the friends which constitute the resemblance. Now, what likeness is there between the doctrine of Epicurus and that of M. Fouquet?"

"This—pleasure gives happiness."

"Next?"

"Well, I do not think we ought to consider ourselves unfortunate, for my part, at least. A good repast—vin de Joigny, which they have the delicacy to go and fetch for me from my favorite cabaret—not one impertinence heard during a supper an hour long, in spite of the presence of ten millionaires and twenty poets."

"I stop you there. You mentioned vin de Joigny, and a good repast; do you persist in that?"

"I persist,—anteco, as they say at Port Royal."

"Then please to recollect that the great Epicurus lived, and made his pupils live, upon bread, vegetables, and water."

"That is not certain," said La Fontaine; "and you appear to me to be confounding Epicurus with Pythagoras, my dear Conrart."

"Remember, likewise, that the ancient philosopher was rather a bad friend of the gods and the magistrates."

"Oh! that is what I will not admit," replied La Fontaine. "Epicurus was like M. Fouquet."

"Do not compare him to monsieur le surintendant," said Conrart, in an agitated voice, "or you would accredit the reports which are circulating concerning him and us."

"What reports?"

"That we are bad Frenchmen, lukewarm with regard to the king, deaf to the law."

"I return, then, to my text," said La Fontaine. "Listen, Conrart, this is the morality of Epicurus, whom, besides, I consider, if I must tell you so, as a myth. Antiquity is mostly mythical. Jupiter, if we give a little attention to it, is life. Alcides is strength. The words are there to bear me out; Zeus, that is, zen, to live. Alcides, that is, alce, vigor. Well, Epicurus, that is mild watchfulness, that is protection; now who watches better over the state, or who protects individuals better than M. Fouquet does?"

"You talk etymology and not morality; I say that we modern Epicureans are indifferent citizens."

"Oh!" cried La Fontaine, "if we become bad citizens, it is not through following the maxims of our master. Listen to one of his principal aphorisms."

"I—will."

"Pray for good leaders."

"Well?"

"Well! what does M. Fouquet say to us every day? 'When shall we be governed?' Does he say so? Come, Conrart, be frank."

"He says so, that is true."

"Well, that is a doctrine of Epicurus."

"Yes; but that is a little seditious, observe."

"What! seditious to wish to be governed by good heads or leaders?"

"Certainly, when those who govern are bad."

"Patience, I have a reply for all."

"Even for what I have just said to you?"

"Listen! would you submit to those who govern ill? Oh! it is written: Cacos politeuousi. You grant me the text?"

"Pardieu! I think so. Do you know, you speak Greek as well as Aesop did, my dear La Fontaine."

"Is there any wickedness in that, my dear Conrart?"

"God forbid I should say so."

"Then let us return to M. Fouquet. What did he repeat to us all the day? Was it not this? 'What a cuistre is that Mazarin! what an ass! what a leech! We must, however, submit to that fellow.' Now, Conrart, did he say so, or did he not?"

"I confess that he said it, and even perhaps too often."

"Like Epicurus, my friend, still like Epicurus; I repeat, we are Epicureans, and that is very amusing."

"Yes; but I am afraid there will rise up, by the side of us, a sect like that of Epictetus; you know him well; the philosopher of Hierapolis, he who called bread luxury, vegetables prodigality, and clear water drunkenness; he who, being beaten by his master, said to him, grumbling a little it is true, but without being angry, 'I will lay a wager you have broken my leg!'—and who won his wager."

"He was a goose, that fellow Epictetus."

"Granted, but he might easily become the fashion by only changing his name into that of Colbert."

"Bah!" replied La Fontaine, "that is impossible. Never will you find Colbert in Epictetus."

"You are right, I shall find—Coluber there, at the most."

"Ah! you are beaten, Conrart; you are reduced to a play upon words. M. Arnaud pretends that I have no logic; I have more than M. Nicole."

"Yes," replied Conrart, "you have logic, but you are a Jansenist."

This peroration was hailed with a boisterous shout of laughter; by degrees the promenaders had been attracted by the exclamations of the two disputants around the arbor under which they were arguing. The discussion had been religiously listened to, and Fouquet himself, scarcely able to suppress his laughter, had given an example of moderation. But with the denouement of the scene he threw off all restraint, and laughed aloud. Everybody laughed as he did, and the two philosophers were saluted with unanimous felicitations. La Fontaine, however, was declared conqueror, on account of his profound erudition and his irrefragable logic. Conrart obtained the compensation due to an unsuccessful combatant; he was praised for the loyalty of his intentions, and the purity of his conscience.

At the moment when this jollity was manifesting itself by the most lively demonstrations, when the ladies were reproaching the two adversaries with not having admitted women into the system of Epicurean happiness, Gourville was seen hastening from the other end of the garden, approaching Fouquet, and detaching him, by his presence alone, from the group. The superintendent preserved on his face the smile and character of carelessness; but scarcely was he out of sight than he threw off the mask.

"Well!" said he, eagerly, "where is Pelisson! What is he doing?"

"Pelisson has returned from Paris."

"Has he brought back the prisoners?"

"He has not even seen the concierge of the prison."

"What! did he not tell him he came from me?"

"He told him so, but the concierge sent him this reply: 'If any one came to me from M. Fouquet, he would have a letter from M. Fouquet.'"

"Oh!" cried the latter, "if a letter is all he wants—"

"It is useless, monsieur!" said Pelisson, showing himself at the corner of the little wood, "useless! Go yourself, and speak in your own name."

"You are right. I will go in, as if to work; let the horses remain harnessed, Pelisson. Entertain my friends, Gourville."

"One last word of advice, monseigneur," replied the latter.

"Speak, Gourville."

"Do not go to the concierge save at the last minute; it is brave, but it is not wise. Excuse me, Monsieur Pelisson, if I am not of the same opinion as you; but take my advice, monseigneur, send again a message to this concierge,—he is a worthy man, but do not carry it yourself."

"I will think of it," said Fouquet; "besides, we have all the night before us."

"Do not reckon too much on time; were the hours we have twice as many as they are, they would not be too much," replied Pelisson; "it is never a fault to arrive too soon."

"Adieu!" said the superintendent; "come with me, Pelisson. Gourville, I commend my guests to your care." And he set off. The Epicureans did not perceive that the head of the school had left them; the violins continued playing all night long.

Chapter LIX.
A Quarter of an Hour's Delay.

FOUQUET, on leaving his house for the second time that day, felt himself less heavy and less disturbed than might have been expected. He turned towards Pelisson, who was meditating in the corner of the carriage some good arguments against the violent proceedings of Colbert.

"My dear Pelisson," said Fouquet, "it is a great pity you are not a woman."

"I think, on the contrary, it is very fortunate," replied Pelisson, "for, monseigneur, I am excessively ugly."

"Pelisson! Pelisson!" said the superintendent, laughing: "You repeat too often, you are 'ugly', not to leave people to believe that it gives you much pain."

"In fact it does, monseigneur, much pain; there is no man more unfortunate than I: I was handsome, the small-pox rendered me hideous; I am deprived of a great means of attraction; now, I am your principal clerk, or something of that sort; I take great interest in your affairs, and if, at this moment, I were a pretty woman, I could render you an important service."

"What?"

"I would go and find the concierge of the Palais. I would seduce him, for he is a gallant man, extravagantly partial to women; then I would get away our two prisoners."

"I hope to be able to do so myself, although I am not a pretty woman," replied Fouquet.

"Granted, monseigneur; but you are compromising yourself very much."

"Oh!" cried Fouquet, suddenly, with one of those secret transports which the generous blood of youth, or the remembrance of some sweet emotion, infuses into the heart. "Oh! I know a woman who will enact the personage we stand in need of, with the lieutenant-governor of the concierge."

"And, on my part, I know fifty, monseigneur; fifty trumpets, which will inform the universe of your generosity, of your devotion to your friends, and, consequently, will ruin you sooner or later in ruining themselves."

"I do not speak of such women, Pelisson; I speak of a noble and beautiful creature who joins to the intelligence and wit of her sex the valor and coolness of ours; I speak of a woman, handsome enough to make the walls of a prison bow down to salute her, discreet enough to let no one suspect by whom she has been sent."

"A treasure!" said Pelisson; "you would make a famous present to monsieur the governor of the concierge! Peste! monseigneur, he might have his head cut off; but he would, before dying, have had such happiness as no man had enjoyed before him."

"And I add," said Fouquet, "that the concierge of the Palais would not have his head cut off, for he would receive of me my horses, to effect his escape, and five hundred thousand livres wherewith to live comfortably in England: I add, that this lady, my friend, would give him nothing but the horses and the money. Let us go and seek her, Pelisson."

The superintendent reached forth his hand towards the golden and silken cord placed in the interior of his carriage, but Pelisson stopped him. "Monseigneur," said he, "you are going to lose as much time in seeking this lady as Columbus took to discover the new world. Now, we have but two hours in which we can possibly succeed; the concierge once gone to bed, how shall we get at him without making a disturbance? When daylight dawns, how can we conceal our proceedings? Go, go yourself, monseigneur, and do not seek either woman or angel to-night."

"But, my dear Pelisson, here we are before her door."

"What! before the angel's door?"

"Why, yes."

"This is the hotel of Madame de Belliere!"

"Hush!"

"Ah! Good Lord!" exclaimed Pelisson.

"What have you to say against her?"

"Nothing, alas! and it is that which causes my despair. Nothing, absolutely nothing. Why can I not, on the contrary, say ill enough of her to prevent your going to her?"

But Fouquet had already given orders to stop, and the carriage was motionless. "Prevent me!" cried Fouquet; "why, no power on earth should prevent my going to pay my compliments to Madame de Plessis-Belliere; besides, who knows that we shall not stand in need of her!"

"No, monseigneur, no!"

"But I do not wish you to wait for me, Pelisson," replied Fouquet, sincerely courteous.

"The more reason I should, monseigneur; knowing that you are keeping me waiting, you will, perhaps, stay a shorter time. Take care! You see there is a carriage in the courtyard: she has some one with her." Fouquet leaned towards the steps of the carriage. "One word more," cried Pelisson; "do not go to this lady till you have been to the concierge, for Heaven's sake!"

"Eh! five minutes, Pelisson," replied Fouquet, alighting at the steps of the hotel, leaving Pelisson in the carriage, in a very ill-humor. Fouquet ran upstairs, told his name to the footman, which excited an eagerness and a respect that showed the habit the mistress of the house had of honoring that name in her family. "Monsieur le surintendant," cried the marquise, advancing, very pale, to meet him; "what an honor! what an unexpected pleasure!" said she. Then, in a low voice, "Take care!" added the marquise, "Marguerite Vanel is here!"

"Madame," replied Fouquet, rather agitated, "I came on business. One single word, and quickly, if you please!" And he entered the salon. Madame Vanel had risen, paler, more livid, than Envy herself. Fouquet in vain addressed her, with the most agreeable, most pacific salutation; she only replied by a terrible glance darted at the marquise and Fouquet. This keen glance of a jealous woman is a stiletto which pierces every cuirass; Marguerite Vanel plunged it straight into the hearts of the two confidants. She made a courtesy to her friend, a more profound one to Fouquet, and took leave, under pretense of having a number of visits to make, without the marquise trying to prevent her, or Fouquet, a prey to anxiety, thinking further about her. She was scarcely out of the room, and Fouquet left alone with the marquise, before he threw himself on his knees, without saying a word. "I expected you," said the marquise, with a tender sigh.

"Oh! no," cried he, "or you would have sent away that woman."

"She has been here little more than half an hour, and I had no expectation she would come this evening."

"You love me just a little, then, marquise?"

"That is not the question now; it is of your danger; how are your affairs going on?"

"I am going this evening to get my friends out of the prisons of the Palais."

"How will you do that?"

"By buying and bribing the governor."

"He is a friend of mine; can I assist you, without injuring you?"

"Oh! marquise, it would be a signal service; but how can you be employed without your being compromised? Now, never shall my life, my power, or even my liberty, be purchased at the expense of a single tear from your eyes, or of one frown of pain upon your brow."

"Monseigneur, no more such words, they bewilder me; I have been culpable in trying to serve you, without calculating the extent of what I was doing. I love you in reality, as a tender friend; and as a friend, I am grateful for your delicate attentions—but, alas!—alas! you will never find a mistress in me."

"Marquise!" cried Fouquet, in a tone of despair; "why not?"

"Because you are too much beloved," said the young woman, in a low voice; "because you are too much beloved by too many people—because the splendor of glory and fortune wound my eyes, whilst the darkness of sorrow attracts them; because, in short, I, who have repulsed you in your proud magnificence; I who scarcely looked at you in your splendor, I came, like a mad woman, to throw myself, as it were, into your arms, when I saw a misfortune hovering over your head. You understand me now, monseigneur? Become happy again, that I may remain chaste in heart and in thought: your misfortune entails my ruin."

"Oh! madame," said Fouquet, with an emotion he had never before felt; "were I to fall to the lowest degree of human misery, and hear from your mouth that word which you now refuse me, that day, madame, you will be mistaken in your noble egotism; that day you will fancy you are consoling the most unfortunate of men, and you will have said, I love you, to the most illustrious, the most delighted, the most triumphant of the happy beings of this world."

He was still at her feet, kissing her hand, when Pelisson entered precipitately, crying, in very ill-humor, "Monseigneur! madame! for Heaven's sake! excuse me. Monseigneur, you have been here half an hour. Oh! do not both look at me so reproachfully. Madame, pray who is that lady who left your house soon after monseigneur came in?"

"Madame Vanel," said Fouquet.

"Ha!" cried Pelisson, "I was sure of that."

"Well! what then?"

"Why, she got into her carriage, looking deadly pale."

"What consequence is that to me?"

"Yes, but what she said to her coachman is of consequence to you."

"Kind heaven!" cried the marquise, "what was that?"

"To M. Colbert's!" said Pelisson, in a hoarse voice.

"Bon Dieu!—begone, begone, monseigneur!" replied the marquise, pushing Fouquet out of the salon, whilst Pelisson dragged him by the hand.

"Am I, then, indeed," said the superintendent, "become a child, to be frightened by a shadow?"

"You are a giant," said the marquise, "whom a viper is trying to bite in the heel."

Pelisson continued to drag Fouquet to the carriage. "To the Palais at full speed!" cried Pelisson to the coachman. The horses set off like lightening; no obstacle relaxed their pace for an instant. Only, at the arcade Saint-Jean, as they were coming out upon the Place de Greve, a long file of horsemen, barring the narrow passage, stopped the carriage of the superintendent. There was no means of forcing this barrier; it was necessary to wait till the mounted archers of the watch, for it was they who stopped the way, had passed with the heavy carriage they were escorting, and which ascended rapidly towards the Place Baudoyer. Fouquet and Pelisson took no further account of this circumstance beyond deploring the minute's delay they had thus to submit to. They entered the habitation of the concierge du Palais five minutes after. That officer was still walking about in the front court. At the name of Fouquet, whispered in his ear by Pelisson, the governor eagerly approached the carriage, and, hat in hand, was profuse in his attentions. "What an honor for me, monseigneur," said he.

"One word, monsieur le goverenur, will you take the trouble to get into my carriage?" The officer placed himself opposite Fouquet in the coach.

"Monsieur," said Fouquet, "I have a service to ask of you."

"Speak, monseigneur."

"A service that will be compromising for you, monsieur, but which will assure to you forever my protection and my friendship."

"Were it to cast myself into the fire for you, monseigneur, I would do it."

"That is well," said Fouquet; "what I require is much more simple."

"That being so, monseigneur, what is it?"

"To conduct me to the chamber of Messieurs Lyodot and D'Eymeris."

"Will monseigneur have the kindness to say for what purpose?"

"I will tell you that in their presence, monsieur; at the same time that I will give you ample means of palliating this escape."

"Escape! Why, then, monseigneur does not know?"

"What?"

"That Messieurs Lyodot and D'Eymeris are no longer here."

"Since when?" cried Fouquet, in great agitation.

"About a quarter of an hour."

"Whither have they gone, then?"

"To Vincennes—to the donjon."

"Who took them from here?"

"An order from the king."

"Oh! woe! woe!" exclaimed Fouquet, striking his forehead. "Woe!" and without saying a single word more to the governor, he threw himself back into his carriage, despair in his heart, and death on his countenance.

"Well!" said Pelisson, with great anxiety.

"Our friends are lost. Colbert is conveying them to the donjon. They crossed our path under the arcade Saint-Jean."

Pelisson, struck as by a thunderbolt, made no reply. With a single reproach he would have killed his master. "Where is monseigneur going?" said the footman.

"Home—to Paris. You, Pelisson, return to Saint-Mande, and bring the Abbe Fouquet to me within an hour. Begone!"

Chapter LX.
Plan of Battle.

THE night was already far advanced when the Abbe Fouquet joined his brother. Gourville had accompanied him. These three men, pale with dread of future events, resembled less three powers of the day than three conspirators, united by one single thought of violence. Fouquet walked for a long time, with his eyes fixed upon the floor, striking his hands one against the other. At length, taking courage, in the midst of a deep sigh: "Abbe," said he, "you were speaking to me only to-day of certain people you maintain."

"Yes, monsieur," replied the abbe.

"Tell me precisely who are these people." The abbe hesitated.

"Come! no fear, I am not threatening; no romancing, for I am not joking."

"Since you demand the truth, monseigneur, here it is:—I have a hundred and twenty friends or companions of pleasure, who are sworn to me as the thief is to the gallows."

"And you think you can depend on them?"

"Entirely."

"And you will not compromise yourself?"

"I will not even make my appearance."

"Are they men of resolution?"

"They would burn Paris, if I promised them they should not be burnt in turn."

"The thing I ask of you, abbe," said Fouquet, wiping the sweat which fell from his brow, "is to throw your hundred and twenty men upon the people I will point out to you, at a certain moment given—is it possible?"

"It will not be the first time such a thing has happened to them, monseigneur."

"That is well: but would these bandits attack an armed force?"

"They are used to that."

"Then get your hundred and twenty men together, abbe."

"Directly. But where?"

"On the road to Vincennes, to-morrow, at two o'clock precisely."

"To carry off Lyodot and D'Eymeris? There will be blows to be got!"

"A number, no doubt; are you afraid?"

"Not for myself, but for you."

"Your men will know, then, what they have to do?"

"They are too intelligent not to guess it. Now, a minister who gets up a riot against his king—exposes himself—"

"Of what importance is that to you, I pray? Besides, if I fall, you fall with me."

"It would then be more prudent, monsieur, not to stir in the affair, and leave the king to take this little satisfaction."

"Think well of this, abbe, Lyodot and D'Eymeris at Vincennes are a prelude of ruin for my house. I repeat it—I arrested, you will be imprisoned—I imprisoned, you will be exiled."

"Monsieur, I am at your orders; have you any to give me?"

"What I told you—I wish that, to-morrow, the two financiers of whom they mean to make victims, whilst there remain so many criminals unpunished, should be snatched from the fury of my enemies. Take your measures accordingly. Is it possible?"

"It is possible."

"Describe your plan."

"It is of rich simplicity. The ordinary guard at executions consists of twelve archers."

"There will be a hundred to-morrow."

"I reckon so. I even say more—there will be two hundred."

"Then your hundred and twenty men will not be enough."

"Pardon me. In every crowd composed of a hundred thousand spectators, there are ten thousand bandits or cut-purses—only they dare not take the initiative."

"Well?"

"There will then be, to-morrow, on the Place de Greve, which I choose as my battle-field, ten thousand auxiliaries to my hundred and twenty men. The attack commenced by the latter, the others will finish it."

"That all appears feasible. But what will be done with regard to the prisoners upon the Place de Greve?"

"This: they must be thrust into some house—that will make a siege necessary to get them out again. And stop! here is another idea, more sublime still: certain houses have two issues—one upon the Place, and the other into the Rue de la Mortellerie, or la Vannerie, or la Tixeranderie. The prisoners entering by one door will go out at another."

"Yes; but fix upon something positive."

"I am seeking to do so."

"And I," cried Fouquet, "I have found it. Listen to what has occurred to me at this moment."

"I am listening."

Fouquet made a sign to Gourville, who appeared to understand. "One of my friends lends me sometimes the keys of a house which he rents, Rue Baudoyer, the spacious gardens of which extend behind a certain house on the Place de Greve."

"That is the place for us," said the abbe. "What house?"

"A cabaret, pretty well frequented, whose sign represents the image of Notre Dame."

"I know it," said the abbe.

"This cabaret has windows opening upon the Place, a place of exit into the court, which must abut upon the gardens of my friend by a door of communication."

"Good!" said the abbe.

"Enter by the cabaret, take the prisoners in; defend the door while you enable them to fly by the garden and the Place Baudoyer."

"That is all plain. Monsieur, you would make an excellent general, like monsieur le prince."

"Have you understood me?"

"Perfectly well."

"How much will it amount to, to make your bandits all drunk with wine, and to satisfy them with gold?"

"Oh, monsieur, what an expression! Oh! monsieur, if they heard you! some of them are very susceptible."

"I mean to say they must be brought to the point where they cannot tell the heavens from the earth; for I shall to-morrow contend with the king; and when I fight I mean to conquer—please to understand."

"It shall be done, monsieur. Give me your other ideas."

"That is your business."

"Then give me your purse."

"Gourville, count a hundred thousand livres for the abbe."

"Good! and spare nothing, did you not say?"

"Nothing."

"That is well."

"Monseigneur," objected Gourville, "if this should be known, we should lose our heads."

"Eh! Gourville," replied Fouquet, purple with anger, "you excite my pity. Speak for yourself, if you please. My head does not shake in that manner upon my shoulders. Now, abbe, is everything arranged?"

"Everything."

"At two o'clock to-morrow."

"At twelve, because it will be necessary to prepare our auxiliaries in a secret manner."

"That is true; do not spare the wine of the cabaretier."

"I will spare neither his wine nor his house," replied the abbe, with a sneering laugh. "I have my plan, I tell you; leave me to set it in operation, and you shall see."

"Where shall you be yourself?"

"Everywhere; nowhere."

"And how shall I receive information?"

"By a courier whose horse shall be kept in the very same garden of your friend. A propos, the name of your friend?"

Fouquet looked again at Gourville. The latter came to the succor of his master, saying, ["The name is of no importance."

Fouquet continued, "Accompany] monsieur l'abbe, for several reasons, but the house is easily to be known—the 'Image-de-Notre-Dame' in the front, a garden, the only one in the quarter, behind."

* [The text in the print copy is corrupt at this point. The suggested reading, in brackets, is by John Bursey.]

"Good, good! I will go and give notice to my soldiers."

"Accompany him, Gourville," said Fouquet, "and count him down the money. One moment, abbe—one moment, Gourville—what name will be given to this carrying off?"

"A very natural one, monsieur—the Riot."

"The riot on account of what? For, if ever the people of Paris are disposed to pay their court to the king, it is when he hangs financiers."

"I will manage that," said the abbe.

"Yes; but you may manage it badly, and people will guess."

"Not at all,—not at all. I have another idea."

"What is that?"

"My men shall cry out, 'Colbert, vive Colbert!' and shall throw themselves upon the prisoners as if they would tear them in pieces, and shall force them from the gibbets, as too mild a punishment."

"Ah! that is an idea," said Gourville. "Peste! monsieur l'abbe, what an imagination you have!"

"Monsieur, we are worthy of our family," replied the abbe, proudly.

"Strange fellow," murmured Fouquet. Then he added, "That is ingenious. Carry it out, but shed no blood."

Gourville and the abbe set off together, with their heads full of the meditated riot. The superintendent laid himself down upon some cushions, half valiant with respect to the sinister projects of the morrow, half dreaming of love.

Chapter LXI.
The Cabaret of the Image-de-Notre-Dame.

AT two o'clock the next day fifty thousand spectators had taken their position upon the Place, around the two gibbets which had been elevated between the Quai de la Greve and the Quai Pelletier; one close to the other, with their backs to the embankment of the river. In the morning also, all the sworn criers of the good city of Paris had traversed the quarters of the city, particularly the halles and the faubourgs, announcing with their hoarse and indefatigable voices the great justice done by the king upon two speculators, two thieves, devourers of the people. And these people, whose interests were so warmly looked after, in order not to fail in respect for their king, quitted shops, stalls, and atliers, to go and evince a little gratitude to Louis XIV., absolutely like invited guests, who feared to commit an impoliteness in not repairing to the house of him who had invited them. According to the tenor of the sentence, which the criers read aloud and incorrectly, two farmers of the revenues, monopolists of money, dilapidators of the royal provisions, extortioners, and forgers, were about to undergo capital punishment on the Place de Greve, with their names blazoned over their heads, according to their sentence. As to those names, the sentence made no mention of them. The curiosity of the Parisians was at its height, and, as we have said, an immense crowd waited with feverish impatience the hour fixed for the execution. The news had already spread that the prisoners, transferred to the Chateau of Vincennes, would be conducted from that prison to the Place de Greve. Consequently, the faubourg and the Rue Saint Antoine were crowded; for the population of Paris in those days of great executions was divided into two categories: those who came to see the condemned pass—these were of timid and mild hearts, but philosophically curious—and those who wished to see the condemned die—these had hearts that hungered for sensation. On this day M. d'Artagnan received his last instructions from the king, and made his adieus to his friends, the number of whom was, at the moment, reduced to Planchet, then he traced the plan of his day, as every busy man whose moments are counted ought to do, because he appreciates their importance.

"My departure is to be," said he, "at break of day, three o'clock in the morning; I have then fifteen hours before me. Take from them the six hours of sleep which are indispensable for me—six; one hour for repasts—seven; one hour for a farewell visit to Athos—eight; two hours for chance circumstances—total, ten. There are then five hours left. One hour to get my money,—that is, to have payment refused by M. Fouquet; another hour to go and receive my money of M. Colbert, together with his questions and grimaces; one hour to look over my clothes and arms, and get my boots cleaned. I still have two hours left. Mordioux! how rich I am." And so saying, D'Artagnan felt a strange joy, a joy of youth, a perfume of those great and happy years of former times mount into his brain and intoxicate him. "During these two hours I will go," said the musketeer, "and take my quarter's rent of the Image-de-Notre-Dame. That will be pleasant. Three hundred and seventy-five livres! Mordioux! but that is astonishing! If the poor man who has but one livre in his pocket, found a livre and twelve deniers, that would be justice, that would be excellent; but never does such a godsend fall to the lot of the poor man. The rich man, on the contrary, makes himself revenue with his money, which he does not even touch. Here are three hundred and seventy-five livres which fall to me from heaven. I will go then to the Image-de-Notre-Dame, and drink a glass of Spanish wine with my tenant, which he cannot fail to offer me. But order must be observed, Monsieur d'Artagnan, order must be observed! Let us organize our time, then, and distribute the employment of it! Art. 1st, Athos; Art. 2d, the Image-de-Notre-Dame; Art. 3rd, M. Fouquet; Art. 4th, M. Colbert; Art. 5th, supper; Art. 6th, clothes, boots, horse, portmanteau; Art. 7th and last, sleep."

In consequence of this arrangement, D'Artagnan went straight to the Comte de la Fere, to whom, modestly and ingenuously, he related a part of his fortunate adventures. Athos had not been without uneasiness on the subject of D'Artagnan's visit to the king; but few words sufficed for an explanation of that. Athos divined that Louis had charged D'Artagnan with some important mission, and did not even make an effort to draw the secret from him. He only recommended him to take care of himself, and offered discreetly to accompany him if that were desirable.

"But, my dear friend," said D'Artagnan, "I am going nowhere."

"What! you come and bid me adieu, and are going nowhere?"

"Oh! yes, yes," replied D'Artagnan, coloring a little, "I am going to make an acquisition."

"That is quite another thing. Then I change my formula. Instead of 'Do not get yourself killed,' I will say,—'Do not get yourself robbed.'"

"My friend, I will inform you if I set eyes on any property that pleases me, and shall expect you will favor me with your opinion."

"Yes, yes," said Athos, too delicate to permit himself even the consolation of a smile. Raoul imitated the paternal reserve. But D'Artagnan thought it would appear too mysterious to leave his friends under a pretense, without even telling them the route he was about to take.

"I have chosen Le Mans," said he to Athos. "It is a good country?"

"Excellent, my friend," replied the count, without making him observe that Le Mans was in the same directions as La Touraine, and that by waiting two days, at most, he might travel with a friend. But D'Artagnan, more embarrassed than the count, dug, at every explanation, deeper into the mud, into which he sank by degrees. "I shall set out to-morrow at daybreak," said he at last. "Till that time, will you come with me, Raoul?"

"Yes, monsieur le chevalier," said the young man, "if monsieur le comte does not want me."

"No, Raoul; I am to have an audience to-day of Monsieur, the king's brother; that is all I have to do."

Raoul asked Grimaud for his sword, which the old man brought him immediately. "Now then," added D'Artagnan, opening his arms to Athos, "adieu, my dear friend!" Athos held him in a long embrace, and the musketeer, who knew his discretion so well, murmured in his ear—"An affair of state," to which Athos only replied by a pressure of the hand, still more significant. They then separated. Raoul took the arm of his old friend, who led him along the Rue Saint-Honore. "I an conducting you to the abode of the god Plutus," said D'Artagnan to the young man; "prepare yourself. The whole day you will witness the piling up of crowns. Heavens! how I am changed!"

"Oh! what numbers of people there are in the street!" said Raoul.

"Is there a procession to-day?" asked D'Artagnan of a passer-by.

"Monsieur, it is a hanging," replied the man.

"What! a hanging at the Greve?" said D'Artagnan.

"Yes, monsieur."

"The devil take the rogue who gets himself hung the day I want to go and take my rent!" cried D'Artagnan. "Raoul, did you ever see anybody hung?"

"Never, monsieur—thank God!"

"Oh! how young that sounds! If you were on guard in the trenches, as I was, and a spy! But, pardon me, Raoul, I am doting—you are quite right, it is a hideous sight to see a person hung! At what hour do they hang them, monsieur, if you please?"

"Monsieur," replied the stranger respectfully, delighted at joining conversation with two men of the sword, "it will take place at about three o'clock."

"Aha! it is now only half-past one; let us step out, we shall be there in time to touch my three hundred and seventy-five livres, and get away before the arrival of the malefactor."

"Malefactors, monsieur," continued the bourgeois; "there are two of them."

"Monsieur, I return to you many thanks," said D'Artagnan, who as he grew older, had become polite to a degree. Drawing Raoul along, he directed his course rapidly in the direction of La Greve. Without that great experience musketeers have of a crowd, to which were joined an irresistible strength of wrist, and an uncommon suppleness of shoulders, our two travelers would not have arrived at their place of destination. They followed the line of the Quai, which they had gained on quitting the Rue Saint-Honore, where they left Athos. D'Artagnan went first; his elbow, his wrist, his shoulder formed three wedges which he knew how to insinuate with skill into the groups, to make them split and separate like firewood. He made use sometimes of the hilt of his sword as an additional help: introducing it between ribs that were too rebellious, making it take the part of a lever or crowbar, to separate husband from wife, uncle from nephew, and brother from brother. And all that was done so naturally, and with such gracious smiles, that people must have had ribs of bronze not to cry thank you when the wrist made its play, or hearts of diamond not to be enchanted when such a bland smile enlivened the lips of the musketeer. Raoul, following his friend, cajoled the women who admired his beauty, pushed back the men who felt the rigidity of his muscles, and both opened, thanks to these maneuvers, the compact and muddy tide of the populace. They arrived in sight of the two gibbets, from which Raoul turned away his eyes in disgust. As for D'Artagnan, he did not even see them; his house with its gabled roof, its windows crowded with the curious, attracted and even absorbed all the attention he was capable of. He distinguished in the Place and around the houses a good number of musketeers on leave, who, some with women, others with friends, awaited the crowning ceremony. What rejoiced him above all was to see that his tenant, the cabaretier, was so busy he hardly knew which way to turn. Three lads could not supply the drinkers. They filled the shop, the chambers, and the court, even. D'Artagnan called Raoul's attention to this concourse, adding: "The fellow will have no excuse for not paying his rent. Look at those drinkers, Raoul, one would say they were jolly companions. Mordioux! why, there is no room anywhere!" D'Artagnan, however, contrived to catch hold of the master by the corner of his apron, and to make himself known to him.

"Ah, monsieur le chevalier," said the cabaretier, half distracted, "one minute if you please. I have here a hundred mad devils turning my cellar upside down."

"The cellar, if you like, but not the money-box."

"Oh, monsieur, your thirty-seven and a half pistoles are all counted out ready for you, upstairs in my chamber; but there are in that chamber thirty customers, who are sucking the staves of a little barrel of Oporto which I tapped for them this very morning. Give me a minute,—only a minute?"

"So be it; so be it."

"I will go," said Raoul, in a low voice, to D'Artagnan; "this hilarity is vile!"

"Monsieur," replied D'Artagnan, sternly, "you will please to remain where you are. The soldier ought to familiarize himself with all kinds of spectacles. There are in the eye, when it is young, fibers which we must learn how to harden; and we are not truly generous and good save from the moment when the eye has become hardened, and the heart remains tender. Besides, my little Raoul, would you leave me alone here? That would be very wrong of you. Look, there is yonder in the lower court a tree, and under the shade of that tree we shall breathe more freely than in this hot atmosphere of spilt wine."

From the spot on which they had placed themselves the two new guests of the Image-de-Notre-Dame heard the ever-increasing hubbub of the tide of people, and lost neither a cry nor a gesture of the drinkers, at tables in the cabaret, or disseminated in the chambers. If D'Artagnan had wished to place himself as a vidette for an expedition, he could not have succeeded better. The tree under which he and Raoul were seated covered them with its already thick foliage; it was a low, thick chestnut-tree, with inclined branches, that cast their shade over a table so dilapidated the drinkers had abandoned it. We said that from this post D'Artagnan saw everything. He observed the goings and comings of the waiters; the arrival of fresh drinkers; the welcome, sometimes friendly, sometimes hostile, given to the newcomers by others already installed. He observed all this to amuse himself, for the thirty-seven and a half pistoles were a long time coming. Raoul recalled his attention to it. "Monsieur," said he, "you do not hurry your tenant, and the condemned will soon be here. There will then be such a press we shall not be able to get out."

"You are right," said the musketeer; "Hola! oh! somebody there! Mordioux!" But it was in vain he cried and knocked upon the wreck of the old table, which fell to pieces beneath his fist; nobody came. D'Artagnan was preparing to go and seek the cabaretier himself, to force him to a definite explanation, when the door of the court in which he was with Raoul, a door which communicated with the garden situated at the back, opened, and a man dressed as a cavalier, with his sword in the sheath, but not at his belt, crossed the court without closing the door; and having cast an oblique glance at D'Artagnan and his companion, directed his course towards the cabaret itself, looking about in all directions with his eyes capable of piercing walls of consciences. "Humph!" said D'Artagnan, "my tenants are communicating. That, no doubt, now, is some amateur in hanging matters." At the same moment the cries and disturbance in the upper chambers ceased. Silence, under such circumstances, surprises more than a twofold increase of noise. D'Artagnan wished to see what was the cause of this sudden silence. He then perceived that this man, dressed as a cavalier, had just entered the principal chamber, and was haranguing the tipplers, who all listened to him with the greatest attention. D'Artagnan would perhaps have heard his speech but for the dominant noise of the popular clamors, which made a formidable accompaniment to the harangue of the orator. But it was soon finished, and all the people the cabaret contained came out, one after the other, in little groups, so that there only remained six in the chamber; one of these six, the man with the sword, took the cabaretier aside, engaging him in discourse more or less serious, whilst the others lit a great fire in the chimney-place—a circumstance rendered strange by the fine weather and the heat.

"It is very singular," said D'Artagnan to Raoul, "but I think I know those faces yonder."

"Don't you think you can smell the smoke here?" said Raoul.

"I rather think I can smell a conspiracy," replied D'Artagnan.

He had not finished speaking, when four of these men came down into the court, and without the appearance of any bad design, mounted guard at the door of communication, casting, at intervals, glances at D'Artagnan, which signified many things.

"Mordioux!" said D'Artagnan, in a low voice, "there is something going on. Are you curious, Raoul?"

"According to the subject, chevalier."

"Well, I am as curious as an old woman. Come a little more in front; we shall get a better view of the place. I would lay a wager that view will be something curious."

"But you know, monsieur le chevalier, that I am not willing to become a passive and indifferent spectator of the death of the two poor devils."

"And I, then—do you think I am a savage? We will go in again, when it is time to do so. Come along!" And they made their way towards the front of the house, and placed themselves near the window which, still more strangely than the rest, remained unoccupied. The two last drinkers, instead of looking out at this window, kept up the fire. On seeing D'Artagnan and his friend enter:—"Ah! ah! a reinforcement," murmured they.

D'Artagnan jogged Raoul's elbow. "Yes, my braves, a reinforcement," said he; "cordieu! there is a famous fire. Whom are you going to cook?"

The two men uttered a shout of jovial laughter, and, instead of answering, threw on more wood. D'Artagnan could not take his eyes off them.

"I suppose," said one of the fire-makers, "they sent you to tell us the time—did not they?"

"Without doubt they have," said D'Artagnan, anxious to know what was going on; "why should I be here else, if it were not for that?"

"Then place yourself at the window, if you please, and observe." D'Artagnan smiled in his mustache, made a sign to Raoul, and placed himself at the window.

Chapter LXII.
Vive Colbert!

THE spectacle which the Greve now presented was a frightful one. The heads, leveled by the perspective, extended afar, thick and agitated as the ears of corn in a vast plain. From time to time a fresh report, or a distant rumor, made the heads oscillate and thousands of eyes flash. Now and then there were great movements. All those ears of corn bent, and became waves more agitated than those of the ocean, which rolled from the extremities to the center, and beat, like the tides, against the hedge of archers who surrounded the gibbets. Then the handles of the halberds were let fall upon the heads and shoulders of the rash invaders; at times, also, it was the steel as well as the wood, and, in that case, a large empty circle was formed around the guard; a space conquered upon the extremities, which underwent, in their turn the oppression of the sudden movement, which drove them against the parapets of the Seine. From the window, that commanded a view of the whole Place, D'Artagnan saw, with interior satisfaction, that such of the musketeers and guards as found themselves involved in the crowd, were able, with blows of their fists and the hilts of their swords, to keep room. He even remarked that they had succeeded, by that esprit de corps which doubles the strength of the soldier, in getting together in one group to the amount of about fifty men; and that, with the exception of a dozen stragglers whom he still saw rolling here and there, the nucleus was complete, and within reach of his voice. But it was not the musketeers and guards that drew the attention of D'Artagnan. Around the gibbets, and particularly at the entrances to the arcade of Saint-Jean, moved a noisy mass, a busy mass; daring faces, resolute demeanors were to be seen here and there, mingled with silly faces and indifferent demeanors; signals were exchanged, hands given and taken. D'Artagnan remarked among the groups, and those groups the most animated, the face of the cavalier whom he had seen enter by the door of communication from his garden, and who had gone upstairs to harangue the drinkers. That man was organizing troops and giving orders.

"Mordioux!" said D'Artagnan to himself, "I was not deceived; I know that man,—it is Menneville. What the devil is he doing here?"

A distant murmur, which became more distinct by degrees, stopped this reflection, and drew his attention another way. This murmur was occasioned by the arrival of the culprits; a strong picket of archers preceded them, and appeared at the angle of the arcade. The entire crowd now joined as if in one cry; all the cries united formed one immense howl. D'Artagnan saw Raoul was becoming pale, and he slapped him roughly on the shoulder. The fire-keepers turned round on hearing the great cry, and asked what was going on. "The condemned are arrived," said D'Artagnan. "That's well," replied they, again replenishing the fire. D'Artagnan looked at them with much uneasiness; it was evident that these men who were making such a fire for no apparent purpose had some strange intentions. The condemned appeared upon the Place. They were walking, the executioner before them, whilst fifty archers formed a hedge on their right and their left. Both were dressed in black; they appeared pale, but firm. They looked impatiently over the people's heads, standing on tip-toe at every step. D'Artagnan remarked this. "Mordioux!" cried he, "they are in a great hurry to get a sight of the gibbet!" Raoul drew back, without, however, having the power to leave the window. Terror even has its attractions.

"To the death! to the death!" cried fifty thousand voices.

"Yes; to the death!" howled a hundred frantic others, as if the great mass had given them the reply.

"To the halter! to the halter!" cried the great whole; "Vive le roi!"

"Well," said D'Artagnan, "this is droll; I should have thought it was M. Colbert who had caused them to be hung."

There was, at this moment, a great rolling movement in the crowd, which stopped for a moment the march of the condemned. The people of a bold and resolute mien, whom D'Artagnan had observed, by dint of pressing, pushing, and lifting themselves up, had succeeded in almost touching the hedge of archers. The cortege resumed its march. All at once, to cries of "Vive Colbert!" those men, of whom D'Artagnan never lost sight, fell upon the escort, which in vain endeavored to stand against them. Behind these men was the crowd. Then commenced, amidst a frightful tumult, as frightful a confusion. This time there was something more than cries of expectation or cries of joy, there were cries of pain. Halberds struck men down, swords ran through them, muskets were discharged at them. The confusion became then so great that D'Artagnan could no longer distinguish anything. Then, from this chaos, suddenly surged something like a visible intention, like a will pronounced. The condemned had been torn from the hands of the guards, and were being dragged towards the house of L'Image-de-Notre-Dame. Those who dragged them shouted, "Vive Colbert!" The people hesitated, not knowing which they ought to fall upon, the archers or the aggressors. What stopped the people was, that those who cried "Vive Colbert!" began to cry, at the same time, "No halter! no halter! to the fire! to the fire! burn the thieves! burn the extortioners!" This cry, shouted with an ensemble, obtained enthusiastic success. The populace had come to witness an execution, and here was an opportunity offered them of performing one themselves. It was this that must be most agreeable to the populace: therefore, they ranged themselves immediately on the party of the aggressors against the archers, crying with the minority, which had become, thanks to them, the most compact majority: "Yes, yes: to the fire with the thieves! Vive Colbert!"

"Mordioux!" exclaimed D'Artagnan, "this begins to look serious."

One of the men who remained near the chimney approached the window, a firebrand in his hand. "Ah, ah!" said he, "it gets warm." Then, turning to his companion: "There is the signal," added he; and he immediately applied the burning brand to the wainscoting. Now, this cabaret of the Image-de-Notre-Dame was not a very newly built house, and therefore, did not require much entreating to take fire. In a second the boards began to crackle, and the flames arose sparkling to the ceiling. A howling from without replied to the shouts of the incendiaries. D'Artagnan, who had not seen what passed, from being engaged at the window, felt, at the same time, the smoke which choked him and the fire that scorched him. "Hola!" cried he, turning round, "is the fire here? Are you drunk or mad, my masters?"

The two men looked at each other with an air of astonishment. "In what?" asked they of D'Artagnan; "was it not a thing agreed upon?"

"A thing agreed upon that you should burn my house!" vociferated D'Artagnan, snatching the brand from the hand of the incendiary, and striking him with it across the face. The second wanted to assist his comrade, but Raoul, seizing him by the middle, threw him out of the window, whilst D'Artagnan pushed his man down the stairs. Raoul, first disengaged, tore the burning wainscoting down, and threw it flaming into the chamber. At a glance D'Artagnan saw there was nothing to be feared from the fire, and sprang to the window. The disorder was at its height. The air was filled with simultaneous cries of "To the fire!" "To the death!" "To the halter!" "To the stake!" "Vive Colbert!" "Vive le roi!" The group which had forced the culprits from the hands of the archers had drawn close to the house, which appeared to be the goal towards which they dragged them. Menneville was at the head of this group, shouting louder than all the others, "To the fire! to the fire! Vive Colbert!" D'Artagnan began to comprehend what was meant. They wanted to burn the condemned, and his house was to serve as a funeral pile.

"Halt, there!" cried he, sword in hand, and one foot upon the window. "Menneville, what do you want to do?"

"Monsieur d'Artagnan," cried the latter; "give way, give way!"

"To the fire! to the fire with the thieves! Vive Colbert!"

These cries exasperated D'Artagnan. "Mordioux!" said he. "What! burn the poor devils who are only condemned to be hung? that is infamous!"

Before the door, however, the mass of anxious spectators, rolled back against the walls, had become more thick, and closed up the way. Menneville and his men, who were dragging along the culprits, were within ten paces of the door.

Menneville made a last effort. "Passage! passage!" cried he, pistol in hand.

"Burn them! burn them!" repeated the crowd. "The Image-de-Notre-Dame is on fire! Burn the thieves! burn the monopolists in the Image-de-Notre-Dame!"

There now remained no doubt, it was plainly D'Artagnan's house that was their object. D'Artagnan remembered the old cry, always so effective from his mouth: "A moi! mousquetaires!" shouted he, with the voice of a giant, with one of those voices which dominate over cannon, the sea, the tempest. "A moi! mousquetaires!" And suspending himself by the arm from the balcony, he allowed himself to drop amidst the crowd, which began to draw back form a house that rained men. Raoul was on the ground as soon as he, both sword in hand. All the musketeers on the Place heard that challenging cry—all turned round at that cry, and recognized D'Artagnan. "To the captain, to the captain!" cried they, in their turn. And the crowd opened before them as though before the prow of a vessel. At that moment D'Artagnan and Menneville found themselves face to face. "Passage, passage!" cried Menneville, seeing that he was within an arm's length from the door.

"No one passes here," said D'Artagnan.

"Take that, then!" said Menneville, firing his pistol almost within an arm's length. But before the cock fell, D'Artagnan had struck up Menneville's arm with the hilt of his sword and passed the blade through his body.

"I told you plainly to keep yourself quiet," said D'Artagnan to Menneville, who rolled at his feet.

"Passage! passage!" cried the companions of Menneville, at first terrified, but soon recovering, when they found they had only to do with two men. But those two men were hundred-armed giants; the swords flew about in their hands like the burning glaive of the archangel. They pierce with its point, strike with the flat, cut with the edge; every stroke brings down a man. "For the king!" cried D'Artagnan, to every man he struck at, that is to say, to every man that fell. This cry became the charging word for the musketeers, who, guided by it, joined D'Artagnan. During this time the archers, recovering from the panic they had undergone, charge the aggressors in the rear, and regular as mill strokes, overturn or knock down all that opposed them. The crowd, which sees swords gleaming, and drops of blood flying in the air—the crowd falls back and crushes itself. At length cries for mercy and of despair resound; that is, the farewell of the vanquished. The two condemned are again in the hands of the archers. D'Artagnan approaches them, seeing them pale and sinking: "Console yourselves, poor men," said he, "you will not undergo the frightful torture with which these wretches threatened you. The king has condemned you to be hung: you shall only be hung. Go on, hang them, and it will be over."

There is no longer anything going on at the Image-de-Notre-Dame. The fire has been extinguished with two tuns of wine in default of water. The conspirators have fled by the garden. The archers are dragging the culprits to the gibbets. From this moment the affair did not occupy much time. The executioner, heedless about operating according to the rules of the art, made such haste that he dispatched the condemned in a couple of minutes. In the meantime the people gathered around D'Artagnan,—they felicitated, they cheered him. He wiped his brow, streaming with sweat, and his sword, streaming with blood. He shrugged his shoulders at seeing Menneville writhing at his feet in the last convulsions. And, while Raoul turned away his eyes in compassion, he pointed to the musketeers the gibbets laden with their melancholy fruit. "Poor devils!" said he, "I hope they died blessing me, for I saved them with great difficulty." These words caught the ear of Menneville at the moment when he himself was breathing his last sigh. A dark, ironical smile flitted across his lips; he wished to reply, but the effort hastened the snapping of the chord of life—he expired.

"Oh! all this is very frightful!" murmured Raoul: "let us begone, monsieur le chevalier."

"You are not wounded?" asked D'Artagnan.

"Not at all; thank you."

"That's well! Thou art a brave fellow, mordioux! The head of the father, and the arm of Porthos. Ah! if he had been here, good Porthos, you would have seen something worth looking at." Then as if by way of remembrance—

"But where the devil can that brave Porthos be?" murmured D'Artagnan.

"Come, chevalier, pray come away," urged Raoul.

"One minute, my friend; let me take my thirty-seven and a half pistols, and I am at your service. The house is a good property," added D'Artagnan, as he entered the Image-de-Notre-Dame, "but decidedly, even if it were less profitable, I should prefer its being in another quarter."

Chapter LXIII.
How M. d'Eymeris's Diamond passed into the Hands of M. d'Artagnan.

WHILST this violent, noisy, and bloody scene was passing on the Greve, several men, barricaded behind the gate of communication with the garden, replaced their swords in their sheaths, assisted one among them to mount a ready saddled horse which was waiting in the garden, and like a flock of startled birds, fled in all directions, some climbing the walls, others rushing out at the gates with all the fury of a panic. He who mounted the horse, and gave him the spur so sharply that the animal was near leaping the wall, this cavalier, we say, crossed the Place Baudoyer, passed like lightening before the crowd in the streets, riding against, running over and knocking down all that came in his way, and, ten minutes after, arrived at the gates of the superintendent, more out of breath than his horse. The Abbe Fouquet, at the clatter of hoofs on the pavement, appeared at a window of the court, and before even the cavalier had set foot to the ground, "Well! Danicamp?" cried he, leaning half out of the window.

"Well, it is all over," replied the cavalier.

"All over!" cried the abbe. "Then they are saved?"

"No, monsieur," replied the cavalier, "they are hung."

"Hung!" repeated the abbe, turning pale. A lateral door suddenly opened, and Fouquet appeared in the chamber, pale, distracted, with lips half opened, breathing a cry of grief and anger. He stopped upon the threshold to listen to what was addressed from the court to the window.

"Miserable wretches!" said the abbe, "you did not fight, then?"

"Like lions."

"Say like cowards."

"Monsieur!"

"A hundred men accustomed to war, sword in hand, are worth ten thousand archers in a surprise. Where is Menneville, that boaster, that braggart, who was to come back either dead or a conqueror?"

"Well, monsieur, he kept his word. He is dead!"

"Dead! Who killed him?"

"A demon disguised as a man, a giant armed with ten flaming swords—a madman, who at one blow extinguished the fire, put down the riot, and caused a hundred musketeers to rise up out of the pavement of the Greve."

Fouquet raised his brow, streaming with sweat, murmuring, "Oh! Lyodot and D'Eymeris! dead! dead! dead! and I dishonored."

The abbe turned round, and perceiving his brother, despairing and livid, "Come, come," said he, "it is a blow of fate, monsieur; we must not lament thus. Our attempt has failed because God—"

"Be silent, abbe! be silent!" cried Fouquet; "your excuses are blasphemies. Order that man up here, and let him relate the details of this terrible event."

"But, brother—"

"Obey, monsieur!"

The abbe made a sign, and in half a minute the man's step was heard upon the stairs. At the same time Gourville appeared behind Fouquet, like the guardian angel of the superintendent, pressing one finger on his lips to enjoin observation even amidst the bursts of his grief. The minister resumed all the serenity that human strength left at the disposal of a heart half broken with sorrow. Danicamp appeared. "Make your report," said Gourville.

"Monsieur," replied the messenger, "we received orders to carry off the prisoners, and to cry 'Vive Colbert!' whilst carrying them off."

"To burn them alive, was it not, abbe?" interrupted Gourville.

"Yes, yes, the order was given to Menneville. Menneville knew what was to be done, and Menneville is dead."

This news appeared rather to reassure Gourville than to sadden him.

"Yes, certainly to burn them alive," said the abbe, eagerly.

"Granted, monsieur, granted," said the man, looking into the eyes and the faces of the two interlocutors, to ascertain what there was profitable or disadvantageous to himself in telling the truth.

"Now, proceed," said Gourville.

"The prisoners," cried Danicamp, "were brought to the Greve, and the people, in a fury, insisted upon their being burnt instead of being hung."

"And the people were right," said the abbe. "Go on."

"But," resumed the man, "at the moment the archers were broken, at the moment the fire was set to one of the houses of the Place destined to serve as a funeral-pile for the guilty, this fury, this demon, this giant of whom I told you, and who, we had been informed, was the proprietor of the house in question, aided by a young man who accompanied him, threw out of the window those who kept the fire, called to his assistance the musketeers who were in the crowd, leaped himself from the window of the first story into the

Place, and plied his sword so desperately that the victory was restored to the archers, the prisoners were retaken, and Menneville killed. When once recaptured, the condemned were executed in three minutes." Fouquet, in spite of his self-command, could not prevent a deep groan escaping him.

"And this man, the proprietor of the house, what is his name?" said the abbe.

"I cannot tell you, not having even been able to get sight of him; my post had been appointed in the garden, and I remained at my post: only the affair was related to me as I repeat it. I was ordered, when once the affair was at an end, to come at best speed and announce to you the manner in which it finished. According to this order, I set out, full gallop, and here I am."

"Very well, monsieur, we have nothing else to ask of you," said the abbe, more and more dejected, in proportion as the moment approached for finding himself alone with his brother.

"Have you been paid?" asked Gourville.

"Partly, monsieur," replied Danicamp.

"Here are twenty pistols. Begone, monsieur, and never forget to defend, as this time has been done, the true interests of the king."

"Yes, monsieur," said the man, bowing and pocketing the money. After which he went out. Scarcely had the door closed after him when Fouquet, who had remained motionless, advanced with a rapid step and stood between the abbe and Gourville. Both of them at the same time opened their mouths to speak to him. "No excuses," said he, "no recriminations against anybody. If I had not been a false friend I should not have confided to any one the care of delivering Lyodot and D'Eymeris. I alone am guilty; to me alone are reproaches and remorse due. Leave me, abbe."

"And yet, monsieur, you will not prevent me," replied the latter, "from endeavoring to find out the miserable fellow who has intervened to the advantage of M. Colbert in this so well-arranged affair; for, if it is good policy to love our friends dearly, I do not believe that is bad which consists in obstinately pursuing our enemies."

"A truce to policy, abbe; begone, I beg of you, and do not let me hear any more of you till I send for you; what we most need is circumspection and silence. You have a terrible example before you, gentlemen: no reprisals, I forbid them."

"There are no orders," grumbled the abbe, "which will prevent me from avenging a family affront upon the guilty person."

"And I," cried Fouquet, in that imperative tone to which one feels there is nothing to reply, "if you entertain one thought, one single thought, which is not the absolute expression of my will, I will have you cast into the Bastile two hours after that thought has manifested itself. Regulate your conduct accordingly, abbe."

The abbe colored and bowed. Fouquet made a sign to Gourville to follow him, and was already directing his steps towards his cabinet, when the usher announced with a loud voice: "Monsieur le Chevalier d'Artagnan."

"Who is he?" said Fouquet, negligently, to Gourville.

"An ex-lieutenant of his majesty's musketeers," replied Gourville, in the same tone. Fouquet did not even take the trouble to reflect, and resumed his walk. "I beg your pardon, monseigneur!" said Gourville, "but I have remembered; this brave man has quitted the king's service, and probably comes to receive an installment of some pension or other."

"Devil take him!" said Fouquet, "why does he choose his opportunity so ill?"

"Permit me then, monseigneur, to announce your refusal to him; for he is one of my acquaintance, and is a man whom, in our present circumstances, it would be better to have as a friend than an enemy."

"Answer him as you please," said Fouquet.

"Eh! good Lord!" said the abbe, still full of malice, like an egotistical man; "tell him there is no money, particularly for musketeers."

But scarcely had the abbe uttered this imprudent speech, when the partly open door was thrown back, and D'Artagnan appeared.

"Eh! Monsieur Fouquet," said he, "I was well aware there was no money for musketeers here. Therefore I did not come to obtain any, but to have it refused. That being done, receive my thanks. I give you good-day, and will go and seek it at M. Colbert's." And he went out, making an easy bow.

"Gourville," said Fouquet, "run after that man and bring him back." Gourville obeyed, and overtook D'Artagnan on the stairs.

D'Artagnan, hearing steps behind him, turned round and perceived Gourville. "Mordioux! my dear monsieur," said he, "there are sad lessons which you gentlemen of finance teach us; I come to M. Fouquet to receive a sum accorded by his majesty, and I am received like a mendicant who comes to ask charity, or a thief who comes to steal a piece of plate."

"But you pronounced the name of M. Colbert, my dear M. d'Artagnan; you said you were going to M. Colbert's?"

"I certainly am going there, were it only to ask satisfaction of the people who try to burn houses, crying 'Vive Colbert!'"

Gourville pricked up his ears. "Oh, oh!" said he, "you allude to what has just happened at the Greve?"

"Yes, certainly."

"And in what did that which has taken place concern you?"

"What! do you ask me whether it concerns me or does not concern me, if M. Colbert pleases to make a funeral-pile of my house?"

"So, ho, your house—was it your house they wanted to burn?"

"Pardieu! was it!"

"Is the cabaret of the Image-de-Notre-Dame yours, then?"

"It has been this week."

"Well, then, are you the brave captain, are you the valiant blade who dispersed those who wished to burn the condemned?"

"My dear Monsieur Gourville, put yourself in my place. I was an agent of the public force and a landlord, too. As a captain, it is my duty to have the orders of the king accomplished. As a proprietor, it is to my interest my house should not be burnt. I have at the same time attended to the laws of interest and duty in replacing Messieurs Lyodot and D'Eymeris in the hands of the archers."

"Then it was you who threw the man out of the window?"

"It was I, myself," replied D'Artagnan, modestly.

"And you who killed Menneville?"

"I had that misfortune," said D'Artagnan, bowing like a man who is being congratulated.

"It was you, then, in short, who caused the two condemned persons to be hung?"

"Instead of being burnt, yes, monsieur, and I am proud of it. I saved the poor devils from horrible tortures. Understand, my dear Monsieur de Gourville, that they wanted to burn them alive. It exceeds imagination!"

"Go, my dear Monsieur d'Artagnan, go," said Gourville, anxious to spare Fouquet the sight of the man who had just caused him such profound grief.

"No," said Fouquet, who had heard all from the door of the ante-chamber; "not so; on the contrary, Monsieur d'Artagnan, come in."

D'Artagnan wiped from the hilt of his sword a last bloody trace, which had escaped his notice, and returned. He then found himself face to face with these three men, whose countenances wore very different expressions. With the abbe it was anger, with Gourville stupor, with Fouquet it was dejection.

"I beg your pardon, monsieur le ministre," said D'Artagnan, "but my time is short; I have to go to the office of the intendant, to have an explanation with Monsieur Colbert, and to receive my quarter's pension."

"But, monsieur," said Fouquet, "there is money here." D'Artagnan looked at the superintendent with astonishment. "You have been answered inconsiderately, monsieur, I know, because I heard it," said the minister; "a man of your merit ought to be known by everybody." D'Artagnan bowed. "Have you an order?" added Fouquet.

"Yes, monsieur."

"Give it me, I will pay you myself; come with me." He made a sign to Gourville and the abbe, who remained in the chamber where they were. He led D'Artagnan into his cabinet. As soon as the door was shut,—"how much is due to you, monsieur?"

"Why, something like five thousand livres, monseigneur."

"For arrears of pay?"

"For a quarter's pay."

"A quarter consisting of five thousand livres!" said Fouquet, fixing upon the musketeer a searching look. "Does the king, then, give you twenty thousand livres a year?"

"Yes, monseigneur, twenty thousand livres a year. Do you think it is too much?"

"I?" cried Fouquet, and he smiled bitterly. "If I had any knowledge of mankind, if I were—instead of being a frivolous, inconsequent, and vain spirit—of a prudent and reflective spirit; if, in a word, I had, as certain persons have known how, regulated my life, you would not receive twenty thousand livres a year, but a hundred thousand, and you would belong not to the king but to me."

D'Artagnan colored slightly. There is sometimes in the manner in which a eulogium is given, in the voice, in the affectionate tone, a poison so sweet, that the strongest mind is intoxicated by it. The superintendent terminated his speech by opening a drawer, and taking from it four rouleaux, which he placed before D'Artagnan. The Gascon opened one. "Gold!" said he.

"It will be less burdensome, monsieur."

"But, then, monsieur, these make twenty thousand livres."

"No doubt they do."

"But only five are due to me."

"I wish to spare you the trouble of coming four times to my office."

"You overwhelm me, monsieur."

"I do only what I ought to do, monsieur le chevalier; and I hope you will not bear me any malice on account of the rude reception my brother gave you. He is of a sour, capricious disposition."

"Monsieur," said D'Artagnan, "believe me, nothing would grieve me more than an excuse from you."

"Therefore I will make no more, and will content myself with asking you a favor."

"Oh, monsieur."

Fouquet drew from his finger a ring worth about three thousand pistoles. "Monsieur," said he, "this stone was given me by a friend of my childhood, by a man to whom you have rendered a great service."

"A service—I?" said the musketeer; "I have rendered a service to one of your friends?"

"You cannot have forgotten it, monsieur, for it dates this very day."

"And that friend's name was—"

"M. d'Eymeris."

"One of the condemned?"

"Yes, one of the victims. Well! Monsieur d'Artagnan, in return for the service you have rendered him, I beg you to accept this diamond. Do so for my sake."

"Monsieur! you—"

"Accept it, I say. To-day is with me a day of mourning; hereafter you will, perhaps, learn why; to-day I have lost one friend; well, I will try to get another."

"But, Monsieur Fouquet—"

"Adieu! Monsieur d'Artagnan, adieu!" cried Fouquet, with much emotion; "or rather, au revoir." And the minister quitted the cabinet, leaving in the hands of the musketeer the ring and the twenty thousand livres.

"Oh!" said D'Artagnan, after a moment's dark reflection. "How on earth am I to understand what this means? Mordioux! I can understand this much, only: he is a gallant man! I will go and explain matters to M. Colbert." And he went out.

Chapter LXIV.
Difference D'Artagnan finds between the Intendant and the Superintendent.

M COLBERT RESIDED in the Rue Neuve des Petits-Champs, in a house which had belonged to Beautru. D'Artagnan's legs cleared the distance in a short quarter of an hour. When he arrived at the residence of the new favorite, the court was full of archers and police, who came to congratulate him, or to excuse themselves, according to whether he should choose to praise or blame. The sentiment of flattery is instinctive with people of abject condition; they have the sense of it, as the wild animal has that of hearing and smell. These people, or their leader, understood that there was a pleasure to offer to M. Colbert, in rendering him an account of the fashion in which his name had been pronounced during the rash enterprise of the morning. D'Artagnan made his appearance just as the chief of the watch was giving his report. He stood close to the door, behind the archers. That officer took Colbert on one side, in spite of his resistance and the contradiction of his bushy eyebrows. "In case," said he, "you really desired, monsieur, that the people should do justice on the two traitors, it would have been wise to warn us of it; for, indeed, monsieur, in spite of our regret at displeasing you, or thwarting your views, we had our orders to execute."

"Triple fool!" replied Colbert, furiously shaking his hair, thick and black as a mane; "what are you telling me? What! that I could have had an idea of a riot! Are you mad or drunk?"

"But, monsieur, they cried 'Vive Colbert!'" replied the trembling watch.

"A handful of conspirators—"

"No, no; a mass of people."

"Ah! indeed," said Colbert, expanding. "A mass of people cried 'Vive Colbert!' Are you certain of what you say, monsieur?"

"We had nothing to do but open our ears, or rather to close them, so terrible were the cries."

"And this was from the people, the real people?"

"Certainly, monsieur; only these real people beat us."

"Oh! very well," continued Colbert, thoughtfully. "Then you suppose it was the people alone who wished to burn the condemned?"

"Oh! yes, monsieur."

"That is quite another thing. You strongly resisted, then?"

"We had three of our men crushed to death, monsieur!"

"But you killed nobody yourselves?"

"Monsieur, a few of the rioters were left upon the square, and one among them who was not a common man."

"Who was he?"

"A certain Menneville, upon whom the police have a long time had an eye."

"Menneville!" cried Colbert, "what, he who killed Rue de la Huchette, a worthy man who wanted a fat fowl?"

"Yes, monsieur; the same."

"And did this Menneville also cry, 'Vive Colbert'?"

"Louder than all the rest; like a madman."

Colbert's brow grew dark and wrinkled. A kind of ambitious glory which had lighted his face was extinguished, like the light of glow-worms we crush beneath the grass. "Then you say," resumed the deceived intendant, "that the initiative came from the people? Menneville was my enemy; I would have had him hung, and he knew it well. Menneville belonged to the Abbe Fouquet—the affair originated with Fouquet; does not everybody know that the condemned were his friends from childhood?"

"That is true," thought D'Artagnan, "and thus are all my doubts cleared up. I repeat it, Monsieur Fouquet may be called what they please, but he is a very gentlemanly man."

"And," continued Colbert, "are you quite sure Menneville is dead?"

D'Artagnan thought the time was come for him to make his appearance. "Perfectly, monsieur;" replied he, advancing suddenly.

"Oh! is that you, monsieur?" said Colbert.

"In person," replied the musketeer with his deliberate tone; "it appears that you had in Menneville a pretty enemy."

"It was not I, monsieur, who had an enemy," replied Colbert; "it was the king."

"Double brute!" thought D'Artagnan, "to think to play the great man and the hypocrite with me. Well," continued he to Colbert, "I am very happy to have rendered so good a service to the king; will you take upon you to tell his majesty, monsieur l'intendant?"

"What commission is this you give me, and what do you charge me to tell his majesty, monsieur? Be precise, if you please," said Colbert, in a sharp voice, tuned beforehand to hostility.

"I give you no commission," replied D'Artagnan, with that calmness which never abandons the banterer; "I thought it would be easy for you to announce to his majesty that it was I who, being there by chance, did justice upon Menneville and restored order to things."

Colbert opened his eyes and interrogated the chief of the watch with a look—"Ah! it is very true," said the latter, "that this gentleman saved us."

"Why did you not tell me, monsieur, that you came to relate me this?" said Colbert with envy; "everything is explained, and more favorably for you than for anybody else."

"You are in error, monsieur l'intendant, I did not at all come for the purpose of relating that to you."

"It is an exploit, nevertheless."

"Oh!" said the musketeer carelessly, "constant habit blunts the mind."

"To what do I owe the honor of your visit, then?"

"Simply to this: the king ordered me to come to you."

"Ah!" said Colbert, recovering himself when he saw D'Artagnan draw a paper from his pocket; "it is to demand some money of me?"

"Precisely, monsieur."

"Have the goodness to wait, if you please, monsieur, till I have dispatched the report of the watch."

D'Artagnan turned upon his heel, insolently enough, and finding himself face to face with Colbert, after his first turn, he bowed to him as a harlequin would have done; then, after a second evolution, he directed his steps towards the door in quick time. Colbert was struck with this pointed rudeness, to which he was not accustomed. In general, men of the sword, when they came to his office, had such a want of money, that though their feet seemed to take root in the marble, they hardly lost their patience. Was D'Artagnan going straight to the king? Would he go and describe his rough reception, or recount his exploit? This was a matter for grave consideration. At all events, the moment was badly chosen to send D'Artagnan away, whether he came from the king, or on his own account. The musketeer had rendered too great a service, and that too recently, for it to be already forgotten. Therefore Colbert thought it would be better to shake off his arrogance and call D'Artagnan back. "Ho! Monsieur d'Artagnan," cried Colbert, "what! are you leaving me thus?"

D'Artagnan turned round: "Why not?" said he, quietly, "we have no more to say to each other, have we?"

"You have, at least, money to receive, as you have an order?"

"Who, I? Oh! not at all, my dear Monsieur Colbert."

"But, monsieur, you have an order. And, in the same manner as you give a sword-thrust, when you are required, I, on my part, pay when an order is presented to me. Present yours."

"It is useless, my dear Monsieur Colbert," said D'Artagnan, who inwardly enjoyed this confusion in the ideas of Colbert; "my order is paid."

"Paid, by whom?"

"By monsieur le surintendant."

Colbert grew pale.

"Explain yourself," said he, in a stifled voice—"if you are paid why do you show me that paper?"

"In consequence of the word of order of which you spoke to me so ingeniously just now, dear M. Colbert; the king told me to take a quarter of the pension he is pleased to make me."

"Of me?" said Colbert.

"Not exactly. The king said to me: 'Go to M. Fouquet; the superintendent will, perhaps, have no money, then you will go and draw it of M. Colbert.'"

The countenance of M. Colbert brightened for a moment; but it was with his unfortunate physiognomy as with a stormy sky, sometimes radiant, sometimes dark as night, according as the lightening gleams or the cloud passes. "Eh! and was there any money in the superintendent's coffers?" asked he.

"Why, yes, he could not be badly off for money," replied D'Artagnan—"it may be believed, since M. Fouquet, instead of paying me a quarter or five thousand livres—"

"A quarter or five thousand livres!" cried Colbert, struck, as Fouquet had been, with the generosity of the sum for a soldier's pension, "why, that would be a pension of twenty thousand livres?"

"Exactly, M. Colbert. Peste! you reckon like old Pythagoras; yes, twenty thousand livres."

"Ten times the appointment of an intendant of the finances. I beg to offer you my compliments," said Colbert, with a vicious smile.

"Oh!" said D'Artagnan, "the king apologized for giving me so little; but he promised to make it more hereafter, when he should be rich; but I must be gone, having much to do—"

"So, then, notwithstanding the expectation of the king, the superintendent paid you, did he?"

"In the same manner, as, in opposition to the king's expectation, you refused to pay me."

"I did not refuse, monsieur, I only begged you to wait. And you say that M. Fouquet paid you your five thousand livres?"

"Yes, as you might have done; but he did even better than that, M. Colbert."

"And what did he do?"

"He politely counted me down the sum-total, saying, that for the king, his coffers were always full."

"The sum-total! M. Fouquet has given you twenty thousand livres instead of five thousand?"

"Yes, monsieur."

"And what for?"

"In order to spare me three visits to the money-chest of the superintendent, so that I have the twenty thousand livres in my pocket in good new coin. You see, then, that I am able to go away without standing in need of you, having come here only for form's sake." And D'Artagnan slapped his hand upon his pocket, with a laugh which disclosed to Colbert thirty-two magnificent teeth, as white as teeth of twenty-five years old, and which seemed to say in their language: "Serve up to us thirty-two little Colberts, and we will chew them willingly." The serpent is as brave as the lion, the hawk as courageous as the eagle, that cannot be contested. It can only be said of animals that are decidedly cowardly, and are so called, that they will be brave only when they have to defend themselves. Colbert was not frightened at the thirty-two teeth of D'Artagnan. He recovered, and suddenly,—"Monsieur," said he, "monsieur le surintendant has done what he had no right to do."

"What do you mean by that?" replied D'Artagnan.

"I mean that your note—will you let me see your note, if you please?"

"Very willingly; here it is."

Colbert seized the paper with an eagerness which the musketeer did not remark without uneasiness, and particularly without a certain degree of regret at having trusted him with it. "Well, monsieur, the royal order says thus:— 'At sight, I command that there be paid to M. d'Artagnan the sum of five thousand livres, forming a quarter of the pension I have made him.'"

"So, in fact, it is written," said D'Artagnan, affecting calmness.

"Very well; the king only owed you five thousand livres; why has more been given to you?"

"Because there was more; and M. Fouquet was willing to give me more; that does not concern anybody."

"It is natural," said Colbert with a proud ease, "that you should be ignorant of the usages of state-finance; but, monsieur, when you have a thousand livres to pay, what do you do?"

"I never have a thousand livres to pay," replied D'Artagnan.

"Once more," said Colbert, irritated—"once more, if you had any sum to pay, would you not pay what you ought?"

"That only proves one thing," said D'Artagnan; "and that is, that you have your own particular customs in finance, and M. Fouquet has his own."

"Mine, monsieur, are the correct ones."

"I do not say that they are not."

"And you have accepted what was not due to you."

D'Artagnan's eyes flashed. "What is not due to me yet, you meant to say, M. Colbert; for if I have received what was not due to me at all, I should have committed a theft."

Colbert made no reply to this subtlety. "You then owe fifteen thousand livres to the public chest," said he, carried away by his jealous ardor.

"Then you must give me credit for them," replied D'Artagnan, with his imperceptible irony.

"Not at all, monsieur."

"Well! what will you do, then? You will not take my rouleaux from me, will you?"

"You must return them to my chest."

"I! Oh! Monsieur Colbert, don't reckon upon that."

"The king wants his money, monsieur."

"And I, monsieur, I want the king's money."

"That may be so; but you must return this."

"Not a sou. I have always understood that in matters of comptabilite, as you call it, a good cashier never gives back or takes back."

"Then, monsieur, we shall see what the king will say about it. I will show him this note, which proves that M. Fouquet not only pays what he does not owe, but that he does not even take care of vouchers for the sums that he has paid."

"Ah! now I understand why you have taken that paper, M. Colbert!"

Colbert did not perceive all that there was of a threatening character in his name pronounced in a certain manner. "You shall see hereafter what use I will make of it," said he, holding up the paper in his fingers.

"Oh!" said D'Artagnan, snatching the paper from him with a rapid movement; "I understand perfectly well, M. Colbert; I have no occasion to wait for that." And he crumpled up the paper he had so cleverly seized.

"Monsieur, monsieur!" cried Colbert, "this is violence!"

"Nonsense! You must not be particular about a soldier's manners!" replied D'Artagnan. "I kiss your hands, my dear M. Colbert." And he went out, laughing in the face of the future minister.

"That man, now," muttered he, "was about to grow quite friendly; it is a great pity I was obliged to cut his company so soon."

Chapter LXV.
Philosophy of the Heart and Mind.

FOR a man who had seen so many much more dangerous ones, the position of D'Artagnan with respect to M. Colbert was only comic. D'Artagnan, therefore, did not deny himself the satisfaction of laughing at the expense of monsieur l'intendant, from the Rue des Petits-Champs to the Rue des Lombards. It was a great while since D'Artagnan had laughed so long together. He was still laughing when Planchet appeared, laughing likewise, at the door of his house; for Planchet, since the return of his patron, since the entrance of the English guineas, passed the greater part of his life in doing what D'Artagnan had only done from the Rue Neuve des Petits-Champs to the Rue des Lombards.

"You are home, then, my dear master?" said Planchet.

"No, my friend," replied the musketeer; "I am off, and that quickly. I will sup with you, go to bed, sleep five hours, and at break of day leap into my saddle. Has my horse had an extra feed?"

"Eh! my dear master," replied Planchet, "you know very well that your horse is the jewel of the family; that my lads are caressing it all day, and cramming it with sugar, nuts, and biscuits. You ask me if he has had an extra feed of oats; you should ask if he has not had enough to burst him."

"Very well, Planchet, that is all right. Now, then, I pass to what concerns me—my supper?"

"Ready. A smoking roast joint, white wine, crayfish, and fresh-gathered cherries. All ready, my master."

"You are a capital fellow, Planchet; come on, then, let us sup, and I will go to bed."

During supper D'Artagnan observed that Planchet kept rubbing his forehead, as if to facilitate the issue of some idea closely pent within his brain. He looked with an air of kindness at this worthy companion of former adventures and misadventures, and, clinking glass against glass, "Come, Planchet," said he, "let us see what it is that gives you so much trouble to bring forth. Mordioux! Speak freely, and quickly."

"Well, this is it," replied Planchet: "you appear to me to be going on some expedition or another."

"I don't say that I am not."

"Then you have some new idea?"

"That is possible, too, Planchet."

"Then there will be fresh capital to be ventured? I will lay down fifty thousand livres upon the idea you are about to carry out." And so saying, Planchet rubbed his hands one against the other with a rapidity evincing great delight.

"Planchet," said D'Artagnan, "there is but one misfortune in it."

"And what is that?"

"That the idea is not mine. I can risk nothing upon it."

These words drew a deep sigh from the heart of Planchet. That Avarice is an ardent counselor; she carries away her man, as Satan did Jesus, to the mountain, and when once she has shown to an unfortunate all the kingdoms of the earth, she is able to repose herself, knowing full well that she has left her companion, Envy, to gnaw at his heart. Planchet had tasted of riches easily acquired, and was never afterwards likely to stop in his desires; but, as he had a good heart in spite of his covetousness, as he adored D'Artagnan, he could not refrain from making him a thousand recommendations, each more affectionate than the others. He would not have been sorry, nevertheless, to have caught a little hint of the secret his master concealed so well; tricks, turns, counsels, and traps were all useless, D'Artagnan let nothing confidential escape him. The evening passed thus. After supper the portmanteau occupied D'Artagnan, he took a turn to the stable, patted his horse, and examined his shoes and legs; then, having counted over his money, he went to bed, sleeping as if only twenty, because he had neither inquietude nor remorse; he closed his eyes five minutes after he had blown out his lamp. Many events might, however, have kept him awake. Thought boiled in his brain, conjectures abounded, and D'Artagnan was a great drawer of horoscopes; but, with that imperturbable phlegm which does more than genius for the fortune and happiness of men of action, he put off reflection till the next day, for fear, he said, not to be fresh when he wanted to be so.

The day came. The Rue des Lombards had its share of the caresses of Aurora with the rosy fingers, and D'Artagnan arose like Aurora. He did not awaken anybody, he placed his portmanteau under his arm, descended the stairs without making one of them creak, and without disturbing one of the sonorous snorings in every story from the garret to the cellar, then, having saddled his horse, shut the stable and house doors, he set off, at a foot-pace, on his expedition to Bretagne. He had done quite right not to trouble himself with all the political and diplomatic affairs which solicited his attention; for, in the morning, in freshness and mild twilight, his ideas developed themselves in purity and abundance. In the first place, he passed before the house of Fouquet, and threw in a large gaping box the fortunate order which, the evening before, he had had so much trouble to recover from the hooked fingers of the intendant. Placed in an envelope, and addressed to Fouquet, it had not even been divined by Planchet, who in divination was equal to Calchas or the Pythian Apollo. D'Artagnan thus sent back the order to Fouquet, without compromising himself, and without having thenceforward any reproaches to make himself. When he had effected this proper restitution, "Now," he said to himself, "let us inhale much maternal air, much freedom from cares, much health, let us allow the horse Zephyr, whose flanks puff as if he had to respire an atmosphere, to breathe, and let us be very ingenious in our little calculations. It is time," said D'Artagnan, "to form a plan of the campaign, and, according to the method of M. Turenne, who has a large head full of all sorts of good counsels, before the plan of the campaign it is advisable to draw a striking portrait of the generals to whom we are opposed. In the first place, M. Fouquet presents himself. What is M. Fouquet? M. Fouquet," replied D'Artagnan to himself, "is a handsome man, very much beloved by the women, a generous man very much beloved by the poets; a man of wit, much execrated by pretenders. Well, now I am neither woman, poet, nor pretender: I neither love not hate monsieur le surintendant. I find myself, therefore, in the same position in which M. Turenne found himself when opposed to the Prince de Conde at Jargeau, Gien and the Faubourg Saint-Antoine. He did not execrate monsieur le prince, it is true, but he obeyed the king. Monsieur le prince is an agreeable man, but the king is king. Turenne heaved a deep sigh, called Conde 'My cousin,' and swept away his army. Now what does the king wish? That does not concern me. Now, what does M. Colbert wish? Oh, that's another thing. M. Colbert wishes all that M. Fouquet does not wish. Then what does M. Fouquet wish? Oh, that is serious. M. Fouquet wishes precisely for all the king wishes."

This monologue ended, D'Artagnan began to laugh, whilst making his whip whistle in the air. He was already on the high road, frightening the birds in the hedges, listening to the livres chinking and dancing in his leather pocket, at every step; and, let us confess it, every time that D'Artagnan found himself in such conditions, tenderness was not his dominant vice. "Come," said he, "I cannot think the expedition a very dangerous one; and it will fall out with my voyage as with that piece M. Monk took me to see in London, which was called, I think, 'Much Ado about Nothing.'"

Chapter LXVI.
The Journey.

It was perhaps the fiftieth time since the day on which we open this history, that this man, with a heart of bronze and muscles of steel, had left house and friends, everything, in short, to go in search of fortune and death. The one—that is to say, death—had constantly retreated before him, as if afraid of him; the other—that is to say, fortune—for only a month past had really made an alliance with him. Although he was not a great philosopher, after the fashion of either Epicurus or Socrates, he was a powerful spirit, having knowledge of life, and endowed with thought. No one is as brave, as adventurous, or as skillful as D'Artagnan, without at the same time being inclined to be a dreamer. He had picked up, here and there, some scraps of M. de la Rochefoucault, worthy of being translated into Latin by MM. de Port Royal; and he had made a collection, en passant, in the society of Athos and Aramis, of many morsels of Seneca and Cicero, translated by them, and applied to the uses of common life. That contempt of riches which our Gascon had observed as an article of faith during the thirty-five first years of his life, had for a long time been considered by him as the first article of the code of bravery. "Article first," said he, "A man is brave because he has nothing. A man has nothing because he despises riches." Therefore, with these principles, which, as we have said, had regulated the thirty-five first years of his life, D'Artagnan was no sooner possessed of riches, than he felt it necessary to ask himself if, in spite of his riches, he were still brave. To this, for any other but D'Artagnan, the events of the Place de Greve might have served as a reply. Many consciences would have been satisfied with them, but D'Artagnan was brave enough to ask himself sincerely and conscientiously if he were brave. Therefore to this:—

"But it appears to me that I drew promptly enough, and cut and thrust pretty freely on the Place de Greve, to be satisfied of my bravery," D'Artagnan had himself replied. "Gently, captain, that is not an answer. I was brave that day, because they were burning my house, and there are a hundred, and even a thousand, to speak against one, that if those gentlemen of the riots had not formed that unlucky idea, their plan of attack would have succeeded, or, at least, it would not have been I who would have opposed myself to it. Now, what will be brought against me? I have no house to be burnt in Bretagne; I have no treasure there that can be taken from me.—No; but I have my skin; that precious skin of M. d'Artagnan, which to him is worth more than all the houses and all the treasures of the world. That skin to which I cling above everything, because it is, everything considered, the binding of a body which encloses a heart very warm and ready to fight, and, consequently, to live. Then, I do desire to live: and, in reality, I live much better, more completely, since I have become rich. Who the devil ever said that money spoiled life? Upon my soul, it is no such thing, on the contrary, it seems as if I absorbed a double quantity of air and sun. Mordioux! what will it be then, if I double that fortune; and if, instead of the switch I now hold in my hand, I should ever carry the baton of a marechal? Then I really don't know if there will be, from that moment, enough of air and sun for me. In fact, this is not a dream, who the devil would oppose it, if the king made me a marechal, as his father, King Louis XIII., made a duke and constable of Albert de Luynes? Am I not as brave, and much more intelligent, than that imbecile De Vitry? Ah! that's exactly what will prevent my advancement: I have too much wit. Luckily, if there is any justice in this world, fortune owes me many compensations. She owes me certainly a recompense for all I did for Anne of Austria, and an indemnification for all she has not done for me. Then, at the present, I am very well with a king, and with a king who has the appearance of determining to reign. May God keep him in that illustrious road! For, if he is resolved to reign, he will want me; and if he wants me, he will give me what he has promised me—warmth and light; so that I march, comparatively, now, as I marched formerly,—from nothing to everything. Only the nothing of to-day is the all of former days; there has only this little change taken place in my life. And now let us see! let us take the part of the heart, as I just now was speaking of it. But in truth, I only spoke of it from memory." And the Gascon applied his hand to his breast, as if he were actually seeking the place where his heart was.

"Ah! wretch!" murmured he, smiling with bitterness. "Ah! poor mortal species! You hoped, for an instant, that you had not a heart, and now you find you have one—bad courtier as thou art,—and even one of the most seditious. You have a heart which speaks to you in favor of M. Fouquet. And what is M. Fouquet, when the king is in question?—A conspirator, a real conspirator, who did not even give himself the trouble to conceal his being a conspirator; therefore, what a weapon would you not have against him, if his good grace, and his intelligence had not made a scabbard for that weapon. An armed revolt!—for, in fact, M. Fouquet has been guilty of an armed revolt. Thus, while the king vaguely suspects M. Fouquet of rebellion, I know it—I could prove that M. Fouquet had caused the shedding of the blood of his majesty's subjects. Now, then, let us see. Knowing all that, and holding my tongue, what further would this heart wish in return for a kind action of M. Fouquet's, for an advance of fifteen thousand livres, for a diamond worth a thousand pistoles, for a smile in which there was as much bitterness as kindness?—I save his life."

"Now, then, I hope," continued the musketeer, "that this imbecile of a heart is going to preserve silence, and so be fairly quits with M. Fouquet. Now, then, the king becomes my sun, and as my heart is quits with M. Fouquet, let him beware who places himself between me and my sun! Forward, for his majesty Louis XIV.!—Forward!"

These reflections were the only impediments which were able to retard the progress of D'Artagnan. These reflections once made, he increased the speed of his horse. But, however perfect his horse Zephyr might be, it could not hold out at such a pace forever. The day after his departure from Paris, his mount was left at Chartres, at the house of an old friend D'Artagnan had met with in an hotelier of that city. From that moment the musketeer travelled on post-horses. Thanks to this mode of locomotion, he traversed the space separating Chartres from Chateaubriand. In the last of these two cities, far enough from the coast to prevent any one guessing that D'Artagnan wished to reach the sea—far enough from Paris to prevent all suspicion of his being a messenger from Louis XIV., whom D'Artagnan had called his sun, without suspecting that he who was only at present a rather poor star in the heaven of royalty, would, one day, make that star his emblem; the messenger of Louis XIV., we say, quitted his post and purchased a bidet of the meanest appearance,—one of those animals which an officer of the cavalry would never choose, for fear of being disgraced. Excepting the color, this new acquisition recalled to the mind of D'Artagnan the famous orange-colored horse, with which, or rather upon which, he had made his first appearance in the world. Truth to say, from the moment he crossed this new steed, it was no longer D'Artagnan who was travelling,—it was a good man clothed in an iron-gray justaucorps, brown haut-de-chausses, holding the medium between a priest and a layman; that which brought him nearest to the churchman was, that D'Artagnan had placed on his head a calotte of threadbare velvet, and over the calotte, a large black hat; no more sword, a stick hung by a cord to his wrist, but to which, he promised himself, as an unexpected auxiliary, to join, upon occasion, a good dagger, ten inches long, concealed under his cloak. The bidet purchased at Chateaubriand completed the metamorphosis; it was called, or rather D'Artagnan called if, Furet (ferret).

"If I have changed Zephyr into Furet," said D'Artagnan, "I must make some diminutive or other of my own name. So, instead of D'Artagnan, I will be Agnan, short; that is a concession which I naturally owe to my gray coat, my round hat, and my rusty calotte."

Monsieur d'Artagnan traveled, then, pretty easily upon Furet, who ambled like a true butter-woman's pad, and who, with his amble, managed cheerfully about twelve leagues a day, upon four spindle-shanks, of which the practiced eye of D'Artagnan had appreciated the strength and safety beneath the thick mass of hair which covered them. Jogging along, the traveler took notes, studied the country, which he traversed reserved and silent, ever seeking the most plausible pretext for reaching Belle-Ile-en-Mer, and for seeing everything without arousing suspicion. In this manner, he was enabled to convince himself of the importance the event assumed in proportion as he drew near to it. In this remote country, in this ancient duchy of Bretagne, which was not France at that period, and is not so even now, the people knew nothing of the king of France. They not only did not know him, but were unwilling to know him. One face—a single one—floated visibly for them upon the political current. Their ancient dukes no longer ruled them; government was a void—nothing more. In place of the sovereign duke, the seigneurs of parishes reigned without control; and, above these seigneurs, God, who has never been forgotten in Bretagne. Among these suzerains of chateaux and belfries, the most powerful, the richest, the most popular, was M. Fouquet, seigneur of Belle-Isle. Even in the country, even within sight of that mysterious isle, legends and traditions consecrate its wonders. Every one might not penetrate it: the isle, of an extent of six leagues in length, and six in breadth, was a seignorial property, which the people had for a long time respected, covered as it was with the name of Retz, so redoubtable in the country. Shortly after the erection of this seignory into a marquistate, Belle-Isle passed to M. Fouquet. The celebrity of the isle did not date from yesterday; its name, or rather its qualification, is traced back to the remotest antiquity. The ancients called it Kalonese, from two Greek words, signifying beautiful isle. Thus, at a distance of eighteen hundred years, it had borne, in another idiom, the same name it still bears. There was, then, something in itself in this property of M. Fouquet's, besides its position of six leagues off the coast of France; a position which makes it a sovereign in its maritime solitude, like a majestic ship which disdains roads, and proudly casts anchor in mid-ocean.

D'Artagnan learnt all this without appearing the least in the world astonished. He also learnt the best way to get intelligence was to go to La Roche-Bernard, a tolerably important city at the mouth of the Vilaine. Perhaps there he could embark; if not, crossing the salt marshes, he would repair to Guerande or Le Croisic, to wait for an opportunity to cross over to Belle-Isle. He had discovered, besides, since his departure from Chateaubriand, that nothing would be impossible for Furet under the impulsion of M. Agnan, and nothing to M. Agnan through the initiative of Furet. He prepared, then, to sup off a teal and a torteau, in a hotel of La Roche-Bernard, and ordered to be brought from the cellar, to wash down these two Breton dishes, some cider, which, the moment it touched his lips, he perceived to be more Breton still.

Chapter LXVII.
How D'Artagnan became Acquainted with a Poet.

BEFORE taking his place at table, D'Artagnan acquired, as was his custom, all the information he could; but it is an axiom of curiosity, that every man who wishes to question well and fruitfully ought in the first place to lay himself open to questions. D'Artagnan sought, then, with his usual skill, a promising questioner in the hostelry of La Roche-Bernard. At the moment, there were in the house, on the first story, two travelers either preparing for supper, or at supper itself. D'Artagnan had seen their nags in the stable, and their equipages in the salle. One traveled with a lackey, undoubtedly a person of consideration;—two Perche mares, sleek, sound beasts, were suitable means of locomotion. The other, a little fellow, a traveler of meagre appearance, wearing a dusty surtout, dirty linen, and boots more worn by the pavement than the stirrup, had come from Nantes with a cart drawn by a horse so like Furet in color, that D'Artagnan might have gone a hundred miles without finding a better match. This cart contained divers large packets wrapped in pieces of old stuff.

"That traveler yonder," said D'Artagnan to himself, "is the man for my money. He will do, he suits me; I ought to do for him and suit him; M. Agnan, with the gray doublet and the rusty calotte, is not unworthy of supping with the gentleman of the old boots and still older horse."

This said, D'Artagnan called the host, and desired him to send his teal, tourteau, and cider up to the chamber of the gentleman of modest exterior. He himself climbed, a plate in his hand, the wooden staircase which led to the chamber, and began to knock at the door.

"Come in!" said the unknown. D'Artagnan entered, with a simper on his lips, his plate under his arm, his hat in one hand, his candle in the other.

"Excuse me, monsieur," said he, "I am as you are, a traveler; I know no one in the hotel, and I have the bad habit of losing my spirits when I eat alone; so that my repast appears a bad one to me, and does not nourish me. Your face, which I saw just now, when you came down to have some oysters opened,—your face pleased me much. Besides, I have observed you have a horse just like mine, and that the host, no doubt on account of that resemblance, has placed them side by side in the stable, where they appear to agree amazingly well together. I therefore, monsieur, do not see any reason why the masters should be separated when the horses are united. Accordingly, I am come to request the pleasure of being admitted to your table. My name is Agnan, at your service, monsieur, the unworthy steward of a rich seigneur, who wishes to purchase some salt-mines in this country, and sends me to examine his future acquisitions. In truth, monsieur, I should be well pleased if my countenance were as agreeable to you as yours is to me; for, upon my honor, I am quite at your service."

The stranger, whom D'Artagnan saw for the first time,—for before he had only caught a glimpse of him,—the stranger had black and brilliant eyes, a yellow complexion, a brow a little wrinkled by the weight of fifty years, bonhomie in his features collectively, but some cunning in his look.

"One would say," thought D'Artagnan, "that this merry fellow has never exercised more than the upper part of his head, his eyes, and his brain. He must be a man of science: his mouth, nose, and chin signify absolutely nothing."

"Monsieur," replied the latter, with whose mind and person we have been making so free, "you do me much honor; not that I am ever ennuye, for I have," added he, smiling, "a company which amuses me always: but, never mind that, I am happy to receive you." But when saying this, the man with the worn boots cast an uneasy look at his table, from which the oysters had disappeared, and upon which there was nothing left but a morsel of salt bacon.

"Monsieur," D'Artagnan hastened to say, "the host is bringing me up a pretty piece of roasted poultry and a superb tourteau." D'Artagnan had read in the look of his companion, however rapidly it disappeared, the fear of an attack by a parasite: he divined justly. At this opening, the features of the man of modest exterior relaxed; and, as if he had watched the moment for his entrance, as D'Artagnan spoke, the host appeared, bearing the announced dishes. The tourteau and the teal were added to the morsel of broiled bacon; D'Artagnan and his guest bowed, sat down opposite to each other, and, like two brothers, shared the bacon and the other dishes.

"Monsieur," said D'Artagnan, "you must confess that association is a wonderful thing."

"How so?" replied the stranger, with his mouth full.

"Well, I will tell you," replied D'Artagnan.

The stranger gave a short truce to the movement of his jaws, in order to hear the better.

"In the first place," continued D'Artagnan, "instead of one candle, which each of us had, we have two."

"That is true!" said the stranger, struck with the extreme lucidity of the observation.

"Then I see that you eat my tourteau in preference, whilst I, in preference, eat your bacon."

"That is true again."

"And then, in addition to being better lighted and eating what we prefer, I place the pleasure of your company."

"Truly, monsieur, you are very jovial," said the unknown, cheerfully.

"Yes, monsieur; jovial, as all people are who carry nothing on their minds, or, for that matter, in their heads. Oh! I can see it is quite another sort of thing with you," continued D'Artagnan; "I can read in your eyes all sorts of genius."

"Oh, monsieur!"

"Come, confess one thing."

"What is that?"

"That you are a learned man."

"Ma foi! monsieur."

"Hein?"

"Almost."

"Come, then!"

"I am an author."

"There!" cried D'Artagnan, clapping his hands, "I knew I could not be deceived! It is a miracle!"

"Monsieur—"

"What, shall I have the honor of passing the evening in the society of an author, of a celebrated author, perhaps?"

"Oh!" said the unknown, blushing, "celebrated, monsieur, celebrated is not the word."

"Modest!" cried D'Artagnan, transported, "he is modest!" Then, turning towards the stranger, with a character of blunt bonhomie: "But tell me at least the name of your works, monsieur; for you will please to observe you have not told me your name, and I have been forced to divine your genius."

"My name is Jupenet, monsieur," said the author.

"A fine name! a grand name! upon my honor; and I do not know why—pardon me the mistake, if it be one—but surely I have heard that name somewhere."

"I have made verses," said the poet, modestly.

"Ah! that is it, then; I have heard them read."

"A tragedy."

"I must have seen it played."

The poet blushed again, and said: "I do not think that can be the case, for my verses have never been printed."

"Well, then, it must have been the tragedy which informed me of your name."

"You are again mistaken, for MM. the comedians of the Hotel de Bourgogne, would have nothing to do with it," said the poet, with a smile, the receipt for which certain sorts of pride alone knew the secret. D'Artagnan bit his lips. "Thus, then, you see, monsieur," continued the poet, "you are in error on my account, and that not being at all known to you, you have never heard tell of me."

"Ah! that confounds me. That name, Jupenet, appears to me, nevertheless, a fine name, and quite as worthy of being known as those of MM. Corneille, or Rotrou, or Garnier. I hope, monsieur, you will have the goodness to repeat to me a part of your tragedy presently, by way of dessert, for instance. That will be sugared roast meat,—mordioux! Ah! pardon me, monsieur, that was a little oath which escaped me, because it is a habit with my lord and master. I sometimes allow myself to usurp that little oath, as it seems in pretty good taste. I take this liberty only in his absence, please to observe, for you may understand that in his presence—but, in truth, monsieur, this cider is abominable; do you not think so? And besides, the pot is of such an irregular shape it will not stand on the table."

"Suppose we were to make it level?"

"To be sure; but with what?"

"With this knife."

"And the teal, with what shall we cut that up? Do you not, by chance, mean to touch the teal?"

"Certainly."

"Well, then—"

"Wait."

And the poet rummaged in his pocket, and drew out a piece of brass, oblong, quadrangular, about a line in thickness, and an inch and a half in length. But scarcely had this little piece of brass seen the light, than the poet appeared to have committed an imprudence, and made a movement to put it back again in his pocket. D'Artagnan perceived this, for he was a man that nothing escaped. He stretched forth his hand towards the piece of brass: "Humph! that which you hold in your hand is pretty; will you allow me to look at it?"

"Certainly," said the poet, who appeared to have yielded too soon to a first impulse. "Certainly, you may look at it: but it will be in vain for you to look at it," added he, with a satisfied air; "if I were not to tell you its use, you would never guess it."

D'Artagnan had seized as an avowal the hesitation of the poet, and his eagerness to conceal the piece of brass which a first movement had induced him to take out of his pocket. His attention, therefore, once awakened on this point, he surrounded himself with a circumspection which gave him a superiority on all occasions. Besides, whatever M. Jupenet might say about it, by a simple inspection of the object, he perfectly well knew what it was. It was a character in printing.

"Can you guess, now, what this is?" continued the poet.

"No," said D'Artagnan, "no, ma foi!"

"Well, monsieur," said M. Jupenet, "this little piece of metal is a printing letter."

"Bah!"

"A capital."

"Stop, stop, stop," said D'Artagnan, opening his eyes very innocently.

"Yes, monsieur, a capital; the first letter of my name."

"And this is a letter, is it?"

"Yes, monsieur."

"Well, I will confess one thing to you."

"And what is that?"

"No, I will not, I was going to say something stupid."

"No, no," said Master Jupenet, with a patronizing air.

"Well, then, I cannot comprehend, if that is a letter, how you can make a word."

"A word?"

"Yes, a printed word."

"Oh, that's very easy."

"Let me see."

"Does it interest you?"

"Enormously."

"Well, I will explain the thing to you. Attend."

"I am attending."

"This is it."

"Good."

"Look attentively."

"I am looking." D'Artagnan, in fact, appeared absorbed in observations. Jupenet drew from his pocket seven or eight other pieces of brass smaller than the first.

"Ah, ah," said D'Artagnan.

"What!"

"You have, then, a whole printing-office in your pocket. Peste! that is curious, indeed."

"Is it not?"

"Good God, what a number of things we learn by traveling."

"To your health!" said Jupenet, quite enchanted.

"To yours, mordioux, to yours. But—an instant—not in this cider. It is an abominable drink, unworthy of a man who quenches his thirst at the Hippocrene fountain—is not it so you call your fountain, you poets?"

"Yes, monsieur, our fountain is so called. That comes from two Greek words—hippos, which means a horse, and—"

"Monsieur," interrupted D'Artagnan, "you shall drink of a liquor which comes from one single French word, and is none the worse for that—from the word grape; this cider gives me the heartburn. Allow me to inquire of your host if there is not a good bottle of Beaugency, or of the Ceran growth, at the back of the large bins in his cellar."

The host, being sent for, immediately attended.

"Monsieur," interrupted the poet, "take care, we shall not have time to drink the wine, unless we make great haste, for I must take advantage of the tide to secure the boat."

"What boat?" asked D'Artagnan.

"Why the boat which sets out for Belle-Isle."

"Ah—for Belle-Isle," said the musketeer, "that is good."

"Bah! you will have plenty of time, monsieur," replied the hotelier, uncorking the bottle, "the boat will not leave this hour."

"But who will give me notice?" said the poet.

"Your fellow-traveler," replied the host.

"But I scarcely know him."

"When you hear him departing, it will be time for you to go."

"Is he going to Belle-Isle, likewise, then?"

"Yes."

"The traveler who has a lackey?" asked D'Artagnan. "He is some gentleman, no doubt?"

"I know nothing of him."

"What!—know nothing of him?"

"No, all I know is, that he is drinking the same wine as you."

"Peste!—that is a great honor for us," said D'Artagnan, filling his companion's glass, whilst the host went out.

"So," resumed the poet, returning to his dominant ideas, "you never saw any printing done?"

"Never."

"Well, then, take the letters thus, which compose the word, you see: A B; ma foi! here is an R, two E E, then a G." And he assembled the letters with a swiftness and skill which did not escape the eye of D'Artagnan.

"Abrege," said he, as he ended.

"Good!" said D'Artagnan; "here are plenty of letters got together; but how are they kept so?" And he poured out a second glass for the poet. M. Jupenet smiled like a man who has an answer for everything; then he pulled out—still from his pocket—a little metal ruler, composed of two parts, like a carpenter's rule, against which he put together, and in a line, the characters, holding them under his left thumb.

"And what do you call that little metal ruler?" said D'Artagnan, "for, I suppose, all these things have names."

"This is called a composing-stick," said Jupenet; "it is by the aid of this stick that the lines are formed."

"Come, then, I was not mistaken in what I said; you have a press in your pocket," said D'Artagnan, laughing with an air of simplicity so stupid, that the poet was completely his dupe.

"No," replied he; "but I am too lazy to write, and when I have a verse in my head, I print it immediately. That is a labor spared."

"Mordioux!" thought D'Artagnan to himself, "this must be cleared up." And under a pretext, which did not embarrass the musketeer, who was fertile in expedients, he left the table, went downstairs, ran to the shed under which stood the poet's little cart, and poked the point of his poniard into the stuff which enveloped one of the packages, which he found full of types, like those which the poet had in his pocket.

"Humph!" said D'Artagnan, "I do not yet know whether M. Fouquet wishes to fortify Belle-Isle; but, at all events, here are some spiritual munitions for the castle." Then, enchanted with his rich discovery, he ran upstairs again, and resumed his place at the table.

D'Artagnan had learnt what he wished to know. He, however, remained, none the less, face to face with his partner, to the moment when they heard from the next room symptoms of a person's being about to go out. The printer was immediately on foot; he had given orders for his horse to be got ready. His carriage was waiting at the door. The second traveler got into his saddle, in the courtyard, with his lackey. D'Artagnan followed Jupenet to the door; he embarked his cart and horse on board the boat. As to the opulent traveler, he did the same with his two horses and servant. But all the wit D'Artagnan employed in endeavoring to find out his name was lost—he could learn nothing. Only he took such notice of his countenance, that it was impressed upon his mind forever. D'Artagnan had a great inclination to embark with the two travelers, but an interest more powerful than curiosity—that of success—repelled him from the shore, and brought him back again to the hostelry. He entered with a sigh, and went to bed directly in order to be ready early in the morning with fresh ideas and the sage counsel of sufficing sleep.

Chapter LXVIII.
D'Artagnan continues his Investigations.

AT daybreak D'Artagnan saddled Furet, who had fared sumptuously all night, devouring the remainder of the oats and hay left by his companions. The musketeer sifted all he possibly could out of the host, who he found cunning, mistrustful, and devoted, body and soul, to M. Fouquet. In order not to awaken the suspicions of this man, he carried on his fable of being a probable purchaser of some salt-mines. To have embarked for Belle-Isle at Roche-Bernard, would have been to expose himself still further to comments which had, perhaps, been already made, and would be carried to the castle. Moreover, it was singular that this traveler and his lackey should have remained a mystery to D'Artagnan, in spite of all the questions addressed by him to the host, who appeared to know him perfectly well. The musketeer then made some inquiries concerning the salt-mines, and took the road to the marshes, leaving the sea on his right, and penetrating into that vast and desolate plain which resembles a sea of mud, of which, here and there, a few crests of salt silver the undulations. Furet walked admirably, with his little nervous legs, along the foot-wide causeways which separate the salt-mines. D'Artagnan, aware of the consequences of a fall, which would result in a cold bath, allowed him to go as he liked, contenting himself with looking at, on the horizon, three rocks, that rose up like lance-blades from the bosom of the plain, destitute of verdure. Piriac, the bourgs of Batz and Le Croisic, exactly resembling each other, attracted and suspended his attention. If the traveler turned round, the better to make his observations, he saw on the other side an horizon of three other steeples, Guerande, Le Pouliguen, and Saint-Joachim, which, in their circumference, represented a set of skittles, of which he and Furet were but the wandering ball. Piriac was the first little port on his right. He went thither, with the names of the principal salters on his lips. At the moment he reached the little port of Piriac, five large barges, laden with stone, were leaving it. It appeared strange to D'Artagnan, that stones should be leaving a country where none are found. He had recourse to all the amenity of M. Agnan to learn from the people of the port the cause of this singular arrangement. An old fisherman replied to M. Agnan, that the stones very certainly did not come from Piriac or the marshes.

"Where do they come from, then?" asked the musketeer.

"Monsieur, they come from Nantes and Paimboeuf."

"Where are they going, then?"

"Monsieur, to Belle-Isle."

"Ah! ah!" said D'Artagnan, in the same tone he had assumed to tell the printer that his character interested him; "are they building at Belle-Isle, then?"

"Why, yes, monsieur, M. Fouquet has the walls of the castle repaired every year."

"It is in ruins, then?"

"It is old."

"Thank you."

"The fact is," said D'Artagnan to himself, "nothing is more natural; every proprietor has a right to repair his own property. It would be like telling me I was fortifying the Image-de-Notre-Dame, when I was simply obliged to make repairs. In good truth, I believe false reports have been made to his majesty, and he is very likely to be in the wrong."

"You must confess," continued he then, aloud, and addressing the fisherman—for his part of a suspicious man was imposed upon him by the object even of his mission—"you must confess, my dear monsieur, that these stones travel in a very curious fashion."

"How so?" said the fisherman.

"They come from Nantes or Paimboeuf by the Loire, do they not?"

"With the tide."

"That is convenient,—I don't say it is not; but why do they not go straight from Saint-Nazaire to Belle-Isle?"

"Eh! because the chalands (barges) are fresh-water boats, and take the sea badly," replied the fisherman.

"That is not sufficient reason."

"Pardon me, monsieur, one may see that you have never been a sailor," added the fisherman, not without a sort of disdain.

"Explain to me, if you please, my good man. It appears to me that to come from Paimboeuf to Piriac, and go from Piriac to Belle-Isle, is as if we went from Roche-Bernard to Nantes, and from Nantes to Piriac."

"By water that would be the nearest way," replied the fisherman imperturbably.

"But there is an elbow?"

The fisherman shook his head.

"The shortest road from one place to another is a straight line," continued D'Artagnan.

"You forget the tide, monsieur."

"Well! take the tide."

"And the wind."

"Well, and the wind."

"Without doubt; the current of the Loire carries barks almost as far as Croisic. If they want to lie by a little, or to refresh the crew, they come to Piriac along the coast; from Piriac they find another inverse current, which carries them to the Isle-Dumal, two leagues and a half."

"Granted."

"There the current of the Vilaine throws them upon another isle, the Isle of Hoedic."

"I agree with that."

"Well, monsieur, from that isle to Belle-Isle the way is quite straight. The sea, broken both above and below, passes like a canal—like a mirror between the two isles; the chalands glide along upon it like ducks upon the Loire; that's how it is."

"It does not signify," said the obstinate M. Agnan; "it is a long way round."

"Ah! yes; but M. Fouquet will have it so," replied, as conclusive, the fisherman, taking off his woolen cap at the enunciation of that respected name.

A look from D'Artagnan, a look as keen and piercing as a sword-blade, found nothing in the heart of the old man but a simple confidence—on his features, nothing but satisfaction and indifference. He said, "M. Fouquet will have it so," as he would have said, "God has willed it."

D'Artagnan had already advanced too far in this direction; besides, the chalands being gone, there remained nothing at Piriac but a single bark—that of the old man, and it did not look fit for sea without great preparation. D'Artagnan therefore patted Furet, who, as a new proof of his charming character, resumed his march with his feet in the salt-mines, and his nose to the dry wind, which bends the furze and the broom of this country. They reached Le Croisic about five o'clock.

If D'Artagnan had been a poet, it was a beautiful spectacle: the immense strand of a league or more, the sea covers at high tide, and which, at the reflux, appears gray and desolate, strewed with polypi and seaweed, with pebbles sparse and white, like bones in some vast old cemetery. But the soldier, the politician, and the ambitious man, had no longer the sweet consolation of looking towards heaven to read there a hope or a warning. A red sky signifies nothing to such people but wind and disturbance. White and fleecy clouds upon the azure only say that the sea will be smooth and peaceful. D'Artagnan found the sky blue, the breeze embalmed with saline perfumes, and he said: "I will embark with the first tide, if it be but in a nutshell."

At Le Croisic as at Piriac, he had remarked enormous heaps of stone lying along the shore. These gigantic walls, diminished every tide by the barges for Belle-Isle, were, in the eyes of the musketeer, the consequence and the proof of what he had well divined at Piriac. Was it a wall that M. Fouquet was constructing? Was it a fortification that he was erecting? To ascertain that, he must make fuller observations. D'Artagnan put Furet into a stable; supped, went to bed, and on the morrow took a walk upon the port or rather upon the shingle. Le Croisic has a port of fifty feet; it has a look-out which resembles an enormous brioche (a kind of cake) elevated on a dish. The flat strand is the dish. Hundreds of barrowsful of earth amalgamated with pebbles, and rounded into cones, with sinuous passages between, are look-outs and brioches at the same time. It is so now, and it was so two hundred years ago, only the brioche was not so large, and probably there were to be seen to trellises of lath around the brioche, which constitute an ornament, planted like gardes-fous along the passages that wind towards the little terrace. Upon the shingle lounged three or four fishermen talking about sardines and shrimps. D'Artagnan, with his eyes animated by a rough gayety, and a smile upon his lips, approached these fishermen.

"Any fishing going on to-day?" said he.

"Yes, monsieur," replied one of them, "we are only waiting for the tide."

"Where do you fish, my friends?"

"Upon the coasts, monsieur."

"Which are the best coasts?"

"Ah, that is all according. The tour of the isles, for example?"

"Yes, but they are a long way off, those isles, are they not?"

"Not very; four leagues."

"Four leagues! That is a voyage."

The fishermen laughed in M. Agnan's face.

"Hear me, then," said the latter with an air of simple stupidity; "four leagues off you lose sight of land, do you not?"

"Why, not always."

"Ah, it is a long way—too long, or else I would have asked you to take me aboard, and to show me what I have never seen."

"What is that?"

"A live sea-fish."

"Monsieur comes from the province?" said a fisherman.

"Yes, I come from Paris."

The Breton shrugged his shoulders; then:

"Have you ever seen M. Fouquet in Paris?" asked he.

"Often," replied D'Artagnan.

"Often!" repeated the fishermen, closing their circle round the Parisian. "Do you know him?"

"A little; he is the intimate friend of my master."

"Ah!" said the fishermen, in astonishment.

"And," said D'Artagnan, "I have seen all his chateaux of Saint Mande, of Vaux, and his hotel in Paris."

"Is that a fine place?"

"Superb."

"It is not so fine a place as Belle-Isle," said the fisherman.

"Bah!" cried M. d'Artagnan, breaking into a laugh so loud that he angered all his auditors.

"It is very plain that you have never seen Belle-Isle," said the most curious of the fishermen. "Do you know that there are six leagues of it, and that there are such trees on it as cannot be equaled even at Nates-sur-le-Fosse?"

"Trees in the sea!" cried D'Artagnan; "well, I should like to see them."

"That can be easily done; we are fishing at the Isle de Hoedic—come with us. From that place you will see, as a Paradise, the black trees of Belle-Isle against the sky; you will see the white line of the castle, which cuts the horizon of the sea like a blade."

"Oh," said D'Artagnan, "that must be very beautiful. But do you know there are a hundred belfries at M. Fouquet's chateau of Vaux?"

The Breton raised his head in profound admiration, but he was not convinced. "A hundred belfries! Ah, that may be; but Belle-Isle is finer than that. Should you like to see Belle-Isle?"

"Is that possible?" asked D'Artagnan.

"Yes, with permission of the governor."

"But I do not know the governor."

"As you know M. Fouquet, you can tell your name."

"Oh, my friends, I am not a gentleman."

"Everybody enters Belle-Isle," continued the fisherman in his strong, pure language, "provided he means no harm to Belle-Isle or its master."

A slight shudder crept over the body of the musketeer. "That is true," thought he. Then recovering himself, "If I were sure," said he, "not to be sea-sick."

"What, upon her?" said the fisherman, pointing with pride to his pretty round-bottomed bark.

"Well, you almost persuade me," cried M. Agnan; "I will go and see Belle-Isle, but they will not admit me."

"We shall enter, safe enough."

"You! What for?"

"Why, dame! to sell fish to the corsairs."

"Ha! Corsairs—what do you mean?"

"Well, I mean that M. Fouquet is having two corsairs built to chase the Dutch and the English, and we sell our fish to the crews of those little vessels."

"Come, come!" said D'Artagnan to himself—"better and better. A printing-press, bastions, and corsairs! Well, M. Fouquet is not an enemy to be despised, as I presumed to fancy. He is worth the trouble of travelling to see him nearer."

"We set out at half-past five," said the fisherman gravely.

"I am quite ready, and I will not leave you now." So D'Artagnan saw the fishermen haul their barks to meet the tide with a windlass. The sea rose; M. Agnan allowed himself to be hoisted on board, not without sporting a little fear and awkwardness, to the amusement of the young beach-urchins who watched him with their large intelligent eyes. He laid himself down upon a folded sail, not interfering with anything whilst the bark prepared for sea; and, with its large square sail, it was fairly out within two hours. The fishermen, who prosecuted their occupation as they proceeded, did not perceive that their passenger had not become pale, neither groaned nor suffered; that in spite of that horrible tossing and rolling of the bark, to which no hand imparted direction, the novice passenger had preserved his presence of mind and his appetite. They fished, and their fishing was sufficiently fortunate. To lines bated with prawn, soles came, with numerous gambols, to bite. Two nets had already been broken by the immense weight of congers and haddocks; three sea-eels plowed the hold with their slimy folds and their dying contortions. D'Artagnan brought them good luck; they told him so. The soldier found the occupation so pleasant, that he put his hand to the work—that is to say, to the lines—and uttered roars of joy, and mordioux enough to have astonished his musketeers themselves, every time that a shock given to his line by the captured fish required the play of the muscles of his arm, and the employment of his best dexterity. The party of pleasure had made him forget his diplomatic mission. He was struggling with a very large conger, and holding fast with one hand to the side of the vessel, in order to seize with the other the gaping jowl of his antagonist, when the master said to him, "Take care they don't see you from Belle-Isle!"

These words produced the same effect upon D'Artagnan as the hissing of the first bullet on a day of battle; he let go of both line and conger, which, dragging each other, returned again to the water. D'Artagnan perceived, within half a league at most, the blue and marked profile of the rocks of Belle-Isle, dominated by the majestic whiteness of the castle. In the distance, the land with its forests and verdant plains; cattle on the grass. This was what first attracted the attention of the musketeer. The sun darted its rays of gold upon the sea, raising a shining mist round this enchanted isle. Little could be seen of it, owing to this dazzling light, but the salient points; every shadow was strongly marked, and cut with bands of darkness the luminous fields and walls. "Eh! eh!" said D'Artagnan, at the aspect of those masses of black rocks, "these are fortifications which do not stand in need of any engineer to render a landing difficult. How the devil can a landing be effected on that isle which God has defended so completely?"

"This way," replied the patron of the bark, changing the sail, and impressing upon the rudder a twist which turned the boat in the direction of a pretty little port, quite coquettish, round, and newly battlemented.

"What the devil do I see yonder?" said D'Artagnan.

"You see Locmaria," replied the fisherman.

"Well, but there?"

"That is Bangor."

"And further on?"

"Sauzon, and then Le Palais."

"Mordioux! It is a world. Ah! there are some soldiers."

"There are seventeen hundred men in Belle-Isle, monsieur," replied the fisherman, proudly. "Do you know that the least garrison is of twenty companies of infantry?"

"Mordioux!" cried D'Artagnan, stamping with his foot. "His majesty was right enough."

They landed.

Chapter LXIX.
D'Artagnan was to meet an Old Acquaintance.

THERE is always something in a landing, if it be only from the smallest seaboat—a trouble and a confusion which do not leave the mind the liberty of which it stands in need in order to study at the first glance the new locality presented to it. The moveable bridges, the agitated sailors, the noise of the water on the pebbles, the cries and importunities of those who wait upon the shores, are multiplied details of that sensation which is summed up in one single result—hesitation. It was not, then, till after standing several minutes on the shore that D'Artagnan saw upon the port, but more particularly in the interior of the isle, an immense number of workmen in motion. At his feet D'Artagnan recognized the five chalands laden with rough stone he had seen leave the port of Piriac. The smaller stones were transported to the shore by means of a chain formed by twenty-five or thirty peasants. The large stones were loaded on trollies which conveyed them in the same direction as the others, that is to say, towards the works, of which D'Artagnan could as yet appreciate neither the strength nor the extent. Everywhere was to be seen an activity equal to that which Telemachus observed on his landing at Salentum. D'Artagnan felt a strong inclination to penetrate into the interior; but he could not, under the penalty of exciting mistrust, exhibit too much curiosity. He advanced then little by little, scarcely going beyond the line formed by the fishermen on the beach, observing everything, saying nothing, and meeting all suspicion that might have been excited with a half-silly question or a polite bow. And yet, whilst his companions carried on their trade, giving or selling their fish to the workmen or the inhabitants of the city, D'Artagnan had gained by degrees, and, reassured by the little attention paid to him, he began to cast an intelligent and confident look upon the men and things that appeared before his eyes. And his very first glance fell on certain movements of earth about which the eye of a soldier could not be mistaken. At the two extremities of the port, in order that their fires should converge upon the great axis of the ellipse formed by the basin, in the first place, two batteries had been raised, evidently destined to receive flank pieces, for D'Artagnan saw the workmen finishing the platform and making ready the demi-circumference in wood upon which the wheels of the pieces might turn to embrace every direction over the epaulement. By the side of each of these batteries other workmen were strengthening gabions filled with earth, the lining of another battery. The latter had embrasures, and the overseer of the works called successively men who, with cords, tied the saucissons and cut the lozenges and right angles of turfs destined to retain the matting of the embrasures. By the activity displayed in these works, already so far advanced, they might be considered as finished: they were not yet furnished with their cannons, but the platforms had their gites and their madriers all prepared; the earth, beaten carefully, was consolidated; and supposing the artillery to be on the island, in less than two or three days the port might be completely armed. That which astonished D'Artagnan, when he turned his eyes from the coast batteries to the fortifications of the city, was to see that Belle-Isle was defended by an entirely new system, of which he had often heard the Comte de la Fere speak as a wonderful advance, but of which he had as yet never seen the application. These fortifications belonged neither to the Dutch method of Marollais, nor to the French method of the Chevalier Antoine de Ville, but to the system of Manesson Mallet, a skillful engineer, who about six or eight years previously had quitted the service of Portugal to enter that of France. The works had this peculiarity, that instead of rising above the earth, as did the ancient ramparts destined to defend a city from escalades, they, on the contrary, sank into it; and what created the height of the walls was the depth of the ditches. It did not take long to make D'Artagnan perceive the superiority of such a system, which gives no advantage to cannon. Besides, as the fosses were lower than, or on a level with, the sea, these fosses could be instantly inundated by means of subterranean sluices. Otherwise, the works were almost complete, and a group of workmen, receiving orders from a man who appeared to be conductor of the works, were occupied in placing the last stones. A bridge of planks thrown over the fosses for the greater convenience of the maneuvers connected with the barrows, joined the interior to the exterior. With an air of simple curiosity D'Artagnan asked if he might be permitted to cross the bridge, and he was told that no order prevented it. Consequently he crossed the bridge, and advanced towards the group.

This group was superintended by the man whom D'Artagnan had already remarked, and who appeared to be the engineer-in-chief. A plan was lying open before him upon a large stone forming a table, and at some paces from him a crane was in action. This engineer, who by his evident importance first attracted the attention of D'Artagnan, wore a justaucorps, which, from its sumptuousness, was scarcely in harmony with the work he was employed in, that rather necessitated the costume of a master-mason than of a noble. He was a man of immense stature and great square shoulders, and wore a hat covered with feathers. He gesticulated in the most majestic manner, and appeared, for D'Artagnan only saw his back, to be scolding the workmen for their idleness and want of strength.

D'Artagnan continued to draw nearer. At that moment the man with the feathers ceased to gesticulate, and, with his hands placed upon his knees, was following, half-bent, the effort of six workmen to raise a block of hewn stone to the top of a piece of timber destined to support that stone, so that the cord of the crane might be passed under it. The six men, all on one side of the stone, united their efforts to raise it to eight or ten inches from the ground, sweating and blowing, whilst a seventh got ready for when there should be daylight enough beneath it to slide in the roller that was to support it. But the stone had already twice escaped from their hands before gaining a sufficient height for the roller to be introduced. There can be no doubt that every time the stone escaped them, they bounded quickly backwards, to keep their feet from being crushed by the refalling stone. Every time, the stone, abandoned by them, sunk deeper into the damp earth, which rendered the operation more and more difficult. A third effort was followed by no better success, but with progressive discouragement. And yet, when the six men were bent towards the stone, the man with the feathers had himself, with a powerful voice, given the word of command, "Ferme!" which regulates maneuvers of strength. Then he drew himself up.

"Oh! oh!" said he, "what is this all about? Have I to do with men of straw? Corne de boeuf! stand on one side, and you shall see how this is to be done."

"Peste!" said D'Artagnan, "will he pretend to raise that rock? that would be a sight worth looking at."

The workmen, as commanded by the engineer, drew back with their ears down, and shaking their heads, with the exception of the one who held the plank, who prepared to perform the office. The man with the feathers went up to the stone, stooped, slipped his hands under the face lying upon the ground, stiffened his Herculean muscles, and without a strain, with a slow motion, like that of a machine, lifted the end of the rock a foot from the ground. The workman who held the plank profited by the space thus given him, and slipped the roller under the stone.

"That's the way," said the giant, not letting the rock fall again, but placing it upon its support.

"Mordioux!" cried D'Artagnan, "I know but one man capable of such a feat of strength."

"Hein!" cried the colossus, turning round.

"Porthos!" murmured D'Artagnan, seized with stupor, "Porthos at Belle-Isle!"

On his part, the man with the feathers fixed his eyes upon the disguised lieutenant, and, in spite of his metamorphosis, recognized him. "D'Artagnan!" cried he; and the color mounted to his face. "Hush!" said he to D'Artagnan.

"Hush!" in his turn, said the musketeer. In fact, if Porthos had just been discovered by D'Artagnan, D'Artagnan had just been discovered by Porthos. The interest of the particular secret of each struck them both at the same instant. Nevertheless the first movement of the two men was to throw their arms around each other. What they wished to conceal from the bystanders, was not their friendship, but their names. But, after the embrace, came reflection.

"What the devil brings Porthos to Belle-Isle, lifting stones?" said D'Artagnan; only D'Artagnan uttered that question in a low voice. Less strong in diplomacy than his friend, Porthos thought aloud.

"How the devil did you come to Belle-Isle?" asked he of D'Artagnan; "and what do you want to do here?" It was necessary to reply without hesitation. To hesitate in answer to Porthos would have been a check, for which the self-love of D'Artagnan would never have consoled itself.

"Pardieu! my friend, I am at Belle-Isle because you are here."

"Ah, bah!" said Porthos, visibly stupefied with the argument and seeking to account for it to himself, with the felicity of deduction we know to be particular to him.

"Without doubt," continued D'Artagnan, unwilling to give his friend time to recollect himself, "I have been to see you at Pierrefonds."

"Indeed!"

"Yes."

"And you did not find me there?"

"No, but I found Mouston."

"Is he well?"

"Peste!"

"Well, but Mouston did not tell you I was here."

"Why should he not? Have I, perchance, deserved to lose his confidence?"

"No; but he did not know it."

"Well; that is a reason at least that does not offend my self-love."

"Then how did you manage to find me?"

"My dear friend, a great noble like you always leaves traced behind him on his passage; and I should think but poorly of myself, if I were not sharp enough to follow the traces of my friends." This explanation, flattering as it was, did not entirely satisfy Porthos.

"But I left no traces behind me, for I came here disguised," said Porthos.

"Ah! You came disguised did you?" said D'Artagnan.

"Yes."

"And how?"

"As a miller."

"And do you think a great noble, like you, Porthos, can affect common manners so as to deceive people?"

"Well, I swear to you my friend, that I played my part so well that everybody was deceived."

"Indeed! so well, that I have not discovered and joined you?"

"Yes; but how did you discover and join me?"

"Stop a bit. I was going to tell you how. Do you imagine Mouston—"

"Ah! it was that fellow, Mouston," said Porthos, gathering up those two triumphant arches which served him for eyebrows.

"But stop, I tell you—it was no fault of Mouston's because he was ignorant of where you were."

"I know he was; and that is why I am in such haste to understand—"

"Oh! how impatient you are, Porthos."

"When I do not comprehend, I am terrible."

"Well, you will understand. Aramis wrote to you at Pierrefonds, did he not?"

"Yes."

"And he told you to come before the equinox."

"That is true."

"Well! that is it," said D'Artagnan, hoping that this reason would mystify Porthos. Porthos appeared to give himself up to a violent mental labor.

"Yes, yes," said he, "I understand. As Aramis told me to come before the equinox, you have understood that that was to join him. You then inquired where Aramis was, saying to yourself, 'Where Aramis is, there Porthos will be.' You have learnt that Aramis was in Bretagne, and you said to yourself, 'Porthos is in Bretagne.'"

"Exactly. In good truth, Porthos, I cannot tell why you have not turned conjuror. So you understand that, arriving at Roche-Bernard, I heard of the splendid fortifications going on at Belle-Isle. The account raised my curiosity, I embarked in a fishing boat, without dreaming that you were here: I came, and I saw a monstrous fine fellow lifting a stone Ajax could not have stirred. I cried out, 'Nobody but the Baron de Bracieux could have performed such a feat of strength.' You heard me, you turned round, you recognized me, we embraced; and, ma foi! if you like, my dear friend, we will embrace again."

"Ah! now all is explained," said Porthos; and he embraced D'Artagnan with so much friendship as to deprive the musketeer of his breath for five minutes.

"Why, you are stronger than ever," said D'Artagnan, "and still, happily, in your arms." Porthos saluted D'Artagnan with a gracious smile. During the five minutes D'Artagnan was recovering his breath, he reflected that he had a very difficult part to play. It was necessary that he always should question and never reply. By the time his respiration returned, he had fixed his plans for the campaign.

Chapter LXX.
Wherein the Ideas of D'Artagnan begin to clear up a little.

D'ARTAGNAN immediately took the offensive. "Now that I have told you all, dear friend, or rather you have guessed all, tell me what you are doing here, covered with dust and mud?"

Porthos wiped his brow, and looked around him with pride. "Why, it appears," said he, "that you may see what I am doing here."

"No doubt, no doubt, you lift great stones."

"Oh! to show these idle fellows what a man is," said Porthos, with contempt. "But you understand—"

"Yes, that is not your place to lift stones, although there are many whose place it is, who cannot lift them as you do. It was that which made me ask you, just now. What are you doing here, baron?"

"I am studying topography, chevalier."

"You are studying topography?"

"Yes; but you—what are you doing in that common dress?"

D'Artagnan perceived he had committed a fault in giving expression to his astonishment. Porthos had taken advantage of it, to retort with a question. "Why," said he, "you know I am a bourgeois, in fact; my dress, then, has nothing astonishing in it, since it conforms with my condition."

"Nonsense! you are a musketeer."

"You are wrong, my friend; I have given in my resignation."

"Bah!"

"Oh, mon Dieu! yes."

"And you have abandoned the service?"

"I have quitted it."

"You have abandoned the king?"

"Quite."

Porthos raised his arms towards heaven, like a man who has heard extraordinary news. "Well, that does confound me," said he.

"It is nevertheless true."

"And what led you to form such a resolution."

"The king displeased me. Mazarin had disgusted me for a long time, as you know; so I threw my cassock to the nettles."

"But Mazarin is dead."

"I know that well enough, parbleu! Only, at the period of his death, my resignation had been given in and accepted two months. Then, feeling myself free, I set off for Pierrefonds, to see my friend Porthos. I had heard talk of the happy division you had made of your time, and I wished, for a fortnight, to divide mine after your fashion."

"My friend, you know that it is not for a fortnight my house is open to you; it is for a year—for ten years—for life."

"Thank you, Porthos."

"Ah! but perhaps you want money—do you?" said Porthos, making something like fifty louis chink in his pocket. "In that case, you know—"

"No, thank you; I am not in want of anything. I placed my savings with Planchet, who pays me the interest of them."

"Your savings?"

"Yes, to be sure," said D'Artagnan: "why should I not put by my savings, as well as another, Porthos?"

"Oh, there is no reason why; on the contrary, I always suspected you—that is to say, Aramis always suspected you to have savings. For my own part, d'ye see, I take no concern about the management of my household; but I presume the savings of a musketeer must be small."

"No doubt, relative to yourself, Porthos, who are a millionaire; but you shall judge. I had laid by twenty-five thousand livres."

"That's pretty well," said Porthos, with an affable air.

"And," continued D'Artagnan, "on the twenty-eighth of last month I added to it two hundred thousand livres more."

Porthos opened his large eyes, which eloquently demanded of the musketeer, "Where the devil did you steal such a sum as that, my dear friend?" "Two hundred thousand livres!" cried he, at length.

"Yes; which, with the twenty-five I had, and twenty thousand I have about me, complete the sum of two hundred and forty-five thousand livres."

"But tell me, whence comes this fortune?"

"I will tell you all about it presently, dear friend; but as you have, in the first place, many things to tell me yourself, let us have my recital in its proper order."

"Bravo!" said Porthos; "then we are both rich. But what can I have to relate to you?"

"You have to relate to me how Aramis came to be named—"

"Ah! bishop of Vannes."

"That's it," said D'Artagnan, "bishop of Vannes. Dear Aramis! do you know how he succeeded so well?"

"Yes, yes; without reckoning that he does not mean to stop there."

"What! do you mean he will not be contented with violet stockings, and that he wants a red hat?"

"Hush! that is promised him."

"Bah! by the king?"

"By somebody more powerful than the king."

"Ah! the devil! Porthos: what incredible things you tell me, my friend!"

"Why incredible? Is there not always somebody in France more powerful than the king?"

"Oh, yes; in the time of King Louis XIII. it was Cardinal Richelieu; in the time of the regency it was Cardinal Mazarin. In the time of Louis XIV. it is M—"

"Go on."

"It is M. Fouquet."

"Jove! you have hit it the first time."

"So, then, I suppose it is M. Fouquet who has promised Aramis the red hat."

Porthos assumed an air of reserve. "Dear friend," said he, "God preserve me from meddling with the affairs of others, above all from revealing secrets it may be to their interest to keep. When you see Aramis, he will tell you all he thinks he ought to tell you."

"You are right, Porthos; and you are quite a padlock for safety. But, to revert to yourself?"

"Yes," said Porthos.

"You said just now you came hither to study topography?"

"I did so."

"Tudieu! my friend, what fine things you will do!"

"How do you mean?"

"Why, these fortifications are admirable."

"Is that your opinion?"

"Decidedly it is. In truth, to anything but a regular siege, Belle-Isle is absolutely impregnable."

Porthos rubbed his hands. "That is my opinion," said he.

"But who the devil has fortified this paltry little place in this manner?"

Porthos drew himself up proudly: "Did I not tell you who?"

"No."

"Do you not suspect?"

"No; all I can say is that he is a man who has studied all the systems, and who appears to me to have stopped at the best."

"Hush!" said Porthos; "consider my modesty, my dear D'Artagnan."

"In truth," replied the musketeer, "can it be you—who—oh!"

"Pray—my dear friend—"

"You who have imagined, traced, and combined between these bastions, these redans, these curtains, these half-moons; and are preparing that covered way?"

"I beg you—"

"You who have built that lunette with its retiring angles and its salient edges?"

"My friend—"

"You who have given that inclination to the openings of your embrasures, by means of which you so effectively protect the men who serve the guns?"

"Eh! mon Dieu! yes."

"Oh! Porthos, Porthos! I must bow down before you—I must admire you! But you have always concealed from us this superb, this incomparable genius. I hope, my dear friend, you will show me all this in detail."

"Nothing more easy. Here lies my original sketch, my plan."

"Show it me." Porthos led D'Artagnan towards the stone that served him for a table, and upon which the plan was spread. At the foot of the plan was written, in the formidable writing of Porthos, writing of which we have already had occasion to speak:—

"Instead of making use of the square or rectangle, as has been done to this time, you will suppose your place inclosed in a regular hexagon, this polygon having the advantage of offering more angles than the quadrilateral one. Every side of your hexagon, of which you will determine the length in proportion to the dimensions taken upon the place, will be divided into two parts, and upon the middle point you will elevate a perpendicular towards the center of the polygon, which will equal in length the sixth part of the side. By the extremities of each side of the polygon, you will trace two diagonals, which will cut the perpendicular. These will form the precise lines of your defense."

"The devil!" said D'Artagnan, stopping at this point of the demonstration; "why, this is a complete system, Porthos."

"Entirely," said Porthos. "Continue."

"No; I have read enough of it; but, since it is you, my dear Porthos, who direct the works, what need have you of setting down your system so formally in writing?"

"Oh! my dear friend, death!"

"How! death?"

"Why, we are all mortal, are we not?"

"That is true," said D'Artagnan; "you have a reply for everything, my friend." And he replaced the plan upon the stone.

But however short the time he had the plan in his hands, D'Artagnan had been able to distinguish, under the enormous writing of Porthos, a much more delicate hand, which reminded him of certain letters to Marie Michon, with which he had been acquainted in his youth. Only the India-rubber had passed and repassed so often over this writing that it might have escaped a less practiced eye than that of our musketeer.

"Bravo! my friend, bravo!" said D'Artagnan.

"And now you know all that you want to know, do you not?" said Porthos, wheeling about.

"Mordioux! yes, only do me one last favor, dear friend!"

"Speak, I am master here."

"Do me the pleasure to tell me the name of that gentleman who is walking yonder."

"Where, there?"

"Behind the soldiers."

"Followed by a lackey?"

"Exactly."

"In company with a mean sort of fellow, dressed in black?"

"Yes, I mean him."

"That is M. Getard."

"And who is Getard, my friend?"

"He is the architect of the house."

"Of what house?"

"Of M. Fouquet's house."

"Ah! ah!" cried D'Artagnan, "you are of the household of M. Fouquet, then, Porthos?"

"I! what do you mean by that?" said the topographer, blushing to the top of his ears.

"Why, you say the house, when speaking of Belle-Isle, as if you were speaking of the chateau of Pierrefonds."

Porthos bit his lip. "Belle-Isle, my friend," said he, "belongs to M. Fouquet, does it not?"

"Yes, I believe so."

"As Pierrefonds belongs to me?"

"I told you I believed so; there are no two words to that."

"Did you ever see a man there who is accustomed to walk about with a ruler in his hand?"

"No; but I might have seen him there, if he really walked there."

"Well, that gentleman is M. Boulingrin."

"Who is M. Boulingrin?"

"Now we are coming to it. If, when this gentleman is walking with a ruler in his hand, any one should ask me,—'who is M. Boulingrin?' I should reply: 'He is the architect of the house.' Well! M. Getard is the Boulingrin of M.

Fouquet. But he has nothing to do with the fortifications, which are my department alone; do you understand? mine, absolutely mine."

"Ah! Porthos," cried D'Artagnan, letting his arms fall as a conquered man gives up his sword; "ah! my friend, you are not only a Herculean topographer, you are, still further, a dialectician of the first water."

"Is it not powerfully reasoned?" said Porthos: and he puffed and blew like the conger which D'Artagnan had let slip from his hand.

"And now," said D'Artagnan, "that shabby-looking man, who accompanies M. Getard, is he also of the household of M. Fouquet?"

"Oh! yes," said Porthos, with contempt; "it is one M. Jupenet, or Juponet, a sort of poet."

"Who is come to establish himself here?"

"I believe so."

"I thought M. Fouquet had poets enough, yonder—Scudery, Loret, Pelisson, La Fontaine? If I must tell you the truth, Porthos, that poet disgraces you."

"Eh!—my friend; but what saves us is that he is not here as a poet."

"As what, then, is he?"

"As printer. And you make me remember, I have a word to say to the cuistre."

"Say it, then."

Porthos made a sign to Jupenet, who perfectly recollected D'Artagnan, and did not care to come nearer; which naturally produced another sign from Porthos. This was so imperative, he was obliged to obey. As he approached, "Come hither!" said Porthos. "You only landed yesterday and you have begun your tricks already."

"How so, monsieur le baron?" asked Jupenet, trembling.

"Your press was groaning all night, monsieur," said Porthos, "and you prevented my sleeping, corne de boeuf!"

"Monsieur—" objected Jupenet, timidly.

"You have nothing yet to print: therefore you have no occasion to set your press going. What did you print last night?"

"Monsieur, a light poem of my own composition."

"Light! no, no, monsieur; the press groaned pitifully beneath it. Let it not happen again. Do you understand?"

"Yes, monsieur."

"You promise me?"

"I do, monsieur!"

"Very well; this time I pardon you. Adieu!"

The poet retreated as humbly as he had approached.

"Well, now we have combed that fellow's head, let us breakfast."

"Yes," replied D'Artagnan, "let us breakfast."

"Only," said Porthos, "I beg you to observe, my friend, that we only have two hours for our repast."

"What would you have? We will try to make two hours suffice. But why have you only two hours?"

"Because it is high tide at one o'clock, and, with the tide, I am going to Vannes. But, as I shall return to-morrow, my dear friend, you can stay here; you shall be master; I have a good cook and a good cellar."

"No," interrupted D'Artagnan, "better than that."

"What?"

"You are going to Vannes, you say?"

"To a certainty."

"To see Aramis?"

"Yes."

"Well! I came from Paris on purpose to see Aramis."

"That's true."

"I will go with you then."

"Do; that's the thing."

"Only, I ought to have seen Aramis first, and you after. But man proposes, and God disposes. I have begun with you, and will finish with Aramis."

"Very well!"

"And in how many hours can you go from here to Vannes?"

"Oh! pardieu! in six hours. Three hours by sea to Sarzeau, three hours by road from Sarzeau to Vannes."

"How convenient that is! Being so near to the bishopric; do you often go to Vannes?"

"Yes; once a week. But, stop till I get my plan."

Porthos picked up his plan, folded it carefully, and engulfed it in his large pocket.

"Good!" said D'Artagnan aside; "I think I now know the real engineer who is fortifying Belle-Isle."

Two hours after, at high tide, Porthos and D'Artagnan set out for Sarzeau.

Chapter LXXI.
A Procession at Vannes.

THE passage from Belle-Isle to Sarzeau was made rapidly enough, thanks to one of those little corsairs of which D'Artagnan had been told during his voyage, and which, shaped for fast sailing and destined for the chase, were sheltered at that time in the roadstead of Locmaria, where one of them, with a quarter of its war-crew, performed duty between Belle-Isle and the continent. D'Artagnan had an opportunity of convincing himself that Porthos, though engineer and topographer, was not deeply versed in affairs of state. His perfect ignorance, with any other, might have passed for well-informed dissimulation. But D'Artagnan knew too well all the folds and refolds of his Porthos, not to find a secret if there were one there; like those regular, minute old bachelors, who know how to find, with their eyes shut, each book on the shelves of their library and each piece of linen in their wardrobe. So if he had found nothing, our cunning D'Artagnan, in rolling and unrolling his Porthos, it was because, in truth, there was nothing to be found.

"Be it so," said D'Artagnan; "I shall get to know more at Vannes in half an hour than Porthos has discovered at Belle-Isle in two months. Only, in order that I may know something, it is important that Porthos should not make use of the only stratagem I leave at his disposal. He must not warn Aramis of my arrival." All the care of the musketeer was then, for the moment, confined to the watching of Porthos. And let us hasten to say, Porthos did not deserve all this mistrust. Porthos thought of no evil. Perhaps, on first seeing him, D'Artagnan had inspired him with a little suspicion; but almost immediately D'Artagnan had reconquered in that good and brave heart the place he had always occupied, and not the least cloud darkened the large eye of Porthos, fixed from time to time with tenderness on his friend.

On landing, Porthos inquired if his horses were waiting and soon perceived them at the crossing of the road that winds round Sarzeau, and which, without passing through that little city, leads towards Vannes. These horses were two in number, one for M. de Vallon, and one for his equerry; for Porthos had an equerry since Mouston was only able to use a carriage as a means of locomotion. D'Artagnan expected that Porthos would propose to send forward his equerry upon one horse to bring back another, and he—D'Artagnan—had made up his mind to oppose this proposition. But nothing D'Artagnan had expected happened. Porthos simply told the equerry to dismount and await his return at Sarzeau, whilst D'Artagnan would ride his horse; which was arranged.

"Eh! but you are quite a man of precaution, my dear Porthos," said D'Artagnan to his friend, when he found himself in the saddle, upon the equerry's horse.

"Yes; but this is a kindness on the part of Aramis. I have not my stud here, and Aramis has placed his stables at my disposal."

"Good horses for bishop's horses, mordioux!" said D'Artagnan. "It is true, Aramis is a bishop of a peculiar kind."

"He is a holy man!" replied Porthos, in a tone almost nasal, and with his eyes raised towards heaven.

"Then he is much changed," said D'Artagnan; "you and I have known him passably profane."

"Grace has touched him," said Porthos.

"Bravo," said D'Artagnan, "that redoubles my desire to see my dear old friend." And he spurred his horse, which sprang off into a more rapid pace.

"Peste!" said Porthos, "if we go on at this rate, we shall only take one hour instead of two."

"To go how far, do you say, Porthos?"

"Four leagues and a half."

"That will be a good pace."

"I could have embarked you on the canal, but the devil take rowers and boat-horses! The first are like tortoises; the second like snails; and when a man is able to put a good horse between his knees, that horse is better than rowers or any other means."

"You are right; you above all, Porthos, who always look magnificent on horseback."

"Rather heavy, my friend; I was weighed the other day."

"And what do you weigh?"

"Three hundred-weight!" said Porthos, proudly.

"Bravo!"

"So that you must perceive, I am forced to choose horses whose loins are straight and wide, otherwise I break them down in two hours."

"Yes, giant's horses you must have, must you not?"

"You are very polite, my friend," replied the engineer, with affectionate majesty.

"As a case in point," replied D'Artagnan, "your horse seems to sweat already."

"Dame! It is hot! Ah, ah! do you see Vannes now?"

"Yes, perfectly. It is a handsome city, apparently."

"Charming, according to Aramis, at least; but I think it black; but black seems to be considered handsome by artists: I am sorry for it."

"Why so, Porthos?"

"Because I have lately had my chateau of Pierrefonds, which was gray with age, plastered white."

"Humph!" said D'Artagnan, "and white is more cheerful."

"Yes, but it is less august, as Aramis tells me. Fortunately there are dealers in black as well as white. I will have Pierrefonds replastered in black; that's all there is about it. If gray is handsome, you understand, my friend, black must be superb."

"Dame!" said D'Artagnan, "that appears logical."

"Were you never at Vannes, D'Artagnan?"

"Never."

"Then you know nothing of the city?"

"Nothing."

"Well, look!" said Porthos, raising himself in his stirrups, which made the fore-quarters of his horse bend sadly,—"do you see that corner, in the sun, yonder?"

"Yes, I see it plainly."

"Well, that is the cathedral."

"Which is called?"

"Saint-Pierre. Now look again—in the faubourg on the left, do you see another cross?"

"Perfectly well."

"That is Saint-Patern, the parish preferred by Aramis."

"Indeed!"

"Without doubt. Saint-Patern, you see, passes for having been the first bishop of Vannes. It is true that Aramis pretends he was not. But he is so learned that that may be only a paro—a para—"

"A paradox," said D'Artagnan.

"Precisely; thank you! my tongue trips, I am so hot."

"My friend," said D'Artagnan, "continue your interesting description, I beg. What is that large white building with many windows?"

"Oh! that is the college of the Jesuits. Pardieu! you have an apt hand. Do you see, close to the college, a large house with steeples, turrets, built in a handsome Gothic style, as that fool, M. Getard, says?"

"Yes, that is plainly to be seen. Well?"

"Well, that is where Aramis resides."

"What! does he not reside at the episcopal palace?"

"No; that is in ruins. The palace likewise is in the city, and Aramis prefers the faubourgs. That is why, as I told you, he is partial to Saint-Patern; Saint-Patern is in the faubourg. Besides, there are in this faubourg a mall, a tennis-court, and a house of Dominicans. Look, that where the handsome steeple rises to the heavens."

"Well?"

"Next, you see the faubourg is like a separate city, it has its walls, its towers, its ditches; the quay is upon it likewise, and the boats land at the quay. If our little corsair did not draw eight feet of water, we could have come full sail up to Aramis's windows."

"Porthos, Porthos," cried D'Artagnan, "you are a well of knowledge, a spring of ingenious and profound reflections. Porthos, you no longer surprise me, you confound me."

"Here we are," said Porthos, turning the conversation with his usual modesty.

"And high time we were," thought D'Artagnan, "for Aramis's horse is melting away like a steed of ice."

They entered almost at the same instant the faubourg; but scarcely had they gone a hundred paces when they were surprised to find the streets strewed with leaves and flowers. Against the old walls of Vannes, hung the oldest and the strangest tapestries of France. From over balconies fell long white sheets stuck all over with bouquets. The streets were deserted; it was plain the entire population was assembled on one point. The blinds were closed, and the breeze penetrated into the houses under the hangings, which cast long, black shades between their places of issue and the walls. Suddenly, at the turning of a street, chants struck the ears of the newly arrived travelers. A crowd in holiday garb appeared through the vapors of incense which mounted to the heavens in blue fleeces, and clouds of rose-leaves fluttered as high as the first stories. Above all heads were to be seen the cross and banners, the sacred symbols of religion. Then, beneath these crosses and banners, as if protected by them, walked a whole world of young girls clothed in white, crowned with corn-flowers. At the two sides of the street, inclosing the cortege, marched the guards of the garrison, carrying bouquets in the barrels of their muskets and on the points of their lances. This was the procession.

Whilst D'Artagnan and Porthos were looking on with critical glances, which disguised an extreme impatience to get forward, a magnificent dais approached preceded by a hundred Jesuits and a hundred Dominicans, and escorted by two archdeacons, a treasurer, a penitent and twelve canons. A singer with a thundering voice—a man certainly picked out from all the voices of France, as was the drum-major of the imperial guard from all the giants of the empire—escorted by four other chanters, who appeared to be there only to serve him as an accompaniment, made the air resound, and the windows of the houses vibrate. Under the dais appeared a pale and noble countenance with black eyes, black hair streaked with threads of white, a delicate, compressed mouth, a prominent and angular chin. His head, full of graceful majesty, was covered with the episcopal mitre, a headdress which gave it, in addition to the character of sovereignty, that of asceticism and evangelic meditation.

"Aramis!" cried the musketeer, involuntarily, as this lofty countenance passed before him. The prelate started at the sound of the voice. He raised his large black eyes, with their long lashes, and turned them without hesitation towards the spot whence the exclamation proceeded. At a glance, he saw Porthos and D'Artagnan close to him. On his part, D'Artagnan, thanks to the keenness of his sight, had seen all, seized all. The full portrait of the prelate had entered his memory, never to leave it. One thing had particularly struck D'Artagnan. On perceiving him, Aramis had colored, then he had concentrated under his eyelids the fire of the look of the master, and the indefinable affection of the friend. It was evident that Aramis had asked himself this question:—"Why is D'Artagnan with Porthos, and what does he want at Vannes?" Aramis comprehended all that was passing in the mind of D'Artagnan, on turning his look upon him again, and seeing that he had not lowered his eyes. He knew the acuteness and intelligence of his friend; he feared to let him divine the secret of his blush and his astonishment. He was still the same Aramis, always having a secret to conceal. Therefore, to put an end to his look of an inquisitor, which it was necessary to get rid of at all events, as, at any price, a general extinguishes a battery which annoys him, Aramis stretched forth his beautiful white hand, upon which sparkled the amethyst of the pastoral ring; he cut the air with sign of the cross, and poured out his benediction upon his two friends. Perhaps thoughtful and absent, D'Artagnan, impious in spite of himself, might not have bent beneath this holy benediction; but Porthos saw his distraction, and laying his friendly hand upon the back of his companion, he crushed him down towards the earth. D'Artagnan was forced to give way; indeed, he was little short of being flat on the ground. In the meantime Aramis had passed. D'Artagnan, like Antaeus, had only touched the ground, and he turned towards Porthos, almost angry. But there was no mistaking the intention of the brave Hercules; it was a feeling of religious propriety that had influenced him. Besides, speech with Porthos, instead of disguising his thought, always completed it.

"It is very polite of him," said he, "to have given his benediction to us alone. Decidedly, he is a holy man, and a brave man." Less convinced than Porthos, D'Artagnan made no reply.

"Observe my friend," continued Porthos, "he has seen us; and, instead of continuing to walk on at the simple pace of the procession, as he did just now,—see, what a hurry he is in; do you see how the cortege is increasing its speed? He is eager to join us and embrace us, is that dear Aramis."

"That is true," replied D'Artagnan, aloud.—Then to himself:—"It is equally true he has seen me, the fox, and will have time to prepare himself to receive me."

But the procession had passed; the road was free. D'Artagnan and Porthos walked straight up to the episcopal palace, which was surrounded by a numerous crowd anxious to see the prelate return. D'Artagnan remarked that this crowd was composed principally of citizens and military men. He recognized in the nature of these partisans the address of his friend. Aramis was not the man to seek for a useless popularity. He cared very little for being beloved by people who could be of no service to him. Women, children, and old men, that is to say, the cortege of ordinary pastors; was not the cortege for him.

Ten minutes after the two friends had passed the threshold of the palace, Aramis returned like a triumphant conqueror; the soldiers presented arms to him as to a superior; the citizens bowed to him as to a friend and a patron, rather than as a head of the Church. There was something in Aramis resembling those Roman senators who had their doors always surrounded by clients. At the foot of the steps, he had a conference of half a minute with a Jesuit, who, in order to speak to him more secretly, passed his head under the dais. He then re-entered his palace; the doors closed slowly, and the crowd melted away, whilst chants and prayers were still resounding abroad. It was a magnificent day. Earthly perfumes were mingled with the perfumes of the air and the sea. The city breathed happiness, joy, and strength. D'Artagnan felt something like the presence of an invisible hand which had, all-powerfully, created this strength, this joy, this happiness, and spread everywhere these perfumes.

"Oh! oh!" said he, "Porthos has got fat; but Aramis is grown taller."

Chapter LXXII.
The Grandeur of the Bishop of Vannes.

PORTHOS and D'Artagnan had entered the bishop's residence by a private door, as his personal friends. Of course, Porthos served D'Artagnan as guide. The worthy baron comported himself everywhere rather as if he were at home. Nevertheless, whether it was a tacit acknowledgement of the sanctity of the personage of Aramis and his character, or the habit of respecting him who imposed upon him morally, a worthy habit which had always made Porthos a model soldier and an excellent companion; for all these reasons, say we, Porthos preserved in the palace of His Greatness the Bishop of Vannes a sort of reserve which D'Artagnan remarked at once, in the attitude he took with respect to the valets and officers. And yet this reserve did not go so far as to prevent his asking questions. Porthos questioned. They learned that His Greatness had just returned to his apartment and was preparing to appear in familiar intimacy, less majestic than he had appeared with his flock. After a quarter of an hour, which D'Artagnan and Porthos passed in looking mutually at each other with the white of their eyes, and turning their thumbs in all the different evolutions which go from north to south, a door of the chamber opened and His Greatness appeared, dressed in the undress, complete, of a prelate. Aramis carried his head high, like a man accustomed to command: his violet robe was tucked up on one side, and his white hand was on his hip. He had retained the fine mustache, and the lengthened royale of the time of Louis XIII. He exhaled, on entering, that delicate perfume which, among elegant men and women of high fashion, never changes, and appears to be incorporated in the person, of whom it has become the natural emanation. In this case only, the perfume had retained something of the religious sublimity of incense. It no longer intoxicated, it penetrated; it no longer inspired desire, it inspired respect. Aramis, on entering the chamber, did not hesitate an instant; and without pronouncing one word, which, whatever it might be, would have been cold on such an occasion, he went straight up to the musketeer, so well disguised under the costume of M. Agnan, and pressed him in his arms with a tenderness which the most distrustful could not have suspected of coldness or affectation.

D'Artagnan, on his part, embraced him with equal ardor. Porthos pressed the delicate hand of Aramis in his immense hands, and D'Artagnan remarked that His Greatness gave him his left hand, probably from habit, seeing that Porthos already ten times had been near injuring his fingers covered with rings, by pounding his flesh in the vise of his fist. Warned by the pain, Aramis was cautious, and only presented flesh to be bruised, and not fingers to be crushed, against the gold or the angles of diamonds.

Between two embraces, Aramis looked D'Artagnan in the face, offered him a chair, sitting down himself in the shade, observing that the light fell full upon the face of his interlocutor. This maneuver, familiar to diplomatists and women, resembles much the advantage of the guard which, according to their skill or habit, combatants endeavor to take on the ground at a duel. D'Artagnan was not the dupe of this maneuver; but he did not appear to perceive it. He felt himself caught; but, precisely because he was caught he felt himself on the road to discovery, and it little imported to him, old condottiere as he was, to be beaten in appearance, provided he drew from his pretended defeat the advantages of victory. Aramis began the conversation.

"Ah! dear friend! my good D'Artagnan," said he, "what an excellent chance!"

"It is a chance, my reverend companion," said D'Artagnan, "that I will call friendship. I seek you, as I always have sought you, when I had any grand enterprise to propose to you, or some hours of liberty to give you."

"Ah! indeed," said Aramis, without explosion, "you have been seeking me?"

"Eh! yes, he has been seeking you, Aramis," said Porthos, "and the proof is that he has unharbored me at Belle-Isle. That is amiable, is it not?"

"Ah! yes," said Aramis, "at Belle-Isle! certainly!"

"Good!" said D'Artagnan; "there is my booby Porthos, without thinking of it, has fired the first cannon of attack."

"At Belle-Isle!" said Aramis, "in that hole, in that desert! That is kind, indeed!"

"And it was I who told him you were at Vannes," continued Porthos, in the same tone.

D'Artagnan armed his mouth with a finesse almost ironical.

"Yes, I knew, but I was willing to see," replied he.

"To see what?"

"If our old friendship still held out; if, on seeing each other, our hearts, hardened as they are by age, would still let the old cry of joy escape, which salutes the coming of a friend."

"Well, and you must have been satisfied," said Aramis.

"So, so."

"How is that?"

"Yes, Porthos said hush! and you—"

"Well! and I?"

"And you gave me your benediction."

"What would you have, my friend?" said Aramis, smiling; "that is the most precious thing that a poor prelate, like me, has to give."

"Indeed, my dear friend!"

"Doubtless."

"And yet they say at Paris that the bishopric of Vannes is one of the best in France."

"Ah! you are now speaking of temporal wealth," said Aramis, with a careless air.

"To be sure, I wish to speak of that; I hold by it, on my part."

"In that case, let me speak of it," said Aramis, with a smile.

"You own yourself to be one of the richest prelates in France?"

"My friend, since you ask me to give you an account, I will tell you that the bishopric of Vannes is worth about twenty thousand livres a year, neither more nor less. It is a diocese which contains a hundred and sixty parishes."

"That is very pretty," said D'Artagnan.

"It is superb!" said Porthos.

"And yet," resumed D'Artagnan, throwing his eyes over Aramis, "you don't mean to bury yourself here forever?"

"Pardon me. Only I do not admit the word bury."

"But it seems to me, that at this distance from Paris a man is buried, or nearly so."

"My friend, I am getting old," said Aramis; "the noise and bustle of a city no longer suit me. At fifty-seven we ought to seek calm and meditation. I have found them here. What is there more beautiful, and stern at the same time, than this old Armorica. I find here, dear D'Artagnan, all that is opposite to what I formerly loved, and that is what must happen at the end of life, which is opposite to the beginning. A little of my old pleasure of former times still comes to salute me here, now and then, without diverting me from the road of salvation. I am still of this world, and yet every step that I take brings me nearer to God."

"Eloquent, wise and discreet; you are an accomplished prelate, Aramis, and I offer you my congratulations."

"But," said Aramis smiling, "you did not come here only for the purpose of paying me compliments. Speak; what brings you hither? May it be that, in some fashion or other, you want me?"

"Thank God, no, my friend," said D'Artagnan, "it is nothing of that kind.—I am rich and free."

"Rich!" exclaimed Aramis.

"Yes, rich for me; not for you or Porthos, understand. I have an income of about fifteen thousand livres."

Aramis looked at him suspiciously. He could not believe—particularly on seeing his friend in such humble guise—that he had made so fine a fortune. Then D'Artagnan, seeing that the hour of explanations was come, related the history of his English adventures. During the recital he saw, ten times, the eyes of the prelate sparkle, and his slender fingers work convulsively. As to Porthos, it was not admiration he manifested for D'Artagnan; it was enthusiasm, it was delirium. When D'Artagnan had finished, "Well!" said Aramis.

"Well!" said D'Artagnan, "you see, then, I have in England friends and property, in France a treasure. If your heart tells you so, I offer them to you. That is what I came here for."

However firm was his look, he could not this time support the look of Aramis. He allowed, therefore, his eye to stray upon Porthos—like the sword which yields to too powerful a pressure, and seeks another road.

"At all events," said the bishop, "you have assumed a singular traveling costume, old friend."

"Frightful! I know it is. You may understand why I would not travel as a cavalier or a noble; since I became rich, I am miserly."

"And you say, then, you came to Belle-Isle?" said Aramis, without transition.

"Yes," replied D'Artagnan; "I knew I should find you and Porthos there."

"Find me!" cried Aramis. "Me! for the last year past I have not once crossed the sea."

"Oh," said D'Artagnan, "I should never have supposed you such a housekeeper."

"Ah, dear friend, I must tell you that I am no longer the Aramis of former times. Riding on horseback is unpleasant to me; the sea fatigues me. I am a poor, ailing priest, always complaining, always grumbling, and inclined to the austerities which appear to accord with old age,—preliminary parleyings with death. I linger, my dear D'Artagnan, I linger."

"Well, that is all the better, my friend, for we shall probably be neighbors soon."

"Bah!" said Aramis with a degree of surprise he did not even seek to dissemble. "You my neighbor!"

"Mordioux! yes."

"How so?"

"I am about to purchase some very profitable salt-mines, which are situated between Piriac and Le Croisic. Imagine, my dear friend, a clear profit of twelve per cent. Never any deficiency, never any idle expenses; the ocean, faithful and regular, brings every twelve hours its contingency to my coffers. I am the first Parisian who has dreamt of such a speculation. Do not say anything about it, I beg of you, and in a short time we will communicate on the matter. I am to have three leagues of country for thirty thousand livres."

Aramis darted a look at Porthos, as if to ask if all this were true, if some snare were not concealed beneath this outward indifference. But soon, as if ashamed of having consulted this poor auxiliary, he collected all his forces for a fresh assault and new defense. "I heard that you had had some difference with the court, but that you had come out of it as you know how to get through everything, D'Artagnan, with the honors of war."

"I!" said the musketeer, with a burst of laughter that did not conceal his embarrassment: for, from those words, Aramis was not unlikely to be acquainted with his last relations with the king. "I! Oh, tell me all about that, pray, Aramis?"

"Yes, it was related to me, a poor bishop, lost in the middle of the Landes, that the king had taken you as the confidant of his amours."

"With whom?"

"With Mademoiselle de Mancini."

D'Artagnan breathed freely again. "Ah! I don't say no to that," replied he.

"It appears that the king took you one morning, over the bridge of Blois to talk with his lady-love."

"That's true," said D'Artagnan. "And you know that, do you? Well, then, you must know that the same day I gave in my resignation!"

"What, sincerely?"

"Nothing more so."

"It was after that, then, that you went to the Comte de la Fere's?"

"Yes."

"Afterwards to me?"

"Yes."

"And then Porthos?"

"Yes."

"Was it in order to pay us a simple visit?"

"No, I did no know you were engaged, and I wished to take you with me into England."

"Yes, I understand; and then you executed alone, wonderful man as you are, what you wanted to propose to us all four. I suspected you had something to do with that famous restoration, when I learned that you had been seen at King Charles's receptions, and that he appeared to treat you like a friend, or rather like a person to whom he was under an obligation."

"But how the devil did you learn all that?" asked D'Artagnan, who began to fear that the investigation of Aramis had extended further than he wished.

"Dear D'Artagnan," said the prelate, "my friendship resembles, in a degree, the solicitude of that night watch whom we have in the little tower of the mole, at the extremity of the quay. That brave man, every night, lights a lantern to direct the barks that come from sea. He is concealed in his sentry-box, and the fishermen do not see him; but he follows them with interest; he divines them; he calls them; he attracts them into the way to the port. I resemble this watcher; from time to time some news reaches me, and recalls to my remembrance all those I loved. Then I follow the friends of old days over the stormy ocean of the world, I, a poor watcher, to whom God has kindly given the shelter of a sentry-box."

"Well, what did I do when I came from England?"

"Ah! there," replied Aramis, "you get beyond my depth. I know nothing of you since your return. D'Artagnan, my eyes are dim. I regretted you did not think of me. I wept over your forgetfulness. I was wrong. I see you again, and it is a festival, a great festival, I assure you, solemnly! How is Athos?"

"Very well, thank you."

"And our young pupil, Raoul?"

"He seems to have inherited the skill of his father, Athos, and the strength of his tutor, Porthos."

"And on what occasion have you been able to judge of that?"

"Eh! mon Dieu! on the eve of my departure from Paris."

"Indeed! tell me all about it!"

"Yes; there was an execution at the Greve, and in consequence of that execution, a riot. We happened, by accident, to be in the riot; and in this riot we were obliged to have recourse to our swords. And he did wonders."

"Bah! what did he do?"

"Why, in the first place, he threw a man out of the window, as he would have flung a sack full of flock."

"Come, that's pretty well," said Porthos.

"Then he drew, and cut and thrust away, as we fellows used to do in the good old times."

"And what was the cause of this riot?" said Porthos.

D'Artagnan remarked upon the face of Aramis a complete indifference to this question of Porthos. "Why," said he, fixing his eyes upon Aramis, "on account of the two farmers of the revenue, friends of M. Fouquet, whom the king forced to disgorge their plunder, and then hanged them."

A scarcely perceptible contraction of the prelate's brow showed that he had heard D'Artagnan's reply. "Oh, oh!" said Porthos; "and what were the names of these friends of M. Fouquet?"

"MM. d'Eymeris and Lyodot," said D'Artagnan. "Do you know these names, Aramis?"

"No," said the prelate, disdainfully; "they sound like the names of financiers."

"Exactly; so they were."

"Oh! M. Fouquet allows his friends to be hanged, then," said Porthos.

"And why not?" said Aramis.

"Why, it seems to me—"

"If these culprits were hanged, it was by order of the king. Now M. Fouquet, although superintendent of the finances, has not, I believe, the right of life and death."

"That may be," said Porthos; "but in the place of M. Fouquet—"

Aramis was afraid Porthos was about to say something awkward, so interrupted him. "Come, D'Artagnan," said he; "this is quite enough about other people, let us talk a little about you."

"Of me you know all that I can tell you. On the contrary let me hear a little about you, Aramis."

"I have told you, my friend. There is nothing of Aramis left in me."

"Nor of the Abbe d'Herblay even?"

"No, not even of him. You see a man whom Providence has taken by the hand, whom he has conducted to a position that he could never have dared even to hope for."

"Providence?" asked D'Artagnan.

"Yes."

"Well, that is strange! I was told it was M. Fouquet."

"Who told you that?" cried Aramis, without being able, with all the power of his will, to prevent the color rising to his cheeks.

"Ma foi! why, Bazin!"

"The fool!"

"I do not say he is a man of genius, it is true; but he told me so; and after him, I repeat it to you."

"I have never even seen M. Fouquet," replied Aramis with a look as pure and calm as that of a virgin who has never told a lie.

"Well, but if you had seen him and known him, there is no harm in that," replied D'Artagnan. "M. Fouquet is a very good sort of a man."

"Humph!"

"A great politician." Aramis made a gesture of indifference.

"An all-powerful minister."

"I only hold to the king and the pope."

"Dame! listen then," said D'Artagnan, in the most natural tone imaginable. "I said that because everybody here swears by M. Fouquet. The plain is M. Fouquet's; the salt-mines I am about to buy are M. Fouquet's; the island in which Porthos studies topography is M. Fouquet's; the garrison is M. Fouquet's; the galleys are M. Fouquet's. I confess, then, that nothing would have surprised me in your enfeoffment, or rather in that of your diocese, to M. Fouquet. He is a different master from the king, that is all; but quite as powerful as Louis."

"Thank God! I am not vassal to anybody; I belong to nobody, and am entirely my own master," replied Aramis, who, during this conversation, followed with his eye every gesture of D'Artagnan, every glance of Porthos. But D'Artagnan was impassible and Porthos motionless; the thrusts aimed so skillfully were parried by an able adversary; not one hit the mark. Nevertheless, both began to feel the fatigue of such a contest, and the announcement of supper was well received by everybody. Supper changed the course of conversation. Besides, they felt that, upon their guard as each one had been, they could neither of them boast of having the advantage. Porthos had understood nothing of what had been meant. He had held himself motionless, because Aramis had made him a sign not to stir. Supper, for him, was nothing but supper; but that was quite enough for Porthos. The supper, then, went off very well. D'Artagnan was in high spirits. Aramis exceeded himself in kind affability. Porthos ate like old Pelops. Their talk was of war, finance, the arts, and love. Aramis played astonishment at every word of politics D'Artagnan risked. This long series of surprises increased the mistrust of D'Artagnan, as the eternal indifference of D'Artagnan provoked the suspicions of Aramis. At length D'Artagnan, designedly, uttered the name of Colbert: he had reserved that stroke for the last.

"Who is this Colbert?" asked the bishop.

"Oh! come," said D'Artagnan to himself, "that is too strong! We must be careful, mordioux! we must be careful."

And he then gave Aramis all the information respecting M. Colbert he could desire. The supper, or rather, the conversation, was prolonged till one o'clock in the morning between D'Artagnan and Aramis. At ten o'clock precisely, Porthos had fallen asleep in his chair and snored like an organ. At midnight he woke up and they sent him to bed. "Hum!" said he, "I was near falling asleep; but that was all very interesting you were talking about."

At one o'clock Aramis conducted D'Artagnan to the chamber destined for him, which was the best in the episcopal residence. Two servants were placed at his command. "To-morrow, at eight o'clock," said he, taking leave of D'Artagnan, "we will take, if agreeable to you, a ride on horseback with Porthos."

"At eight o'clock!" said D'Artagnan; "so late?"

"You know that I require seven hours' sleep," said Aramis.

"That is true."

"Good-night, dear friend!" And he embraced the musketeer cordially.

D'Artagnan allowed him to depart; then, as soon as the door closed, "Good!" cried he, "at five o'clock I will be on foot."

This determination being made, he went to bed and quietly, "put two and two together," as people say.

Chapter LXXIII.
In which Porthos begins to be sorry for having come with D'Artagnan.

SCARCELY had D'Artagnan extinguished his taper, when Aramis, who had watched through his curtains the last glimmer of light in his friend's apartment, traversed the corridor on tiptoe, and went to Porthos's room. The giant who had been in bed nearly an hour and a half, lay grandly stretched out on the down bed. He was in that happy calm of the first sleep, which, with Porthos, resisted the noise of bells or the report of cannon: his head swam in that soft oscillation which reminds us of the soothing movement of a ship. In a moment Porthos would have begun to dream. The door of the chamber opened softly under the delicate pressure of the hand of Aramis. The bishop approached the sleeper. A thick carpet deadened his steps, besides which Porthos snored in a manner to drown all noise. He laid one hand on his shoulder—"Rouse," said he, "wake up, my dear Porthos." The voice of Aramis was soft and kind, but it conveyed more than a notice,—it conveyed an order. His hand was light, but it indicated danger. Porthos heard the voice and felt the hand of Aramis, even in the depth of sleep. He started up. "Who goes there?" cried he, in his giant's voice.

"Hush! hush! It is I," said Aramis.

"You, my friend? And what the devil do you wake me for?"

"To tell you that you must set off directly."

"Set off?"

"Yes."

"Where for?"

"For Paris."

Porthos bounded up in his bed, and then sank back down again, fixing his great eyes in agitation upon Aramis.

"For Paris?"

"Yes."

"A hundred leagues?" said he.

"A hundred and four," replied the bishop.

"Oh! mon Dieu!" sighed Porthos, lying down again, like children who contend with their bonne to gain an hour or two more sleep.

"Thirty hours' riding," said Aramis, firmly. "You know there are good relays."

Porthos pushed out one leg, allowing a groan to escape him.

"Come, come! my friend," insisted the prelate with a sort of impatience.

Porthos drew the other leg out of the bed. "And is it absolutely necessary that I should go, at once?"

"Urgently necessary."

Porthos got upon his feet, and began to shake both walls and floors with his steps of a marble statue.

"Hush! hush! for the love of Heaven, my dear Porthos!" said Aramis, "you will wake somebody."

"Ah! that's true," replied Porthos, in a voice of thunder, "I forgot that; but be satisfied, I am on guard." And so saying, he let fall a belt loaded with his sword and pistols, and a purse, from which the crowns escaped with a vibrating and prolonged noise. This noise made the blood of Aramis boil, whilst it drew from Porthos a formidable burst of laughter. "How droll that is!" said he, in the same voice.

"Not so loud, Porthos, not so loud."

"True, true!" and he lowered his voice a half-note.

"I was going to say," continued Porthos, "that it is droll that we are never so slow as when we are in a hurry, and never make so much noise as when we wish to be silent."

"Yes, that is true; but let us give the proverb the lie, Porthos; let us make haste, and hold our tongue."

"You see I am doing my best," said Porthos, putting on his haut de chausses.

"Very well."

"This is something in haste?"

"It is more than that, it is serious, Porthos."

"Oh, oh!"

"D'Artagnan has questioned you, has he not?"

"Questioned me?"

"Yes, at Belle-Isle?"

"Not the least in the world."

"Are you sure of that, Porthos?"

"Parbleu!"

"It is impossible. Recollect yourself." "He asked me what I was doing, and I told him—studying topography. I would have made use of another word which you employed one day."

"'Castrametation'?"

"Yes, that's it; but I never could recollect it."

"All the better. What more did he ask you?"

"Who M. Getard was."

"Next?"

"Who M. Jupenet was."

"He did not happen to see our plan of fortifications, did he?"

"Yes."

"The devil he did!"

"But don't be alarmed, I had rubbed out your writing with India-rubber. It was impossible for him to suppose you had given me any advice in those works."

"Ay; but our friend has phenomenally keen eyes."

"What are you afraid of?"

"I fear that everything is discovered, Porthos; the matter is, then, to prevent a great misfortune. I have given orders to my people to close all the gates and doors. D'Artagnan will not be able to get out before daybreak. Your horse is ready saddled; you will gain the first relay; by five o'clock in the morning you will have traversed fifteen leagues. Come!"

Aramis then assisted Porthos to dress, piece by piece, with as much celerity as the most skillful valet de chambre could have done. Porthos, half stupefied, let him do as he liked, and confounded himself in excuses. When he was ready, Aramis took him by the hand, and led him, making him place his foot with precaution on every step of the stairs, preventing him running against door-frames, turning him this way and that, as if Aramis had been the giant and Porthos the dwarf. Soul set fire to and animated matter. A horse was waiting, ready saddled, in the courtyard. Porthos mounted. Then Aramis himself took the horse by the bridle, and led him over some dung spread in the yard, with the evident intention of suppressing noise. He, at the same time, held tight the horse's nose, to prevent him neighing. When arrived at the outward gate, drawing Porthos towards him, who was going off without even asking him what for: "Now, friend Porthos, now; without drawing bridle, till you get to Paris," whispered he in his ears; "eat on horseback, drink on horseback, but lose not a minute."

"That's enough; I will not stop."

"This letter to M. Fouquet; cost what it may, he must have it to-morrow before mid-day."

"He shall."

"And do not forget one thing, my friend."

"What is that?"

"That you are riding out on a hunt for your brevet of duc and peer."

"Oh! oh!" said Porthos, with his eyes sparkling; "I will do it in twenty-four hours, in that case."

"Try."

"Then let go the bridle—and forward, Goliath!"

Aramis did let go, not the bridle, but the horse's nose. Porthos released his hand, clapped spurs to his horse, which set off at a gallop. As long as he could distinguish Porthos through the darkness, Aramis followed him with his eyes: when he was completely out of sight, he re-entered the yard. Nothing had stirred in D'Artagnan's apartment. The valet placed on watch at the door had neither seen any light, nor heard any noise. Aramis closed his door carefully, sent the lackey to bed, and quickly sought his own. D'Artagnan really suspected nothing, therefore thought he had gained everything, when he awoke in the morning, about half-past four. He ran to the window in his shirt. The window looked out upon the court. Day was dawning. The court was deserted; the fowls, even, had not left their roosts. Not a servant appeared. Every door was closed.

"Good! all is still," said D'Artagnan to himself. "Never mind: I am up first in the house. Let us dress; that will be so much done." And D'Artagnan dressed himself. But, this time, he endeavored not to give to the costume of M. Agnan that bourgeoise and almost ecclesiastical rigidity he had affected before; he managed, by drawing his belt tighter, by buttoning his clothes in a different fashion, and by putting on his hat a little on one side, to restore to his person a little of that military character, the absence of which had surprised Aramis. This being done, he made free, or affected to make free with his host, and entered his chamber without ceremony. Aramis was asleep or feigned to be so. A large book lay open upon his night-desk, a wax-light was still burning in its silver sconce. This was more than enough to prove to

D'Artagnan the quiescence of the prelate's night, and the good intentions of his waking. The musketeer did to the bishop precisely as the bishop had done to Porthos—he tapped him on the shoulder. Evidently Aramis pretended to sleep; for, instead of waking suddenly, he who slept so lightly required a repetition of the summons.

"Ah! ah! is that you?" said he, stretching his arms. "What an agreeable surprise! Ma foi! Sleep had made me forget I had the happiness to possess you. What o'clock is it?"

"I do not know," said D'Artagnan, a little embarrassed. "Early, I believe. But, you know, that devil of a habit of waking with the day, sticks to me still."

"Do you wish that we should go out so soon?" asked Aramis. "It appears to me to be very early."

"Just as you like."

"I thought we had agreed not to get on horseback before eight."

"Possibly; but I had so great a wish to see you, that I said to myself, the sooner the better."

"And my seven hours' sleep!" said Aramis: "Take care; I had reckoned upon them, and what I lose of them I must make up."

"But it seems to me that, formerly, you were less of a sleeper than that, dear friend; your blood was alive, and you were never to be found in bed."

"And it is exactly on account of what you tell me, that I am so fond of being there now."

"Then you confess, that it is not for the sake of sleeping, that you have put me off till eight o'clock."

"I have been afraid you would laugh at me, if I told you the truth."

"Tell me, notwithstanding."

"Well, from six to eight, I am accustomed to perform my devotions."

"Your devotions?"

"Yes."

"I did not believe a bishop's exercises were so severe."

"A bishop, my friend, must sacrifice more to appearance than a simple cleric."

"Mordioux! Aramis, that is a word which reconciles me with your greatness. To appearances! That is a musketeer's word, in good truth! Vivent les apparences, Aramis!"

"Instead of felicitating me upon it, pardon me, D'Artagnan. It is a very mundane word which I had allowed to escape me."

"Must I leave you, then?"

"I want time to collect my thoughts, my friend, and for my usual prayers."

"Well, I leave you to them; but on account of that poor pagan, D'Artagnan, abridge them for once, I beg; I thirst for speech with you."

"Well, D'Artagnan, I promise you that within an hour and a half—"

"An hour and a half of devotions! Ah! my friend, be as reasonable with me as you can. Let me have the best bargain possible."

Aramis began to laugh.

"Still agreeable, still young, still gay," said he. "You have come into my diocese to set me quarreling with grace."

"Bah!"

"And you know well that I was never able to resist your seductions; you will cost me my salvation, D'Artagnan."

D'Artagnan bit his lips.

"Well," said he, "I will take the sin on my own head, favor me with one simple Christian sign of the cross, favor me with one prayer, and we will part."

"Hush!" said Aramis, "we are already no longer alone, I hear strangers coming up."

"Well, dismiss them."

"Impossible; I made an appointment with them yesterday; it is the principal of the college of the Jesuits, and the superior of the Dominicans."

"Your staff? Well, so be it."

"What are you going to do?"

"I will go and wake Porthos, and remain in his company till you have finished the conference."

Aramis did not stir, his brow remained unbent, he betrayed himself by no gesture or word; "Go," said he, as D'Artagnan advanced to the door. "A propos, do you know where Porthos sleeps?"

"No, but I will inquire."

"Take the corridor, and open the second door on the left."

"Thank you! au revoir." And D'Artagnan departed in the direction pointed out by Aramis.

Ten minutes had not passed away when he came back. He found Aramis seated between the superior of the Dominicans and the principal of the college of the Jesuits, exactly in the same situation as he had found him formerly in the auberge at Crevecoeur. This company did not at all terrify the musketeer.

"What is it?" said Aramis, quietly. "You have apparently something to say to me, my friend."

"It is," replied D'Artagnan, fixing his eyes upon Aramis, "it is that Porthos is not in his apartment."

"Indeed," said Aramis calmly; "are you sure?"

"Pardieu! I came from his chamber."

"Where can he be, then?"

"That is what I am asking you."

"And have you not inquired?"

"Yes, I have."

"And what answer did you get?"

"That Porthos, often walking out in a morning, without saying anything, had probably gone out."

"What did you do, then?"

"I went to the stables," replied D'Artagnan, carelessly.

"What to do?"

"To see if Porthos had departed on horseback."

"And?" interrogated the bishop.

"Well, there is a horse missing, stall No. 3, Goliath."

All this dialogue, it may be easily understood, was not exempt from a certain affectation on the part of the musketeer, and a perfect complaisance on the part of Aramis.

"Oh! I guess how it is," said Aramis, after having considered for a moment, "Porthos is gone out to give us a surprise."

"A surprise?"

"Yes; the canal which goes from Vannes to the sea abounds in teal and snipes; that is Porthos's favorite sport, and he will bring us back a dozen for breakfast."

"Do you think so?" said D'Artagnan.

"I am sure of it. Where else can he be? I would lay a wager he took a gun with him."

"Well, that is possible," said D'Artagnan.

"Do one thing, my friend. Get on horseback, and join him."

"You are right," said D'Artagnan, "I will."

"Shall I go with you?"

"No, thank you; Porthos is a rather remarkable man: I will inquire as I go along."

"Will you take an arquebus?"

"Thank you."

"Order what horse you like to be saddled."

"The one I rode yesterday, on coming from Belle-Isle."

"So be it: use the horse as your own."

Aramis rang, and gave orders to have the horse M. d'Artagnan had chosen saddled.

D'Artagnan followed the servant charged with the execution of this order. When arrived at the door, the servant drew on one side to allow M. d'Artagnan to pass; and at that moment he caught the eye of his master. A knitting of the brow gave the intelligent spy to understand that all should be given to D'Artagnan he wished. D'Artagnan got into the saddle, and Aramis heard the steps of his horse on the pavement. An instant after, the servant returned.

"Well?" asked the bishop.

"Monseigneur, he has followed the course of the canal, and is going towards the sea," said the servant.

"Very well!" said Aramis.

In fact, D'Artagnan, dismissing all suspicion, hastened towards the ocean, constantly hoping to see in the Landes, or on the beach, the colossal profile of Porthos. He persisted in fancying he could trace a horse's steps in every puddle. Sometimes he imagined he heard the report of a gun. This illusion lasted three hours; during two of which he went forward in search of his friend—in the last he returned to the house.

"We must have crossed," said he, "and I shall find them waiting for me at table."

D'Artagnan was mistaken. He no more found Porthos at the palace than he had found him on the sea-shore. Aramis was waiting for him at the top of the stairs, looking very much concerned.

"Did my people not find you, my dear D'Artagnan?" cried he, as soon as he caught sight of the musketeer.

"No; did you send any one after me?"

"I am deeply concerned, my friend, deeply, to have induced you to make such a useless search; but, about seven o'clock, the almoner of Saint-Patern came here. He had met Du Vallon, who was going away, and who, being unwilling to disturb anybody at the palace, had charged him to tell me that, fearing M. Getard would play him some ill turn in his absence, he was going to take advantage of the morning tide to make a tour of Belle-Isle."

"But tell me, Goliath has not crossed the four leagues of sea, I should think."

"There are full six," said Aramis.

"That makes it less probable still."

"Therefore, my friend," said Aramis, with one of his blandest smiles, "Goliath is in the stable, well pleased, I will answer for it, that Porthos is no longer on his back." In fact, the horse had been brought back from the relay by the direction of the prelate, from whom no detail escaped. D'Artagnan appeared as well satisfied with as possible with the explanation. He entered upon a part of dissimulation which agreed perfectly with the suspicions that arose more strongly in his mind. He breakfasted between the Jesuit and Aramis, having the Dominican in front of him, and smiling particularly at the Dominican, whose jolly, fat face pleased him much. The repast was long and sumptuous; excellent Spanish wine, fine Morbihan oysters, exquisite fish from the mouth of the Loire, enormous prawns from Paimboeuf, and delicious game from the moors, constituted the principal part of it. D'Artagnan ate much, and drank but little. Aramis drank nothing, unless it was water. After the repast,—

"You offered me an arquebus," said D'Artagnan.

"I did."

"Lend it me, then."

"Are you going shooting?"

"Whilst waiting for Porthos, it is the best thing I can do, I think."

"Take which you like from the trophy."

"Will you not come with me?"

"I would with great pleasure; but, alas! my friend, sporting is forbidden to bishops."

"Ah!" said D'Artagnan, "I did not know that."

"Besides," continued Aramis, "I shall be busy till mid-day."

"I shall go alone, then?" said D'Artagnan.

"I am sorry to say you must; but come back to dinner."

"Pardieu! the eating at your house is too good to make me think of not coming back." And thereupon D'Artagnan quitted his host, bowed to the guests, and took his arquebus; but instead of shooting, went straight to the little port of Vannes. He looked in vain to observe if anybody saw him; he could discern neither thing nor person. He engaged a little fishing boat for twenty-five livres, and set off at half-past eleven, convinced that he had not been followed; and that was true, he had not been followed; only a Jesuit brother, placed in the top of the steeple of his church, had not, since the morning, by the help of an excellent glass, lost sight of one of his steps. At three quarters past eleven, Aramis was informed that D'Artagnan was sailing towards Belle-Isle. The voyage was rapid; a good north north-east wind drove him towards the isle. As he approached, his eyes were constantly fixed upon the coast. He looked to see if, upon the shore or upon the fortifications the brilliant dress and vast stature of Porthos should stand out against a slightly clouded sky; but his search was in vain. He landed without having seen anything; and learnt from the first soldier interrogated by him, that M. du Vallon had not yet returned from Vannes. Then, without losing an instant, D'Artagnan ordered his little bark to put its head towards Sarzeau. We know that the wind changes with the different hours of the day. The breeze had veered from the north north-east to the south-east; the wind, then, was almost as good for the return to Sarzeau, as it had been for the voyage to Belle-Isle. In three hours D'Artagnan had touched the continent; two hours more sufficed for his ride to Vannes. In spite of the rapidity of his passage, what D'Artagnan endured of impatience and anger during that short passage, the deck alone of the vessel, upon which he stamped backwards and forwards for three hours, could testify. He made but one bound from the quay whereon he landed to the episcopal palace. He thought to terrify Aramis by the promptitude of his return; he wished to reproach him with his duplicity, and yet with reserve; but with sufficient spirit, nevertheless, to make him feel all the consequences of it, and force from him a part of his secret. He hoped, in short—thanks to that heat of expression which is to secrets what the charge with the bayonet is to redoubts—to bring the mysterious Aramis to some manifestation or other. But he found, in the vestibule of the palace, the valet de chambre, who closed his passage, while smiling upon him with a stupid air.

"Monseigneur?" cried D'Artagnan, endeavoring to put him aside with his hand. Moved for an instant the valet resumed his station.

"Monseigneur?" said he.

"Yes, to be sure; do you not know me, imbecile?"

"Yes; you are the Chevalier d'Artagnan."

"Then let me pass."

"It is of no use."

"Why of no use?"

"Because His Greatness is not at home."

"What! His Greatness is not at home? where is he, then?"

"Gone."

"Gone?"

"Yes."

"Whither?"

"I don't know; but perhaps he tells monsieur le chevalier."

"And how? where? in what fashion?"

"In this letter, which he gave me for monsieur le chevalier." And the valet de chambre drew a letter form his pocket.

"Give it me, then, you rascal," said D'Artagnan, snatching it from his hand. "Oh, yes," continued he, at the first line, "yes, I understand;" and he read:—

"Dear Friend,—An affair of the most urgent nature calls me to a distant parish of my diocese. I hoped to see you again before I set out; but I lose that hope in thinking that you are going, no doubt, to remain two or three days at Belle-Isle, with our dear Porthos. Amuse yourself as well as you can; but do not attempt to hold out against him at table. This is a counsel I might have given even to Athos, in his most brilliant and best days. Adieu, dear friend; believe that I regret greatly not having better, and for a longer time, profited by your excellent company."

"Mordioux!" cried D'Artagnan. "I am tricked. Ah! blockhead, brute, triple fool that I am! But those laugh best who laugh last. Oh, duped, duped like a monkey, cheated with an empty nutshell!" And with a hearty blow bestowed upon the nose of the smirking valet de chambre, he made all haste out of the episcopal palace. Furet, however good a trotter, was not equal to present circumstances. D'Artagnan therefore took the post, and chose a horse which he soon caused to demonstrate, with good spurs and a light hand, that deer are not the swiftest animals in nature.

Chapter LXXIV.
D'Artagnan makes all Speed, Porthos snores, and Aramis counsels.

From thirty to thirty-five hours after the events we have just related, as M. Fouquet, according to his custom, having interdicted his door, was working in the cabinet of his house at Saint-Mande, with which we are already acquainted, a carriage, drawn by four horses steaming with sweat, entered the court at full gallop. This carriage was, probably, expected; for three or four lackeys hastened to the door, which they opened. Whilst M. Fouquet rose from his bureau and ran to the window, a man got painfully out of the carriage, descending with difficulty the three steps of the door, leaning upon the shoulders of the lackeys. He had scarcely uttered his name, when the valet upon whom he was not leaning, sprang up to the perron, and disappeared in the vestibule. This man went to inform his master; but he had no occasion to knock at the door: Fouquet was standing on the threshold.

"Monseigneur, the Bishop of Vannes," said he.

"Very well!" replied his master.

Then, leaning over the banister of the staircase, of which Aramis was beginning to ascend the first steps,—

"Ah, dear friend!" said he, "you, so soon!"

"Yes; I, myself, monsieur! but bruised, battered, as you see."

"Oh! my poor friend," said Fouquet, presenting him his arm, on which Aramis leant, whilst the servants drew back respectfully.

"Bah!" replied Aramis, "it is nothing, since I am here; the principal thing was that I should get here, and here I am."

"Speak quickly," said Fouquet, closing the door of the cabinet behind Aramis and himself.

"Are we alone?"

"Yes, perfectly."

"No one observes us?—no one can hear us?"

"Be satisfied; nobody."

"Is M. du Vallon arrived?"

"Yes."

"And you have received my letter?"

"Yes. The affair is serious, apparently, since it necessitates your attendance in Paris, at a moment when your presence was so urgent elsewhere."

"You are right, it could not be more serious."

"Thank you! thank you! What is it about? But, for God's sake! before anything else, take time to breathe, dear friend. You are so pale, you frighten me."

"I am really in great pain. But, for Heaven's sake, think nothing about me. Did M. du Vallon tell you nothing, when he delivered the letter to you?"

"No; I heard a great noise; I went to the window; I saw at the foot of the perron a sort of horseman of marble; I went down, he held the letter out to me, and his horse fell down dead."

"But he?"

"He fell with the horse; he was lifted, and carried to an apartment. Having read the letter, I went up to him, in hopes of obtaining more ample information; but he was asleep, and, after such a fashion, that it was impossible to wake him. I took pity on him; I gave orders that his boots should be cut from off his legs, and that he should be left quite undisturbed."

"So far well; now, this is the question in hand, monseigneur. You have seen M. d'Artagnan in Paris, have you not?"

"Certes, and think him a man of intelligence, and even a man of heart; although he did bring about the death of our dear friends, Lyodot and D'Eymeris."

"Alas! yes, I heard of that. At Tours I met the courier who was bringing the letter from Gourville, and the dispatches from Pelisson. Have you seriously reflected on that event, monsieur?"

"Yes."

"And in it you perceived a direct attack upon your sovereignty?"

"And do you believe it to be so?"

"Oh, yes, I think so."

"Well, I must confess, that sad idea occurred to me likewise."

"Do not blind yourself, monsieur, in the name of Heaven! Listen attentively to me,—I return to D'Artagnan."

"I am all attention."

"Under what circumstances did you see him?"

"He came here for money."

"With what kind of order?"

"With an order from the king."

"Direct?"

"Signed by his majesty."

"There, then! Well, D'Artagnan has been to Belle-Isle; he was disguised; he came in the character of some sort of an intendant, charged by his master to purchase salt-mines. Now, D'Artagnan has no other master but the king: he came, then, sent by the king. He saw Porthos."

"Who is Porthos?"

"I beg your pardon, I made a mistake. He saw M. du Vallon at Belle-Isle; and he knows, as well as you and I do, that Belle-Isle is fortified."

"And you think that the king sent him there?" said Fouquet, pensively.

"I certainly do."

"And D'Artagnan, in the hands of the king, is a dangerous instrument?"

"The most dangerous imaginable."

"Then I formed a correct opinion of him at the first glance."

"How so?"

"I wished to attach him to myself."

"If you judged him to be the bravest, the most acute, and the most adroit man in France, you judged correctly."

"He must be had then, at any price."

"D'Artagnan?"

"Is that not your opinion?"

"It may be my opinion, but you will never get him."

"Why?"

"Because we have allowed the time to go by. He was dissatisfied with the court, we should have profited by that; since that, he has passed into England; there he powerfully assisted in the restoration, there he gained a fortune, and, after all, he returned to the service of the king. Well, if he has returned to the service of the king, it is because he is well paid in that service."

"We will pay him even better, that is all."

"Oh! monsieur, excuse me; D'Artagnan has a high respect for his word, and where that is once engaged he keeps it."

"What do you conclude, then?" said Fouquet, with great inquietude.

"At present, the principal thing is to parry a dangerous blow."

"And how is it to be parried?"

"Listen."

"But D'Artagnan will come and render an account to the king of his mission."

"Oh, we have time enough to think about that."

"How so? You are much in advance of him, I presume?"

"Nearly ten hours."

"Well, in ten hours—"

Aramis shook his pale head. "Look at these clouds which flit across the heavens; at these swallows which cut the air. D'Artagnan moves more quickly than the clouds or the birds; D'Artagnan is the wind which carries them."

"A strange man!"

"I tell you, he is superhuman, monsieur. He is of my own age, and I have known him these five-and-thirty years."

"Well?"

"Well, listen to my calculation, monsieur. I send M. du Vallon off to you two hours after midnight. M. du Vallon was eight hours in advance of me; when did M. du Vallon arrive?"

"About four hours ago."

"You see, then, that I gained four upon him; and yet Porthos is a staunch horseman, and he has left on the road eight dead horses, whose bodies I came to successively. I rode post fifty leagues; but I have the gout, the gravel, and what else I know not; so that fatigue kills me. I was obliged to dismount at Tours; since that, rolling along in a carriage, half dead, sometimes overturned, drawn upon the sides, and sometimes on the back of the carriage, always with four spirited horses at full gallop, I have arrived— arrived, gaining four hours upon Porthos; but, see you, D'Artagnan does not weigh three hundred-weight, as Porthos does; D'Artagnan has not the gout and gravel, as I have; he is not a horseman, he is a centaur. D'Artagnan, look you, set out for Belle-Isle when I set out for Paris; and D'Artagnan, notwithstanding my ten hours' advance, D'Artagnan will arrive within two hours after me."

"But, then, accidents?"

"He never meets with accidents."

"Horses may fail him."

"He will run as fast as a horse."

"Good God! what a man!"

"Yes, he is a man whom I love and admire. I love him because he is good, great, and loyal; I admire him because he represents in my eyes the culminating point of human power; but, whilst loving and admiring him, I fear him, and am on my guard against him. Now then, I resume, monsieur; in two hours D'Artagnan will be here; be beforehand with him. Go to the Louvre, and see the king, before he sees D'Artagnan."

"What shall I say to the king?"

"Nothing; give him Belle-Isle."

"Oh! Monsieur d'Herblay! Monsieur d'Herblay," cried Fouquet, "what projects crushed all at once!"

"After one project that has failed, there is always another project that may lead to fortune; we should never despair. Go, monsieur, and go at once."

"But that garrison, so carefully chosen, the king will change it directly."

"That garrison, monsieur, was the king's when it entered Belle-Isle; it is yours now; it is the same with all garrisons after a fortnight's occupation. Let things go on, monsieur. Do you see any inconvenience in having an army at the end of a year, instead of two regiments? Do you not see that your garrison of to-day will make you partisans at La Rochelle, Nantes, Bordeaux, Toulouse—in short, wherever they may be sent to? Go to the king, monsieur; go; time flies, and D'Artagnan, while we are losing time, is flying, like an arrow, along the high-road."

"Monsieur d'Herblay, you know that each word from you is a germ which fructifies in my thoughts. I will go to the Louvre."

"Instantly, will you not?"

"I only ask time to change my dress."

"Remember that D'Artagnan has no need to pass through Saint-Mande; but will go straight to the Louvre; that is cutting off an hour from the advantage that yet remains to us."

"D'Artagnan may have everything except my English horses. I shall be at the Louvre in twenty-five minutes." And, without losing a second, Fouquet gave orders for his departure.

Aramis had only time to say to him, "Return as quickly as you go; for I shall await you impatiently."

Five minutes after, the superintendent was flying along the road to Paris. During this time, Aramis desired to be shown the chamber in which Porthos was sleeping. At the door of Fouquet's cabinet he was folded in the arms of Pelisson, who had just heard of his arrival, and had left his office to see him. Aramis received, with that friendly dignity which he knew so well how to assume, these caresses, respectful as earnest; but all at once stopping on the landing-place, "What is that I hear up yonder?"

There was, in fact, a hoarse, growling kind of noise, like the roar of a hungry tiger, or an impatient lion. "Oh, that is nothing," said Pelisson, smiling.

"Well; but—"

"It is M. du Vallon snoring."

"Ah! true," said Aramis: "I had forgotten. No one but he is capable of making such a noise. Allow me, Pelisson, to inquire if he wants anything."

"And you will permit me to accompany you?"

"Oh, certainly;" and both entered the chamber. Porthos was stretched upon the bed; his face was violet rather than red; his eyes were swelled; his mouth was wide open. The roaring which escaped from the deep cavities of his chest made the glass of the windows vibrate. To those developed and clearly defined muscles starting from his face, to his hair matted with sweat, to the energetic heaving of his chin and shoulders, it was impossible to refuse a certain degree of admiration. Strength carried to this point is semi-divine. The Herculean legs and feet of Porthos had, by swelling, burst his stockings; all the strength of his huge body was converted into the rigidity of stone. Porthos moved no more than does the giant of granite which reclines upon the plains of Agrigentum. According to Pelisson's orders, his boots had been cut off, for no human power could have pulled them off. Four lackeys had tried in vain, pulling at them as they would have pulled capstans; and yet all this did not awaken him. They had hacked off his boots in fragments, and his legs had fallen back upon the bed. They then cut off the rest of his clothes, carried him to a bath, in which they let him soak a considerable time. They then put on him clean linen, and placed him in a well-warmed bed—

the whole with efforts and pains which might have roused a dead man, but which did not make Porthos open an eye, or interrupt for a second the formidable diapason of his snoring. Aramis wished on his part, with his nervous nature, armed with extraordinary courage, to outbrave fatigue, and employ himself with Gourville and Pelisson, but he fainted in the chair in which he had persisted sitting. He was carried into the adjoining room, where the repose of bed soon soothed his failing brain.

Chapter LXXV.
In which Monsieur Fouquet Acts.

IN the meantime Fouquet was hastening to the Louvre, at the best speed of his English horses. The king was at work with Colbert. All at once the king became thoughtful. The two sentences of death he had signed on mounting his throne sometimes recurred to his memory; they were two black spots which he saw with his eyes open; two spots of blood which he saw when his eyes were closed. "Monsieur," said he rather sharply, to the intendant; "it sometimes seems to me that those two men you made me condemn were not very great culprits."

"Sire, they were picked out from the herd of the farmers of the financiers, which wanted decimating."

"Picked out by whom?"

"By necessity, sire," replied Colbert, coldly.

"Necessity!—a great word," murmured the young king.

"A great goddess, sire."

"They were devoted friends of the superintendent, were they not?"

"Yes, sire; friends who would have given up their lives for Monsieur Fouquet."

"They have given them, monsieur," said the king.

"That is true;—but uselessly, by good luck,—which was not their intention."

"How much money had these men fraudulently obtained?"

"Ten millions, perhaps; of which six have been confiscated."

"And is that money in my coffers?" said the king with a certain air of repugnance.

"It is there, sire; but this confiscation, whilst threatening M. Fouquet, has not touched him."

"You conclude, then, M. Colbert—"

"That if M. Fouquet has raised against your majesty a troop of factious rioters to extricate his friends from punishment, he will raise an army when he has in turn to extricate himself from punishment."

The king darted at his confidant one of those looks which resemble the livid fire of a flash of lightning, one of those looks which illuminate the darkness of the basest consciences. "I am astonished," said he, "that, thinking such things of M. Fouquet, you did not come to give me your counsels thereupon."

"Counsels upon what, sire?"

"Tell me, in the first place, clearly and precisely, what you think, M. Colbert."

"Upon what subject, sire?"

"Upon the conduct of M. Fouquet."

"I think, sire, that M. Fouquet, not satisfied with attracting all the money to himself, as M. Mazarin did, and by that means depriving your majesty of one part of your power, still wishes to attract to himself all the friends of easy life and pleasure—of what idlers call poetry, and politicians, corruption. I think that, by holding the subjects of your majesty in pay, he trespasses upon the royal prerogative, and cannot, if this continues so, be long in placing your majesty among the weak and the obscure."

"How would you qualify all these projects, M. Colbert?"

"The projects of M. Fouquet, sire?"

"Yes."

"They are called crimes of lese majeste."

"And what is done to criminals guilty of lese majeste?"

"They are arrested, tried, and punished."

"You are quite certain that M. Fouquet has conceived the idea of the crime you impute to him?"

"I can say more, sire; there is even a commencement of the execution of it."

"Well, then, I return to that which I was saying, M. Colbert."

"And you were saying, sire?"

"Give me counsel."

"Pardon me, sire; but in the first place, I have something to add."

"Say—what?"

"An evident, palpable, material proof of treason."

"And what is that?"

"I have just learnt that M. Fouquet is fortifying Belle-Isle."

"Ah, indeed!"

"Yes, sire."

"Are you sure?"

"Perfectly. Do you know, sire, what soldiers there are in Belle-Isle?"

"No, ma foi! Do you?"

"I am ignorant, likewise, sire; I should therefore propose to your majesty to send somebody to Belle-Isle?"

"Who?"

"Me, for instance."

"And what would you do at Belle-Isle?"

"Inform myself whether, after the example of the ancient feudal lords, M. Fouquet was battlementing his walls."

"And with what purpose could he do that?"

"With the purpose of defending himself someday against his king."

"But, if it be thus, M. Colbert," said Louis, "we must immediately do as you say; M. Fouquet must be arrested."

"That is impossible."

"I thought I had already told you, monsieur, that I suppressed that word in my service."

"The service of your majesty cannot prevent M. Fouquet from being surintendant-general."

"Well?"

"That, in consequence of holding that post, he has for him all the parliament, as he has all the army by his largesses, literature by his favors, and the noblesse by his presents."

"That is to say, then, that I can do nothing against M. Fouquet?"

"Absolutely nothing,—at least at present, sire."

"You are a sterile counselor, M. Colbert."

"Oh, no, sire; for I will not confine myself to pointing out the peril to your majesty."

"Come, then, where shall we begin to undermine this Colossus; let us see;" and his majesty began to laugh bitterly.

"He has grown great by money; kill him by money, sire."

"If I were to deprive him of his charge?"

"A bad means, sire."

"The good—the good, then?"

"Ruin him, sire, that is the way."

"But how?"

"Occasions will not be wanting; take advantage of all occasions."

"Point them out to me."

"Here is one at once. His royal highness Monsieur is about to be married; his nuptials must be magnificent. That is a good occasion for your majesty to demand a million of M. Fouquet. M. Fouquet, who pays twenty thousand livres down when he need not pay more than five thousand, will easily find that million when your majesty demands it."

"That is all very well; I will demand it," said Louis.

"If your majesty will sign the ordonnance I will have the money got together myself." And Colbert pushed a paper before the king, and presented a pen to him.

At that moment the usher opened the door and announced monsieur le surintendant. Louis turned pale. Colbert let the pen fall, and drew back from the king, over whom he extended his black wings like an evil spirit. The superintendent made his entrance like a man of the court, to whom a single glance was sufficient to make him appreciate the situation. That situation was not very encouraging for Fouquet, whatever might be his consciousness of strength. The small black eye of Colbert, dilated by envy, and the limpid eye of Louis XIV. inflamed by anger, signalled some pressing danger. Courtiers are, with regard to court rumors, like old soldiers, who distinguish through the blasts of wind and bluster of leaves the sound of the distant steps of an armed troop. They can, after having listened, tell pretty nearly how many men are marching, how many arms resound, how many cannons roll. Fouquet had then only to interrogate the silence which his arrival had produced; he found it big with menacing revelations. The king allowed him time enough to advance as far as the middle of the chamber. His adolescent modesty commanded this forbearance of the moment. Fouquet boldly seized the opportunity.

"Sire," said he, "I was impatient to see your majesty."

"What for?" asked Louis.

"To announce some good news to you."

Colbert, minus grandeur of person, less largeness of heart, resembled Fouquet in many points. He had the same penetration, the same knowledge of men; moreover, that great power of self-compression which gives to hypocrites time to reflect, and gather themselves up to take a spring. He guessed that Fouquet was going to meet the blow he was about to deal him. His eyes glittered ominously.

"What news?" asked the king. Fouquet placed a roll of papers on the table.

"Let your majesty have the goodness to cast your eyes over this work," said he. The king slowly unfolded the paper.

"Plans?" said he.

"Yes, sire."

"And what are these plans?"

"A new fortification, sire."

"Ah, ah!" said the king, "you amuse yourself with tactics and strategies then, M. Fouquet?"

"I occupy myself with everything that may be useful to the reign of your majesty," replied Fouquet.

"Beautiful descriptions!" said the king, looking at the design.

"Your majesty comprehends, without doubt," said Fouquet, bending over the paper; "here is the circle of the walls, here are the forts, there the advanced works."

"And what do I see here, monsieur?"

"The sea."

"The sea all round?"

"Yes, sire."

"And what is, then, the name of this place of which you show me the plan?"

"Sire, it is Belle-Ile-en-Mer," replied Fouquet with simplicity.

At this word, at this name, Colbert made so marked a movement, that the king turned round to enforce the necessity for reserve. Fouquet did not appear to be the least in the world concerned by the movement of Colbert, or the king's signal.

"Monsieur," continued Louis, "you have then fortified Belle-Isle?"

"Yes, sire; and I have brought the plan and the accounts to your majesty," replied Fouquet; "I have expended sixteen hundred livres in this operation."

"What to do?" replied Louis, coldly, having taken the initiative from a malicious look of the intendant.

"For an aim very easy to seize," replied Fouquet. "Your majesty was on cool terms with Great Britain."

"Yes; but since the restoration of King Charles II. I have formed an alliance with him."

"A month since, sire, your majesty has truly said; but it is more than six months since the fortifications of Belle-Isle were begun."

"Then they have become useless."

"Sire, fortifications are never useless. I fortified Belle-Isle against MM. Monk and Lambert and all those London citizens who were playing at soldiers. Belle-Isle will be ready fortified against the Dutch, against whom either England or your majesty cannot fail to make war."

The king was again silent, and looked askant at Colbert. "Belle-Isle, I believe," added Louis, "is yours, M. Fouquet?"

"No, sire."

"Whose then?"

"Your majesty's."

Colbert was seized with as much terror as if a gulf had opened beneath his feet. Louis started with admiration, either at the genius or the devotion of Fouquet.

"Explain yourself, monsieur," said he.

"Nothing more easy, sire; Belle-Isle is one of my estates; I have fortified it at my own expense. But as nothing in the world can oppose a subject making an humble present to his king, I offer your majesty the proprietorship of the estate, of which you will leave me the usufruct. Belle-Isle, as a place of war, ought to be occupied by the king. Your majesty will be able, henceforth, to keep a safe garrison there."

Colbert felt almost sinking down upon the floor. To keep himself from falling, he was obliged to hold by the columns of the wainscoting.

"This is a piece of great skill in the art of war that you have exhibited here, monsieur," said Louis.

"Sire, the initiative did not come from me," replied Fouquet; "many officers have inspired me with it. The plans themselves have been made by one of the most distinguished engineers."

"His name?"

"M. du Vallon."

"M. du Vallon?" resumed Louis; "I do not know him. It is much to be lamented, M. Colbert," continued he, "that I do not know the names of the men of talent who do honor to my reign." And while saying these words he turned towards Colbert. The latter felt himself crushed, the sweat flowed from his brow, no word presented itself to his lips, he suffered an inexpressible martyrdom. "You will recollect that name," added Louis XIV.

Colbert bowed, but was paler than his ruffles of Flemish lace. Fouquet continued:

"The masonries are of Roman concrete; the architects amalgamated it for me after the best accounts of antiquity."

"And the cannon?" asked Louis.

"Oh! sire, that concerns your majesty; it did not become me to place cannon in my own house, unless your majesty had told me it was yours."

Louis began to float, undetermined between the hatred which this so powerful man inspired him with, and the pity he felt for the other, so cast down, who seemed to him the counterfeit of the former. But the consciousness of his kingly duty prevailed over the feelings of the man, and he stretched out his finger to the paper.

"It must have cost you a great deal of money to carry these plans into execution," said he.

"I believe I had the honor of telling your majesty the amount."

"Repeat it if you please, I have forgotten it."

"Sixteen hundred thousand livres."

"Sixteen hundred thousand livres! you are enormously rich, monsieur."

"It is your majesty who is rich, since Belle-Isle is yours."

"Yes, thank you; but however rich I may be, M. Fouquet—" The king stopped.

"Well, sire?" asked the superintendent.

"I foresee the moment when I shall want money."

"You, sire? And at what moment then?"

"To-morrow, for example."

"Will your majesty do me the honor to explain yourself?"

"My brother is going to marry the English Princess."

"Well, sire?"

"Well, I ought to give the bride a reception worthy of the granddaughter of Henry IV."

"That is but just, sire."

"Then I shall want money."

"No doubt."

"I shall want—" Louis hesitated. The sum he was going to demand was the same that he had been obliged to refuse Charles II. He turned towards Colbert, that he might give the blow.

"I shall want, to-morrow—" repeated he, looking at Colbert.

"A million," said the latter, bluntly; delighted to take his revenge.

Fouquet turned his back upon the intendant to listen to the king. He did not turn round, but waited till the king repeated, or rather murmured, "A million."

"Oh! sire," replied Fouquet disdainfully, "a million! what will your majesty do with a million?"

"It appears to me, nevertheless—" said Louis XIV.

"That is not more than is spent at the nuptials of one of the most petty princes of Germany."

"Monsieur!"

"Your majesty must have two millions at least. The horses alone would run away with five hundred thousand livres. I shall have the honor of sending your majesty sixteen hundred thousand livres this evening."

"How," said the king, "sixteen hundred thousand livres?"

"Look, sire," replied Fouquet, without even turning towards Colbert, "I know that wants four hundred thousand livres of the two millions. But this monsieur of l'intendance" (pointing over his shoulder to Colbert, who if possible, became paler, behind him) "has in his coffers nine hundred thousand livres of mine."

The king turned round to look at Colbert.

"But—" said the latter.

"Monsieur," continued Fouquet, still speaking indirectly to Colbert, "monsieur has received, a week ago, sixteen hundred thousand livres; he has paid a hundred thousand livres to the guards, sixty-four thousand livres to the hospitals, twenty-five thousand to the Swiss, an hundred and thirty thousand for provisions, a thousand for arms, ten thousand for accidental expenses; I do not err, then, in reckoning upon nine hundred thousand livres that are left." Then turning towards Colbert, like a disdainful head of office towards his inferior, "Take care, monsieur," said he, "that those nine hundred thousand livres be remitted to his majesty this evening, in gold."

"But," said the king, "that will make two millions five hundred thousand livres."

"Sire, the five hundred thousand livres over will serve as pocket money for his royal highness. You understand, Monsieur Colbert, this evening before eight o'clock."

And with these words, bowing respectfully to the king, the superintendent made his exit backwards, without honoring with a single look the envious man, whose head he had just half shaved.

Colbert tore his ruffles to pieces in his rage, and bit his lips till they bled.

Fouquet had not passed the door of the cabinet, when an usher pushing by him, exclaimed: "A courier from Bretagne for his majesty."

"M. d'Herblay was right," murmured Fouquet, pulling out his watch; "an hour and fifty-five minutes. It was quite true."

Milton Keynes UK
Ingram Content Group UK Ltd.
UKHW030836021124
450589UK00006B/761